IN DEFENSE OF SCHREBER
SOUL MURDER AND PSYCHIATRY

Family Portrait of the Schrebers, 1851 (courtesy Jung family)

IN DEFENSE OF SCHREBER

SOUL MURDER AND PSYCHIATRY

Zvi Lothane

THE ANALYTIC PRESS

1992   Hillsdale, NJ   London

Portions of texts by Paul Schreber quoted herein are reprinted from *Psychosis and Sexual Identity: Toward a Post-Analytic View of the Schreber Case* (Allison et al., 1988) by permission of the State University of New York Press.

The Analytic Press
365 Broadway
Hillsdale, New Jersey 07642

Set in Bem by Lind Graphics, Inc., Upper Saddle River, NJ

Library of Congress Cataloging-in-Publication Data

Lothane, Zvi, 1934–
   In defense of Schreber : soul murder and psychiatry / Zvi Lothane.
       p.   cm.
   Includes bibliographical references and index.
   ISBN 0-88163-103-5
   1. Schreber, Daniel Paul, 1842–1911—Mental health.   2. Schreber,
Daniel Paul, 1842–1911—Influence.   3. Paranoia—Patients—Germany—
Biography.   4. Paranoia—Case studies.   5. Schreber, Moritz,
1808–1861.   I. Title.
   RC520.S33L68   1992
   616.89'7'0092—dc20
   [B]   92-16302
                                                                           CIP

Printed in the United States of America
10 9 8 7 6 5 4 3 2 1

To the Women in My Life

CONTENTS

Acknowledgments ix

List of some abbreviations used in this book xi

1. Man in Search of a Soul 1

2. Paul Schreber's Story 13

3. The Life and Legacy of Moritz Schreber 106

4. Moritz Schreber's Philosophy of Medicine and Education 147

5. Paul Flechsig and the First Biological Psychiatry 199

6. Guido Weber and the First Antipsychiatry 260

7. How Others Interpreted Schreber 317

8. Schreber as Interpreter and Thinker 375

9. The Dreams and Dramas of Love 429

Appendix: Paul Schreber's Clinical Chart 469

References 485

Index 524

ACKNOWLEDGMENTS

I would like to thank the people who participated in the process of writing this book. I am grateful to Martin Schulman and Lloyd deMause, who published my first essays on Schreber that became the seed of this book.

Dr. W. G. Niederland, the doyen of Schreber studies, was helpful with advice and archival and bibliographic materials pertaining to the Schreber Case. Similarly generous was my friend Professor Uwe Peters of Cologne, currently the President of the German Psychiatric Association.

My thanks go to the descendants of Schreber on the side of his sister Anna Jung: Mr. Dieter Jung and his mother, Mrs. Ruth Jung née Beyse, Miss Renate Jung, Mrs. Maria Schultheiss, Dr. Friedrich and his wife, Mrs. Ursula Friedrich, Mr. Reinhardt Röder, and, above all, Mrs. Brigitte Wienstein. In Germany I was also helped by Dr. Ruth Rank, at that time the director of the Dösen Hospital, the hospital librarian, Mrs. Heidrun Smers-Zimmermann and Gerd Zimmermann, and Mr. Römer.

In the early phases I was helped by Professor Han Israëls of Amsterdam and Dr. Gerhard Busse of Berlin, whom I met through the Freud historian Peter Swales, and with whom I have had both personal and written exchanges of ideas and sources.

My good friends Dr. Thomas Szasz from Syracuse, Dr. John Hickman Phillips, Dr. Martin Schulman, and Dr. Anthony Stern were patient readers of the various versions of the manuscript. I received generous scholarly help and materials from university departments of history of medicine: Professor Harig in Berlin, Professor Gerhard Fichtner and Dozent Albrecht Hirschmüller in Tübingen, and Professor Achim Thom and Drs. Gilardon and Kästner in Leipzig. Dr. Volker Friedrich from Hamburg was also a source of inspiration and support.

Scholarly hints of various kinds and materials were generously offered by Dr. Daniel Devreese from Ghent, Dr. Leo Ikelaar of the Duits Seminariam of Amsterdam University, Martin Stingelin of the Deutsches Seminar of Basel University, Dr. Joachim-Ernst Meyer of Göttingen, Professor David Allison of Stony Brook, Luis Eduardo Prado de Oliveira in Paris, Mr. David Toren of New York City. I corresponded with Dr. Kurt Eissler of New York, Professor Klaus Dörner of Gütersloh, Professor Peter Gay of New Haven, Professors Paul Roazen and John O'Neal from Toronto, Dr. Elisabeth Schreiber of Berlin, Dr. John Nemiah, Dr. John Mack, Dr. Morton Schatzman, and Mr. Henry Cohen.

My research was done in a number of archives and libraries: In Germany, the State Libraries of Berlin; libraries of Leipzig, Warsaw, and Kraków Universities; Sächsische Landesbibibliothek in Dresden; the State Archives in Dresden (Drs. Brichzin and Gross), and the State Archives in St. Petersburg. In the United States I had continuous support with interlibrary loans at the Mount Sinai School of Medicine Library (Mrs. Celia Soto) and the following: the Library of the New York Academy of Medicine (Mrs. Gams); the National Library of Medicine, History Section (Ms. Ann Toohey); the Special Collections, Millbank Memorial Library, Teachers College of Columbia University (Dr. Mind); the College of Physicians and Surgeons of Philadelphia; and the Alan Mason Chesney Medical Archives of Johns Hopkins University.

I am grateful to the Editor-in-Chief of The Analytic Press, Dr. Paul Stepansky, for his unflagging support of this book from the word go. Dr. John Kerr, my editor, has shown a profound understanding of the subject matter as well as a superb sense of proportion and style. My manuscript editor, Toby Troffkin, lavished meticulous attention to detail on every page, saving me from many a pitfall. I am grateful to Eleanor Starke Kobrin, Managing Editor, for her loving care and devotion at every step of the production process, and to Nancy Liguori for her meticulous proofreading.

Finally I want to give most generous thanks to Dr. Karl Golling and Mr. Brett Singer, who taught me how to use the word processor; without their patience and steadfast help this manuscript could not have been completed.

LIST OF SOME ABBREVIATIONS USED IN THIS BOOK

AKAK   *Archiv für Kriminal-Anthropologie und Kriminalistik.*

AP   *Archiv für Psychiatrie und Nervenkrankheiten*, continued as *Archiv für Psychiatrie*; also referred to as *Archiv*.

AZP   *Allgemeine Zeitschrift für Psychiatrie und psychisch-gerichtliche Medicin*, renamed *Allgemeine Zeitschrift für Psychiatrie und ihre Grenzgebiete*, and then *Zeitschrift für Psychiatrie*; also referred to as *Zeitschrift*.

CNP   *Centralblatt für Nervenheilkunde und Psychiatrie*, a continuation of *Centralblatt für Nervenheilkunde Psychiatrie und gerichtliche Psychopathologie*. Later spelling: *Zentralblatt*.

DMW   *Deutsche Medizinische Wochenschrift.*

DMZ   *Deutsche Medizinal-Zeitung.*

DZN   *Deutsche Zeitschrift für Nervenheilkunde.*

JKPE   *Jahrbuch für Kinderheilkunde und physische Erziehung.*

JPPF   *Jahrbuch für psychoanalytische und psychopathologische Forschungen*; also referred to as *Jahrbuch*.

LNN   *Leipzig Neuste Nachrichten.*

MPN   *Monatschrift für Psychiatrie und Neurologie.*

MMW   *Muenchener Medizinische Wochenschrift.*

NC   *Neurologisches Centralblatt* (later: *Zentralblatt*).

NJT   *Neue Jahrbücher für die Turnkunst.*

PMW   *Prager Medizinische Wochenschrift.*

PNW   *Psychiatrisch-Neurologische Wochenschrift*, continuation of *Psychiatrische Wochenschrift*.

PW   *Psychiatrische Wochenschrift*, renamed *Psychiatrisch-Neuro-
          logische Wochenschrift.*
RFP   *Révue Française de Psychanalyse.*
SANP   *Schweizer Archiv für Neurologie und Psychiatrie.*
SJIAGM   *Schmidt's Jahrbücher der in- und ausländischen gesammten Me-
          dicin.*
ZPPS   *Zeitschrift für die Psychologie und Physiologie der Sinnesorgane.*

1

MAN IN SEARCH
OF A SOUL

And so I believe I am not mistaken in expecting that a very special palm of victory will be mine. . . . I close in the hope that favorable stars will watch over the success of my labour.

D. P. Schreber, 1903

It remains for the future to decide whether there is more delusion in my theory than I should like to admit, or whether there is more truth in Schreber's delusions than other people are as yet prepared to believe.

Freud, 1911a

He who wants to understand the poet must travel to the land of the poet.

Goethe, West-East Divan

WHY READ SCHREBER?

It is now a century and a half since Daniel Paul Schreber J.D. was born in 1842. It is but one year short of a century since he was admitted as a patient to the Hospital for Psychiatric and Nervous Diseases of Leipzig University[1] for what was to be a prolonged confinement during which he wrote the memoirs of his experience, *Denkwürdigkeiten eines Nerven-kranken*, published in 1903. The title means: "the great thoughts of a

1

nervous patient"—that is how Schreber meant it. However, the title *Memoirs of My Nervous Illness*,[2] is the one that persists.

Schreber's book can be viewed on many levels: as an autobiography; as an account of his mental illness, involuntary hospitalization, and the legal battle to regain his civil liberties; as a document about psychiatry in Germany; and as a commentary on contemporary culture. It is also a work of art, a uniquely crafted narrative. Taking its place beside Clifford Beers's *The Mind that Found Itself* (1908) and Perceval's *Narrative* (1838-40), Schreber's tome shines as one of the most glorious books ever written by a psychiatric patient. After all, nervous illness, madness, madhouses and mad doctors are forever fascinating.

Among Schreber's meditations were thoughts about the soul. It was already clear to Heraclitus (Fragment 45) that one cannot find the boundaries of the soul, no matter which path one follows, for it is so profound. The very words soul, spirit, and God, owing to their metaphysical and theological accretions down the ages, are no longer respectable concepts in scientific and philosophical discourse, as they were in the generation of Schreber's father and his own. This is especially so in modern English, but less so in German. For example, whereas Freud still used the term *seelisches Apparat* (mental apparatus), in modern English, soul and spirit have been replaced with mind and mental. To the modern reader God and soul may suggest a proximity to suspect occult preoccupations and pathology, especially in a text primarily identified as psychotic, such as the *Memoirs*. However, we are well advised to remember the two basic pragmatic meanings of soul, both still in German and English usage: Soul means a person, and it means the feeling, thinking, moral, and acting center of the person. Otherwise, we will not be able to understand one of Schreber's central concepts, that of soul murder. Schreber's soul murder is not a psychotic neologism but a term with a long history, used for a specific purpose. God, spirit, soul and immortality will always fascinate.[3]

In 1911 Freud, inspired by Jung,[4] published his epochal analysis of the *Memoirs* in his essay, "Psycho-analytic Notes on an Autobiographical Account of a Case of Paranoia (Dementia paranoides)."[5] Since then Schreber and Freud are indissolubly conjoined in the history of psychiatry and psychoanalysis. Freud's essay made history because of the causal connection between paranoia and repressed homosexuality, which became the cornerstone of Freudian psychoanalytic approaches to psychosis. On this view, the sexual desire of the child for the parent of the same gender, repressed and sublimated in the course of development, can break through in adulthood as a transference toward a significant other. The overt sexual desire in the present, conflictual and unacceptable, leads to two consequences: a detachment of libido from people and the world, with regression to a more primitive state of withdrawal, and a projection of the desire onto the other, with a secondary turning of love into hate, that is, a complete delusion of persecution. While the generality and universality of this theory has since been challenged, the essay is rich in many other, even more important, insights.

Were it not for Freud, Schreber's would have been a forgotten book, collecting dust in a library. In the *Memoirs*[6] Schreber expresses the belief that great fame would be his "surpassing that of thousands of other people much better mentally endowed," owing to the spread of his religious ideas, which would "lead to a fundamental revolution in mankind's religious views unequalled in history" (*M*, pp. 293-294). But it is sex and psychosis, not religion, that have made Schreber—and Freud—famous. Sex is a most important ingredient in any *succès de scandale*.

It is therefore not surprising that even today the Schreber story and Freud's essay retain a remarkable vitality, attracting an ever-increasing interest among professionals, scholars and the reading public. In addition to its many interesting ideas, articulated with intelligence and style, the story has drama and poignancy. It touches on some perennial themes in psychiatry, including the nature of mental illness, psychiatric hospitalization, and methods of treatment. Today, as one hundred years ago, psychiatrists are still grappling with the same problems: competing concepts of cause and cure of mental illness; the importance of psychological versus biological and the cultural versus constitutional factors; the doctor-patient relationship; involuntary hospitalization and the abuses of the civil rights of institutionalized patients; the boundary between the normal and the abnormal. Similarly, the psychoanalytic interpretations that sprung up around Schreber, both in Freud's time and thereafter, are as passionate today as they were then.

Le style c'est l'homme, style is the man himself. Just prior to publication of the *Memoirs* Schreber realized that he "might perhaps have formulated some passages of [the] Memoirs differently." But he resisted the impulse to rewrite: "Nevertheless I have left them mainly in the form in which they were written originally. To change certain points now would only prejudice the freshness of the original descriptions" (*M*, p. iv). His instinct was right. The bane of madness turned into the boon of magic: it is the poetic power of his writing in the *Memoirs* that has made it into a profound text, inviting exegetes and interpreters to ponder its mysteries.

Thanks to Freud Schreber became a paradigmatic case and passed into the writings of other psychoanalysts.[7] Modern debate broke out all over when the American psychiatrist and psychoanalyst W. G.

Niederland (1974), the doyen of Schreber studies in our time, created a sensation in 1959 by publishing his landmark paper, "Schreber: father and son," which, he believed, contained the key to the puzzle, that is, the key to explaining the content of Schreber's famous hallucinations and delusions. Niederland's (1959) mind-capturing thesis, which earned him a *succès d'estime* among his colleagues, was that the images and sensations in Paul Schreber's psychosis were derivatives of the way his father, Daniel Gottlob Moritz Schreber, M.D., tortured his son by means of posture-improving orthopedic appliances and other educational methods, described in Moritz Schreber's books on child rearing, notably the *Kallipädie* (1858a). Like sex, sadism is a fascinating subject. Niederland's writings revolutionized Schreber studies. Before them and under the influence of Freud there were scattered contributions on the Schreber case to the literature. After Niederland the interest in Schreber mushroomed and is still growing. The important consequence of Niederland's conception for received psychoanalytic theory (such as structural ego psychology with its focus on intrapsychic id-ego conflicts), was his emphasis that adult psychopathology is determined by childhood trauma, be it sexual or sadistic. Niederland's trauma perspective both challenged the structural theory and, when it became as exclusionary as the genetic fallacy, it tended to deemphasize historical, social and current reality factors.

While Niederland published in the professional literature, it was another American psychiatrist, Morton Schatzman, whose book achieved best-seller status. Schatzman (1973) used all of Niederland's ideas but claimed to have presented a radically new theory in his book, *Soul Murder: Persecution in the Family*.[8] However, the innovation was only terminological: persecution was the new word for trauma. The book, however, was impassioned and made Schatzman famous and Schreber a popular subject. This is to Schatzman's credit, even though his claim of an original theory about Schreber is not justified. Appearing in 1973, in the aftermath of the youth revolt of the late sixties against a generation of fathers and the Vietnam War, it seemed to hit a nerve. Mix together the idea of parental sadism, rename it persecution, add a dash of Freud bashing (the perception was that Schatzman was attacking Freud for not reading his books before attempting an analysis of the son's *Memoirs*, an "omission" already made evident by Niederland, even though Freud actually knew some of Moritz Schreber's ideas), and you have the recipe for a *succès de scandale*. Schatzman's perspective became the popular one, and Niederland's reputation suffered as a result. One can now read papers and books about the victimization of Paul Schreber by his allegedly sadistic father based solely on the authority of Schatzman, either misrepresenting Niederland's contribution or without even mentioning Niederland at all.[9] Compared with Niederland, Schatzman had no interest in the contemporaneous background to Schreber's story. Even though billed as anti-Freudian and anti-psychiatric, Schatzman's idea of sadistic parental persecution was not only derived from Niederland but, ironically, from Freudian geneticism as well. Schatzman invoked interpersonal dynamics, but limited them to the childhood trauma only.

A recent biographical contribution is the doctoral thesis of Han Israëls in 1980, published in book form in English and German in 1989. It bears Niederland's title: *Schreber: Father and Son* and is a detailed documentary, bibliographic and archival study about the Schreber family. It sheds no new light on the actual father-son relationship, for the simple reason that no documents directly bearing on their relation have survived. Israëls did not formulate a method of interpretation. I both respect his work as an important source book and take issue with his misleading interpretations and arguments (Lothane, 1991b).

MY APPROACH TO SCHREBER

For years Schreber was for me mostly a matter of hearsay, one of those classics much quoted but never read. I was acquainted with Freud's essay and found Niederland's papers convincing when I first read them; I did not see Schatzman's book until the summer of 1988.

In the summer of 1987 I wrote a methodological analysis of the concept of self and searched for the occurrence of self in Freud. There are only three or four places where Freud uses the word *Selbst*. One of these rare times is in a quotation from Schreber. Finding this quotation stimulated me to read on. I was inspired by Freud's (1911a) recommendation to his readers in the introductory remarks preceding his case history of Paul Schreber "to make themselves acquainted with the book [by Schreber] by reading it through at least once beforehand" (p. 10).

When I finally immersed myself in Schreber's *Memoirs*, both in German and English, and then compared what Schreber said with what Freud said, I came to question Freud's reading of Schreber. First, I approached Schreber at eye level, so to speak, as if I had entered into a dialogue with a friend. I was also mindful of the historiographic method advocated by R. G.. Collingwood (1946), which is in consonance with the psychoanalytic method. I was putting mental questions to my protagonist, trying to put myself in his shoes, thinking his thoughts, and imagining what it must have felt like to be in his situation. The more I read and the more I compared Freud's great interpretation with what Schreber said, the more it struck me that Freud was not listening to Schreber, not, as he would say later (Freud, 1933, p. 12), interpreting *from* Schreber but interpreting *into* Schreber, projecting his ideas into him. This raised questions about method.

An essential piece of the puzzle was missing: the awareness of the *reality* of Schreber's long years in mental hospitals and how important this was in itself. For the *Memoirs* are about his adult life, illnesses and hospitalizations. It was as if, *for Freud*, Schreber's life had existed in a vacuum, unaffected by his life in the institutions. But this could not be so. How were aspects of daily life affecting the patient? How were they reflected in his hallucinations, delusions and bodily sensations? This connection had not been previously acknowledged and seemed to be a glaring omission.[10] It was as if Schreber's illness had existed as a static fact, as if Schreber were a "windowless monad," to use Leibniz's expression. After all, in medicine there is recognition of the iatrogenic effects of the doctor and his treatments on the patient and the course of an illness. Why was this not acknowledged in the case of Schreber? Why did he complain so bitterly about Professor Flechsig, his first psychiatrist? Was it all a delusion? Why did Dr. Weber, his other psychiatrist, fight so hard in court to keep Schreber under lock and key, even as the patient improved? How did this opposition affect the patient's mental state? Who were Flechsig and Weber? What were their personalities, backgrounds, theories and practices? How did these affect the patient and how did he portray this in his story? My next step was to immerse myself in reading the writings of Flechsig and Weber and what was said about them by their contemporaries and later generations.

In the summer of 1988 I traveled to Dresden and searched in the Dresden State Archives.[11] I reviewed the Flechsig personal and hospital files and found the files of Guido Weber, Schreber's psychiatrist from 1894 to 1902. In the summer of 1989 I went again to Dresden. This time I found legal records of court proceedings and decisions (in Chemnitz, Freiberg and Dresden) in which Paul Schreber participated and interviewed descendants of Paul Schreber's elder sister Anna both in both what was then East and West Germany.

As informative as the discussions with the descendants had been, along with information gathered by biographers, there remained un-explored areas in the *Memoirs* themselves. The legal proceedings and the court decisions in Schreber's own court case, appended to the *Memoirs*, are more important than has been thought until now. The *Denkwürdigkeiten* in Germany, as well as the *Memoirs* in the English-speaking countries, was published under an abridged title. Only the French version bears the complete title. True, the full title of the original is reproduced on the page facing the preface in the English translation but is left untranslated and thus lost on the average reader. The full title, in my translation, is *Great Thoughts of a Nervous Patient with Postscripts and an Addendum Concerning the Question: "Under what Premises Can a Person Considered Insane be Detained in an Asylum Against His Own Declared Will?"* by Daniel Paul Schreber, J.D., Formerly *Senatspräsident* at the Royal Superior Appellate Court in Dresden. For this addendum is no mere disposable appendage to the book: it is an integral part of it. Schreber's long detention was an injustice and an infringement on his civil liberties. Writing the book and getting it published were integral parts of the fight for his freedom and self-vindication.

In addition to the issues ignored in the methodology of my predecessors, another dimension of the story kept nagging at me with increasing insistence: the ethical implications of the Schreber literature. It comes to this: Moritz Schreber and Paul Schreber, father and son, have been the target of gross distortions. The father was made to look like a crank, the son queer and crazy.[12] Both are gross distortions. Both caricatures stem from prejudice and ignorance of historical facts. Some of these distortions were partially corrected by Israëls while others were maintained unmodified.

Moritz Schreber has been written off as a serious scientist owing to the combined influence of Niederland and Schatzman and the uncritical secondary literature that has burgeoned as a result of their misrepresentations. Israëls has gone a certain distance in correcting in a qualified way some of these gross misrepresentations, for example, the view of the father as sadistic. However, Israëls paid scant—and in a few places tendentious—attention to Moritz Schreber's place in the history of medicine and education. Nevertheless, Moritz Schreber's achievements as an orthopedist, pediatrician and an early advocate of *Naturheilkunde*, or holistic medicine, have been recognized by experts and historians.[13] His educational methods have also been positively appraised and deserve to be reappraised. I will try to shed more light on some of these issues.

Paul Schreber has been branded as a paranoiac and a homosexual. Paranoia as a discrete nosological entity has been repeatedly debated ever since it was introduced into German psychiatry in the mid-19th century. When used properly, the term serves a phenomenological purpose. When abused, *paranoia* and *paranoid* become terms of abuse, stigmas, and slurs. I will argue that Paul Schreber did not suffer from paranoia and that this was a misdiagnosis fashioned by his psychiatrist, Weber, which was then uncritically repeated by Jung, Bleuler, and Freud. This misdiagnosis cost Schreber his freedom for a number of years. These issues of diagnosis and treatment inspired me to study the history of psychiatry, hospital practices and the legal aspects of incompetency rulings in Germany.

HOW TO READ SCHREBER

Heretofore, interpreters of Schreber took Schreber's encoded productions, his now-famous hallucinations and delusions, those multitudinous "miracles" that were wrought in his mind and body by a malevolent God, as the essential content of his book. Some came to regard Schreber's text as nothing but hallucinations and delusions with little else in it to merit attention: "word salad," much morbid fantasy, and little respectable fact. Furthermore, the fact of his living in the asylum colors everything he says. Therefore, any hallucination or delusion immediately leads to the question: is Schreber using this medium to talk about his past or about his present?

The Factual and the Fantastic

I propose to reverse the priorities in reading Schreber or, to use Marx's phrase, to put the pyramid back on its base. For Schreber did not primarily live in the "miracled up"[14] world of the "fleetingly improvised men"[15] of his hallucinations and delusions. He was first and foremost a person who lived, loved, and suffered in the real world of people, one who had a profession and a marriage, family, and friends. His dramas preceded his dreams. He reacted to his life events in ordinary ways and spoke of them in ordinary language; but he also reacted and spoke in some very extraordinary ways. Some of the extraordinary reactions took the shape of dream formations: that is, hallucinations and delusions.

Thus it can be said that the same life events were thought of and spoken of in two distinct modes of representation—the factual, or prosaic, and the fantastic, or poetic—even as reality and the dream, the factual and the fantastic, the mundane and the miraculous, are the perennial polarities that characterize the life of every person, in health and disease. And it is the fantastic that has always been the more fascinating.

Schreber was also fascinated by the fantastic and expounded on it at great length. For example, he regarded the characterization of himself as a "Prince of Hell" a "fantastic term" (*M*, p. 163), in contrast with the reality of his surroundings. He also called his fantastic terminology "basic language" (*Grundsprache*) and "soul language" (*Seelensprache*). In his narrative he used both modes of representation as a running counterpoint. In the various chapter titles of his book the phrase "personal experiences" is a recurrent motif among locutions referring to the fantastic. Schreber wrote to tell the story of his life, and he employed two styles: ordinary realism and magical realism. In addition to the autobiographical passages, he also expressed psychological, philosophical and religious ideas, also clothed in the ordinary and the magical styles.

In keeping with the primacy of the lived personal experience, in Chapter 2 we first focus on the events in Paul Schreber's life. We shall first read Schreber's factual descriptions of these events and then correlate them with their fantastic representations. In this we will be true to Freud's perennial insight into the nature of the dream: a formation instigated by reality (the day residue) that, under the sway of the laws of dream life (i.e., through the operation of unconscious mental processes), becomes a dream representation of that reality.

We shall review the life of Moritz Schreber in chapter 3 and devote chapter 4 to a discussion of his ideas as expounded in his various books and pamphlets. This will be preparatory to tracing the influence of the father's ideas on those of the son, which will be left until chapter 8.

Chapter 5 is devoted to the life and work of Paul Flechsig, neuroanatomist turned psychiatrist, declared by Schreber to be his archenemy. This influential man of science and colorful personality played his own historical role in German organic psychiatry and in the history of the localization of mind in brain. We are heirs to the mind-brain debate almost a century after the publication of Flechsig's *Gehirn und Seele* (Brain and Soul).

Chapter 6 is devoted to Schreber's second important psychiatrist, Guido Weber—Schreber's real opponent—superintendent of the prestigious Sonnenstein Asylum, dean of Saxony's institutional psychiatrists, and noted forensic expert. In addition to reviewing his life and work, I also describe the background to the first antipsychiatry movement in Germany a century ago and locate Schreber's legal case in it.

Chapter 7 is a review of the writings inspired by the *Memoirs* and the Schreber case from the beginning to our day. It can be said that the *Memoirs* became a scripture leading to a multifarious exegetical literature that is still growing.

Chapter 8 honors Paul Schreber's as a thinker in his own right. Here it is important to trace the delusions, i.e., the dream theories of Schreber, to the doctrines, be they scientific, cosmological or mystical, that formed the climate of opinion during his lifetime. The net effect will be to dispel the impression of mere madness from some of his views.

The aforementioned chapters are left to speak for themselves, with a minimum of commentary. The final chapter provides a concluding statement of my own views of this remarkable story.

At the end of Chapters 2, 3, 5, and 6 I have provided chronological tables of the life and work of Paul Schreber, Moritz Schreber, Paul Flechsig and Guido Weber, respectively, to make their stories easier to follow. A list of abbreviations of some of the books, journals, and other materials cited in this work is also provided.

Unless otherwise indicated, the translations of all the German texts are my own.

NOTES

1. The hospital has been given a number of different names since its founding in 1882, two years prior to Schreber's first admission. In the Macalpine and Hunter translation of the *Memoirs* it is referred to sometimes as a clinic and sometimes as an asylum. In Germany a university hospital is traditionally designated as a clinic; this is an accurate translation of this hospital's first official name, *Die Irrenklinik der Universität Leipzig*, but it may be misleading, since in American usage today *clinic* refers to an outpatient, not an inpatient, setting. Thus, the institution to which Schreber was first admitted was a city asylum, as against a provincial or outlying rural asylum, equivalent to the American state hospital, where he was transferred later. And since the former was attached to an academic center, it carried less stigma than the state public asylum and was a place where people admitted themselves voluntarily. At a later date its name was changed to a more prestigious one: *Die Psychiatrische und Nervenklinik der Universität Leipzig*, The Hospital for Psychiatric and Nervous Diseases of Leipzig University.

2. This is the title of the first full English translation of Schreber's book by Ida Macalpine and Richard A. Hunter in 1955, reissued by Harvard University Press, 1988. I will use the abbreviation *Memoirs* from here on. However, I consider this title a mistranslation. According to *Webster's* (1971), memoir means "(1) an autobiographical account, (2) an account of something regarded as noteworthy." Dr. W. G. Niederland called to my attention that in Schreber's title the second meaning is intended in the German word *Denkwürdigkeiten*. Indeed, Paul Schreber was consistent in making a distinction between accounts of noteworthy things, such as his reflections about theology, religion, and psychology and accounts of his personal experiences. The German title, *Denkwürdigkeiten eines Nervenkranken*, thus means memoirs, in both senses of the word, of a nervous person. Thus the Macalpine and Hunter title depersonalizes by narrowing the focus to the illness and away from the person. Their version contains a number of mistranslations; I quote the original and provide my own version in brackets next to the disputed translation.

3. In Paul Schreber's time in the United States, the concepts of soul and spirit found a protagonist in the United States in William James. Inspired by the Leipzig mystical philosopher and scientific psychologist Gustav Theodor Fechner (1801-1887)—who would have been known to both Schreber and his father and was cited by Freud—James wrote a preface to the 1905 American edition of Fechner's *The Little Book of Life After Death*. Idealism and materialism

form a chain of thesis, antithesis and various syntheses in the history of European thought. James (1904) writes:

> Little by little the materialistic generation that called his [Fechner's] speculations fantastic has been replaced by one with greater liberty of imagination. Leaders of thought, such as Paulsen [1892], . . . treat Fechner's panpsychism as plausible . . . and it is easy to believe that consciousness or inner experience . . . are co-eternal aspects of one self-same reality, much as concave and convex are aspects of the same curve. . . . God for Fechner, is the totalized consciousness of the whole universe, of which the Earth's consciousness forms an element, just as in turn my consciousness and yours form elements of the whole earth's consciousness [pp. x-xvi].

This spiritual monism has been paralleled by the materialist monism that is the metaphysical foundation of modern science. Some of Schreber's delusions cannot be understood without spiritual monism as a background.

4. Freud's understanding of Schreber was influenced by C. G. Jung's *Über die Psychologie der Dementia Praecox*, 1907 (of which the first English translation by A. A. Brill, *The Psychology of Dementia Praecox*, was published in 1909), by the Freud-Jung correspondence and by numerous personal communications between them (Kerr, personal communication, 1991).

5. First published in the *Jahrbuch für psychoanalytische und psychopathologische Forschungen*, from here on abbreviated as *JPPF* and *Jahrbuch*, when Jung was its editor.

6. Hereafter *Memoirs* will be abbreviated in parenthetical in-text citations as *M* followed by page numbers of the 1903 German original. Paul Schreber's footnotes will be capitalized as follows: "Foot Note." Translated passages from the *Memoirs* are from Macalpine and Hunter (1955), in which the original page numbers are printed in the margins.

7. Although the descendants of Schreber destroyed copies of the book, apparently the *Memoirs* did not totally disappear from the shelves of booksellers. The *Bericht über die Fortschritte der Psychoanalyse in den Jahren 1914-1919* (Report on Advances in Psychoanalysis) of 1921, published by the International Psychoanalytic Association in Leipzig, Vienna, and Zurich, carried an advertisement that the *Memoirs* were obtainable through the International Psychoanalytic Publishers.

8. The book was an expanded version of Schatzman's (1971) "Paranoia or Persecution: The Case of Schreber."

9. For example, in Alice Miller (1986) we can read:

> Freud traced all Schreber's fears of persecution back to resistance against a homosexual love for his father. Schatzman carries his investigation an important step beyond Niederland's, comparing passages from the son's memoirs with the father's pedagogical writings and discovering some startling connections. It turns out that even the ill son's most absurd ideas, fantasies and fears of persecution are a retelling,

without realizing it, of the story of persecution he was subjected to in early childhood (p. 186).

But there is no such step beyond Niederland in these comparisons. That step has to do with the idea in Miller's title: The parent mistreats the child and also issues a command to forget and repress the mistreatment. But that is a different issue, and whether it applies to Paul Schreber is an open question. Miller does not quote Niederland's literature on Schreber in her bibliography. Her description of Schatzman's discoveries thus is a misrepresentation.

10. Schatzman alluded to such matters in a footnote but did not pursue them in his study of Schreber.

11. Dr. Gerd Busse was helpful in orienting me how to gain access to the Archives.

12. For example, Macalpine and Hunter say this about Moritz Schreber in their introduction to the *Memoirs*:

He was also an educationalist and a social reformer with an apostle-like mission to bring health, happiness and bliss to the masses through physical culture. . . . He published a number of books of which the titles alone, quite apart from the text, show that he was an eccentric, not to say a crank ["Translators' Introduction," p. 1].

Did the translators read any of those texts?

13. For example, in Sudhoff (1922), Schreber is cited on p. 432; Sudhoff's is the third edition of J. L. Pagel's (1898) *Introduction to the History of Medicine*, where Schreber and his coworker and successor Schildbach are cited on pp. 452, 495.

14. *Angewundert*, "caused by miracles," is Schreber's word for that which was beyond his control and against his will, and therefore seemed to be produced by supernatural, divine, or miraculous causes. He did not have Freud's term for unbidden thoughts, feelings, or bodily sensations unconsciously caused. In the Middle Ages such miraculous phenomena were seen as caused either by the devil or by the deity. Latter-day organic psychiatry believed them to be caused by disordered brain metabolism. Freud (1893) saw them as a special manifestation of the mind and "replaced the 'demon' of clerical phantasy by a psychological formula" (p. 22); he exchanged the "religious terminology of the dark and superstitious age for the scientific language of to-day" (p. 20), that is, for the concept of causation by unconscious mental processes.

15. *Flüchtig hingemachte männer* is, literally, "fleetingly made up men." The other known translation is "cursorily improvised men," by Strachey. Since Schreber does not intend real people but only the unreal creatures of his day dreams, I propose that one should not speak of men but of phantoms, the shadowy, incorporeal creatures of reverie. These phantoms express, for example, Schreber's strong but controlled emotions, such as rage, in a disguised way.

2

PAUL SCHREBER'S
STORY

I believed the whole of mankind to have perished . . . the impressions which rushed in upon me were such a wonderful mixture of natural events and happenings of supernatural nature, that it is extremely difficult to distinguish mere dream visions from experiences in a waking state, that is to say to be certain how far all that I thought I had experienced was in fact historical reality. It is unavoidable, therefore, that my recollections of that time must in some measure bear the stamp of confusion.

D. P. Schreber, 1903

Any one who was more daring than I am in making interpretations, or who was in touch with Schreber's family and consequently better acquainted with the society in which he moved and the small events of his life, would find it an easy matter to trace back innumerable details of his delusions to their sources and so discover their meaning. . . . But as it is, we must necessarily content ourselves with this shadowy sketch of the infantile material which was used by the paranoic disorder in portraying the current conflict.

Freud, 1911a

Paul Schreber's life[1] can be divided into six periods: (1) 1842-1863, childhood and youth, to the end of his law studies; (2) 1864-1885, from the start of his legal career to the end of the first illness and hospitalization at Flechsig's Psychiatric University Hospital; (3) 1886-1893, the zenith and end of his legal career; (4) 1893-1902, the second illness

13

and the years of hospitalization at Sonnenstein Asylum; (5) 1903–1907, the last good years; (6) 1907–1911, the last illness and death in the Leipzig–Dösen Asylum.

FIRST PERIOD: 1842–1863

Paul Schreber was born in Leipzig on July 25, 1842, the third child of Daniel Gottlob Moritz Schreber (1808–1861) and Louise Henriette Pauline Schreber née Haase (1815–1907). The couple were married in 1838. The firstborn was Gustav (1839–1877) and the first daughter was Anna (1840–1944). By 1839 Moritz Schreber had already spent three years in a successful practice; and that year wrote his first large book, *Das Buch der Gesundheit* (The Book of Health). The other daughters were Sidonie (1846–1924) and Klara (1848–1917), who both maintained a contact with the Sonnenstein Asylum (Baumeyer, 1956). Gustav and Sidonie never married and Klara was childless. All the descendants, dead and still living, come from Anna Jung née Schreber.[2]

Father

Daniel Gottlob Moritz Schreber was the grandson and nephew of the illustrious Schrebers, Gottfried and Johann Christian Daniel, respectively. Moritz's father died in 1837 and his mother in 1846, the latter fact interpreted by Niederland (1974) as follows: "It is likely that this was for our 41/2 year old patient [i.e., Paul Schreber] a first experience with death of a close family member" (p. 97). The salient facts in the history of Moritz are a ladder accident he suffered in 1851, at age 43, when Paul was 9 years old, and his untimely death when Paul was 19. The accident caused head trauma and the sequelae were headaches and depressions that changed Moritz Schreber's personality and life. It deeply affected the whole family. Fifty-four years after the event Paul (1905) remembered the effects on his mother and himself in a poem written in celebration of her 90th birthday:

> But then suddenly the sky darkened
> Long drawn out illness gnawed at your husband;
> From then on it threw deep shadows on life's path,
> At the same time being a test of your love.
> What you suffered and did without in those days—
> The world was avoided, even in the house there were
> off-limits areas—
> Truly, no one else need say it,
> You yourself often linger there in your thoughts.
> And finally, just when you were allowed to hope,

Recovery, as the reward for sacrifice, seemed to beckon,
Then you were hit the hardest:
You saw him suddenly swallowed up in an early grave.
[D. P. Schreber, 1905; lines 280-292 in Israëls, 1988]

Are the words "you yourself" directed at mother only, or do they refer to Paul's own thoughts?

In Schreber's hospital chart there is a notation by an unknown psychiatrist that has been quoted repeatedly: "The father (originator of the Schreber gardens in Leipzig) suffered from obsessive ideas of murderous impulses" (see Appendix).[3] This description of such ruminations fits a person suffering from depression. Depressions run like a crimson thread among the Schrebers.[4]

The story of Moritz Schreber is told in chapter 3. In that story one fact towers above all the others: in Paul's lifetime the father was recognized as an authority in medicine and education and revered as a celebrity in Leipzig. He must have influenced his son by virtue of this recognition and also by the ideas in his writings.

Mother

Pauline Schreber was the daughter of Juliana Emilie née Wenck (1789-1841) and Leipzig professor of medicine and pharmacology Wilhelm Andreas Haase (1784-1837), son of Johann Gottlob Haase, professor of anatomy and surgery at Leipzig University School of Medicine. University professors and scholars were both on her mother's and father's sides, the Haases and the Wencks,[5] "connected through blood relations or friendship with the most distinguished families of her homeland" (Hartung, 1907, p. 2). Her maternal grandfather was Friedrich August Wilhelm Wenck (1741-1810), professor and judge with the rank of Royal Saxon Court and Justice Councillor. Her father died in 1837, her mother in 1841.

In the initial phases of his second illness (1893) Paul spends time with his mother (*M*, p. 39). "In the last two weeks before Christmas I spent part of every day at my mother's house" (p. 43). In his stream of consciousness he names his "mother, wife and father-in-law" (p. 51), and mentions mother once again upon his temporary transfer to Pierson's hospital (p. 103), a time of great stress.

She will not be heard from until shortly before Paul's release from the asylum in 1902. What was the contact between mother and son all these years? We do not know. We read in Weber's last report that "mother and sister took up residence in Wehlen nearby [near Sonnenstein], as planned and arranged by President Schreber himself" (*M*, p. 464). After his discharge Paul went to stay with his mother.

The great influence Pauline Schreber had on her son has not yet been fully acknowledged. She was not taken into account by Freud. I regard her as a matriarch of towering strength. She lived 92 years, happy at first and full of sorrows later. Married at 23, a widow at 46, she lived through many losses (among which were the suicide of her firstborn son, the illnesses of the second, and the death of her son-in-law Theodor Krause a year before her own death) and endured "cloudy, troubled days of existence, poor in joys, rich in pain and sorrows" (D. P. Schreber, 1905; lines 12–13). She gave support and solace to her husband during his bouts with illness. She helped Moritz in the publication of his books but as the housewife remained in her husband's shadow; after his death she participated actively in the "Schreber movement" (Schilling, 1960). More importantly, following Moritz Schreber's death she held the family together. As a woman of intellect, esthetic sensibility, and high moral standards, she was a tremendous inspiration to all her children, especially to her firstborn daughter, Anna, and to her second son, Paul. The profound identification between mother and son, or a very special bond, is also suggested by their names: Pauline and Paul.[6]

In that poem of 1905 son Paul remembers his parents' marriage:

> You were bound to each other in love and faithfulness,
> Together you bore every happiness and sorrow;
> If ever two hearts had found each other,
> Then yours did, for all time and eternity.
> Alas, that only modest duration of untroubled
> Marital happiness was granted this union!
> [D. P. Schreber (1905), lines 177–182 in Israëls, 1988].

Paul's daughter (adopted after his release from the hospital in 1902) remembered her as a person who had suffered from depressions.[7]

The Atmosphere in the Schreber Household

The first nine years of Paul's life, until 1851, may have been the happiest period of the Schreber's family life. When Paul was four years old, his second sister, Sidonie, was born and when he was six years old, the last Schreber child, sister Klara, was born. During those years, Moritz Schreber was active as director of his Orthopedic Institute and a founding member of the Leipzig Turnverein.

In the few sources that have come down to us, the emphasis is on the father and little about the mother.[8] As noted earlier, in those days mother stood in the shadow of the father. An important source is "*Interesting Reports by the Daughters of Dr. Schreber about Their Father*," recorded by Siegel (1909) in the periodical *Freund der Schreber-Vereine*,[9] henceforth abbreviated as *"Interesting Reports."*

In this report the atmosphere in the home was described by the daughters as a children's "paradise that was destroyed" by the death of the father. Moritz Schreber's own childhood and youth were happy ones, and therefore "as reflected in his writings (especially *The Book of Child Rearing*) [a later edition of the Kallipädie], he regarded 'the intimacy of family life as something sacred,' and life in the family, this 'thinking and acting with each other and for each other 'has always been the joy of his life" (*Interesting Reports*,[10] p. 11). Thus:

> Every free moment he could allow himself, he gave to his family. Before dinner, he would sometimes play pool for an hour at the 'Harmonie' club [at the Kramerstrasse, not far from Schreber's house at 10 Zeitzerstrasse; Schilling, 1960], spending the rest of the evening in the family circle. . . . Our father led a clean, strict and strong life, as the core of health and vital energy. Movement in clean open air, bathing, swimming and other kinds of athletics were for him a life requirement. . . . He hated comfort and called it softening [*Verweichlichung*] of the body. . . . Our father never let himself go and exercised strong self-discipline and self-control in the face of physical and mental temptations [p. 11].

This word *softening* has the additional connotations of delicacy, weakness, and effeminacy. Moritz Schreber both lived this idea and promulgated it as an educational principle. His son cultivated feminine feelings as a cure for his illness.

The Schreber daughters reminisced about their family life:

> Father advocated "bodily health before everything else, because it is a precondition of the health of the soul," and in our upbringing he was guided by this principle. He exercised with us and in the winter, at dusk, he practiced indoor gymnastics with us . . . he regretted that public bathing was not allowed in those days to women. However, he taught us skating; very often the whole family went skating . . . He was simple in matters of food and clothing. For health reasons, no meat was served, at least once a week, at the mid-day meal and usually none evenings, except Sundays and holidays. . . as prizes for good achievements, exams etc we never received sweets, at most a beautiful toy [pp. 12-13].

The children were encouraged to participate in household chores, in order to learn to respect the work of the servants. Both parents taught them charity towards the less fortunate in life, and this was practiced. But play was also important.

In every way he encouraged our playing and romping in our big yard and garden; with the boarders of the Orthopedic Institute we were altogether about ten to twelve children. He was for the gaiety of youth and encouraged our cheerfulness and liveliness, as long as it remained within proper limits. In the garden every boarder was allotted a bed to plant and cultivate as he liked it; we were also encouraged to join in gardening projects. In the course of frequent joint walks he drew our attention to nature. . . . During holiday trips we had to walk a lot [p. 12].

Consistency in child rearing and truthfulness were especially important to Moritz Schreber:

As father and as concerned with the upbringing of the children he was always kind in spite of his strictness. It was easy for us to obey him because he was "truthful, consistent, and abiding in his love." What father bade and forbade stood firm, things were not once forbidden, once allowed. For example, once during cherry season we were allowed to pick our own cherries for the evening meal such that the three oldest siblings climbed the trees and we two youngest sisters were allowed to eat the allotted number of thirty cherries, even though nobody counted the numbers. When we let ourselves eat the thirty-first cherry, we were already tasting "bad conscience." Lies were punished severely, including so-called society lies, which our parents never practised [p. 12]

Father taught the children to see no evil and to speak no evil, and always stick together. An important trait of the father was practising stoicism and contentedness and a belief in God's love for mankind. "He often admonished us: 'Be contented, always of good cheer! Do not look up above yourselves to those blessed with happiness but to those down, below yourselves! Be virtuous and strong in God!'" (*Interesting Reports*, p. 12).

The daughter offered the following tribute to their father:

In this way, in faithfully following his own hygienic (i.e., preventive) and ethical principle: "Live moderately, calmly and contentedly! Fight for full dominion over yourself!", and in his trust in God, our beloved father gave us a live example of his "art of living," that is the art of living a right and happy life [p. 12].

The deep ethical religiosity is in evidence in the family ethos. The mother was eulogized as a "devout Christian." The father would not have been a devout churchgoer but a person imbued with an ethical and spiritual kind of religiosity. All this may have had an effect on Paul's own religious sentiments.

The year 1851, Paul's ninth year, was an important watershed in his life; that year the father suffered his head injury. The incident not only changed Moritz Schreber's life but for the next ten years, until his death, cast a shadow on the life of the family.

The family is immortalized that year in an oil portrait by August Richter.[11] It may well have been a moment frozen in time before the ladder accident. The painting shows the parents and their five children in a pose that may strike some as romanticized or idealized; yet there is something paintings and drawings project that is beyond what is captured in a photographic reproduction.

The composition of the painting shows the parents seated, Pauline on the left and Moritz on the right of the canvas, with four of the children standing to the sides and in between them, so that each parent is flanked by a child on both sides. The eldest girl, Anna, is on her mother's right; the youngest, Klara, is to the father's left. To the right of the father is the firstborn, Gustav, and to his right Sidonie. Paul is standing above the group, which forms a pyramid, or an isosceles triangle, of which Paul's head is the apex. The left side of the triangle is formed by the heads of Anna, Pauline and Paul, the right side, by the heads of Klara, Moritz and Paul. Thus the impression is created, at least spatially but maybe also spiritually, of a closeness between Pauline, Anna and Paul. The deep brooding expression on Paul's face is striking compared with the open simplicity of the elder son. Anna looks serious and self-possessed.

Striking also is the closeness between Pauline and Anna. We will follow Anna through her long life, long like her mother's, and in her regal and matriarchal splendor in the midst of her children and grand-children down to the fourth generation.

Both parents look serene in this painting. Moritz is 43 years old, his wife 36. Both parents appear to be in excellent health and both look youthful and vigorous. She will live to be 92 and he will be dead ten years after the painting, at the end of a decade marked by intermittent depressions and gastrointestinal disorders. In photographs taken after 1851 Moritz Schreber's face looks much older, showing the wear and tear of life and the ravages of suffering.

As a result of the ladder accident, Moritz Schreber underwent what Ellenberger (1964) called a "creative illness," amounting to a change of character and a change of career: his interests shifted from orthopedics to orthopediatrics and, to some degree, to orthopsychiatry, that is, child rearing and education. For the last ten years of his life, while Paul was between nine and nineteen, Moritz devoted most of his creative efforts to writing and speaking on these subjects. Moreover, as Moritz became more reclusive in the house due to his headaches his wife was "the only person whose presence he could stand" (Schilling, 1960).

This implies that the children were excluded from his presence. His wife became the dominant person in the Schreber household.

In 1909 the Schreber daughters remembered:

> He [our father] discussed everything with mother; she took part in all his ideas, plans and projects, she also read the galleys during the publication of his writings. And after a ladder fell on the head of our beloved father, as a result of which his year-long chronic head illness would often banish him for half-a-day at a time into painful quiet and loneliness, his wife stood by him in these dark hours as a devoted mate. . . . He bore his severe head malady with patience and manly composure, remaining friendly and never cranky, and even comforting the wife who took great pains to look after the sick man: 'We must leave everything to God. The sun of mercy will yet shine upon us.' He kept up this 'God-oriented' spirit ('*gottwärts' gerichteten Sinn*) all his life; and this was the wellspring of his calm, constancy, assurance, contentedness, and quiet joy [*Interesting Reports*, pp. 11, 12].

Moritz Schreber died suddenly of an acute intestinal illness in 1861.

The years 1851 through 1861, Paul's years from nine to nineteen, were the time of his puberty and adolescence. As with the previous period of his childhood, there is no direct evidence of the nature of Paul's relationship to his parents or to his brother and sisters.

There are some documents about Paul's and his elder brother, Gustav's, high school and university education. Between 1853 and 1855 Paul was a student at the Leipzig high school of sciences and then transferred to the famed *Thomasschule*. He graduated from the latter in 1860 with "honors grades in science, being fourth at the top of the list" and was among those who received an excellent grade for conduct (Schreiber, 1987, p. 159).

From 1860 to 1863 Paul studied law at Leipzig University. The dean of the law faculty was Law Professor Carl Joseph Georg Sigismund von Wächter (1797-1880),[12] who appears as a departed soul "Dr. Wächter" in Paul's stream of consciousness in the *Memoirs* (p. 50). There Paul also mentions his activity in the various student societies: he himself was a member of one of them—*Burschenschaft Wartburg*.[13] It later changed its name to *Germania*. Later Paul became an honorary member (Israëls, 1989, pp. 133, 136).

Students often engaged in brawls and duels. But more than brawling and beer drinking, the students participated in political debate and action. Paul gained prominence early on as a serious student who was socially active and identified with pro-Prussian and pro-Bismarck attitudes and politics.

An interesting glimpse into the mores of students is offered by a history of the aforementioned student organizations. Paul Schreber was very active in his *Burschenschaft* in a number of committees, and excelled as a mediator and speaker. The students met during so-called *Kneipabende* (pub evenings) during which scientific, economic, political, legal, patriotic, philosophical, and moral issues, in an atmosphere of "high-minded conviviality," were pursued in a lively spirit of debate. They discussed the various interpretations of the principle of morality (*Sittlichkeitsprincip*), which also included the principle of chastity (*Keuschheitsprincip*) (Hirschfeld and Franke, 1879), which probably meant abstaining from premarital sex and prostitutes. Moritz Schreber would have approved.

According to reminiscences of one of the members of the Wartburg, Hans Blum (who was a law student at the time), Paul and other students were avid followers of the pro-Prussian professor of history von Treitschke. Blum and Paul collaborated on the statutes of the society (Israëls, 1989, p. 134-135). In 1862 they disagreed about students participating in festivities to honor the Saxon king's visit in Leipzig: Paul was in favor of complying and his group lost to the opposition led by Blum. (Hans Blum was the son of the ill-fated left-wing politician Robert Blum, mentioned in history books, who was the bearer of a congratulatory message from the National Assembly to the Viennese during their uprising and was executed in Vienna in 1849 on charges of high treason).

Hans Blum's career was in some respects similar to Paul's: he also obtained a doctoral law degree and served in France in the Franco-Prussian war. Later he became active as contributor to a number of well-known newspapers, among them the *Gartenlaube,* where Moritz Schreber's article (1860a) was first published. From 1867 to 1870 he was the representative of the 15th Saxon electoral district in the German *Reichstag,* and from 1875 to 1878 a city councillor in Leipzig. Blum also wrote a number of historical books, among which were the story of his father (*Robert Blum, Ein Zeit und Charakterbild für das deutsche Volk,* 1878) and *Die Lügen unserer Socialdemokratie* ("The Lies of Our Social Democrats," 1891). His younger sister Ida Blum was also an author (*Das litterarische Leipzig,* 1897, pp. 79-80).

On December 2, 1863, Paul took the first bar examination and passed it with honors, "Censur: ausgezeichnet,- I" (Devreese, 1981a, p. 20).[14] He was at the top of the list of the 19 candidates examined (Busse, 1990, p. 19). That same year he became an intern in the firm of the Leipzig lawyer Moritz Hennig.

Brother

In the *Memoirs* Paul does not say that his brother Gustav was three years older than himself. Neither does he mention his brother's career choice or his suicide (in 1877). It may be assumed that the suicide of this older brother by gunshot,[15] one year before Paul's marriage, played an important role in Paul's life. Paul may be referring to this fact by indirection and by means of displacement in the *Memoirs* when he writes that he "had visions according to which Professor Flechsig had shot himself either in Weissenburg in Alsace or in the police station in Leipzig" (p. 82). Many times, early on in his illness, Paul "wished to put a bullet through [his] head or chest" (p. 290). He also remembers a "cousin of [his] wife who had shot himself early in 1887" (p. 105); this cousin has not been identified.

We have scant information about Gustav from other sources.[16] He was born on July 27, 1839 and received his high school diploma from the *Thomasschule* in 1857, with the grades "imprimis digni" in science and "raro" for conduct, apparently not as high as his brother's. At first he studied in Leipzig under teachers such as Weber in anatomy and Erdmann in chemistry. He then transferred to the University of Heidelberg and later to Göttingen, where he studied under the world-famous professor Wöhler (who was the first to synthesize an organic compound, urea, in the laboratory), finally returning to his native Leipzig to study organic and practical chemistry under Erdmann. In Göttingen he was a member of the Hildeso-Guestphalia student organization (Schreiber, 1987, pp. 158-159). At the ripe age of 22, upon the death of his father in 1861, he became the male head of the Schreber family.

By 1866, the year of Austria's defeat by Prussia in the historic battle of Königgrätz and the first step toward the unification of Germany under Bismarck, he was an owner of a chemical factory in Leipzig and pro-Prussian in his politics, at a time when Saxony was pro-Austrian. By 1869 he was following in the footsteps of his younger brother Paul: he studied law, graduated with the highest grade and rose to the rank of appeals judge (*Apellationgerichtsrath*).[17] He may have been, like his brother, called to the *Reichsjustizamt*, the Supreme Legislative Court of the German Empire, in Berlin to work on the unification of the laws of the Empire. The brothers shared a lot in common: not only Gustav's final choice of career but also their pro-Bismarck views (Israëls, 1989, pp. 146-147).

Gustav was involved in a campaign to promote *Der Hausfreund*, his father's book on education, a popularized version of the *Kallipädie* published in 1861, which Moritz Schreber sent to all the German states for cost-free distribution by secular and religious bodies (Israëls, 1989, p. 122). A year after his father's death Gustav wrote about the matter in response to a letter from the Ministry of Coburg.[18] Toward the end of his stay at Sonnenstein, Paul also worked on legal arrangements with publishers concerning his father's books. In addition to the choice of career by Gustav, these facts suggest that the brothers may have shared more interests with their father than we shall ever know of.

On May 7, 1877, Gustav wrote a postcard to his mother from the Saxon city of Bautzen, where he worked as judge:

Dear Mother! I assume the contemplated party [which can refer to a *Heiratspartie*, a marriage match, or to a *Lustpartie*, a fun party] has been dropped, with which I am in full agreement, and will therefore journey to Leipzig Wednesday evening. As I will probably arrive at night, please send me the keys to the house. With best wishes, your G.

We are in the dark about the exact reference of *"Partie,"* but the sentence construction supports the hypothesis that the reference is to marriage.[19] Why else would he need to say he is in full agreement, and why would it follow he had to see mother in Leipzig?[20] He never got to Leipzig. An obituary notice in the *Chemnitzer Tageblatt* read: "Bautzen. On May 7 the recently appointed appeal judge at the district court, Dr. Schr., put an end to his own life by a shot through the head. It is to be assumed that a strong tendency to melancholy is the cause of the sad event."[21] He never married, there were no children. The body was later brought for burial in Leipzig.[22]

Niederland also found a notation about the suicide in the *Stadtarchiv* of Bautzen: "Schreber. Daniel Gustav, Doctor of Law,[23] Royal Judge in Bautzen, according to the register of St. Peter's, Bautzen, died on May 8, in the morning, 38 years old, unmarried. Suicide by gunshot" (Niederland, 1974, p. 97). Niederland was impressed with Paul Schreber's identification with this event as alluded to in the *Memoirs*: "I recollect that in the middle of March 1894 when communication with supernatural powers was well underway, a newspaper was put in front of me in which something like my own obituary notice could be read" (*M*, p. 81). Later he refers to *Selbstmord* and *Entleibung* (*M*, p. 177), both words meaning suicide, of which the latter is used in the aforementioned St. Peter's church records.

In Paul Schreber's hospital chart there is a notation about "one brother paralytic [paretic, i.e., a sufferer from tertiary syphilis], committed suicide" (see Appendix). In a letter to the Sonnenstein administration in 1900 one of the sisters wrote: "The developing psychosis of our dear eldest brother had already been recognized at that time, but that the doctor, who had already thought of placing him in an asylum, did not consider the poor man to be ill enough" (Baumeyer, 1956, p. 68). According to another opinion, Gustav "committed suicide because he was afraid to become psychotic."[24] Might the condition alluded to in these comments have also caused the abandonment of the *"Partie"*?

Gustav's suicide cast a shadow on both his mother[25] and brother. Sometime during the year he got married, 1878, Paul suffered from a bout of hypochondria, known to be a manifestation of depression. Was this guilt about survival and success where his brother failed?

Gustav's paresis, whose mental manifestations may be diverse, running the gamut from depression to elation and including hallucinations and delusions, is a more complex issue. As today with the threat of AIDS, sexual promiscuity in those days carried the risk of venereal infection, mostly gonorrhea or syphilis, the latter in those days classified as a lust plague (*Lustseuche*) and also nicknamed the new plague (Liebreich, 1900). In the *Memoirs* there are both indirect and direct references to syphilis ("syphilitic epidemic" p. 74) and to unbridled sexual gratification. In another place Schreber feels that "the inner table of my skull was lined with a different brain membrane" (*M*, p. 95), a possible allusion to disease in the brain membranes in tertiary syphilis. During his first admission Paul Schreber himself "was given pot[assium] iod[ide] since syphilis was suspected" (Appendix). A "dissolute life" (p. 95) and sexual promiscuity (or "excesses", as they are referred to in the *Memoirs*) in those days involved servants and brothels (which were outlawed in the late 1880s), i.e., situations at high risk for sexually transmitted diseases.[26] Of the two brothers, Paul as a bachelor stayed in Leipzig, close to the parental home, while as a student Gustav lived away from home in other cities, an arrangement conducive to promiscuity. However, the details of the sexual habits of the Schreber brothers remain a mystery.

There are no documents about the relationship of the brothers. I believe Paul experienced his brother's suicide as a major trauma, both as a personal loss and as a reminder of the problems and conflicts about life and sex he may have shared with him, or his own. There is reason to suspect a measure of identification with Gustav's alleged syphilis and mental symptoms.

Sisters

Of the three sisters—Anna, Klara and Sidonie—Anna is clearly the most impressive. Paul was apparently the match-maker between Klara and his colleague Theodor Krause, who like Paul, was *Landgerichtsdirector* in Chemnitz. Krause died in his retirement in Leipzig on July 4, 1906, eleven years before his wife. Their marriage was childless (Friedrich, 1932). Sidonie never married and kept her mother company until her death in 1907; Sidonie died in 1924. Sidonie was the last bearer of the name Schreber and the sister who visited Paul at Sonnenstein. Klara corresponded with Weber (Israëls, 1989, p. 180).

Sister Anna grew up to resemble her mother. When she was born, it was said "for one hundred years there has been no Mamsel Schreber" (Friedrich, 1932). Like her mother, Anna had longevity, dying at age 104, and raised five children (the firstborn only lived three years, from 1865 to 1868). Anna was the other matriarch of the family, for many years presiding at family gatherings. More devout than her mother, of reformed Lutheran-Evangelical confession, she created a strong spiritual presence and remained lucid till her dying day.

Anna Jung née Schreber was interviewed by reporters on her 98th, 99th, and 100th birthdays.[27] The interviewers were impressed with her physical appearance. She was thin and frail (for years she suffered from stomach symptoms) but held herself erect. She had no fear of the cold. She was somewhat hard of hearing but her eyesight was still excellent for she was able to read without glasses. Her letters show a strong and steady hand. She was quoted as saying, "It is not easy to get old, but it can be beautiful." All her life she had kept very busy with crafts, correspondence, and charitable work.

The reporters were also impressed with her memory, her alertness, and her penchant for aphorisms. Her inspiration came from the Bible, pietistic and mystical authors, such as Count Zinzendorf, church fathers like Augustine, and spiritual-mystical writers like Thomas à Kempis.[28] She was seen as possessed of inner purity, an embodiment of the philosophy and attitudes of her father Moritz. The reporters quoted her as saying: "It is only in the last years of his life that I correctly grasped the ideas of my father and realized his greatness. . . . This was a great loss for me."

Anna's strong spiritual qualities, which I believe came from both parents, shine in the many surviving letters to different members of the family.[29] This family spirit, characterized by a nobility of bearing, an essential and unaffected truthfulness, and an adherence to ethical principles, as well as a measure of reserve, impressed me in all the descendants I have personally interviewed. I see these family qualities as confirming the self-description of Paul Schreber.

In 1864 Anna married Carl Ferdinand Jung (1839-1912), who was one of Paul's character witnesses in his case at appeals and may have played an important role in Paul's fate. After Moritz Schreber's death in the years of Pauline's widowhood, Carl Jung, as the husband of the oldest daughter, may have assumed the role of the family patriarch and reinforced the aloofness the family maintained toward the hospitalized Paul.

Carl Ferdinand Jung, a scion of a family that included merchants and physicians, inherited a soap and perfume factory, Friedrich Jung and Company, from his father and amassed a sizable fortune. He was remembered by his grandson as an imposing presence, a kindly, lively and jovial elderly gentleman, who wore huntsman's garb, smoked cigars, and enjoyed the game of skittles. In contrast to the proverbial easygoing lifestyle of the Saxons, Carl Jung presided over a household ruled by order and discipline. He was good-humoredly tolerant of his wife's devout practices. He did not suffer loiterers gladly and would react to them with irascibility, in contrast to his usual joviality. He sold his factory early on, as he did not trust any of his children with money.[30] His son Carl Friedrich (Fritz) Jung appeared to Schreber as a vision, "my nephew Fritz" (M, p. 106). Carl Jung died one year after Paul.

As recalled by Renate Jung (1989), Anna Jung never brought up the subject of her brother Paul. According to Brigitte Wienstein (1989), Carl Jung out of concern for his reputation as merchant insisted on the deletion of the famous Third Chapter from the Memoirs and was also behind the effort to buy up and destroy the printed copies.

SECOND PERIOD: 1864-1885

In the second period of Paul Schreber's life two major developments took place: the flowering of his career and his marriage. In June of 1865 Paul took the Richtereid, or judicial oath. Thus began a long, steady, and distinguished legal career.

In 1865 Schreber began work in the Landesgericht (district court) of the provincial city of Chemnitz, passing through the junior grades (Hilfsaktuar, Referendar, Assessor) and in 1867 he became a public servant in the employ of the Ministry of Justice. By 1869 he obtained his doctorate in law and in 1870 passed his second state bar examination. From 1870 through 1877 he was assigned to a number of judicial posts in various courts in Leipzig.

During the Franco-Prussian War of 1871 Paul worked as judge in Strasbourg. References are made to Alsace in the Memoirs (pp. 82, 85). In September of 1872 he returned to Leipzig, living in his mother's house. In 1878-1879 he was summoned to work on the laws of the Empire at the Reichsjustizamt in Berlin.

For some time, Paul's adult life was intertwined with that of his older brother, Gustav. In 1872 both brothers and the two younger sisters lived in Leipzig with their mother, while Anna and her family lived nearby (Israëls, 1989, pp. 148-149). After a stint in the court in Zwickau (Paul Flechsig's birthplace), Gustav returned to Leipzig in 1874 and again lived with Paul at their mother's. In 1877 Gustav moved to Bautzen, some 30 miles east of Dresden, where he ended his life.

In 1879 Paul was appointed to the position of *Landgerichtsdirector*, that is, administrator and judge presiding over a three judge panel of the First Civil Chamber in the district court of Chemnitz. This was an intermediate level court, above a county court, for trials and appeals having to do with financial and property issues (*Verwaltung des Landgerichts Chemnitz*, 1881). He stayed in Chemnitz until his first illness (Devreese, 1981a, p. 22). One year prior to the move and and the year following his brother's suicide he married Ottilie Sabine Behr. It must have been a rough time, for, as mentioned earlier, "at the time of his marriage in 1878 [the patient] expressed hypochondriacal ideas" (Appendix).

The Marriage

We know nothing about how Sabine and Paul met, how they fell in love, and why they chose each other. They may have met in Leipzig—after Sabine's father, Heinrich Behr, moved to that city in 1875 (Peters, 1990)—or in Berlin. When they married on February 6 of 1878, one year after Gustav's suicide, Sabine was 21 and Schreber 36. Apparently, in the family tradition, the marriage was seen as a mésalliance, "*nicht Standesgemäss*" (Renate Jung, 1989). Theater people might have been seen in those days as beneath the status of doctors, judges, and professors. But this may not have been the opinion of the Behrs.

We do not know if the Behrs were against the union. According to poems seen by Busse (1990, pp. 23-24) that Paul wrote to her, Sabine left the parental home some months before the marriage ceremony, which may mean that she and Schreber lived together as an unmarried couple.

The marriage remained childless after "six fetuses born dead or miscarriages" (Baumeyer, 1970). We will recall this fact in connection with the background of the second illness. Two of the miscarriages occurred before the first illness, and the exact month of their occurrence or their precise causes remain unknown. We know nothing about the nature of the sexual relations between the spouses. We do have a statement from Schreber about his attitude toward sex. "Few people have been brought up according to such strict moral principles as I, and have throughout life practised such moderation [*Zurückhaltung*, reserve] especially in matters of sex, as I venture to claim for myself" (*M*, p. 208). If we take this statement at face value, it would suggest that Schreber remained celibate until his marriage. Such an assumption might also be in consonance with the ideas of Schreber's father on the sanctity of marriage and of the importance of male continence. We shall return later to the possible role of such attitudes in the genesis of Schreber's conflicts about sexuality.

An interesting glimpse into the marriage is offered in the reminiscences of the adoptive daughter (Niederland, 1969).[31] The daughter remembered that the adoptive father "loved his wife a great deal, the marriage was good and harmonious. There was occasional bickering, but no big fights." She described her adoptive mother, "as a diabetic (*Zuckerkranke*) [who] was often irritated and angry" (Niederland, 1969).[32] It is suggested by Paul's statements in the *Memoirs* that she did not have a higher education. The photograph of the youthful Sabine shows a somewhat plump girl with a pretty face and a sweet smile.[33] She looks less refined than her husband or the other Schreber offspring or the brother-in-law. In later photographs she shows signs of overweight.

Wife

Ottilie Sabine Behr was the third child of Heinrich Behr, born on June 19, 1857, and preceded in birth by Heinrich Behr, junior (1859-1897) and sister Albertine, and followed by Therese Emilie (1876-1959).[34] Sabine's attention to the latter competed with Schreber's interests in 1902: Sabine put off her husband's journey from Sonnenstein to his mother because she herself had to travel "to Vienna for the confinement of her youngest sister" (Baumeyer, 1956, p. 68).

Sabine is the most frequently mentioned relative in the *Memoirs*, though not by name. She was the most important next of kin. Besides his career, Schreber's relationship with his wife was the most important issue in his life. His book was written so that his wife, and others close to him, would get "an approximate idea at least of my religious conceptions, . . . some understanding of the necessity which forces me to various oddities of behavior" (*M*, p. 1).

In connection with Paul's recovery from his first illness, Sabine "felt even more sincere gratitude and worshipped Professor Flechsig as the man who had restored her husband to her; for this reason she kept his picture on her desk for many years" (*M*, p. 36). Like the mother, she played an important role in the initial phase of the second illness, during Paul's stay at Flechsig's hospital. Paul's deep love for and dependence on Sabine lasted throughout his life. But the relation between the spouses was not always happy and harmonious: money conflicts were present and Paul felt that he did not get back the interest on the emotional capital he had invested in Sabine.

Independent confirmation of marital tensions came from Sabine's correspondence with the Sonnenstein administration, as documented by Baumeyer (1956). Baumeyer was impressed with "her primitive, almost childish writing," noting that

> her attitude toward her husband who had become psychotic is one of helpless anxiety. In many letters she inquires about his condition but puts off her announced visits, often referring to external reasons. When her father [who died in Leipzig in 1897] fell ill she wrote: "My heart is drawn to my dear husband and yet is restrained by the love and duty of a child" [p. 68].

While Sabine was torn by these emotions, her husband may have felt that his father-in-law was coming between him and his wife. We also read in Sabine's letter that "Professor Flechsig, who treated me, forbade me, at my father's request, to spend too much time with the patient [i.e., Paul]" (Baumeyer, 1956, p. 68).

Sabine was a sickly woman.[35] Her main illness was diabetes, but it cannot be precisely dated. In 1901 she suffered from chorioretinitis. In a letter Schreber's sister referred to "her usual ailments . . . at present aggravated by the effects of influenza" (Baumeyer, 1956, p. 68). Her miscarriages could have also been complicated by emotional conflicts. From her letters it also appears, although the period is not clearly specified, that there was marital discord and threats of divorce were often heard by Sabine. Thus, when Sabine hesitated in 1901 about her husband coming home from Sonnenstein for a trial of leave from the hospital, "her husband has threatened her, 'If you will not agree, I shall sue for divorce'. She adds to this, 'How often I have had to yield to this threat!' " (Baumeyer, 1956, p. 68).

Sabine's Family

In his *Memoirs* Schreber mentions three events that were instrumental in his recovery from the acute psychosis by making him doubt the reality of his dream experiences and reaffirming his belief in the reality of the world as it exists. One of these events was "a letter from my sister-in-law in Cologne on the Rhine addressed to [him] and bearing the postmark of Cologne" (*M*, p. 202). This must have been Sabine's sister Albertine, married to Dr. Rückel, an appeals judge in the Superior Court in Cologne, a highranking judge like Schreber himself.[36]

Father-in-Law

Heinrich Eucharius Behr, Sabine's father, is mentioned by Schreber in his very first footnote of the *Memoirs* as a fleeting phantom, perhaps indicating by this the importance of the role Behr played during his second hospitalization. Later Behr played a part in the fateful sequence of February 15, 1894, when Sabine traveled to her father in Berlin for four days, precipitating a deterioration in her husband's mental state. Thus Schreber may have perceived an important bond between daughter and father and may have been affected by it. Later still, he once "saw" Behr "on the drive leading to the Asylum" and Schreber explains: "About that time I also had a number of his nerves in my body and from their behavior in conversation by way of nerve-contact I clearly recognized my father-in-law's nature [*Sinnesart*, also way of thinking and feeling]" (*M*, p. 107). What were they conversing about in his head? What influences and identifications with his father-in-law is he hinting at? What possible conflicts of interest?

Heinrich Behr was born on June 2, 1821, in Rostock and died on March 13, 1897 in Leipzig, having lived there since his retirement in 1875. This means that from that point on he was in the same city as Schreber and near the scene of his daughter's marriage in 1878 and his son-in-law's first two illnesses and hospitalizations.[37] A photograph shows him as a man of patriarchal and dominant bearing, balding and with a long beard. He married Ottilie Benedix (1828-1893), the sister of the then-famous playwright Roderich Benedix (1811-1873), author of some 100 plays. The death of Sabine's mother in 1893, the year Paul became depressed again, and the death of both her father and brother in 1897, should be seen as additional life events that added more stress to the Schrebers.

At first intending to become a sculptor, Behr later decided in favor of singing, and after studying with the then-famous Eduard Mantius and Theodor Teschner in Berlin, he became a basso. In 1841 he joined the Berlin Court Opera on the recommendation of Meyerbeer and Felix Mendelssohn-Bartholdy. Five years later, in 1846, he was first basso at the Municipal Theater of Leipzig and two years after that he started a career as artistic director in opera houses in Leipzig, Bremen, Rostock, Rotterdam, Berlin (one month in 1871), and finally, in 1872, in Cologne. He became known for his productions of Wagner's operas, such as "*Die Meistersinger von Nürnberg*" and others.

The huge retributions paid by France to Germany after the Franco-Prussian war contributed to the flowering of the arts. By the time he retired in 1875, Heinrich Behr was a rich man, probably a millionaire. He went to live in Leipzig, became a professor at the Leipzig School of Music, excelled as a drama and opera coach and sang occasionally.

A number of details about Heinrich Behr's attitude toward his son-in-law deserve attention. One has already been noted: his request that his daughter stay away from the patient. We do not know if

Sabine sought her father's support in her disagreements with Paul. Nor do we know the nature of the relations between Paul and his father-in-law. What seems to stand out is the considerable importance of money in the marriage, since Sabine was the daughter of a rich man. This throws new light on the money disputes between the spouses that took place toward the end of Paul's second stay at Flechsig's hospital.

The relative prominence of the family of Sabine Behr is an important fact. Until now, the impression has prevailed that Schreber married a woman from a family much beneath his own in social status. This assumption can no longer be held. While in the 18th century actors and singers were still considered on a par with other servants of the aristocracy, in the 19th century, with the rise in the importance of the professional bourgeoisie, performers were becoming powerful and prominent players on the social scene.

German Society at the Time of the First Illness

Schreber's remarks about the growth of rail and steamship travel hint at the tremendous changes in society as a result of industrialization and the growth of the bourgeoisie. Moritz Schreber's roots were still in the era of transition between the 18th and the 19th centuries. The transformations during his sons' generation are tellingly portrayed by Max Nordau, a German physician of Jewish-Hungarian extraction, born in 1849, who became an author and philosopher. Like Moritz Schreber before him, medical moralist Nordau became a doctor to the new "sick" society and the sick individual in it; he described, diagnosed and dispensed remedies. The disease was degeneration, the title of his best-seller (both in Europe and in the United States), written in 1893.

The 1840s, at the time Moritz Schreber was at the high point of his life, was described by Nordau (1895) as a period that has

> witnessed the irruption of new discoveries in every relation of life, and thus personally experienced those transformations. . . . Its own new discoveries and progress have taken civilized humanity by surprise. . . . The sum of work of civilized humanity has increased during the half-century. . . . It has become a commonplace to speak of the constant increase in crime, madness and suicide. . . . The new nervous diseases . . . [are] states of fatigue and exhaustion [pp. 38-42].

One of the most formidable new transformations, which did not much affect Moritz Schreber but impinged powerfully on the life of his son, was the emergence of German socialism. The struggles for constitutional liberty from 1848 to 1849 were paralleled by the publication of Marx's *Communist Manifesto* of 1848, the growth of the socialists, and the subsequent unification of the factions of Lassalle and Marx in 1875 (*Protokolle*, 1971). Political life in Germany was marked by the struggles between Bismarck and the socialists. After the attempt by a socialist to assassinate the Kaiser, repressive laws against socialists were enacted in 1878, eased in 1881, and repealed in 1890. In his book Paul Schreber identifies only one socialist, the Catholic Canon Mou-fang, but no Jewish socialists. It was socialist Bruno Geiser (mentioned in the *Protokolle*) who played a role in his first illness.

The Story of the First Illness

After the termination of Schreber's legal assignment in Berlin, the newlyweds came to live in the provincial city of Chemnitz, where Paul was appointed *Landgerichtsdirector*, or administrative director, of the district court.[38] In 1864, a year before Schreber arrived for his first stint there, Chemnitz was a city of some 54,827 inhabitants, increasing to 110,808 by 1885 and to 138,954 by 1890 (*Brockhaus Konversations Lexikon*, 14th edition). Its claim to fame was that it was the first industrial city of Saxony, home to a number of industries.[39] With its many textile and appliance factories, Chemnitz was a working-class city and a stronghold of the Social Democratic party.

We do not have an account of what a day in Schreber's life in Chemnitz was like. We can imagine Schreber pursuing, day in and day out, "the strenuous profession of a judge" (Foot Note #36). There were the evenings at home with his wife, all the reading he had to do, and maybe occasional visits to the local theater and concert hall. Attempts to start a family ended in two miscarriages. By this time, his sister Anna had five children.[40]

At some point in the midst of this seemingly unheroic existence, Paul was bitten by the bug of political ambition. He decided to run for election to the *Reichstag* on the ticket of the National Liberal Party. Perhaps he was tired of life in the provinces, or the memories of Berlin were haunting him. Was this a manifestation of the same restless spirit as in the father, who also longed for a spot in the limelight? But was it folly or courage? For the chances of Paul Schreber's winning this election were very slim.

His opponent at the polls was none other than the socialist Bruno Geiser, a newspaper editor from Stuttgart,[41] for many years an active member of the Social-Democratic party and a veteran of many of its congresses (*Protokolle*, 1971). He had won the seat in the 1881 elections and was thus the incumbent in the 16th electoral district of Chemnitz.[42] In an editorial of the local newspaper, *Chemnitzer Tageblatt und Anzeiger*, Schreber was "generally recognized as eminently suited to run [on the combined ticket of the Conservatives and the National Liberals] owing to the honesty of his convictions, vast knowledge in many areas and an unusual talent for oratory."[43] The party was promoting workers' rights, such as health and sick-leave insurance—though more in appearance than in substance, for it was simultaneously supporting the continuation of Bismarck's repressive antisocialist laws as protection against unrest and revolution.[44] Schreber's campaign thus stood against radical socialism. Constituting a symbolic presence in the campaign were the Jewish socialists, the founders Marx and Lassalle, and many lesser-known adherents in Germany. By 1890 there were 953 Jews in Chemnitz, and while we have no knowledge of what they felt about Schreber's candidacy, we know from his remarks in the *Memoirs* something about what Schreber Paul felt about the Jews.[45]

Schreber's party and like-minded citizens promoted him in huge advertisements on the pages of the local newspaper. A second editorial, favoring Paul, was printed on October 26, two days before the election day. All this was to no avail: the socialists won in Chemnitz by a sweep, whereas in most of the surrounding districts the National Liberals, favoring Bismarck's policies both at home and abroad, carried the day.

It was Goliath who won; Schreber may have felt he was defeated by the Jews and the Catholics. In fact, the election was a crushing defeat for him. When the results of the voting were published in the *Chemnitzer Tageblatt* only the figures for the 16th district were omitted. Who decided this omission?[46] The defeat ushered in Schreber's first depressive illness: "I have twice had a nervous illness, each time as a consequence of mental overstrain; the first . . . was occasioned by my candidature for parliament" (*M*, p. 34). Note the mention of life stress, its social and political setting, and the breakdown as a result of an inability to cope with the stress. "The first of the two illnesses commenced in the autumn of 1884 and was fully cured at the end of 1885, so that I was able to resume work . . . on 1st January 1886" (*M*, p. 34). Thus, the first episode lasted for almost a year and a half. He also says that he "was eventually cured (after a prolonged convalescence)" (*M*, p. 35). Other than the terse reference to the candidacy, Schreber does not tell us anything more about the circumstances or the causes of his first illness. Candidacy means he did not get beyond being a candidate, that is, that he lost the election. Paul does not say a word about losing the election; this is noteworthy in itself. Similarly, we are not told what emotional reaction he had to the defeat. He tells nothing about the hopes he had, the dreams he wanted to realize, the possible conflicts or doubts. His reticence suggests a pain that is passed over in silence, a high sensitivity about frustrated ambitions. Is there a connection here to what his father discussed in *Gymnastics,* frustrated high ambition, a disproportion between performance and ability, and the crash of defeat?

Prior to coming to Flechsig Schreber was treated by another physician, Dr. R. in S., later identified as Dr. Richter at the Sonneberg spa (Israëls, 1989, p. 163). I found an advertisement for it: "Hydropathic establishment Sonneberg in Thuringia. A health resort for nervous patients (*Nervenkranke*). Dr. med. Banke, director and owner. Founded by *Sanitätsrath* Dr. Richter" (*CNP* for 1892). Like his father some 25 years earlier, he first traveled to take the waters. We are not told why the waters he took at Sonneberg, a favorite cure for hypochondria and a host of other maladies, and the course of bromides and other tranquilizers prescribed by Dr. Richter—morphine and chloral hydrate—were not effective in curing him of his symptoms, but the threat of suicide may have weighed in the decision to become Flechsig's patient.

Bromides (largely of potassium but also of sodium) were the most frequently used tranquilizers of the day: "in states of nervous hyperirritability due to hard mental work potassium bromide (3.0g) can procure a most pleasant peace of mind" (Nothnagel and Rossbach, 1894). It was a major central nervous system depressant drug (in addition to narcotics), used as a tranquilizer and sedative. As a depressant, it had been used as an antiepileptic medication since 1851. Among its side effects are lowering of sex drive, dryness of mouth, weakness and physical and mental depression, headache, tremors, weakness, transient paralyses, a peculiar unpleasant smell on the breath and a skin rash (Nothnagel and Rossbach, 1894; Liebreich, 1900). It also caused the symptoms of a toxic delirium, such as hallucinations and delusions. It is unclear if Schreber had any of these side effects, but some of his delusional complaints in the *Memoirs*, in the course of his second illness, both at Flechsig's and at Sonnenstein, might be read as suggesting reminiscences about such possible side effects, as for example, "I particularly remember the foul taste and smell which such *impure* souls cause in the body of the person through whose mouth they have entered" (*M*, p. 83).

Due to a suspicion of syphilis, at Sonneberg Schreber was also treated with the antisyphilitic agent potassium iodide, also known for its unpleasant side effects, including "a state of intoxication known as an iodine high, tinnitus, painful sensations, palpitations, even convulsions" (Nothnagel and Rossbach, p. 296). Another disturbing side effect was a condition of a "nasal catarrh, called an iodine catarrh . . . [and] cough causing pain in the chest that could lead to pneumonia and pleuritis" (p. 295), possibly hinted at in Foot Notes #70 and #71. Potassium iodide was also a common medicine for a variety of tumors not due to syphilis, especially in glandular organs. It was also given in asthma and various forms of neuralgia. In the poem written in 1888 (Busse, 1990) Schreber alluded to a mysterious physical ailment, in addition to his mental condition, which may have been treated with potassium iodide.

Schreber's decision to put himself in the hands of Professor Flechsig was a fateful one. We do not know who referred him for further treatment at Flechsig's, but on the day of admission he came accompanied by his wife. This is especially interesting in view of another choice that was available to him, that of the psychiatric hospital for wealthy patients at Thonberg near Leipzig. The name Thonberg is mentioned by Schreber in Foot Note #52.

The Thonberg Asylum was also known in Leipzig as the Güntz Hospital. It was founded in 1836 by Dr. Eduard W. Güntz, taught by Pietro Pisani of Palermo, who was also an inspiration for John Conolly, the father of the no-restraint approach in the treatment of the mentally ill. In 1839 the hospital was moved to a hill in Thonberg, between the rivers Elster and Mulde, half an hour southeast of Leipzig, amidst parks and woods. The place was noted for its beautiful architecture and furnishings. It catered to both neurotic and psychotic patients and had rooms for violent patients. Treatments were individualized and included, "Among others, all manner of conversations in the house, musical and theater performances, lectures and exhibitions, paintings exhibitions, instruction in music and drawing and other crafts" and a host of outdoors activities such as "garden and field work, walks and excursions, carriage and sleigh rides, trips into town with visits to the theater, concerts, museums, and collections" (Lochner, 1891, pp. 318-319). It sounds like an almost ideal milieu therapy setting.[47]

Speculating about future events, it is a moot point how Schreber's life would have progressed had he chosen Thonberg over Flechsig's Asylum for his second hospitalization. He might have recovered there; he might have been better treated by the doctors and staff there than at Flechsig's. Often the success of a treatment depends to quite an extent on the doctor-patient relationship; any number of subtle but momentous interactions may spell the difference between success and failure. Schreber might have been able to stay at Thonberg for as long as he wished, until his recovery, without having to be transferred to Sonnenstein. Instead, both times he chose Flechsig. Compared to Thonberg, Flechsig's asylum was a "dungeon, cells, window gates, straight jackets, hammocks and forever fear of the patients."[48]

The only description Schreber gives of his symptoms during the first illness is the following: "certain hypochondriacal ideas with which I was preoccupied at that time, particularly concern over loss of weight" (*M*, p. 35). We are not told why the possible weight loss was a cause for concern or what disease was feared. But it is a well-known clinical fact that hypochondria is often prima facie an indication of depression. It was also viewed then, as today, as one of the hard-core manifestations of psychosis, which will be the case in his next hospitalization. Here it is important to note that depression, along with the other basic painful emotion, anxiety, is often repressed or masked in the sufferer. To become fully aware of the painful feelings is to face all the other unbearable thoughts and realizations that go with them. Depression and anxiety wear many masks, the so-called depressive and anxiety equivalents.

Schreber reminisced about his first stay at Flechsig's, fourteen years after the event:

> In each case when first I entered the Asylum I had not the faintest idea of an antagonism existing between the Schreber and the Flechsig families. . . . The first illness passed without any occurrences bordering on the supernatural, and while it lasted I had on the whole only favorable impressions of Professor Flechsig's methods of treatment [although] some mistakes were made . . . [and] had at the time no reason to be other than most grateful to Professor Flechsig; I gave this special expression by a subsequent visit and in my opinion an adequate honorarium. My wife felt even more sincere gratitude and worshipped Professor Flechsig as the man who had restored her husband to her; for this reason she kept his picture on her desk for many years [*M*, pp. 35-36].

This honorarium seems to have been a private fee paid on top of the cost of hospitalization.

Already during the first admission Schreber had doubts about Flechsig. Flechsig is accused of telling him

> *white lies* [Schreber's emphasis], which a nerve specialist may perhaps not be able to dispense with altogether in the case of some mental patients . . . [but which are] hardly ever appropriate in my case, for he must have soon realized that in me he was dealing with a human being of high intellect, of uncommon keenness of understanding and acute powers of observation [*M*, p. 35].

Thus, "Professor Flechsig wanted to put down [his] illness solely to poisoning with potassium bromide, for which Dr. R[ichter] in S[onneberg], in whose care I had been before, was to be blamed," for which he still found extenuating circumstances: "perhaps it is unreasonable to expect the Director of a big Asylum with hundreds of patients to concern himself in such detail with the mental state of a single patient" (*M*, p. 35). The other white lie, also excusable, was treating him for syphilis, which Paul did not have, unless it was given for a different reason at Flechsig's.

Schreber knew better, even as intoxication with potassium bromide, or bromism, is known for its aforementioned pharmaco-psychological side effects. For the depression he suffered following the defeat at the polls was not caused by the drug. Flechsig's white lie was maintained with the help of the new piety: the belief in that mind is caused by brain, that all mental illness is brain illness, for which the cure is drugs, not dialogue. This basic discord between the patient and the doctor is going to dog them both from here to the very end.

The excerpts from the hospital chart (Appendix, December 10, 1884, through June 1, 1885), referring to the first illness, are quite sketchy. They are quoted here because they confirm Paul's description of his illness and add a few very significant details.

He was transferred from Sonneberg[49] to Flechsig's psychiatric hospital in Leipzig on December 8, 1884. On admission he was afraid of imminent death due to heart attack. On subsequent days his mood went up and down, with teariness and restlessness. His thoughts were melancholy, he felt incurable. He required potassium bromide and paraldehyde for sleep. At other times he complained of hypersensitivity to the slightest noise, asked to be carried as he was too weak to walk, asked to be photographed repeatedly, suspected his wife would be sent away never to return. It is striking that even though Flechsig felt Schreber had been overmedicated with bromides by the previous physician, he continued to prescribe bromides, which were now combined with paraldehyde.

The suspicion of syphilis in Schreber is an interesting issue, since, as noted in connection with Gustav, a number of Paul's hypochondriacal complaints are consistent with the fears of a person suspecting he might be harboring the deadly disease. In those days, even before the discovery of the treponema pallidum (in 1905 by Schaudinn and demonstrated in the brain of general paralytics only by 1913), it was erroneously believed that syphilis could be transmitted to the fetus by the infected sperm of the father alone (Liebreich, 1896-1900, vol. 3, p. 756). However, if indeed the Schreber fetuses were stillborn due to syphilis, it would have to be caused by syphilis in the wife, and she could have been infected by another man.

On the last day of his stay he "imagined" he lost 30-40 pounds, when in fact he gained 2kg, and insisted he was being deceived on purpose. Earlier it was noted that he ate a lot. That day he left the hospital for convalescence in Ilmenau, also in Thuringia.

The striking difference between the self-description and the hospital chart is the prominence of the mood disorder, with lability of mood, with clinically evident anxiety and depression, agitation, disturbed sleep, a history of two suicidal attempts prior to admission to Flechsig's and one in the course of his stay there. There is a mild paranoid flavor. The significant precipitating factor, the defeat of his bid for the *Reichstag*, is described as "actively involved in the election campaign" (Appendix).

The profound dependency on the wife is suggested by the almost panicky-paranoid fear of losing her. This goes hand in hand with the regressive behavior of childlike helplessness to the point of asking to be carried.

Schreber is silent about the extent of his depression. But so is Flechsig: his diagnosis was "(hyponchondria) chronic bromide intoxication?" However, this diagnosis comes from the log-book of admissions, where Schreber is case #350, and it may have been Flechsig's diagnostic impression at the time of admission only. A discharge summary could not be found. The patient left the hospital as improved (Flechsig, 1882-1885) for the Ilmenau spa.

My conclusion is that the diagnosis was a moderate to severe depressive illness which did not come to full remission until the end of that year, 1885. It should be noted it was the clinical diagnostic custom of the day to view anxiety and depression as accompaniments rather than phenomena in their own right. Such a bias would naturally predispose the clinician towards linking hypochondriasis with paranoia rather than with depression, a common practice. Here we have a good example of how a theoretical bias might tip the scales toward a skewed perception. And when a theoretical-diagnostic bias is present, a therapeutic bias may not be far behind.[50]

These diagnostic considerations are not only important for the understanding of Schreber's personality and the nature of the first illness but also for the correct understanding of his second illness. Schreber saw his second illness as a return of the first. So did many others. The question is, a return of what illness: depression or schizophrenia?

THE THIRD PERIOD: 1886-1893

"After recovering from my first illness I spent eight years with my wife, on the whole quite happy ones, rich also in outward honors and marred only from time to time by the repeated disappointments of our hope of being blessed with children" (*M*, p. 36).

After his recovery from the first illness Schreber worked from 1886 to 1889 in Leipzig, to be transferred for his first appointment as Präsident, or presiding judge of a three judge panel in a district court of appeals. He thus became the *Landgerichtspräsident* of the Royal Landgericht in Freiberg, from 1889 to 1893 (Files of the Ministry of Justice; Devreese, 1981, 1986a). He heard cases in the I civil chamber (*Civilkammer*). Freiberg was a smaller provincial city than Chemnitz.[51] Scanning through the volumes of the *Freiberger Anzeiger und Tageblatt*, the local newspaper, I did not find Schreber's name mentioned: no more splashy advertisements, no more tributes in the editorial columns. There are to be found frequent reports of the legal decisions of the Chairman of the second criminal court chamber, Herr Landgerichtsdirektor v. Wolf. Then as now crime was newsworthy, civil cases much less.[52]

Devreese (1981a, p. 20; 1986a) is impressed that already in Freiberg Schreber experienced the honor of being called president. This is how Schreber is also listed in the Dresden State Archives: Director of the Landesgericht in Leipzig, and president of the court in Freiberg. Additional honors included receiving the cross of the Knight of the Order of Merit, first class, in 1888, and being chosen twice in a row, in 1891 and 1892, as member of the council of the Freiberg district magistracy (*Amtshauptmannschaft*). Schreber's youngest nephew Felix Jung wrote in 1955: "Professionally too my uncle was held in high regard, and more than one of his colleagues saw in him the future minister of justice in Saxony. However, that was not to be, on account of the outbreak of his illness" (Israëls, 1989, p. 170).

In the *Memoirs*, Schreber is reticent about the causes of the repeated disappointments to have children, but details of two of Sabine's stillbirths (Schilling, 1964, p. 5) are recorded in the family tree: a stillborn girl on October 30, 1888, and, later, a stillborn boy on January 6 of 1892 (Leipzig Genealogy Office, the Niederland Collection). It is not clear whether at this point Sabine was already suffering from diabetes (Baumeyer, 1956), an important cause of fetal mortality. In comparison, by that time his sister Anna, two years older than he, had given birth to six children, the last in 1882, of whom five were still living at the time of his writing.

In 1888 Paul wrote a poem in honor of his wife. The poem is titled "To my dear Sabchen on the tenth anniversary of the marriage the 6th of February 1888 dedicated by her Paul." I quote from Busse (1990) in my own prose translation:

> I have not written poetry for you for some time now. . . . Maybe it was the dust of files that lay heavy on my soul, maybe life with its hefty storms has hurt the little plant [of poetry]. . . . Ten years have passed.

Then a rosy glow shone upon our lives; a picture of a future of un-clouded happiness presented itself to love's trusting gaze. . . . We were blessed with honor, friendship and love. The home was pleasant, you gave joy to many a guest. . . . The source of your deepest sorrow, now as in earlier years, often presents itself to memory's eye. Your ardent desire has gone unfulfilled four times! . . . Sweet motherhood was not your share. The fate hit you with an even harder blow. I myself fell ill; out of seeds (*Keimen*) hardly noticed an illness grew and hard days followed. Not only the body was affected; also the mind was disturbed . . . a mixture of joys and sorrows . . . let us be both enveloped by love until the hues of silver appear on our heads, until—and may it last long—death us part [pp. 334-335].

Note that Schreber is reticent in this poem about his own suffering because of the loss of parenthood. We have no clue about the nature and the chronology of the bodily ailment he is alluding to; perhaps he means the physical complaints that Flechsig diagnosed as hypochon-dria.

In 1889 Paul composed a "Poem for the Silver Wedding of His Sister Anna" (D. P. Schreber, 1889). In it are these lines:

Many a wish for blessings will ring in your ears,/ Many a good word will sound at the festive table,/ But none of them will bring you such joy/ As this first greeting from the mouths of your children . . . You can certainly be satisfied with destiny; You are surrounded by a lively throng of children,/ So that in almost everything happiness smiles on you [Israëls, 1988; lines 6-8, 32, 35-36).

This picture contrasts starkly with Paul and Sabine's sorrows.

Another event during this period, important for Schreber's life after 1902, is the birth of his future adoptive daughter Fridoline[53] in Austria, on December 15, 1890. Fridoline's origins remain veiled in mystery. I mention this event here because it may have also played a role in precipitating the second illness. According to Felix Jung, Anna Jung's youngest son, "[Fridoline's] father was . . . an opera singer in Cologne by the name of Petter, who must in some way be related to my aunt [i.e., Sabine], for I can remember that a small photograph of him had a place on my aunt's bedside table" (Israëls, 1989, p. 167). Thanks to Professor U.H. Peters (1990), we have learnt more about the Wagne-rian tenor Franz Petter. Based on his extensive correspondence with Felix Jung, Baumeyer suspected that Sabine may have been an un-faithful wife and Fridoline an illegitimate child of hers, born on De-cember 15, 1890 (Busse, 1990, pp. 44-45). This is still an open issue.[54]

If Franz Petter was indeed the father of Fridoline and the lover of Sabine, than the romance must have taken place while he studied in Berlin as a 21-year-old. But somebody else could have been Sabine's lover, if indeed she had one. I pursued this guess for a short distance (Lothane, 1989a), because of the fact that soul murder, so prominent in Schreber's account of his second illness, was also a term used by Strindberg, whose plays were known in Germany. As traced by Donald Burnham, Strindberg (1887) used the term "psychic murder" in discussing Ibsen's *Rosmersholm*, the drama of a hero driven by his mistress's power of suggestion to murder his wife in pursuit of political ambition. Strindberg saw mental illness as resulting from a battle of wills between man and woman in which woman has the upper hand. In his play *The Father*, the hero is driven mad by a wife who casts doubts on the paternity of their daughter, and he ends up being hauled off to the asylum in a straightjacket by his wife and an old nurse.

Whether or not Sabine was the mother of this child, it appears that Fridoline was born out of wedlock. My guess is that at some point between the birth of Fridoline and the outbreak of Schreber's second illness, Sabine may have suggested to her husband the idea of adopting this child, a suggestion which he rejected out of hand because it was not his child, and that may have been the unacknowledged element in his "mental overstrain."

From this provincial milieu of Freiberg Schreber was catapulted to Dresden, the capital of the Kingdom of Saxony, having been appointed as *Senatspräsident* as of October 1st 1893, by a decree signed July 5 by Albert King of the Saxons. He was to preside over a five-judge panel in the Third *Civilsenat* of the Dresden *Oberlandesgericht*.

The early 1890s of the century is the time when, according to the contemporary social critic Nordau, the disease of society finally yielded its bitter fruit, the advanced stage of degeneration in civilized society, the fin de siècle syndrome, the dusk of the nations. The decadence of society suppposedly revealed itself in many forms: on the personal level, in egotism and the pursuit of pleasure in drugs and sex; in aesthetics, in the morbid emotionalism of hysteria and exaltations of artistic activity, notably Wagner's music; in the literary works of the likes of Nietzsche, Tolstoy, and Ibsen; in the coprolalia (feces-talk), or blasphematory mania, that is, the urge to utter obscenities, of a Zola and the degenerate literary forms of Wilde, Verlaine, Rimbaud and other French *symbolistes*. All these phenomena Nordau subsumed under the main manifestation of degeneration, namely, mysticism. Nordau described mysticism in its most general terms as "musing and dreaming, the free range of imagination, disporting itself at its own sweet will along the meandering paths of association, [that] demand less exertion and will therefore be widely preferred to the hard labor of observation and intelligent judgment" (Nordau, 1895, p. 67).

According to other views, by contrast, such dire diagnoses were still far in the offing. Indeed, the German Empire was built by Bismarck into a world power. Gone were the days of the revolutionary unrest in Saxony in the mid and late 1840s; Bismarck's *Kulturkampf*, the fight against Catholics and the dogma of papal infallibility; the repressive laws against the socialists. And Bismarck himself had been removed from power in 1890. On any day, sipping his morning coffee, Paul Schreber might open his copy of the *Freiberger Anzeiger und Tageblatt*, the official royal and municipal paper, and read the news, reviews of arts and sciences, the latest decisions of the criminal chamber of the Freiberg *Landesgericht,* discussions of books about modern civilized nervousness, or the occasional exposé of a fake medium. On new year's day of 1893 he would have read the lead article—"What Will the New Year Bring Us"—which was filled with high-sounding patriotic greetings for the new year. After rhapsodizing in purple prose about the Janus-faced life with its joys and sorrows and invoking Ulrich von Hutten's "O, century now it's such fun to be alive!" the author exhorts the reader to lead a life based on fear of God, discipline and tradition and respect for law and the authorities and to avoid the kind of ruthless politics that leads to the crudest forms of materialism, ending with the words of Philipp Heinrich Welcker about the wondrous aurora shining upon the blessed German Reich.

THE FOURTH PERIOD: THE SECOND ILLNESS, 1893-1902

Paul saw his second illness as caused "by the extraordinary burden of work on taking up office" as President of a Senate of the Superior Court of Appeals in Dresden, "to which [he] was newly appointed"[55] (*M*, p. 34). "In June 1893 I was informed (in the first place by the Minister of Justice, Dr. Schurig in person) of my impending appointment" (p. 36). The keynote is identified by Schreber in the naming of two major stresses in his life: the old one, mentioned earlier, of the missed opportunities to become a father and continue the name Schreber, since he was the only surviving son, and the new one, of conflicts about his career.

During this time, says Schreber, "I dreamt [*es träumte mir*, it came to me in a dream] several times that my former nervous illness had returned; naturally I was as unhappy about this in the dream, as I felt happy on waking and that it had only been a dream" (p. 36). Schreber's phrase is a more precise description of the preconscious gestation of the idea of the return of the illness and its irruption into consciousness than the active meaning conveyed by the English verb *to dream*. It also suggests a supernatural visitation "from out there," but Schreber's preoccupation with the supernatural began many months later.

It is not uncommon to experience the foreboding of a recurrence of an episode of illness in a dream: such foreboding suggests the breakthrough of repressed conflicts and fantasies past the barriers of defense, lowered in the state of sleep. This is the price one pays for using repression as a defense against the awareness of disturbing facts and feelings. The past refuses to remain repressed; like a ghost, it comes back to haunt us.

Schreber's own initial diagnosis was that it was not a new illness coming upon him but the old one, the one that was filled with memories of defeat, depression, hypochondriacal anxiety, fears of dying, and suicidal attempts. How was his new situation similar to the old one? On first blush, it is strange, if not paradoxical, to think of defeat at a time of professional promotion. Nevertheless, promotion may be stressful, as Schreber himself explained.

But a stranger dream was yet to come.

Furthermore, one morning while still in bed (whether still half asleep or already awake I cannot remember), I had a feeling which, thinking about it later when fully awake, struck me as highly peculiar. It was the idea [*Vorstellung*] that it really must be rather pleasant to be a woman succumbing to intercourse. This idea was so foreign to my nature that I may say I would have rejected it with indignation if fully awake [*M*, pp. 36-37].

This hypnopompic dream has the full quality of an unbidden emergence and its unconscious provenance cannot be doubted. It is a harbinger of Schreber's future fantasies of turning into a woman. Note that Paul says how nice it would be to submit to intercourse *as a woman*, whereas Freud and many others read this dream as a wish to submit *as a man,* that is, to be sodomized. The manifest content of the dream concerns both sexuality and feminization. But what is the latent content? Is it desire or defense? Is the thought concrete or metaphorical? We shall continue with these issues when the dream progresses to thoughts of unmanning and ignominious homosexual abuse.

Schreber's social anxieties continued.

On the 1st of October 1893, I took up my office as *Senatspräsident* to the Superior Court in Dresden. I have already mentioned the heavy burden of work I found there. I was driven, maybe by personal ambition, but certainly also in the interests of the office, to achieve first of all the necessary respect among my colleagues and others concerned with the Court (barristers, etc.) by unquestionable efficiency. The task was all the heavier and demanded all the more tact in my personal dealings with the members of the panel of five judges over which I had to preside, as all of them were much more senior to me (up to twenty years), and anyway they were much more intimately acquainted with the procedure of the court, to which I was a newcomer. It thus happened that after a few weeks I had already overtaxed myself mentally. I started to sleep badly at the very moment when I was able to feel that I had largely mastered the difficulties of settling down in my new office and in my new residence, etc. I started taking sodium bromide. There was almost no opportunity for social distraction which would certainly have been very much better for me—this became evident to me when I slept considerably better after the only occasion on which we had been asked to a dinner party—but we hardly knew anybody in Dresden. The first really bad, that is to say almost sleepless nights, occurred in the last days of October or the first days in November [*M*, p. 37].

This is a factual, lucid, and eloquent description of Schreber's predicament in the prodromal period of his second illness. He was 51 years old to his wife's 36. After 15 years of marriage, there were still no children, and the pressure of time's running out was undoubtedly felt. Schreber was torn between conscientiousness and ambition and he now feared failure. He also felt estranged and isolated in Dresden, the seat of the powerful Ministry of Justice, with its royal palace and its aristocracy. He felt intimidated by older colleagues and potential rivals and by Dresden high society, where he was possibly hamstrung by other people's perception that his wife was a far cry from a high-society lady.[56] The memories of loss and of loss of face came back as a dread of the return of his previous depression, with feelings of rejection, despair, desperation and suicide, but with a difference. This was incipient melancholia, seen retrospectively as caused by *"an intention . . . to prevent my sleep and later my recovery from the illness"* (*M*, p. 38; emphasis Schreber's).

THE COURSE OF THE SECOND ILLNESS

As with Job, what Schreber feared came to pass. According to Freud (1916), and echoed by Baumeyer (1956), Schreber was wrecked by success. A month and a week had passed since his coming to work in Dresden. His anxiety increased and so did the sleeplessness. "It was then when an extraordinary event occurred. During several nights when I could not get to sleep, a recurrent crackling noise in the wall or our bedroom . . . it woke me as I was about to go to sleep" (*M*, p. 38). By the 8th or 9th of November the "illness . . . began to assume a menacing character" (p. 38). This looked much more severe than the first illness.

"Doctor Ö., whom *I had* consulted made me take a week's sick leave, which *we were* going to use to consult Professor Flechsig, in whom *we placed all our faith* since his successful treatment of my first illness" (p. 38; emphasis added). Paul explains: "[Traveling back from Dresden to Leipzig,] because it was Sunday and Professor Flechsig would not be available, we (my wife and I) [made a stopover in] Chemnitz and spent the night from Sunday to Monday with my brother-in-law" (p. 38). Note the possible implication of this transition from "I" to "we": as Paul became increasingly helpless, Sabine was a strong advocate of the decision to go back to Flechsig.[57]

The brother-in-law was the aforementioned Theodor Krause, a friend and former colleague in the Chemnitz judiciary and husband of sister Klara. The atmosphere should have been conducive to peace of mind, but the memories of the electoral defeat in Chemnitz may have been too much.

> That evening [on Sunday] I was given an injection of morphine, and for the first time chloral during the night—perhaps accidentally not in the dosage ordered right away; the previous evening I suffered as severely from palpitation as in my first illness, so that walking up only a moderate incline caused attacks of anxiety. The night in Chemnitz was also bad [*M*, p. 39].

Schreber's predominant symptoms were anxiety, which was not calmed by medication, and a feeling of constriction and squeezing in the heart.[58] This feeling of constriction is both a symptom of angina pectoris, or coronary heart disease, an illness marked by suffocating chest pain and dread of impending death, and also of the psychobiological syndrome of anxiety. We are reminded, as was Schreber himself, more acutely than anyone else, of his fears of dying of a heart attack during his first illness. Now the memory of the first illness was no longer a fear and a foreboding: the first illness had returned.

> Early the following day (Monday) we traveled . . . to Professor Flechsig at the University Clinic. . . . A long interview followed in which . . . Flechsig developed a remarkable eloquence which affected me deeply. He spoke of advances made in psychiatry since my first illness, of newly discovered sleeping drugs, etc., and gave me hope of delivering[59] me of the whole illness through one prolific sleep, which

was to start if possible at three o'clock in the afternoon and last to the following day [*M*, p. 39].

Aside from lacking treatments for depression known today, Flechsig's eloquence amounted to a misunderstanding of Schreber's illness. It was a continuation of the basic misunderstanding from before. More was required by Schreber than a knowledge of diagnoses and drugs. He wanted his doctor to be personally interested in him, to know the intimate details of his life, to care for him in a personal way. Flechsig had no concept of the true nature of his patient's illness, of its psychogenic causation, and thus no corresponding concept of a psychotherapeutic cure through confession and conflict resolution. As we shall see later, this was not due to Flechsig's lack of opportunity to know better: he had made a fateful choice himself.

True, the main presenting symptom was insomnia. For Flechsig, this was clearly an organic disease of the brain requiring the best available new sleeping drugs: "one prolific sleep" would do it. Flechsig believed this could be achieved on an outpatient basis, and no recommendation for inpatient treatment was given at that point. Also, the professor might have said to himself, never mind the psychological reasons for the sleeplessness: if there are any, they will right themselves automatically once the organic cause of the insomnia is properly treated. Schreber knew Flechsig's approach was a "white lie," but the eloquence has its soothing influence. It was a transference effect, a placebo effect, or a cure by faith. Schreber's mood was temporarily lifted.

However, a cure by faith requires meticulous attention to the details of the treatment ritual. If the professor said three o'clock, the sleep had to begin at three o'clock or the treatment would lose its effectiveness:

> We went right away to the chemist to fetch the sleeping drug prescribed, then had a meal with my mother at her house, and I spent the rest of the day quite bearably, going for a little walk, amongst other things. Naturally I did not get to bed (in my mother's house) as early as 3 o'clock, but (possibly according to some secret instruction my wife had received) it was delayed until the 9th hour" [*M*, p. 39].

Something was terribly amiss with the initial treatment and communications. Instead of being soothed, Schreber's irritation mounted; his condition went from bad to worse.

> More serious symptoms developed again immediately before going to bed. Unfortunately, the bed was cold because it was aired too long, with

the result that I was immediately seized by a severe rigor [the shivers] and was already in a state of great excitement [*Aufregung*, which also connotes agitation and irritation] when I took the sleeping drug. Because of this the sleeping drug failed almost entirely in its effect, and after one or more hours my wife also gave me the chloral hydrate which was kept in hand in reserve. Despite this I spent the night almost without sleep, once even left the bed in an attack of anxiety in order to make preparations for a kind of suicidal attempt by means of a towel or suchlike; this woke my wife who stopped me. The next morning my nerves were badly shattered; the blood had gone from my extremities to the heart, my mood was gloomy in the extreme and Professor Flechsig, who had been sent for early in the morning, therefore advised my admission to the Asylum for which I set out immediately by cab accompanied by him [*M*, pp. 39-40].

According to Flechsig's log book of admissions, where Schreber is case #488, he was delivered by "the spouse of the patient." The admission diagnosis was "sleeplessness" (Flechsig, 1892-1894). The suicide attempt was both an act of desperate self-directed violence and a shot at his wife. Was mother, in whose house it happens, targeted as well? It was correctly perceived as a cry for help and it ushered in Schreber's nine long years in institutions, from November 21, 1893, to December 20, 1902.

THE STAY IN FLECHSIG'S HOSPITAL

In describing the chronology of the second illness I will correlate notations in Schreber's hospital chart with his own statements, both factual and fantastic, in the *Memoirs*.

1893

From the hospital chart on November 21. "Very depressed. Believes that as his luck would have it, they made him crazy, that he is suffering from softening of the brain. Inaccessible" (Appendix).
Schreber's version of the early days of this hospitalization:

My illness progressed rapidly during the following days; the nights passed mostly without sleep because the weaker sleeping drugs-
. . . failed to act. I could not occupy myself in any way; nor did I see anybody of my family. I passed the days therefore in endless melancholy; my mind was occupied almost exclusively with thoughts of death. It seems to me in retrospect that Professor Flechsig's plan of curing me consisted in intensifying my nervous depression [*Nervende-pression*] as far as possible, in order to bring about a cure all at once by

sudden change of mood. At least this is the only way I could explain the following event, which I could otherwise only attribute to malicious intent [*M*, p. 40].

The degree of depression is striking, as is its agitated quality. Schreber is sitting on a powder keg. He correctly diagnoses his condition as psychobiological, a *Nervendepression*, a nervous depression, which calls for a multilevel treatment approach. What he says about Flechsig's treatment method is interesting in connection with the so-called opium-bromides regimen, a kind of chemical shock treatment, which was Flechsig's method of treating epilepsy. Schreber's idea of softening of the brain may be an allusion to the treatment with potassium iodide for alleged syphilis, a known cause of brain lesions, or to an identification with his brother's paresis.

The following very disturbing event took place on the fourth or fifth night of Schreber's admission to Flechsig's hospital, that is, on November 24 or 25:

I was pulled out of bed by two attendants in the middle of the night and taken to a cell fitted out for dements (maniacs) to sleep in. I was already in a highly excited state [*aufgeregtester Stimmung*, a most agitated mood], a fever delirium so to speak, and was naturally terrified in the extreme of this event, the reasons for which I did not know. The way led through a billiard room . . . a fight started between myself, clad only in a shirt, and the two attendants, during which I tried to hold fast to the billiard table, but was eventually overpowered and removed to the above mentioned cell. There I was left to my fate; I spent the rest of the night sleepless in this cell, furnished only with an iron bedstead and some bedding. Regarding myself as totally lost, I made a naturally unsuccessful attempt during the night to hang myself on the bedstead with the sheet. I was completely ruled by the idea that there was nothing left for a human being for whom sleep could no longer be procured by all the means of medical art but to take his life. I knew this was not permitted in asylums, but I labored under the *delusion* that when all attempts at cure had been exhausted, one would be discharged—solely for the purpose of making an end to one's life either in one's own home or somewhere else [*M*, pp. 40-41; emphasis added].

From the chart for November 24: "At night very agitated, screams for help, throws table and chair around. Attempts to hang himself in the isolation cell. Then tearful, promises to be obedient."

Maybe his screams were disturbing other patients, and maybe the attendants were harsh and punitive because he refused to to submit to their control. In those days there was no legal ground to commit a person to an asylum because of suicidal risk, unless the suicide endangered other people (Flechsig, 1888). It was either the patient or the family who could not take the suicidal threats any longer. Schreber himself felt that as much as he longed for death, it was a delusion to think he might be released for the purpose of killing himself, a remarkable insight for someone afflicted with delusions of persecution. He was probably neither delusional nor dishonest when he described the rough melee with the attendants.

Schreber deplored Flechsig's reaction to his complaint: "Professor Flechsig denied the whole occurrence in the billiard room and all connected with it, and tried to make out that it was only a figment of my imagination—this by the way was one of the circumstances which from then on made me somewhat distrustful of Professor Flechsig" (Foot Note #23).

Even while laboring under delusions, patients do not lose all contact with reality, and certainly this was true of Schreber. He does not mention his screaming. The doctor was possibly annoyed by the patient's unruly behavior and was compelled to whitewash the violent behavior of his attendants. After all, attendants were more important to the director of a hospital than troublesome patients.[60] Schreber was a rebellious patient, who also wanted fair treatment and encouragement. This he could not get from Flechsig, only from the good soul Dr. Täuscher (actually Teuscher), Flechsig's assistant:

> [He reassured me the next morning] that there was no intention of giving up treatment; and coupled with the manner in which he tried to raise my spirits again—I cannot deny him also my appreciation of the excellent way he spoke to me on that occasion—had the effect of a very favorable change in my mood. I was led back to the room I had previously occupied and spent the best day of the whole of my second stay in Flechsig's Asylum, that is the *only day on which I was enlivened by a joyful spirit of hope*. Even the attendant R. behaved most tactfully and skillfully . . . [*M*, p. 42; emphasis Schreber's].

Following that memorable night and day Schreber's depression and anxiety went up and down.

> From then on I was regularly given chloral hydrate every night, and the following weeks were at least outwardly a little calmer, because in this way moderate sleep was usually procured. My wife visited me regularly and in the last two weeks before Christmas I spent part of every day at my mother's house. But the hyperexcitability [*Überreizung*, hyperirritability] of my nerves remained and got worse rather than better. . . . In other respects too my whole nervous system was in a state of utter laxity

[*tiefster Erschlaffung*, deepest enervation]. I could hardly, if at all, manage any intellectual occupation such as reading newspapers. . . . The laxity of my nerves increased with the simultaneous reappearance of states of anxiety, whenever they again tried giving me weaker sleeping drugs instead of chloral hydrate, which, although it strengthens the nerves temporarily, nevertheless damages them if used for any length of time. My will to live was entirely broken [*M*, pp. 43-44].

Laxity suggests not only lesser nervous tonus while the added meaning of *Erschlaffung*, enervation, also hints at a weakness and passivity with overtones of effeminacy, an exhaustion to the point of prostration. Schreber's self-descriptions are consistent with his self-diagnosis as a *Nervenkranker*, a person suffering from a nervous illness. There were no effective drugs to cure his sleeplessness, which was refractory even to the best efforts at Flechsig's. He was appropriately worried about chloral hydrate, in use since 1869, for prolonged or heavy doses were known to be a cause of unpleasant side effects (redness of skin, rashes and exanthems) and death (Lückerath, 1901). Schreber was under influences beyond his control and beyond consolation. His despair was profound.

1894
February

A further decline in my nervous state *and an important chapter in my life commenced about the 15th of February 1894* when my wife, who until then had spent a few hours every day with me and had also taken lunch with me in the Asylum, undertook a four-day journey to her father in Berlin, in order to have a holiday herself, of which she was in urgent need. My condition deteriorated so much in these four days that after her return I saw her only once more, and then declared that I could not wish my wife to see me again in the low state into which I have fallen. From then on my wife's visits ceased; when after a long time I did see her again at the window of a room opposite mine, such important changes had occurred in my environment and in myself that I no longer considered her a living being, but only thought *I saw in her a human form produced by miracle in the manner of the 'fleeting-improvised-men'* [or fleeting phantoms]. Decisive for my mental collapse was one particular night; during that night I had quite an unusual number of pollutions (perhaps half a dozen) [*M*, pp. 44; emphasis added].

Sabine's journey was a crucial milestone in the course of both the illness and Paul's life. It was a trauma within a trauma, this four-day absence of his wife. Fortunately, thanks to the findings of Uwe Peters

(1990), we now know a bit more about Schreber's in-laws even as many unanswered questions remain. Sabine's journey to Berlin was not only a vacation but possibly a turning to father for help with her husband. Schreber perceived it as an abandonment. He subsequently reacted to his wife with total rejection, expressed by seeing her as a fleeting phantom, which suggests rage at her. The half-dozen pollutions hint at a connection to their sex life[61] and possibly to the childbearing issue. This crisis coincided with a turning point in the nature of Schreber's symptoms: depression progressed to hallucinations and delusions, sleeplessness seemed to become schizophrenia:

> From then on appeared the first signs of communication with supernatural powers, particularly that of nerve-contact which Professor Flechsig kept up with me in such a way that he spoke to my nerves without being present in person. From then on also I gained the impression that Professor Flechsig had *secret designs against me* [*nichts Gutes mit mir im Schilde führe*, did not have good intentions; emphasis added]; this seemed confirmed when I once asked him during a personal visit *whether he really honestly believed that I could be cured* [emphasis added], and he held out certain hopes, but *could no longer*—at least so it seemed to me—*look me straight in the eye* [M, pp. 44-45; emphasis Schreber's].

Note the concern with being incurable. But whose doubt is it, the patient's or the doctor's? In Foot Note #103 Schreber also dates the onset of the first visions, which he discussed with Flechsig, as the beginning of March, the time of the appearance of the feeling that Flechsig had given up on him and that he was being persecuted by Flechsig. Schreber suspected Flechsig had some secret designs on him and he tied it to the issue of whether he was curable or not.

There was thus double trauma and double conflict: the other major conflict was with his wife. As Schreber was given to "sad memories of my wife who was much in my mind during that time" (M, p. 73) and to the "idea that the world has perished away" and also pictured having "crossed my own wife's grave" (p. 74).

The medical chart entry for February 12, 1894 corroborates Paul's story: "Visual hallucinations." This means that for about three months, since Schreber's admission to the hospital on November 21, the clinical picture had been essentially a severe agitated depression without frank hallucinations and delusions. The big change in the clinical picture is the beginning of the shift toward "communication with supernatural powers," with the "inner voices" (p. 45). Schreber then perceived the world around him through a consciousness altered by the psychotic process. His wife was now a "fleeting phantom," not a real person. Flechsig, the other significant person in his life, was perceived to relate to him as a soul that had divided into many parts and ascended to heaven to turn God against him. Schreber now considered himself a "seer of spirits" who, once he enters "into indissoluble contact with divine nerves or rays," must be "'unmanned' (transformed into a woman)" (*M*, p. 45).

Psychotic or perceptive? Crazy or clever? For Schreber wears many hats. The fantastic content of the *Memoirs* is not of one piece. It is primarily a stream of consciousness, an interior monologue, a stream of reverie that, like the dream, becomes a vehicle for any number of reminiscences and observations about the past, present, and future.

March

March was the month during which Schreber began to believe the practice of soul murder was occurring. "March 1. Believes he is a young girl, fears indecent assaults" (Appendix). According to Schreber,

> ever since the beginning of my contact with God (mid–March 1894) . . . somebody . . . *committed soul murder*; at first Flechsig was named as the instigator of soul murder [*M*, p. 23].
>
> In this way a plot [*Komplott*] was laid against me (perhaps March or April 1894), the purpose of which was to hand me over to another human being after my nervous illness had been recognized as, or assumed to be, incurable, in such a way that my soul was handed to him, but my body—transformed into a female body—. . . was then left to that human being for sexual misuse and simply "forsaken," in other words left to rot. . . . I have not the slightest doubt that this plot really existed, with the proviso always that I do not dare maintain that Professor Flechsig took part in it in his capacity as a human being. Naturally such matters were not mentioned by Professor Flechsig when he faced me *as a human being*. But the purpose was clearly expressed in the *nerve-language* [*Nervensprache*], . . . that is in the nerve-contact which he maintained *at the same time as a soul* [*M*, pp. 56–57]
>
> Always the main idea . . . was to "forsake" me, that is to say, abandon me; at the time I am now discussing it was thought that this could be achieved by unmanning me and allowing my body to be prostituted [*Preisgebung*, also means surrender] like that of a female harlot, sometimes also by killing me and later by destroying my reason (making me demented) [*M*, pp. 94; emphasis Schreber's].

For Schreber soul murder is the essence of his mistreatment as an inpatient first at Flechsig's and later at Sonnenstein. It is primarily taking possession of his soul: not just an imagined sexual rape, but a rape of his mind and his person. Besides, in Schreber's delusion, prior to sexual abuse, he is transformed into a woman, a harlot at that, who is then handed over to be abused. This transformation begins with a plot masterminded by Flechsig himself. (In old English, "plot" meant a scheme to accomplish any goal. Under the influence of the French *complot*, Germanized as *Komplott*, it acquired the legal meaning of complicity in a crime.) No crime was being committed, but a plan turned into a plot; for at this time negotiations were conducted behind Schreber's back, involving his doctor, his wife and others (as described on page 56, this volume), about which he was apparently not told, unless he was being disingenuous. Schreber was surely entitled to feel, at least retrospectively, that these negotiations were not in his best interest, thus his notion of a plot.

The hospitalization itself was a double edged-sword for Schreber: it was a safe haven from life's conflicts and stresses but also a living hell, because of restrictions of freedom and the deprivations (*M*, p. 132) imposed by hospital rules and order.

The way I was treated externally seemed to agree with the intentions announced in the nerve language; for weeks I was kept in bed and my clothes were removed to make me—as I believed—more amenable to voluptuous sensations, which could be stimulated in me by the female nerves which had already started to enter my body; *medicines, which I am convinced served the same purpose* [emphasis added], were used; these I therefore refused, or spat out again when an attendant poured them forcibly into my mouth. Having, as I thought, definitely come to realize this abominable intention one may imagine how my whole sense of manliness and my manly honour, my entire moral being, rose up against it, all the more so as I was stirred at that time by the first revelations about divine affairs which I had received through contact with other souls, and was completely filled by holy ideas about God and the Order of the World. Completely cut off from the outside world, without any contact with my family, left in the hands of rough attendants with whom, the inner voices said, it was my duty to fight now and then to prove my manly courage, I could think of nothing else but that any manner of death however frightful, was preferable to so degrading an end. I therefore decided to end my life by starving to death and refused all food. . . . This resulted in the so-called *"feeding system"* being started: attendants . . . forced food into my mouth, at times with the utmost brutality [*M*, pp. 57-58; emphasis Schreber's].

It is a perennial professional conflict for psychiatry that coercion must be used in order to help a person in the throes of acute delirium or psychosis. It is not always possible to persuade a delusional and self-destructive patient to accept food and to be reasonably cooperative. But neither can one deny the patient's perception of the often-gratuitous brutality of the system and the personnel. And in Schreber's case the system was operating with the full approval of the director of the institution, and his personal doctor. Later he would have other reasons for being suspicious of Flechsig.

During this time Schreber was treated with enforced bed rest and with sedatives, "opium and morphine" (Appendix, May 5, 1894). The opiates had their side effects too, among them, in susceptible persons, paradoxical "excitement, sleeplessness, restless tossing and turning, and sometimes even hallucinations" (Nothnagel and Rossbach, p. 713). In some patients even small doses could be fatal. He may have given vent to his opposition to the drugs he was given and his fear of them in inventing the curious drug name "*Nekrin*" (*M*, p. 42), which will not be found in any pharmacopoeia; spelled *necrin*, a possible variant, it suggests the Greek word *necros*, meaning dead body; however, there was an opium derivative in use, *Narcein*, an opium preparation (Nothnagel and Rossbach, 1894, p. 736). Another medication he objected to was "a white ointment which may have been bismuth" (Foot Note #32); it may be a delusional allusion to some event. Actually a bismuth compound in powder form occasionally replaced iodoform in the treatment of the soft chancre, or chancroid, that is, a nonsyphilitic genital ulcer, and gonorrhea. Was this the physical illness Schreber had in 1884?

Schreber's other major experience at this time was, as he puts it, "the notion [*Vorstellung*] of an approaching *end of the world*, as a consequence of the indissoluble connection between God and myself. Bad news [*Hiobsbotschaften* in the Ullstein edition, *Hiobsposten* in the Focus edition; Job's tidings] came in on all sides" (*M*, p. 70; emphasis added). The depressive ring in this fantasy is unmistakable. Furthermore, says Schreber, "If these and other occurrences were really visions, there was *method* in them, i.e., they were connected in a certain way which enabled me to see what one had in store for me" (p. 81; emphasis Schreber's). We shall see how Schreber's use of Hamlet's famous phrase correctly refers to events surrounding his removal from Flechsig's.

The depressive mood is reflected in the chart entries of March 15, the date of onset of soul murder: "Promises attendant 500 marks for digging a grave." Schreber singles out the period between April 2 or 4 to 19 as one he calls "the 'first Divine Judgment'. . . a series of continuous visions by night and by day, all based . . . on one common basic *general idea*. . . . the conflict between Professor Flechsig and myself" (p. 83; emphasis Schreber's). The hospital chart entry of April 16 reads: "Suicide attempts in the water of the bathtub." On April 21: "Disconnected delusions. During every visit says he is ready to die, demands the glass of potassium cyanide earmarked for him" (Appendix).

Among the symptoms that caused Schreber's concern at this time, and related to the dream of the end of the world, is the "peril of a syphilitic epidemic" (*M* p. 74). Flechsig is implicated again: "In the modern world something in the nature of a wizard had suddenly appeared in the person of Professor Flechsig . . . ; this had spread terror and fear amongst the people, destroying the bases of religion and causing general nervousness and immorality. In its train devastating epidemics had broken upon mankind. This last idea was supported by the fact . . . of . . . leprosy and plague [*Pest*]" (*M*, p. 91). On the day of admission Schreber thought he was suffering from "softening of the brain," a possible allusion to syphilis, his own, his brother's, or another patient's. Since the sixteenth century leprosy and bubonic plague were eclipsed by the terror of the "new plague," syphilis, as viewed by the professional and the popular mind (Liebreich, 1900).

The chart entry of May 5 mentions "Numerous auditory and olfactory hallucinations. . . . there is a patient stricken with the plague. He asks whether he has been dead for a long time" (Appendix). And in the *Memoirs*: "The souls considered the plague a disease of nerves [*Nervenkrankheit*] and hence a 'holy disease' "(p. 93). This description does not apply to either leprosy[62] or bubonic plague, because central nervous system disease is not a classical manifestation of either disease. It does, as noted earlier, apply to syphilis, especially the mental disorders of tertiary syphilis, presumably the dual disease of his older brother and many other prominent persons of that period, who, like "a certain R., a fellow student and member of Students' Union, . . . had led a rather dissolute life" (p. 95). Schreber is undoubtedly alluding to syphilis, or lues, when he says, "the inner table of my skull was lined with a different brain membrane [Foot Note #49A] in order to extinguish the memory of my own ego" (p. 95). Luetic meningitis, inflammation of the membranes (meninges) of the brain and spinal cord was a common complication of syphilis, while swings of depression and elation, with delusions and hallucinations, were the common mental manifestations. Luetic meningitis was also the topic of Flechsig's (1870) doctoral dissertation. No traces of the disease would be found in Schreber at autopsy.

On May 24 he is given "Opium and morphine. Severe hallucinations continue." It is surprising that later, as Schreber tells us, "I took no sleeping drugs at all for several weeks at the end of my stay in Flechsig's Asylum. I slept—though in part restlessly and always with more or less exciting visions—without any artificial help" (*M*, p. 89).

The other change was Schreber's release from enforced bed rest which was "followed, at the end of [his] stay in Flechsig's Asylum, by a time when [he] walked regularly in the garden" (p. 88). It was a mixed state: progress alternating with regress, the calm before the storm.

There are four brief notes in the hospital chart for the month of June. On the 5th we read: "Visit of his wife. Later asks the attendant whether this was his wife in the flesh, believes she arose from the grave." The rage toward his doctor and his wife is strongly suggested in these statements, and it is appropriate to correlate these angry reactions—as well as the dating of the onset of soul murder some time in March or April of 1894—with crucial decisions that were being made about Schreber's fate around that time.

At this point Flechsig would have decided to transfer Schreber based on the assessment that the patient was incurable and on the limits on length of stay at his institution, as defined by his bylaws (Flechsig, 1882b). In addition, the situation was complicated by money disputes between Sabine and Paul Schreber, in which the Ministry of Justice, Schreber's employer, became involved. For some reason Schreber was in a rage toward Sabine and refused to sign remittances against which she could collect his monthly paycheck. The Ministry of Justice refused to accept Sabine's signature in lieu of her husband's and the bickering between the spouses continued. Flechsig recommended that the patient should not be further disturbed by these clashes, while Schreber's boss, Carl Edmund Werner, the president of the entire Dresden *Oberlandesgericht*, possibly with Flechsig's approval, decided to cut the Gordian knot by recommending that Schreber be *"entmündigt,"* that is, legally certified as "mentally incompetent to manage his affairs" by virtue of insanity, thus committable to a public asylum, such that the court-appointed guardian and Sabine would get control of Schreber's assets. This method of prosecution of spendthrifts and social parasites was commonly practised throughout the Empire, as written into law in the *Bürgerliches Gesetzbuch*, or the Civil Code. It was a reflection of the bourgeois credo of productivity, prudence, and providence and it empowered the ministries of justice, internal affairs and the police to intervene in the private lives of the citizenry in the name of curing social ills. In accordance with the law (Brockhaus' *Conversations Lexikon*, 1898, entry *"Entmündigung"*; Hoche, 1909), Sabine made the application and proceedings for a temporary declaration of incompetency were instituted. It was finalized by November 27 of 1894, five months after the transfer to Sonnenstein, and at Sabine's request the administration of the guardianship was trasferred to the County Court in Leipzig. Wittingly or unwittingly, Sabine collaborated with the psychiatric and legal systems against her husband. But it was Weber's report of November 7, 1894, that was used by the lower court judge to certify the incompetency status (Devreese, 1981a, pp. 66, 68, 70). In retrospect, Schreber had good reason to feel unmanned and raped. But in the meantime, he may have had at least a vague inkling that something was being plotted behind his back.

By June 14th the jig is up: three attendants appear in his cell to take him to Lindenhof, a private insane asylum in Coswig. Schreber says: "My only reaction at first was a feeling of *liberation*. . . . The journey's goal left me indifferent; I felt *only* that I could not fare worse anywhere in the world than I had fared in Flechsig's Asylum; . . . I left . . . without seeing Professor Flechsig again" (*M*, p. 99; emphasis added). We can believe that this was Schreber's feeling for the moment. But it was premature joy, for a fate much worse lay ahead at his eventual destination, Sonnenstein. The unpleasant foretaste was already evident soon after his transfer as "uncured to the Private Asylum Lindenhof" (Flechsig, 1892-1894), run by Dr. Pierson, for Paul nicknamed the place the "Devil's Kitchen."

THE STAY AT LINDENHOF

In retrospect, Schreber was as baffled by the transfer as he was critical of it.

> Why I was taken to Pierson's Asylum—temporarily, for 7 to 14 days— is still inexplicable when I try to view these things in a human, natural light. My transfer from the University Clinic in Leipzig to the present Country Asylum (Sonnenstein) once decided upon, it would after all have been far simpler to set it in motion direct, without a stay somewhere else in between; if suitable rooms were not ready for my reception at Sonnenstein my stay in the Leipzig Asylum would have been better prolonged by a week or two, instead of entrusting a fairly dangerous patient, as I certainly was at the time, to the care of a Private Asylum [Schreber's Foot Note #53].

The transfer was, however, part of a scheme to get him out of Flechsig's in a hurry, a scheme that required the collaboration of all three psychiatrists who presided over the fate of Schreber: Flechsig, Pierson and Weber. Flechsig repeatedly complained about how cumbersome and lengthy such transfers were. Indeed, Flechsig (1888) noted the special arrangement with Sonnenstein required for speedy transfers of acutely ill patients. At the time of his discharge from Flechsig's, Schreber was no longer an acute patient; while after two weeks at Lindenhof that was perhaps a fair description of him. He arrived at Lindenhof in such a desperate and suicidal mood that, he says, "I would have been ready any moment . . . to throw myself on the railway line or to jump into the water while crossing the Elbe" (p. 100). The remedy for this despair was a frantic flight into fantasy: "The time I spent in Pierson's Asylum was when the wildest mischief through miracles was carried on. . . . At no time were [fleeting phantoms] set down so extravagantly as then" (p. 102). He describes his experiences with such qualifiers as Hamlet's phrase, "I witnessed [*gesehen*, saw] with my mind's eye" (p. 110), or "the picture which I have in my mind," or "it appeared that" (p. 111). The latter is an inexact translation: Schreber says "*es schien als ob*" ("it appeared *as if*") such and such were taking place. This 'as if' quality of the delusion/dream state is further accentuated by his stating, that the "[miracles] also provoked some amusing effects, even lending to my otherwise gloomy existence, if I may put it like this, a touch of the comic" (p. 113).

In this waking dream ". . . *almost all the patients in the Asylum,*" says Schreber, "looked like persons who had been more or less close to me in my life" (*M*, p. 103-104; emphasis Schreber's). In his distress, he dreams of his parents. Thus, in one of the ladies he sees his own mother. One could read this as a expression of his loneliness and helplessness and, thus, either as a turning to her for help in this night of the soul or perhaps as a silent reproach to her for forsaking him. He also imagines his father, he says, "as a soul in my body or belly. . . . I recognized in him flesh of my own flesh and blood of my own blood" (pp. 115-116).

Schreber cannot stop thinking of Flechsig and mocks him, as a court jester might, as an apostle of the new materialistic religion, that is, brain mythology, placed in a historic taproom, the Gosenschänke in Eutritzsch near Leipzig, and endows him with "professorial arrogance" (*M*, p. 113). Flechsig is further derided as a phantom maid who has to serve him: "in expiation for the wrong he has done to me. It seems that some mildly mocking humiliation was to be the lot of those who had sinned in life" (M Schreber's Foot Note #56).

Schreber was not impressed with the owner and director of this private asylum for the well-to-do. "A gentleman appeared occasionally—mostly in the evening hours—who was supposed to be the Medical Director of the Asylum . . . and I must now presume that it was Dr. Pierson; his conversation was regularly confined to a few empty words" (p. 103). The decision to send him to Sonnenstein had already been made. It happened in no time.

THE STAY AT THE SONNENSTEIN ROYAL STATE HOSPITAL

The stay at Sonnenstein has made the greatest impression on the students of Schreber and the "miracles" that took place there have come to be regarded as the core of his psychosis. Here is how Schreber begins this part of his chronicle:

> I was taken . . . to this Country Asylum Sonnenstein near Pirna . . . on the 29th of June 1894. I do not know the reason for my transfer. . . . When I first arrived the voices called the place "The Devil's Castle." I still occupy the same rooms I was given then —number 28 on the first floor of the Elbe wing, with an adjoining bedroom. . . . In contrast to the fairly elegantly furnished Asylum of Dr. Pierson, the rooms struck me as rather poor at first [M, p. 117].

Upon the transfer to Sonnenstein, a highly traumatic event, Schreber was extremely frightened, as noted in the following passage from the chart:

> It was striking that beads of sweat were continuously seen on his forehead, as well as fibrillary twitchings of the face muscles and marked tremor of his hands. He was markedly agitated, at first quite inaccessible, sullen, almost melancholy. . . . He hallucinated severely . . . In the garden it was noticed that he held his hands to his ears as if listening [Appendix].

It is difficult to tell where the observed hallucinations end and the inferred ones begin. They must have something to do with the causes of his fright and the excitement that suggest the desperation of a cornered man. For we cannot deny that Schreber, in addition to being depressed and agitated as a result of his illness, had the ability to realize what has been done to him and where he was: in a scary place, with little hope for a quick solution and with irreversible damage to his professional career.

The chart records a significant event for the month of July: "Made an attempt to escape, he threw his coat away and ran to the gate. Stool sluggish, appetite poor. From time to time clearly molested by voices, but never said anything about them. Once a short fainting fit , which was probably caused by the patient withholding an urge to pass stool" (Appendix). I see a connection between the fainting and the attempt to escape, expressing Schreber's opposition to his involuntary confinement at Sonnenstein, in complete contrast to the voluntary way he entered Flechsig's hospital. His rage, suggested by his excitement and his fainting, is both hopeless and helpless. There was absolutely nothing he could do but resign himself to his captivity. His future experiences and thoughts would be colored by this fundamental fact of his existence at Sonnenstein.

I can divide the time of my stay at Sonnenstein into two periods, of which the first on the whole still retained that serious, holy and sometimes awesome quality which characterized my life in the latter part of my stay at Flechsig's Asylum and Dr. Pierson's Asylum; in contradistinction the second period merged gradually more and more into ordinary [everyday](not to say vulgar[ordinary]) channels. The first period lasted for about a year; the second period continues, modified of late only by becoming less vulgar in some respects. In the first period the miracles were still terrifying and threatening in their bodily and mental effects, so that for a long time I was most seriously concerned for my life, my manliness and my reason; in the second period—naturally very gradually and not without some setbacks—the miracles became increasingly more harmless, not to say senseless and childish, although to some extent still repugnant [M, pp. 117-119).

First Period: 1894-1895.

Of his experience during the first period of his confinement at Sonnenstein, Schreber says: "In the first period I was still convinced that I was dealing not with real human beings but with . . . [fleeting phantoms]. For this reason I kept almost total silence" (p. 119, Foot Note #59). He also kept an emotional distance from the superintendent of the asylum, Dr. Weber, from his assistants, and from the other patients ("Other patients did not seem to exist in the Asylum at the time"); and he hated the attendants: "The voices called the attendants 'rascals'" (M, p. 120). He also kept aloof from his wife:

[She] visited me at Sonnenstein at longish intervals—probably of a few months. I was petrified when I saw her the first time entering my room on such a visit; I had long believed she was no more among the living. . . . [I] felt the nerves belonging in my wife's soul in my body [and it was my dream-wish that] such soul parts were filled with the devoted love which my wife has always shown me" [p. 121].

How could he be loving toward a wife who may have played a role in having him confined at Sonnenstein? The conflict between love and rage went on.

Schreber states these facts directly: "On one of her visits—probably on my birthday in 1894 [July 25, thus 26 days after admission]—my wife brought me a poem, which I reproduce here word for word because it made such a deep impression on me at the time." The poem went as follows:

Ere true peace can embrace you—
God's still and silent peace—

The peace life never giveth
Nor worldly joys beneath,
It needs God's arm must strike
A blow and wound you deep,
So that you cry: Have mercy,
God have mercy on my days;
It needs a cry must ring,
Ring from your soul
And darkness be within you
As 'fore the world's first day.
It needs that crushing pain
Must wholly vanquish you,
And not a lonely tear be left
In your poor wretched soul.
And when you've done with weeping
And weary art, so weary,
Then comes to you a faithful guest
God's still and silent peace [M, p. 122].

Schreber says: "This poem, by an unknown author, made such a singular impression on me because the phrase 'God's peace,' which recurs in it, is *the expression used in basic language for sleep produced by rays* [i.e., God]" (M, pp. 122-123; emphasis Schreber's). I strongly suspect that the poet is Schreber himself. He says about himself that he used to write poems for family occasions (I quoted from one of them earlier). The poem is the only factual and direct depiction of his profound depression. It renders beautifully the long dark night of the soul and the suffering he must endure before peace comes. It evokes the dual image of Job and Jesus (a man of sorrows, despised and rejected of men) in Handel's *Messiah*, whom Schreber quotes. It is the only place in the *Memoirs* where tears and crying are mentioned. It strikes the keynote of "the sufferings and privations of the *last seven* years" (p. 292; emphasis Schreber's) at Sonnenstein: the long torment and the recovery.

Schreber's torment was twofold: struggling with the demons within, that is, his psychological conflicts, and without, that is, the conflict with his wife and his doctors and "the restriction of freedom" (M, p. 132). The conditions of his confinement were both consequence and continuation of Flechsig's soul murder. The "mental torture" (M, p. 132) was portrayed as punishing "miracles" inflicted by a hostile God (rays), who was, as in the case of Job, seduced, in this case by Flechsig, to visit upon innocent subject, Schreber, a host of painful symptoms of illness, most acutely in the "second half of the year 1894 and perhaps the first half of the year 1895" (p. 151), that is, the period following the transfer to Sonnenstein.

These "miracles," that fill Chapter 11 of the *Memoirs*, are the very ones that sent Niederland on the quest to find evidence of Schreber's allegedly evil father and the traumas inflicted on him as a child, thus starting a myth that is still with us. Of the "miracles" Schreber writes:

> If I wanted to describe all these miracles in detail I could fill a whole book with them alone. . . . I may say that hardly a single limb or organ in my body escaped being pulled by miracles, . . . the first year of my stay at Sonnenstein the miracles were of such threatening nature that I thought I had to fear almost incessantly for my life, my health or my reason. . . . Contrary to the Order of the World . . . [my body] . . . has been destroyed by impure rays . . . [and] . . . later . . . built up or mended again by pure rays [*M*, p. 148-149].

Schreber is here describing sensations accompanied by great anxiety, a kind of anxiety hysteria. They are not simply automatic transpositions of his alleged childhood experiences into his hospital life but portrayals in dream language and postperceptual metaphor of his unresolved conflicts, moods, and reactions to the hardships of a life of involuntary confinement. Jung has rightly said, following Freud, that such symptoms are explicable by the dynamics of hysteria.[63]

While Flechsig is portrayed repeatedly as an evil spirit, the allusions to Weber in Schreber's fantasies are few and far between. Thus, during these first weeks at Sonnenstein, Schreber notices important changes with the sun: "I recollect that for a longish period there appeared to be a *smaller* sun. This sun, as mentioned in the end of Chapter 8, was first led by Flechsig's soul but later by a soul whose nerves I identified as those of the Director of the present Asylum, Dr. Weber" (*M*, p. 135; emphasis Schreber's). Freud (1912b) wrote an entire "Postcript" about the sun as a symbol of a male God, even though *sun* is feminine in German. I believe Schreber is here punning on the name Sonnenstein, literally "sun stone," and poking fun at the superintendent of Sonnenstein, Weber, a very common name in Germany. (Instead of using his Christian name, Weber used to sign his publications in the psychiatric journal as "Weber-Sonnenstein.")

Other fantastic terms are used to describe visions of awe-inspiring magnificence. Again, these visions might be seen as Schreber's attempts to use the medicine of the magnificent and the magical to soothe the misery of his daily existence.

> For several days and nights I had at that time the most wonderful and magnificent impressions . . . I believe I may say that at that time and at that time *only* I saw God's omnipotence in its complete purity. During

that night—and as far as I can remember in one single night—the lower God (Ariman) appeared. The radiant picture of his rays became visible to my inner eye (compare Foot Note #61), while I was lying in bed not sleeping but awake . . . my impression was not one of alarm and fear but largely one of admiration for the magnificent and the sublime; the effect on my nerves was therefore beneficial . . . [*M*, pp. 136-138].

This is a visionary description of Biblical or Blakean grandeur. Schreber continues: "After a few days the miraculous phenomena of which I have spoken were over; the sun assumed the shape which she has since then retained without interruption" (*M*, p. 139).

In contrast to these heavenly visions, Schreber describes the more ordinary aspects of his life:

My *outward life* was extremely *monotonous* during that time—the first months of my stay at Sonnenstein. Apart from daily morning and afternoon walks in the garden, I mainly sat *motionless* the whole day on the chair at my table. . . . All the same the main reason for my immobility was not so much the actual lack of means of occupation but that I considered absolute passivity almost a religious duty" [*M*, pp. 140-141; emphasis Schreber's].

Schreber continues:

It goes without saying that my behaviour as described above could not be correctly judged by my environment, least of all by my physicians and attendants . . . they could hardly see in me anything but a stuporous dullard. And yet the real situation towered sky high above this appearance: I lived in the belief—and this is still my conviction that this is the truth—that I had to solve one of the most intricate problems ever set for man and that I had to fight a sacred battle for the greatest good of mankind. Unfortunately my deceiving appearance to the contrary brought with it innumerable indignities in the way I was treated; for years I suffered from them severely, and it seemed that one had altogether forgotten my standing and the high position I had occupied in life. . . . Sometimes I opposed such indignities with actual resistance . . . [as] when one tried to move me from my own bedroom to sleep in cells fitted out for raving madmen. Later on I desisted from all opposition because it led to senseless scenes of violence; I kept silent and suffered [*M*, p. 146-147].

The other torment was loneliness and isolation from the outside world, which Schreber depicted as God's desire to withdraw time and "again as far as possible from the power of attraction of my over-excited nerves. . . . To that end one first considered my *unman-*

ning . . . an intended insult, for in a peculiar way it was imagined, or perhaps wishfully thought, that an unmanned body would lose its power of attraction for the rays [of God]" (p. 127; emphasis Schreber's). This unmanning, "contrary to the Order of the World," was, Schreber says, "[a] threatening ignominy, especially while there was the possibility of my body being sexually abused by other people" (p. 128), in contrast to the unmanning "consonant with the Order of the World" that expressed feminine identification and led to useful psychological work.

> For over a year therefore . . . I suppressed every feminine impulse by exerting my sense of manly honour . . . [not to appear as] a human being trembling with feminine anxiety. On the other hand, my will power could not prevent the occurrence, particularly when lying in bed, of a sensation of voluptuousness which as so-called "soul–voluptuousness" exerted an increased power of attraction on the rays [of God]; this expression used by the souls meant a voluptuousness sufficient for the souls but felt by human beings only as a general bodily well-being without real sexual excitement [*M*, p. 129].

Viewed as an adaptive response, as a strategy of coping with a traumatic situation, illness is both a reaction to trauma and an attempt at self-cure. For Schreber, feminine anxiety due to loss of manly pride, surrender and "feminine impotence" was painful. But the creation of the concept of feminine voluptuousness was turning the liability into an asset: it produced peace of mind.

A change in "these conditions" became noticeable to Schreber toward "the end of 1894 or early 1895:

> It coincided with . . . an influence by miracles on one's mood . . . [like] morphine which has the effect of producing a relatively serene [*heiter*, also cheerful], in any case indifferent mood, in a person who is harassed by bodily pain or in the throes of a depression. . . . as time went by I found it easier to allow its influence, because I noticed that subjectively I really felt less unhappy . . . [*M*, p. 145].

Further mention of the change in his conditions is found in the following passage:

> *My outward living conditions* have in some respects at least become more bearable since about the first half of the year 1895. . . . Most important was that I started to occupy myself in different ways. It is true that I still declined to write to my relatives, in particular to my wife, although the attendant M. tried to persuade me. I did not believe in the existence of a real mankind outside the Asylum. . . . during my wife's visit, a small

piano was put into my room in the Spring of 1895 for my regular use. The feelings aroused in me when I resumed this occupation which in days of health I enjoyed, I can best describe by a quotation from *Tannhäuser*: "Total forgetting descended between today and yesterday. . . . I could only remember that *I had lost all hope of ever greeting you again* [*M*, p. 167; emphasis Schreber's].

November of 1895

November 1895, the anniversary of Schreber's father's death at age 53 and the month of Paul's own 53d birthday, was also a harbinger of change:

> The month of November of 1895 marks an important time in the history of my life and in particular in my own ideas of the shaping of my future. I remember the period distinctly. . . . During that time the signs of transformation into a woman became so marked on my body that I could no longer ignore the *immanent*[64] [emphasis Schreber's] goal at which the whole development was aiming. . . . Soul-voluptuousness had become so strong . . . and that therefore it was common sense . . . to . . . reconcile myself to the thought [*mich zu befreunden*, to make friends with the thought] of being transformed into a woman. Nothing of course could be envisaged as a further consequence of unmanning but fertilization by divine rays for the purpose of creating new human beings. . . . that behaviour . . . I had come to recognize as essential and curative for all parties—myself and the rays [i.e., God]. Since then I have wholeheartedly inscribed the cultivation of femininity on my banner, . . . *The pursuit of my previous profession, which I loved wholeheartedly, every other aim of my manly ambition, and every other use of my intellectual powers in the service of mankind, are now all closed to me through the way circumstances have developed* [emphasis added]; . . . I must follow a healthy egoism, unperturbed by the judgment of other people, which prescribes for me the cultivation of femininity . . . In this way only am I able to make my physical condition bearable during the day and at night . . . obtain the sleep necessary for the recuperation of my nerves; *high-grade voluptuousness* [emphasis Schreber's] eventually passes into sleep [*M*, pp. 177–178].

We note that the "immanent goal" is a shift toward identification with woman and mother, with its inherent self-healing properties. It is also a change toward becoming reconciled to a milestone in his life: the ending of his judicial career because of his institutionalization. However, he bought whatever safety the hospital walls gave him at a dear price. At the same time, he paid off his conscience for giving up a high pressure public office.

By the end of 1895 the first cracks appeared in Schreber's conviction that a malevolent God was persecuting him. As healing soul-pleasure,

the notion of femininity became an antidote to the noxious impure rays
he believed were issuing from God (in the twin shape of Ariman and
Ormuzd). Schreber now believed that when upon entering his body
the rays find it in a state of enjoyment and pleasure, they accept it as a
substitute for their own lost heavenly blessedness, or bliss, and dis-
solve, that is, dissipate. As a result of this steady process of dissipation
the previously hostile Ariman now becomes friendly, and the upper
Ormuzd became temporarily so. Thus, a further increase in God's
benevolence results in "certain changes in heavenly conditions,
. . . mainly [in] the fate of 'tested souls,'" that is, the impure souls, like
that of Flechsig, hostile to Schreber. These inimical souls, says
Schreber, "eventually become a nuisance to God's omnipotence itself.
After I succeeded in drawing down to myself a considerable part of
them, God's omnipotence started a raid among them . . . [and gradu-
ally] the previous 'tested souls'[Flechsig's and v. W.'s] vanished from
the scene" (M, pp. 191-193).

1896

The hospital-chart entry for November of 1895 reads: "More talkative
and more accessible. Reads more" (Appendix). From November 1894
to November 1896 the chart mostly documents manifestations of
excitement, agitation, laughing, and raging and is meager in describing
his fantastic productions ("Refuses to talk about his delusional phan-
tasies"). By July 1896 "the attacks of laughing and bellowing [Brüllen,
the word used by Schreber himself] are less frequent, but more severe
and last longer." There is an interesting notation in regard to his sexual
feelings: "Is very much under the sway of sexual ideas, eagerly scans
illustrated periodicals for nude pictures and makes drawings of those.
In a letter to his wife written in Italian, he says that the nights are very
pleasant because he always has *un poco di volupta feminae*" (Appendix).
   Schreber notes the following facts about his existence during the
year 1896:

> My outward life was no longer quite as monotonous . . . yet there was
> little variety, as may be expected from living in an Asylum. . . . I started
> to make written notes . . . my circumstances were so pitiful that even a
> pencil or a rubber were guarded by me like a real treasure. . . . in 1896—
> I was limited to meagre entries in a small calendar [M, p. 195].

Recounting experiences that occurred at the end of 1895 or the
beginning of 1896, Schreber writes:

I had a number of experiences which led me to a critical examination of my ideas. . . . In particular I remember three events which made me hesitate whether what I had considered true and correct [e.g., the notion of fleeting phantoms] was really so: firstly, taking part in the Christmas festivities of the family of the Director of the Asylum Dr. Weber; secondly receiving a letter from my sister-in-law in Cologne on the Rhine addressed to me and bearing the postmark of Cologne [the aforementioned Albertine, the judge's wife]; thirdly a children's procession celebrating the twenty-fifth anniversary of the Peace of Frankfurt [imposed by Germany upon France, defeated in the war of 1871]—10th of May 1896—which I saw from my window passing along a street in Pirna which runs below it. After these and similar events—soon regular correspondence was added and reading newspapers which were subscribed for by my relatives—I could no longer doubt that a real race of human beings in the same number and distribution as before did in fact exist [*M*, pp. 202-203].

1897-1898

In addition to becoming more receptive to outward reality, Schreber intensified his note taking, a labor of self-revelation, even a kind of self-analysis.

Beginning with the year 1897—*I started to keep regular diaries* . . . [a] sketch [of] my future "Memoirs," . . . entitled "From My Life"; . . . it was immeasurably richer than what I could incorporate in the limited space of the "Memoirs." Finally—since the late autumn of 1897—I have written down certain observations mentioned in footnote 80 and the Little Studies in small note-books B, C, and I [*M*, pp. 194-195; emphasis added].

In the chart, we read that while still shouting furiously during his "bellowing states" ("*Brüllzustände*") and still occasionally "screaming, bellowing and grimacing," all the while lacking any "sensitivity for the disturbance he causes," Schreber is also now engaged in a "lively correspondence with his wife and relatives, written quite properly and without any trace of morbidity. Apparently speaks with full insight about his illness." This opinion of full insight was later contradicted by Weber.

What is the sum and substance of Schreber's paranoid illness at this point? The content of Schreber's preoccupations had undergone a marked and significant change. The idea that Flechsig committed soul murder, that is, the principal persecutory manifestation of the alleged paranoia, had been replaced, in July of 1896, by Schreber's acting out, by means of cross-dressing, his fantasy of turning into a woman. According to the hospital chart entry for that month, Schreber, "dressed incompletely, shows the doctor his bared chest, 'now he has almost a woman's breasts.' The only actual change was a more pronounced fatty deposit." At the same time, he was much preoccupied with sexual ideas and pictures of nudes. And, in March 1898, this entry: "Religious delusions. Adorns himself with multicolored ribbons, at times engages in really petty games," and later, for January 22, 1899, the entry reads: "For the first time writes a detailed letter to his wife in which he describes his delusions." Schreber's sexual preoccupations perhaps reflect in part the lack of any sexual outlet for this heretofore fully heterosexual man, while their content, so shocking to his doctors, can be seen as a consolation and an attempt at magical restitution of the missing element of the feminine. Then, too, there is a latent element of defiance here, both toward his wife, who continues to be less indispensable, and to his doctors, whose tolerance for these ideas is understandably low. As for Schreber's religious delusions, his redeemer fantasies, spelled out in the drafts of the future *Memoirs*, were being composed at this time.

It is not clear whether at this point he asked his wife or other members of his family to take him home. Nor do we know what fantasies or feelings prompted the behavior described in the October 1897 entry: "During visits of his wife he often has to go [to] the window and roar out and laugh, and then resume the conversation as if nothing happened." Schreber objected to his wife's many trips and threatened to withhold moneys, or even divorce, if she would not take him home (Baumeyer, 1956, p. 68).

Two and a half years of nightly isolation in a cell (Foot Note #63), one of his "mental tortures," have now (December, 1898) ended. Schreber notes in the *Memoirs*: "[this fact of] how unbearably I suffered during this stay in cells belongs to the story of the complete picture of my sufferings (*M*, pp. 198-199).

The March 1898 entry in the chart reads: "Amiable upon approach, even though quite reserved and aloof, well oriented about current events, reads a lot and discusses legal issues. . . . Religious delusions. . . . really petty games." This may seem quite confusing.

On one hand, Schreber appeared normal; on the other hand, he was exasperating the doctors and attendants—"really petty games"—with his undescribed antics. A patient in Schreber's position would know that he was being constantly watched and assessed; it is more than conceivable that he was responding to this constant scrutiny with that combination of heightened self-consciousness and hostility that characterizes tomfoolery in schoolboys, military recruits, and others faced with a constantly watching authority that will not go away. While still emotionally labile at this point, his response to his circumstances was not itself altogether mad or crazy.

> It is obstinately held that I have become stupid to such a degree that day after day one doubts whether I still recognize people around me, whether I still understand ordinary natural phenomena, or articles of daily use or objects of art, indeed whether I still know *who I am* or *have been* [emphasis Schreber's]. The phrase 'has been recorded' with which I was examined . . . for example when I saw the doctor my nerves immediately resounded with "has been recorded"[65] . . . or the senior attendant . . . I would like to add . . . the idea that *God is totally incapable of judging a living human being correctly;. . .*" [*M*, p. 246; emphasis added].

Here, I submit, Schreber is referring to his continuous preoccupation with the fact of having been admitted to the hospital as a mental patient and to mental status examinations to which he must have been subjected at Sonnenstein, while "God" refers to Schreber's veiled scorn of the omniscience and arrogance of doctors, in this context, Weber, who at this time was not visiting the patient and would soon be rendering damaging reports about Schreber's mental status to the courts, which I will discuss in greater detail later.

Schreber shows compassion toward his earthly examiners:

> One might of course doubt whether I can or will speak the truth, in other words whether I exaggerate or suffer from self-deception. But I may say—whatever one may think of my mental faculties, that I can claim two qualities for myself without reservation, namely *absolute truthfulness* and *more than usually keen powers of observation*; no one who knew me in the days of health or witnessed my behavior now would dispute this [*M*, pp. 246-247; emphasis Schreber's].

1899

The year 1899 was one of decision. The hospital chart entry of January 22, 1899, is most instructive from the point of view of his self-diagnosis: "His 'nervous illness' was not a disorder of his mental functions but was a deep affective depression" (Appendix). In these few words is contained Schreber's own understanding of his condition conceived of solely from a medical standpoint. Implicit in this statement is that he disagreed with the official diagnosis: he maintained that he was depressed; the doctors insisted that he was a paranoiac. There was no overlap, no point of contiguity, between these two competing assessments and seemingly no way of settling the question. Accordingly, Schreber attempted to provide one by specifically maintaining that his "mental functions" were undisturbed, a fact, ironically, not contested by Weber himself. Were he dealing with a modern-day psychiatrist, Schreber might have found other grounds, and other diagnostic categories, such as "psychotic depression," upon which to forge some mutual point of departure for brokering his fate. But in terms of the medical-forensic discourse of his age, his particular choice was both astute and certain to be contested.

In the note of October 1899 Schreber challenges the legal contradictions of his case: the public prosecutor was duty-bound either to rescind the now illegal temporary incompetency status or make application for a permanent status and guardianship. "On the 9th of October personal discussion with his guardian, at which time he tendered a paper he had written about his incompetency status, whose skillful and strongly logical form is brilliant in many ways" (Appendix, October 1899). Schreber's legal essay (*M*, pp. 363–375) had little practical effect: following Weber's first report of December 9, 1899 the permanent incompetency status was instituted.

The patient and the doctors were indeed talking past each other. According to the patient:

> I really belong among educated people, not among madmen; as soon as I move among educated people, as for instance at the table of the Director of this Asylum where I have taken meals since Easter of 1900, many of the evils caused by miracles fade away, particularly the bouts of so-called bellowing, because during such times I have the opportunity to prove to God that my mental powers are undiminished. Although I have a nervous illness [*nervenkrank*], I do not suffer in any way from mental illness [*Geisteskrankheit*, psychosis] which would make me incapable of looking after my own affairs. . . . Contrary to my expectation, a formal order for my tutelage [i.e., the permanent incompetency status] was made in March 1900 by the District [County] Court in Dresden, based on a medical expert's report from this Asylum and a court hearing of January of that year [*M*, p. 268].

This first confrontation marked the beginning of a nearly three-year-long legal battle between Schreber and Superintendent Weber, who used all the forensic weapons at his disposal to prevent Schreber's discharge from the asylum.

The negative attitude of Weber is in evidence in the first of his three psychiatric opinions about Paul, dated 9 December 1899 (*M*, Addendum A), in response to Schreber's initial petition for rescission. The texts marked Addenda A to E in the Macalpine-Hunter translation, which contain Webers reports and excerpts from the court proceedings, were appended to the *Memoirs* by Schreber himself (following his discharge and prior to publication) and they are treated here as an integral part of the *Memoirs*.

In his first report, Weber recapitulated the findings in Flechsig's report dated June, 25, 1894 (see Appendix), added his own—some of which Schreber was contesting—and made two diagnoses:

> From the early, more acute psychosis . . . called hallucinatory insanity, the *paranoid form of illness* became more and more marked, crystallized out so to speak, *into its present picture.* This kind of illness is well known, characterized by the fact that next to a more or less fixed elaborate delusional system there is complete possession of mental faculties and orientation, . . . Thus President Schreber now appears *neither confused, nor psychically inhibited, nor markedly affected in his intelligence, apart from the psychomotor symptoms* which stand out clearly as pathological even to the casual observer: he is circumspect, his memory excellent, he commands a great deal of knowledge . . . and little would be noticeable in these directions to an observer not informed of his total state [*M*, pp. 385-386; emphasis added].

The early hallucinatory psychosis and the ideas of persecution by Flechsig were gone, and what counted as paranoia in Weber's eyes had to do with Sehreber's ideas of being changed into a woman and redeeming the world, and his cross-dressing. But he was a different person now. To be sure, there were those psychomotor symptoms, the bellowing and the banging on the piano, but there was a reason for them: it is very likely that Schreber worried whether he would prevail in the court battle and whether his wife would eventually take him back home. Why, then, was Dr. Weber not happy with the positive changes in his patient? Why did he not recommend taking a calculated risk, for example, a trial leave for a man possessed of so many excellent qualities? His objections were these:

> Nevertheless, the patient is *filled with pathological ideas, which are woven into a complete system,* more or less fixed, and not amenable to correction by objective evidence and judgment of circumstances as they really are; the latter still less so as hallucinatory and delusory processes continue to be of importance to him and *hinder normal evaluation of sensory impressions.* As a rule the patient does not mention these pathological ideas or only hints at them, but it is evident how much he is occupied by them, *partly from some of his writings* (extracts of some are added), partly it is easily seen *from his whole bearing* [*M*, p. 386; emphasis added].

Schreber certainly was not filled with pathological ideas, for these, by Weber's own account, were circumscribed and his intelligence was unaffected. Furthermore, as documented in the hospital chart, these ideas were neither being broadcast by Schreber, nor disguised: they were set forth in great detail in the early drafts of the *Memoirs* (on pp. 194-195), which Weber had taken possession of as a matter of asylum censorship and was now using as ammunition against Schreber. Weber was also careless in reporting the facts: he stated that Schreber was segregated in an "isolated room . . . for a number of months" (*M*, p. 383). This is contradicted by the *Memoirs* and by the entries in the chart: Schreber had been kept in the isolation room for two and a half years running. In his written report Weber damns Schreber with praise and destroys him with pathological palaver. He justifies his stand by recourse to the brain mythology of his day: "The delusory processes . . . hinder normal evaluation of sensory impressions." Hallucinations were then called in German *Sinnestäuschungen*, sensory illusions, as they are also called in Strachey's translation in the *Standard Edition*. At that time, however, false sensory impressions were the diagnostic keystone of an organicist and quasi-neurological conception of paranoia; the sensory illusions both indicated that the illness was indeed a disease of the brain and provided a rationale for Weber's prognostic assessment that Schreber's illness was chronic and incurable. But here is the rub: self-determination is not a medical but a social and ethical issue, to be decided by the court. Weber both passed this responsibility to the court and brought the weight of his forensic expertise and quasi-judicial power to bear upon the judges:

> Whether President Schreber is to be considered deprived of the use of reason in terms of the law by virtue of the above exposition of his pathological mental state, which must be labelled paranoia, is a question for the Court to decide. . . . clearly in this case the existing hallucinations, the delusions connected with them and built into a system, and the *irresistible impulses* which rule the patient, amount to a considerable degree of impairment and continue to do so [*M*, p. 389; emphasis added].

Eleven days after the County Court ruled on March 13, 1900 to uphold Schreber's incompetency and guardianship and to continue his incarceration at Sonnenstein, Schreber informed Weber—in letters of March 24, 26 and 30—of his intention "to contest this decision": "as . . . the Director of the Asylum would be asked for a further expert report about me . . . it was . . . important to acquaint him with the nature of my illness, so as to draw his attention to certain points before the report is made" (*M*, pp. 273-274).

As Paul Schreber, J.D., predicted, the court indeed asked Weber for a new report. Accordingly, to acquaint Weber better with the nature of his illness, Schreber handed him the text of the 22 chapters of the *Memoirs* newly completed in September of 1900, in the hope of gaining Weber's understanding and support before Weber wrote the new report. Weber handed in his second report on November 28, 1900 (Addendum B), *following* a perusal of the *Memoirs*. After rehashing arguments from his first published report (*M*, p. 393) and the second unpublished report of November 7, 1895, Weber reaffirmed his opinion: "A *favorable outcome* of the illness . . . must be abandoned. . . . there is a *total lack* . . . of . . . insight . . . he adheres firmly to the reality of his delusional ideas and declares the most *monstrous* of the events described by him as facts" (M, p. 396; emphasis added).

Instead of trying to see the positive, Weber went out of his way to exaggerate the negative to the point of monstrosity. He continued confidently to use the text of the future *Memoirs* as his trump card: "From them [the *Memoirs*] the Judge will readily obtain a clear picture of the author's mental state without any further comments [and without further ado, *ohne weiteres*, omitted in the Macalpine translation] (*M*, p. 394). According to Weber, these *Memoirs* were the best proof

> that he lacks insight into the pathological nature of the hallucinations and the ideas that influence him; what objectively are delusions and hallucinations are to him unassailable truth *and adequate motive for action. It follows from this that the patient's decisions at a given moment are quite unpredictable*; he may follow and turn into action what his relatively intact mental powers dictate or *he may act under the compulsion of his pathological mental processes*. In this connection I wish to draw particular attention to a very pregnant example and for this reason I enclose the patient's 'Memoirs' [*M*, pp. 401–402; emphasis added].

However, in the *Memoirs* Schreber repeatedly qualifies his voices as nonsense, he displays great insight, and there is no proof that the voices are instigators of irresistible actions save for the bellowing. Nevertheless, Weber was scandalized and revolted by the *Memoirs*:

> When one looks at the content of his writings, and takes into consideration the abundance of indiscretions relating to himself and others contained in them, the unembarrassed detailing of the most doubtful and aesthetically impossible situations and events, the most offensive vulgar words, etc., one finds it quite incomprehensible that a man otherwise tactful and of fine feeling could propose an action which would compromise him so severely in the eyes of the public, were not his whole attitude to life pathological, and he unable to see things in their total perspective, and if the tremendous overvaluation of his own person

caused by lack of insight into his illness had not clouded his appreciation of the limitations imposed on man by society [M, p. 402].

It does not matter that by Weber's own earlier admission ("The undersigned has for nine months had the most thorough opportunity of discussing all sorts of subjects with President Schreber during daily meals at the family table") Schreber "was well-behaved and amiable" (M, p. 397), or that "he dealt with safeguarding his family's copyright in his father's book in an altogether professional manner" (M, p. 401). To Weber, Schreber was a paranoiac, an *Untermensch* (a subhuman species), a devil quoting the Scripture.

In the next sentence Weber rushes to prognosticate that because "in the face of the grand mission" of publishing the *Memoirs* "pecuniary interests naturally recede into the background . . . it must be regarded as doubtful [*zweifelhaft*, also precarious] how far the striving for pathological hopes and wishes for the future . . . would lead him to material expenses far beyond his means" (M, p. 401). Pathological squandering of one's fortune was a recognized forensic-psychiatric criterion of craziness and grounds for depriving a person of civil rights and personal freedom on grounds of incompetency.

Weber was also identified with the interests of Sabine Schreber, who had acted both fearful and overly cautious toward her husband. Thus the second report continues: "[Because of the] considerable concern owing to his conduct until now [and] reasonable concern of his family [his wife or members of his own family?] . . . it has not been possible to extend the trials [of functioning outside the asylum]" (M, pp. 392-393). This conclusion suggests undue caution, since Schreber was no longer suicidal, nor was he ever a threat to another person. It also means that in the absence of trial leaves, Weber had no data to conclude that Schreber, because of his delusions, was incapable of handling his affairs, a finding that would later impress the judges at appeal.

Weber's final thrust relates to Schreber's ongoing symptom of bellowing, or vociferation. By 1900 the stormy hallucinations and delusions were long gone. Schreber now experienced periods of relief that alternated with recurrent attacks of anxiety. (He may be anxious about the success of his attempts to get out of Sonnenstein alive.) The "miracles" he now experienced were described as follows:

> [I suffer] all manner of painful states [which] occur alternately (namely when God withdraws again), almost without exception quite suddenly and vanishing equally regularly after a short time. [for example] . . . sciatica, cramp in the calves, states of paralysis, sudden attacks of hunger, and suchlike. . . . Sometimes the lumbago was so painful . . . I

could only lift myself from the bed with the simultaneous cries of pain—
half *voluntarily* uttered. . . . Even now I suffer from almost uninterrupted
headaches of a kind certainly unknown to other human beings, and
hardly comparable to ordinary headaches. They are tearing and pulling
pains. . . . My sleep is on the whole very much better than before; I have
already mentioned that sometimes I cannot remain in bed because of the
persistent states of bellowing (which alternate with high-grade sensuous
pleasure). . . . Rarely do dreams have character of visions, i.e., the peculiar vividness of impressions. The talk of voices has slowed down even
more since my description in chapter XVI, so that it is almost nothing
more than a *hissing* in my head. . . . Most troublesome now are the states
of bellowing—next to an occasional bad head—by which I have been
visited for two or three years, and which have in the last year been an
almost unbearable plague. Whether one can expect them to improve in
the future I dare not prophesy; but if I could take up residence outside the
Asylum I believe, for reasons given earlier, that these things would
improve [*M*, pp. 270-272; emphasis Schreber's].

This prophecy would be fulfilled in due course. But in the meantime
Weber offered dire prognoses, still protecting Sabine:

It is the patient's opinion that these attacks of bellowing might improve
after eventual discharge from the Asylum; . . . [that] he can avoid the
resulting disturbances of peace and quiet . . . his . . . statements are naturally illusory, . . . the patient in his morbid egoism does not even
consider how his wife would have to suffer from all this; in fact married
life with him would be almost impossible for her; [he] . . . complains
only of *his own* suffering. The ill-effect of the illness on marital relations
is according to his wife's information, also noticeable in other ways.
Earlier on, the patient had offered his wife a possible divorce in view of
his expected unmanning; even now when she demurs and contradicts his
ideas and behavior, he is quick to hint that she could leave him if she
wished. Therefore in this respect also one must not overlook the impact
of the pathological process [*M*, p. 400; emphasis added].

This is not a friendly opinion. Schreber is damned either way:
should he want to expose the poor wife to his bellowing, then he is a
monster of selfishness; should he offer her a divorce and live by himself
in an isolated house, then his offer of divorce is proof of the impact of
pathological processes. Weber ended his reports with confidence that
the judges would have no trouble endorsing his conclusion that "the
present mental illness is sufficient in extent and severity to prevent the
patient from looking after his affairs in the widest sense" (*M*, p. 403).

On the basis of this report, on April 13 of 1901, the intermediate
court, the Dresden District Court, upheld the earlier decision of the

County Court to maintain Schreber under guardianship and behind the walls of Sonnenstein. This decision Schreber proceeded to appeal to the highest court, the *Oberlandesgericht* of Dresden, the very same court of appeals where he had served as president of the Third Chamber eight years earlier, prior to falling ill the second time in 1893.

SCHREBER'S WRIT OF APPEAL

The writ of appeal (*Memoirs*, Addendum C), dated July 23 1901 (two days before his 59th birthday), is a moving act of self-defense. Schreber had decided to dismiss his lawyer, whom he found inept, and handle his own appeal. He argued both factually and cogently and did a much better job than his principal opponent, Weber. While Weber's arguments show many gaps and contradictions, Schreber was in full command of his facts and drove his point home consistently and inexorably.

Having dismissed the *Memoirs* as worthless, Weber also overlooked Schreber's essay on forensic psychiatry, written at Sonnenstein in early 1900 and reflected in the book's complete title, "In what circumstances[66] can a person considered insane be detained in an asylum against his declared will?" (p. 268, Foot Note #107). The legal principles Schreber nails down in this essay are both cogent and valid, and he knew the pertinent paragraphs by heart. They also were the basis for his own pleadings before Weber and in the courts. In the essay Schreber made it clear that a psychiatrist acting as director of a public asylum is not so different from a policeman. A person may be deprived of his liberty only if he is a danger to himself or to others. These are the only legal grounds for involuntary confinement, Schreber argues, and they have to be established on the basis of documented unreasonable action and so proven in court. The various ordinances were merely administrative procedures regarding admission and as such, devoid of any legal principle, which Schreber was at pains to define.

While respectful of the rights of a psychiatrist to confine a person who may be prone to irresistible impulse in the acute phase of an illness, Schreber argues that "the mere subjective opinion of the chief physician that the patient would be better left in his hands than anywhere else, would not entitle the former to restrict the patient in any way in the choice of his future residence" (*M*, p. 365), or be "transferred to another asylum" (p. 371). Schreber agrees that "incurable cases, deeply demented and abhorrent to look at" do belong in the custodial asylum "*Landesversorganstalt zu Colditz*"[67] (Did he know Weber first worked there?) (*M*, p. 368). Regarding such cases as the exceptions, Schreber continues:

All the other cases of mental illness . . . showing perhaps a few delusions—of whom it cannot be said that being at liberty would be dangerous either to themselves or others . ... I would like to designate as cases of *harmless insanity* for the purpose of their position in *administrative law*—irrespective of how these diseases are classified by *scientific psychiatry* [added in Foot Note #127 on that page]. The writer of this essay counts himself amongst the harmless mental patients in the sense described above; it is said of him that he is possessed by religious hallucinations, whereas in his own opinion these contain objective truth unrecognizable by other people. He trusts in particular to have proved with this essay that cases do in fact exist, in which clarity of logical and particularly juristical thinking is unimpaired by the presumed hallucinations, so that one cannot maintain the existence of a morbid mental derangement excluding free determination of will *in the direction of unreasonable action* . . . nor an inability to look after his own affairs . . . [*M*, p. 368; emphasis Schreber's].

With these points in mind, Schreber argues he was entitled to the status of a "voluntary boarder" (*M*, p. 375), which he was when he first entered Flechsig's asylum until he was declared psychotic and legally incompetent. Toward a harmless and voluntary patient, both Flechsig and Weber could "essentially only [be] a medical adviser; *on the question of deprivation of liberty* his relation. . .[would be] in no way different from that of any private practitioner towards his patient" (p. 371; emphasis Schreber's). This was his contract with Flechsig. With Weber this contract became null and void. For with the help of the existing laws Weber became empowered by the state, as "the Director of a Public Asylum [acting as] an organ of security police" to deprive Schreber of his liberty, such that this deprivation of liberty assumed the character of an "*illegal incarceration* [*den Charakter einer widerrechtlichen Freiheitsberaubung*]" (p. 371; emphasis Schreber's).

In the essay Schreber then begins his appeal by correcting two of his lawyer's fundamental errors: (1) the endorsement of Weber's idea that he is psychotic, that is, suffering from "paranoia [*Verrücktheit*, craziness], an idea that is, says Schreber, "a blow in the face of truth, which could hardly be worse . . . where the recognition of my legal capacity is at stake . . . " (*M*, p. 405) and (2) the following assumption

[that] I myself consider my stay in the Asylum as one which could only be to the advantage of my mental well-being. This is not quite true. . . . I do not expect any advantage to my health by extending my stay in this Asylum. . . . I do not wish to spend the rest of my life in an institution. . . . Should certain nuisances (like the bellowing) continue to give concern as regards my appearing in public, I would know how to restrain myself in such circumstances [*M*, pp. 406-407].

The main purpose of the appeal was to refute the district court judgment that upheld the recent incompetency ruling. But since that judgment was entirely based on Weber's second report, Schreber's appeal became a matter of refuting that report. This Schreber does in a number of well-thought-out steps.

1. "I accept entirely the remarks in the judgment referring to the fact that there is no reason for concern about my endangering my life if freedom over my person were granted to me" (M, p. 408).

2. "The so-called attacks of bellowing can remain out of consideration because pure police matters could not furnish grounds for upholding my tutelage" (M, p. 408).

3. "[As to] hallucinations: it is a question only of earlier phases of my illness" (M, p. 409).

4. One's religious convictions are one's right, beyond the pale of science, and are not to be reduced to pathology. Against any detractor, Schreber argues, he would echo "Huss's cry to the wretched peasants who were carrying wood for his stake: *Oh sancta simplicitas!* [holy naïveté]" (p. 410). He, too, is willing to suffer for his "insight into the true state of divine matters," which, he says, "accounts for my continual serenity" (p. 411). Schreber is acutely aware of the risk he is taking: for "[by voicing my] so-called delusions or . . . religious beliefs . . . the attention of the Court might be diverted from the decisive and only question in their competence, namely, *whether I possess the capacity for reasonable action in practical life*" (p. 412; emphasis Schreber's).

5. He takes an even greater risk by continuing to maintain that his uncontrollable psychomotor symptoms, such as banging on his piano, noisy outbursts of bellowing, and involuntary grimacing, are caused by "influences which can only be ascribed to forces working from the outside, in other words . . . divine miracles" (p. 417). Of course, Schreber does not have recourse to the notion of unconscious processes as causing unbidden behavior, but he does argue that the difference between himself and the expert is due to their assuming different beliefs of causality, due, that is, to a difference in the climate of opinion or, as Shaw said, of credulity. *"In essence it is one assertion versus another"* (p. 419; emphasis Schreber's); he claims for himself the same right as enjoyed by Weber—to maintain his own beliefs.

6. As to Weber's ability to assess his capacity for self-determination, Schreber says, "[he] has only come to know me really well in the last year, that is since I have taken my meals regularly at his family table. . . . Before that time . . . the medical expert only became acquainted with the pathological shell, as I would like to call it, which concealed my true spiritual life" (p. 424). If Weber wanted to, he could have tried, Schreber insists, "to get to know me sooner as a human

being in full power of his mental powers . . . at least [since] the beginning of the year 1897" (p. 425). Schreber asserts, "[It is] not quite
correct . . . that I showed no inclination . . . to move outside the Asylum" (p. 424). He continues: "On 8th October 1899 I complained
to . . . Schmidt my official guardian that for five years I had not been
allowed outside the walls of the Asylum even for the small walks
allowed to many other patients. In order to be loyal I sent a written
copy of this exposition to Dr. Weber in a letter of November 27th
1899" (p. 425), that is, just prior to Weber's first negative report of
December 9, 1899.

7. Schreber presses his point relentlessly; he insists he is capable of
acting reasonably: "The *onus of proof* lies with my opponent, the Public
Prosecutor, . . . [because it is] the duty of him *who requests* that a person
be placed under tutelage to furnish the Judge with the required factual
proofs [instead of] vague generalities" (*M*, p. 427; emphasis Schreber's), such as those offered by Weber. Schreber argues, "It is *not my
fault that for years I have been detained in the Asylum and denied leave*, after
the real reason, that is, to safeguard myself and other people from
danger, had passed (*M*, p. 428; emphasis Schreber's) and treated "legally like a child under seven" (p. 427).

8. "The *only thing* which could be counted as somewhat unreasonable in the eyes of other persons is as mentioned by the medical expert,
that at times I was standing in front of the mirror or elsewhere with
some female adornments . . . I have *very good and important reasons* for
this behaviour, . . . Even if people think the advantage exists in my
imagination only, . . . they can at worst see in it an incomprehensible
whim, the *absolute harmlessness* of which cannot be denied" (pp. 429, 430;
emphasis Schreber's). This is the only perversion of Schreber's: cross-
dressing, not homosexuality.

9. Claiming that he has "never given occasion for doubt in the
sincerity of [his] love of truth," Schreber maintains that there would be
no danger of his behaving recklessly in money matters or with regard
to his wife, effectively rebutting Weber's claims about his "pathologically increased egoism." And if he were unable to control his outbursts, Schreber says, "I would be sufficiently sensitive to the impossibility of staying outside of a closed institution and would return to it
of *my own free will* without there being any necessity for compulsion on
police grounds" (p. 439; emphasis Schreber's).

10. Schreber insists on his right to publish his memoirs and assures
the Court he "will not necessarily give them to the printer *in their
present form without changes* . . . without detracting from the whole"
(pp. 440–441; emphasis Schreber's). He will consider his family: "My
father's and my brother's memory as well as my wife's honour are as

sacred to me as anyone in similar circumstances who has the reputation of his near relatives at heart" (p. 442).

He apologizes that "sexual matters are widely discussed," explaining, "this is not due to my taste or predilection, but rests entirely on the fact . . . that voluptuousness is closely related to the state of Blessedness of departed spirits . . . I am sure nobody could say I have shown particular pleasure in vulgarities; on the contrary, one cannot miss the moral seriousness which pervades my whole work and which seeks no other goal but the achievement of truth . . . " (p. 443). As it is, Schreber already knows that he has been "treated very *much more respectfully* in [the] Asylum since the contents of [his] "Memoirs" became known and [his] intellectual and moral personality appreciated differently than had perhaps been possible before" (p. 444; emphasis Schreber's).

11. Schreber dismisses the danger of being accused of libel because of the way he writes about Flechsig. He had to write about him, he says, for two reasons: it is important for his story and it also proves that he is capable of managing his affairs. Flechsig is not likely to bring action against him, and were he to do so, he notes with irony, it would be better to endure a "few months' imprisonment at the most" than be locked up "in an Asylum *for a lifetime* deprived of freedom and fortune" (p. 448; emphasis Schreber's).

12. He ends with a promise to stay in the asylum for as long as is necessary for his health but that the guardianship ought to be rescinded: "As long as I am under tutelage [I] have to fear being sent from pillar to post with my request" (p. 451).

WEBER'S LAST STAND AND SCHREBER'S VICTORY

Eight months after Schreber's appeal Weber agreed reluctantly to furnish a supplementary report on Schreber, since "the appellant has been able to move about more freely since the last report and had command over larger sums of money" (*M*, p. 454).

In Weber's supplementary report the old arguments are rehashed: "[we are dealing with] diseases of the human brain" (p. 454); "scientifically . . . the appellant's mental illness and its peculiarities . . . clearly belong to a well-known and well-characterized form of mental illness, paranoia" (p. 456). Before long Weber begins to speak of "partial insanity" in this case (p. 457). Thus, gradually, the lofty scientific discourse begins to show cracks: "The well-known complicated delusional system has crystallized out and become fixed and the patient has come to terms with it . . . [and] being less affect-laden it only acts and reacts little on the rest of his mind, particularly on that part concerned with daily life, and does not influence his actions significantly" (p. 463).

And there is a new development altogether, as revealed in the following passage:

> [With] gradually increasing freedom of movement in view of his general improvement . . . since the summer of this year [1901] he has been allowed out unaccompanied. At that time the appellant's mother and sister took up residence in Wehlen nearby, as planned and arranged by President Schreber himself. For a number of weeks he visited them almost daily. . . . Since then the appellant has been granted absolute freedom of movement outside the Asylum without restriction . . . [*M*, pp. 464-465]

Weber begins to yield: "One must testify that in the appellant's behavior on all these occasions there was never anything unreasonable or unfitting . . . [and his] conduct in the outside world was never incorrect" (p. 465); consequently, "from the medical side in agreement with the apellant's legal adviser and with himself, . . . at present the pathological manifestations noticeable *outwardly* concern mostly relatively unimportant fields, . . . Only . . . his efforts to get his Memoirs published [can] be regarded as a harmful action" (p. 470; emphasis Schreber's).

Weber began by saying he would not comment on Schreber's ability to act rationally but only on the nature of the illness; he ended by saying, in favor of Schreber, that there was no substantive ground for a ruling of legal incapacity. After a few more back-and-forth exchanges he reached a conclusion: "Apprehension for the future, therefore, need not weigh as heavily to-day as previously in judging the over-all situation" (p. 472).

THE APPEAL JUDGES' VERDICT

As a result of Schreber's action, on July 14, 1902, his appeal was allowed and both the previous decisions of the lower courts upholding the guardianship were overturned. The noteworthy fact is that whereas during the hearings in the lower court Schreber was damned both by Weber's report and by his personal appearance, now he was both impressive and persuasive. The judges upheld Schreber's basic contention against Weber:

> A person who is capable of dealing with so involved a legal matter in self-composed representations with circumspection and expert knowledge, and is tactful and discreet where other people's opinions are

concerned, should be trusted to be capable also of managing the simpler and less important matters of ordinary life in a competent way [*M*, p. 479].

Some of the judges' arguments in favor of Schreber are of interest and also a source of historical information. The justices upheld Schreber's right to his idiosyncratic religious beliefs, no matter how pathological they appeared to Weber:

> Dr. Weber stands with his feet firmly planted in rationalism, which denies out of hand the possibility of supernatural happenings. In opposition to him the plaintiff champions fundamentally the contrary point of view. . . . One does not usually and without further reason declare the adherents of spiritualism mentally ill and put them under a guardian, although their way of looking at things supernaturally is also neither shared nor comprehended by the vast majority of their fellow men [*M*, p. 481].

Regarding the persistence of pathological symptoms, that is, the bellowing, the court was also on Schreber's side: "He has observed that the bellowing occurred only while he was in the Asylum but almost never outside, when travelling, etc." (*M*, p. 489). Furthermore, "in point of fact, in the last two years not a single instance of unreasonable action could be proved against him" (p. 490). Moreover, Schreber could now name a number of character witnesses in his favor, among them the following: "his brother-in-law, the merchant Karl Jung in Leipzig and his wife, his eldest sister [Anna, the only time she is mentioned]; his brother-in-law, the Country Court Judge Krause in Chemnitz [where Schreber worked prior to his first illness] and his wife; . . . Dr. Hennig [?the editor of his father's *Kallipädie*]; the publisher Nauhardt, the possible publisher of his "Memoirs," all in Leipzig. They would all confirm that during their meetings with him they received the impression of a completely reasonable person capable of every demand of social and business life, in whom they as laymen did not notice the least sign of mental illness, let alone one making him incapable of managing his affairs" (pp. 491-492).

In overturning the incompetency ruling the judges did note "that there is no doubt that the appellant is insane [*geisteskrank*]. One would not wish to argue with him whether he suffers from a mental illness [*Geisteskrankheit*, psychosis] known as paranoia. . . . But it is not sufficient ground for placing plaintiff under tutelage . . . " (*M*, p. 494). They noted that in his last report Weber left the question of incompetency open and the decision to the court's discretion; the judges reached the following conclusion: "The progress of recent legislation lies precisely in the fact that it is now possible to leave such more or less harmless persons in possession of their legal capacity of free disposition necessary for their progress in life. . . . only one single field of plaintiff's mental life is affected, the field of religion" (pp. 497-498).

The judges also ruled—and this was a benchmark decision (Hoche, 1909)—that those who requested the upholding of the incompetency, Dr. Weber and the Public Prosecutor, had not positively established the existence of incapacity on the basis of actual observation; that Dr. Weber's report suggested that at best the patient was suffering only from "partial insanity," so that "the pathological ideas . . . withdraw to a certain circumscribed field and within these limits maintain a kind of 'separate existence'" (M, p. 499); and that in the meantime the patient's condition had improved and that Weber's findings were "altogether favorable to the plaintiff" (M, p. 502). The judges noted that Dr. Weber agreed in principle to the patient's discharge from the Asylum, with certain precautions, and had "no hesitation in returning plaintiff to free congress with human society" (p. 508).

Even as the judges slightly embellished Weber's opinions, they duly noted that Schreber also showed excellent judgment in managing his finances, had expressed due concern for his wife's interests and his intention to improve marital relations, and had gained the approval of his brother-in-law Karl Jung, the merchant in Leipzig, for the way he managed "the extraordinarily difficult question of making further use of his father's book 'Medical Indoor Gymnastics' after its publisher had gone into liquidation"(M, p. 510)

The judges overruled the finding of the lower court that the "Memoirs" were defamatory and "damaging the honor of the family." Instead, they reached the following conclusions:

> It is a fact that nothing of this kind can be found in the manuscript. One also cannot maintain the contents of the "Memoirs" are such as to compromise plaintiff himself. The manuscript is the product of a morbid imagination and nobody reading it would for a moment lose the feeling that its author is mentally deranged. But this could not possibly lower the patient in respect of his fellow men, particularly as no one can miss the seriousness of purpose and the striving after truth which fill every chapter. As Dr. Schreber remarks correctly, the worst that could happen to him would be that one consider him mad, and this one does in any case [M, pp. 513-514].

Nor was there any danger of Schreber's being sued for defamation by Professor Flechsig, who was accused of soul murder and worse.

Schreber was protected under paragraph 51 of the Criminal Code, because—and this is the only cutely quaint reason given by the judges—"here the plaintiff is not in any way talking for himself or acting on his own behalf, but only reporting what the voices of miraculous spirits told him, with whom in his opinion he was in communication." Similarly: "One cannot be offended by the strong language in the book. It is not plaintiff's; he only repeats what the voices of spirits spoke into him in earlier years when he was most severely hallucinated" (*M*, p. 514).

This is quite remarkable: here the good judges have not only canceled their previous opinion that Schreber was suffering from even partial insanity: they even went so far as to agree with the appellant that those voices were every bit as real as Schreber himself had believed them to be. They also ruled that the book was not only worth publishing but that since it was to be published on a commission basis, it did not represent a ruinous expenditure of money. The judges may have rescued the book from destruction.

At the end of two and a half years of litigation Schreber emerged victorious. The judgment was signed on July 26, 1902, one day after Schreber's 60th birthday. Since the judgment was not appealed, it became valid on the 1st of September of 1902. Yet Schreber stayed at Sonnenstein until the 20th of December of that year. Why did he tarry? For his own sake or to impress Weber? He was discharged in time to celebrate Christmas and the New Year with his loved ones.

THE FIFTH PERIOD: 1903–1907, BEFORE THE THIRD ILLNESS

The few facts we have about Schreber for the period 1903–1907 are useful historically and for contemplating his diagnosis. As far as the latter is concerned, Schreber showed adequate social performance, and there was no overt evidence of mental disorder.[68] None can be found in the poems he wrote during that time (D. P. Schreber, 1904, 1905, 1907). There is no direct evidence (Israëls, 1989, agrees) for Niederland's assertions that Schreber held on "to the conviction that he was a woman with female breasts and with feminine attributes" (Niederland, 1974, p. 7).

Schreber's nephew remembered that after his release Paul called at various family members to present himself as recovered (Israëls, 1989, p. 189). Weber's son, who became a specialist in nervous diseases in Dresden, described him in those years as "outwardly normal and in good spirits." According to the testimony of Schreber's adopted daughter Fridoline (Niederland, 1969), her father did not show morbid symptoms or disturbances. There was a hint of some short-lived moments of bellowing (Niederland, 1969); sometimes he held his head askew and often sat with his eyes closed (Baumeyer, 1970, p. 244). As recalled by his sister prior to his last admission, "The voices never completely disappeared. But he did not speak at all about the illness. When questioned, he said there was a spot at the back of his head where he experienced a constant buzzing noise, as if a thread were pulled. The voices were now only an unintelligible noise. He said nothing about his delusions, did not even mention them once to his wife" (Appendix).

At first Paul went to live with his mother and sister. Attempts to find employment with the Ministry of Justice came to naught. According to the existing laws, a jurist with a history of mental illness, unlike a doctor, could no longer work again in his profession: Schreber had the bridges burned behind him (Hoche, 1909). As remembered by a descendant, "Paul Schreber dressed in woman's clothing, in private, to be sure" (Wienstein, 1989). The perception was that Schreber had disgraced himself by conduct unbecoming to a judge and had thus forfeited the chance of getting his job back. He did, however, do private legal work for the family and lived on his pension. It must have been ample enough to permit the construction of a new house in Dresden:

> During the construction of the house he was interested and took care of everything. . . . At home he played the piano a lot and was a good chess player. Twice a week he went downtown and there he played both chess parties with the aid of a chess journal. He read a lot and showed interest in everything that had to do with culture. Everyone who knew him was impressed with his personality and warm humanity" [Baumeyer, 1973, p. 244].

When the house was ready in 1905, he moved there not only with his wife, but with a 13-year-old foster daughter Fridoline. He formally adopted the child in 1906, arguably the sunniest event of his life at this time.[69]

At this time Schreber also gave expression to his feelings for his wife in a poem, "To his dear Sabchen [diminutive of Sabine] for the nineteenth of June dedicated by her Paul" (D. P. Schreber, 1907), composed in honor of her 50th birthday and in celebration of the 30 years of their marriage, only two months after his mother's death at age 92 and a few months before Sabine's stroke and his final decompensation. It refers to his second illness. Let me quote a few lines.

> Should I speak to you of things past—
> Not joy alone is there to relate in verse.

Not only about happiness and cheer can I sing.
Several times we closed up our hope in a coffin.
Some of those dear to us have been lowered into the grave.
Both of your parents have long since perished.
Nor have I remained son to a mother.
The full force of youth, which may not know
Limits for its goals and wishes,
Oh, it sometimes even wavered,
And suffered now and then because of little things.
And worse yet: my mind, disturbed for a second time,
Was in the bonds of heavy illness;
The bitter cup of separation and sorrow,
Full of grief and suffering, was yours again.
Nine heavy years passed in that way,
You could almost consider yourself a widow;
Hope of returning hardly came to mind.
Prospects for recovery hardly seemed to beckon;
But for that very reason we mustn't complain,
Since much changed for the better;
We once again saw light after troubled days,
Old love's bonds were newly knotted. . . .

So let a grain of joy be scattered now and then
On our path in the evening of life.
But if nothing else remains according to our wishes,
May one thing stand beyond all time:
That you keep your past love for me
As mine is faithfully dedicated to you
       [D. P. Schreber, 1907, lines 10–32, 51–56].

These lines are suffused with bittersweet sadness and yearning for love. There is no doubt that Schreber loved his "dear Sabchen." The poem also clarifies important aspects of Paul's character. He reflects on the many losses in their lives: the most recent death of his mother and others "dear to us" who "have been lowered into the grave." He mentions his sensitivity to frustrations of "limits for . . . goals and wishes, . . . [having] suffered now and then because of little things . . . The bitter cup of separation and sorrow" (lines 18–22). These have been his sensibilities and frustrations throughout his life. It also points to a great need in him to love and to be loved in return; note his having found lost love again.

We first encountered the adoptive daughter, Fridoline, in describing Paul's marriage and the theory that the birth of the child may have been a precipitating factor in the onset of the second illness. She was born in

1890 in Wilten, then a village in the vicinity of, now a part of, Innsbruck, Austria, to Franz Petter, a Wagnerian Heldentenor and a mother who has not been identified.[70] According to Fridoline's testimony, since she lost her mother (we do not know when), Sabine, who knew Franz Petter through her connections with theater people in her father's circle, offered to adopt the child. Paul agreed. If true to fact, it is noteworthy that the adoption of Fridoline was not formalized until 1906. Why so late? This may have some connection with the presence up to that point of her own father, Franz Petter, in Dresden, where he came in 1899 to sing at the Royal Opera House. According to the information supplied by Dr. Uwe Peters (1990), he officially assumed the position of the "youthful hero tenor" at the Cologne Opera House on September 1, 1904. What negotiations had gone on, and since when, between the father of the child and the Schrebers? Why did not the daughter choose to live with her father? How did all this affect Paul? All these are unanswered questions.

The three-story townhouse built for the Schrebers in Dresden still stands in all its splendor, untouched by age, at the corner of Angelika street 15a, surrounded by a garden with tall pines. The letter *S* is seen in the grillwork. Above the entrance, in musical notation, is the Siegfried motif from Richard Wagner's *Siegfried* (the other Wagnerian hero Schreber mentions in the *Memoirs* being Tannhäuser). We cannot know with certainty whose idea it was to put it there.[71] Sabine's father and Fridoline's father both sang Wagner roles.

"We once again saw light after troubled days,/Old love's bonds were newly knotted" says Paul in the poem on his wife's 50th birthday (Schreber, 1907). Had Paul finally found peace with Sabine? Fridoline described her as a "charming, spoilt, selfish woman, with many connections in the theatre world and to the stage manager Levinger" (Niederland, 1969).

Paul most certainly found solace in raising his adoptive daughter. Father and daughter became friends. Fridoline got along very well with her adoptive father but had problems with her mother. For example, Sabine insisted that she change her religion from Catholic to Evangelical Lutheran and threatened to return her to her humble surroundings in Innsbruck, but Paul insisted she be left alone. Fridoline Hammer described herself at her arrival at the Schrebers' as a country girl, speaking the Tyrol dialect and quite an *enfant terrible*. She was well received by her aunts but with considerable reserve by her grandmother Pauline. In his patience toward her, Paul Schreber was, Fridoline told Niederland, "more of a mother to me than my mother." Niederland wrote of his interaction with Fridoline:

She also gave me letters and poems written by Schreber, details on his personal warmth and kindness, told me how he helped her with her school work, took her on hikes through the forests and mountains surrounding Dresden. . . . Schreber's letters and poetry disclose his personal sensitivity and a quality of genuine tenderness, over and above that creative ability which found expression also in the writing of the *Memoirs* [Niederland, 1974, pp. 31-32].[72]

"In my entire life I have not encountered a man nobler than him [i.e., Paul Schreber]: he was loving, just and kind and extremely knowledgeable" (Niederland, 1969). He spoke Latin, Greek, French, English and Italian. He was musical, was interested in history, geography and religion, but was at the same time liberal minded and not a devout church goer. He never mentioned his experiences at Sonnenstein.

Trouble came again in 1907, from two sources: rivalries and squabbles amongst the various Schreber associations regarding bequests and death and illness in the family. Schreber's sister recalled that "After mother's death he busied himself with many calculations of the many bequests, was somewhat overworked and therefore [*daher*, missing in Baumeyer, 1955] slept poorly some nights" (Appendix). Paul's mother Pauline Schreber became an honorary member of the oldest Schreber associations and left in her bequest 500 marks apiece to a number of Schreber Associations (Israëls, 1989, pp. 207-209, 261-264). The rivalries and squabbles that developed between the legatees may have compounded Paul's sorrows in the wake of his mother's death. His wife's stroke, however, hit him much harder.

SIXTH PERIOD: 1907-1911, SCHREBER'S LAST ILLNESS AND DEATH

It will be remembered that during his defense at appeals Schreber had maintained against Weber that if he ever needed psychiatric help, he would know where to find it. He kept his word. He himself instructed his daughter to summon the physician, Dr. Dannenberg, should anything go wrong with him. He was ready to be readmitted.

The emotional pressure on Schreber due to the problems in connection with the death of his mother and the rivalries among the various Schreber associations pale in comparison with the sudden and profound effect upon him of his wife's illness, which struck on November 14, 1907. Sabine suffered a sudden brain hemorrhage and stroke that left her with disturbances of vision and loss of speech. She recovered, but, according to Fridoline, "remained very irritated and exceedingly irritable, so that it was very difficult to stay around her. From 1907 on she became more and more difficult to live with" (Niederland, 1969).

Of her adoptive father Fridoline said: "The illness of my mother upset him very much and he became agitated" (quoted in Niederland, 1969). With one stroke, literally and figuratively, the fragile equilibrium Paul Schreber had achieved was shattered. Once more loss struck. The end-of-the-world mood was upon Schreber again. He gave up his interest in life and the urge to fight for it.

The psychiatric scene had changed since 1902. Sonnenstein was now full to capacity. New cases were routed to the new asylum (opened in 1901) in Dösen, then a village (now a suburb) in the south of Leipzig, which Schreber entered on November 27, 1907, for the last leg of his journey on earth. Once again it was November: the month his father died, the month of his second admission to Flechsig's, and now the month of his wife's apoplexy.

The narrative at this point is no longer Schreber's own, except for a few notes and scribbles in his own hand: we rely on the clinical record from the Dösen Asylum (see Appendix). There, he withdrew entirely from relating to the world and his loved ones. He became a regressed, incontinent, care-dependent, mostly bed-ridden psychiatric-geriatric inmate, waiting to die, living out his last years in an intermittent depressive stupor, punctuated by outbursts of screaming and laughter.

On admission, Schreber was inaccessible, looked pale, stiff in posture and gait; he opened his eyes only seldom during closed questioning, and exhibited a twitching of his raised eyebrows and the corners of the mouth. He was oriented to his surroundings and his answers were correct, but nothing about his immediate past could be elicited—he did not want to be bothered. His attitude toward the attendants was "domineering and haughty" and he was described as "melancholy." I submit that it is psychotic depression and despair that are again the central clinical findings, of which the central features, from now to the end, are gloominess, withdrawal, poor appetite and stubborn constipation, smearing himself with feces, suicidal gestures, and poor sleep. The delusional depressive ideas of "The odor of corpses, rotting [*Leichengeruch, Verwesung*]" (December 1, 1907) are repeated on December 5, 1907:

> Food intake very limited. He maintains he has no stomach any more, that he lost an intestine in a "miraculous way" [*auf wunderbare Weise*]. It will happen that "the body will begin to rot" while "the head will keep on living." He refuses to answer further questions. "I cannot express any opinion about that now." "You will not be able to understand this" [Appendix].

Schreber asked about arrangements for his burial and once said to his doctor, cast in the role of executioner: "If you want to kill me, do it already" (August, 1908). The word *rotting* echoes the accusation for which Schreber would become famous in our own age, that of "soul murder." Prominent also were anxiety attacks with violent outbursts, punctuated by groans and screams of "Ha-ha-ha" (August, 1908, Appendix).

This description of his condition runs through the entire hospital chart until his death. We find in it repeated conclusions by the psychiatrists about alleged hallucinations and delusions. The few documented delusions echo the ones described at Sonnenstein and are typically congruent with his depressed mood. The psychotic mode of expression has returned in force, but the morbid, depressive content is more pronounced as compared to the exalted flights of fancy of the second episode. There was no notation found of any visits by Sabine or other relatives.

However, some very telling statements, the last before his death, were scribbled in pencil on scraps of paper. In the chart we read: "Now and then writes in barely legible characters, 'Miracle'(after he was asked the cause of his groaning) or 'Tomb' or 'No food'." The pieces of paper are kept in a special envelope, attached to the chart at the Dösen psychiatric hospital.[73]

The last intact text of Paul Schreber from December 11, 1907, written shortly after his admission, reads as follows:

> I am ready to sign a declaration with a firm hand, which, as has somehow become known to me, is required of me by the supervising authorities of the Dösen Hospital concerning the special form of burial that will be carried out, and to this effect I request to be acquainted with the essential content of such an ordinance. D. Schreber, Senatspräsident, retired [hospital chart from the former Leipzig-Dösen Asylum].

Later came fragments of thought, like leaves drifting on water, scribbled by Scheber almost illegibly: "9/8/09. stays eternally trust our Lord;" "11/13/1910. do research on causes"; "11/13/1910 am eternally damned am wrong? [I] suffer don't know how to continue" (from pieces of paper attached to the chart). These fragments are evocative of his mood and lifelong conflicts.[74]

As the darkness was closing in on him, Schreber gave expression to matters of great personal relevance, to which his doctors were naturally oblivious. What would Freud have thought of them? What guilt was he referring to? What was he innocent of? What could he not tell his sisters? What sexual excesses still haunted his conscience? The conflicts seem to reflect a lifelong concern, heavily influenced by the precepts of his father. He took the answers with him to his grave.

In 1909 there was a first sign of deteriorating physical health: a painfully swollen hand. In March of 1911 the heart and lungs began to fail. In a letter attached to the chart of April 13, 1911, a Dr. Rösler who was called to his bedside found a "gangrenous lung process openly communicating with the pleural cavity. The only treatment that might save the patient's life is surgery. However, I believe this is pointless given the dreary condition of the patient."

The wish Schreber once harbored, "that when my last hour strikes I will no longer find myself in an Asylum but in the orderly domestic life surrounded by my near relatives" (M, p. 338), was denied him by fate. Paul Schreber died in heart failure, gasping for breath, on April 14 of 1911, one year before his wife, three years before Weber.

SYNOPSIS OF PAUL SCHREBER'S LIFE AND WORK

1842, July 25: Birth in Leipzig to Daniel Gottlob Moritz Schreber (born 1808) and Pauline née Haase (born 1815). Both families belong to the upper middle class and among their ancestors are scholars, university professors, lawyers, and a noble.

1846: Death of paternal grandmother, Friederike Schreber née Grosse.

1842-1865: Life in parental home in Leipzig.

1851: Father's ladder accident and the beginning of father's head complaints, intermittent depressions, and his withdrawals from active life and his children.

1860, Easter: Graduation from the *Thomasschule* in Leipzig.

1861, November 10: Death of father.

1860-1863: Law studies in Leipzig.

1863: First bar examination, "grade: excellent." Beginning of work as law intern in the law office of Hennig in Leipzig.

1864: Marriage of elder sister Anna (born 1840) to factory owner Karl Jung.

1865: Judicial oath.

1865-1869: Work in various legal capacities, including *Landesgericht* (district court) in Chemnitz, Saxony.

1865-1882: Six children born to sister Anna, five of whom married and four of whom left descendants.

1867: Official start of career in civil service, in the employ of the Ministry of Justice.

1869: Earns doctorate in law in Leipzig.

1870: Passes state bar exam.

1871-1872: During the Franco-Prussian War, service in the Civil

Administration of Alsace-Lorrraine: first in the prefecture, then as investigating judge in the court martial in Strasbourg.

1872-1877: Work in various courts in Leipzig, culminating in the position of appeals judge.

1877: Suicide by head gunshot of brother Gustav (born 1839), at that time appeals judge in Bautzen, Saxony.

1878-1879: Temporary service in the *Reichsjustizamt* in Berlin, work on the laws of the German Empire.

1878: Marriage to Ottilie Sabine Behr (born 1857), daughter of theater director Heinrich Behr.

1878: First episode of hypochondriasis.

1879-1884: Service as *Landgerichtsdirector* (administrative director) of the District Court in Chemnitz.

1884, October 28: Defeat as candidate for the *Reichstag* from the 16th electoral district of Chemnitz.

1884-end of 1885: First illness; treatment first at the Sonneberg Spa, then hospitalization at Flechsig's Psychiatric Hospital of Leipzig University (December 8, 1884 to June 1, 1885), and finally convalescence at Ilmenau Spa.

1885: January 1, appointment as *Landgerichtsdirector* at Leipzig.

1886, January 1-1889: Service as *Landgerichtsdirector* of the District Court in Leipzig.

1889, January 10-1893: *Landgerichtsspräsident* (administrative judge presiding) of the District Court in Freiberg, Saxony.

1892: reelected as member of the Freiberg magistracy.

1893: July 5, nomination as *Senatspräsident* in Dresden.

1893, October-November: Serves as *Senatspräsident* of the 3rd *Civilsenat* at the *Oberlandesgericht* (Supreme Court of Appeals of the Kindgom of Saxony) in Dresden.

1893, November 9, 10: Consultations with Flechsig in Leipzig, suicide attempts, and emergency admission to Flechsig's Hospital.

1893-1902: Second illness; hospitalization in Flechsig's Hospital November 21, 1893-June 14, 1894, then at Pierson's Asylum, June 14-June 29, 1894, and finally, at the Royal Public Asylum at Sonnenstein (June 29, 1894-December 20, 1902).

1893: Death of Sabine Schreber's mother.

1894, January 4: Notification by Sabine of Carl Edmund Werner, Schreber's superior at the *Oberlandesgericht*, that Paul will require a longer leave of absence. Werner's recommendation to put a cap on such a leave.

1894, June 15: Werner's recommendation to Sabine, in view of money disputes, to institute a temporary incompetency status for Paul.

1894, November 21: Weber's first unpublished psychiatric report to C. E. Werner and the Ministry of Justice.

1894, November 26: Based on Weber's report, Werner's instruction to the Dresden County Court to declare Schreber temporarily incompetent.

1894, November 27: Sabine's request for and official instruction to institute temporary incompetency and retirement for Schreber approved by the Ministry of Justice.

1895, November 7: Second unpublished psychiatric report of Weber to the Ministry of Justice.

1895, November 16: Permanent retirement instituted.

1897: death of Sabine's father, Heinrich Behr, and brother.

1897-1900: Writing of the *Memoirs* at Sonnenstein; expresses wish to be discharged.

1899, December 29: Weber's first report to the court.

1900, March 13: Failure of first attempt to contest his incompetency and the lower County Court's ruling to make it permanent.

1900, November 28: Weber's second report to the court.

1901, April 13: Incompetency confirmed by the intermediate Dresden District Court.

1901, July 23: Schreber's writ of appeal to the Dresden *Oberlandesgericht*.

1902, April 5: Weber's third and last report to the court.

1902, July 14: Decision of the Sixth *Civilsenat* of the Dresden *Oberlandesgericht* to rescind incompetency and guardianship.

1902, December 20: Release from Sonnenstein, at first to stay with mother.

1903: Publication of the *Memoirs*, with new preface and "Open Letter to Professor Flechsig."

1903-1907: The last good years. The couple move to a newly built house at 15 Angelikastrasse, in the new Dresden suburb. Functions well socially. Does private legal work. Involved with the Schreber Association and legacy disputes. Adoption of daughter, Fridoline.

1907, May 14: Death of Pauline Schreber at age 92.

1907, November 14: Sabine suffers stroke and has speech disturbances.

1907-1911: Third illness, admission (November 27) to newly opened (1901) Leipzig-Dösen Asylum, then the District Psychiatric Hospital of Leipzig and now Park Krankenhaus Leipzig-Dösen.

1911, April 14: Death at Leipzig-Dösen of cardio-pulmonary complications.

1912: Death of wife, Sabine.

NOTES

1. The sources for this account of Schreber's life are Baumeyer (1956, 1970), Tabouret-Keller (1973), Niederland (1969, 1974), Schilling (1950, 1964), Devreese (1981a, b; 1986a, b), Israëls (1989), Schreiber (1987), Busse (1989a, b; 1990), Peters (1990), interviews with the descendants of Anna Jung née Schreber and other sources, and the *Memoirs*. The *Memoirs* are an important source, although they suffer from deletions imposed on them by members of Paul Schreber's family, such as the entire chapter 3 (*M*, p. 33).

2. Anna became the wife of Carl Jung. Five of Anna and Carl Ferdinand Jung's six children were long-lived (the first, Friedrich Moritz Heinrich, lived from 1865 to 1868).

Friedrich or Fritz (1867-1937) was a farmer and later owner of the family manor in Mühlbach; he is mentioned in the *Memoirs* (p. 106). Fritz's first-born son, Carl-Heinz Jung (1900-1943), was the father of Mrs. Brigitte Wienstein née Jung (born 1934), whom I met in 1989, interviewed at length, and have corresponded with since. Two middle children of Fritz Jung were: Ilse Jung (born 1904), who married Dr. Röder, whose son Reinhardt, along with his wife Maria, I interviewed in Kühren in 1989; and Reinhard Jung (1906-1944), whose widow Ruth and children Maria Schultheiss and Dieter Jung and his wife Carmen I also had conversations with in 1989 (the last two also in 1988). Fritz's youngest daughter, Renate Jung, born in 1907, I interviewed twice in 1989. Carl-Heinz and Reinhard died as soldiers in the second World War.

Helene (born 1868) married first Hans, then Hermann Cunio, both jurists.

Paula, or Pauline (1870-1925) married Dr. Friedrich from Kiel, mentioned in the *Memoirs* (p. 89), whose youngest son Günther (born in 1900), along with his wife Ursula, I also interviewed in the summer of 1989. Dr. Friedrich was trained as a pathologist and after the war he was ordered by the British occupation authorities to become a psychiatrist. He impressed me as a kind person and as a humane and compassionate psychiatrist with his own patients. Career choice was a problem in his own family and tragedy struck. He died later that year, on his birthday.

Wilhelm (born 1872) was a doctor of law and a choir master and music critic. His second wife was a concert singer.

The youngest was Felix (1882-1957), a lawyer, who had one son, Karl Ottokar. He corresponded with Franz Baumeyer.

3. *"litt an Zwangsvorstellungen mit Mordtrieb."* In the published English translation of the chart (Baumeyer, 1956) it is translated: "suffered from obsessional ideas with homicidal tendencies." This chart was first mentioned by Baumeyer in 1952 and published in 1955. It is now kept in the Park Hospital, formerly in the GDR the Bezirkkrankenhaus für Psychiatrie, and originally the Leipzig-Dösen Asylum, where Schreber died. I visited the hospital in 1988 and 1989, and gave a presentation about Schreber. The former director, Dr. Ruth Rank, the librarian Mrs. Heidrun Smers and Mr. Römer were of assistance in making me a copy of the clinical chart and its contents. Who would Moritz Schreber have told about such ruminations?

This is a mystery, too. The late Dr. Günther Friedrich (1900-1989) attributed this assessment to the delusions of Paul (Israëls, 1989, pp. 178-179). I wonder if Paul's sister Klara Krause refers to this description in a letter to Weber:

> A letter (of 21 March, 1900). . . .: "It is incomprehensible to me how he ([Paul]Schreber) mixes up facts with misstatements and obscurities, for example in what he said about the illness of our good father and brother, just because they fit in with his present delusions; and he does not mention in these notes things which he knew earlier when he was well. For instance, he does not mention the incident in the gymnasium when an iron ladder fell on father's head, which started his peculiar head complaints which started a few months later . . ." [Baumeyer, 1956, pp. 67-68].

What *delusions* did Paul voice about his father's illness and what was the kernel of truth in them? Are "these notes" by any chance part of the famous expurgated third chapter of the *Memoirs*? If indeed Paul was the source of the information about his father noted in the hospital chart, it would indicate an important insight on his part about his father's obsessional character, or about his overt or covert rage—and also about himself. It may have be an insight of the psychiatrist who took the history from either Paul or his family.

4. One third-generation descendant and one fourth-generation descendant of Anna Jung told me about their depressions. Three of Anna's grandchildren, two sons and one daughter, were described as having suffered from anxiety and depression, based on statements of the descendants. Even though a precise pedigree cannot be established at this time, these findings suggest both a biological predisposition and depressive reactions to environmental factors among a number of the Schrebers, more in the men than in the women. I could not get a clear picture of the chronic mental illness in the son of Felix Jung, Otto Karl Jung, who was marginally socially adjusted. Mrs. Wienstein (1989) told the poignant story of the suicide in 1968, at age 27, of a male cousin who had insoluble career conflicts.

5. Israëls (1989) claims that Pauline "came from a family of considerably higher standing than her future husband" (p. 21). This claim has been disputed by Mrs. Brigitte Wienstein née Jung. I concur with her perception that there was no difference between the social status of the Schrebers and the Haases, except that the Schrebers were more illustrious while the Haases had more money and property. Mrs. Wienstein corresponded with Israëls extensively, corrected a number of factual errors in his writings, and was invited by him to attend the public defense of his doctoral thesis, "Schreber: Father and Son" in 1981 in Amsterdam.

6. This was pointed out by Niederland (1974, pp. 96-97) and also discussed by Dr. Mortimer Ostow (1989).

7. The daughter was the late Mrs. Fridoline Hammer, born 1890, who knew Pauline Schreber until her death in 1907. Mrs. Hammer's testimony is found in Niederland (1969) and also in Baumeyer (1970).

8. The sources about the mother, father and the family I had access to are Hartung (1907), Siegel (1909), A. L. (1938, 1939, 1940), Richter (1914, 1928,

1939), Schilling (1964), Niederland (1969) and the Niederland Collection in the Library of Congress, and Baumeyer (1970). Some were given to me by the descendants and they have also been used by Israëls (1989, pp. 65-66). Israëls first offered but later refused to send me copies of some of these hard-to-find sources. I was fortunate to find A. L. and the texts by Richter in the library of Leipzig University.

9. I am quoting from the text of this 1909 Siegel interview as printed on pages 10 - 14 from an unidentified book (given to me by Reinhardt Röder, grandson of Anna Jung). The footnote on page 10 states: "These reminiscences have already been published once before in an overview by Richard Siegel (*Freund der Schrebervereine*, Volume V, Issue X, 1909)". It is possible that these pages come from a 1925 book by Richter, but I have not seen it (Israëls, 1989, p. 103). The text is identical with the typescript sent to Niederland by Dr. Kurt Schilling in a letter of 5.4.1960 (the Niederland Collection, Library of Congress). Dr. Schilling added a postscript to the text: "This report comes perhaps from Anna Jung," which may explain all the fuss Israëls (1989) made about Niederland's mistake of misattribution. Schilling was also the source of the famous advertisement, according to him placed by the Freisinnige Party, "Wer kennt schon den Dr. Schreber?" (Who has ever heard of Dr. Schreber), which Israëls could not find in the *Chemnitzer Anzeiger*.

10. Some of the statements are in quotation marks, but it is unclear who is being quoted.

11. For details, see Israëls (1989), pp. 49-51.

12. Wächter was a friend of Paul's parents. I found a list of his works in B. Windscheid (1880) and one work by him from 1835: *Essays on the penal code*, vol. 1, which deals with crimes of seduction and of sexual assault and includes an elaboration on so-called carnal crimes in a narrower sense. In chapter 3 section 5 Wächter discusses various forms of rape, incest, sodomy, and masturbation according to Roman, German and Saxon law. Paul omits the prefix indicating nobility from his name. Could this be the mysterious v. W.? Another biography is by Oskar von Waechter (1881), which I did not see.

13. Daniel Devreese sent me a copy of Hirschfeld and Franke (1879) about Paul's activity in the various student bodies.

14. The details of Paul's legal career became known following the publication by Daniel Devreese (1981a) of Paul Schreber's personal file from the Ministry of Justice. This citation refers to that file.

15. The first to publish the fact was Niederland (1974). Gustav shot himself in Bautzen in 1877.

16. Based on information gathered by Niederland (1974), Israëls (1989), Schreiber (1987) and Busse (1990), the latter since published in 1991 as a book by Peter Lang in Frankfurt, which I have not seen.

17. Busse (1990), quoting the work of Kris Vermeiren, from his dissertation at the Ghent University, Belgium, and The Dresden State Archives.

18. The letter and other archival materials pertaining to this were found by Gerd Busse (1990) in the Coburg State Archives.

19. I have written to the Stadtarchiv Bautzen enquiring if there was any record of Gustav's betrothal, but received no answer.

20. Maria Schultheiss, a descendant, also gave me a copy of this postcard. My translation differs from that of Israëls (1989, p. 149).

21. Niederland (1974, p. 97) quoted from this notice. Israëls (1989) reproduced it in full.

22. From Israëls, quoting G. Friedrich's citation of the *Stadtarchiv Bautzen*.

23. The same was confirmed in a letter dated 3.6.60 from Dr. Schilling (see note 1) to Niederland. The notation in the church registry read: "*Hat sich selbst entleibt*," "killed himself."

24. Niederland, unpublished, interview with Fridoline Schreber-Hammer on July 30 and 31, 1969 (see note 7). The assumption that Gustav had syphilis was also expressed by Schilling (letter of March 6, 1960).

25. Mentioned by pastor Hartung on May 17, 1907, in the funeral speech for Pauline Schreber. He also mentioned Paul's recovery and homecoming. Paul must have been present at the ceremony. Source: Reihardt Röder.

26. Ellenberger (1970, p. 291) notes the importance of syphilis in the life of Nietzsche and in literary works, such as Ibsen's drama *Ghosts,* which was known all over Europe. Leo Ikelaar (1989) mentioned the preoccupation with the femme fatale, both as a vamp and a carrier of the disease.

27. The clippings from two newspapers were given to me by Mr. Reinhardt Röder and Miss Renate Jung. They come from the *Neue Leipziger Zeitung* and *Leipzig Neuste Nachrichten* and are available in the library of Leipzig University. One, signed A. L., is dated December 30, 1938; another, signed dt, is dated December 30, 1939; and a third, signed A. L. and H. B., is dated December 30, 1940 (see References).

28. Israëls erroneously copied "St. Thomas Aquinas" (1989, p. 222).

29. Copies of letters, written to various family members, were given to me by Miss Renate Jung, Mrs. Ruth Jung, and Mrs. Brigitte Wienstein. Contrary to the assertion of Israëls (1989a, p. 222), these letters do not consist "solely of religious passages." They are sparing in self-descriptions and largely addressed to the situations and needs of the correspondents. They contain many encouragements and homilies about "faith, love, hope, comfort, and patience" (from a November 1, 1943 letter to Reihard Jung). He was the father of Dieter Jung—born in 1943 (shortly after his father was killed in Poland)—whom I interviewed in Zschölkau near Leipzig in the summer of 1988.

30. This portrait is based on a letter written by Carl Jung's grandson, Carl-Heinz Jung (1900-1943), the father of Mrs. Brigitte Wienstein, who kindly gave me copies of excerpts from her father's letter written on Christmas of 1942 from Norway, where he was killed. He also had memories of his grandmother Anna Jung and his assessment of her is rather critical:

> Her instinct has led her to live a life of a pietistic Christian. With this strong support she is able to hold off the demonic powers to which her brothers had succumbed. . . . Religious, confessional, social and political issues still capture her undivided attention. Her books, her collection of newspaper clippings and apothegms reflect her interests. She combines an earnestness with an archness that has an educational-moral impact. . . . She showed particular love toward my mother, the widow of her worry-

child Fritz [the second son, born 1867]. . . . Her circumstances offered her a devout and contemplative peace. This narrow view may have been an essential requirement for her existence. But for her children this resulted in a life-alien upbringing, against which worldly-wise grandfather [i.e., Carl Jung] must have fought in vain and for which we had to pay in one way or another. The children were not used to hold their own, and this had a deleterious influence not only on material success in life.

This excerpt should give pause to consider the ideas, habits, and character identifications that shape the fates of a family across generations. The question is how much of these were the legacy of the spirit of Moritz Schreber himself, a man of vision more than a hero of worldly success?

31. She is referred to on line 44 of a poem written on the 50th birthday of his wife (D. P. Schreber, 1907): "A child is permitted to accompany us into our new house," the house Paul built in Dresden after his release from Sonnenstein. This suburban townhouse, at the corner of Angelikastrasse 15a, with its garden and trees, can still be admired today. According to the interview with Niederland (see next footnote), Sabine Schreber travelled to Innsbruck to meet the future foster child in 1902 and the adoption date was 1906, rather late, at which point the daughter assumed the name Schreber.

32. According to Dr. Niederland's (1969) unpublished notes of interviews (which he kindly gave to me), that took place on July 30 and 31 of 1969, in Freiburg-im-Breisgau, where Mrs. Schreber-Hammer lived. She was 79 years old at that time, having been born in 1890. Niederland (1974, p. 31), refers to an interview in 1972, citing the same age; there is some error here. She was described by Niederland as a "very gentle, lively, cooperative person, younger looking than her chronological age, answered all my questions promptly and clearly, person of good memory and manner."

33. Israëls (1988) prints this photograph on p. 296 with the legend indicating that this is Sabine Behr Schreber. In the German translation of Israëls (1989) the caption on p. 134 says "Fig. 30 (probably) Sabine Behr." Another likeness is reproduced by Franz Baumeyer from a somewhat later time. A different Sabine looks at us from an oval joint portrait reproduced by Israëls on the frontispiece of the German version. Sabine is standing fourth from the left in a family portrait taken around 1905 (Israëls, 1988, p. 290).

34. The biographical data about the wife's family are to my knowledge presented here for the first time. They have been found by my friend Prof. Dr. Uwe Henrik Peters from Cologne, who kindly permitted me to use them. He presented them on May 12, 1990, at the panel discussion "The Schreber Case—New Insights," which I organized and chaired, at the annual meeting of the American Academy of Psychoanalysis in New York. These data are recorded in the archives of the Köln (Cologne) Theatermuseum.

35. This fact is disputed by Israëls (1989, p. 182), based on the testimony of Felix Jung.

36. The other sister, Therese Emilie or Helene was a famous concert singer. She married Vienna born Josef Nesper (1844-1929), a famous actor at the court of the duchy of Meiningen. The brother was an actor, active in Halle,

Magdeburg and Aachen. Both he and father died in 1897, within three months of each other, the brother first.

37. Dr. Uwe Peters mentions two letters in the manuscript division of the Cologne Theater Museum dated in 1878 and sent by Heinrich Behr from a Leipzig address.

38. The tiers in the German judiciary system were, from lowest to highest, the *Amtsgericht* (county court), the *Landesgericht* (the district court), and the *Oberlandesgericht* (the highest court of appeals of the country, in this case the Kingdom of Saxony). The *Oberlandesgericht* had its seat in the capital, Dresden. Thus, in Saxony there was one *Oberlandesgericht*, 7 *Landsgericht*s and 105 *Amtsgericht*s. The highest court of appeals at the top of the system, that is the *Reichsgericht* for the entire German Empire, was for historic reasons located in Leipzig. The office that dealt with writing the laws for the German Empire was the *Reichsjustizamt* in Berlin, where Paul Schreber worked in 1879. The massive, ornate building that housed the *Reichsgericht* survived the World War and is now the seat of government and city offices and the Leipzig Museum. One can still admire the allegories of justice and the statues of supplicants and judges that adorn the portico. During the ceremonies for the departing rector of the Leipzig University, on October 31, 1895, departing *rector magnificus* Paul Flechsig (1895) noted: "On the 26th of this month we witnessed the laying of the keystone of the edifice of the *Reichsgericht*. In this way, the city of Leipzig has won the eternal honor as the law capital of the German Empire" (p. 7). That year, among those elevated to the rank of honorary law lecturers was one Harald Arthur Wolf von Wolff. Was he perchance the mysterious v. W mentioned in the *Memoirs*?

39. According to the *Brockhaus Konversations Lexikon*, 14th edition. Chemnitz celebrated its 750th anniversary in 1893. The opening invocation to *Der Stadt der Arbeit!* (the worker city) (Uhle, 1893).

40. Fritz was born in 1867, Helene in 1868, Paula in 1870, Wilhelm in 1872 and Felix in 1882.

41. According to File #257 of the Chemnitz District Court, in 1882 a criminal case was instituted by the public prosecutor against the "Redacteur Rudolf Maximilian Bruno Geiser." It is unclear what emotional impact the matter had on Schreber when he confronted Geiser at the polls.

42. Israëls (1989, Chapter 12) quotes extensively from the *Chemnitzer Tageblatt*, first used as a source by Niederland, and corrects a number of errors that crept into Niederland's account. Geiser (1846-1898), editor in Stuttgart of the popular illustrated journal *Die Neue Welt*, had been the winner in the 1881 elections, and in the same issue of the *Chemnitzer Tageblatt* from which Israëls quoted he was named as the current representative to the *Reichstag* from the 16th electoral district (*Wahlkreis*), thus the incumbent. Some of his output can be seen in the New York Public Library: "The Demands of Socialism toward the Future and the Present," in 1876, and "The Aims of Social Democracy Illuminated by the Delusions of Eugen Richter," in 1891.

43. *Chemnitzer Tageblatt*, # 253 of October 19, 1884. According to the paper, Schreber did not make public speeches but was personally introduced to the constituency. The editorial in #259, on October 26, 1884, avoided

recommending a specific choice for the voters while urging the readers to think "of the loyal man of conviction, who has true love of his fatherland, a shining star firm in the sky of his heart and pointing the right way." For other quotes from that newspaper, see Israëls, 1989, pp. 160-163.

44. The program of the National-Liberals is described in detail in Specht and Schwalbe (1904) and reflects the politics of industrialists, merchants, owners of property and lands, artisans and professionals like Schreber himself. Such people were pro-Empire and pro-Bismarck but against Bismarck's anti-Church politics known as *Kulturkampf*, Bismarck's protectionism, and centralization of power by the Empire. These views the National-Liberals shared with their partner in 1884, the Conservative Party. In the *"Heidelberger Erklärung"* (the Heidelberg Explanation) part of the platform of 1881 was a plank regarding protecting the interests and welfare of the working class. But this support paled in comparison with the support shown for workers by the socialists and, surprisingly, by the Catholics, in the form of Christian Socialism. By 1884 the rivals of Schreber's conservative faction of the National-Liberals also included the new secessionist liberal faction of the original National-Liberal party, a faction that joined forces with the *Freisinnige*. These alignments underscore the weakness of Schreber's candidacy.

45. I do not know how the Jews in Chemnitz stood politically. There are a number of instances of anti-Semitic and anti-Catholic sentiments expressed in the *Memoirs*. They may well be epitomized in the nonsensical bird-talk phrase, quoted by Freud (1911, p. 36), "'Santiago' or 'Carthago',", opposing a catholic symbol (i.e., the world-famous cathedral of Santiago de Compostela) to the ancient Semitic kingdom of Hannibal. Schreber imagined that like with the Catholicizing of his mother, "[he was himself] the object of attempts at conversion" (*M*, Foot Note #38), while at another time he believed his own stomach was miraculously replaced for "a very inferior so-called 'Jew's stomach'" (p. 151). In Paul's stream of consciousness of hundreds if not thousands of names we encounter many "Catholics who expected a furtherance of Catholicism," amongst them "the Cathedral Dean (*Domkapitular*) Moufang, the Cardinals Rampolla, Galimberti and Casati" (*M*, p. 49). Canon Moufang was a historical figure, a German Catholic socialist. In his electoral address in Mainz in 1871 he condemned economic liberalism, dear to Schreber, while promulgating legal protection for the workers in such areas as hours of labor, wages, labor of women and children, sanitation, lowering of taxes and greater burdens on the rich (*Encyclopedia Britannica*, 9th American Edition, New York: Werner, 1899, 22:215). It should be pointed out that the ruling royal Saxon family, the Wettins, were Catholic while the overwhelming majority of their subjects were Protestant. On the same page Schreber refers to a mysterious "Viennese nerve specialist . . . a baptised Jew and Slavophile, who wanted to make Germany Slavic through me," reflecting views already current in the 1880s and especially the 1890s, of the ambitions of the Jews to achieve world domination. Such ideas were held, for example, by the anti-semite Carl Paasch, at one time a patient in Flechsig's hospital, and will be discussed in chapter 5. Here I will dwell briefly on the Italian Major Casati, who was known in Germany. Niederland, who realized that there was

no Cardinal Casati (Niederland, 1974, pp. 87), drew fanciful son-and-father parallels between Paul and Moritz Schreber on one hand, and Casati (1838-1902) and Emin Pasha, whose dates he does not cite. Emin Pasha (in German Pascha), alias Eduard Schnitzer, was a Jew born in 1840 (and assassinated in 1892), a colorful adventurer who became governor of the Sudan and was later asked by the government to secure more colonies for Germany in equatorial Africa. It is clear that Emin Pasha and Major Casati were peers. Said Niederland: "Both [i.e., Casati and Schreber] were imprisoned and tortured, the one in the African jungle, the other—according to his thinking—in the Sonnenstein sanatorium" (p. 88). Niederland's comparison is self-contradictory—Casati's torture was real, Schreber's in his mind only (another delusion?)—and is heightened by the irony of calling Sonnenstein a sanatorium (a designation usually reserved in the United States for health resorts), which Niederland may have read in the older version of Freud (1911a) in volume 3 of the 1925 Hogarth Press edition of Freud's *Collected Papers*.

I found Major Casati mentioned in connection with an anti-semitic rally in Leipzig, described by Paasch (1892a). Major Casati is mentioned by Paasch as siding with Stanley, the famous explorer of Africa, against Emin Pasha the Jew, accusing the latter of being a treacherous Judas who committed political assassinations in Africa and other misdeeds (Paasch, 1891, "Open Letter to His Excellency the Reichskanzler von Caprivi," pp. 43-45). A few pages later Paasch blames the Jews for seducing children to alcoholism and spreading syphilis in Russia. I am therefore inclined to regard as anti-semitically tinged (thus, not as blandly as Israëls [1989, p. 44] has it), Schreber's invoking the "Wandering Jew" and "the legend . . . of the Jew Ahasver [*der ewiger Jude*]" (*M*, p. 53), that is, the hated and accursed Jew amongst the nations. Schreber's notion of the Eternal Jew as unmanned I interpret as both an admiring and contemptuous view of the Jew in that he is both without worldly power but bearing eternal spiritual messages.

Racial anti-semitism (beginning in France with Voltaire and reaching a high water mark in 1851 with Gobineau's epoch-making *Essai sur l'Inegalité des Races Humaines*) and political anti-semitism are inextricably woven into European and especially German history of the 1880s and 1890s, starting with Napoleon's emancipation of the Jews and the 1848 revolution. Jews were not only prominent as socialists but, more importantly for Schreber, some (for example, the Jews Eduard Lasker and Ludwig Bamberger, among the heroes of the 1848 revolution) were the founders of his own original National Liberal party. That party had an up-and-down course with Bismarck. Once his staunch supporter, the party seceded to oppose him, whereupon he then courted the Catholic Centre, starting the "journey to Canossa," and even considered launching a *Kulturkampf* against the Jews. It did not stop Bismarck from employing as his financial wizard the Jewish financier Gerson von Bleichröder, for which Bismarck came under severe attack, for example, by the anti-semitic Dr. Erwin Bauer (1891), the editor-in-chief of the *Leipziger Tages-Anzeiger*, in his defamatory pamphlet about Bleichröder. Jews were numerous in the liberal professions but were excluded from the army, the church and the student fraternities. In the *Reichstag* there was an official Anti-Semitic Party (*Die Fraktion der Antisemiten im Reichstage*). Anti-semitic pamphlets by the preacher to the Imperial Court, Adolf Stöcker, and Rektor Hermann Ahlwardt (n.d.), author of *The Desperate Struggle of the Aryan Peoples with Jewry*, sold in the tens of thousands of copies, and were provided with such slogans as: "The rampant spread of Jews are the shame of Germany, *Finis Germaniae*"(the end of Germany)."

In 1891 the officially anti-semitic *Dresdener Nachrichten* of October 24 favorably reviewed a book that had a printing of 60,000 copies entitled *Rembrandt as Educator*. It was an anti-semitic tract that juxtaposed Germans, the "amor generis humani" (the love of mankind) with Jews, the "odium generis humani" (horror of mankind): the source of crass "Jewish materialism, skepticism, democratism and the German Social Democracy," and urged the student bodies to close the door to Jews. In 1892 Saxony was regarded as one of the hotbeds of anti-semitic agitation in Germany, even though there were so few Jews in it ("so wenig verjudet"), and especially since the "Saxon officer corps and administration . . . the nobility, judiciary, academia, commerce and press were virtually free of Jews [Judenrein]" (article in the *Freiberger Anzeiger und Tageblatt* of May 31, 1892, quoting a report from the anti-semitic newspaper "Der Reichsbote"). Hitler was born in 1889. Perhaps Paul Schreber was uncannily ironic when he called both Jews and Germans examples of God's chosen people (*M*, p. 14).

46. According to *Chemnitzer Tageblatt und Anzeiger* (No. 283, Erste Beilage, of November 22, 1884), the comparison of the election results of 1881 and 1884 showed that in 1881 there were 5,097,760 as against 5,662,066 votes cast in 1884. In 1881 the National Liberal Party received 642,718, compared with 979,430 in 1884, thus an increase of more than 50% of the votes. The Social-Democrats received 14,398 votes in 1881 and 14,477 in 1884, thus an increment of less than 1% nationwide. One should view Schreber's defeat against the background of these singular statistics. The voting results of 1881 in the Saxon voting district #16, where Schreber ran, showed the Social-Democrat Bruno Geiser winning with a total of 10,256 votes as against 6,301 cast for his opponent Hecker. In 1884, Geiser received 14,512 votes, Schreber 5,762 votes, and the candidate for the Deutsche Freisinnige 4,123 (Files of the Ministry of the Interior in the Dresden State Archives). The *Chemnitzer Tageblatt* # 262 of October 30, 1884 showed the voting results for 23 voting districts, with the omission of the 16th. The National-Liberals won in 7 other districts.

47. The hospital was still active and advertised in the *PNW* [vol. 13 (1911), issue #1] the year Schreber died: "For patients suffering from nervous and mood disorders . . . 12 min. by electrical train from Leipzig. Details in brochures. Hofrat Dr. Lochner."

48. As recorded by Flechsig's successor in the years 1921-1924, Oswald Bumke (1953). The hospital was rebuilt after Bumke's departure.

49. Misprinted in the English translation of Baumeyer (1956) as "Sonnenstein Asylum" but correctly stated in the original (Baumeyer, 1955). The mistake is repeated in the *Standard Edition*.

50. In a conversation with Dr. J.-E. Meyer in Göttingen in the summer of 1988 he quoted a saying by Rümke: "The empirical [data] are seen differently when our theoretical [viewpoints] change."

51. According to the 14th edition of the Brockhaus, Freiberg, 20 miles WSW of Dresden, had 116,328 inhabitants in 1890 and its main industry was mining. There were only 53 Jews in the city.

52. Could this be the mysterious "v. W" that hounds Schreber in the *Memoirs?*

53. Fridoline Schreber became a nurse and married doctor Hammer. It is known who her father was, but the mother remains unknown. I looked in vain for a girl Fridoline in the church birth registries of Innsbruck parishes in 1989. In response to my letter of inquiry of April 11, 1990, the Standesamt at City Hall in Freiburg-im-Breisgau, where Mrs. Hammer lived (and died on May 10, 1981) sent me this reply of May 4, 1990: " Mrs. Fridoline Josefine Hammer née Schreber died in F.i.B. on the 10th of May 1981. Frau Hammer was born on December 15, 1890 in Innsbruck, Austria, and married Dr. med. Hugo Alexis Max Hammer on the 6th of February 1913, in Dresden. There are no further documents." The quoted maiden name is, of course, not true because she was adopted by Paul Schreber. Mrs. Hammer had a daughter with whom I have not been able to establish contact.

54. When I interviewed Mrs. Ursula Friedrich (now the widow of Dr. Günther Friedrich) in 1989 and asked her specifically if she had heard rumors about an illegitimate child of Sabine Schreber she would neither confirm nor deny but smiled and remarked that such matters were in those days often referred to euphemistically as *"ein Malheurchen,"* (a "little mishap"). Mrs. Wienstein felt this could have never happened, because Sabine would not have risked losing everything in the marriage as a result of such an indiscretion. If Paul's illness was a disgrace to himself and the family, then this issue would also have been a touchy subject *("die Angelegenheit sehr heikel ist")*, as stated by Felix Jung to Baumeyer (Busse, 1990, pp. 44-45).

55. Corrects the mistranslation of Macalpine and Hunter. The Court of Appeal was composed of a number of senates, or chambers. Schreber was the president of the third *Civilsenat.* I found in the *Staatsarchiv Dresden* the records of some of his decisions in that court in *Urtheilbücher* M: # 790, 792; a week after his last decision, dated November 14, 1893, Schreber was admitted to Flechsig's hospital.

56. The issue of the social inequality of the spouses, noted by Baumeyer, is underscored even more in his correspondence with Felix Jung (Busse, 1990).

57. L. E. Prado de Oliveira (1990) called my attention to this fact.

58. Macalpine and Hunter mistranslate Schreber's word. He was suffering then, as in his first illness, not from palpitations (*'Herzklopfen'*) but from *"Herzbeklemmungen"* (i.e., a feeling of constriction; *Memoirs*, p. 39).

59. Lacan singled out Ida Macalpine (omitting R. A. Hunter), to tease her for having supplied the missing verb *delivering* because of her feminine hermeneutic bias of stressing procreation fantasies.

60. See Forel's letter about the attendant situation at Flechsig's, cited in Chapter 5.

61. As suggested by Schreber's way of citing page 102 in his father's *Gymnastics* and by the fact that on that page measures against pollutions are discussed.

62. It was a belief among the ancients that leprosy was a venereal disease (Rosenbaum, 1955).

63. For Jung's opinions, see chapter 7; for Freud's, see *Standard Edition,* 12:77.

65. A misleading translation for "*Fand Aufnahme* (was received)" but also a pun on "*Aufnahme* (admission to a hospital)."

64. Emphasis added; the Macalpine version says "imminent".

66. "*Unter welchen Voraussetzungen,*" which means under what premises, is translated by Macalpine and Hunter as "Under what circumstances," missing the wider implication of the legal principles involved, which were Schreber's interest.

67. That is, the provincial custodial asylum in Colditz, not, as translated by Macalpine and Hunter, "the Country *Home* at Colditz."

68. Most of the information about this period of Schreber's life comes from the two publications of Baumeyer (1956, 1970); interesting documents from a nephew, Felix Jung; and from a friend of the family, Herr Troitzsch (Israëls, 1989); and from the poems written by Schreber (1904, 1905, 1907) during that time (Israëls, 1988). Dr. Niederland's unpublished interview of Fridoline Schreber-Hammer in 1969 is also very important.

69. The date of the adoption is given by Niederland (1974, pp. 31-32) as 1903, based on interviews in 1972, but according to Niederland's notes (1969) the adoption date was 1906. In the Niederland Collection, kept in the Manuscript Division of the Library of Congress, I found four short letters from Fridoline to Niederland. I believe they show a continuity of the gentle Schreber spirit that combines a touching simplicity and depth of feeling. I offer the translation of one of them in full:

Freiburg, 22. Dec. 69.

Esteemed Herr Professor Niederland:

How can I thank you for your friendly lines of 24. Oct. 69 and the great pains you took with the Schreber family tree, which requires a great deal of research. I have not yet given it its due, since I was unable to find the time needed for it. But it interests me greatly, since there is so much in it that is new to me. What effort it must have been to put together all these names and dates! I immediately paid attention to the reprint you sent me and read it with utmost interest. There, too, I learned something I have never known. How much empathy on your part is to be found in all of this! But also, what unending pain was the lot of the patient all these long years.

Concerning the dates of the Schreber siblings of the father it is stated that the dates for Anna Jung were 1840-1914. However, she died on 23.11.1944 having almost completed her 104th year, in case this should be of interest.

My heartfelt thanks for everything. With good wishes and best regards, also from my daughter, I am

your
Fridoline Hammer.

On January 25, 1970, Fridoline tells Dr. Niederland that she cannot be more than a few hours on her feet due to low blood pressure. Her husband is also not feeling well. On January 13, 1971 she reports that toward the end of November her husband died at the age of 91. The last is a postcard of December 29, 1972.

70. According to data supplied by Dr. Uwe Peters (1990), Franz Petter was born in Innsbruck, Austria, on June 4, 1869 and died there on September 11, 1943, the son of carpenter Adolf Petter and Josefa Schranz. The following facts also come from Dr. Uwe Peters. At first, after his father's death, he ran the carpentry shop. After his voice was discovered, he became, in 1890, a student of the well-known singer Schultze-Strelitz in Berlin. From 1890 on, he sang as a tenor in Berlin and Dresden and in other opera houses of Germany and Europe. He was called to sing in the Dresden Hofoper. In 1901 he was singing in Richard Strauss' opera "Feuersnot" and the same year in Beyreuth in Wagner's "Rheingold" and "The Flying Dutchman." From 1904 to 1911 he was known as a "Jugendlicher Heldentenor" at the Cologne Opera, although he continued to live in Dresden and to sing the heroes of Wagner, Verdi, and others (as stated in the correspondence with the Cologne Opera pension fund). He died in Innsbruck in 1943.

71. Israëls quotes this from Mrs. Hammer's letter (p. 195), but this does not exclude Schreber's possible input.

72. It is difficult to reconcile these statements by Niederland with his assertion: "Nonetheless, one serious vestige of his illness remained: the conviction that he was a woman with female breasts and other feminine attributes" (Niederland, 1974, p. 7); the evidence for this assertion was not cited by Niederland.

73. These lines have been reconstructed anonymously from the scribbles: some are clear but others are ambiguous. They are also reproduced in Israëls, 1989, pp. 274-280.

74. It is difficult to decide how much here is authentic reconstruction and how much lucky guessing: "Habe doch recht gutes in mir war immer *Ehrlich* u ha[be] *rechtschaffen* mich ergeb[en] *Pflichtstreuer Beamter* / auch nicht wollustigen Ausschweifungen / habe mit meinen Schwestern nicht sprechen können weil mir der [?] sehe ein dass ich mit diesen *unschuldig* / nur Gottes Allmacht schauen [in my translation: have so much good in me was always *honest* and have given of myself with uprightness dutiful employee (or civil servant) / and neither lustful excesses / have been unable to speak to my sisters because [I] see that with these *innocent* / only to contemplate God's omnipotence;" from "fragments of thought" scribbled on pieces of paper and kept in an envelope attached to Schreber's hospital chart].

3

THE LIFE AND LEGACY
OF MORITZ SCHREBER

My father's and my brother's memory . . . are . . . sacred to me.

D. P. Schreber, 1903

Strive after full command over thyself, over thy spiritual and bodily
weaknesses and wants. . . . Dare to be wise (*sapere aude*)—at whatever
period of life you may have arrived, it is never too late—and persevere unweariedly in the struggle for this true (inward) freedom, for
the perfection of the self.

D. G. M. Schreber, 1899

The first person to be acutely aware of the lack of historical knowledge
about Moritz Schreber was the first psychoanalyst. But Freud took few
pains to discover historical facts about the Schrebers.[1] Even as Freud
claimed to have made "use of no material in this paper that is not
derived from the actual text of the *Denkwürdigkeiten*" (Freud, 1911, p.
46, note 1), he cited some biographical data supplied to him by Dr.
Arnold Georg Stegmann, a psychiatrist from Dresden, who was acquainted with all three of Paul's psychiatrists (Flechsig, Pierson, and
Weber) and an early follower of Freud. In an unpublished letter to
Ferenczi of October 6, 1910, Freud says: "I have now asked Stegmann
to find out all kinds of details about Schreber senior. It depends on
these reports how much I will say about it publicly." It is not known
how much information Stegmann provided.

Freud did cite the October 1908 issue of the periodical of the

106

Schreber Associations, *Der Freund der Schrebervereine* (Friend of the Schreber Associations). On the basis of his sources Freud came out with a positive appraisal of Paul's father.

> Now the father of Senatspräsident Dr. Schreber was no insignificant person. He was the Dr. Daniel Gottlob Moritz Schreber whose memory is kept green to this day by the numerous Schreber Associations which flourish especially in Saxony; and, moreover, he was a physician. His activities in favour of promoting the harmonious upbringing of the young, of securing coordination between education in the home and in the school, of introducing physical culture [*Körperpflege*] and manual work with a view to raising the standards of health—all this exerted a lasting influence upon his contemporaries. His great reputation as the founder of therapeutic gymnastics [*Heilgymnastik*] in Germany is still shown by the wide circulation of his *Ärztliche Zimmergymnastik* in medical circles and the numerous editions through which it has passed [Freud, 1911, p. 51 and note 2].

Freud's main interest in the father was to show that he was an admired physician, capable of miraculous cures, and the source of Paul's positive transference to Flechsig as physician, father and God figure. It is a pity Freud did not quote from the *Zimmergymnastik* or any of Moritz Schreber's views on philosophy of medicine or child rearing, for he correctly identifies Schreber's contribution to "education in the home and in the school." Nor did he mention any of the educational works reviewed or excerpted in that 1908 issue of the *Freund der Schrebervereine* (Israëls, 1989, p. 265); for, contrary to an entrenched false notion, Freud was acquainted with some of those ideas and had an essentially realistic impression of Schreber's actual achievement. Thus, he understood that as a physician Moritz Schreber had made a contribution to the therapeutics and prevention of illness and to the promotion of health by means of the harmonious development and integration of body and mind. He also knew that Schreber was a physician turned pedagogue.

I stress this aspect because opinions about Moritz are at the heart of the current controversy about his effect on his son Paul and because the real achievements of Moritz have been either ignored or distorted in the course of time. It is the interpretation of these educational works of Moritz Schreber, first by Niederland (1959a, b), and their subsequent popularization by Schatzman (1973), that procured for Moritz the sinister reputation of a tyrannical and sadistic child abuser whose alleged tortures caused the son's delusions.

The legacy of Moritz Schreber can be organized under five headings: (1) exercising the body, or *Turning* (athletics, gymnastics, and calisthenics); (2) orthopedics and therapeutic gymnastics; (3) philosophy of medicine, therapeutics and dietetics (i.e., prevention); (4) ethics of education; and (5) the Schreber gardens—the greening of Germany. The last achievement was posthumous, and for this reason we shall survey it first.

SCHREBER ASSOCIATIONS AND SCHREBER GARDENS

The word *Schrebergarten* is a common word in the German language.[2] Like the word *sandwich* in English, *Schrebergarten*, or—as the English call it, an allotment garden—is an eponym. When you mention *Schrebergarten* to persons, they may proceed to tell you something about the joys of city gardening. The word has even become a verb: some people talked to Niederland of *"schrebern"*, that is, gardening (Beeck, 1982). However, the word *Schrebergarten* was not coined by Moritz Schreber.[3] Like Amerigo Vespucci, who did not discover America but whose name America bears, Schreber neither wrote about Schreber gardens nor founded the Schreber associations. The eponym and the associations were created posthumously. Two issues need to be underscored: first, it was the Schreber gardens and the Schreber associations that made Schreber a household word, whereas his contributions to orthopedics, gymnastics, medicine, and education secured him a place in history books; second, it behooves us to trace briefly the history of these Schreber associations, for Moritz's stature in Leipzig and his educational ideas had an influence on Paul's ideas and character.

It is an oft told story (e.g., Schilling, 1950, 1964) how three years after Moritz Schreber's death a number of Leipzig educators gathered around Moritz's friend Ernst Innozenz Hauschild[4] and came up with the idea to call their newly founded educational association a *Schreber-Verein*, to enshrine the memory of physician and educator Moritz Schreber and his inspiring ideas about children's education. Although the name "Hauschild associations" was initially proposed, the educators ultimately selected "Schreber associations," a name more euphonious and appropriate as a tribute to their spiritual father. Others who became connected with this idea and its perpetuation (all in Ritter, 1936) were Eduard Mangner, L. Mittenzwey, Richard Siegel, Hugo Fritzsche, Gerhard Richter, and Karl Gesell, all teachers or school directors.[5]

It was Schreber's concern with children's play and playgrounds, in the last decade of his life, that so impressed the educators[6] in Leipzig. A playground, or *Spielplatz*, was initially nicknamed a *"Schreberplatz"* or "Schreber recreational ground."[7] It was later that people also thought of leasing from the city of Leipzig small plots of land for the purpose of planting small flower and vegetable lots.[8] As a further development, some of the original educational Schreber associations were transformed over the years from education promoting organizations into clubs devoted to amateur gardening and small-animal husbandry.[9] Another later incarnation was the Schreber youth movement. With the passage of time, it was the idea of city gardens that seemed to eclipse everything else Schreber stood for, as well as the original aims of the Schreber associations. This fact has served Israëls to make Schreber's fame look like notoriety and to unfairly trivialize his place in the history of medicine and the recognition Schreber achieved in his time as educator in the eyes of teachers and as physician among his medical colleagues.[10]

MORITZ SCHREBER'S LIFE AND ACHIEVEMENT

In an 1861 autobiographical statement Moritz Schreber summed up the essential facts of his life and career as follows:[11]

> Dr. med. Daniel Gottlob Moritz Schreber was born in Leipzig in 1808, where he received his elementary and high school education; he began his studies at the University there in 1826, devoted himself to practical and literary activities from 1831 on, and graduated as a medical doctor in 1833. In order to further his education in the greater medical education centers such as Berlin, Prague Vienna etc, he accepted a position of a traveling private physician which took him to the principal cities of Germany as well as various parts of Russia. Back in 1836, he settled in Leipzig and engaged in the practice of medicine, literary activity and medical teaching with the rank of *Docent* [lecturer] at the University. He married in 1838 the oldest daughter of the deceased Professor of medicine Haase and fathered five children. Since 1844 he was the director of the Institute for Orthopedics and Therapeutic Gymnastics of Leipzig. Later he undertook two scientific travels through Belgium, England, France, part of Italy and Switzerland. In addition to collaborating in various medical periodicals, encyclopedias and contemporary yearbooks etc, in the course of his literary activity he produced the following [Schreber lists 13 of his works: 1839, 1840, 1842, 1843, 1846, 1852a, b, 1853, 1855a, 1858a, b, and 1859a, and Schreber and Neumann, 1858] [Kloss, 1862, pp 11-12].

These are the bare bones of a life, fit for an entry in an encyclopedia; they do not reflect the joys and sorrows of the child, the youth, and the man; the unfulfilled dreams and ambitions; the crises in his life. We can divide this life into three periods: (1) 1808-1837, birth through graduate and postgraduate studies, and beginning of medical practice; (2) 1838-1850, marriage, birth of his children, founding of the Orthopedic Institute, production of medical writings and first works on therapeutic and educational gymnastics; (3) 1851-1861, the final decade ushered in by the head trauma accident, the personality change and shift from orthopedics to pedagogics, writings on gymnastics, child rearing and education.

FIRST PERIOD: 1808-1837

Moritz was a scion of an upper middle class family among whose members were illustrious men of learning. This created a cultural climate that fostered the attitudes of Moritz, his son Paul, and other descendants.[12]

A daughter of Hans Schreber the Old, Barbara, married Master Valentin Braun, born in 1498, who lived to the age of 103 and served as the amanuensis of Martin Luther. He was minister in Döbeln and at one point was "distraught by Satan," of whose wiles he was freed by the intercession of Luther himself. Braun converted to Protestantism the last bishop of Meissen and "thus . . . gradually cleansed the whole Meissen bishopric of the egregious papist errors" (G. Friedrich, fragment of unpublished biography, pp. 80-81; see preceding footnote 12). The Schrebers were proud of their antipapist sentiments all the way down to Paul Schreber.[13]

Moritz's great grandfather Johann David Schreber (born 1669) was a vice-principal (*Conrector*) of a school in Meissen and later a principal (*Rector*) of a school in Pforta and married Martha Maria Jakobi[14] of Meissen. Two of his writings are extant. The first was a dissertation in Latin of 1688 (reissued in 1690, a rare event): *De Libris Obscoeniis* (On Obscene Books). There Johann David seeks to protect "chaste ears and eyes" from "authors who openly speak of things lascivious, vigorously discuss parts that differentiate between the sexes, describe men that are salacious and impure" (quoted in Tabouret-Keller, 1973). Among the authors he inveighs against are Catullus, Ovid, Juvenal, Horace, and Petronius, but also Anacreon and Aristophanes. He calls on Christians to reject such works, to burn the books rather than roast in hell; it is only physicians, scientists and philosophers who are permitted to treat of these subjects. This essay also drew the attention of Bloch (1908, p. 794), who notes that in it Johann David Schreber lumps together the obscene and the erotic; but the former, argues Bloch, is used exclusively in the service of sexual excitement, while the latter serves the purpose of sensuality as an aspect of love, and is a subject that merits discussion in letters, arts, and sciences. Johann David's other work (1736) testifies to his concerns with reforming education: *Lines of Doctrines of Faith, that is Articles of Positive Theology so that it Can Be More Easily Extracted from the Summary of Hutter, Firm Directions of Right Pedagogics.*[15] The Latin text is interspersed with quotations from the Bible in German; one portion—Article 21 (*De conjugio*, On Marriage)—is dedicated to the sanctity of marriage, to which is appended a verse from the Apocrypha (Tob. 8:9): "At present, O Lord, you know that it is not out of evil lust [*nicht böser Lust halber*] that I took my sister as my wife but in order to father children, so that thy name be exalted and praised for ever." The issue of lust, or voluptuousness, meaning both desire and gratification, was very much on the mind of both Moritz and Paul.[16]

The reference to Hutter is important in establishing the connection between reformist ideas in education and pietistic and other reform movements in the Lutheran church, active in the 17th and 18th centuries, and their influence on the educational and ethical ideas of Moritz and the spiritual ideas of father and son. This spiritual legacy was later visible in the inspirational and devotional readings of Paul's elder sister Anna Jung. Paul identified with one of the earliest protestant reformers and mystics, John Hus,[17] and a spiritual conception of the deity.

Johann David's son and Moritz's grandfather, Daniel Gottfried Schreber (1708-1777), was trained as a jurist but distinguished himself as professor of economics in Jena, Halle, and Leipzig. He was a prolific writer[18] with a lively style. He revealed his vision of the future in a treatise on economics (1764):

> We work for posterity. . . . How much more important it is to be the father of a people rather than its hero; how much more does a state prosper by means of economics and its applications than as a result of war-mongering: the latter draws sighs from the breasts and tears from the eyes of unhappy citizens, the former fosters the sweet sentiments of love and gratitude [translated from Tabouret-Keller, 1973].

Moritz expressed similar ideas about education; he knew a number of languages and was a skillful translator.

Gottfried's son of the first marriage was the apple of his eye, the illustrious Johann Christian Daniel *Edler* (noble) von Schreber (1739-1810), a student of Carl Linné and editor of his works. He was the only Schreber to be ennobled in recognition of his scientific writings and services as professor of medicine and physician to the court.[19] His two treatises on insects (J. C. D. Schreber, 1759, 1770) reverberate in Paul's delusions. The work on medicinal plants may have inspired Moritz's (1840) book on pharmacology while the volumes on mammals, published between 1774-1846 and with later editions (1855), may have contributed to Moritz's interest in anthropology and the allusions to mammals in the *Memoirs*. He had no wife and no issue.

After the mother of J. C. D. Schreber died the year her son was born, Gottfried remarried and at age 46 fathered his second son, Johann Gotthilf Daniel Schreber (1754-1837), the father of Moritz, 15 years younger than his illustrious half-brother and totally undistinguished. In 1802 he married Friderike Grosse (1779-1846), whose name appears in distorted form in Paul's reveries (Niederland, 1974, p. 97). Moritz was born in 1808, when Gotthilf was 54 and his wife 29 (thus, as with Freud, to an old father and a young mother). According to Schilling (1964), this may account for Moritz's weak constitution as a child and compensating by developing into an athlete only in his youth and manhood, and may be reflected in the advice Moritz offered in the *Kallipädie* (1858a) against marriages too early or too late in life. Four years after Moritz another boy, Gustav, was born who lived only four years. This means that Moritz lived through the death of his brother at age 8, his father at age 29, and his mother at age 38.

In his autobiography written in old age, Gotthilf comes through as a crotchety, selfish old man beset with numerous ailments (Israëls, 1989, pp. 5-6). He settled in Leipzig as a "legal practitioner, lawyer and notary" (Schilling, 1964). His father Gottfried left all his estate to the half-brother Johann Christian, leaving Gotthilf with only a pittance, which was quickly spent. Since Gotthilf later made a modest living as a lawyer, Moritz studied with the help of scholarships (Schreber, 1833b).

The facts about Moritz's childhood are few. Daughter Anna described his childhood as filled with the sunshine of parental love. As a five year old, Moritz looked for bullet casings and other war memorabilia with his father on the battlefield of the Battle of the Nations in Leipzig (Ritter, 1936). This battle was an all-European historical event: it was followed by the defeat of Napoleon, the overthrow of the French occupation of German lands, and the prelude to the emergence of German nationhood and statehood and the post-Napoleonic Reaction, beginning in 1815, that is, the Metternich-led Holy Alliance and the political reactionary spirit that swept through Europe and Germany and lasted until the 1848-1849 Revolution. These events continued to play a role in Moritz's life. Early on in the history of modern Germany Leipzig earned the reputation of a city of political ferment and turmoil.

"After imbibing the rudiments of literature and religion in a public school, [Moritz] was transferred to the *Thomasschule*" (Schreber, 1833b), the famed high school from which he graduated at the end of seven years. An important event in those years was the *Turnsperre*, the ban on athletics and gymnastics, first instituted in Prussia in 1819 and extended to the other German states. The ban was imposed as a reaction to the politicization of the university athletic clubs. Many of their members belonged to the *Burschenschaften* or student fraternities that championed liberal and democratic reforms, clearly not to the liking of the reactionary authorities in the post-Metternich era. Thus, when the dramatist A. F. F. von Kotzebue, at one time a spy in the Czar's employ and detested by the libertarians among the students, was assassinated by the student Carl Ludwig Sand in 1819, the German government used the event as a pretext to clamp down on the universities, and *Turning* (athletics) became an outlawed activity and word.

A high school classmate of Moritz Schreber reminisced about clandestine *Turning* activities at the *Thomasschule*, accompanied by singing of patriotic songs (Israëls, 1989, p. 18). Schreber may have taken part in such activities in high school and later at the university, where he began his medical studies at age 18. As later recalled by C. H. Schildbach, his friend, associate, successor and spiritual heir, during his years at the university athletics transformed Moritz's body from "a small and puny shape into such height and breadth that when he left the university he surpassed the average size of the male body build" (Schildbach, 1862a). "To the very end of his life, Schreber remained a most skillful, vigorous, elegant and correct athlete. In body building he took pains to give a well-proportioned shape to body and limb. Even in his later years diligent working-out was discernible in his physique and posture" (Schildbach, 1862b). This devotion to athletics remained a life-long activity, up to the time of the second and last physical illness of his life (Schildbach, 1862b).

Equally important are the autobiographical data, hitherto unnoticed, regarding Moritz's intellectual development, his philosophical beginnings. "At first I devoted myself to the study of philosophy and anthropology, and audited the lectures of the excellent Richter and the illustrious Heinroth" (Schreber, 1833b). Heinroth became an important influence on Moritz. By the time Moritz graduated in 1833, J. C. A. Heinroth—a friend and colleague of Moritz's in-laws, the Haases), the first professor of psychiatry in Leipzig from 1811 to 1843, and the future godfather of his firstborn son, Gustav—had already published historical textbooks on psychiatry and a textbook on anthropology.

Moritz passed the theoretical and practical examinations in medicine "with honors (*prima censura*) from the medical faculty" (1833b), followed, as was the custom in those days, by a public examination, and received his M.D. degree with his dissertation on the *Therapeutic Use of Ammonium Tartarate in Inflammations of Respiratory Organs* (Schreber, 1833a). Following graduation and after stints as assistant in a number of hospitals (Schilling, 1964), Moritz, as others have done before him, embarked on a career as a private physician to a wealthy Russian nobleman, residing on his estate near the historic Ukrainian city of Chernigov (Schilling, 1964). He also accompanied the Russian on his many travels in Russia and Europe. It appears that in the course of country living and traveling, eating well was a major pastime and athletics fell by the wayside, so much so that

> His limbs have gotten so rounded that folds of fat were showing on his arms. Twenty-five years later he described to me in vivid colors the horror he felt upon this discovery. He immediately had horizontal and vertical bars put up in the garden and exercised daily to the astonishment of the dumbfounded local denizens (Schildbach, 1862b).

SECOND PERIOD: 1838-1850

In the fall of 1836 Moritz returned to Leipzig where he settled to pursue a private general medical practice. He also became a private fees earning lecturer at Leipzig University, teaching internal medicine and pharmacology (Hirsch, 1887), and publishing a text on pharmacology: *The Normal Dosages of Medications* (Schreber, 1840). This was followed two years later by another medical text: *The Cold Water Therapeutic Method* (1842).

In the aforementioned 1861 autobiographical sketch Moritz tells that in 1838 he married "the oldest daughter of the deceased Professor of medicine Haase and fathered five children" and stresses his literary activity. This implies that he valued it highly. Moreover, this facet of Moritz Schreber has not been given its due. In 1839 he fathered his first son and wrote his first book.

He read widely and wrote in preparation for his first book, *Das Buch der Gesundheit* (The Book of Health, henceforth abbreviated as *Health*; the first edition was printed in 1839, when he was 31. The book contains all his seminal ideas, including ideas on child rearing. Other early writings, or unpublished manuscripts have been lost.

The personal and family life does not seem to show any overt crises. However, in this period Moritz experienced two disappointments. In 1843 he was denied a permit by the city fathers to found a children's hospital (Schilling, 1964). He may not have fared better with the bureaucrats in the appropriate ministry, as implied by Kleine (1942). He also failed in his bid for a professorship (Israëls, 1989, pp. 28-28). This steered him to orthopedics (Friedrich, 1932).

Whether Moritz reacted to these failures with depressions is not known. However, chapter 11 of *Health* ends with a story about a learned man whom Moritz says he met on one of his travels in South Germany and who as a youth suffered from depression with obsessional ruminations. Moritz retells it in the first person. Niederland (1974, p. 64) believed this to be a story about Moritz himself. It is an oft used ploy for an author to disguise his own autobiographical data as someone else's case history. However, it may also have been constructed as a parable to demonstrate Schreber's views on the cause and cure of mental disorder. It has a beauty of its own and I reproduce it here in its entirety and in my translation.

A Confession of a Former Melancholic[20]

Born of upright parents I was given a good education, which in some respects may have been improved by a stronger discipline. An inborn tendency to melancholy manifested itself, in an otherwise happy mental frame, as an almost uncontrollable drive to anxious rumination and a disgruntled mood. Towards the twelfth year I was especially much tormented by a detail—otherwise insignificant—of a nuisance which recurred often, which I could neither avoid, nor ignore, nor say something about, and which gradually turned into an idée fixe. Feeling how oppressive and unnatural my situation was, I still could not convince myself of the insignificance of my idée fixe. As my will power and my free judgment continued to decline, my brooding became more unbridled, and as early as by my 16th or 17th year I was suffering from occasional, although still weak, attacks of melancholy, such that I was tortured by *all manner of black thoughts and especially a temptation to commit criminal acts*, which stood all the more in contradiction to my otherwise good natured character. I took flight as best as I could every time I was threatened by being taken over by my idée fixe. The unavoidable consequence of all this was an occasional unkindness towards my loved ones and frequent neglect of my professional duties. The bitter remorse which I experienced on account of this in my quieter moments made recovering my mental strength [*Ermannung*] more and more difficult every time. I did manage to regain some happiness by putting up a stronger fight, but had neither courage nor strength enough to weed out completely my simply overpowering melancholy. It finally broke through as soon as I reached manhood, after I became involved in circumstances which more and more, and more so than usually, drove the circle of my thoughts away from the world around me and into myself. My beclouded imagination caused me to see my gloomy memories of the past and my own guilt connected with them in a light perhaps all too black. This crippled the resistance powers of my will more and more and the melancholy reached its highest degree. Mad thoughts raged in my brains day and night. The quite strange and most hurting headache caused by the above increased my suffering in repeated attack. I was able to procure sleep with great difficulty and the hellish thoughts continued in sleep. The impulsion to evil became more and more appalling and was fanned by every occasion which presented to the eye a possibility of realizing the temptation. Briefly, my whole mood was devilishly depressed. [original footnote: It reminds one of the Biblical stories of possession—sui generis cases of melancholy, which recur ever so often also in our times.] The painful uncertainty whether during an attack I would really be capable of committing anything so gruesome caused in me an unrest which brought every mood elevation crushing to the ground. The torments were all the more great as I otherwise retained almost all my wits which made me realize the awfulness of my situation all the more clearly. I pined for God but could not reach him any more, whereas before, even when it was possible, I never had the courage to abandon him. Nothing could bring me joy; because of the stark contradiction to the inner events, joyous events—instead of lifting my mood—brought me down even more deeply. Finally my thinking capacity became affected by the shattering of my mood and only seldom did a faint spark of reason shine through the black clouds of melancholy. Therefore it cost an indescribable effort to keep myself on the track of my ordinary life and professional business given the extent of my inner state of terror, which would have been ripe enough for quite some time now to land me in an insane asylum but which did not become public knowledge. I can still hardly fathom how I managed such a high degree of needed mental.effort given the weakening of my will power through my morbid urges. People in my environment noticed a certain decline in my otherwise iron-strong body and at times more absent-mindedness and gloominess than usual, but ascribed it to bodily malaise. I could hardly see the way to my recovery, I often lacked the desire and inclination to pursue this road seriously. I found myself in a state of complete annihilation. How often I wished to exchange my indescribable sufferings with the most painful and terrible bodily illnesses!—This gruesome state lasted for many years, during which, in addition to looking up Heavenward, I was also sustained and saved from utter despair by the thought that an insane person, since he is no longer lord of his feelings and thoughts, cannot be held fully responsible for those. True, I have fought the delusions a thousand times but mostly in vain, as I could not resist the strong drive; the more I tried to follow the conviction I gained regarding the irrationality of my delusional ideas, the more I was overtaken by renewed thought confusion. Then I finally managed to gather the remains of my mental powers and decided to forcibly repress every crooked thought at the point of its emergence and to force my mind to turn Heavenward; I was fighting a life and death fight. True, many of these attempts remained unsuccessful, but I would not allow the perseverance of my striving—my only salvation—to become confused and thus came to experience the inexpressible joy that gradually the struggle became easier and that it began to dawn inside me. I redoubled my efforts and regained, God be praised, the long lost love of God and the world and with it the joy and the happiness of my life [*Health*, 1839, pp. 213-216; emphasis added].

That cautionary tale may have been a lesson to Paul Schreber to fight, by means of will power, melancholy and the false ideas that instigate it, lest they become overpowering. This is both a Kantian and a Christian idea in Schreber, fully espoused by Heinroth (Sänger, 1963; Kesting, 1987). If this is indeed Moritz's own story, then it refers to his depressions at an early age and to his struggles with them and would also be the precursor of his depressions in later life.

Niederland (1974, p. 62) correlated the description in the story of black thoughts and the temptation to commit criminal acts with the notation in Paul's chart: "The father . . . suffered from obsessional ideas of murderous impulses [*Zwangsvorstellungen mit Mordtrieb*]" (Appendix). The informant remains unknown, but tormenting ruminations are certainly in keeping with a picture of depression.

Let us recall that the confession of the melancholic was written down by Moritz at the age of 31, the year his first son Gustav was born. It was at least 12 years later, within the last decade of his life, following a head concussion in 1851, that Moritz suffered from bouts of headaches and depressions. At any rate, Moritz Schreber suffered from depressions in later life, which Paul witnessed between the ages of nine and nineteen.

There is yet another possibility: that this tale was read by Paul later in life and had an effect on him. There are some striking similarities between the learned man and Paul. The urge to commit murder, *Mordtrieb*, is ambiguous in the story: it could also refer to *Selbstmordtrieb*, the urge to commit self-murder or suicide. The latter was very much on Paul's mind. His torments were also described in the imagery of the devil and hell. There is at first a distance from God and then a reconciliation. The idea of self-cure through willpower, of being active in the process of recovery and returning to society, is also seen in Paul. The delusional and fantastic mode of representation predominate in Paul's descriptions, but the phenomenology and dynamics of the depressions are similar. One word leaps from the page of the story in *Health—Ermannung*, becoming manly and strong, regaining strength— in contrast to *Entmannung* (unmanning, emasculation or depotentiation), a concept often on Paul's mind.

Two successes stand out in this period of Moritz's life: becoming the director of the Orthopedic Institute and cofounding the *Leipzig Turnverein*. In 1844 he took over the Orthopedic Institute, a facility for inpatients but mostly for outpatients, the first in Leipzig, founded in 1829 by E. A. Carus, who was called to a post in Dorpat, in Estonia, a place of emigration for a number of German doctors. With the growth of the family and an increase in the number of orthopedic inpatients, mostly children and adolescents, the Schrebers moved in 1847 to a newly built, most spacious building at number 10 Zeitzerstrasse (Schilling, 1964), an event later commemorated by Paul (D. P. Schreber, 1905, lines 251-262).

Moritz acted as director of the Orthopedic Institute until 1859. He was later joined in running it by his colleague, collaborator, and successor, C. H. Schildbach. (The Institute later became, under Schildbach in 1876, the Orthopedic Hospital of Leipzig University.) These two were credited by a medical historian with "great achievements . . . in leading the Orthopedic Institute, . . . both of them made efforts in addresses and writings to move orthopedic gymnastics, especially as applied to scoliosis, in the right direction" (Valentin, 1961, p. 57).[21] However, the Institute was not only a place for practicing orthopedics: it was also a place of education and even a kind of psychotherapy.

EXERCISING THE BODY OR TURNING: MENS SANA IN CORPORE SANO

Even though Moritz Schreber established himself as a specialist first in internal medicine and later in orthopedics, it was the practice and philosophy of gymnastics as sport and therapy that made him famous. *Turnen* and *Turning*, Americanized as turning, was the name given to bodily exercises (*Leibesübungen*) by Friedrich Ludwig Jahn (1778-1852), who as a result earned the nickname of *Turnvater*, the father of exercising, in Germany. It should be emphasized, that many among those concerned with exercising were teachers and educators, for the concern for body exercises was part of education. The other national promoters of German *Turning* (a word more inclusive than gymnastics, because it also referred to athletics, games and sports), were the following: Johann Bernhard Basedow (1723-1790), who combined body culture with the ideas of the enlightenment ethics, and philanthropism; Guts Muths (1759-1839), active in the Schnepfenthal school called the Philanthropinum, in Saxony; and Adolf Spiess (1810-1858), the founder of German school *Turning* (Spiess, 1840, a, b; 1842). The word *Turnen* was made popular in the United States by German immigrants through the founding of many turnvereins, or athletic clubs, and "turnhalls," where turners pursued their activities.

Here is how in 1816 Jahn described the aims of his system of physical education for the people:

> The turning system would reestablish the lost symmetry of human development; would connect a proper bodily training with mere exclusive intellectual cultivation; would supply the proper counteracting influence to the prevailing overrefinement and would comprehend and

influence the whole man by means of a social mode of living for the young. Every turning institution is a place for exercising the bodily powers, a school of industry in manly activity, a place of chivalrous contest, an aid to education, protection to the health and a public benefit. It is constantly and interchangeably a place of teaching and learning. In an unbroken circle follow constantly after each other direction, exemplification, instruction, independent investigation, practice, emulation, and further instruction. Thus the turners do not learn their occupation from hearsay. They have lived in and with their work, investigated it, proved it, and perfected it. It awakens all dormant powers and secures a self-confidence and readiness which are never found at a loss [Monroe, 1918, p. 200].

Guts Muths listed the effects produced by gymnastics and athletics as follows: health of the body led to peace of mind; hardening of the body to manliness; power and dexterity to presence of mind and courage; bodily activity to mental activity; good body building to beauty of the soul; acuity of the senses to acuity of thinking (Cotta, 1902).

The word gymnastics is, of course, the legacy of ancient Greece where physical education and all other education formed a harmonious whole, an idea immortalized by the Roman poet Juvenal in the motto *mens sana in corpore sano* (a sound mind in a sound body). In Greece gymnastics was also employed as a treatment for many diseases and as a means of preventing illness. This application of gymnastics is mentioned in the works of the Roman physicians Celsus and Galen. Thus from very early on bodily exercise penetrated into two domains: medicine and education. A third domain was that of social *Turning*, as practised in the various Turnvereins. It cannot be overly stressed that the traditional view of bodily exercises is that it is inherently pleasant and joyful, not torture.

The educational value of exercising the body was recognized in modern times by, among others, John Locke; in *Some Thoughts Concerning Education* (1693), he viewed exercise as a method for hardening body and mind. He also recommended gardening. Locke's reputation rests on his contribution to philosophy, but his work on education, relatively unknown, has a permanent place in the history of education. Also prominent are two other promoters of body exercises: Jean-Jacques Rousseau in his *Émile ou sur l'Éducation"* (1762), and the educator Pestalozzi (1746-1827) in his work of 1807. The philosopher Fichte, an influence on Schreber, also advocated physical culture.

In 1843 Moritz Schreber published his essay *Turning Presented from the Medical Point of View and as a Matter of State*, abbreviated as *Das Turnen*. The book is addressed to both chambers of the House of

Representatives of the Kingdom of Saxony. It appears barely one year after the lifting of the government ban on *Turning*. Having defined *Turning* in the introduction, Schreber refers to this fact in the "Short Historical Overview." He names as his predecessors Jahn, Eiselen, Werner, Guts Muths, Koch and Klumpp. In Section VII he presents his "Ideas about the advisability of building turning grounds and turning as a whole," while Section VIII, "Appeal to State Governments and Agencies," pleads for public moneys for the implementation of his ideas. During the *Turnsperre* (prohibition of *Turning*), which had lasted from 1820 to 1842, and in the course of the heated debates in favor and against *Turning*, a number of physicians, among them doctors Koch[22] and Lorinser, took positions in favor of the medical and pedagogical value of *Turning*. In 1843 Moritz Schreber was already a second-generation medical champion of bodily exercises as education for the people. Another noteworthy medical predecessor of Schreber in championing exercises in Saxony during the *Turnsperre* was Dr. Johann Adolf Ludwig Werner (1794-1866), born near Zwickau, in Saxony. He was at first against Jahn, even as he was indebted to him, and he wrote about the three uses of exercises: in the school, in medicine, and in the military.[23]

Thus, Moritz Schreber's activity was firmly located within a medically inspired humanistic tradition of education. In this he had both predecessors and followers. His appeal of 1843 in *Das Turnen* was cold-shouldered by officialdom. Although this early appeal to the authorities shows him to be a man of daring and of progressive views, it may have jeopardized forever any future attempts on his part to gain official support.[24]

Schreber was not alone in his attempts to secure government support. His advocacy of *Turning* as progressive was echoed by other writers around the end of the next decade. Medically trained and other promoters of physical culture attempted to rouse the nation from its apathy towards *Turning* in fiery appeals. This can be seen, for example, in Oswald Faber's (1859) pamphlet, *Turning in its Relations to State and Nation, a Timely Question, an Epistle to Supporters and Opponents, for the Benefit of the Jahn Monument in the Hasenhaide*. Faber was then Turner-in-chief of the General Leipzig Turnverein and praised Schreber's achievement. Or consider *A Call to Turning. Open Letters to Everyman* by Eduard Ferdinand Angerstein (1859), doctor of therapeutics, practising physician surgeon and obstetrician, member of the Berlin Medical Society, president of the Berlin Turn Council, honorary member of the Berlin Turner-Verein, member of the Turngemeinde, of the Eiselen Turn-Verein and the Association of Turnteachers of Berlin, of which the opening paragraph in the introduction reads:[25]

In many places of the German fatherland there is a awakening to noble Turning. Maybe a spring-tide will come that will break the winter sleep of indolence and prejudice and propagate new life's blooms. Indeed, things are still not well with the cause of Turning; oft rejected, it still eaks out a miserly existence. But the forecast seems to be brighter, here and there Turning is calling attention to itself, the forces of the Turners, while still small, seem to be growing [1859].

Moritz Schreber's dedication to *Turning* and his civic functions were important aspects of his prominence in Leipzig among his contemporaries. This reputation of Schreber in Leipzig during his lifetime and the posthumous veneration may have shaped Paul's aspirations to become a public figure himself, as in his candidacy for the Reichstag. Moritz was active in the militia called the "communal guards" (*Leipzig Communalgarde*, 1843). His participation in the activities of this militia force in the turbulent year 1848 was later vividly recollected by his daughter Anna (A. L., 1940).

In 1845 Moritz was one of the cofounders of the "*Allgemeiner Turnverein zu Leipzig*," along with two other Leipzig professors of medicine, Karl Ernst Bock (1809-1874) and Karl Biedermann (1812-1901). This was duly recognized by another follower, Georg Hirth (1865),[26] who penned a brief biography of Moritz Schreber to precede excerpts from his *Gymnastics*. He credited Schreber's chairmanship of the Leipzig Turnverein between the years 1847 and 1851 with the happy overcoming of the difficult years of 1848 and 1849, the years of the Spring of Nations and the political unrest in Leipzig, thus echoing a sentiment similar to one expressed earlier by Schildbach (1862b). Bock also wrote about education in a manner reminiscent of Schreber.[27]

Endowed with a strong sense of a calling and mission, Schreber dreamt of official recognition of his efforts but never received it. This discrepancy between high ambition and insufficient recognition may have contributed to his depressions during the last ten years of his life. The same sense of mission was also discernible in his sons, especially Paul, who doubtless acquired it from their high-striving father. As an adolescent, Paul would have been exposed to his father's depressions, and he would thus have learned early that long suffering and a lack of recognition may be combined with that inner, almost secret, sense of self-exaltation and higher worth that is the melancholic's chief recompense for his fate.

THERAPEUTIC GYMNASTICS

The idea of the medical application of gymnastics, one of the mainstays of modern rehabilitation medicine, was powerfully stated in modern times by the Swede Per Henrik Ling (1776-1839), who was an influence on Moritz Schreber. At first a student of divinity and languages, Ling elaborated a system of gymnastics that was divided into four branches (pedagogical, medical, military, and aesthetic). The centerpiece of Ling's method was passively exercising the body with the help of an assistant, which at that time was referred to in German as *duplicirte* or assisted (i.e., passive) exercises. He not only obtained official support to found in 1813 the Royal Gymnastic Central Institute for the training of gymnastic instructors but became a member of the Swedish Medical Association: passive exercises and massage became a respected medical treatment.

Schreber at first borrowed ideas from Ling.[28] Ling's writings were based on a rational approach to exercising and replete with philosophical and anthropological learned quotations, adhering to the aforementioned four divisions of gymnastics. Schreber went on to develop his own method of active exercises and engaged in polemics with Ling and Ling's German followers, especially A. C. Neumann, on the pages of the *Neue Jahrbücher für die Turnkunst* (henceforth abbreviated as *NJT*).[29]

Schreber (1855b) set the tone in reviewing a book by the Dresden physician E. Friedrich, *Therapeutic Gymnastics in Sweden and Norway*, by endorsing Friedrich's opinion that one should speak of "one therapeutic gymnastics, that incorporates what is good and useful" (p. 90). Friedrich (1855) had cited Schreber (1852a). In his review of one of Neumann's books (1855e), Schreber was critical of Neumann's "Swedish-gymnastic idioms, jarring to the German ear" and of his adherence to the occult ("v. Reichenbach Od-theory," an "eccentric direction in science"). Schildbach (1859), reviewing Neumann's (1859a) *Haus Gymnastik*, was much more caustic toward this apparent rival of Schreber's, also scoffing at his mystical ideas (Schildbach, 1859).[30] This debate resulted in work written by Schreber and Neumann (1858) in epistolary form: *Controversies about German and Swedish Therapeutic Gymnastics*. Neumann succeeded with the authorities, achieving what was denied to Moritz Schreber: an official post and recognition by the Prussian King.[31] In the standard reference books there is little mention of Neumann, while Schreber is regarded as the founder of German therapeutic gymnastics and a man who achieved posthumous fame.

This controversy about active and passive methods in therapeutic gymnastics may have been fueled by rivalry and patriotism. There are three varieties of movements used in therapeutic gymnastics, the passive (in which the therapist manipulates the muscles and the patient remains passive), the active (initiated by patient without other aids), and the oppositional (a combination of the first two one, where the patient opposes the manipulation of his muscles by the therapist). Which variety of movement is not a question of either-or but of what is indicated for the patient. Ling's method is suitable for the very incapacitated (and is still in use by physical therapists), while the more active forms are not.

The other issue has thematic importance: Moritz's great emphasis on German active exercise, as against the Swedish passive method, reverberates with themes of activity and passivity in his son Paul's *Memoirs*.

In the history of therapeutic gymnastics, a number of other names, in addition to Ling, precede Moritz Schreber both in Germany and in the Austro-Hungarian Empire. We know from his aforementioned autobiographical sketch about his travels in Vienna, Prague and Berlin and the various institutions. We are also told of later travels to Belgium, England and France, where he studied the methods of others.

He may have read a work on orthopedics by J. Hirsch (1845),[32] who is addressing in Prague issues that occupy Schreber in Leipzig. They share a common interest and are exposed to the same influences, but Schreber already shows a greater refinement, relying less and less on the use of cumbersome orthopedic machines made of metal and leather—the assorted iron corsets, belts, buckles, and braces—and moving towards free exercises and more holistic conceptions.

ORTHOPEDICS, THERAPEUTIC GYMNASTICS AND PREVENTION

Today orthopedists are known as surgeons who treat broken bones, deformities and other disorders. In Schreber's day and his own practice there was no orthopedic surgery in the modern sense (Uibe, 1959). For a long time orthopedists treated functional disorders of the spine with varieties of machinery, earning the appellation of the "belts and buckles doctors." The domain of functional disorders has been largely taken over by chiropractors and osteopaths.

From its inception, however, since the Frenchman Nicolas Landry[33] coined the word *orthopédie* (from *orthos*, straight and *paidos*, child), orthopedics dealt with the correction and prevention of deformities in children, either from birth or acquired as a result of tuberculosis or rickets, for whom treatment included exercising (with and without machinery), and the natural virtues of air, water and sunlight. Tuberculosis was a common disease, and rickets were due to poor nutrition (vitamin D deficiency). The discovery of vitamins was still in the future, but Schreber in his article "On the Therapeutic Use of Sunbathing, Especially Against Certain Chronic Diseases of Children"

(1858c), was already empirically aware that sunlight was an effective medicine against rickets.

Schreber's first work dealing with issues of treatment and prevention of deformities was a 39-page-long essay published in 1846, two years into his work as director of the Orthopedic Institute, entitled *On the Prevention of Spine Deformities or Scoliosis, Well-Intentioned Advice to Parents, Teachers and Educators*, henceforth abbreviated as *Scoliosis*.[34] In *Scoliosis* Schreber distinguishes between spine deformities as a health hazard (*Gesundheitsfehler*) and as a cosmetic defect (*Schönheitsfehler*) and states his purpose as follows:

> Since generally speaking it is easier and surer to *prevent* an ill than to *cure* an existing one, this also especially applies here. Consequently, *prevention* should be our first and foremost task. By virtue of my profession as director of an orthopedic hospital I felt obligated to call *this* matter to the attention of parents and educators in my essay specially devoted to this topic, hoping that I would be making a humble contribution to meeting an urgent need of our times. And an urgent need it is, when one sees that with each new generation among the civilized nations there is an increase in the incidence of this disorder, and especially in the female gender, where such disorders are of the greatest importance [*Scoliosis*, p. 6; emphasis Schreber's].

Treatment of existing deformities meant the use of stretching apparatuses, which earned orthopedists the reputation of torturers. Schreber defended their necessary use, but as a humane and public health-minded physician he entered a plea for preventive measures, which were included in the so-called dietetic prescriptions. The adjective *dietetic*, from the now obsolete '*Diätetik*', does not refer here to the science of nutrition, as in English, but to the notion of health regimens, already practiced in antiquity. A further meaning of the term appears in Kant, when he discusses the two main concerns of medicine, therapeutics and dietetics (that is, prevention). Dietetics means proper regimens for the health of body and mind. As defined in *Scoliosis*, it includes measures for "the removal and the prevention of a weak and sickly bodily constitution" (p. 17)—thus dietetics of the body. It also includes nutrition,[35] the proper metabolism of noxious substances, the right proportion of movement and rest, and, finally, the proper age-appropriate training of the child, that is, dietetics of the mind.

We see here the beginnings of the transition from orthopedics to pediatrics. Thus, in the section of *Scoliosis* dealing with motion and rest Schreber says this about the rearing of infants:

> Already the suckling infant feels the need to give his body a workout by means of thrusting and kicking movements of his arms and legs, so that

the swaddling of infants should be *completely free from restraints*. When the child has reached the capacity for independent movement, it should be afforded the opportunity to exercise freely, to be able to give unrestrained expression to his lust for movement, and indeed as far as possible outdoors. Later, towards the fifth or seventh year, the age appropriate use of *bodily exercises* [*Turnen*] will best fulfill all the conditions required for the growth and strengthening of the body from the side of muscle activity. . . . One should protect the mind of the child from premature strain, for it inhibits the development of the body, . . . Regular school education should start at age seven. Should any learning be undertaken earlier, then it should proceed at least in no other fashion than uncoercively and playfully [pp. 21-22; emphasis Schreber's].

In the last section of *Scoliosis* Schreber discusses the body in movement and at rest and practical steps for the prevention of deformities. Thus, he stresses the importance of symmetry in movements and proper body carriage, as well as desirable body postures in lying and sitting. For the school-age child—sitting, writing, or reading—he recommends a prototype of the future *Geradehalter*, or straight-holder, the famous contraption that would later allow first Niederland and then Schatzman to portray Moritz Schreber as a malefactor. Here it is a piece of board with a toothed edge placed below the chin to prevent the child from lurching forward, used only for as long as it is necessary to condition the child to develop a proper posture habit at the table. Another conditioning device, consisting of belts loosely applied to the arms and legs of a sleeping child, affording free play to the extremities, is used to promote the habit of a supine sleeping posture (*Scoliosis*, pp. 30, 31). Of course, these concerns for the prevention of disease and the proper rearing of children are not specifically orthopedic. Prevention is basic in medicine today, but in the generations preceding Schreber and in Schreber's time it was a relatively new idea.[36]

The next book Schreber wrote about gymnastics was a slim volume of 92 pages published in 1852, *Kinesiatrics or the Gymnastic Treatment Method*, here abbreviated as *Kinesiatrics* (the word *kinesiatric* is derived from the Greek, the root words meaning movement and physician). This work was Schreber's main contribution to the professional literature on therapeutic gymnastics. According to Cyriax (1909), the book was translated into Spanish in 1899.

To begin with, Schreber moved away from the use of machines and orthopedic mechanical contraptions worn by the patient.[37] Schreber went beyond the usual applications of orthopedic gymnastics to find a wider scope in a "*gymnastische Heilmethode*" (therapeutic gymnastics), that is, exercising as a kind of medical therapy for a variety of chronic disorders, both functional and organic. Thus, the method of kinesiatrics, that is, the "gymnastic or movement therapeutic method,"[38] was to be distinguished both from *Turngymnastik* (i.e., exercises for the healthy), and from orthopedic kinesiatrics (i.e, the use of orthopedic machines), marking a departure from the method of Ling. Whereas Ling prescribed passive muscle exercises and massage administered by a physical therapist, Schreber advocated simple active gymnastic exercises, with and without exercise aids or machines.

According to Schreber, increasing muscular activity has the effect of stimulating metabolism and making the body younger. In this he declared himself to be a follower of the Berlin physician Schultz-Schultzenstein (1842), author of *The Rejuvenation of Human Life*, citing the second edition of the book of 1850. Due to its effect on physiological processes in the nerves, Schreber held, muscular activity can alleviate "nervous congestion," "excessive nervous excitability," and "excitation in nerves transmitting sexual stimuli" (*Kinesiatrics*, p. 28) and is thus indicated in hypochondria and hysteria. For muscle activity, Schreber believed, has important psychic effects:

> Inherent in the vigorous use of the body, and the ensuing growing awareness of bodily power, and the accompanying consistent overcoming of ... bodily limpness and softness goes the psychologically inevitable strengthening of the will power, activeness in general, self-confidence, decisiveness, courageousness etc, ... so important in the treatment of the chronically ill [*Kinesiatrics*, pp. 28-29].

Schreber recommended the method as treatment for a host of so-called paralyses, that is, functional disorders thought to be caused by "spinal irritation," and chronic disorders, such a tuberculosis, asthma, rheumatism and gout. While he was aware of J. Traugott (1850) who published a book on the use of gymnastics and athletics in the treatment of psychotic disorders, interestingly conducted on patients at the Sonnenstein Asylum, Schreber advised caution against unwarranted extensions of the method. He recommended individualized treatment plans.

Kinesiatrics contains information about patients and their treatments at the Orthopedic Institute. Schreber described his procedure as follows:

> Prior to admission, every patient was subjected by me to a thorough medical examination to determine the need for the [kinesiatric] treatment. Following admission, every patient received a written treatment plan detailing the indicated gymnastic exercises, manipulations, or other

necessary orders. . . . The treatments are carried out directly by me . . . as required . . . or by aides trained by me. I follow the progress of each case during the treatment by frequent and thorough examinations . . . and daily visits [pp. 73–74].

Kinesiatrics, the book and the method, had its heyday in mid-century and for the next few decades. Thus it appeared in the second edition of Eulenburg's *Real-Encyclopädie* (1885–1891), but was no longer mentioned in the third.[39] Ling's idea of the passive massages and manipulations—and a voluminous literature in that spirit, more in keeping with the methods of traditional medicine—carried the day.[40]

The promotion of kinesiatrics was continued in Schreber's second book of 1855 and his most famous, *Gymnastics*,[41] which we have seen mentioned by Paul, largely aimed at the general public but also acknowledged in the professional literature.[42]

His last book on exercises, conceived as the second part of *Gymnastics*, was *The Pangymnastikon, or the whole Turn System Based on the use of a Single Appliance without Space Requirement as a Simple Aid for the Development of the Highest and Versatile Muscle Power, Body Building and Proficiency: for Schools, Home Turners and Turnvereins*, published posthumously in 1862. The "pangymnastikon" was Schreber's name for that universal appliance—the dumbbell.[43]

THIRD PERIOD: 1851–1861

In 1851 he suffered head trauma, followed by a somewhat mysterious posttraumatic syndrome with recurrent depressions. "The brain congestions that filled the last ten years of life with bitterness, were supposedly due to an external wound, caused by a heavy object that fell on his head, half a year prior to the beginning of the illness [i.e, the brain congestions]" (Schildbach, 1862b, p. 17).

Brain congestion is both a medical term and a euphemism for depression. What happened during the hiatus of six months between the head wound and the onset of the illness? Was there a hemorrhage into the meninges? Did the external trauma mask an internal, or psychological, trauma?

"During the last ten years of his life he was often interrupted in his customary activities due to illness [*durch Leiden*]" (Schildbach, 1877, p. ix). Although it resulted in a curtailment of his professional, familial, and social activities, the illness ushered in the most prolific period of writing on the subject of education. According to Ellenberger (1964), it qualifies as Schreber's creative illness. He emerged from this illness with a new identity and a new direction to his creativity: writing books on education.

Schreber's Orthopedic Institute

In gymnastics Schreber found both a personal solution and a pragmatic and theoretical principle in his practice of medicine. Something similar occurred in relation to his educational principles: applying them and writing about them came together for him in the manner in which he ran his orthopedic institution. How much he practised on his children of the educational methods he wrote about is an open question. It is plausible to assume that at least in the Schreber household, he would not have been the only disciplinarian: his wife would have lent a helping hand, or would be the source of authority and discipline in infancy and early childhood. There is no doubt that discipline and obedience to rules had to prevail in his institution for things to run efficiently. It was not a hospital in the usual sense of the word: it was an arrangement half way between a medical and a psychiatric residential treatment unit, and in it at any one time lived between 7 to 15 children. Furthermore, as testified by Schreber's daughters, the patients and the Schreber children mingled freely.

Schreber's Gymnastic-Orthopedic Therapeutic Institute (*Gymnastisch-Orthopädische Heilanstalt*) in Leipzig was described by Schreber in *Kinesiatrics* and in three reports of its operations by Schildbach.[44] Schildbach bought the Institute from Schreber in the fall of 1858 and took it over in May of 1859. I believe that since Schildbach was a true follower, what he writes can serve as a description of how the place was run by Schreber himself.[45]

The first report (Schildbach, 1861) covers a period of 20 months, through the end of 1860, a period following the retirement of Schreber from the institute and thus still reflects his influence and practices. The patients came from all over Germany, Russia, Western Europe, North America, South America, West Indies, Egypt, and Java. It was not strictly speaking a hospital with sick and bedridden patients but a boarding house that was an "extended family" of Schreber and, later, Schildbach. The inmates or boarders were treated for a variety of musculoskeletal problems: scoliosis, kyphosis, lordosis, clubfoot (varus, valgus, and varo-equinus), paralyses, malformed breastbones. However, others were treated for "hernias, internal chronic disorders of the spinal cord and neurasthenia (*Nervenschwäche*), one case of generalized nerve-irritability, one case of epilepsy-like illness, abdominal and hemorrhoidal ailments, hypochondria, liver swelling, stomach and intestinal catarrh" (Schildbach, 1861, p. 9). This variegated list is thus seen to include nonspecific functional disorders strongly indicative of emotional and behavioral dysfunction. Of particular interest is the mention of a disorder called *"Kopfleiden,"* or head ailment, a name like the one Schreber himself suffered from after the accident in 1851.

The Institute was located in the house that Schreber moved into in 1847. It was built on "free and high ground, with large and well lit rooms and anterooms, and [a] magnificent and spacious gymnasium (*Turnsaal*)" (Schildbach, 1877, p. vii), the house flanked by gardens on two sides. The *Turnsaal* was on the ground floor, equipped with a variety of exercise appliances, and it was the place where the actual treatments of inpatients and outpatients took place. In the elevated basement there were all manner of showers. The second floor housed female boarders and the third floor the residence of the director and had space for male boarders. The treatment modalities were appliance exercises, free exercises, bed rest and water treatments. Schildbach reaffirms that while the founder, Dr. Carus, stressed the use of mechanical aids, Schreber had moved toward a specific and scientific therapeutic gymnastic method. The exercises usually took half a day. They were carried out in an atmosphere of patience, attention and care, with an emphasis on elegance, calm and beauty. While Ling's method was used in some cases (paralyses and foot deformities), most were treated with the "the German method": "long before people in Germany knew anything about Ling, Dr. Schreber treated the deformed and the sick in his fashion . . . [a method] that is quicker, cheaper and combined with a greater general gain for body and character of the patient" (Schildbach, 1861, p. 9).

Schildbach thus continued procedures already in existence during Schreber's tenure, including providing personal attention: "The patients were under the direct supervision of myself and my wife." The goal was "the development of mind and character [and] an educational influence" (Shildbach, 1861, p. 14). The two doctors were dealing with a group of schoolchildren, an assembly of different personalities with different needs, who had to be managed, controlled, and guided from day to day.

The institution was "less restrictive than the usual educational boarding houses" (Schildbach, 1877, p. viii). There were "few directives but unconditional obedience" was required of all, though not to excess, but the infractions were listed on a special board (*Strafenrügen*). But there was not too much fussing with punishments. "I find that I can achieve much more if I impose my will thoroughly once and then leave the child to itself as much as possible" (Schildbach, 1877, p. IX). An atmosphere of joy was stressed: "The exercises hours were not viewed as a burdensome duty but as a pleasure . . . meant to enliven hope and further independence" (Schildbach, 1877, p. xi). The idea was to teach the youthful patients how to experience beauty, how to develop the faculties of perception and attention, and how to "strengthen the will and keep alive the devotion to duty." The young boarders also attended school or were privately tutored. "I fought hypersensitivity, softness, laziness and cowardice in every fashion and sought—through safe encouragements, insistence on unflagging adherence to the laws and the establishment of few but strongly maintained rules and active willpower—to build a self-disciplining character" (Schildbach, 1861, p. 15).

These ideas of Schildbach might have been direct quotes from Schreber's *Kallipädie* (1858a) on child rearing and discipline. Moreover, the fact that Schreber lived with these children under one roof for many years may have provided him with experiences and observations that inspired many of his educational ideas; thus, there existed the potential for a reciprocal and ongoing interaction between practice and philosophy, experience and theory building.

THE SUDDEN END

Tracing Moritz Schreber's career has been at the expense of considering his personal fates. Both are important, for both shaped the character of the son by way of imitation, identification and counteridentification.

Disappointments and depressions run like a crimson thread through Moritz Schreber's life, from the early resonance with the melancholic described in *Health* to his last ten years. The heaviness of those last ten years is revealed in the likenesses of Schreber that have survived. In the family portrait painted in oil in 1851 we still see the lineaments of a youthful, tranquil paterfamilias, surrounded by wife and children. A studio photograph of Schreber in an orator's pose, probably taken in the last decade of his life, shows a markedly aged person.

> Even as his face showed, in the somewhat pinched parts around the eyes, the signs of having undergone severe bodily suffering and lacked fullness and a healthy color, . . . his lean and strong body . . . did not presage an early death. Who would have thought of it during the last summer of his life, when in the company of his Dresden friend Kloss he travelled to Berlin to participate in the dedication of the monument to *Turnvater* Jahn on the Hasenhaide field. And when he died in his 54th year, a few may have said: 'It was of no use to him; he lived a moderate life, exercised diligently and still died so young!" [Schildbach, 1862b, p. 16].

"Pure and noble of character, . . . indefatigable in the search for truth" (Schildbach, 1862b, p. 17), Moritz Schreber was unable to carry out high ambitions into achievements according to his wishes. Even as late as the winter of 1861 he was still trying to find recognition in the eyes of the state by submitting a four-page letter addressed to the "High Ministry of Education" (Schreber, 1861d): in it he states, at the outset, that national education and social hygiene are both the highest ethical goal of mankind and the concern of the state, for these determine the fate of the state. He returns to his first theme: the harmony of body and mind, and finds that modern culture, in spite of its progress, is still lacking in this essential balance, with undue emphasis on intellect and not enough on the body. Furthermore, Schreber continues, contemporary religious and moral life has split into two extremes: "rigid and sinister dogmatism" and "bottomless materialism." Both are enemies of the true spirit of Christianity and the laws of man's spiritual life. Without coming into conflict with established churches, the solution should be sought, Schreber suggests, in understanding human nature in the light of an anthropology that unifies body and mind. Pragmatically, this should be achieved through education. As an example of enlightened social action he cites the recent founding in England of "Ladies' Sanitary Associations" with the participation of physicians and men of science, organizations whose purpose, says Schreber, is to disseminate popular writings and organize public lectures addressed to all the social classes on subjects like hygiene and diet, as is done in London, Manchester, America, Holland, and Hungary. It is a good beginning, acknowledges Schreber, but it still lacks the integration of the whole, the physical and the ethical parts of mankind. Schreber then proposes for the various German states that his own attached pamphlet be distributed at government cost to school authorities, community leaders, agencies for the poor, and so forth. It should reach the masses, he asserts; thousands will remain unaffected, but other thousands will respond. The message is urgent, he insists, and is needed by the German nation and all the other civilized nations that seek rejuvenation and a harmonious culture.

Like the appeal of 1843, this one was cold-shouldered as well. Was this man a realist or a naïve dreamer? Did he really believe that the existing secular and religious powers would rush to embrace a program both humanistic and messianic? It is tempting to wonder how much more Moritz Schreber would have achieved had he lived, but maybe he believed that he had said it all.

Yet, this would-be healer of a sick society could not heal himself. The healthy, well-exercised body was powerless to provide him with the much needed personal harmony of body and mind. His head ailment may have abated during the treatments he took at the spas of Gastein, Carlsbad and Heligoland (Israëls, 1989, p. 125). In

Carlsbad—a story that impressed Niederland—he even defeated an old gentleman in a race (Schildbach, 1862a, Israëls, 1989, p. 125). But there was also talk of another reason for visiting the spas: "an intestinal disorder" (Richter, quoted by Israëls, 1989, p. 125).

In 1861 the "Second All-German Turning Festival and Jubilee" was held in Berlin with great pomp, in commemoration of Jahn's centenary. Festive speeches and patriotic songs resounded. Among the members of the festival committee were Friedrich from Dresden and F. Götz from Leipzig. Kloss and Schreber were among the visitors but Schreber made no speech (Angerstein, 1861).

"It was only last year," writes Kloss in his obituary of Schreber, echoing the sentiments of Schildbach,

> that the lead-off in the first issue of the preceding volume of the *Jahrbücher* [*NJT*] was the vigorous "Appeal and international New Year's greetings to the student youth at all the German universities" by our former collaborator. When during the Berlin Jahn Centenary last summer we walked together outside the city on our way to the Hasenhaide, to participate with German athletes in raising the monument to the Great Master Jahn, we had no inkling that in the first issue of the current year we would be publishing the obituary of a man who only months before moved hale and hearty alongside German athletes, celebrating the new life that has come to German national Turning.
>
> During the festivities in Berlin Schreber told the writer his ideas about introducing *Turning* in public schools on a much wider basis and of the plan of the book that since appeared under the title "*Pangymnastikon.*" Only days before his death he sent us this book with a note: "Here is what I promised you. I am anxious to hear your opinion. If you do not object, the three first pages might be published as a separate small article, with something like this for a title: "The close connection between the art of Turning and the development of German national life," or however you see fit. Cordial greetings to Professors Richter and Friedrich. Keep in good remembrance
>
> your
> Dr. Schreber [Kloss, 1862, pp. 10-11]

The worm within kept gnawing at his insides. At some point, against the backdrop of the ups and downs in the functional intestinal disorder, he developed acute appendicitis. He died suddenly on November 10, 1861, of complications of an inflamed and ruptured appendix, confirmed by autopsy performed by Professor Wagner.[46] It seemed as if the thread of his life was suddenly cut in midstream. The excerpt from the *Pangymnastikon*, under Schreber's suggested title, was printed in the issue of the *NJT* following Schildbach's postscript to Kloss's obituary.

SYNOPSIS OF MORITZ SCHREBER'S LIFE AND WORK

Family tree traceable to the 15th century.

1808, October 15: Born in Leipzig to lawyer Johann Gotthilf Daniel Schreber (1754-1837), age 54, and mother Friederike née Grosse (1779-1846), age 29.

1812: Birth of brother Friedrich Gustav Daniel, who died 1816.

Until 1826: Elementary and high school studies (at the famous *Thomasschule*) in Leipzig.

1826-1833: Medical studies at Leipzig University.

1831: Self-dated beginning of literary activities.

1833: Graduates with the thesis, *Therapeutic Use of Ammonium Tartarate in Inflammations of Respiratory Organs*.

1833-1836: Personal physician to a Russian nobleman, travels in spas of Germany, central and southern Russia; study travels in Vienna, Prague, and Berlin.

1836: Starts medical practice in Leipzig, *Privatdozent* (lecturer) at Leipzig University. Continuation of literary activities (books, professional and popular journals).

1837: Death of father, age 82.

1838: Marriage to Pauline Haase, oldest daughter (born 1815) of Wilhelm Andreas Haase, professor of medicine at Leipzig University, and Juliane Wenck, also from a family of professors.

1839: Writing, first period: first published book, *The Book of Health*, his first contribution to medical pedagogics.

1839-1848: Birth of the Schreber children: Gustav, 1839; Anna, 1840; Paul, 1842; Sidonie, 1844; Klara, 1848.

1846: Death of mother.

1840-1842: Writings, second period, on medical subjects: *The Normal Dosages of Medications* (1840) and *The Cold Water Therapeutic Method* (1842).

1843: Member of the Communalgarde in Leipzig.

1843: First writing on the educational importance of gymnastics: *Turning Presented from the Medical Point of View and as a Matter of State*. Unsuccessful in his bid to found a hospital for sick children.

1844: Takes over as director of the orthopedic clinic and hospital of Dr. Carus in Leipzig. Scientific travels in Belgium, England, France, Italy, and Switzerland. Contributor to various medical periodicals, encyclopedias, contemporary yearbooks.

1845: Cofounder, with Drs. Biedermann and Bock, of the Leipzig *Turnverein* (athletic club).

1846-1855: Writings, third period—therapeutic applications of gymnastics: *On the Prevention of Spine Deformities or Scoliosis* (1846); *Kinesiatrics or the Gymnastic Treatment Method* (1852a); *The Injurious Body Postures and Habits of Children and the Means to Prevent Them* (1853); and his most famous, *Medical Indoor Gymnastics* (1855a); also one work on pediatrics: *The Characteristics of the Child's Organism in Health and Disease* (1852b).

1847: Builds a spacious new house to which he moves his clinic, hospital, and residence.

1851: Ladder accident and head trauma; beginning of chronic head complaints alternating with depressions.

1858: Polemical work on medical applications of gymnastics, in collaboration with Neumann: *Controversies about German and Swedish Therapeutic Gymnastics* (1858).

1858-1861: Writings, fourth period, works on education: *Kallipädie* (1858a); *A Medical Perspective on School Affaires* (1858c); *Anthropos: The Wonderful Structure of the Human Organism* (1859a); *The Methodical Training of the Acuity of Sense Organs* (1859b); *On National Education* (1860).

1859: Gives up directorship of the orthopedic clinic and hospital to successor C. H. Schildbach.

1860-1861: Gastrointestinal ailments, treatments at Carlsbad.

1861: Petition to the Ministry for recognition of his educational ideas, with a disappointing response.

1861, August: In Berlin for the all-German Jahn jubilee and festivities; not honored as a national figure.

1861: Second Edition of *The Book of Health* (1839) and *The Family Friend*. Edits Hartmann's fourth edition of *The Doctrine of Happiness*.

1861, November 10: Death from paralytic ileus due to peritonitis caused by an acute perforating appendicitis.

1862: Posthumous publication of *Pangymnasticon*, the second part of *Medical Indoor Gymnastics*.

1882: Second edition of the *Kallipädie*, now called *The Book of Child Rearing*.

1875: Second edition of the *Pangymnasticon*.

1885: Second edition of Schreber, 1842, *The Water-Therapy Method: Its Limitations and True Worth*.

1889: 26th edition of *Gymnastics*.

1891: The second edition of *The Book of Child Rearing*.

NOTES

1. In addition to the information in *Freund der Schrebervereine* (Friend of the Schreber Associations), the basic data about Moritz Schreber's life and work

were already in print when Freud was writing his essay: the autobiographical sketch in Moritz Schreber's (1833b) doctoral thesis (a universal procedure); the obituaries by Politzer and Kloss (both from 1862, the latter with additions by Schildbach); entries about Moritz Schreber in Schmidt's and Schulze's (1891) *Allgemeine Deutsche Biographie* (Universal German Biography), with the rare spelling, "Gottlieb" (also in Schreber, 1852a, whereas elsewhere the spelling is "Gottlob"), citing two earlier sources (Heindl, 1859, and Pierer's *"Jahrbücher* vol. 3, [p.] 380"); Hirsch's (1887); and in the standard 19th-century encyclopedias, *Brockhaus* and *Meyer.* None of these sources was noted by Freud; they, along with Moritz Schreber's own works, were sources for other dictionaries, encyclopedias, and reference works in other languages (Russian, Polish, Czech), for example in Brockhaus and Efron (1903).

2. It is translated as allotment garden in Klatt et al. (1983).

3. The entry on Schreber in the 1954 edition of *Der Grosse Brockhaus* tells that it was school director Hauschild who founded the first Schreber Association. Israëls is justified in his efforts to dispel the still popularly held idea that Schreber was the originator of the idea of city gardening. He shows a photograph of the sign of a street in Leipzig, the *Schreberstrasse,* which states: "Founder of the Schreber Gardens," also shown in Schilling (1964).

4. Hauschild was not only an admirer and follower of Moritz Schreber but an expert on children's upbringing in his own right. The first (1858) edition of his work, *The Bodily Care of Children,* appeared in the same year as the *Kallipädie* (1858a); the motto is that teacher and physician are natural friends in this endeavor. In this work Hauschild used the concept of *Kinderdiätetik,* the system of the right living for children, quoting the physician Lorinser as his inspiration and citing his earlier work of 1855: *Leipziger Blätter für Erziehung und Unterricht* (Leipzig Gazette on Education and Instruction). He developed his own ideas, without citing Schreber as reference, not even the *Gymnastics,* even as he mentioned exercise as a method for combating masturbation (which was Schreber's idea too). Educator Hauschild, in the manner of a pediatrician, devoted many sections to bodily functions and bodily care. In the section entitled "The Sexual Parts" he gave much attention to the role of the teacher in catching children masturbating in class (with a zeal that far surpasses that of Schreber), warning against the danger of sexual seduction of children by each other, the temptations of masturbation, and of lounging too long in bed after awakening.

5. All but the last have been important sources of information for Israëls. A number of them contributed articles about Moritz Schreber to *Der Freund der Schrebervereine.* Israëls errs in identifying these men with the Schreber gardens movement only, instead of also locating them in the field of education.

6. One of them was Eduard Mangner, whose essay of 1876, *Dr. D.G.M.S., a Fighter for National Education* (author's reprint from the periodical *Cornelia;* source: dr. Niederland) is a well-balanced tribute to Schreber. This assessment of Moritz is endorsed by Bornstein (1931), a physician.

7. The story is told by L. Mittenzwey (1891, pp. 251-254) in "22. Schrebervereine," in the Festschrift *The City of Leipzig and Hygiene* (courtesy of Dr. Gilardon of the Karl-Sudhof-Institute, Leipzig). Mittenzwey himself wrote on the importance of play ("*Das Spiel im Freien* [Play Outdoors]" and "*Das*

Spiel im Zimmer [Play Indoors]") and cites two works by Mangner, of 1884 and 1889(?): "Playgrounds and Educational Associations" and "The Importance of Children's Games and their Introduction in Middle and Elementary Schools." The first association was founded in 1865 by Hauschild (who died a year later) in West Leipzig, to be followed in 1874 by another in the south and in 1881 by one in the north of the city. By 1891 there were six associations in Leipzig with a membership of 2,500. From there the idea spread to the other cities of Germany and became a movement. In his chapter Mittenzwey connects the spirit of the *Schrebervereine* with Schreber's idea from the second (1882) revised edition of the *Kallipädie* (1858a), now called *The Book of Child Rearing*: "Bodily health before all else, because it determines the health of the mind, i.e., joy [*Frohsinn*]." The third edition of the *Kallipädie* was published in 1891.

8. According to the late Dr. Günther Friedrich, during the Nazi era the name Schreber was obliterated and the eponym *Schrebergarten* was changed into *Kleingarten*. It is remarkable, however, that transitory tyranny did not change the popular sentiment and the name *Schrebergarten* is still with us.

9. This is called in Germany *Schrebergärten und Kleintierzucht* (Schreber Gardens and Small-Animal Husbandry). In the library of the University of Wrocław, formerly Breslau, I found this obscure journal from 1917: *Schrebergärten und Kleintierzucht, offizielle Wochenzeitschrift der Schrebergärtner Kreisverband Glogau, Fraustadt und Umgegend und des zusammengeschlossenen Verein Glogau 1917, Jahrgang 1* (S. G. S.-A. H. Official Weekly of the Schreber Gardeners of the District Associations G., F., and Environs, 1917, vol. 1). These topics were also featured in the Sunday magazine of the *Niederschlesiche Anzeiger*.

Israëls (1989) thoroughly traced the latter-day fate of the Schreber movement, up to our own time. However, he has misleadingly lumped together the *Schrebervereine*, as associations devoted to education with the garden associations and has given them the collective name of the "allotment tradition," described in the "allotment literature" (p. 65). The injury of conflation has been compounded by the insult of misattribution: for example, an author like Brauchle (1937), an authority on naturopathy (holistic medicine), has been incorrectly classified as belonging to the allotment tradition. Nor do Ritter (1936), Kleine (1942), or the recent writers like Peiper (1957), Kilian and Uibe (1958) and Bethge (1981), belong to this tradition (Lothane, 1991b).

10. Thus, Schreber is mentioned in Pagel (1898) and Sudhoff (1922), and has an entry in Eulenburg's (1880-1911) *Real-Encyclopädie* and in Hirsch (1887, vol. 5, pp. 279-280) and the later edition of Hirsch (1931, vol. 3, pp. 135-136): he "won justified recognition in the widest circles" for his contributions to orthopedics and therapeutic gymnastics. The provenance of the remark in Hirsch "In the late 1840's he first advanced the idea of the allotments of land which bear his name" is unclear. It is hard to imagine that Schreber's name was included in Hirsch, next to his illustrious kin, Johann Christian Daniel von Schreber, as a result of his connection with gardens and the same goes for Schreber's inclusion in Schmidt and Schulze's (1891). In the first three decades following Moritz Schreber's death, the *Schrebervereine* had grown to a membership of 2,500, modest compared to the enormous popularity in the twen-

tieth century. Nevertheless, Israëls came to "believe that he [Moritz Schreber] was not so well known in his own day . . . [later] it must have been the fame acquired as a consequence of the Schreber Associations and the Schreber gardens" (1989, p. 249). Israëls lumps the latter two together as the "allotment literature" and asserts that "Moritz Schreber's 'ordinary reputation'" [that is, the] "reputation won independently of the allotments and the work of later psychiatrists . . . was always grossly exaggerated" (p. 231). Israëls levels the same criticism at L. M. Politzer who was so impressed with Schreber's paper *Children's Games* (Schreber, 1860a), published in a popular magazine *Gartenlaube*, that he reprinted it in the pediatric journal of which he was one of the editors and later wrote Schreber's obituary (Politzer, 1862). Israëls (1989) did catch (p. 232) one gross mistake in L. M. Politzer's much quoted obituary: except for *Gymnastics*, Schreber's books did not go "through many editions and translations in almost all languages in a short time" (Politzer, 1862, quoted in Schatzman, 1973, p. 142)," as written by Politzer. But with this exception I disagree that Politzer's assessment "is far from reliable": it conveys correctly the thrust of Schreber's thought. The identity of these gross exaggerations of Schreber's achievement as physician and educator found in the allotment literature (or elsewhere) is not stated by Israëls. This has led Israëls to fashion an unwarranted generalization equating "two sorts of literature: idealizing accounts by authors connected with the Schreber Associations named after Moritz Schreber and demonizing accounts in modern psychiatric writings . . . drawing on Schreber's educational publications . . . paint[ing] him as a domestic tyrant (p. 225), which "reached its peak in the work of the psychiatrist Morton Schatzman" (Israëls, p. 63). But this is comparing apples and oranges, for there is this essential difference between these two literatures: whereas the early "idealizing" appraisers of Schreber, even if guilty of adulation, at least wrote about the man whose work they knew (Hauschild, Kloss, Schildbach), and the next generation authors (Mangner, Mittenzwey, Siegel, Fritsche) were still close enough to the time when Schreber was rather well known in Leipzig; the "demonizing" psychiatrists and others indulged in guesses and inferences derived from reading Schreber's books, that is, fictions made into facts (Lothane, 1991).

11. From the autobiographical sketch included in the obituary by Kloss (1862). Additional facts are mentioned in the autobiography (1833b) at the end of Schreber's (1833a) medical dissertation.

12. The family biography and pedigree were researched by Günther Friedrich (1932), Ritter (1936), Schilling (1964), Niederland (1974), Tabouret-Keller (1973), This (1973, 1974), Israëls (1989), and Busse (1990). G. Friedrich compiled a great deal of materials on the history of the Schrebers, of which I was given a small fragment.

13. Moritz gives expression to this sentiment in the introduction to his posthumously published *Pangymnastikon* (1862): "For centuries the lively German spirit of the nation fought the sinister power of medieval popism and jesuitism both overtly and covertly, without . . . being defeated by this power" (quoted in the *NJT*, 8:19, for 1862). In Saxony the issue of Catholicism was tied to the royal family and the connections to Catholic Poland. The elector of

Saxony Friedrich Augustus II converted to Catholicism and became king of Poland from 1694 to 1733. He had a reputation for prodigious eating and drinking. His son was also a king of Poland, from 1733 to 1763. The ruling house of Saxony, the Wettins, were Catholic. The issue of Protestants versus the pope erupted in Paul's life with Bismarck's *Kulturkampf,* the historic dispute about papal infallibility. Conversion to Catholicism (for himself and his mother) and the ambitions and designs on Germans of Jesuits and Slavophiles were on Paul's mind during his second illness.

14. The last name Jakobi was also borne by Jews, but I have no knowledge of Martha Maria Jakobi being Jewish. Biblical first names were, of course, given to Protestant children in Germany as well as in England and America. Jews and Jewish ambitions toward Germans, as well as his feelings toward the Jews, were subjects voiced by Paul during his second illness.

15. Quoted by Tabouret-Keller and in the *British Museum General Catalog of Printed Books,* vol. 216 p. 128.

16. In this connection it is of interest to recall that Freud's textual analysis of Paul's literary allusions to soul murder leads him to Byron's *Manfred* : "The essence and the secret of the whole work lies in—an incestuous relation between a brother and a sister" (Freud, 1911, p. 44). This theme is developed at great length by Devreese (1990a).

17. The Hutterian Brethren, who lived in communes, were first in Switzerland, then moved to Moravia, and then, after joining the Mennonites, came to the United States. The Bohemian Jan (John) Hus, burned at the stake in 1414, was the spiritual father of the Moravian Church and later of the Moravian Brethren, or Herrnhutters. The last Moravian bishop, Johann Amos Comenius, is honored as an important early educator who inspired the giants in the history of education. Pietism was a spiritual movement in the Lutheran Church begun by Philipp Jacob Spener, who at one time was active in Dresden. It proposed living according to rules of the Bible and a religion of the heart instead of the prevailing intellectual dogmas of the ruling church. The writings of his student August Hermann Francke inspired many educational ideas of Moritz Schreber (Schilling, 1964; Devreese, personal communication, 1990). In the entry "Fehler Der Jugend [The Defects of Youth]" (Rein, 1895, vol. 2), the author credits Francke with the saying, "To prevent is better than to improve," which Moritz also derived from his experience as physician. Spener and Francke were an influence on Count Zinzendorf, the reorganizer of the Moravian Brethren in the 18th century. On his estate, Berthelsdorff in Saxony, the city of Herrnhut was built, and from there many Hernhutters moved to America. Pfister (1910) analyzed Zinzendorf the way Freud analyzed Schreber, connecting aspects of his life and teachings with repressed homosexuality.

18. The *National Union Catalog* lists fifteen works by Daniel Gottfried Schreber and many works by his noble son, Johann Christian Daniel. In the British Museum catalog the latter's books are lumped together with those of Johann David's. I have also found them in the library of the Jagiellonian University in Kraków and in the National Library of Medicine, History Section, in Rockville, MD.

19. Cited in Kneschke (1868). See the family pedigree and information found by Niederland (1974).

20. *"Geständniss eines wahnsinnig Gewesenen"*—the words *Wahnsinn, wahnsinnig* (the noun and the adjective) have a general meaning, that is, madness and mad, and a special meaning, that is, delusion, delusional. *Madness* and *mad* are popular usages (compared with the psychiatric terms *psychosis* and *psychotic*), whereas *delusion* and *delusional* are technical ones. I believe that my translation, "a former melancholic," reflects the clinical facts whereas the one in Israëls, "former lunatic" distorts the facts. Niederland's (1974, p. 64) translation, "Confessions of One Who Had Been Insane." while true to the original, also obscures the salient clinical facts: the patient in the story was neither diagnosed as psychotic nor committed to an asylum; the clinical picture was predominantly melancholia, with an admixture of tormenting idées fixes, that is, obsessive–compulsive behavior in the form of ruminations and horrific temptations, not delusions, the latter defined as false beliefs refractory to correction by evidence and common sense. The patient had insight concerning the absurdity of his ruminations but fluctuated in his capacity to oppose them or master them or extinguish them completely. Also, melancholia was then called *stiller Wahnsinn* (the calm insanity) and *manisch-depressives Irresein* (manic-depressive insanity).

21. As I have shown in my review of Israëls (Lothane, 1991b), Israëls misquoted Valentin (1961), thus belittling Moritz Schreber's achievement.

22. Carl Friedrich Koch (1802-1871) wrote *Gymnastics from the Viewpoint of Dietetics and Psychology and a Report on the Gymnastic Institute of Magdeburg* in 1830. It is cited in Schreber's *Kinesiatrik* (1852a). Note the term dietetics, which means life philosophy and prevention of illness, beloved of Kant and Moritz Schreber.

23. J. A. L. Werner, cited by Schreber (1852a, p. 6), was the author of the following books: *Medical Gymnastics or the Art of Strengthening and Restoring to Their Original Lines of Parts of the Human Body Deformed or Departing from the Natural Form and Position, Based on Anatomical and Physiological Principles and Explained by Means of 100 Illustrations* (1838). Werner was a Lieutenant in the Royal Saxon Army, director of a gymnastic and orthopedic institute, corresponding member of the Society for Science and Therapeutics, and honorary member of the Dresden Pedagogical Institute. This is a neat example of the florid book titles of the period. Notice the connection between Werner's interest in gymnastics and therapeutics, as well as his recognition by educators, both interests strongly represented in Moritz Schreber. Werner also wrote *All About Gymnastics or a Complete Textbook of Exercises According to the Principles of Better Education for Public and Private Instruction* (1834), *The Gymnastic-Orthopedic Therapeutic Institute in Dessau, its Structure and Functioning* (1843), *Twelve Life-Questions or Is the Happiness of a Cultured and Well-Run State to be Founded on a Regulated Mental Education Alone or Should the Physical Education Also Be Bound up with It*, and *Amona, or the Surest Means to Build and Strengthen the Female Body for its Natural Purpose* (1837). He was also cited in the *Kinesiatrik* (1852a) and for a good reason: so many of his ideas are found and continued in Schreber. Among the illustrations supplied by Schwarz (1973a) to Niederland there is

one derived from Werner's book of 1833, which I did not see, entitled *Gymnastik für die weibliche Jugend* (Gymnastics for Girls), which shows shoulder bed-straps applied to a sleeping, supine school-age girl, presumably recommended for the correction of small curvatures of the spine. They would have been a model for similar straps recommended by Schreber for the maintenance of correct body postures (illustrated in the *Kallipädie*, 1858a), which so horrified Niederland (1959, a, b) and Schatzman (1973).

24. Israëls tends to minimize this risk and to belittle the reputation of Schreber's progressive spirit by attributing it to the flattering, and exaggerated, attitudes of the members of the Schreber movement or to the arrogance of biographers. I disagree with this perception. Israëls (1989), in spite of noting on p. 18 "how treasonable (because it was nationalist in spirit) gymnastics was considered to be in Saxony of 1825," dismisses as "rubbish" the perceptions of Schilling (1964) and Kleine (1942) that Schreber's pursuit of gymnastics was politically courageous and potentially risky conduct in 1843. He does so solely on the basis of a quotation from the *Sächsische Vaterlands-Blätter* (Israëls, 1989, p. 53). We are not told the political orientation of the *Blätter* and how it stood in relation to the government. That Schreber's pursuit was risky is indicated by the fact that another physician in 1843 wrote anonymously about gymnastics (see Anonymous, 1843) and by the following confession of Moritz's friend, Karl Biedermann: In a preface to his *Education to Work: what Life Requires from the School* (1883), Biedermann remarks that back in the 1850's he signed his works on education with the alias Karl Friedrich, to disguise his identity, so as to avoid being noticed by the reactionary authorities. This sheds light on Schreber's daring in openly publishing his progressive ideas and lends credence to the perception that he was not viewed favorably by the officials. Israëls himself writes that politically Moritz Schreber was a "moderate left-winger" (p. 224), which would have also been known to the authorities.

25. Eduard Ferdinand Angerstein (1830-1896) also edited, with C. Eckler (1887), a tome entitled *House Gymnastics for the Healthy and the Sick. Advice to Every Age and Gender How by Means of Bodily Exercises to Preserve and Increase Health and to Remove Morbid States.* In the introduction the authors refer to Schreber's *Medical Indoor Gymnastics* as a work that "cannot be overlooked." The contribution of physicians to the promotion of body exercises is discussed in another work by E. F. Angerstein (1897), *Fundamentals in the History and Development of Bodily Exercises.* We find there mention of Schreber, Bock, and of

Hermann Eberhard Richter (born on 14 of May 1808 in Leipzig, Professor at the Surgical-Medical Academy in Dresden), one of the first in Germany to call attention to Swedish gymnastics. By means of inspiring essays and lectures about *Turning* he was successful in promoting of *Turning* in general and especially of the Dresden *Turnverein*, which thanks to Richter's activity until 1849 was the most important one in Germany [p. 128].

In the same paragraph Angerstein mentions "D. G. M. Schreber . . . the actual founder of German *therapeutic gymnastics* and widely known through his

Turning medical writings. Among those one should single out are the *Kinesia-trik* and the *Medical Indoor Gymnastics* (Leipzig, Fleischer), which went through many editions and translations." H. E. Richter (1845, 1850) is cited by Schreber (1852a) in his bibliography.

26. Hirth also stresses Schreber's *Turning* activity as a student, his resuming *Turning* upon the takeover of the Carus Orthopedic Institute and mentions Schreber's 1843 writing to the Parliament in Saxony about making *Turning* a matter for the people. Hirth was himself the author of a similar writ of 1860: *How to Raise Turning to a National Issue: An Urgent Question for All Turners, Turnvereins and Friends of Turning Placed Close to the Heart by a Member of the Gotha Turnverein.* Hirth also wrote that before Swedish gymnastics were known in Germany, Schreber already laid the foundation for German therapeutic gymnastics, especially the treatment of spine deformities through corresponding muscle exercises. Similar admiration for Schreber's daring, courage and calm leadership in 1843 and 1845-1847 (the years of the return of the reaction) were later expressed by Brauchle (1937) and Kleine (1942). Israëls is inclined to dismiss such praise.

27. Bock published in 1871 *On the Care of the Bodily and Mental Health of the School Child: An Appeal to Parents, Teachers and School Authorities* and in 1891 *The Structure, Life, and Care of the Human Body in Word and Pictures*, a popular textbook for schools, that went through numerous editions, on the physiology and care of the body.

28. "Prof. Ling" is cited on p. 3 of the introduction to the *Kinesiatrik*, Moritz's only book on therapeutic gymnastic written for professionals (1852a), and the only one provided with a reference list, that includes E. F. Koch (1830) and the followers of Ling, H. E. Richter, Rothstein in Germany (1847), and Georgii (1847) in France, the latter also translated and published in England. According to K. A. Schmid (1881-1887), Professor Massmann called attention to Ling's work in Germany as early as 1830, but it was Hugo Rothstein (1810-1865) who did a lot to promote Ling in Prussia. According to Cotta (1902), Rothstein traveled to Stockholm in 1843 and published the first instalments of his magnum opus, *Die Gymnastik nach dem System des schwedischen Gymnasiarchen P. H. Ling* (Gymnastics According to the System of the First Gymnast, P. H. L.), in 1847-1851. Rothstein soon rose to influence as head of the Royal Central Turn Institution in 1851. But Rothstein also became an opponent of Turnvater Jahn and this in turn created considerable opposition, owing to patriotic sentiments. A polemic ensued between the Swedish and the German views on exercising, which culminated in the so-called "*Barrenstreit*," the 'parallel bars debate', in which Rothstein was against the horizontal and parallel bars, and his opponents were in favor of them. Among the latter were a number of influential men: Angerstein; the famous professor of physiology Du Bois Reymond in Berlin; Moritz Kloss from Dresden, important for his connections to Schreber; and the Dresden physician Koch (1830), author of *Gymnastics from the Viewpoint of Dietetics and Psychology* (see footnote 22). Naturally, the German point of view prevailed, and Rothstein was fired from office, to die two years later.

29. Schreber was on the editorial board of the *NJT*, edited by Moritz Kloss,

Dr. Phil., a prominent Dresden authority on the educational aspect of gymnastics, Director the Royal Physical Education Teachers Training Institute in Dresden (the NJT were also known as *Kloss's Jarhbücher*), and a friend of Schreber's who cited him early on (Kloss, 1862, 1873), but later neglected Schreber's legacy (Kloss, 1887, 1889), except for a long entry, "Bodily Exercises," in Schmid (1881-1887). On the pages of the *NJT* Schreber published a number of book reviews and short articles, including the following: "On Therapeutic Gymnastics in General" (1855c), claiming the need for medical supervision of *Heilgymnastik*, as distinct from *Turngymnastik*; "Truths and Untruths about the Radical Treatment of Hernia by Means of Gymnastics (1855f); "On the Health and Educational Value of Skating and Stilt-Walking" (1857); and "The *Turn* Institution as a School of Manliness" (1858d). Among the reviews was one of his friend Professor C. E. Bock's (1855) *The Book of the Healthy and Sick Person*, a tome 537 pages long, written in a spirit like his own (Schreber, 1855d), of which the 13th edition appeared in 1884. Another was devoted to a report of a director of a gymnastic therapeutic institute in Bonn (Schreber, 1856b). A number of Schreber's books were given lengthy reviews: *Anthropos*, by Friedrich (1859); *Ueber Volkserziehung*, also by Friedrich (1860). Gymnastics was also on the mind of a German *Psychiker*, or soul-psychiatrist, Karl Wilhelm Ideler (1795-1860), who wrote *Über die Anwendung der Heilgymnastik auf Seelenleiden ausserhalb der Irrenanstalten* (On the Application of Therapeutic Gymnastics on Mental Illness Outside Mental Hospitals), reviewed in *NJT* for 1856 (2:30ff), an excerpt from which was reprinted—along with excerpts from Moritz Schreber—in Hirth (1865). A review of Ideler's *Handbuch der Diätetik* ("Textbook on Dietetics") of 1855, with its emphasis on exercising, appears in *NJT*, 1(1855):172.

30. Schildbach (1859) claims Neumann is merely a Schreber imitator. His review is followed by an even more corrosive postscript by Kloss, *NJT*, 5(1859):138-139, in which Kloss attacks Neumann for his "jeremiads" and "Donquixotiads," inspired by "confused Swedish fancies," that cast aspersions on German active exercising by calling it "crude."

31. A. C. Neumann published in 1859 his *Home Gymnastics. Instruction How to Keep Healthy in Body and Soul Until Old Age and to Be Cured of Many Diseases by Means of Dietetic Limb Movements and Breathing Exercises, Done Easily Any Day and in Any Room. With 102 Woodcuts in the Text*. Neumann does not mention Schreber's *Gymnastik* nor any other work by him. He lists his own previously published works: *A Short Exposition of the Nature of Swedish Gymnastics and Its application to Most Chronic Illnesses, Namely of the Chest and Abdomen, etc, for the Educated Layman* (1852a); *Therapeutic Gymnastics or the Art of Bodily Exercises Applied to the Treatment of Diseases etc. A Report at the Expense of the Prussian State of Travels to Stockholm, London and St. Petersburg, Undertaken at the Behest of the Minister for Medical Affairs* (1852b), second edition titled *Therapy of Chronic Diseases* etc. 1857; *Textbook of Exercising* two volumes, 1856; *The Art of Breathing in Man* (1859b). Neumann's official title was Royal Prussian District Physician, Director of the Institute for Therapeutic Gymnastics in Berlin, Ritterstrasse No. 60; he was a practicing physician, surgeon, and obstetrician.

He also wrote *The Muscle Life of Man in Relation to Therapeutic Gymnastics and Turning*, which Schreber reviewed (1855e).

32. *Orthopedics in its Special Relation to Defects of Carriage and of Growth and the Special Gymnastic and Mechanical Aids.* Hirsch, doctor of medicine and surgery, was the founder of the first Gymnastic-Orthopedic Institute in Prague. He was interested in reaching not only the professional but also the lay public. In his books he invokes his own extensive travels in Germany, France and England from which he learned a great deal. Among the causes of defects he lists bad carriage during standing, sitting and walking; bad posture during writing, drawing, sewing, and knitting; unsuitable beds and faulty positions during sleep; and constraining clothing. At the end of the book there are illustrations of mechanical aids and apparatuses, which are meticulously described. We see girls in various bed straps while lying on their back or sides, girls in corrective corsets, and girls in swings. Hirsch also devotes a chapter to the mental attitudes of the young, invoking the idea that "mind and body are twins" (p. 36). He has recommendations for the mental development of children between the ages of five and seven. We can see here both similarities and differences as compared to the approach of Moritz Schreber. For names of other predecessors of Moritz Schreber see Eulenburg's *Real-Encyclopädie* (1880-1911) and E. F. Cyriax (1909). A word should also be said about the many followers of Schreber, or those who pursued similar aims, for example Gruber (1862), "the founder and director of the Orthopedic Institute of the Royal Bavarian District Capital Regensburg," who provided his work "Therapeutic Gymnastics as Orthopedics in Comparison with Apppliances Orthopedics . . . ," with this long subtitle: "With special explanations on the origin of deformities, the use of exercises for healing deformities of the human body and special observations and remarks for lay persons during treatment in popular language for the use of physicians and families."

33. Valentin (1961) quotes Landry's book of 1741: *L'Orthopédie ou l'Art de prévenir et de corriger dans les Enfants les difformités du corps. Le Tout par les moyens à la portée des Pères et des Mères, et des toutes les Personnes qui ont des Enfants à élever* (Orthopedics or the Art of Preventing and Correcting in Children of Deformities of the Body. All by Means Within Reach of Fathers and Mothers and All Other Persons who Raise Children), 2 volumes. Uibe spells the name *Andry*, and notes that the symbol of the new profession was a crooked little tree, suggesting that "the hand of a skilled gardener would straighten [it] by firmly tying it to strong trunk . . . for as the twig is bent so the tree will grow" (Uibe, 1959, p. 216).

34. "By Dr. med. D. G. M. S., practicing physician and director of the Orthopedic Institute in Leipzig." I found the book in 1988 in the Jagiellonian Library of the Kraków University, which has books by Moritz Schreber and his 18th-century forefathers in its holdings.

35. Moritz Schreber also wrote not only about dietetics but about healthy diets, and is cited by Ernst (1886, p. 685), in her *Book of Correct Nutrition for the Healthy and the Sick, A Cook Book*, a supplement to a later edition of Bocks's *Book of the Healthy and Sick Person*.

36. Schreber's ideas about child care and prevention of disease were further developed in a book on pediatrics published in 1852: *The Characteristics of the Infantile Organism in Health and Disease* (1852b). And in 1853 there appeared another work devoted to the fostering of proper body carriage and postures: *Injurious Body Postures and Habits and the Means to Combat Them. For Parents and Educators.* A lengthy discussion of the subject appears in the *Kallipädie* (1858a). For illustrations of the various devices, both as treatments and as means of prevention Schreber used, see Lothane, 1989b.

37. The book is subtitled as follows: "For physicians and educated laymen, based on his own experiences by Dr. Daniel Gottlieb [sic] Moritz Schreber, practising physician and Director of the Leipzig Orthopedic Institute. With 210 illustrations." Some of the illustrations are reproduced by Israëls (1989). The bulk of the illustrations show free gymnastic exercises and light athletic exercises performed with the help of chairs, horizontal bars, rings, and swings. There are only three machines: one was designed by Schreber himself, a large screw turned by means of T-shaped lever, for exercising arms and spine; the others were harnesses—Kunde's stretch machine using pulleys and Glisson's swing—were used for correcting spine curvatures, these belonging to the domain of orthopedic kinesiatrics.

38. In the original, *"die Kinesiatrik, die gymnastische oder Bewegungs-Heilmethode"* (1852a, p. 5; emphasis Schreber's).

39. The entry *Heilgymnastik* (Therapeutic Gymnastics) heavily leans toward Ling (Eulenburg, 1880-1911, second edition, pp. 247-249). The third edition of Eulenburg, where the entry was called *Mechanotherapie* (p. 53), cites two works by Schildbach: "Report on Newer Methods of Therapeutic Gymnastics and Orthopedics" (1865), and *Gymnastics for the Nursery* (1880). I did not see the latter work. The former (1865) is a detailed review of educational gymnastics as advocated by Schreber, Kloss, and Hauschild and of orthopedic gymnastics for specialists, with an emphasis on history and a rich bibliography.

40. The new trend is in evidence, for example, in Dr. B. Fromm's (1887), *Die Zimmergymnastik*, in whose preface we read: "No doubt, there is Schreber's "Zimmer-Gymnastik", popular in numerous circles, which is limited to active exercises, whereas for a great number of cases there is an indication for the duplicated or resistance-exercises and the passive movements" (page iv).

41. *Gymnastics* was published in England in 1856. The term *medico-hygienic* was used to refer to the treatment and prevention aspects of kinesiatrics. A new English translation appeared in the United States in 1899. The book went through 30 editions in Germany (33, by 1913 according to the Brockhaus's encyclopedia), and was translated into many languages: for example, Dutch, by Willink in Arnhem, in 1857; Swedish, by Ewerflof in Gefle, in 1865; French by Masson in Paris, fifth edition in 1883; Spanish, by Bailly-Balliere, in Madrid, in 1899; Russian, which I did not see; and Italian, cited in Cyriax (1909). There were three Polish editions, of which the second, of 1897, was based on a combination of the systems of Dr. Schreber and Dr. Eduard Angerstein. In 1909 appeared a translation of a 1907 work by R. Kochendorf,

Lungen-Gymnastic ohne Geräte: nach dem System von Dr. med. Daniel Gottlob Moritz Schreber (lung gymnastics without apparatus according to the system of D. G. M. S.) Kochendorf, *Gimnastyka płuc bez przyrządów/ podług układu Dr. D.M. Schrebera / opracowana przez Dr. R. Kochendorfa / przełożyt niemieckiego Dr. I.P.*, Warsaw: M. Arct. Another work of R. Kochendorf, inspired by Schreber, was *Heilgymnastik gegen Nervosität* ("Therapeutic Gymnastics To Cure Nervousness"; Cyriax, 1909, in section "Hysteria and neurasthenia. Neuroses in general").

42. *Gymnastics* had two publishers in the United States: the one noted in the previous footnote, and another by Charles Russell Bardeen in Syracuse who published it in 1890 under the title *Home Exercises for Health and Cure*. In 1901 Bardeen published *Note Book of the History of Education* which includes 400 portraits of pioneers in educational work, arranged chronologically. The note on Schreber is reproduced here in its entirety:

DANIEL GOTTLIEB [sic] MOR. SCHREBER (German, 1808-1861), noted for his services in behalf of physical education, after being educated at Leipzig was from 1843 to 1859 physician in the Carus orthopedic hospital. He exerted great influence in the reform of educational methods, especially in the direction of physical education. He made the expression "health gymnastics" (*Heilgymnastik*) a familiar word. His most famous work is *Ärztliche Zimmergymnastik* (24th ed. 1890), of which an American translation under the title *Gymnastics for Health and Cure* is in common use. Other books are [he lists Schreber 1839, 1852a, 1853, 1858a, 1859c, 1891].

43. Schreber's system was made popular in the United States in a translation by Dio Lewis, M.D., in a volume that contained two works: *The New Gymnastics for Men, Women and Children: With a Translation of Prof. Kloss's Dumb-bell Instructor* and *Prof. Schreber's Pangymnastikon* (Boston: Ticknor & Fields, 1862). Another edition, the 25th, revised and "greatly" enlarged, was printed in New York by Fowler & Wells, in 1891. There was also an English edition, illustrated with 107 woodcuts: *The Parlour Gymnasium; or, All Gymnastic Exercises Brought Within the Compass of a Single Piece of Apparatus, as the Simplest Means for the Complete Development of Muscular Strength and Endurance According to the System Devised by D. G. M. Schreber* (London: G. W.. Bacon, 1866). Another likely contemporary example of a follower of Schreber's methods are Trall (1857) and Watson (1864).

44. Schildbach wrote three reports (1861, 1864 and 1877) about the Institute's functioning. The first two are thin brochures that are quite rare (Tabouret-Keller, 1973, Israëls, 1989). I located the first report of 1861, 16 pages long, and the third from 1877 in the New York Library of Medicine.

45. Carl Hermann Schildbach (1824-1888), a son of a merchant from Schnecberg in Saxony, lost his father at birth. He graduated from Leipzig University with an M.D. dissertation in obstetrics (1848), *Childbirth with Face Presentation*. In 1876 he founded the Orthopedic Hospital of the Leipzig University, the first in Germany to certify orthopedists. He also published a

book on indoor gymnastics (1880). He wrote quite a bit about scoliosis (1862c, 1872b, 1886). His pedagogical identification with Schreber is expressed in his having edited E. I. Hauschild's 1858 book, whose second edition was printed by M. G. Prieber in Leipzig.

46. The condition caused paralytic ileus and in the autopsy the term *Darmverschlingung* or intestinal obstruction appears (G. Friedrich), echoed in "*Darmverschlingungen*" in Foot Note #72 of the *Memoirs*, another instance of the son's identification with the father.

4

MORITZ SCHREBER'S PHILOSOPHY OF MEDICINE AND EDUCATION

In its original meaning soul conception is I think a somewhat idealized version which souls had formed of human life and thought. One
must remember that souls were the departed spirits of erstwhile
human beings . . . [and] had a lively interest . . . in the fortunes of
their still living relatives.

D. P. Schreber, 1903

Wouldst thou want to plumb life's sense in all its depth,
To make the art of life all clear to thy perception,
Wouldst thou imitate the pinnacle of God's creation,
All thou needst, man, is to probe thy heart's conception!
And shouldst thou walk along this path reflecting,
The more wilt thou know God, thyself perfecting.

D. G. M. Schreber, 1859a

PHILOSOPHY OF MEDICINE: THERAPEUTICS AND DIETETICS OF THE MIND

I discuss Moritz Schreber's ideas for two reasons: they are interesting
in their own right, vindicating his importance in the history of medicine and education, and they may shed light on the influences that
helped shape Paul's character during childhood, adolescence, and
adulthood.

Moritz Schreber's first book (1861a), referred to here as *Health*,
concerns the hygiene of body and mind and was originally published in
1839 (when he was 31), three years after he established himself as a

147

practitioner in Leipzig. Its full title was *The Book of Health, an Orthobiotics according to the Laws of Nature and the Structure of the Human Organism.* The key word, orthobiotics,[1] meant right living (from the Greek *orthos*, right and *bios*, life). Its second edition in 1861 bore a new title, *The Book of Health or the Art of Living According to the Organization and Laws of Human Nature*, was 20 pages longer than the first one, and included illustrations of human anatomy. Except for additions, the texts of the two editions are the same. The title of 1839 reflects the influence of Leipzig psychiatrist Heinroth, that of 1861 the ideas of the Viennese physician Carl Philipp Hartmann, whose book Schreber edited the same year. (Unless otherwise indicated, the quotes are from the second edition.)

It should be helpful to locate Moritz Schreber historically and trace his forerunners. Orthobiotics in the original title of *Health* is conceptually related to "macrobiotics" (from *macros*, long) in the title of a book written by Hufeland in 1796: *Makrobiotik oder die Kunst das menschliche Leben zu verlängern* (published a year later in London as *The Art of Prolonging Life* and abbreviated in the following discussions as *Macrobiotics*).

Christoph Wilhelm Hufeland (1762-1836), a contemporary of Heinroth (1773-1843), born in Langensalza in Thuringia and the grandson and son of physicians to the Weimar Court, became one of the most famous and respected physicians of his time. His idea of individual health and prevention derived from ideas about public health and prevention, the latter having been powerfully stimulated by his experiences with infectious diseases, specifically smallpox.[2] In 1788 he published his *Notes on Natural and Inoculated Smallpox* (abbreviated here as *Smallpox*). The second edition of *Smallpox* (Hufeland, 1793) contains a chapter entitled "A Memoir on Very Important and Yet Neglected Aspects of the Physical Upbringing in the first Period of Childhood". In that chapter Hufeland is concerned with a "respect for the rights of nature and of children" (p. 428). He is against mollycoddling (*Verzärtelung*) and spoiling (*Verwöhnung*) and in favor of hardening (*Abhärtung*). He expresses the importance of "maintaining the splendid equilibrium of energies and movements, of soul and body, which are the basis of the body's and soul's health" (p. 435) and recommends washing the child every morning with cold water, from head to toe, as well as plenty of air and sunbathing. Children, he says, should be bathed more and given laxatives less, methods that were observed and applied to his own children with happy results.

For the concept of preventive medicine for the individual, we should also give credit to another predecessor of Schreber (and contemporary of Hufeland himself), the pediatrician Dr. Bernhard

Christoph Faust, best known for his work *Health Catechism for the Use in Schools and in Home Instruction* hereafter called *Catechism*.[3] The book is in two parts: the first devoted to general principles of health and diet and the second to the treatment of specific diseases, a model that was a convention. Of interest to us are the chapters on the following topics: the care of young children, the physical education of children, movement and rest, and the beauty and perfection of the human body. According to Faust, the greatest need of the child is love and care from the mother, who also meets his physical needs. Faust recommends exercises for the health of the body and God-given values of nature and order for the health of the soul and he stresses the importance of work and the fulfillment of duties, the latter being a guarantee of happiness.

I believe that Hufeland's ideas and the ideas of Faust in his *Catechism* on the proper child rearing and wholesome living for children and adults were an inspiration for Moritz Schreber, even though he did not directly acknowledge his debt to them. However that may be, the works of these authors were part and parcel of the climate of opinion in matters of child rearing in which Schreber also participated. To be noted here is Hufeland's (1836) *Good Advice to Mothers*, a book on the physical education of children (the first edition of which appeared in 1795). It was sold in the United States (Steiger's Catalog). The structure of this book is the same as that of Schreber's *Health*, while the ideas about deformities in children, expounded in the addendum to Hufeland's book,[4] are similar to those that Schreber pursues in *Scoliosis*.

The Ideas in Hufeland's Macrobiotics

The goal of macrobiotics is to prolong life, as distinguished from that of medicine, which is to insure health through diagnosis, treatment and prevention of diseases. Being concerned with dietetics, that is, the field of prevention, Hufeland realized that it is more effective to point out which life habits prolong or shorten life than to say which are healthy or unhealthy. *Macrobiotics* was also important in pioneering a respectable tradition of popular works in medicine to serve as health guides for the general public.

One of Hufeland's main ideas was that in health and disease, medical issues cannot be separated from moral issues, because in the person the moral and the physical cannot be separated and the moral has an effect on the prolongation and preservation of life. Hufeland stressed how crucial is the *"drive to preserve [life] and to save it at a moment of crisis"* [Hufeland, (1796), p. 19; emphasis Hufeland's], anticipating both Darwin and Freud. This drive is also the main guarantor of inner happiness or eudaimonism (*Glückseligkeit*). In this Hufeland adheres to the Aristotelian concept of happiness in contrast to hedonism, which equates happiness with pleasure. The eudaimonist system of ethics stresses the duty to pursue the happy frame of mind that goes hand in hand with well-being.

In *Macrobiotics* Hufeland invokes the physical and moral health precepts of Hippocrates and his school: "*moderation, enjoyment of open clean air, baths and preferably daily rubbings and exercising of the body . . . [that is] gymnastics*" (p. 20; emphasis Hufeland's) are connected with the powers of nature, "the benevolent mother who loves and rewards him who seeks her" (p. 29). "*Undoubtedly the life-energy is the most fundamental, the most inexplicable and the most awesome of the powers of nature. It fills, it moves everything, it is most probably the wellspring of all the other energies of the physical . . . world. She is inexhaustible, infinite—a true and eternal breath of the deity*" (p. 30; emphases Hufeland's). Life energy is the means of the preservation of the body. It is a defense against decay, inclemencies of weather and frost. It is destroyed by cold and concussions. It is fed by light, air, and rest. It is important not to consume it too quickly, not to lead a "fast life"(p. 39), to have enough sleep. Thus squandering of life energy shortens life.

From such precepts follow principles for the upbringing of children. From the very beginning, according to Hufeland, one should avoid "pampering, overstimulation and physical and moral softness" (p. 116). Among the chief causes of loss of life energy, due to overconsumption, are sexual excesses leading to squandering of the energy of procreation. This affects the stomach, spinal cord and the lungs. This danger can be caused by the most horrible of poisons, venery in extramarital activity. The danger is related to premature arousal of physical love and to the evils of masturbation in both genders, a deadly sin and vice that makes the sinner look like a "faded rose, a tree dried up in its bloom, a walking corpse" (p. 120). And it is not only physical onanism but mental onanism as well that is dangerous and becomes a true mental illness when fancy is filled and made hot with lustful and lascivious images. A cardinal virtue is *Enthaltsamkeit*, or continence, which means temperance in food and drink and in sex, both in the young and in marriage. This temperance also applies to excessive straining of mental faculties. It is thus dangerous to expose the child to too strenuous studying, to boring subjects taught without love, to cramped sitting in closed, airless rooms.

Among the causes that shorten life Hufeland cites the drive to suicide, listed both as a violent act and as a manifestation of self-destructive activity. Other causes are indulging in imaginary illnesses (i.e., hypochondriasis) and in sentimentalism, the romantic way of thinking. Among the cures Hufeland sees a strong moral upbringing, the inherent ennobling values of suffering and of temperance and the daily exercising of body and mind. The summit of the good and long life is reached in the happiness of marital life.

The book ends with an invocation of the "two golden words" spoken by "our Sages: . . . pray and work—God will do the rest. For it cannot be otherwise but that the peace of God inside and useful work outside are the only true foundations of all happiness, all health and a long life" (p. 290).

Kant's reaction to Macrobiotics

Kant, Hufeland's contemporary, was both an influence on him and influenced by him. Upon reading Hufeland's *Macrobiotics*, sent him by the author, Kant (1798a) wrote a response in the form of an essay, *On the Power of the Mind to Master Morbid Feelings by Mere Resolution* (abbreviated here as *Mind*).[5] Having divided medicine into its two main branches, therapeutics and dietetics (i.e., prevention), in *Mind* Kant declares that Hufeland's idea is indeed the "supreme dietetic task" (i.e., the mastery of one's feelings) and that the main dietetic principle is stoicism, which belongs not only in philosophy but also in medicine. As a prescription for moderation in life, it ranks, says Kant, as a therapeutic agent in addition to medications and surgery. Kant discusses many bad and good habits pertaining to diet and sleep. He discusses hypochondria at some length, and tells how he overcame his own.[6]

Schreber did not directly state his indebtedness to Hufeland, but there is indirect evidence of this influence: Schreber's mention in *Kinesiatrics* (1852a) of a predecessor named Schultz-Schultzenstein (1798-1871) and the second edition (1850) of his work of 1842, *On the Rejuvenation Human Life and the Ways and Means to Its Cultivation*. In paragraph #8 Schultz-Schultzenstein invokes Hufeland's *"Macrobiotik"* (1842, p. 11).[7]

Hartmann's Prescription for Happiness

The other contemporary of Hufeland whose influence on Schreber is no mere supposition but documented fact is Philipp Carl Hartmann (1773-1830). Schreber (1861b) was the editor of the "fourth edition (fully revised and augmented by Moritz Schreber)" of Hartmann's *A Happiness Doctrine for the Physical Life of Man. A Dietetical Guide for Living,*[8] and here abbreviated as *Happiness.* For this reason, the quotes from Hartmann below are referenced under Schreber (1861b).

Hartmann was born in Germany, studied medicine and philosophy in Göttingen and later in Vienna with J. P. Frank to become a professor of medicine at Vienna University. He was dubbed the "Kant of the new medicine" and wrote on the practice and theory of medicine as well as popular works on medicine, such as the aforementioned book.[9] An aphorism of Hartmann's, "theory without experience is empty, experience without theory is blind, action without principle is stupidity," echoes Kant's famous dictum "Concepts without percepts are empty, percepts without concepts are blind." In an early essay of 1805, "The Influence of Philosophy on Medicine and Therapeutics," Hartmann came out against Schelling's *Naturphilosophie* and his identity theory. He taught that functional differed from organic disorders, because in the former one could not show a physical substratum (Winternitz, 1860, pp. 3-5).

While Hufeland's popular book lives on, Hartmann's has been relegated to oblivion. Hartmann, however, was a natural extension of Hufeland. Like Hufeland's, Hartmann's leading idea was to combine Kant's rationalism and ethics into the guiding principle of eudaimonism, that is, the theory of a happy and balanced life. This was also the leading interest of Moritz Schreber. Philosophically, Hartmann, Hufeland, and Schreber were Kantians, that is, rationalists and empiricists (and against mysticism and occultism). Ethically, they believed in subordinating the passions, including the sexual instinct, to the dominance of reason.

Like his predecessor Hufeland and his follower Schreber, in *Happiness* Hartmann was also concerned with prolonging and preserving life by means of proper bodily hygiene and physical exercise. He recommended the balanced use of all the body muscles, laying stress on breathing and exercising abdominal muscles. He devoted an entire chapter to sexual relations, in which he distinguished between sexual love and love writ large. Raw animal instincts and sexual pleasure (*Wollust*, the same word later used by Paul Schreber), should not lead to sexual excesses (*Ausschweifungen*, also used by Paul Schreber), while chaste love (*keusche Liebe*, reverberating to the chastity principle on the minds of students at Leipzig University) "should make the young man and woman happy" (p. 159). One should be guided by moderation and "put prudent limits on pleasure" (p. 165). The passions, that is, powerful and passionate emotions (anger, fear, jealousy, sadness), should also be controlled (p. 166).

Moritz Schreber added a section of his own on "Pollutions and Menstruation" to *Happiness*. Schreber (1861b) says in his addendum that "the semen, in the absence of a successful procreation act, is either absorbed in the body and used for the strengthening of one's body or is excreted from time to time in the course of spontaneous nightly emissions" (p. 170). A frequency of such pollutions exceeding two to four weeks, caused by "unchaste trends of the imagination, previous masturbation and other sexual excesses, and, in general, a sybaritic [*üppige*] and soft life, hot spices and drinks," will result in the depletion of nervous energy (Schreber, 1861b, p. 170). The antidote is avoidance of excess body heat, regular bowel and bladder movements, and baths at about 66 degrees.

These remarks are in keeping with Hartmann's own recommendations. His rhetoric includes expression like "excessive lust" (*unmässige Wollust*), "unnatural self-abuse" (*unnatürliche Schändung*), and "animal drives" (*thierische Triebe*). Says Hartmann in *Happiness*: "[The rational man] will not act on feeling alone but on the basis of rational choice; his happiness requires that he know law and order" (p. 174). He admonishes against the premature arousal of the "sexual drive" in children by nursemaids and servants should parental vigilance slacken. This premature arousal by servants may become further reinforced by fantasy-arousing smut produced by novelists, painters, and ballet dancers. Exposure to this creates the future voluptuary (*Wollüstling*) and drives him to pursue the "purchased lust" of prostitution, both male and female, "the black vice" of the age. The price to pay is "an extreme overstrain or weakening of the nerves [including exhaustion of the brain], a cause of sad diseases, such as tormenting hysteria and hypochondria, black melancholy, madness and epilepsy" and impotence (p. 177-178). The list would be incomplete, says Hartmann, without warning against the poison of venereal diseases, "the slow pest."

Another section is devoted to marriage problems, and a whole chapter is devoted to the overcoming of passions; the positive ones (love, hope, joy, courage) should be used in overcoming the negative ones (fear and spasms, anger with its show of "bellowing and shouting [*brüllende Geschrei*]," hatred, revenge, remorse and sadness, envy and doubt). In this way one achieves physical well-being and happiness in accordance with the laws of nature. This is also the foundation of upbringing and education.

Modern education, criticizes Hartmann, is entirely based on rote memorizing of empty abstract concepts of religion and morality from books. Against this he pits the ideal of raising the whole person. Such a whole person, active rather than passive, can be developed by the education of the senses, the imagination, and reason through observation of nature; by joyful physical activity and games in the open; by the avoidance of premature sexual arousal; and good habits, all based on a recognition of what is appropriate to each age and developmental stage.

These ideas constitute the Kantian zeitgeist, anchored in the ideals of the Enlightenment rather than in the romantic ideas of many of Hartmann's and Schreber's contemporaries. We encounter them in Moritz Schreber's health and educational ideals and their echoes in the conflicts and symptoms of his son Paul.

Schreber's Ideas in Health

Health (Schreber, 1861a) was subtitled "the art of living according to the structure and laws of human nature" and bore a motto from the poet Fr. Rückert: "Consider that a God dwells in your body, And may that temple be preserved from desecration." In this book Schreber expresses ideas similar to those of Hufeland and Hartmann. In the introduction he describes some basic facts about human anatomy, physiology, and development. Part 1 is devoted to a delineation of the rules of healthy life: air, light, diet, drinking, evacuations, skin care, washing and bathing, and, of course, exercising the body. The plan of the book also imitates Hufeland's: after describing the conditions of health in Part 1, he devotes a short part (three chapters only) to discussing certain diseases and treatments.

He also shows the development of a philosophy of health and disease: animals pursue health by instinct but man is incapable of achieving this goal simply, in spite of his superior endowment. Thanks to reason and the trials life presents, mankind can exercise the capacity for free choice and responsible action in order to realize the supreme earthly good, that is, health. But this ideal condition of health is constantly under attack from forces that oppose it. The pure and noble attitude of the mind and the physical strength achieved in the process of hardening the body are opposed by a tendency to live softly and indolently. There is therefore a need for the discipline called dietetics (now called by Schreber hygiene), or the preventive science of rational living and health preservation. From there Schreber goes to formulate a number of hygienic prescriptions. Quoting Rousseau, he reaffirms the need for a healthy body, strengthened by exercises, to prevent premature aging, hemorrhoids, gout, diseases of the chest and abdomen, hypochondria, and melancholia. His definition of *Turning* as including swimming, skiing, fencing, wrestling and throwing (i.e, as athletics, with or without appliances). A good substitute, says Schreber, is indoor gymnastics. All these are means for the strengthening of body and mind. He believes that the sureness and dexterity thus achieved will protect against falls, blows and concussions. He also mentions his mentors: Basedow, Salzmann, Guts Muths, Jahn and Spiess. Like Hufeland, Schreber devotes many pages to the subject of sleep. He argues against soft bedding and recommends sleeping on the back and changing positions often.

The Ethics of Child Rearing and Sexuality

Chapter 9 in Part 1 of *Health* is devoted to sexual relations. Schreber sees the cosmic polarity of attracting and repulsing forces mirrored in the sexual polarities of man and woman, in the tension and attraction between the sexes. The sexual drives first serve the more general purpose of procreation, which is the goal of man and woman throughout life. However, "Unlike in animals, the sex drive in man is not blind instinct but one transformed into a cultivated (*veredelter*) natural drive when subjected to the rule of reason and moral sentiment. In it there is a most intimate melding of pure spiritual love and carnal love, of the divine and the sensual" (Schreber, 1861a, p. 174). Such love is the foundation of life within the family and the nation and its actualization is to be found in marriage, a sanctum in the order of the world.

Schreber, like Hufeland, upholds the idea of marital fidelity and abhors gratification of love's crude sensuality outside the marriage. One good reason is the prevention of "malignant infections," which "destroy not only life's happiness of the individual but also that of entire families". Of course, he has in mind venereal disease—in particular syphilis, although he avoids mentioning the horrible word. He also prescribes abstinence before the age of sexual maturity (22-25 in man, 20-22 in woman). Like Hufeland, he is against masturbation. These matters will also preoccupy his son Paul on the pages of the *Memoirs*.

In *Health* Schreber formulates ideas about sex hygiene. He insists on a certain measure of chastity and moderation even between husband and wife. Some people, he says, believe marriage gives them the right to indulge in sensual lust (*Sinnenlust*). Man and wife should both be physically healthy, the man older than his wife by some five to ten years, and genuinely attracted to each other. The sex act is basically meant for procreation and should be undertaken in a mood of mutual peace and happiness; enjoyment should be kept within bounds of moderation, because any excess "unnerves man and woman." A woman given to sexual excesses is in danger of developing cancer of the womb (p. 179). The sex urges should not be aroused by artificial means, such as the "arousal of phantasy through lascivious literature and paintings, love dalliance etc" (p. 180). The recommended frequency of intercourse is two, at most three, times a week, preferably in the morning hours, and never during the menstrual period, in the late months of pregnancy, or during breast feeding. Following these rules, Schreber believes, will prevent infertility in the couple, although he concedes in a footnote that infertility has so many causes that a thorough medical examination is necessary to determine the proper cause and cure. He condemns childlessness by choice.

Another aspect of sex hygiene covered in Health is the natural regulation of the sex drive. In man, Schreber says, it is achieved by nocturnal seminal emissions. The normal frequency is at intervals of two, three, or four weeks. Any higher frequency means either a "generalized weakness or a lustful turn of the imagination, or sexual excesses, or a generally immoderate, voluptuous and soft way of life" (p. 182). The countermeasures are exercise, hard mattresses, regular bowel and bladder movements, cold baths and washings of the small of the back and under the genitals, and early rising. According to Schreber, the woman during her period should be treated as half sick and vulnerable to morbidity. She should be spared all manner of bodily or emotional stresses.

We will postpone discussing Moritz Schreber's ideas about mental health till later and mention now some of his ideas about child rearing. Although the Kallipädie (1858a) has come to be viewed by modern commentators as his principal text about child rearing, the basic ideas were already expressed in Health, where chapter 12 is devoted to "life rules in regard to the upbringing of children." In these remarks good pediatric practices are combined with sound educational principles. For example, Schreber stresses the helpless infant's need for its mother's true love and tender loving care with respect to its basic bodily needs for food, warmth, cleanliness. He warns against rushing to overmedicate children with emetics and laxatives at the first sign of such normal reactions as rattling breathing shortly after birth.

Weaning should be gentle and gradual (p. 220), and every effort should be made by the mother to nurse her child. Otherwise, wet-nurses should be chosen carefully: they must be of good temperament and compassionate character, for the cases are not rare when "mean-spirited wet-nurses or mothers, who first stirred violent emotions in the child and then gave it the breast, either held a dead child in their lap or saw it die soon of cramps"(p. 222). One should avoid premature (i.e., before the end of the first year), stuffing of children with food adults eat.

Schreber goes on to advise that the child should be protected from too strong stimuli of light, and noise, and smell. Infants should be allowed freedom of independent motion and mothers should not resort to "most pitiless swaddling (einzuschnüren) and gagging (zusammen-zuknebeln), which leads to countless bodily defects"(p. 230). Children should learn to walk by themselves and be allowed to crawl and slide and avoid artificial means of support.

On the other hand, warns Schreber, the tendency to scream unnec-

essarily should be curbed or it might become a defect of the temperament. Not every crying should be managed by excessive attention,
picking the child up, petting it, and so forth. The danger Schreber sees
here is that the child will grow up selfish. Let it cry itself out, he
advises. If it shows stubbornness, it should be subjected to "repeated
threatening gestures, which a child already months old [four, six, or
eight] can understand, or if needed, dampen such small whims even by
means of mild bodily punishments (*leichte fühlbare Züchtigungen*) and
persistent refusal to gratify them"(p. 234). Here we see a degree of
severity not encountered in Hufeland and one that might raise eyebrows.

Schreber prescribes rules for the spiritual upbringing of children.
Since the intellectual powers are the later ones to develop, during the
earlier periods efforts should be directed at emotional development,
the virtues of diligence and order; the taste for the good, the beautiful,
the noble, and the sublime; a rejection of the evil, the low, the shameless, and the selfish—briefly, child rearing efforts should attempt to
inculcate in the child the "steadfast habit of the good in feeling,
thinking and acting" (p. 246).

> Such ethical foundations of character are seen as the best remedy against
> all those afflictions which so heavily embitter and shorten human
> life . . . anxious worrying for the most insignificant reasons, despon-
> dency, hopelessness in misfortune, discontent, hypochondria, etc.
> . . . By learning in early youth to subordinate sensuousness to higher
> moral considerations, by making moderation and continence into ha-
> bitual virtues, in later periods of his life man will be spared all difficulty
> and torment in his struggle against the passions that assail him and
> threaten to destroy his better I or self (*besseres Ich*). Briefly, by means of a
> thorough moral upbringing we sow in the child's heart the seed of
> unshakable peace of mind in all life's circumstances, of contentedness, of
> a steadfast and decisive character, of an energetic, active life [p. 247].

Schreber preaches strength based on love, and the need to make the
child's heart open to love, benevolence, and forgiveness.

For the child of seven and older, the principles remain the same, but
from now on "one should strive to change the [child's] ways of
thinking and acting, which until now were based on blind obedience,
gradually into willing and doing based on [the child's] own conviction,
to lay the foundation for the steadfastness and independence indispensable in later life"(p. 254). Therefore, toward the ages of ten to twelve
one should dispense with corporal punishment and gain entry into the
child's mind by appealing to his self-respect by means of rebuke and
reprimand. Thus it is

the duty of the parents to inculcate in the sons the truly manly virtues: indefatigable work and steadfast striving after one's chosen profession, courage and energy to achieve good, strength of the will, decisiveness and fearlessness and in the daughters the virtues that adorn the woman: domesticity, delicacy of feeling, gentleness, mildness [p. 257].

These prescriptions would not be complete without repeating the warning against the dangers of "self-pollution, onanism," the "sad vice," the "secret plague of the young" (p. 258), the cause of "mental dullness, fatigue . . . abdominal disorders and nervous disorders" (p. 259).

Schreber on Mental Illness

Already exemplified in the "Confessions of a Former Melancholic," Moritz Schreber's views on mental illness deserve special attention. They also reflect his ethical views, deriving from the philosophy of Kant, whose name is mentioned in passing in *Health*. These ideas would have had an effect on his son Paul, who also read Kant: on Paul's self-diagnosis and coping with illness.

Kantian ideas on emotional health and disease were an influence not only on Schreber but also on a prominent group of German psychiatrists known as the *Psychiker*—that is, the soul, or humanistic (as I would like to call them) psychiatrists—who became vocal around the 1830s (Ackerknecht, 1968; Dörner, 1984; Kesting, 1987; Thom, 1987). They held to the idea of psychological causation of illness, in opposition to the *Somatiker*, whom we would today call the biologists, the believers in organic causation. Among the humanistic psychiatrists was J. C. A. Heinroth whose use of the word orthobiotics in his titles (see footnote 1) justifies the assumption of an influence on Moritz. The soul psychiatrists also became identified with German romanticism (*Sturm und Drang*) and with romantic medicine and *Naturphilosophie*, a metaphysical and mystical conception of nature. Some commentators saw this influence reflected in Heinroth and Moritz Schreber.[10] The net thrust of such views was to substitute a metaphysics of nature for the scientific observation of nature, an idea furthest from Kant's philosophy.[11]

Heinroth occupied the first chair of psychiatry at Leipzig University, created in 1811 and at first called psychic therapy, rooted in Kant's anthropology.[12] Heinroth's concept of mental health (like Moritz Schreber's later writings), was imbued with ethical, rather than ecclesiastical, religious ideas; Christ was seen as an ideal of mankind, healthy and wholesome and without evil or sin but possessed of freedom of will. Free man, Heinroth believed, is also responsible man, one who opts for good over evil, who masters stimuli both from within, such as instincts and passions, and from without, such as fear and hate. Organic diseases have organic causes, mental illness has moral causes—succumbing to passions, vice and unreason. Thus, mental health is freedom, illness a reduction of freedom due to *Ich-Sucht*, or self-love, and other passions. Ellenberger (1970) thought that if we substitute guilt for sin in Heinroth's equation—especially if we find sin too close to religion—then this idea makes good psychological sense. According to Heinroth, disordered passions lead to a disturbance of reason and to delusions, the main feature of madness. Indirect psychic methods of treatment included the use of tranquilizing restraints, such as the famous chair, which Heinroth regarded as dubious compared to the direct moral treatment, which is defined as follows:

> If an impure soul can corrupt the pure soul, then a pure, God-energized soul can heal a sick soul. The medium is the will. This has to first become energy, to be able to energize. Thus, everyone should strive to strengthen his will, to purify it and to make it holy, and thus he will acquire an energy that is capable of causing what used to be called miracles, which come about due to the will enlivened by faith [Heinroth quoted in Sänger, 1963, p. 53].

The Kant–Heinroth influence on Moritz Schreber is discernible in the 11th chapter in *Health*, devoted to "life rules in regard of the mental side of man, insofar as it has an influence on the bodily state of health." Thus, Schreber here treats not only of mental phenomena as such but also of their psychosomatic and somatopsychic connections, a topic that was also on Kant's mind. The opening remarks in the chapter are the following:

> Mind and body are so closely fused in man that between the two there is the most direct and reciprocal influence from the state of one onto the other. . . . From this intimate reciprocal influence of mind and body stems also the close kinship between the science of morals and the science of health. Full health can only be enjoyed by man when mind and body stand to each other in a proper relationship, in true harmony [p. 201].

Schreber follows Kant's division of the faculties into understanding, feeling, and willing. He believes these need to be maintained in a state of equilibrium. He augments Kant's system by saying that these powers should also have a true direction and steadiness and that such direction and steadiness can only be achieved by the human mind when it is inspired through and through by a pure and noble purpose, true all-embracing love (that is, joyful action for the overall world purpose), the supreme guiding star of its whole thinking and doing, likened to a sun whose rays (*Strahlen*) permeate and illuminate the thinking of its reason and intellect, the sensing of its emotions, the desiring of its will-power [p. 202].

The antithesis of such love is limiting one's striving to "one's own I (*Ich*)," or to selfishness (*Selbstsucht*). Cultivation (*Veredlung*) means seeking such love. (Rays is a locution beloved of Paul Schreber and comes up in many of his daydreams and delusions.)

Schreber puts greater stress on the life of the emotions (*das Gemüth*).[13] Good emotions or a good mood prevail "when our inner voice, our conscience, furnishes evidence that we have lived true to the fulfilling of our obligations and given our energies to creating goodness" (p. 208). But the manifestations of the life of the emotions, feelings and passions can easily overthrow reason and intellect if not held in check, fought against and destroyed in the germ. Thus, emotions that cause

excitement (*joy, hope, sexual love, anger* etc.), when in excess, can cause, among others, empty day dreaming, feverish states, cramps, apoplexy or psychosis, whereas an excess of depressing emotions (*fear, anxiety, panic, worry, rage, despondency, sadness, remorse, jealousy, envy, stinginess, hatred, vengefulness*, etc.) can cause mental and nervous weakness, paralyses, inhibition of life activities, wasting, melancholia and despair [p. 209; emphasis Schreber's].

Schreber regards the will as a power to influence the mood and direction of the mind and, like Kant, he believes that it can control the states of the body, as a means of mitigating, making more treatable, and preventing many illnesses. A strong and decisive effort of the will may, he says, not only control the whims and tempers in hypochondriacal men and hysterical women but also be the glimmer of hope in the dark night of delirium and delusion.

From Health To Gymnastics

Gymnastics, our abbreviation for *Medical Indoor Gymnastics*, is most often mentioned in connection with those much maligned Schreber gymnastic exercises. Yet, this thin volume deserves our close attention for the following reasons: it deals not only with exercises but contains some of Schreber's seminal ideas about physical and mental health and sexuality,[14] and it is explicitly cited by Paul in the *Memoirs*. For example, while delving into the idea of "soul conception" (see epigraph of this chapter), which is his way of referring to his father's system of education, Paul brings up the differences between female and male gender characteristics and sexuality and notes "that a man lies on his side in bed, a woman on her back (as the 'succumbing part,' considered from the point of view of sexual intercourse)" (M p. 166). On that same page Paul says that he read his "father's *Medical Indoor Gymnastics* (23rd Edition, p. 102)."[15]

Section 6 of Moritz Schreber's *Medical Indoor Gymnastics* (1899; Day's translation) is entitled: "Prescription for unhealthy, weakening, frequency of pollutions" (p. 79). After providing a list of exercises to counteract the effects of pollutions (i.e., involuntary, not masturbatory, seminal emissions), Moritz adds:

> When cases such as these are persistent, it is also advisable before going to bed (and therefore in every case, some time after the exercises, which should generally never be performed later than before the evening meal) to take a hip-bath of a temperature between 54 and 60 Fahr., and lasting from 6 to 8 minutes, or a simple injection [*Wasserklystier*, water enema] of the same temperature, which should be retained for as long as possible, and therefore not too abundant; and at night, in this case, as an exception, instead of lying on the back, make a habit of lying on each side alternately; and in the morning, not at night, wash the parts about the sexual organs and the perineum with cold water [p. 80].

Moritz's concern here is placing limits on the amount of sexual enjoyment as such, not just illicit or perverse sexuality; he considered excessive sexual discharge a health hazard. Freud was similarly concerned. The pietistically and puritanically bent Schreber and the sexually restrained and not so puritanical yet rationally inclined Freud did share a common moral code and similar etiological views: Freud regarded neurasthenia, an exhaustion disorder, as due to excessive masturbation. Freud departed from Schreber in his views on the causes of anxiety neurosis: intoxication with undischarged sexual libido caused by excessive continence (Freud, 1895a).[16]

Yet *Gymnastics* has a broader philosophical-moral medical underpinning. The motto defines a holistic therapy: "It is a surer method, more fruitful of results, and more worthy of man, to develop and to *earn* Health as far as possible by personal activity, than when it is lost to *look* passively to nature, or to drugs to bring about its slow return" (Schreber, 1899; translator's emphasis). This approach is of Hippocratic inspiration: disease is disequilibrium, be it excess or lack, and cure is regulation: "the endeavor to harmonize the powers that lie within our organism" (p. v).

These ideas are developed in the first entitled "The value of medical gymnastics in general."

> Man is a twofold being, and consists of a marvelously [*wunderbaren*] intimate union of two natures, mental and physical; and he should keep both of these in activity, in order to use to the fullest both his mental and physical powers. His whole being is constituted for this end. . . . The want of this brings on dullness of the whole organism, disturbance of its action, then disease and early death [Schreber, 1899, p. 1].

It is the ancient idea of *mens sana in corpore sano* (sound mind in a sound body) extended to achieving a higher mental culture by the methods of physical culture. Using the simile of horticulture, Schreber (p. 8) sees civilized man as ascending from an *Urzustand*, a primitive state, which is "unconscious and uncultivated" (*das Unbewusst- und Rohnatürliche*) to an evolved "conscious and cultivated" state (*Bewusst- und Edelnatürliche*) (p. 8; German in Schreber, 1889, p. 16). Freud, another Kantian, applied similar antinomies to sexuality and opposed the unconscious id to the conscious ego: where id was there shall ego be. Schreber's concept of *Veredlung* (ennoblement, cultivation)—literally turning something rough and raw into something noble and cultured—also reverberates with kindred comparisons of weeds and tares and cultivated plants, wild horses and thoroughbreds, primitive man and civilized man, thus, cultivation.[17] Human development should culminate, says Schreber, in a harmony and balance between the laws of nature and the highest ethical goals of life. One of the means to achieve this harmony is to practice *medical* gymnastics, which comprises *therapeutic* gymnastics, for the "removal of certain diseases and states of failure and deficiency" and *hygienic* (Schreber's other term for preventive) gymnastics.

Nor is medical gymnastics a panacea. But it is, asserts Schreber, an important method of natural healing and prevention, avoiding the use of pharmacological agents. Exercising the muscle masses of the body has a direct physiological effect on blood flow and hence ensures the proper circulation of bodily juices, renewal of substances (my translation for *Stofferneurung*; Schreber, 1889, p. 19), his term for a balanced metabolism, the basis of freshness and youthful vigor and the elimination of used-up and unusable matter particles, a cause, among others, of fat deposits. An unbalanced metabolism in later years is one of the leading causes of the usual chronic gastrointestinal "ailments . . . and their various consequences: indigestion, constipation, congestion of the liver and the spleen . . . with their consequent painful affections of the brain [*rührende Kopfbeschwerden*, hefty head complaints], especially congestion and hypochondriacal and melancholy humours [moods]" (p. 8).

Another important equilibrium is "between the nerves of movement and the nerves of sensation" with regard to their excitability and state of activity. A hyperexcitation [*Überreizung*] of the nervous system can cause "nervous overstrain" [*Nervenspannung*] (Schreber, 1889, p. 22; 1899 p. 9) and also "extreme excitability [*reizbare Schwäche*] . . . of the nervous system, nervous hypochondria and hysteria, unhealthy enfeebling pollutions, [and] diseases of the mind . . ." (p. 9). Other causes of ill health, says Schreber, are the adverse effects of "the constant use of hot condiments, spirituous drinks, coffee and tea, . . . sexual exhaustions, indulgence in too great luxury of the mind *[Verweichlichung*, which also carries the connotation of effeminacy], laziness and surfeiting of the senses, want of balance between our powers and the demands we make on them, and the want of harmonious physical and moral energy, which is due to our faulty up-bringing" (p. 16).

We have seen how gastrointestinal disorders and depressions were Moritz's lot in the years preceding his death, how melancholy moods befell him in his youth and were prominent in Paul's illness, and how pollutions were seen as a cause of illness. Compare these difficulties with Paul's recurrent concern with blessedness as both happiness and pleasure (M p. 31), the bases of health, and his concern with their opposites, "poison of corpses and other putrid matter (*Fäulniss*)" (*M*, p. 129), and the juxtaposition of "moral decay [*sittliche Fäulniss*, voluptuous excesses]" (*M*, p. 52) and of blessedness. It is both an identification with and a departure from father. For, as Paul says (p. 51), *Seligkeit* is also "connected with the nature of God's nerves, through which Blessedness . . . is felt, if not exclusively as, at least accompanied by, a greatly increased feeling of voluptuousness" (*M*, p. 51). The son both agreed and disagreed with his father. Like the early Freud and like Reich *(Function of the Orgasm)*, Paul also underscores the healing and redemptive power of sexuality. Such a conception was alien to his father.

Noteworthy are Moritz's ideas about the reciprocal influence of body and mind and the relation between medical and ethical precepts. A central idea is that hygiene, or prevention, is easier than cure. This is how prevention, according to Moritz (1899) works:

> To live *soberly, actively* and *contentedly*, are the three rules of the Philosophy of Health, and if we obey them we may hope for a contented old age. And in the closest connection with them are the commands of the Ethical Philosophy of life—
> > Strive after full command over thyself, over thy spiritual and bodily weaknesses and wants. . . . Dare to be wise [*Sapere aude*, the quote is from Horace]—at whatever period of life you may have arrived at it is never too late—and persevere unweariedly in the

struggle for this true (inward) freedom, for the perfection of the self. By this means, within the limits which are marked out for this earthly life by a Higher Power, thou shalt go on from victory to victory until thou comest to the final goal with the blissful consciousness that thy life-task has been worthily performed.

For in the true performance of these two commands—of the hygienic and of the ethical—lies the whole secret of the most difficult, but the most noble and most important of all sciences—the science of life, the science [*Kunst*, art] of living *well* [*richtig*, right] [p. 17].

Schreber's dynamic approach reflects the dynamic psychiatry of the humanistic Heinroth and others of that time. The principle of wholeness and harmony is extended from medicine to education, as affirmed by Moritz in an autobiographical sketch in Heindl (1859). One would look in vain here for Freud's dynamic psychiatry, his idea of conflict as the root of illness and conflict resolution as a key to health; Freud had his own prescription for the right life.

SCHREBER'S PHILOSOPHY OF EDUCATION

Moritz Schreber's later writings as educator, that is, a propounder of a practical philosophy and method of child rearing, are important for two reasons: to locate him in the history of education and to understand the character and personality of his son Paul, his conduct and some of the statements in the *Memoirs*. Schreber's ideas on child rearing and education survive in his works and in encyclopedias and textbooks on the history of education.[18]

Schreber began as a physician. His starting point was the healthy and normally functioning body, energized and nurtured by mother nature, and the *joie de vivre* inherent in the enjoyment of nature's bounty. But as health is often a native metaphor for virtue, the healer is never too far from the moralist, the educator, and the reformer. The healthy and the good were combined for Schreber in dietetics,[19] or the science of prevention. We now add the other meaning of dietetics: the art of living in accordance with reason and the higher feelings, which rule body and soul and strengthen the personality as a whole. This meaning is also a manifestation of nature and an extension of it. It inheres in the proper functioning of the senses. It is a guarantor of conduct that will ensure the pursuit of health, the good life, and happiness.

This naturalism of medicine contributed to philosophical, social, and cultural naturalism in modern times and challenged the asceticism promulgated by the church. Its wellsprings were ancient Greek ideals that were brought back to life by the humanists of the Renaissance. It was continued by Hobbes and Locke in England; by leaders of the French Enlightenment, including Rousseau; and then through Kant, Fichte, Pestalozzi, and Basedow to Schreber. Kant and Rousseau were direct influences on Johann Gottlieb Fichte, an important inspiration for Schreber. Another line of development has to do with the effect of Rousseau on Pestalozzi, the latter's influence on Fichte and Froebel, and theirs on Schreber.[20] From Kant, Fichte got his ideas about the active ego and ethics; from Rousseau he took the concepts of liberty, individuality, and the importance of feelings, and combined these in an education toward moral freedom and independence, in a process that led from the concept of life ruled by instincts to that ruled by morality based on reason. A prerequisite for such education was training in obedience, seen as a means to a higher end. This conception of education was also used by Fichte in developing his ideas about the role of the state in a system of national education.[21]

Schreber's naturalism inspired his ideas on education. The methods he recommended were qualified by him as *"naturgemäss,"* according to nature. The antagonist of the natural and the rational is, for Schreber, *"widernatürlich,"* against nature, such as unnatural habits of body and mind and the unnatural vices, that is, those that destroy health. Schreber was intent on promulgating the natural and decrying the antinatural and did so with an insistence that strikes some modern readers as preachy and fanatical. I am impressed with the sobriety and the matter of factness of his arguments, devoid of condescension.

A further corollary of this naturalism is not only natural ethics but natural religion. Schreber's God is more in the nature of the Greek Logos and of Spinoza's *Deus sive natura* (God, that is nature), that is, of the deity as the repository of reason and the higher spiritual values. Christianity is occasionally mentioned by Schreber; these are still the days prior to the conquest of Germany by Darwinism. The God of enlightened Lutheranism and the god of philosophical deism are still seen as the creator of nature and in harmony with her. That God could become inimical to man, that he could be the creator of good and evil, was a notion foreign to Schreber but one very much on his son's mind. With this deism went the rational rejection of everything supernatural and occult. In Schreber's day it was still permissible to use the God-term as an embodiment of the true, the good, and the ethical; it was not until the post-Darwininian generations that God became for some an antiquated embarrassment.

The concept of the natural life of the organism led Schreber early on to his main educational idea: the child is not just born healthy but has the potential for healthy growth and development if this is not inhibited or destroyed (*Health,* p. 242). One of the causes of faulty growth and development, says Schreber, is faulty education. With the knowledge we have won in pediatrics, child psychology, psychiatry, and psychoanalysis this seems self-evident. But child psychology was almost unknown in Schreber's days: in *Health* he speaks with a foresight rare for his times.

Growth and development of the individual and society go hand in hand: therefore, for Schreber, health, education, and ethics formed an organic whole.

Schreber's Kallipädie

The *Kallipädie* (1858a)[22] is Schreber's largest book on education, bearing the dedication "To the welfare of future generations." It has a long title: *Callipedia, or Education Towards Beauty by Means of the Natural and Even Promotion of Normal Body Growth, Life-Sustaining Health and Spiritual Cultivation and in Particular Through the Optimal Use of Special Educational Aids: For Parents, Educators, and Teachers.* In the preface Schreber refers to ideas in his earlier works (1852b, 1853, 1855) and explains that it is his aim now, based on years of experience with body and mind, to suggest ways to promote the harmony between the body, the emotions—the most important being love—mind, and character.

In the introduction of *Kallipädie* Schreber stresses the importance of a thorough knowledge of physiology and psychology. The new emphasis was for this knowledge to become the foundation of a systematic science of education (*Erziehungswissenschaft*), one still young in Schreber's day, except for Herbart, who was yet to become popular. Universities did not yet have chairs of education, and educators were only taught how to teach, that is, methods of instruction of various subjects but nothing about the physiology, psychology and development of children. To us the importance of these subjects to educators seems obvious, but in 1858 Schreber was ahead of his time. He viewed the growing child as an organism containing cultivated (*edle*) and base (*unedle*) seeds (*Keime*). This is a mixed metaphor, referring to noble plants versus weeds, and noble versus base metals. It reverberates with Rousseau's statement in *Émile*[23] about the innate goodness of man, but it also goes beyond it and points to the need to correct, from the beginning, bad dispositions and faulty habits. Using Schreber's terms, education should promote the good and remove the bad seeds.

Education, says Schreber (1858a), should be based on the principle of individualization, on a recognition of the personal needs of the child. He makes a plea to the parents as well. They should rear their children by acting as "living examples and models" for the child. If you want to be such a model, Schreber informs parents, then be true to your own example, because "the natural instinctive gaze of the child penetrates deeper, feels the true and the hidden motives of its environment better than our own mental eyes, spoiled and dulled by the varnish of the world" (p. 30). He demands of parents the qualities of truthfulness, consistency, and love. What he says about the roles of the mother and father is enlightening: Mother and father "have equal rights in the family circle," even though there is an edge to a man's knowledge. Child rearing should not be left to mothers alone; fathers should participate and help out, show understanding toward weaknesses of mothers, and strive to strengthen and empower the mothers. Speaking in the name of fathers, Schreber says, "We have no justification to act superior towards the other sex, because we too, the best of us, have weaknesses that are more injurious than the weaknesses of mothers . . . husband and wife should complement each other" (pp. 31-32).

The pediatric guidelines in the *Kallipädie* regarding kind and gentle infant care are as sound today as they were in Schreber's day. Infants should be optimally stimulated to grow, he says, neither understimulated nor overstimulated. In the first months of life the infant should be allowed complete freedom of movement. If he hollers out of hunger, do not immediately reach out for food but see if after a brief pause he calms down on his own.

Schreber insists on early moral training of the infant, which raises some difficulties for modern sensibilities. He feels that by the third or the fourth month the infant is already capable of responding to love; modern infant observation has confirmed this. By the fifth or sixth month, says Schreber, the infant is already capable of a dawning awareness of right and wrong. This is an area where eyebrows might be raised, though, to be sure, some contemporary psychoanalytic theorists would correlate this period with the beginning of what Melanie Klein called the "depressive position" and thus with the beginnings of such feelings as concern and guilt. Schreber reasons as follows: "By developing in the child good and right habits, we prepare it to pursue good and right later in life, with awareness and free will. . . . [For which] the habit is but the necessary precondition . . ." (p. 60). Therefore, when faced with

> groundless screaming and crying . . . the first manifestations of selfishness . . . one should no longer adopt a wait-and-see attitude but respond in a positive manner: by means of a quick diversion of attention, serious words, threatening glances, rapping the bed (as a result of which the child will check itself and stop), or when all this is to no avail, then consistently, by means of repeated, of course, appropriately mild bodily admonitions, in small intervals, until the child calms down or falls asleep. . . . in this way . . . the child learns to obey. Half-measures (i.e.,

letting go before achieving the goal) excite rather than calm. Such a procedure is needed only once or at most twice—one is master of the child forever. From then on, one gaze, one word, one threatening mien will suffice to rule the child. Think that with this you offer the child the greatest benefit . . . you free him from inner torment. . . . A further corollary of this important rule is the following: that the permissible desires of the child are to be granted only when the child is acting in a calm and friendly and harmless manner, never as a result of screaming or unruly conduct. . . . [in order to develop] the art of waiting . . . the art of self-abnegation [pp. 61-63].

Is this sadism or salutary strictness? The concept of ruling the child is an idea that preceded Schreber.[24] For infants near the end of the first year Schreber recommends education of the emotions and of the will. He recommends treating the child with cheerfulness and training the child to " unconditional obedience . . . what you once demand, you should insist it be done in every case, as insignificant as it may be, if necessary by use of force. The idea should never cross the child's mind that his will might prevail . . . a precondition of all subsequent education" (p. 66). This is referred to as breaking the child's spirit, or taming untamed nature.

Following his recommendations for infants Schreber addresses the issues for the next three age groups: the age of play, from 2 to 7, the age of learning, 8 to 16, and the age of youth, 17 to 20. In the play age the emphasis is on using play as an essential educational method, preparatory to later learning. In this Schreber is quite modern in spirit. However, he is against stimulating the imagination prematurely with scary fairy tales, which excite the child unduly. He believes in showing the child at this age reality, not fantasy. Governesses should have the right to use corporal punishment but are not to use intimidation by fear and threats to discipline their wards.

Parents, says Schreber, should bestow on their children the rays of "glory of cheerfulness . . . the sun of the spiritual life" (p. 130). "The daughter of cheerfulness is love, . . . the mainspring of the whole business of education, down to all its details" (p. 131), not the blind, doting kind of love (*Affenliebe*), but the one tied to respect, the one that insists on what is good, right, and true. "One of the many rays of love is gratitude in the narrow sense" (p. 132), to which the child is led by "gentle indirection" (p. 133). A most important place is given to the training of "moral will power."

Schreber recommends that in the first year the child be trained in the habits of "unconscious obedience . . . [so that] this habit is now raised to the level of an act of free will, . . . of self-aware obedience. The child should not be the slave of somebody else's will, but be raised to a noble independence and the fullness of his own will. The previously acquired habit makes this transition easy" (p. 135). On the other hand, Schreber appears ruthless in insisting that "spitefulness should be broken, on the spot, until complete obedience is achieved, if needed through corporal punishment. This way you get rid of the problem once and for all . . ." (p. 137).

He also warns against "too much reprimanding, too much ordering-about, too much mothering—the mistake of many worrying mothers" (p. 140). He insists on truthfulness, is against the naked lie and against "white lies or the use of the fascinating garb of jest or slyness to dress up half untruths, tall stories, exaggerations, distortions, deceptions, partial or complete concealments" (p. 144).[25]

Schreber warns against the arousal of sensuality in children, such as when "fondness for delicacies is used as a means to procuring joy and as a preferred gift. The children become greedy [*lüstern*, a word which in an adult can mean 'lascivious'] and tend to become grossly sensual in other respects" (p. 149). Such spoiling destroys character: therefore, in child rearing one should strive for an equilibrium between gratification and deprivation; the mother should not indulge indolence or weakness.

Children should be taught to bear losses. Parents, says Schreber, should not conceal their own troubles from the children but set an example of fortitude. Children should also be taught how to bear insignificant discomfort and pain and how to overcome them quickly.

In regard to mental activity Schreber points emphatically to a need to hold to a unity of perception, clear speech, to connect concepts to percepts,and to refrain from all extrasensory and supersensory images and representations. As to religiosity, the longing for God and religious education, should not be prematurely fostered or forced. The child should be made aware of God through the contemplation of nature, not through drumming into his head *"religious concepts and religious exercises for show only"* (p. 155; emphasis Schreber's).

During the earlier ages, Schreber says, the foundations of good habits are laid down. If this has not happened, then during the next age of learning, ages 8 to 16, efforts should not be spared to have the child unlearn the bad habits. Such unlearning should proceed in a mild fashion. In the sphere of physical health, Schreber recommends the use of posture-improving aids, which have, in our day, procured for him the macabre reputation of a sadistic tormentor. This unjustified horror-mongering will be discussed later. Many pages of the *Kallipädie* are devoted to free body exercises.

In the sphere of the mind, Schreber suggests resorting to reason and the child's sense of honor, in a relationship based on mutual respect and trust between the child and the educator. Now that the brain has reached full maturity, school instruction should begin. It is also the age of sexual maturation and the "sad sexual straying of boys and girls. Therefore, over and above general health considerations, if it had not been done earlier, one should absolutely recommend from here on sleeping in *unheated* rooms" (p. 173, emphasis Schreber's). Similarly, children should be encouraged to get out of bed on awakening and discouraged from lounging in bed "*whether awake or half awake*" (p. 172, emphasis Schreber's). (Paul's hypnopompic dream of what it would feel like to submit to intercourse like a woman occurred in a state of semisleep.)

The sense organs and their functions should be trained as well as the correct use of the organs of speech and expression. Good elocution is important, clear end vowels and clear consonants are the goal. Facial grimaces should be discouraged. (Remember that grimacing and inarticulate bellowing were distressing behaviors of Paul.)

Discussing school instruction from the standpoint of the medical psychologist, Schreber believes, that teaching methods should, above all, be based on the principle of "*awakening in the child and continually keeping alive the desire, the full interest and the joy in learning a given subject. . . .* Instruction devoid of the fun (*Lust*) in learning is a torture for the teacher and student alike" (pp. 228–229; emphasis Schreber's). "*Overwhelming the student with too much classroom and at-home work* [might result in] *using the subjects of instruction as means of punishment. . . .* This is a psychological impossibility. . . . *Work should be joy, and where it is not it should become!*" (pp. 229–230; emphasis Schreber's).[26]

Another principle of Schreber's educational philosophy is the importance of developing

> self-creating thinking (instruction that fosters growth, excitement and discovery). . . . Conviction should not be won by means of passive following of authority, but through finding the truth by means of one's own mental activity, . . . [and] disputation. . . . A mechanical filling with information . . . the overloading of the mind with unfruitful stuff kills the spirit, the overfilling of . . . memory with crude and dead stuff crushes independent thinking [p. 232].

Schreber has two special wishes: that "*No child should be kept uninterrupted sitting and being mentally occupied for more than two hours at a stretch*" (p. 233) and that "*No school omit basic courses in human anatomy and physiology*" (p. 234; emphasis Schreber's).

In the relationship with the parents Schreber wants love and respect. "Therefore, obedience should now be based more on free choice and self-awareness" (p. 235). Direct coercion should now be avoided, and obedience is now secured through an appeal to love: "If you want to prove your love to me, do this and do not do that" (p. 236). Inculcate the gentle emotions of love, gratitude, compassion, and generosity as well as the virtues of courage, will power, truthfulness, steadfastness and keeping promises. Teach the child not to give in to anything ignoble or immoral, advises Schreber, and teach him to suppress or nip in the bud (*im Keime*) all the negative passions and emotions, such as sadness, rage, irritability, selfishness, bitterness and worry.

> It is important not to leave a trace in the depths, for all, even the dormant, germs of spiritual weeds (*Seelenunkrautes*), can easily become dangerous, if not early then later in life, should they receive nourishment from one circumstance or another and proliferate once again. The insane asylums could furnish countless examples if one were to trace the individual disease histories to their last root fibers [p. 242].

In the area of thought and judgment Schreber is interested in the fostering of self-knowledge, the basis of life wisdom:

> In the main, it is the task of the parents to show children the way. This can be achieved without difficulty if one takes pains, as the occasion allows it, to analyze with the participation of the child certain points of the child's thought processes, individual actions, in order to throw light on essential inner motives, to direct attention to their purity or impurity, to uncover the inner truth of the thoughts, their flaws and defects, but also to bring out the unlimited power of his will power and thus as far as possible to direct his gaze to the complete mirror of his interiority [pp. 244-245].

Of considerable interest is Moritz Schreber's philosophical analysis of words and concepts. He states that learning must not be a mere passive process of reception. The distinction between words and concepts is Kantian in origin. Schreber holds that the word cannot completely express the concept that points to mental states, emotions, or abstract and supernatural notions. Connecting words and concepts is always an individual affair. In every person the connection between word and concept is individual, as between body and mind. This is especially noted in the attempt to develop and clarify religious concepts.

> Therein lies the innermost essence of our spiritual life . . . Not the word, but the spirit which each man should seek out in the word, the Christian concept of God, the Christian moral law which is the only unassailable

and divine element in the teaching of Christ . . . Any externally imposed coercion of belief is the death knell of true religiosity. Thousands of people are in this way driven to open or secret irreligiosity and many of the susceptible people—to religious insanity [pp. 254-255].

Following these ideas on religion in the *Kallipädie* Schreber once again addresses the ethics of sexual conduct. He warns against disorders due to the premature arousal of drives attached to sexual maturation; the danger is to give in to the satisfaction of sensual desires (*Wollust*).

Schreber devotes some paragraphs to the issue of the choice of career, viewing this as one of the most important tasks in life. He argues in favor of parental permissive guidance.

The following remark, seemingly out of nowhere, deals with the role of fate in the life of individuals and families. In that context, Schreber speaks of the "apparent enigmas and contradictions in the order of the world (*Weltordnung*)" (p. 260) that may trouble the child's half-mature mind. God acting according to the order of the world is very much on his son's mind at Sonnenstein. For example, the child may be confused by the "concomitant presence of contradictions in the world, of the beautiful and the ugly, of fortune and misfortune, of good and evil" which are related to each other as "light and shadow" (p. 261). These dualisms were on Paul's mind when he spoke of the corresponding attributes of the ancient Persian Zoroastrian gods, Ormuzd and Ariman, that were so prominent in his dreams and delusions.

Schreber's Last Educational Works

Anthropos: The Wonderful Structure of the Human Organism, Its Life and Its Health Rules. An Easily Comprehensible Whole Picture of Human Nature for Teachers, Students and Everyman Who Strives After a Thorough Education and the Health of the Body and Soul (Schreber, 1859a) deserves special attention. It continues the ideas about human anatomy, physiology, and psychology begun in *Health*.[27] The pages on the anatomy of the brain and the central and autonomic nervous systems in *Anthropos* and in the two versions of *Health* are of particular importance. I believe that Paul learned about human anatomy from his father before he read anything on the brain by Flechsig.

In the 1839 edition of *Health* Schreber states that

The nerves are thread like structures spread throughout the entire body . . . those in the brain and spinal cord under the control of the will and those in the abdominal nerves (ganglia) outside the influence of the will . . . Those delicate little threads are composed of solid skin-like sheaths and the enclosed nerve marrow, a whitish pulp-like matter [p. 12].

Schreber is correctly referring to the myelin sheaths of nerves, which will become the centerpiece in Flechsig's neuroanatomical system. "The nervous system is the connecting link between mind and body" (p. 12). Discussing nerve physiology, Schreber notes that "once a nerve is cut, all life in it suddenly ceases." Nerves transmit sensation ("reception of stimuli", *Reizempfänglichkeit*) and "vital activities"; the nerve activity consists of "electrical processes." Nerves are conductors and the "central organs," or "focal points" (*Brennpunkte*), of nerve-life are the brain, the spinal cord and the abdominal nerve system. "These organs are the main work sites (*Hauptwerkstätte*) of the soul" (Schreber, 1839, p. 48). They also control metabolism, removing the wastes and replacing them with fresh matter "in one continuous cycle" (pp. 47-49). This description is repeated, with minor additions, in the second edition of *Health*. Efferent nerves are now compared to telegraph wires conducting telegrams (*Depeschen*), i.e, "excitations, sensation, voluntary acts." The central organs are indeed the work sites of the soul,

but are in no way an exclusive seat of same [i.e., the soul]: the soul is intimately melded with the whole [body], in a manner concealed from our sight, not just with one body part. The nerve activity regulates all the activities of the organism. Through it are mediated the reception, storage and revival of ideas [*Vorstellungen*] (brain pictures, *Gehirnbilder*), as well as their infinitely multifarious binding to thoughts (brain sparks, *Gehirnfunken*), feelings, and voluntary acts [Schreber, 1861a, pp. 50-52].

These ideas are still with us, and neuroscientists, before and after Flechsig, have but added details, leaving the mind-body mystery untouched.[28]

The remarks on the brain in *Anthropos* accompany an anatomical table in which Schreber says that in the "nervous system we have the miracle of all miracles" (p. 51). It is the carrier of all vital activities, formerly called the "nerve spirit" (*Nervengeist*). Through it we also achieve the "feeling of our self [*unserer selbst*], become conscious of bodily sensations [*Allgemeingefühl*] and mental states. We stand at the border between the world of the senses and the thickly veiled mental world." He is aware the spinal cord is not just fatty bone marrow but "a thick nerve trunk . . . the collecting organ for most body nerves, to conduct them to the brain" (Schreber, 1859a, pp. 51-52). The brain is concerned with "representational and memory pictures (*Vorstellungs- und Erinnerungsbilder*). All mental activity springs from this organ:

> Accordingly, it can raise our personal existence to high Heaven or plunge it into Hell. Every life-state of which our ego becomes conscious—the highest joy, the most blessed happiness (*das seligste Glück*), as well as the most tormenting pain (physical or mental)—takes place in this organ . . . the deepest sorrow may be caused due to an inhibited or untoward excitation in it. A bad stimulus, a false pressure upon certain fibers of this organ—which may even escape the eye aided by a microscope—and you—the most wretched of men!—are lost in madness, have ceased being human! [Schreber, 1859a, p. 53].

Schreber also mentions the skins, or coverings of the brain (*Häuten*); the frontal, middle and posterior lobes of the brain; and its convolutions. And he is even amazingly prescient about the importance of the "brain stem, the innermost kernel, the most central part of the entire nerve center (brain), nay, maybe the actual carrier of self-consciousness" (1859a, pp. 54-55).[29] He also speaks of the maturation of the brain, the end point occurring at age seven.

Schreber combines the conventional brain physiology of the day with an epistemology of a clearly Kantian inspiration. Thus he divides thought activity into the categories of reason (*Vernunft*), intellect (*Verstand*), and feeling (*Gemüth*). He discusses imagination (*Bildungskraft, Phantasie*), talent and genius. But he warns:

> Even though through investigation we know that the separate mental acts in the realm of thinking, feeling and willing are tied and transmitted through certain parts of the brain, we should not therefore regard these acts as material components or achievements of the brain. They are the insubstantial, unseen and imponderable purely mental achievements of an endlessly free motion capacity of the brain, a capability of the freest reciprocal connection and transformation of the materials of representation rather than transformation flashes of brain particles, like the ability of the speech organs to create, out of sounds, ever new words and out of the words, new sentences [1859a, p. 59].

Compared to this enlightened stance, Flechsig's views will appear as crude materialism.

Finally: "What is the relationship between all this and what we call our ego (*Ich*), our very Self (*Selbst*), our inner personality (*Persönlichkeit*), the innermost kernel of our self-consciousness, our mind (*Geist*)? This ego, our spirit, has its abode in the brain. . . . but our mind is something different from the body, something standing over the body" (1859a, p. 59). After a life-long detour, Flechsig will also return to this essential Platonic-Aristotelian-Kantian point of view. Schreber's concept goes one step further: even as our mind is bound to the body, our ego makes contact with the "divine spark in us," capable of a "god-oriented [gottwärtsgerichtet][30] soaring that should lead us to an ever higher and purer development of the self (Selbstheit), the focal point of our immortal ego. We cannot mathematically prove the existence of this ego or grasp it through our senses, no more than God. But it exists as certainly as God exists . . ." (p. 60). Moritz has come quite close to a metaphysical conception of the deity, but not mystical-religious, as did his son Paul. Moritz ends by noting the importance of sleep and dreams and rejects as "superstition, and as incommensurate with a noble God-concept and proper education of mankind, any idea that God could choose the unconscious and irresponsible state of dreaming as a means of bringing influence to bear on mankind" (1859a, pp. 60-61). This is also very much like the anthropology of Heinroth.

The ideas expounded in the Kallipädie were presented in a more popular form in Family Friend as Educator and Guide to Family Happiness, Health of the People, and Ennoblement of Mankind, for the Fathers and Mothers of the German Nation (Schreber, 1861c). In 1861 this book had already gone through three editions. According to Ritter (1936), the title was inspired by Basedow.

On National Education

The following paragraphs, concerning Moritz Schreber's ideas on national education, are based on his book On National Education and Its Timely Development Through Raising the Standards of the Teaching Profession and the Rapprochement Between School and Home—an Urgent Task for Civilized Nations (1860b), briefly, National Education.

In that book Schreber sees the physician, alongside the statesman and the philosopher, as the educator of a nation. In this he is clearly inspired by Fichte and his "Addresses to the German Nation." He also has high hopes that in addressing "these pages to the public and to the high national governments who oversee the well-being of Europe's civilized peoples" he will have contributed to the harmonious blending of the natural-scientific, religious-ethical, and social-political foundations of education. Education, he says, should be based on fostering the required qualities of character. Even as the natural body is a God-given sacred temple and the crown of creation, it carries within itself both crude and noble seeds. Those that are raw, crude, and undeveloped include the negative emotions of hatred, animosity, revenge, mendacity, cowardice, moroseness, selfishness, and low sensuousness; these are also the seeds of degeneration and death. The noble seeds contain love, friendship, truthfulness, faithfulness, reason, courage, joyfulness, mastery of the physical and sensual side, and hopefulness. At the top of the list he also places these two opposite tendencies: respect for and striving toward God (*Gottesverehrung und gottwärts gerichtetes Streben*) and its opposite, contempt for God and downward-directed trends (*Gottesverachtung und abwärts gerichteter Sinn*). This religiosity of Schreber's is not strictly church-oriented, it points to an amalgamation of philosophical and deistic views, as in Fichte[31] and in Heinroth.

Schreber believed that national education is the most important function of the state, barring none. His approach recognized three goals: (1) the thorough and rational training of teachers; (2) a rational foundation for the school system of education; (3) close emotional connections between home and school.

For the second of these goals Schreber developed an anthropological-pedagogic program—which he called pedology, or the science of children—based on a knowledge of the anatomy, physiology, and hygiene of the child. He stressed the importance of the knowledge of the psychology of the child. In connection with educating the teachers in the knowledge and appreciation of the anatomy and functioning of the human body, he referred to the *Anthropos*.

In *National Education* Schreber (1860b) states that the knowledge of the body should lead one to an idea of a scientific psychology, not just an "empty speculative psychology" (p. 27). It is of interest to note this emphasis; his successor in delineating a scientific psychology was Herbart, whose major work is devoted to defining psychology as a science.[32] The Herbartian system, with its emphasis on mathematics and metaphysics, took over German education in the last third of the 19th century, when Schreber was all but forgotten.

Schreber's anthropologically informed psychology also requires the appreciation of the "*psychology of the child in its various developmental phases*" (p. 19; Schreber's emphasis). We saw this idea developed in the *Kallipädie* (1858a). It is still far from our modern knowledge of developmental child psychology, but the germ of the idea is already there.

In *National Education* Schreber (1860b) addresses the required attitudes toward the child. Here he emphasizes the need to gain the "love and trust of the children" (p. 22). A rational psychology of children requires awakening in them a love of learning and helps avoid overloading them with too much studying. He also comes back to the issue of character training, or the broader task of educating to become a "whole person" (p. 19), to become human. And, of course, this psychology would be incomplete without mentioning active bodily exercises.

Schreber's educational principles lead logically to his recommendations for the training of a good teacher and for what the nation should do for its teachers. Like physicians, teachers should be taught the fundamentals of anatomy, physiology, disease prevention, and child psychology. One way to achieve this education, says Schreber, is to engage in preparatory fieldwork and "observation in children's residences, orphanages, kindergartens, and similar institutions" (p. 20), for "in many respects the foundations of normal life are recognizable in the shadows of abnormal life" (p. 21). He is here very much ahead of his time: he recommends that pedagogics be an independent chair at the university, that teacher training—of those with a humanistic and a scientific orientation alike—be an advanced discipline, and that the university be the place to train teachers of elementary, middle, and high schools. The currently existing so-called teacher seminaries should be elevated to the rank of pedagogical academies.

Thus, the main idea that emerges in *National Education* is the need to raise not only the professional standards of teachers but also teachers' pay and the budgets of schools, as befits the needs of a healthy nation. Schreber (1858b) briefly mentions the requirements for a good physical plant for the school. He recommends a better use for monies that are being "swallowed by the military budget, since by raising the standard of national education, the independence of a nation grows both inwardly and outwardly, so much so that it makes the need for standing armies superfluous" (p. 14) and raising taxes to pay for education.

The establishment of parent–teacher contacts and meetings to discuss the students is also a novel idea for those days. Schreber suggested special "school evenings" to foster good relations between parents and teachers. Freud, too, was impressed with this aspect of Schreber's approach (Freud, 1911a, p. 51).

Since bodily health and fitness are "the soul of learning" (*der Nerv des Lernens*, literally, the nerve of learning), it is important, says Schreber, for children to engage in active bodily exercises but in play and games as well. Such play and games should be the required counterweight to dry, abstract subjects and long hours of studying. Schreber (1860a) develops these ideas in an article entitled "The importance of children's games from the point of view of health and pedagogics and from the point of view of school education." It was first published in a popular magazine and so impressed the Viennese pediatrician Politzer that he reprinted it in his journal of pediatrics. In this paper Schreber touches upon a number of ideas already discussed here and also stresses the importance of "large open playgrounds for school-age children" (p. 252). This idea, so self-evident to us, was innovative in Schreber's day.

Over the decades since Moritz Schreber's death the citations of his works in the pedagogical literature steadily diminished; Ritter (1936) could rightly claim that Schreber's achievement as an educator had been all but forgotten. Yet I have documented above the posthumous awareness of him in medicine, orthopedics, pediatrics, gymnastics (both orthopedic and therapeutic), and education. It is, of course, not possible to know how wide Schreber's influence was, since many authors would have used his ideas without mentioning his name, as was habitual in the 19th century. But it is sufficient to realize that even though he did not become one of the greats in the history of education and was eclipsed by later academic educators, especially the Herbartians, he made a profound impression on his contemporaries and on his own sons.

Niederland was the first in our generation to rediscover the importance of Moritz Schreber's ideas on education, through the *Kallipädie* and the influential dissertation by Ritter (1936). It is interesting that Ritter, a teacher, understood so well Schreber the physician; this is in keeping with the fact that teachers were the principal propagators of Schreber's ideas. However, Niederland was not concerned with Schreber's ideas as such but only as pathogens for Paul's hallucinations and delusions,[33] and the principal pathogens Niederland singled out were those legendary "torture machines."

SCHREBER'S "TORTURE MACHINES": NEITHER SADIST NOR CHILD ABUSER

It is the posture-improving appliances that have procured for Schreber the reputation of a malevolent and sadistic educator. It is due to the horrific imagery created by the exaggerated descriptions of these allegedly immobilizing and pain-producing appliances by Niederland, and the even greater distortions by Schatzman, that this legend about Moritz Schreber arose and took root in the popular imagination. When I ask people at random, both in the field of psychiatry and among the cultured laymen, for their first idea in connection with the name Schreber, I very often see a smile accompanying the response "Oh yes, the guy who tied up his son and tortured him with those machines." Of course, these beliefs were fostered by yet another association: the interpretation of the content of certain hallucinations and delusions experienced by Paul at Sonnenstein during his second hospitalization. The exaggerations about the father fed into the constructions about the son; the constructions about the son became proof of the behavior of the father. The hermeneutic vicious circle seemed to be both plausible and satisfying: in the process, fictions became historical facts. It is a fact, nevertheless, that appliances were only a small facet of Moritz Schreber's medical philosophy and educational writings, just as the alleged parallels to them in the *Memoirs* are but a fraction of the content of the son's experiences. Both Niederland and Schatzman correlated the alleged parallel experiences of Paul at Sonnenstein with the alleged tortures that took place in childhood—but not with events that took place at Sonnenstein.[34] Thus, for example, the experience described by Paul Schreber as "compression-of-the-chest-miracle" was said to be caused by the father using on him an appliance called the straight-holder. How did it come about that the pyramid was made to stand on its tip?

To trace this, we shall reexamine the ways in which Moritz Schreber described and prescribed these notorious "instruments of torture" and what was made of them. The posture-improving aids were first illustrated in *Postures* (1853) and later in the *Kallipädie*; and the illustrations of them in these books excited all the heated imaginings about father and son, beginning with the tendentious representations by Niederland, who first commented on them, on down to the sundry Schreber commentators.[35]

There are 16 illustrations in *Postures*, depicting the following: a brace for clubfoot; bed straps for sleeping flat on the back; a device for holding the body erect; and the famous *Geradehalter*, or straight-holder,[36] a device used to foster the habit of sitting straight at the table. The bed straps are again shown in the *Kallipädie*, now simplified as one strap across the shoulders. Five figures depict the correction of bow-legs in different ages. One figure depicts a head-holder. Two figures depict a chin-band for prognathous jaws. The balance of the figures illustrate gymnastic exercises. And that is the entire "torture" inventory; this is what all the noise has been about. Let us compare what Moritz Schreber said about these appliances and how they were seen by others.

The best known of the postural aids was the straight-holder, which Schreber (1858a) describes in the *Kallipädie*:

Placed just at the *level of the shoulders*. . . . [t]his bar foils every attempt to sit askew because it is positioned across the clavicles and the shoulder bones in front. However, due to the unpleasant feeling quickly caused by the *pressure of the hard body on the bones*, the child will not maintain such a leaning posture for a long time and will *revert by itself to a free erect posture* [p. 204; emphasis added].

The following facts stand out in this description: The aid is described in the section of the *Kallipädie* dealing with children aged eight to sixteen and was thus recommended for use in school age children—not as implied by Niederland (1974), "between two and eight years of age" (p. 51). The aid is leaned against; it does not surround or compress the chest. When its present shape was described by Schreber, in 1853 and 1858, his son Paul was 11 and 16 years old, respectively, thus also of school age. Therefore, it is neither proven nor plausible that Moritz Schreber used the straight-holder on his son when he was a young child and in the manner described by Niederland (1974):

> The father, obsessively preoccupied with the children's postural system, invented a series of orthopedic apparatus, the so-called *Schreber'sche Geradehalter* . . . to secure a straight and upright body posture day and night. One of these contraptions consisted of a system of iron bars fastened to the chest of the child as well as to the table near which the child was sitting; the horizontal bar pressed against the chest and prevented any movement forward or sideward, giving only some freedom to move backward to an even more rigidly upright position. I believe that this device, apparently applied for several hours every day, constitutes the fragment of historic truth recognizable in the "compression-of-the-chest" delusion [p. 77].

This cannot be the only explanation of this delusion. We do not know whether the aid was used on Paul, his elder brother, or his sisters (girls are shown in the pictures); Moritz Schreber says that he conducted "many trials on [his] own children and on the patients in [his] orthopedic institute" (1858a, p. 203). Trials are not the same as steady use. Nor were these measures "aimed at physical and emotional restraint" (Niederland, 1974, p. 50). These appliances were no more menacing than braces for the teeth.[37]

These points present a challenge to a crucial argument of Niederland's:

> One can assume that by the time the child Schreber entered his third or fourth year of life, he had already undergone a notable degree of traumatization. At about that time the father, bent as he was on his stated goal "to eradicate the child's crude nature . . . and to put down its ignoble parts" embarked on a more complex and more ambitious program of regimented upbringing. He brought to bear on the child the whole system of medical gymnastics, calisthenic exercises, orthopedic appliances, and other regulatory practices which he had invented . . . The young boy seems to have been subjected to what Sylvester has named "gadget experience," that is, a combination of ego-disruptive

experiences that come from the application of mechanical contraptions on the child's body, for orthopedic or other purposes, and that can result in serious distortions of the child's body image, ego structure, reality testing, and object relations [1974, p. 72].

Again, let us note that Niederland supposes that the posture improving regime was initiated when Paul was in his "third or fourth" year of life, which is at variance with Moritz's specific recommendation that it be used for children aged 8 to 16. Moreover, Niederland indiscriminately generalizes the use of the gadgets to include the "whole system . . . and other regulatory practices," even though methods of education and the use of gadgets are in altogether different realms. It should be obvious that subjecting a young child to the use of appliances is not the same as with an older child. The young child is in danger of being traumatized by a procedure for which he cannot comprehend the reasons whereas an older child who is capable of understanding the reason for enduring a boring posture-improving device and accepting it temporarily as a necessary evil. The same objections apply to Schatzman's (1973) assessment of the effect of these gadgets, since he used the same arguments as Niederland.

These gadgets were meant to be used for limited periods of time as aversive conditioning aids to inculcate the proper postural habits; once such habits were established, after some months, their use was discontinued. Moritz Schreber believed that such use was a simpler and more effective method than nagging the child with rebukes and admonitions. Furthermore, Schreber was explicitly against using bodily restraints. He says this about infants in an already quoted passage in *Scoliosis* (1846): "Already the suckling infant feels the need to give his body a workout by means of thrusting and kicking movements of his arms and legs, so that the wrapping of infants should be done *completely free from restraints* (p. 21; emphasis Schreber's).

Similar views were expressed six years later. Since muscular growth is essential for the normal development of the child,

> every opportunity should at all times be given to the child to have freedom to move his limbs at will, at first when lying on its back (therefore it should be swaddled loosely and left unbound altogether at frequent intervals during the day); also later, when crawling, running and bustling about; and from the age of four or five on, when given to more vigorous and yet balanced gymnastic exercises, such as jumping, climbing, working out, swimming, etc. [Schreber, 1852b, p. 35].

These recommendations for unhampered movement for infants and children are even more noteworthy when one considers the practice of swaddling infants that was widespread at that time. Schreber was against swaddling. Niederland and Schatzman are silent on this issue. But if traumatic immobilization in infancy was so important for the shaping of the adult delusion, then it is important to know if it was practiced in the Schreber household. Such information is not available.

Schreber's attitude against physical restraint appears in *Postures* (1853) in connection with a discussion on the effect of tight clothing on the posture habits of boys and girls:

> Generally, the principal condition for all kinds of clothing is the following: that *the clothed body part is in no way pressed or narrowed thereby but allowed to maintain completely free and easy motion.* Holding fast to this condition should never be abandoned throughout the *entire* growing *period* [p. 78; emphasis Schreber's].

After discussing the untoward effects of tight clothing on the chest and armpits and circulation and respiration, Schreber (1853) discusses girls' corsets. While corsets are fine, he says, for grown women, in obedience to the dictates of fashion,

> it is in fact irresponsible, as happens so often, when young girls are allowed to be prematurely turned into fashion dolls and coerced to wear the usual corsets. This not only inhibits the free movement so necessary for the unhampered development of the whole body, but also, due to pressure and change of position, negatively affects the noblest inner organs of the chest and abdomen which have not yet attained their full development. This is also the only reason that spine deformities are not prevented, as some believe, but rather facilitated by the currently used corsets [p. 82].

If the case for the orthopedic appliances has been overstated and misstated, the presentation of Schreber's educational methods has not fared much better. Niederland described Schreber's child rearing methods as "studiously applied terror"; Schatzman renamed them "persecution." Yet in the *Kallipädie* are repeated statements about loving and humane attitudes in the rearing of children. Even if one were to take exception to the harsh suppression of what Schreber saw as wanton crying and screaming at the age of five to six months, one should not overlook his positive statements about rearing of children of ages of two to seven: "A cheerful, talkative, laughing, singing, playful conduct towards the child, without becoming excessively exhausting or numbing, is the true life balm for the child" (1858a, p. 65): "Nay, the only prize consistent with the aims of education for the good attitudes and actions of the child is *a word of recognition, a higher grade of satisfaction and friendliness coming from the parents, and occasionally also a loving playing-together and joking-together"* (p. 139, emphasis Schreber's). When speaking of children aged eight to sixteen, Schreber lays great stress on inculcating the values of responsibility, consistency, fairness, forgiveness, and independence.

Niederland's solution to the contradiction between the imputed malevolence and the stated benevolence was to postulate that

> another relevant factor ... connected with the father's psychopathology in a more direct way. His defensive struggle against his own sadism is frequently manifest in his texts on child care; for instance, he insists that all manipulative practices and coercive actions on the child's body be performed "iucunde," that is in a manner pleasurable and enjoyable to the child. The impact of this procedure on the child's psychosexual development, the intense overstimulation thus produced, the premature interference with libidinal needs in general, and the emphasis on homosexual libido in particular, the peculiar mixture of brutally enforced, then again pleasurably induced passivity—all these require little further analytic elaboration. Nor is it surprising to find among the elder Schreber's prescriptions such additional suggestions as his recommendation of enemas "as the most subtle of laxatives" [p. 73].

I have not seen the expression *"iucunde"* (enjoyably) in Schreber's text. However, such a cynical dressing up of pain as pleasure is not suggested by Moritz himself. Nor is he covering up his severe manner of subduing a screaming six-month-old, nor is his attitude hypocritical. Niederland's reference to "emphasis on the homosexual libido" is unclear. If the argument is meant to save the sadistic father hypothesis from collapse and at the same time to pay homage to Freud's theory about repressed homosexual desires of the son toward the father, then this strategy fails on both counts. On one hand, even hypocritical benevolence—forgetting for the moment the deus ex machina quality of this construction—would have the effect of mitigating the sadism, even as it might create the preconditions for the future sexual masochist (which, at any rate, Paul Schreber was not). On the other hand, Niederland's argument does not do much for salvaging Freud's theory about a son's passive erotic longings for the father; such longings, according to the classical formulation of the negative (inverted) oedipal attitude of the son toward the father, were the son's ineluctable destiny, a product of the son's worshiping adoration of the father and in no way provoked by the father's behavior, whether seductive or sadistic.

On the other hand, the strategy used by Schatzman was not to try to reconcile the obvious contradictions in Schreber's text but to expunge them, to doctor quotations or to fall into mistranslations, thus creating an impression of coercive manipulation, cruelty, and ruthlessness in Moritz.[38]

In addition to the *Kallipädie*, Schatzman dismissed another work of Moritz Schreber, *The Methodical Training of the Acuity of Sense Organs* (1859c), as an example of the irrational persecution of the child, allegedly at some point applied to little Paul Schreber. When quoting from that essay of Schreber's Schatzman (1973) says:

> He insists on eye exercises for children in his booklet the *Systematically Planned Sharpening of the Sense Organs*: to distract quickly a child's visual attention, to force him to estimate dimensions of similar objects at different distances, to judge various distances, etc. (1859, p. 11). In another book, in a section called "The Care, Education, and Sharpening of the Sense Organs," he recommends "the proper alternation between looking near and far . . . (1858, p. 215) [p. 35].

In that essay Moritz Schreber does not mention any forcing or distracting quickly of "a child's" visual attention. He is discussing training the acuity of visual perception in school children for the purpose of observing and appreciating nature, as a total body and mind activity, and encourages teachers to take walking tours with their students, to engage them in friendly conversations, and to show them an appreciation of details and how they fit into the whole. In the other work alluded to by Schatzman, the *Kallipädie*, eye exercises are discussed only in two paragraphs in a section entitled "The Training and Care of Individual Parts," starting on page 214, and there is no section with the title indicated by Schatzman. The same ideas are discussed at greater length in yet another work, *A Medical Perspective on School Affairs with the Purpose to Heal and Not to Hurt* (1858b), in a section simply entitled "The Care of Vision." Again, speaking of school children, Schreber pleads for training eyesight at school, both indoors and outdoors, on objects far and near, and warns that such eye exercises should not be pursued beyond the physiological limits but should alternate with periods of rest.

As a result of another mistranslation Moritz Schreber is portrayed as a father who "may have wished to penetrate children sexually. Possibly he sometimes experienced his sons as women and somehow conveyed it to them. Perhaps the author of the *Memoirs* [i.e, his son Paul] understood this and, in ascribing to God certain wishes and motives towards himself, was remembering wishes and motives he once had ascribed to his father" (Schatzman, 1973, p. 84).[39] Again, this is not only unproven, but highly improbable. Schatzman's tendentiously sexual reading, more Freudian than Freud, hangs in thin air; its only proof derives from a mistranslation. It is due to Schatzman inability to appreciate the nature metaphors and similes that are in frequent use in the writings of Moritz Schreber and his contemporaries and that abound in authors such as Herder. Thus, when Schreber talks of the seeds (*Samenkorn*) and germs (*Keim*), he does not mean sperm or female gonads.[40]

The wrong-headed insistence on an explicitly sexual, and sexualized, reading of Moritz's words reaches its uppermost limits with deMause's (1987) work. Endorsing the views of Casper Schmidt and extrapolating from Paul's adult experiences to sexual abuse in childhood—"considering these delusions as real memories"—deMause concludes that Moritz Schreber seduced his son, committing both oral and anal sexual acts upon him. What is the limit of absurdity?

It was Freud (1911a) who first felt "justified in . . . introducing Schreber's father into his delusions . . ." because "such a father as this was by no means unsuitable for transfiguration into a God in the affectionate memory of the son from whom he had been so early separated by death" (p. 51). Freud also saw the father behind the figure of Flechsig. The justification was provided by Paul's own talk of " 'God Flechsig' " and because " 'Flechsig' and 'God' belonged to the same class" (Freud, 1911a, p. 49). In spite of these delusional splittings and condensations, however, it was clear to Freud that Paul was quite able "to distinguish the 'soul Flechsig' from the living man of the same name, the Flechsig of his delusions from the real Flechsig" (p. 40). It is the real Flechsig who will be the subject of our next chapter.

NOTES

1. *Orthobiotics*, a word meaning "the right and harmonious life," was also used by Heinroth, a psychiatrist of the school of the *Psychiker*, or the soul psychiatrists, in a book he published in 1839, *Orthobiotik oder die Lehre vom richtigen Leben* (Orthobiotics or the Science of Right Living). In 1827 Heinroth, who was inspired by Kant, published *Psychologie als Selbsterkenntnislehre oder die Lehre vom richtigen Leben* (Psychology as a Science of Self-Knowledge or the Science of Right Living). He was a friend of the Schreber family, a godfather to Moritz Schreber's firstborn, Gustav, and until 1843 chair of the department of psychiatry of Leipzig University, a position that remained unoccupied until 1882, when Flechsig arrived. I was able to find an English translation of Heinroth's (1838) work on education, but not the German original. The anonymous author of the preface quotes Heinroth as saying, "In Education, as in every thing else, much depends on unity and connexion. . . . [Heinroth] discovered . . . that Education considered as comprehensive—not merely a part, but of the entire Life and Being of Man, in which way it can alone fulfil its complete destination—is still an uncultivated field, which would repay

culture with an abundant harvest." Moritz Schreber may have been inspired by these words. The book contains 16 sections; one, entitled "Preliminary Education" is about infant care, and includes the following passages:

> To the Infant, three things are necessary: Care and Nursing, Regularity, and Protection [p. 71].
> The life and welfare of the new-born infant require the constant protection of a guardian genius; and this guardian genius is maternal love. This is what makes its existence no isolated being but a spiritual life within that of the mother. Fanned by this breath of life, the infant bud unfolds itself most favorably and when deprived of it, is exposed to frost and blighting mildew. The waking heart of the infant, losing its pole of attraction, is forced to learn betimes to exist alone; and desertion is death to the heart. Maternal love, too, is the food of the developing moral powers, even when the infant seeks its bodily nourishment, at its mother's breast; and happy they who find it there; for an instinct then exists between mother and child, which is nothing less than an opening—though, in the child, as yet unconscious, Love [pp. 71-72].
> The child has a natural desire of loving and of being loved [p. 90].
> Ignorant servants may exercise very injurious influence on the tender, undeveloped minds of children, by frightening them, when noisy and troublesome, by violent scolding, or the infliction of actual pain, which drives the defenseless beings to a gloomy feeling of irritation, and embitters their lives, before they have attained distinct self-consciousness. Self-preservation prompts them to offer an ineffectual resistance by redoubled cries; but the more they scream, the more severely are they chastised by their cruel tormentors; and thus the scarcely awakened life is wounded and torn asunder in its inmost depths of feeling, and the foundation laid of an irritable, hostile, disposition. It is the sacred duty of the parents to protect their children against both these kinds of mismanagement, and they cannot be too careful or watchful of those to whom they entrust the charge, where they are unable to take it upon themselves [p. 76].

The last point is offered for future comparison with one of Moritz's recommendations as to how to deal with a naggingly screaming child.

2. Hufeland was also influenced by the great Austrian physician, Johann Peter Frank (1745-1821), an important pioneer of public health and prevention whose teachings were followed by Heinroth and must have been known to Moritz Schreber as well. "The whole field of public health was surveyed in the basic and monumental work of Johann Peter Frank. . . . His six-volume *Complete System of Medical Policy* [was] published between 1777 and 1817" (Ackerknecht, 1955, p. 129). He is also credited with being "interested in methods of physiotherapy" and was thus a pioneer in the promotion of "massage and gymnastics, both closely allied to orthopedics" (p. 183). Frank is quoted in the anthology of quotable quotes on the educational value of gymnastics in Stephany (1848), along with Plato, Rousseau, Koch (1830), and

the noted Swiss professor of anatomy, Meckel (who edited a work by Clias, 1829). Hufeland's influence on ideas about gymnastics entertained by educators is perhaps reflected in *Turning according to Medical and Pedagogical Principles* by the Deputirten (1869), that is the Delegates of Berlin Teacher Associations and the Hufeland Medical–Surgical Society.

Although credit for discovering the smallpox vaccine goes to the Englishman Edward Jenner, in 1796, Hufeland wrote about smallpox as early as 1787, following an epidemic in Weimar; in *Ueber die Ausrottung der Pocken* (On Eradication of Small Pox) Hufeland advocated isolation as the only method known at that time. Although the second edition (1931) of Hirsch's (1887) *Lexikon* cites Hufeland's 1787 work, there is no mention of a 1788 work, *Observations on Natural and Inoculated Small Pox*, which had a second edition (1793), both preceding Jenner's 1798 *Inquiry into the Causes and Effects of the Variolae Vaccine*.

3. B. C. Faust (1755-1842), was a prominent physician of his day. The original *Catechism* was first published in 1792 in Bückeburg by Johann Friedrich Althaus; by 1830 it was in its 11th edition, selling some 150,000 copies. It was reissued in facsimile in 1925 by Dr. Martin Vogel. It was translated into many languages, including English: *A New Guide to Health Compiled from the Catechism of Dr. Faust with Additions and Improvements Selected from the Writings of Men of Eminence/ Designed for the Use of Schools and Private Families* (Newburyport, MA: W. & J. Gilman). Another work by Faust is from 1791: *How to Regulate the Sex Drive of People and How to Make People Better and Happier*. Note the concern for happiness and improvement, as well as the concern for sex, a whole century before Freud. *Catechism*, so named because its chapters are composed of questions and answers, obtained the official imprimatur of the Great Hochfürst (Prince) of Schaumburg-Lippe and the School Board.

4. The full title of Hufeland's (1836) book is, *Good Advice to Mothers on the Most Important Points of the Physical Education of Children in the First Years and on Teaching Young Couples How to Care for the Unborn*. Hufeland was at that time councillor of state and private physician to the King and Queen of Prussia, to whom the book is dedicated. According to Hirsch (1887), the first edition of the book appeared in 1799, following an earlier work of 1794: *Memoir to Mothers who Have the Health of Their Children Close at Heart*, in which Hufeland describes humane, enlightened, and rational methods of child rearing and discusses the main childhood diseases. There is a special addendum with the title "Deformities in Children, Their Prevention and Cure," which anticipates many of Schreber's ideas.

5. The influence of Immanuel Kant (1724-1804) on his contemporaries and the generations that came after him is immeasurable. In connection with *Mind* (1798a), compare "*On the Power of the Mind to Master Morbid Feelings by Mere Resolution*, #63 in Gabriele Rabel, *Kant* (Oxford: Clarendon Press, 1963), pp. 350-355, an exchange between Kant and Hufeland from 1797. See also his *Anthropology from a Pragmatic Point of View* (1800), and *Lectures on Ethics* (1779-82). *Mind* was in Freud's library. The opening remark in Hufeland's preface to *Mind* reads: "The mind (*Geist*) alone lives—the life of the mind is alone the true life. The life of the body is forever subordinated to it and the mind is its master,

not the other way around, that the mind should be subordinated to the whims, moods and drives of the body, if true life is to be preserved" (Hufeland, 1824, in Kant, 1798a, p. 9).

6. Kant also wrote a small treatise on education, *Über Pädagogik*. Kant was influenced by Rousseau's *Émile* and the pietists (see chapter 3), by his experience as a private tutor and by his own moral philosophy, to conclude that education was necessary for the perfection of mankind. He accepted Rousseau's optimism and expressed a respect for the child's liberty. He was more in favor of training mental faculties than in the amassing of information. In matters of religion he combined the idea of the deity with moral principles. He was against corporal punishment and punishing the child out of rancor and conceived a "Moral Catechism," which dealt, among others, with the rights of man (based on Compayre, 1889).

7. According to Hirsch (1887, second edition 1929), Schultz-Schultzenstein did his first researches in plant physiology, became professor of medicine in Berlin and was also president of the Society for Garden Architecture. He believed in a kind of vitalism, such that the life processes were not maintained by chemical metabolism alone but by the appearance and disappearance of "rejuvenated structures" and enhanced by muscular activity, which was viewed as independent of nerves. He also wrote of the importance of correct body posture and of good breathing and against the use of corsets. He extended the notion of rejuvenation to the psychological sphere, as in "the nutrition of the senses," the "assimilation of sensory impressions," and the "education of the sense organs." As vitalist, he later clashed with the foremost exponents of more scientific views, such as Du Bois Reymond and Virchow.

8. In their "Translators' Introduction" to the *Memoirs* the otherwise careful Macalpine and Hunter vilified Moritz Schreber as having "published a number of books of which the titles alone, quite apart from their text, show that he was eccentric, not to say a crank." This is a sweeping statement by people who apparently did not bother to read what Moritz Schreber really said. They also mistranslated the title of one of his book as *How to Achieve Happiness and Bliss by Physical Culture* (M, Introduction, footnote, p. l). First, there is nothing about physical culture in the title, and second, '*Glückseligkeit*' is simply the early 19th-century term for inner happiness and adding the word bliss works as an innuendo ("Certain passages in the Memoirs bring home how much our author was a chip off the old block," p. 1), implying a connection between "crank" Moritz's disquisitions and crazy Paul's delusions about voluptuous and heavenly bliss.

The first edition of Hartmann's *Happiness* was printed in 1808 by Voss of Dessau and Leipzig. The third revised edition was published by Voss in 1841. Moritz Schreber (1861b) used the text of the third edition to bring it out as the revised fourth (published by Geibel in Leipzig) in the last year of his life. The seventh edition was published in 1865. The 13th edition of the book, by Georg Reichardt of Leipzig, came out in 1892. All these editions had a preface by Moritz Schreber. The third edition was also printed in Berlin by Elwin Staude, in 1872 and 1887, under a new title: *Die Kunst des Lebens froh zu werden und dabei Gesundheit, Schönheit, Körper, und Geistesstärke zu erhalten und zu vervollkomnen.*

Eine Glückseligkeitlehre für das physische Leben des Menschen (The Art of Being Happy in Life and How to Preserve and Perfect Health, Beauty, and Strength of Body and Mind. A Happiness Doctrine for the Physical Life of Man). The new German title created a verbal bridge to Hufeland's *Art of Preserving Life.* Hartmann (1820) acknowledges his roots in Kant, Fichte, Schelling and Reil, among others, in his book *The Mind of Man in its Relations to Physical Life, or the Outline of a Physiology of Thinking. For physicians, philosophers and people in the higher sense of the word.*

9. This brief sketch is taken from Dr. David Winternitz (1860), Hirsch (1887), and from the *Neue Deutsche Biographie* (Berlin: Duncker & Humblot, 1965).

10. Thus Ritter (1936) wrote that Moritz was influenced by Schelling (my only disagreement with him) while Ackerknecht (1968) classes Heinroth with romantic physicians and Dörner (1969) sees in him a theological psychiatrist. An opinion that the *Psychiker* were more in harmony with the ideas of enlightenment than romanticism was expressed in a letter to me from Dr. J. E. Meyer of Göttingen of June 12, 1989.

11. Thus Schelling viewed nature as a besouled and creative organism, as a living process of becoming. He taught that self and nature are identical and that nature is ruled by the tension between polarities, or opposites; he argued for an affinity between the philosophy of nature and the philosophy of religion. Schelling and his followers, such as the mystical and pantheistic Fechner in his earlier days, may have been a source for some of the ideas of Paul Schreber.

12. The new department was at first considered as part of medicine (Sänger, 1963, p. 18). Heinroth was a physician's son and, like Moritz, he was first a personal physician to Count Rasumovsky. He studied medicine in Vienna under J. P. Frank and was later in charge of the St. Georgen, an orphanage, correction, and chronic city hospital in Leipzig. His interest in anthropology may also have been inspired by the philosopher E. Platner (1744–1818), who wrote *Anthropologie.*

13. Gemüth has a number of meanings that in German are given by the context. It also means the emotions in general, and refers to feeling or affect. Thus, *Gemüthskrankheiten* are affective disorders, usually considered to be in the neurotic rather than the psychotic, range of disorders.

14. Until now the ideas in *Gymnastics* have not been discussed in the Schreber literature, except for some that are taken up by Schreiber (1987).

15. The 23rd edition of this most popular book by Moritz was revised and enlarged by Rudolf Graefe and printed in 1889, when Paul was 47 years old, four years after his first illness and four years before his second. The 26th edition was translated into English by H. A. Day and published in New York in 1899. The quoted passages are identical with those in the German 23rd edition, and I am using H. A. Day's translation, unless otherwise indicated.

16. In the second edition of his book Niederland (1984) added a section in the epilogue concerning the "anti-masturbatory instructions and devices of Schreber's father" (p. 169), an assertion that gained acceptance among psychoanalysts. The fact is that although Moritz Schreber was concerned with the

supposed dangers of masturbation, there is no mention of such devices in any of Schreber's books nor evidence that he recommended such use in children. Thus, a caveat is in order. To make his point, Niederland reproduced a number of illustrations supplied by the National Library of Medicine (figure 14, Niederland, 1984, p. 170, a device that received an American patent in 1905) and a few others, taken from a Gerhart S. Schwarz (1973b), which also come from a time after Moritz Schreber. Thus, figures 15 and 16 in Niederland (1984, p. 171), which are figures 5 and 7 in Schwarz (1973b), are illustrations of so-called spermatorrhea rings recommended for adult masturbators and described by a J. L. Milton in *Lancet*, 1854; figure 18 (Niederland, 1984, p. 172), the same as figure 11 in Schwarz, dates from 1917. The evils of masturbation at school and at home were on the minds of many physicians at that time, as expressed, for example by Lion (1863, p. 20).

17. Schreber's concept of ennoblement (or cultivation, in the sense of cultured and civilized) is paralleled by Freud's concept of sublimation, which combines the alchemic simile of converting dross into gold, the chemical simile of passing from solid to gas (i.e., spirit), and the culture metaphor of passing from the base to the sublime.

18. Israëls (1989) claims that "books on the history of education . . . contain no mention of him [Moritz Schreber] at all" (p. 243), citing (p. 239) only one work—Schmidt (1867)—without any such mention. The statement is sweeping and untrue. In chapter 3 I have quoted a number of works of predecessors, contemporaries and followers of Schreber in the subject of athletics and gymnastics—that is, physical education—which is an essential part of education, as, for example, expressed in Cotta (1902). Israëls himself cites the reference works of Heindl (1859), Hirth (1865), and Euler (1895) on physical education, all of which contain mention of Moritz Schreber. He also appears in the second, expanded edition of Hirth's encyclopedia, edited by F. Rudolf Gasch (published in Hof by Rud. Lion, 1893). Schreber's works (1853, 1858b) were also cited by the Viennese educator Burgerstein (1887), writing on "Cultivation of Health in the Middle School." Schreber was also mentioned by Angerstein (1859, 1897) and Angerstein and Eckler (1887). However, Schreber's was seen as a *medical* authority, and as such he was subsequently eclipsed by the nonmedical specialized experts both in physical education (e.g., Kloss, J. C. Lion) and general education.

Contrary to Israëls's assertion, Schreber had entries in the standard encyclopedias of the 19th century: Brockhaus and Meyer. For the entry "Schreber (Daniel Gottlieb [one of the rare occasions with this spelling] Moritz)" in the 13th (1886) edition of Brockhaus's *Konversations-Lexikon* we read: "To his great credit are many publications about the reform of education, especially physical education," repeated in the 14th edition of 1898. The entry "Schreber, Daniel Gottlieb Moritz" in *Meyer's Neues Konversations-Lexikon*, second edition in 1867 (reprinted unchanged in 1871), we read: "held lectures on pediatrics . . . became known as a reformer, especially in physical education." Schreber (1855a) is cited in Schmid (1881-1887), in an article coauthored by Kloss (p. 607) and other works (Schreber, 1858a, b) in Schmid (1883-1885, pp. 796, 964). Baginski (1898, 1900) has multiple citations of

Schreber as well as Schildbach. Mentions of Schreber can be found in Lindner (1884), on pages 847 and 921.

Schreber (1891) is also cited in the influential encyclopedia of education of W. Rein (1895, p. 375) in the entry *Hauspädagogik* (home pedagogics) but is curiously missing from entries on body posture and boys' exercises. Rein was a Herbartian. The ninth volume of this encyclopedia, published in 1909, has Schreber's *Über Volkserziehung* (1860b) in the bibliography of the *"Kindergarten-Literatur"* compiled by Hermann Beyer. Schreber (1891) is also invoked by Ackermann (1895). Vogel, author (1877) of "The History of Education as a Science," cites the second (1875) edition of Schreber's *Pangymnastikon* in his "Systematic Encyclopedia of Education" (1881), in the index and in bibliographies of chapters on school dietetics (p. 38) and physical culture (p. 161). E. Steiger, a major publisher in the field of education (for example, Barnard, 1872), also printed *Steiger's (n.d.) Catalog,* in New York, in the latter part of the 19th century. In the section *Pädagogik,* Schreber (1860) is listed under "Miscellaneous works on general pedagogics" and under "Physical education—School dietetics" listed Schreber (1858b) and (1861c). Educated people in America in the 19th century read German, and German education was world-famous. This is by no means a complete list, but it suggests that even though Schreber was gradually being displaced by new currents, he did not disappear completely. Thus, he is described as a trailblazer in the 1917 *Lexikon der Pädagogik* of O. Willmann, edited by E. M. Roloff (Freiburg: Herder). As correctly indicated by Israëls, Schreber's educational works were only translated into Dutch, for example, his 1858b, by J. L. Dusseau as *Genesekundige wenken het schoolwezen* (Utrecht: C. vand der Post).

19. Eisler (1928) defines dietetics as the art of living a right and purposeful life of the mind, especially through a discipline of body and mind under the rule of reason. In this context Eisler also mentions Hufeland's *Macrobiotics,* Hartmann's (1841) *Glückseligkeitslehre,* and E. v. Feuchtersleben's *Zur Diätetik der Seele,* translated into English in 1910 as *Health and suggestion: The dietetics of the mind* (New York: B. W. Huebsch). V. Feuchtersleben is also the author of the influential *Lehrbuch der Ärztlichen Seelenkunde* (Textbook of Medical Psychology), published in 1845. The latter book was in Freud's library, but he did not mention Feuchtersleben in his writings.

20. Jean Jacques Rousseau (1712-1778) wrote *Émile ou Traité de l'Éducation* in 1762. The work influenced Kant's small treatise on education. Although Rousseau's style has led to his being viewed as a romantic, the ideas are mainly those of enlightenment. Pestalozzi (1746-1827) made a major impact with his novel *Leonard and Gertrude,* published in 1781, in which he spoke of the power of education in social renewal. Pestalozzi (1807) also wrote about gymnastics: *On Body Building; as Introduction to a Trial of Elementary Gymnastics in a Series of Body Exercises.* F. W. A. Froebel (1782-1852), born in Thuringia, was founder of the kindergarten system; in his philosophy he was heavily influenced by Fichte and Schelling. He believed in the unity of nature and God and expanded Fichte's idea of self-activity. His most important book was *Menschenerziehung* (1826). Another important work of Froebel was *Mutter and Koselieder* published in the United States in 1895 in a translation by Susan E. Blow, as *The*

Mottoes and Commentaries of Friedrich Froebel's Mother Play (New York: Appleton, 1909). Compared to Moritz Schreber, Froebel placed enormous emphasis on the role of the mother.

21. Fichte's ideas, especially in his *Addresses to the German Nation* (1808), were also important in rousing the Germans to nationalism and patriotism against the French following the conquest of Germany by Napoleon. Fichte's ideas were sadly misrepresented by Schatzman (1973), who proclaimed him to be "a philosophical forefather of Nazism" (p. 136) on the basis of a number of random doctored quotations from Fichte. In his "Theory of State" (a series of lectures delivered in 1813 shortly before his death), Fichte used Plato's idea about education in an ideal state, the kingdom of reason, in which educators, not the home, would be the leaders of a national education. This idea Fichte combined with ideals of Christianity: "The kingdom of justice demanded by reason and the kingdom of heaven on earth promised by Christianity is one and the same. The latter therefore guarantees the former. This *fact* is undoubted" (Fichte quoted in Turnbull, 1926, p. 272). Of the ideal education Fichte wrote the following:

> This education is easily determined by its general aim. Everyone is to understand clearly God's will with him and subordinate himself in clear self-perception, which can represent no difference in it, to that universal law of the spiritual world. This presupposes the clear general view, that man is subject to the will of God and that without obedience he is nothing and does not really exist at all. Now this view is that of Christianity or of philosophy, which are synonymous in this connection. The necessary education must, therefore, possess the art of bringing all men without exception infallibly to this view and, in order that this may be possible, of forming men from the beginning out of what is common to all, in such a way that this knowledge may be imparted to them with certainty [quoted in Turnbull, 1926, p. 273].

Note the use of the concept of God in the ethical–philosophical, rather than ecclesiastical, manner. Ideas about national education were also on the mind of J. Scheinert (1845-1846), a member of the Historical-Theological Society of Leipzig, author of *Education of the People*.

22. The word *Kallipädie*, came into German from French. Like *orthopédie*, *callipédie* was a Greek hybrid (from *kalos*, beautiful, and *paidos*, child), and it appears in the title *Callipédie* by Claude Quillet (1602-1661), as cited by Peiper (1957).

23. "*Tout est bien sortant des mains de l'auteur des choses, tout dégenere entre les mains de l'homme* [Everything that comes from the hand of the creator of things is good, everything degenerates in the hands of man]."

24. In Rein (1895), in the entry "Ruling of Children" (*Regierung der Kinder*), the post-Herbartian view of ruling and punishment methods is explicated. Herbart divided education into instruction (didactics), and guidance (hogedetics), the latter further subdivided into ruling and punishment. This, of course, applied to the school, not the home. Compare with similar ideas in Spock (1945): not fussing too much over the baby, letting the baby cry itself out.

25. This reverberates with Paul's concern that Flechsig has told him white lies (*Memoirs*, p. 35).

26. Thoughts on education in the school were developed by Schreber in his *Medical Perspective on School Affairs with the Purpose to Heal and Not to Hurt* (1858b) and *The Methodical Training of the Acuity of Sense Organs* (1859c), both highly regarded and cited by experts in school hygiene and instruction. They qualify as examples of what Schreber viewed as a "rational science of education," aimed at the integration "not only of the physical but also of the disciplinary, doctrinal and moral aspects . . . aimed at human nature as a *whole*, that is the unification of the physical and the mental" (as rendered by Heindl, 1859, p. 397). No doubt, this rational attitude is also of Kantian inspiration. For Kant's ideas about education, see footnote 6.

27. In the summer of 1989, in the library of the Karl Marx University in Leipzig, I found a separate *Supplement zum "Anthropos." Entwickelungsleben des menschlichen Organismus* (Development of the Human Organism). This supplement deals with the anatomy and development of the sexual organs. In it Schreber repeats his ideas about sexual continence.

28. This conception of the mind–body connection is in the main expounded by Kant in his 1766 work, *The Dreams of a Seer Explained through the Dreams of Metaphysics* (Kant, 1766). Similar ideas were held by Friedrich Paulsen, a contemporary of Paul Schreber.

29. The role of the brain stem in awareness became known thanks to the work of the American neurophysiologist Magoun around 1950. Flechsig had not dreamed of it.

30. The expression *gottwärtsgerichtet* (turned toward God) was also used by the Schreber daughters in the much quoted Siegel (1909) interview. Israëls (1989, p. 69) believed to have disposed of the alleged distortions of many authors (most cuttingly of Niederland's, but also of Croufer's and Schilling's) to conclude: "I do not think religion played a very dominant role in the Schrebers' life: Moritz Schreber wrote little on religion and expressly warned . . . against too early religious instruction," referring to Schreber's remark in the *Kallipädie* (p. 154). But Israëls missed the point entirely. Schreber on that page warns against a "premature start" (*vorzeitiges Beginnen*) in teaching the child about God, declaring that "the awareness of God" is innate to the spirit of man but that teaching about it should be postponed till age 8 or 9, rather than forcing (*Zwang*) the child by demands to participate in devotional activities, such as churchgoing and praying.

Schreber's religiosity was thus a deep theologico-mystico-philosophical deism, as was characteristic of Fichte (see note 21). Compare also the statement by Carl Hennig, professor of gynecology and director of the Women and Children Institute in Leipzig and the editor of the famous third edition of the *Kallipädie* (1891), in his preface to the earlier edition of 1882: "In the realm of religion, Schreber is moved by the great sages of all times and nations. In every relationship, he wants the generation bearing Christianity to show it in deeds, not words alone" (Schreber, 1891, p. ix), and Schreber's appeal to the Ministry of Education (1861d).

This same spirit was characteristic of Anna Jung, who read the Psalms,

Thomas à Kempis, and Zinzendorf. Frau Brigitte Wienstein (1989) also characterized the religious attitude in the family as ethical rather than devout, but Frau Friedrich felt there may have been an element of the strict and devout early on in Anna Jung.

31. I have in mind here Fichte's (1806) *Suggestions for a Happy Life, or also the Teaching of Religion.* Fichte's obsolete word for happy is *seelig,* which today is rendered as "blessed." It was also part of *glückselig,* innerly happy. This locution *selig,* with its multiple reverberations that include both happiness and pleasure, is very frequent in the *Memoirs.*

32. Johann Friedrich Herbart (1850), *Psychology as a Science, Newly Founded on Experience, Metaphysics and Mathematics.* Herbart's ideas were an important precursor of Freud's dynamic psychology; see Rosemarie Sand, "Early Nineteenth Century Anticipation of Freudian Theory, *International Review of Psycho-Analysis* 15 (1988):465. *General Pedagogics* by Heinrich Gräfe (1845) may have been read by Moritz Schreber.

33. Ritter, who was able to locate Moritz Schreber's thought in the march of ideas of 19th century German philosophy, was denounced by Schatzman (1973) as a Nazi "who saw in [Moritz Schreber] a spiritual precursor of Nazism" (p. 144), an accusation of which Israëls cleared Ritter. But then Israëls also attributed to Ritter a racist remark, which I could not find. However, even as he was indebted to Ritter for a number of crucial bibliographic sources, Israëls also did his share to belittle Schreber's ideas and to discredit Ritter in the process. Israëls lumped this dissertation together with what he called the self-serving Schreber garden literature. This error may have been facilitated by the fact that after the official publication of the thesis (defended in 1935) by the Erlangen University Press in 1936 it was reissued that year by the publisher Ohlenroth in Erfurt for the *Reichsbund der Kleingärtner und Kleinsiedler Deutschlands* (Federation of Small Gardeners and Homecrofters of Germany).

Ritter was a person versed in the history of education in Germany who was able to trace the further development of Schreber's educational ideas. Having corrected a number of Ritter's mistakes, Israëls overshot the mark: "Ritter *cunningly managed to suggest* that Moritz Schreber was closely involved with the associations and gardens: 'Enthusiastic supporters saw to his success *even* after his death. Schreber Associations were founded and Schreber gardens were laid out everywhere. . .'" (Israëls, 1989, pp. 255–256; emphasis added). This quote is mistranslated. Ritter meant to convey that Schreber had enthusiastic supporters both before and after his death. In fact, he (Ritter, 1936) first mentions Schreber's last works from 1861, then his many lectures and speeches delivered in medical societies, and continues: "In this way his fame spread. His influence after his death was continued by enthusiastic followers [*Dadurch war sein Namen rühmlich bekannt. Für seine Wirkung über seinem Tod sorgten begeisterte Anhänger*]" (p. 22). The little word 'even' has been insinuated into Ritter's text to reinforce the innuendo that Ritter "cunningly managed to suggest" something. But where is the cunning? By mere contiguity Israëls wants to insinuate that the enthusiastic supporters *were* members of the Associations, and nobody else. It is a historical fact that teachers in Leipzig—Hauschild, Mangner, Mittenzwey, Fritzsche, Gesell, Richter, Siegel—were indeed enthusiastic supporters of Schreber! (See also Lothane, 1991.)

34. The idea that the father terrorized his son was created in its entirety by Niederland; what Schatzman did was to call the terror "persecution" and to suggest that this terror/persecution was transformed in Paul's adulthood into paranoia. Both Niederland and Schatzman invoked interpersonal conceptions of paranoia, the former citing Ehrenwald, the latter Lacan and Szasz, but none applied it to the adult situation and the here-and-now. In their conceptions it is as if the childhood trauma traveled across intervening time and one day landed on Paul Schreber's head. Schatzman (1973) even stated in a footnote "Many experiences and acts of patients in mental hospitals seen by staff as symptoms of a 'disease process' can also be seen as patient's response to staff behavior; for an example of this, see Schatzman, 1970" (p. 101).

35. I have reproduced all but two pictures of the appliances in a journal article (Lothane, 1989b). Since I did not get to proofread that paper, a number of errors crept in, which are corrected in the present work.

Following the appearance of Schatzman's book, Gerhart S. Schwarz, M.D., then chairman of the Section of Historical Medicine of the New York Academy of Medicine, wrote to the editor of the London Times in reaction to the review of Schatzman (1973) by Gillie, in order to protest that some ideas were not true to fact (Schwarz, 1973a). Dr. Schwarz stated that "the statements in this enclosed letter are based upon the many publications by Dr. William G. Niederland." As historian of medicine, Dr. Schwarz objected to the description of the appliances as "Germanic," for "they were 'Victorian' and used everywhere in the Western world." In America, as described by Consuelo Vanderbilt Balsan (1952) in her autobiography, she used "a shoulder harness attached to a head-band by means of a rod, which she had to wear while writing and reading. Though she did not like it, she concludes that she owes her much admired neck and good posture to it . . . "; and in England, "a British book of 1870 extols in glowing colors the virtues of a shoulder harness (made in Vienna, to boot) which was far more formidable than Schreber's" (Schwarz, 1973a). Many of the illustrations that were attached to the Schwarz's letter, from an unnamed German book, can be found in Valentin (1961). Dr. Schwarz forwarded a copy of this letter to Dr. Niederland, who later gave it to me. The impression I get is that Dr. Schwarz did not view such methods as unduly repressive. Niederland (1984) thanked Dr. Schwarz for "making these illustrations available to [him]" and quoted another passage from Consuelo's autobiography where, in referring to her training in "lady-like behavior," she was subjected to

> "A horrible instrument . . . a steel rod which ran down my spine and was strapped to my waist and over my shoulders—another strap went around my forehead to the rod. I had to hold my book high when reading, and it was almost impossible to write in so uncomfortable a position" [Balsan, 1952]. Her description fits so completely the picture of Schreber's Geradehalter or body straightener (see pp. 53 and 54 of this book) that it appears certain that the apparatus she wears was modelled on one of Schreber's orthopedic inventions [p. 169].

Clearly, Niederland selected a much darker view of these matters. However, differences between Schwarz and Niederland in quoting Consuelo aside, two facts stand out: neither does the description of the "horrible instrument" fit Moritz Schreber's "straightener," for in the latter there was no steel rod running down the spine nor was any part of it fastened to the body; nor was Consuelo's horror modelled on Moritz's *Geradehalter*, but rather on devices like the *"Krückenfauteuil* (crutch-chair)" created in 1832 by the Swiss orthopedist Matthias Louis Mayor (1775-1847), who was in turn inspired by the French orthopedist Jean-André Venel (as per the illustrations sent by Schwarz to Niederland).

36. In my papers I used the translation "straightener" but now prefer "straight-holder." The prototype of the straight-holder was first described in *Scoliosis* (1846):

> [Parents and teachers are to] emphatically remind the child [to maintain] a straight posture of the spine and the head especially during writing, drawing or similar activities. Should such efforts fail, the following artificial means is recommended: one screws on the edge of the table, at a suitable height, a piece of toothed board, so that the toothed edge comes to be placed under the child's chin. It will not be long before the habit of sitting straight establishes itself so that the use of artificial means can be dispensed with [p. 27].

The use of the definitive form of the straight-holder is described in *Postures* (1853). Schreber believed that this was a simpler and gentler method of education, for it eliminated the burden of "reminders, reprimands and punishments, which only disturb the child in its work and achieve nothing" (*Postures*, p. 56). The aid is recommended for adults as well.

37. The straight-holder had a mixed reception by Dr. Lion senior, whose "School Hygiene," appears in *Deutsche Klinik*. That medical journal, 8(1856):509-510, earlier favorably reviewed Schreber's *Gymnastic* but in 1863, Dr. Lion (1863), writing in the journal's supplement nos. 2 and 3, says the following about the straight-holder depicted in Schreber (1858b): "We cannot hold brief for the device invented by Schreber, the *Geradehalter*. However, we do not want to ignore it, because some people speak well of it. . . . Such an implement looks almost like a punishment, a torture, it would not look well in the school and end up being a drudgery. It should rather be tried at home" (p. 19). It is self-contradictory that a torture implement at school should still be recommended for home use. The straight-holder was modified by Dr. Carl Hennig around 1880 and depicted in Schreber (1891) and in Niederland (1974). It has survived to our own time and was recommended in former East Germany (Bethge, 1981).

38. Thus, when quoting from page 135 of the *Kallipädie*, Schatzman, on his page 15, omits the mitigating phrase "The child should not be made into a slave of another's will." He translates *"Roheit"* (p. 136 of *Kallipädie*), the child's raw or untamed nature, as "innate barbarity." *"Mit Rastlosigkeit und Nachdruck"* (p. 140) becomes "ruthlessly and vigorously," where one could also say "indefatigably and firmly" (Lothane, 1989a).

Similarly, Schatzman's way of quoting Fichte is tendentious. This is how

Schatzman (1973, p. 137) uses the Fichte quotation (reproduced in Turnbull, 1926, p. 273) mentioned in footnote 19:

> Man is subject to the will of god . . . without *obedience he is nothing and does not really exist at all.* Now this view is that of Christianity or of philosophy *which are synonymous in this connection* [!] The necessary education must, therefore, possess the art of bringing all men without exception infallibly to this view . . .

Schatzman does not indicate that the emphases are his own, nor the context of these ideas, or—forgivably—make allowances for Fichte's style, known for its proneness to exaggeration, emphasis, and self-contradiction. That is still minor. However, Schatzman believes such a passage is sufficient grounds to advance the notion that "Fichte is considered a philosophical forefather of Nazism" (p. 136) and from this to conclude:

> *Remember,* Hitler and his peers were raised when Dr. Schreber's books, preaching household totalitarianism, were popular. I am not alone in intuiting a possible link between microsocial despotism in the Schreber family and the macrosocial despotism of Nazi Germany. Elias Canetti, a novelist and sociologist also did [p. 143].

This surely goes too far: it has the net effect of taking Hitler and his peers off the hook. As far as forefathers of Nazism are concerned, why single out Fichte and spare Hegel and Nietzsche? Why blame it on the alleged Schreber's "household totalitarianism"—not to be found in Schreber's books—and not on the reigning Herbartian variety and books that were much more popular than Schreber's at the time when Hitler (born 1889) and his peers were reared? As to Canetti (who will be discussed again in chapter 8), he did not say a thing about Moritz Schreber but reduced Hitlerism to Hitler's paranoia, and in turn explained Hitler's paranoia with the help of ideas about Paul Schreber's paranoia. We might as well blame Moritz Schreber for Stalin, for his books were also read in St. Petersburg and Moscow, should we follow this kind of logic.

Schatzman also quotes from Fichte's early writings on education, from the year 1789, reproduced by Turnbull (1926, pp. 129-130). Fichte is quoted as saying:

> It is the duty of parents to limit the freedom of children insofar as its use might be detrimental to the aim of education; but only so far . . . Parents ought not to forbid their children anything from mere caprice and in order, as they say, to break their will. It is only the will that runs counter to the aim of education that ought to be broken. Will in general, however, they ought to have; we are educating free beings, not will-less machines [Fichte, quoted in Turnbull, 1926, pp. 128-129].

These quotations are for Schatzman an example of Fichte's despotism in education. However, even without the mitigating qualifications from page 128 in Turnbull, Fichte advocates authoritarianism tempered by parental conscientiousness and religious ethics. This is not the same as a Hitler or a Stalin, as godless despotic leader, being deified by the masses.

True, authoritarianism in education has been and still is a problem that calls for solutions. But despotism and dictatorships have many complex causes. Furthermore, according to Turnbull, the quotations on pages 128-130 belong to Fichte's *Leben und literarischer Briefwechsel* (vol. 2, pp. 3-10), published in 1862, one year after Moritz Schreber's death. Unless they were published earlier, there is no way Moritz Schreber could have read these words; I am not critical of Schatzman for not having known this. The other set of quotations is from the *Addresses to the German Nation*. In his treatment of Fichte, as in the case of Moritz Schreber, Schatzman employed the technique of accentuating negative statements that were torn out of context.

Israëls (1989) has this to say about Schatzman's method: "Despite his severely moralistic view, Schatzman did not allow himself to be beguiled into making many factual errors" (p. 340). If "factual errors" refers to an improper presentation of quotations, then we cannot endorse this encomium.

39. Having "guessed" such desires in the father towards the son, Schatzman (p. 84) finds them validated in this passage on page 235 of the *Kallipädie*: "*Ist das kindliche Gemüth von Liebe, Achtung and allen den daraus hervorquellenden Wärmestrahlen vollständig durchdrungen, so wird nunmehr auch von dieser Seite her der Wille des kindes immer mehr regiert and der reinen und edlen Richtung allmälig zugeführt*" (entire emphasis Schreber's). Schatzman translates: "Once the childlike mind is completely *penetrated* by love and respect and all the *warm rays* that *gush forth* from them, the will of the child is ruled more and more from this perspective and is led gently towards the pure and noble direction" (Schatzman, 1973, p. 84). Now this passage is taken from the chapter dealing with spiritual life of the young, between ages 8 and 16. Having translated *durchdrungen* as "penetrated," rather then "permeated," or simply "filled," Schatzman (1973) concludes:

> The context of the passage makes it clear that it is parents who must "completely penetrate" children—boys and girls—with "warm rays" that "gush" [the more exact translation is: that well up]. An adolescent boy, hearing these terms from his father, might guess they refer to and reflect events the father was experiencing in his penis whether or not the boy was guessing it "consciously." The boy also might experience corresponding, *reciprocal* events in *his* body" [p. 84; emphases Schatzman's].

This is rampant sexual projection, as Schatzman himself admits: "My impression, based on knowing well many families (including my own). . . ." After reading Schatzman's argument, an American father asked, "Does this mean that when I say to my adolescent son, when will I ever be able to penetrate your thick skull, I am seducing him?"

40. As inferred by Schatzman (1973, p. 81). He also says that "*Keim* as a feminine noun means gonad," but *Keim* usually means "ovule," not the "ovary." The nonspecific meaning of *Keim* is seed, a common metaphor for "cause."

5

PAUL FLECHSIG AND THE FIRST BIOLOGICAL PSYCHIATRY

If psychiatry is not flatly to deny everything supernatural and thus *tumble with both feet into the camp of naked materialism*, it will have to recognize the possibility that occasionally the phenomena under discussion may be connected with real happenings, which simply cannot be brushed aside with the catchword "hallucinations."

D. P. Schreber, 1903

Even in recent times the authors of best-selling psychiatric textbooks have flouted their disdain for brain anatomy as a useful principle for the understanding of morbid mental states . . . More than ever before I am convinced that the brain as an organ fully covers mental phenomena and that we are in a position to unfold their causes with the same exactitude as applies to any natural happening available to our observation.

Flechsig, 1896a

We turn now to Flechsig, Schreber's first psychiatrist, whose actions had a momentous and long-lasting effect on him. Schreber's hospital chart (see Appendix), contains only one mention (November, 1894) of Flechsig, remarkable when compared to the prominence of Flechsig as a central dramatis persona in the *Memoirs*. Flechsig was a prominent neuroscientist who did pioneering work in the neuroanatomy of the central nervous system; according to Schreber, an authoritarian, sometimes self-serving, god-like "Herr Professor"; a highly prestigious

199

psychiatrist (and thus one able to foster both a real and a transference dependence in both Paul Schreber and his wife); and, in a hitherto little known role, a forensic expert and participant in the antipsychiatry scene in Germany. We will see how the initial trust placed in him by Schreber was shattered as a result of how he intervened in the lives of Paul and Sabine Schreber.

FLECHSIG'S LIFE

The psychiatrist's full name was Paul Emil Flechsig, which appears on his doctoral dissertation, published in 1870. After that, he was known the world over as Paul Flechsig. He was five years younger than his famous patient. In his doctoral dissertation (1870) he included the following "Vita":

> I was born on June 29, 1847 in Zwickau, where my father is Protodiaconus of St. Mary's; may he, as well as my dear mother, live long and healthy.
>
> From Michaelmas 1856 till Easter 1865 I was a student in the Gymnasium of my native city. On April 22, 1865 I registered as a student at [Leipzig] University.
>
> I participated in the lectures and departments of professors and lecturers . . . Erdmann, Kolbe . . . Ed. Weber, E. H. Weber, . . . Ludwig, Thiersch, Wunderlich, Wagner, Coccius, Credé, Sonnenkalb, . . . On December 28, 1867 I stood the baccalaureate examination and on April 22, 1870 the Examen rigorosum [doctoral exam].
>
> I thank all my esteemed teachers but especially Hofrath Professor Ludwig for the many inspirations and expressions of benevolence shown to me in the course of my studies. I am aware that it is him I will owe thanks above all should I be able to contribute anything to science [Flechsig, 1870, p. 43].

At the age of 80, two years before his death, Flechsig (1929) published his autobiography, *My Myelogenetic Brain Science with an Autobiographical Introduction,* which will serve us as an important source of information. (I will refer to it as *Myelogenesis.*)[1]

Like Schreber, Flechsig came from an upper-middle-class family, although one less illustrious than the Schrebers. His forebears in the century preceding his birth functioned as county judges and jury foremen. There were no men of science in the family. His father, Emil, broke with this judicial tradition and became a theologian and Protestant minister. The son broke tradition again and became a brain anatomist. In his choice of career Paul Flechsig not only challenged his father's spirituality, that is, his theological and philosophical beliefs in

God and soul but embraced science and scientism, the new god of the liberated bourgeoisie. In brief, he lost the soul and found the brain. The repudiated soul, the ghost in the brain, would haunt him all his life.

The maternal grandfather was an estate owner and justiciary who became impoverished during the Napoleonic wars. In his autobiographical sketch he does not mention his mother's name; he only describes his father (but his name, too, remains unmentioned):

> My father, a high-minded person both spiritually and morally, was theologically moderate; he strove . . . to contribute to the education of the poor, which he was able to do as an inspector of girls' schools. . . . He was a cofounder . . . of the *Zwickau Volksschriften-Verein* [Association for Popular Literature] which through the portrayal of exemplary personalities, paragons of simple life etc., sought to further contentment with the humbler life circumstances. The march of socialism has no doubt displaced such more peaceful forms of social action [*Myelogenesis*, p. 4].

Certain similarities can be seen in the educational strivings of the fathers of Flechsig and Schreber. Flechsig's father had a keen interest in world literature and was a bosom friend and soul mate of Robert Schumann.[2] They were buddies at the Lyzeum and later roommates at Leipzig University. Emil Flechsig is mentioned in Schumann's early letters, and he translated texts that were later set to music by Schumann. The family was proud of this friendship, and Paul Flechsig drew from it inspiration to love music and play the piano. His esthetic sensibilities and imagination may have also been inspired by having been "raised in the parish house of the awe-inspiring Church of St. Mary's, a late Gothic church adorned inside by works of contemporary Nürnberg wood carvers, such as Michael Wohlgemut and Veit Stoss" (*Myelogenesis*, p. 5).

His earliest memory was from the times of the 1848–1849 Revolution, that is, at age one to two: "A squadron of Prussian dragoons was bivouacked in front of our house and one of them jokingly pointed his rifle at me, an impression which still remains fresh, even as more than 78 years have passed since" (*Myelogenesis*, p. 6).

In accordance with the family tradition, Flechsig began his studies at age nine at the Zwickau high school, from which he graduated in 1865. At Easter of that same year, unlike some of his friends who studied law or theology, Flechsig chose to join those who were studying medicine and matriculated as a medical student at the University of Leipzig. He quickly realized why his friends were so excited about medicine: they were all inspired by the remarkable person of Professor Ernst Heinrich Weber, a professor of anatomy, a master of science, and a highly moral individual. Weber published what is probably the earliest autobiography of Moritz Schreber.[3]

Following the conclusion of the Austrian-Prussian war, which established Prussian hegemony over all of Germany, the Saxon King Johann, originally allied with Austria, received a delegation of Leipzig students, among whom was Flechsig. Flechsig later noted that this siding with Austria cost Saxony 10 million thalers in war tributes to Prussia, which delayed the long-awaited construction of the new university psychiatric hospital until 1882. The King greeted the young Flechsig with warm words of recognition of his family. As a result, Flechsig was given a microscope as a gift, which set him on a course of histological researches.

As attested by Flechsig, the man who was to have the most profound effect on Flechsig's career was the Viennese professor of physiology Carl Ludwig, who settled in Leipzig and contributed to the world fame of Leipzig University. Like Brücke, Helmholtz, and Du Bois-Reymond, Ludwig was part of the famed Helmholtz school, which in mid-century broke with the tradition of the soul and blazed the trail for the sciences of the brain and a psychology dominated by physiology. While materialism is native to the methods of medicine, in mid-century it was significantly reinforced by the positivism of Comte in France, the evolution theories culminating with Darwin in England, the erosion of the authority of the Bible and the churches, the reaction to the extremes of philosophical idealism, and the rising star of neuroanatomy. (It was the Helmholtz group that also served as inspiration for young Freud when he, too, first embarked on the career of brain anatomy.) Of Ludwig Flechsig (1927) wrote: "Through an unusual chain of circumstances, which would be fateful for the course of my career, I soon became acquainted with Carl Ludwig" (p. 6); Ludwig became Flechsig's lifelong mentor and champion.

Flechsig passed his medical examinations in 1870 and received his doctorate in medicine with his thesis *Remarks on Syphilitic Meningitis and a Case Report*. This dissertation is remarkable in that it is one of three instances in Flechsig's entire corpus that he discusses a clinical case and the only time he describes the patient's life circumstances. The case report was of a young man of 19 who suffered from both meningitis and a depressive syndrome. Central nervous system syphilis and paresis and the psychosis of the syphilitic were dominant themes in 19th century psychiatry. In fact, syphilitic psychosis was seen as the paradigm of all mental illness.

The following year Flechsig was a physician on active duty during the Franco-Prussian War, which was a prelude to the establishment of the German Empire. Upon his return to Leipzig on January 1, 1872,

Flechsig started work as an assistant to Professor Ernst Wagner,[4] head of the Pathological Institute of the university, where Flechsig deepened his knowledge of medicine and anatomy. The following year Ludwig appointed him chief of the histological section of the Physiological Institute he chaired. At that time appeared the epoch-making essay of Theodor Meynert (a brain researcher, psychiatrist, and Freud's teacher in Vienna), *Vom Gehirn der Säugethiere* (On the Mammalian Brain), recommended to Flechsig's attention by his chief. In this work Meynert developed ideas about the phylogeny and ontogeny of the mammalian brain based on dissections of brains of various species. At the suggestion of Wagner, Flechsig worked on histological sections of the human brain.

A fateful event occurred on the fifth of May, 1872, when, still at Wagner's, Flechsig dissected the brain of a five-week-old boy with the unusual—and symbolic—name of Martin Luther. The coincidence seemed to suggest to Flechsig that this event, like the birth of the famous Luther, would also mark the beginning of a reform. The section of the infant's brain did not appear white but grey with a few white patches. Wagner thought the patches were signs of neonatal encephalitis, but Flechsig realized that this was a sign of a normal process of development, not an illness. This chance finding led Flechsig to the discovery of the process of myelination of nerve fibers (i.e., the acquisition of a myelin sheath by nerve fibers in the course of intrauterine development and after birth). He turned this discovery into the foundation of his research methodology and his entire neuroanatomical as well as psychiatric system. Flechsig was able to demonstrate that myelination of nerve fibers was a lawful and sequential process in the development of the nervous system of man, reflecting the maturation of various neural systems. Marie (1929) correctly defined the myelogenetic method as an embryological method of tracing the course of nerve tracts.[5] The word *myelogenetic* also seemed to reverberate with *biogenetic*, that is, Haeckel's law of ontogeny recapitulating phylogeny, suggesting to Flechsig a law-like hypothesis that contained a promise of having solved the perennial riddle of the soul.

After three more months of investigation, in August of 1872, at the age of 25, Flechsig triumphantly lectured "On the development of myelin in the central nervous system of man" at the meeting marking the 50th anniversary of the founding of the Association of German Scientists and Physicians. The discovery impressed such luminaries as Ludwig, Helmholtz, Meynert and Hitzig[6]—an "assembly of kings," as Flechsig described them. At that stage in the history of medicine "the bacteria were hardly noticed; people smiled at the attempts to prove their enormous importance for medicine, which occasionally led to violent scenes" (*Myelogenesis*, p. 10). Flechsig remained indifferent to the "triumphant march of the bacteria" that shaped the course of medicine, and his only memory of the pesky microbes was a severe bout of typhoid he developed following his brilliant lecture. His true love was the brain: "As a scientist born of passion, I did not allow myself to be diverted from studying the brain, for what was always present to my mind, even if not altogether clearly, was the greater task: the relations between brain and soul" (footnote, p. 10).

In the course of the next five years Flechsig continued to apply his myelogenetic method, later combined with old and new histological techniques, to tracing the course of a number of structures and tracts in the spinal cord and their end stations in the brain. He discovered a number of structures, which were eventually named after him.[7] This work won him recognition among scientists, including Freud,[8] and as such remains of lasting value in the history of neuroanatomy. However, very few scientists replicated Flechsig's studies using the myelogenetic method; it was cumbersome and time-consuming. Over the years Flechsig's results and conclusions were frequently challenged by other scientists.[9] [10]

A fateful turn in Flechsig's life took place in 1877: he was elevated by the medical faculty to the rank of "professor extraordinarius" (equivalent to associate professor) and was recommended to the Ministry of Education as the next professor of psychiatry at Leipzig University. Some of his former teachers, Wunderlich, Credé, Wagner, Thiersch, and Dean Coccius, recommended Flechsig over the other candidates, Hitzig and Forel. This was to be a momentous nomination. Established in 1409, Leipzig University (until the unification of Germany, Karl Marx University, now again Leipzig University) went through a renewal in 1811, when a number of chairs in medicine were established. Among them was the professorship (*extraordinariat*) in "*psychische Therapie*,"[11] the current official name for psychiatry. The professor of psychiatry was the "psychologist and anthropologist" Johann Christian August Heinroth, whom we have already encountered as a teacher of Moritz Schreber, a friend of his in-laws, and godfather of Paul's elder brother, Gustav (Busse, 1990). Heinroth was in the tradition of Kant and the German soul psychiatrists, or *Psychiker*, the humanistic psychiatrists of the first half of the 19th century. Following his death in 1843, the chair "remained vacant . . . for a whole generation" (*Myelogenesis*, p. 22), until it was occupied by Flechsig, who wrote of his nomination as follows:

Naturally this measure provoked an unpleasant uproar in psychiatric circles, since a goodly number of very competent psychiatrists were

waiting to be called, especially where the Leipzig position was concerned. It meant a break with custom, for a person was being considered
who had never done any work in a psychiatric institution and it is well
known that psychiatry is an eminently practical and empirical discipline
which requires experience of many years [1927, pp. 22-23].[12]

This was indeed an extraordinary break with custom and was entirely
due to the enormous prestige as scientist and harbinger of a new era
that Flechsig had in the eyes of the Leipzig medical faculty. The
negative reactions to this appointment were to hound Flechsig for
many years.[13] It was a sign of the times: in one fell swoop, through
Flechsig's nomination, the tradition of the soul ended and the reign of
the brain began.

While the new psychiatric wing of Leipzig University was being
built, over the next four years, Flechsig was sent by the university on a
study tour of various institutions from Berlin to Paris. In Berlin he
visited the famous Wilhelm Griesinger, already known at that time as
a bridge builder between the then-unpopular soul psychiatrists and the
up-and-coming brain psychiatrists. In 1845 he coined the slogan
"mental disorders are brain disorders." The eminent neuropsychiatrist
and brain anatomist Franz Nissl later called this approach *Hirnmytholo-
gie*, or "brain mythology", a "trend to describe psychological and
psychopathological phenomena in terms of real or hypothetical brain
structures" (Ellenberger, p. 434). According to Oswald Bumke, Flechsig's successor as chair of psychiatry in Leipzig, Nissl applied brain
mythology to Flechsig's approach.[14] For while the brain is not a myth,
brain mythology is an ideology, or belief system, not a methodology.
It is rooted in philosophical reductionism which views mind as caused
by the brain as against mind acting *in* the brain. It also ignores the
reality of the *tertium quid*, the third given, or the person. The other
aspect of brain mythology is its speculative nature in reverse, in which
"the conception of the functioning of the brain [is] . . . patterned on the
picture of psychological processes given by Herbartian and associa-
tionist psychology" (Andersson, 1962, p. 11), or any other psychology, for that matter. This trend led to picturing various parts of the
brain as personified agents, a variety of anthropomorphism.

In spite of his slogan, the humanist Griesinger (1867) also upheld the
principles of dynamic psychiatry and unconscious processes and was
so acknowledged by Freud (1911b, p. 218). But Flechsig heard the beat
of a different drummer. What he took from Griesinger was mainly the
administrative idea of establishing a psychiatric hospital within the
inner city. This was the beginning of a new trend of moving away from
provincial, or rural, asylums (*Landesasyle*) to city asylums (*Stadtasyle*).
This was also the beginning of the tradition of a psychiatric inpatient

service as part of a teaching university hospital center, to look like any other teaching clinical service. For Flechsig, "the main purpose was to maximize the thorough study of mental illnesses and the discovery of medical treatment methods, for which the admission of the greatest number of 'fresh' cases was indispensable. An asylum for incurable patients was not planned" (p. 24).[15] This definition of the plan and purpose of the new hospital was to become fateful in the life of Paul Schreber. The course of his life at a certain critical point hinged on the question of whether he was suffering from a curable or an incurable illness.

Flechsig's voyages took him through institutions in Germany, Austria, Switzerland, Belgium, and France, especially Paris, where he met the great Charcot. In Paris in 1878 his fame preceded him:

> When in 1878 I visited the auditorium at the Salpêtrière, where I was received in the most friendly manner, I found there, to my great surprise, a more than 2 m tall copy of a figure from my work of 1876 with a legend visible from afar: Coup de Flechsig . . . this exhibit offered me some measure of satisfaction as compared to the many times I was either ignored or attacked by German neurologists [*Myelogenesis*, p. 18].[16]

Flechsig was impressed with Charcot and with the many mistakes Charcot had made in neuroanatomy. What a different lesson would be learned in the presence of the same Charcot in 1885 by another traveling neuroanatomist—Freud!

On his way back from his travels Flechsig "wandered on foot from Bonn on the Rhine over Basel into Switzerland in order to learn how to sleep again; I was accustomed to work until 2 o'clock in the morning and have completely lost the ability to fall asleep sooner. In Heppenheim I regained normal sleep—I was in fact saved by my appointment in psychiatry" (*Myelogenesis*, p. 24). Was the sleeplessness just a work habit or a sign of emotional disease? Did the memory of his own sleeplessness make him more sympathetic toward the same symptom in his patient?

"Early in 1882, I was able to move into my hospital and on the second of May the festive opening took place," wrote Flechsig, and on March 4, 1882, he read his inaugural speech "On the Physical Basis of Mental Diseases" (Flechsig, 1882a).[17] The speech contained Flechsig's manifesto and the direction of the new psychiatry:

> Naturally I made reference to Heinroth and stressed the differences between him and the new psychiatry. Heinroth saw the causes of mental disorders mainly in moral factors: sin, forsaking God, and arbitrary

falling into spiritual unfreedom, etc., of which, of course, hardly anything can be yet found in modern psychiatry; it would imply that alcoholism, venereal infections, and so forth, were to be appreciated from the purely moral viewpoint [*Myelogenesis*, pp. 25-26].

That "purely" is the question. For alcohol and venereal infections are quite importantly related to moral factors in behavior, even as the bodily consequences of alcohol and infection are due to the presence of alcohol and bacteria in the body. The point here is that Flechsig was espousing an either-or approach, instead of a this-and-that approach.[18]

The official name of the hospital was *Irrenklinik*, or asylum. (*Klinik* was the name give to university departments or hospitals.) It was later changed to *Psychiatrische und Nervenklinik* (Hospital for Psychiatric and Nervous Disorders), as was the practice in Vienna and Berlin. It functioned essentially as a psychiatric institution and had only a few neurological beds. In popular parlance it was somewhat affectionately called, at least in Flechsig's mind, "at Flechsig's" (*"bei Flechsig"*). From the beginning, Flechsig prided himself that treatment could be found there at affordable prices: The per diem cost in the hospital was "at all times kept commensurate with that in the provincial state hospitals" (*Myelogenesis*, p. 27). He also took great pains to demonstrate that the institution compared favorably with the existing provincial state hospitals.[19] The hospital was described by Flechsig (1888a) in *The Psychiatric Hospital of Leipzig University and its Operation in the Years 1882-1886* (for the sake of brevity, referred to here as the *Report*). This work became a source of information for many authors.[20] It is worth spending some time on the architecture of the hospital.

The hospital was set in a two hectare (i.e., almost five acres) park and comprised five buildings: (1) the central building, built on two floors, which contained most of the patient rooms as well as administrative offices; (2) the building that housed the maintenance services; (3) the engine house; (4) an isolation pavilion for patients with infectious diseases; and (5) the director's villa. The rooms, wrote Flechsig, were nicely and comfortably appointed. There is no indication that the hospital provided space for either psychotherapy or activities and recreational therapies.

The first floor of the central building deserves special mention. It housed "the auditorium and scientific laboratory (1 microscope room, 1 chemical work room, 1 room for the brain collection, the office of the director, in which were housed scientific apparatus, instruments, models) . . . and a by now well-stocked library" (Flechsig, 1888a, p. 12). (The brain collection may have inspired Paul's famous delusion that

God related only to corpses.) The hospital was officially opened for service on May 2, 1882, and was capable of treating up to 135 patients at any one time.[21]

FLECHSIG'S PSYCHIATRIC HOSPITAL

Flechsig's hospital was from the beginning set up as a showcase institution for the purpose of treatment, teaching, and research. It was, according to Flechsig, the first of its kind in Germany. Administratively, the hospital was under the control of the Royal Ministry of Public Worship and Education[22] (*Königliches Ministerium des Cultus und öffentlichen Unterrichts*), later renamed Ministry of National Education (*Ministerium für Volksbildung*), and not under the Royal *Landes-Medicinal-Collegium* (the Health Board for the Kingdom of Saxony), the latter being the supervisory body for the state hospitals, such as Sonnenstein.

Under these auspices, Flechsig drew up the bylaws of the hospital (Flechsig, 1882b). In the first bylaw it is stated that "as a clinical institution [the hospital] is preferentially geared toward the admission of mental patients who are either curable or capable of considerable improvement" (Flechsig, 1882b). According to the bylaws, Flechsig carved out for himself administrative powers that "indeed exceeded those of an average director of a public state hospital" (Flechsig, 1888a, p. 22). He had the ultimate power of decision for the admission, treatment, and discharge of patients, as well as for everything that had to do with the running of the hospital. Admissions were often decided upon following personal interviews or arranged by contact with Flechsig by telephone or telegraph. Flechsig did not have to report the details of treatment to the Ministry of Education, only statistical monthly reports (Flechsig, 1882–1885, 1892–1894) of patient lists of admissions and discharges, diagnoses and prognoses, results, dispositions, and essential demographic data.

At the beginning the doors of the hospital were opened wide to all kinds of patients to insure occupancy and sufficiently varied clinical material. Flechsig had a special predilection for sufferers from paresis, since these patients showed most clearly the "somatic bases of the mental disorders" (Flechsig, 1888a, p. 52, footnote 1). He was more interested in showing the student the initial phases, rather the end phases, of a disorder. With time, Flechsig became more concerned about the curable/incurable ratio and the reputation of the hospital as a successful treatment center in the eyes of the public. In this context two criteria came to play a decisive role in determining the hospital population: curability and availability of beds to insure sufficient admissions of suitable teaching material. Thus, the discharge policy, too, acquired an important regulatory role. One of the bylaws (no. 21) reads as follows: "The discharge from the hospital takes effect following the assessment which is the sole responsibility of the Direction of the Hospital as soon as the patient is (a) cured or (b) is incurable or incapable of further improvement and thus does not appear suitable for being kept in the hospital" (Flechsig, 1882b).[23]

In order to have beds available for new admissions, Flechsig resorted to two methods: either early discharge of patients to their homes, with subsequent readmissions, or transfers *(Evacuationen* in the *Report)* to the Saxon provincial state hospitals. Such transfers were usually a matter of considerable red tape and shortcuts were desirable. One such shortcut was available by a special arrangement with Sonnenstein for an immediate and direct transfer of acute admissions.

The first six months of a patient's stay constituted the critical period. During this time, various forms of treatment would be tried and, more importantly, an assessment would be made as to the patient's ultimate prognosis. A favorable prognosis might enable one to stay beyond the customary six-month deadline. In certain situations, "persons with an illness of one year's duration were allowed to stay until a definitive resolution if there was a well-founded outlook for a cure" (Flechsig, 1888a, p. 26). Thus, as the sole arbiter and potentate of the institution, Flechsig was able to (and did) use discretionary powers. Thus, for instance, in the *Report* we read about a demented patient who had been kept in the hospital for two years (Flechsig, 1888a, p. 18). Flechsig also notes in the *Report* that chronic male patients who make no progress and cannot be usefully employed on the premises should be "evacuated as soon as possible" (pp. 45–46); by contrast chronic female patients stayed longer because they could be used in various household chores. Other chronic patients were kept longer if they were suitable illustrations of the course and outcome of particular disorders. It can be safely assumed that such considerations, and many others besides, were applied to Paul Schreber.

Some of the statistics of the hospital are of interest. In the four-year period 1882–1886 some 2,100 patients were admitted, from which a subgroup of 1,708 admissions was separated. Among the latter were the following diagnostic categories: 22 were pure neurological cases and 2 were found to be healthy following a diagnostic workup. The remainder were divided into three groups (1) "anatomo-pathologically defined brain disorders (e.g., senile brain atrophy, brain trauma, focal lesions of the brain); (2) toxic brain changes (alcoholism, lead intoxication, etc.); (3) ('functional') brain disorders of a doubtful nature (simple psychosis, simple mental defect, disorders secondary to epilepsy)"

(Flechsig, 1888a, pp. 29–33). Of the above number, 730 were men and women, in almost equal ratios, suffering from simple functional psychoses. Flechsig held the improvement rate to be 45 percent, due, he thought, to the fact that there was an increasing number of patients admitted who were not very sick.

Of the treatment methods in use Flechsig had a preference for bed rest, as recommended by the Göttingen psychiatrist Ludwig Meyer, in contrast to the policy of open-air activity (e.g., gardening), practiced in the rural state hospitals. Flechsig thus stressed the importance of the Weir-Mitchell rest cure for exhaustion. The cuisine offered at the clinic was much more varied than that offered in the state hospitals. Therapeutic tepid baths were used frequently. Conolly's no-restraint policy was adhered to in principle but breached in practice. Thus, the old-fashioned straitjacket was never used in the hospital, but leather gloves, canvas suits, and restraints made of bandages were used to control violent patients. A special bed, the Güntz strap bed, with high rails and crossed straps, was used in some cases instead of padded cells, and it was credited with saving lives.

Besides defending the moderate use of physical restraints, Flechsig was an ardent advocate of what would now be called "chemical straitjackets." Among these the most important were sedatives to insure adequate sleep. Narcotic drugs were heavily used, under strict medical supervision. Surgical treatments for mental illness were used on female patients only, such as the removal of ovaries, and uterus (later described in Flechsig, 1884).

The hospital attendants and their activities were also considered to be part of the treatment armamentarium, although in the *Report* Flechsig does not spell out how attendants were therapeutic agents. Attendants have always been a problem for administrators of psychiatric facilities, and Flechsig was no exception. His attendants had the run of the place, and he had to side with them against the patients, a matter about which Schreber would complain bitterly.[24] Flechsig apparently also had problems with his physicians.[25] Kraepelin had to this say about Flechsig's troubles:

> Otherwise, in the meantime Flechsig had to fire his first assistant, a certain Dr. . . . , a man of shabby exterior, almost demented, because of his very crazy conduct (sexual relations with a wife of a patient and similar things), which was very hard on him. However, purely out of fear of people he gave the man a very good recommendation and stated that the man had resigned voluntarily, a plain and evident lie! Now he has a very young physician, straight from the state exam, who has no idea about psychiatry. That could turn jolly! [Kraepelin's letter of February 22, 1883, in Forel, 1968, p. 167].

As far as a philosophy of psychiatry is concerned, Flechsig adhered to a strict organic (i.e, physical), conception of mental disorders. He believed such a conception provided "the most detailed knowledge of the brain mechanism as well as of the entire organism" and elaborated in the *Report*:

> The undeveloped state of psychology deprived psychiatry of a secure footing. . . . Undoubtedly, the psychiatrist has the task to use all the means at his disposal in order to gain an understanding of the mental state of his patients. . . . in order to understand the motives of their actions. . . . But it should be clear to the physician that such psychological analyses are but a small part of his task, and in my opinion in no way the most important, because it is the most negligible as far as specific therapy is concerned. The specific-medical thinking begins only when the physical factors are kept in mind which are the cause of the psychological changes. And it is on this ground that one should seek the key to psychiatry remaining counted amongst the rest of the medical disciplines.[26] . . . The proper object of investigation is the localization and nature of the underlying somatic processes or factors, completely in the spirit and meaning of modern scientific pathology—not more and not less. It is enough to demonstrate strong and lawful, even if remote, relations between the physical and the psychical. The most exact knowledge of the brain mechanism and of the entire organism is indispensable [Flechsig, 1888a, p. 60-61].[27]

These bylaws, policies, and philosophies were still in effect five years later, in 1893, when Paul Schreber was admitted to Flechsig's for the second time. The problems that they were supposed to remedy were, however, proving intractable. This is revealed by the reports Flechsig sent to the Ministry of Education. The matter of transfers kept plaguing Flechsig and crops up in a number of reports sent to the Ministry of Education.[28] Since by virtue of a contract with the city government of Leipzig, Flechsig had to reserve a number of beds for city cases, problems arose in connection with admissions to observation wards of the poor and the homeless, some of whom were persons with infectious diseases, and "*unanständige Elemente*" (i.e., the social dregs, such as "prostitutes, criminals, etc."). It was relatively easy to put the infectious ones in the isolation ward, but the need for "fresh cases" for "teaching and therapy" (such as the epilepsy studies that Flechsig later published), and competing successfully with the Thonberg *Privatanstalt* (private asylum) for wealthy patients, necessitated speedy transfers of patients out of Flechsig's asylum, a privilege enjoyed by the Charité hospital in Berlin.

SCIENTIFIC CONTRIBUTIONS IN THE YEARS
1882 TO 1896

The first period of Flechsig's neuroanatomical researches was concentrated on the spinal cord (see the sources listed in footnote 20). This lasted until 1893, when Flechsig began delving into the structure of the cerebrum, specifically the cerebral cortex and its connections. As he tells in *Myelogenesis*, "The scientific researches during the first period of the hospital were naturally overwhelmingly devoted to the *pathology* of the nervous system. Myelogenesis took a back seat for the time being" (1927, p. 28; emphasis Flechsig's).

Following clinical work on acute psychoses due to chemical intoxications in industrial workers, Flechsig devoted passing interest to two diseases: hysteria and epilepsy. The first interest earned him a poor reputation among latter-day psychiatrists, the second is of little historical interest, but of importance to the fates of Paul (*M*, pp. 39-40).

At this time, it was still believed by some doctors that hysteria was caused by disease in the uterus and ovaries, or by other unspecified processes in the female reproductive system. Flechsig was not the first to advocate castration, that is, surgical removal of the ovaries, as a treatment for hysteria: "I have convinced myself that this therapy can be useful in cases in which there is disease in the inner sexual organs, whereas following removal of healthy ovaries unpleasant consequences predominate" (*Myelogenesis*, p. 28). This method was described in two papers (Flechsig, 1884, 1885), which clearly show Flechsig's reductive organic approach to emotional disorders.[29] The 1884 paper was first cited by Niederland to suggest that Schreber might have read it and, if so, would have feared castration at the hands of Flechsig. This idea was later touted by Masson (1988). Attractive as this theory seems, it is too literal, and I do not believe it was important in stirring up Schreber's castration fears. Furthermore, this widely discussed form of treatment for hysteria was also mentioned in the sixth edition of Kraepelin's *Lehrbuch der Psychiatrie* of 1899, the famous *Textbook*, another work cited in the *Memoirs*.

The Flechsig method of treating epilepsy was called by him the opium-bromide treatment (*Opium-Brom-Kur*). Narcotics and bromides were essential in the pharmacological treatment of sleep and other disorders at that time. Flechsig claimed therapeutic success in controlling epileptic seizures by first giving opium, then abruptly discontinued, to be followed by high doses of bromides.[30] This regimen induced a kind of chemical shock, which helped some patients but caused death in others. Flechsig made self-laudatory remarks about his regimen but omitted responding to criticism in the literature of the day. The other disorders that were of interest to Flechsig were paresis—for which he mentions treatment with mercury compounds in the form of salves and pastes—and tabes dorsalis, both late sequelae of syphilis. Another disease he was interested in was chorea and the acute delirium states associated with it.

The striking fact in all this is that there is neither awareness nor interest on the part of Flechsig in anything remotely related to psycho-therapy, that is, treatment of mental disorders by psychological means. In this regard Flechsig remained an organicist to the very end.

In the eight-year period between 1885 and 1893 Flechsig's fame grew steadily, attracting many students both at home and abroad.[31] A major honor was bestowed on him with his appointment as rector magnificus of the University of Leipzig for the year 1894-1895. Flechsig celebrated his achievement with another festive oration. This speech (1894a),[32] entitled "*Gehirn und Seele* (Brain and Soul)," was held on the 31st of October of 1894; due to renovations the ceremony was moved to the university's old Dominican Church. Flechsig's podium was placed directly at the altar. One could not have chosen a more symbolic location. The speech, his second manifesto, was a paean to the brain and the new triumphant brain science. It marked the apogee of the theory of localization of the soul in the brain; as noted by Bumke, it was also a triumph for brain mythology.

Shortly after the first printing of Flechsig's oration, he was show-ered with the critical reactions, many in favor and some against. "Of importance for me was only the reaction of Carl Ludwig, who said the speech had impressed him greatly but that I should be careful" (*Mye-logenesis*, p. 40-41). Flechsig understood Ludwig's admonition to mean he should be careful not to antagonize the reactionary authorities. Indeed, some church officials strongly objected to this attack on state and religion from the altar. Flechsig did much better with King Albert, the current ruler of Saxony. The king had already been shown an almost seven-foot-tall diagram of the brain being readied for an exhi-bition in Chicago. The king was so impressed by the similarity be-tween the tracts in the brain and the vast network of railway tracks of the Kingdom of Saxony that he couldn't hold back the question, "How many kilometers long are these brain tracks?" (*Myelogenesis*, p. 41).[33]

Flechsig was most pleased with this royal approval and seemed unmoved by criticism of some of his neurological colleagues who accused him of "crude materialism" or of some Herbartian philoso-phers who protested vocally against his anatomical theories. Some among the latter actually pleased him in pointing to a parallelism between Kant's separation of the faculties into perception and sensa-tion and the structure of the brain as elucidated by him. The lecture was reissued, with slight changes and very extensive footnotes under the same title in 1896 as a monograph, some 106 pages long; I shall refer to it as *Brain and Soul* (1896a). This monograph spread Flechsig's reputation in Europe and in the United States.[34]

In 1896 Flechsig produced two more major essays on the correlation between mental functioning and brain structure, each based on lectures (one was given at the 68th meeting of the German Scientists and Physicians in Frankfurt; the other was in honor of the birthday of King Albert of Saxony): *The Localization of Mental Processes in Particular the Sensations in Man* and *The Boundaries of Mental Health and Disease* (abbreviated as *Localization*, 1896b, 1896c, and *Boundaries*, 1896d, respectively). The theme of these essays was what came to be known as the system of localization of mental functions in the various structures of the brain (or briefly, localization).

Flechsig's interest in cerebral localization dated back to 1893 (Schröder, 1930), but the recorded story of the theories of localization of the soul is more than 2,000 years old (Revesz, 1914). It begins with the ancient Greeks, with Plato and Aristotle, who placed intelligence in the heart, and Erasistratos, who placed it in the brain; the story is still going on. The concern with this problem received new impetus from the spectacular developments in neuroanatomy in the second half of the 19th century. When Flechsig entered the scene, he was joining a number of illustrious predecessors, including, among others, during the 19th century, Karl Friedrich Burdach, Franz Josef Gall, Emil Huschke, Charles Bell, François Magendie, Paul Broca, Hermann Munk, Carl Wernicke, and Theodor Meynert. All of these, in one form or another, localized the soul in the cerebral cortex. The most important immediate precursors of Flechsig were Broca, Meynert,[35] and Wernicke.[36] Another predecessor of paramount importance in terms his neurological publications, especially the monograph on aphasia (1891), was none other than the as yet unknown Sigmund Freud.

In *Brain and Soul* Flechsig (1896a) began with the statement that the brain is the organ of the soul. This slogan had been already sounded by the popular materialist philosophers of the mid-century, such as Büchner, Moleschott, and Vogt, who, in reaction to the preceding idealists and their rhapsodies about the soul, simply stated that the brain produces thought the same way the kidney produces urine. Of course, Flechsig's statement, coming from a physician, was backed up by the knowledge of the ability of brain lesions to cause disorders of mental functioning. However, like other medical men, Flechsig was engaging not only in neurology but in the philosophy of brain and mind. He also knew his philosophy, even as he opted to deny it in various ways.

Meynert was the first to describe the shape of cells in the cerebral cortex and was thus a pioneer of cytoarchitectonics in neuroanatomy. He was also the first to refer to the delayed maturation of the myelin sheaths, thus blazing a trail for Flechsig (Kolle, 1956). He held that the cortex is the seat of the ego. He traced the course of stimuli from the organs of sensation to the brain and distinguished two kinds of nerve fibers, common knowledge today: the projection fibers, that is, those conducting incoming stimuli from the sense organs to the so-called projection fields in the cortex, and association fibers, that is, those connecting the various projection fields within the cortex.

Another predecessor of note whose ideas Flechsig incorporated was Munk, who described a large sensory projection field for stimuli coming in from inside the body. This area of awareness of internal bodily stimuli was called by Munk the *Fühlsphäre*, which Flechsig renamed *Körperfühlsphäre*, or the somatosensory area.

Flechsig combined Meynert's differentiation of projection and association fibers, Munk's somatosensory area, and his own myelogenetic method. His central innovation was to lay an even greater emphasis on the association fibers and centers. He felt that by means of myelogenesis he had established that the bulk of the silent areas of the brain, especially the posterior cortex, is made up of association centers that are the seat of higher neural functions, that is, thinking. In *Brain and Soul* Flechsig (1896a) described his "theory of 'mental' [literally, 'spiritual,' *geistigen*] centers" as the

> shape of the psychology of the future . . . the analysis of functions of . . . specific soul organs in man . . . The human brain cortex, like the surface of the earth divided into continents and oceans, comprises at least seven anatomically distinct provinces [*Gebiete*]. The organ of the mind clearly shows a collaborative constitutional organization; in the two senates the two councils are set up; then come the members of these senates, which are no longer known under the names of the old phrenology—such as friendship, serenity, wit, perseverance, and so forth— but under their new names—the seeing-, hearing-, smelling (and tasting)-, touching-, and somatosensory-areas. . . . [then come] the coagitation[sic][37]—or association-centers; . . . Provisionally, with respect to their location, we will distinguish a frontal or *fore,* insular or *middle*, and parieto-occipito-temporal or *hind* association centers [pp. 24-25; emphasis Flechsig's].

While Flechsig (1896a) saw in this division the foundation of the "statics and mechanics of the soul organ" (p. 33), Schreber would later pun on the upper, middle, lower and small Flechsig, or on Flechsig's God's provinces (*Gottesreiche*). The main point is this: Flechsig put Kant and Schopenhauer into the cortex.

In the association centers the impressions of the senses, the images of memory, and imagination were transformed into reason and understanding. Thus, a thoroughgoing and exact parallelism was postulated between the functioning of the brain and the functioning of the mind. The very term *association centers* harks back to the notion of association of ideas. The faculties of the psychologists and the metaphors of the metaphysicians have been neatly and concretely converted into myelinated fibers.

From this psychology of the future there is only one step to the psychiatry of the future: "Diseases in the association centers [i.e., the thought centers] are the foremost cause of mental diseases, they are the proper object of psychiatry" (Flechsig, 1896a, p. 24). Correspondingly, disease in the sensory and association centers, that is, the functions of sense perception and judgment, leads to disorders of identity, and a variety of illusions, hallucinations, and delusions.

The point in all this is not, of course, to deny the fact that lesions in the brain cortex will cause disturbances of performance: this is a basic clinical fact; the correlation of structure and function is also a fact, although some localizations are more controversial than the effects of lesions. The point here is that Flechsig (1896a) converted the facts concerning lesions and localizations into an overriding philosophy that applied to *all* disorders of behavior and performance, including those he himself classified as functional (p. 92), that is, disorders in which no focal, that is, specific, lesion could be demonstrated. Freud broke with the concept of cerebral localization,[38][39] but he did not give up the organic conception of instinctual drives. The latter was also on the mind of Flechsig, this time not via Kant but via Schopenhauer.

Flechsig (1896a) began by considering the decerebrate animal as described by Goltz. Such an animal responds both to external stimuli and to its internal bodily states. It is moved by needs that require gratification, which occur in both animals and man:

> At the beginning of his life upon earth man resembles a decerebrate being and yet he feels the power of the drives even as he takes his first breath and screamingly demands gratification of his bodily needs. [Flechsig goes on to note with a measure of irony that] the valid observations of Goltz in animals apply to the adult man as well, when we consider him in the throes of a pathological condition. We know innumerable states in which the awareness of the outside world and of one's own person seems to be fully extinguished and yet the body performs all kinds of motions subserving the expression of powerful feelings . . . in the absence of any participation of an intelligent consciousness [p. 18].

An important precursor in this connection is Munk and his afore-mentioned notion of the somatosensory field. Flechsig (1896a) considered the somatosensory projection area to be both important and extensive:

> It is the basis of awareness of sexual pleasure [*Wollustgefühle; Wollust* is also a frequent term in Schreber], to the extent to which they are transmitted by the skin and mucosa of the external genital organs and localized in the somatosensory field. . . . It is unclear so far whether the sexual drive which is determined by the inner sexual organs, especially the sexual glands . . . is also represented in the somatosensory area" (p. 67).

This is quite prescient for those days. Flechsig also noted that this area is of importance for the awareness of the emotions and moods (p. 68) and in certain forms of mental illness:

> [in the] curable "functional" forms of mental disease, predominantly caused by states of exhaustion, . . . we see . . . a strong irritation in the sexual organs next to an exhaustion of the brain. Due to the numerous associative connections between the somatosensory area with *all* the association centers, this intense excitation exercises such a harmful influence on the centers that its presence either inhibits or stimulates to an enormous extent. As a result, such persons, in extreme cases, lose not only the awareness of their own person (to the point of forgetting their own sexual-character), but also to a point of a completely confused conception of their environment and interpretation of it exclusively in terms of the overpowering drive. Given the ebb and flow of the intensity of the sexual excitation, the emotional state swings back and forth, in multifarious nuances, between the most raw and naked sensuality and the most sublime metaphysical ecstasy. When this occurs in persons marked by a greater degree of refinement, we see a series of mental states whose inner connection (to one and the same drive) can be understood only by someone who has directly witnessed its metamorphoses. . . . In some cases, the morbid sexual excitation produces a clinical picture, not, as usually seen, of a manic symptom complex, but of hallucinations of all the senses and confused delusions (hallucinatory insanity). . . . An effect similar to the sexual drive upon the somatosensory area is produced by morbidly excited anxiety feelings. In the face of a feeling of impending annihilation of the individual's existence, it happens . . . that the person imagines supernatural powers, metaphysical events which are alien to the healthy individual, but here, too, the brusque, purely organically based feeling of endangered existence simply acts inhibitingly and confusingly upon the awareness of one's own person and of the external world [pp. 92-93].

Did Flechsig have Schreber in mind when he wrote this?

Similar ideas about the somatosensory area are expressed in *Localization* (Flechsig, 1896c), based on a lecture delivered in Frankfurt (1896b).[40] After restating his myelogenetic principle, Flechsig defines the somatosensory area as the most important of the sensory centers, concerned with consciousness of sensations of "hunger, thirst, and libido sexualis," those sensations localized in the throat and abdomen, which he calls "localized drive-feelings" or "the local signs of the drives." These can cause

> a generalized restlessness, which is not of a psychological nature and which may be due to a direct (automatic) excitation of the motor central apparatuses. . . . It is these drive-feelings which clearly point to phenomena which are designated as the "feeling tones" of sensations, the inner states that move between pleasure and unpleasure. Pleasure and unpleasure are still being separated these days by famous psychologists from their organ sensations . . . a part of the organ sensations is most probably exclusively mediated through the lower brain parts [pp. 10-11].

As to Flechsig's localizing these drives exclusively in the lower brain parts, we should note that he is weak on localization and strong on metaphor: his designation has more to do with viewing sexuality as low, compared to the higher functions of the mind.(Paul Schreber was similarly metaphorical when he spoke of the lower god Ariman and the higher god Ormuzd.)

In the midst of the organicist preoccupation, Flechsig is analyzing a morbid situation in terms of a dynamic disturbance of forces and the dynamic impact of drives, even though he ends up viewing it purely organically. In this he is presciently Freudian, even though he is unaware of the full psychoanalytic implication of what he is saying. But then, since he invokes Schopenhauer, an unacknowledged influence on Freud himself, maybe he is dimly aware of just this dynamic importance. Two questions arise: Did Flechsig apply these dynamics to Paul Schreber? did Paul Schreber read these lines? Again, in *Brain and Soul*, Flechsig (1896a) adds the following to round out his clinical analysis:

> Delusional systems also result from combined diseases of association centers and sensory centers. An important point of origin seen particularly in numerous cases of hypochondriacal insanity is once more the somatosensory area. . . . Seeing that the centers of all the common sensations lie close to each other within the somatosensory area, it is not unusual to see erotic delusions as part of hypochondriacal insanity, as, for example, seen when nymphomania results in a fixed delusion of

persecution; thus here, too, we can find no sharp boundary between certain "manic" forms, on the one hand, and paranoid forms, on the other [pp. 94-95].

Here Flechsig anticipates my own differential diagnosis: Paul's severe hypochondriasis in the second illness, itself a manifestation of depression, included both manic and paranoid features. Besides, it is impressive that Flechsig continued to assign causal importance to the sexual drive in hypochondriasis. As if this weren't enough, Flechsig (1896a) titillates us with more interesting ideas. He notes that

The activity of the association centers is undoubtedly for the most part unconscious. From the structure of the brain I gain the impression that the conscious processes in the nervous system are to some extent connected between two kinds of unconscious processes, which could be termed supraconscious and subconscious. To the former belong the highest associations, to the latter the simple reflexes [p. 99].

This is, of course, a static, not a dynamic conception of the unconscious. Flechsig was also aware of symbolic substitutions in the thinking of the mentally sick, such as the mechanism of "pars pro toto (e.g., unconsciousness-death, warm-fire)" (p. 100). However, this is only important to Flechsig as a matter of representational mechanics (*Vorstellungsmechanik*), not in a psychodynamic sense.

The ethical stance taken by Flechsig is given in his thoughts about the relationship between the drives and the mind. Here his viewpoint is not only Kantian but is in harmony with similar views expressed by Moritz Schreber in his writings:

However, the pathways of conduction between the centers of the drive-nerves and the mental centers of the cerebral cortex are not only called upon to clothe sensuality in representations [*Vorstellungen*], to idealize it, not only to facilitate its gratification through the perception of suitable objects; but also . . . of an exchange, of that work of representations which our self-awareness allows us to grasp as the struggle between sensuality and reason. Next to the driving representations [there are] inhibiting emotions. . . . [the] most noble brain parts [*edelsten Hirntheilen*] . . . a strong cerebrum . . . guarantees the ability to control the lower drives . . . a weakness of the cerebrum . . . may become hidden behind the mask of a condition presently of interest to psychiatry, known as moral insanity [Flechsig, 1896a, pp. 30-32].

In his last major essay of 1896, *Boundaries*, Flechsig continues his ideas about the role of the cerebral cortex as the organ of self-identity and drive regulation. He now expands the role of the cortex and calls it the central organ of character. In referring to the struggle between sexuality (which he calls sensuality) and reason Flechsig uses a term beloved of Moritz Schreber: '*Veredlung*', or refinement, ennoblement, cultivation (what Freud will later call sublimation). Even more tellingly, he builds bridges between brain morality, sublimated sexuality, and education:

> Insofar as the science of the brain [*Hirnlehre*] investigates the conditions which lead to the ennoblement of sexual [*sinnlichen*] drives, be it directly through bodily influences, be it through intellect; insofar as it has the converse conception of the ennoblement of the intellect through refined sexual drives, brain science comes in direct contact with the basic problems of a scientific pedagogy and the goals of a true culture. In this it provides the indispensable preconditions for a *physiological ethic* [Flechsig, 1896d, pp. 4-5].

The more correct term would be: *anatomical ethics*, for Flechsig did not engage in physiology or animal experimentation. But it is an aspect of his complex nature: no matter how much he was tied to anatomical reductionism, he was still able to relate on some level to the complexities of human life. The riddle of sexuality was very much on his mind. And so was the problem of all aberrant behavior, rooted in the central manifestations of character pathology: abnormalities of the emotions and of the moral sense.

Flechsig (1896d) sought the solution to the problem of genius, both creative and criminal, and to moral insanity (coined by Prichard in 1835) in brain anatomy, "in . . . a character center . . . in the brain . . . equivalent to what we call the somatosensory area of the cortex" (p. 35). Such theorizing had become fashionable in the wake of the writings of the Italian Lombroso, translated in Leipzig in the 1880s and widely admired. (Nordau dedicated his *Degeneration* to Lombroso.)

Indeed, this "character center" is no more than localization rhetoric and is not based on any anatomical proof. This is not to deny that a legitimate contribution can be made by neurobiology. But here Flechsig is playing a conceptual game: a complex concept is reduced to an anatomical structure, or part, and then the part is expanded so that its anatomical limits burst to include more and more functions, until at last it becomes as large as the whole person, that is, in his own words, a *pars pro toto*, a part for the whole. Such conceptual problems are the recurrent fate of all reductionists, both physical and mental. Thus, according to Flechsig (1896d):

> *This* [character] *center is influenced by almost every part of the body*; in it are summated nerve stimuli from all the body organs to create feelings; from

it issue all the impulses. . . . The intellect is mainly determined by a few brain parts, and character by other parts. Therefore intellect and character are to some extent independent of each other; therefore, diseases do not damage to the same degree the light of reason and the fullness of the heart. Therefore, the ability to retain ethical principles in memory in a purely conceptual form is not the same as keeping them in flesh and blood. . . . These brain parts are also the principal seat, the *principal point of origin* of important nervous diseases, epilepsy and hysteria [pp. 35-36; emphasis Flechsig's].

We have reached the limits of brain anatomy and of the brain as metaphor: after having gone full circle, from Kant to cortex, we have returned to Kant in the cortex, in the shape of a fully anthropomorphized brain metaphor.

What is, for Flechsig, the proper antidote to the morbid excitation of the brain, the "heat of drives and feelings" (p. 39)? It is to be found in the mental-spiritual thought centers, the very ones that reside in the association centers, whose size and form determine performance. Thus, smallness of the hindbrain association centers in particular (such that the brain comes to assume an animal or simian shape) is the anatomical predisposition (*Keimanlage*; p. 32) in individuals given to criminal recidivism, aggressive behavior and the crudest sensual impulses. By contrast, asserts Flechsig, the mental centers were of enormous size in Bach and Beethoven. Often individuals with a low brain type show arrested development: "As far as brain form is concerned, they are in a state of continuous childhood, and maybe for this reason disease-producing factors deprave their character with particular ease, as actually happens in children" (p. 34). We can see how brain rhetoric can slide into morality rhetoric.

The aforementioned predispositions are also under the influence of the "milieu . . . the physical and bodily vicissitudes and experiences. The younger the child, the more injurious will be the effect of unhealthy influences on character" (p. 33). Among the injurious agents, including "bad diet, exhausting excesses, infectious diseases, painful affections, . . . brain diseases, poisonings and nervous diseases" (p. 34), Flechsig also lists narcotics, and, last but not least, hypnotic states: "Hypnosis is dangerous, for many of the habitual criminals, such as swindlers and confidence men, are hypnotists. The same can be said of many of the '*most dangerous*' inmates of insane asylums. . . . It is possible that even *artificial* hypnosis, i.e. the one used for *therapeutic* purposes, has a similar effect!"(p. 37; emphasis Flechsig's).

Is this prejudice or naïveté? Of course, *hypnosis* (as Flechsig uses the term) also implies suggestion, or simply influence, the influence people have on each other in any human interaction as agents who want to create belief, conviction, and compliance in others. Flechsig did not understand the universality of suggestion, as shown by Bernheim, or as intuitively understood by Paul Schreber. It is not that hypnosis and suggestion are evil but that they can be means to evil ends. Flechsig was mistaken in his wholesale rejection of hypnosis but prescient about the way hypnotic suggestion can be abused for personal, commercial and political gain.

However, all the talk about nerve centers had an added motive: it was Flechsig's groping for an answer to a burning issue of the day—the mounting attack on the credibility of psychiatry. His arguments about the brain were meant to bolster the tainted moral image of psychiatry by enhancing its status as a brain science. The real issue is raised by Flechsig (1896d) in the opening remarks in *Boundaries*. Speaking as a psychiatrist, not as brain anatomist, he observed: "Almost daily we are hearing that psychiatry (*Irrenheilkunde*) is not doing what is required by public interest. Insofar as these complaints are directed at certain alienists (*Irrenärzte*) and certain insane asylums (*Irrenanstalten*) they hardly deserve general attention, even if they were found to be justified" (p. 8). Flechsig's position was that even if some psychiatrists failed, there was no justification to indict the whole profession. True, but in fact the profession had been under attack for quite some decades now. Brochures by former mental patients, who saw themselves as victims and prisoners of an oppressive and arbitrary psychiatric establishment, were multiplying like mushrooms. The public outcry culminated in debates in the *Reichstag* in Berlin in 1897, calling for a revision of the insanity laws and commitment procedures, for improvements in the conditions in institutions, and for the supervision of psychiatrists and lawyers by lay review boards.

The core of *Boundaries* was the idea of

the real or supposed border lands of insanity. Among the alleged victims of the psychiatrist, who in the last years have mightily stirred public opinion, there is one group of persons occupying a prominent place, who live in a continuous state of war with the courts and the authorities . . . These individuals, upon whose mental equilibrium state order and valid laws in many ways act as a poison, are commonly qualified as litigious (*Querulanten*). . . . [or as sufferers from] litigious paranoia [*Querulanten-wahnsinn*] . . . this question is of a predominantly practical importance also in the political sense. . . . Even as I know of no case in which a mentally healthy person has been declared mentally incompetent (*entmündigt*) on the basis of litigious paranoia, . . . the psychiatrists are guilty of the error . . . of unjustifiably generalizing single observations. The so-called querulants are in no way uniformly afflicted by *psychosis* (*Wahnsinn*), they are not all of them driven by delusional *ideas*! Barring those individuals to whom at least some *injustice* had really been done, it is only some querulants that belong to those afflicted with fixed delusions of the chronically crazy psychotics as defined by scientific psychiatry. These individuals that show all manner of hallucinations (*Sinnestäuschungen*) and fantastic persecutory ideas revel in their role as redeemers of their brethren oppressed by the law. . . . Another group of querulants does not show *anomalies of intellect*, but *defects of character*. One of the groups that belongs here suffers from pronounced moral insanity [in English in the original], . . . morally defective and with a perversely eccentric way of feeling . . . to whom the *biologico-pathological* [i.e, brain anatomy] method of investigation should be applied [pp. 22-25; emphasis Flechsig's].

The remaining arguments expressed in *Boundaries* are of interest for a number of reasons. Flechsig, the redeemer of psychiatry in the name of brain science, declares his interest in forensic psychiatry, which has hitherto been unknown (and to which we shall return at the end of this chapter). He does admit that there is something wrong with psychiatry, that some injustice has been done. He also says that delusions are organically caused by hallucinations, viewed as organic disorders of the sense organs, an opinion endorsed by Kraepelin and Weber and shared by today's *Diagnostic and Statistical Manual* of mental disorders of the American Psychiatric Association (DSM-III). (By this time, 1896, the delusional redeemer Paul Schreber was already declared legally incompetent and was lingering at Sonnenstein.)

After 1896 Flechsig participated in a number of international congresses and in the international Brain Commission, received honorary degrees from a number of universities, and was feted by royalty. In 1901 he took part in the international congress of physiologists in Turin, where he demonstrated his division of the cortex into myelogenetically derived areas. In 1903 the international Brain Commission was formed, of which Flechsig became a member.[41] In 1907 he was elected to membership in the Conseil d'administration de l'Institut général psychologique de Paris ("Personalnachrichten," *PNW*, 8:386). He was honored by his students with two festschrifts: the first in 1909, coinciding with the 500th jubilee of his alma mater Lipsiensis (i.e., Leipzig University) and the bestowal of an honorary doctorate in philosophy; and the second in 1927. However, he did not receive permission from the Ministry of Education to travel as an invited guest in the United States. In 1920, at age 73, he retired from his duties. The last time Flechsig took part in a public affair was in 1922, the year of the 100th anniversary of the Society of German Scientists and Physicians. This was only four years after the ending of the Great War, a depressing time. The interest shown in "brain and soul" was moderate, nothing compared to the great reception 50 years earlier, "when a Helmholtz and a Carl Ludwig sat at my feet" (*Myelogenesis*, p. 55).

In 1922, at the age of 75, Flechsig married again, a woman 29 years his junior. We are not told whether he was happy with his first wife who had been an invalid for many years; his second marriage was said to be harmonious. Seven years later he died, following a short heart illness accompanied by anxiety states. His pupil Pfeifer recalled a conversation he had with Flechsig one day before his death: "'You have had beautiful times in your life. Do you still think about your old teacher Ludwig? Do you remember when you were rector and read your great speech?' 'Yes,' he replied, 'those were great and splendid times!' And these were his last words" (Pfeifer, 1930, p. 262). On the 24 of July, 1929, the rector of Leipzig University reported to the Ministry of Education:

> On July 22 of this year died due to heart failure professor of psychiatry, Privy Councillor, doctor of medicine and honorary doctor of philosophy Paul Flechsig at age 82. The cremation will take place on Friday the 26 at 11 a.m. at the South Cemetery (Flechsig, 1877-1931).

Between 1896 and 1927 Flechsig did not produce much new material. The publications of the last period were mainly variations on neuroanatomical themes derived from the idea of myelogenesis, brain sections and brain slides. These are mostly of interest to the basic science of neuroanatomy and its history. There exists a small literature about the importance of Flechsig in the history of neuroanatomy[42] and in it there is a number of statements about his character. The latter is of relevance to the fate of Paul Schreber.

FLECHSIG'S PERSONALITY

Flechsig himself offers a rare self-revelation in letters to V. M. von Bechterew, whom he addressed as "Dear and esteemed friend" (Flechsig, 1893-1899).[43] It shows his need for approval as well as his sense of self-importance. In these letters I found in St. Petersburg, Flechsig reiterates expressions of gratitude for Bekhterev's appreciation for his work, for example: "The less we can count in general on thanks in our practical and theortical work, the more this proof of your devotion has touched me and I drew from it new courage to continue along the path I have been pursuing" (Letter of May 7, 1893). He also offers excuses for his being a "lazy correspondent," explaining this habit as follows:

> The delay derives from a fault in my nature which is probably my most pronounced trait. I always want to do everything myself in a most

thorough fashion and therefore wait for the longest time until I find truly sufficient time to complete the task. . . . Great thanks for a very friendly dedication! It was enormously gratifying to receive such an ovation from your hand! In regard to the developmental-historical school [i.e, the myelogenetic method] you have earned the greatest merit; you are our Apostle Paul who helps to spread the teaching in the wide world . . . [Letter of January 15, 1894].

In response to congratulations from the Minister of Education on his eightieth birthday, Flechsig had this to say about himself:

I always strove to find an objective basis for truth, but in the process I have come into conflict with reigning maxims without the opportunity to prove my integrity. From your letter, your Excellency, it appears that such prejudices no longer prevail and I thus thank you for your encouragement to persevere in my quest for truth [Letter of July 22, 1922; Flechsig, 1877-1931].

These lines suggest pride and pain alike, Flechsig's external and internal conflicts and his sensitivity to criticism. On the other hand, Flechsig's domineering personal style became a legend in his own day.

A typical Voigtländer, Flechsig was a big, broad, bulky individual with a tendency to be abrupt and dogmatic. He frequently declared that it is the duty of a Professor to think 'other than others.' His students did not consider him their friend, but conceded than he was extraordinarily erudite.

He tended to have a poor memory for the discoveries of others; Oscar Vogt tells the story that back in 1894 he showed a newly found group of fibers . . . to Flechsig and that three weeks later Flechsig demonstrated them to him as his (Flechsig's) discovery [Haymaker and Schiller, 1970, pp. 26-27].

A similar accusation against Flechsig was recorded by Auguste Forel following complaints by von Gudden (Forel, 1935).

People who knew Flechsig regarded him as an "odd fish." "Of big body build, he was dressed in all weather in a broad overcoat, a wide brimmed hat and galoshes, and armed, even in sunshine, with an unsheathed umbrella. Following him at a distance of a few feet was his servant, a former patient called Janitzschke, similarly attired, and in addition equipped with a large shopping bag" (Sachse, 1955, pp. 14-15). At other times he was seen dressed in a "silk waistcoat with big glass buttons and a wide-brimmed hat on his head, looking the part of a village mayor more than a man of science."

According to Sachse, he was overbearing with visitors, even high ranking ones, and kept them waiting, with the excuse that they wanted something from him, not he from them. One day an official from the Ministry, His Excellency Mr. Schmaltz, called and was kept waiting for half an hour; when told that the man was impatient, "like a tiger in a cage," Flechsig said calmly, "Give him potassium bromide," a frequently used tranquilizer in those days, also given to Schreber. Toward the end of an agitated conversation, as he was reaching for his galoshes looking backward over his shoulder, Flechsig spoke to His Excellency: "Don't take it amiss, but jurists know nothing about such matters, they should leave this to physicians." His Excellency left beet red and beside himself. Later Flechsig commented: "The armchair-warmer/farter wanted to talk me into some plan at my hospital, he wanted everything cheaper, he is totally crazy." People put up with his eccentricities and his insistence on speaking the Saxon dialect because he projected an enormous presence and exuded self-confidence in his personality and his scientific achievements.

Another trait was Flechsig's expression of strong likes and dislikes toward certain classes of people. According to one anecdote, he evinced a particular dislike toward jurists and theologians, both targets for his barbs (not an auspicious attitude as far as Paul Schreber was concerned): "When you face a man who roars so loud [*so laut brüllenden Menschen*], you should think of religious ideas. It is well known that those roar the loudest." On another occasion he was heard to reply, "Agreed, but what do jurists have to do with the brain?" (Sachse, 1955, pp. 14-19).

His pupil Pfeifer (1930) described him as a pyknic body type with a cyclothymic temperament.

Flechsig's life shows phases during which he was in top form, when he stood crowned in glory and appeared able to enjoy every aspect of life. His head was then full of good ideas; and if genius be defined by the reliability of his observations and the infallibility of his conclusions, then Flechsig was undoubtedly a genius. He not only was a wellspring of stimulation, but he also swept his coworkers along with him by dint of his work drive. His students were inspired by him ... However, we also knew Flechsig during phases of depression, when he tended to act unfairly, when he spoke in exalted tones and only about himself, when he behaved tyrannically toward his subordinates. . . . Such an intolerance was not, however, the result of an emotional lability . . . but was a manifestation of sullenness that in Flechsig could last for years and at times led to states of lethargy, during which he would withdrew completely from the outside world and lie on the couch behind locked doors. He would doze off, read no books and do no work, and it would cost him a considerable effort to hold a lecture, which he read in a soft, barely audible voice. He was capable of falling asleep during a conversation with a person he just met, or during an examination; and he would leave the hospital in the hands of his head attending [p. 261].

Another former student of Flechsig's during 1917-1918,[44] when Flechsig was in his early seventies, remembered him as

an elderly man of athletic build and robust appearance for his age, erect and noble of bearing; his face was broad, the head hair still abundant, with beard and glasses. I never saw him dressed other than in a black frock coat, looking solemn and clean. His gait was springy. . . . He was relatively taciturn and engendered a continuous feeling of a certain anxiety. As witnessed by his longtime attendants in his hospital, he was very stingy, loved money and feared he might lose it in Leipzig either due to the war or because of the rise of the communists. As this danger became real, he used to say to me: "Just let them come, I have got this iron bar in my bed." Retrospectively, this could be read as a sign of senile dementia at that time [letter of Dr. Shilo, 1966].

The remarks about the communists made Dr. Shilo think of delusional propensities in Flechsig. "At that time he also suffered from prostatitis accompanied by uremia. As an examiner during exams in medicine, Flechsig fell asleep and did not seem to hear the answers. Dr. Shilo also recalled that Flechsig was an "authoritarian man, a quality to which he was entitled by virtue of his vast knowledge. . . . The quarters of the private patients in the hospital were very comfortably appointed and the use of the straitjacket eschewed. Flechsig was not known for his art of detailed written mental status examinations of patients." Flechsig does not appear to have mentioned Schreber to his former student.

A story that has surfaced recently is told by Kraepelin (1987) in his posthumously published *Memoirs*. Kraepelin, an authority for both Weber and Freud, born in the same year as Freud, came to work for Flechsig in 1882. At that time Kraepelin was also working in the psychology laboratory of Wilhelm Wundt, the first modern experimental psychologist. Since Wundt could not pay much to the recently married Kraepelin, he suggested to the struggling physician that he might be able to make a living by working in Flechsig's newly opened hospital. Kraepelin had previously met Flechsig in von Gudden's hospital in Munich in 1881, where he heard von Gudden accuse Flechsig of having plagiarized a discovery of his. Shortly after he started his job, Kraepelin was suddenly dismissed by Flechsig. Trenckmann (1982) tells a much more innocent version of this story.

It is possible that Flechsig was jealous of Kraepelin's allegiance to Wundt,[45] or that he was angered by Kraepelin's acting on Wundt's suggestion to request a commitment in writing to ensure his future promotion. Kraepelin later learned, through his highly placed connections, that Flechsig had falsely accused him of professional misconduct to the Ministry. Kraepelin was saved by the personal intervention of the Minister of Education.

Kraepelin's initial impression of Flechsig was positive: "Flechsig wrote to me some days ago from Berlin. . . . A promising young devil, this Flechsig" (Letter of December 29, 1878; in Forel, 1968, p. 146). But after the disappointment, and when Flechsig was in power, Kraepelin acknowledged, "Through my experiences here and in spite of an unaltered penchant for scientific work I have developed a very strong *dégout* [distaste] for academic relations and am inclined, in my present mood, to take the first best second assistantship elsewhere. . ." (Kraepelin on January 16, 1883; in Forel, 1968, p. 161).[46] In the end Kraepelin became the reigning psychiatric authority of his time.[47] Four editions of his *Textbook* are quoted and debated by Paul Schreber. It became the foundation of the *Diagnostic and Statistical Manual* (DSM-III and DSM-IV) of mental disorders of the American Psychiatric Association.

In contrast to Flechsig's poor relationship with Kraepelin, he maintained friendly ties with another of psychiatry's greats, Adolf Meyer, prior to the latter's emigration to the United States. This is reflected in letters written to Meyer in 1890 that are cordial, light-hearted and witty.[48]

Flechsig expressed his feelings about psychiatry in a statement he made to his successor at Leipzig, Oswald Bumke: "You know, said Flechsig, I have never had an interest in psychiatry, which at any rate I consider a hopeless science. The [Leipzig University] Hospital reflected this, too. One abandoned cells, grates, straight jackets, hammocks but one was still afraid of the patients" (Flechsig, quoted in Trenckmann, 1982). What an anticlimactic summing up from a lifelong apostle of brain psychiatry!

There was one more retreat or, more precisely, a return. Toward the end of his career Flechsig recalled where he came from: Kant the philosopher and Gall the phrenologist. He mentioned them in the last section, entitled *"Anthropologisches,"* of his last work, *Myelogenesis*. Gall has been often derided for having dressed up the discredited faculty psychology by finding correlations between faculties and bumps on the skull. In *Myelogenesis* Gall is embraced by Flechsig as the man who had the correct intuition about the importance of the cerebral hemispheres and the localization of mental processes in them, which is valid.

At the same time, Flechsig took offense that in America they refer to his anatomical divisions of the cortex as "Leipzigian or Flechsigian phrenology." But the shoe fits, for the theory of cerebral localizations, for all its anatomical refinements, inevitably harks back to the anthropomorphic statements of faculty psychology. After having for years localized the "feeling soul and the thinking mind" in the associations centers of the posterior parts of the hemispheres, Flechsig now claims to have found the frontal brain, an area that had not been his interest, to be the seat of "mental centers" (geistige Zentren). In what reads like his testament, Flechsig invokes Kant's Anthropology:[49]

> Man is capable of entertaining the idea of the I, and in this he is *infinitely* above all the creatures upon earth. Thanks to this he is a person . . . "This I-ness . . . this faculty (that is, to think) is reason" . . . the brain part to which the "I"-idea is attached is *the one most developed in man* . . . one cannot imagine a more perfect agreement than that between introspective observation and biology . . . I must say that of all my discoveries none has given me more joy than this apotheosis of our Kant . . . the frontal lobe is the seat of logic and the totality of all ideas . . . The ancient fable that the *whole* cortex participates in *every psychical act* appears so erroneous in the light of myelogenetic brain theory and pathology, that I . . . hope that present brain investigators will labor to breathe new life into the legacy of a now surpassed phase of research [*Myelogenesis*, pp. 119-122; emphasis Flechsig's].

These are Flechsig's last published words.[50] More than a century later the mind-body junction is still as sealed as it was in his day, and neither findings of neuropathology nor the sophisticated methods of the neurosciences can interpret one psychical act of introspection. The rising tide of holistic conceptions of brain functioning in the 1920s was refuting the theory of localizations, not to mention Kant and psychoanalysis. Originally, myelogenesis was but one of the laboratory methods for tracing pathways and structures in the central nervous system. For Flechsig, a "scientist out of passion," the structures turned into an all-encompassing system. They were for him a heroic struggle against mysticism. But he protested too much: the structures were but anatomical allegories of the soul. In the end he went back to his spiritual and Kantian roots:[51] he found again the repudiated soul.

FLECHSIG AS FORENSIC EXPERT

We saw earlier that in discussing litigious querulants in *Boundaries* Flechsig (1896d) noted that in the case of those "alleged victims of the psychiatrists who in the last years have mightily stirred public opinion," the psychiatrists were "guilty of the error of unjustifiably generalizing single observations" and "at least some injustice had really been done" (p. 24). That year Flechsig was officially named legal medical officer (*Gerichtsarzt*) of the county court for the Leipzig University Psychiatric Hospital (Flechsig, 1877-1931).

In these remarks in *Boundaries* Flechsig was referring to the antipsychiatry reaction in Germany coeval with the rise of institutional psychiatry in mid-nineteenth century. The public outcry against abuses of psychiatry, or the first antipsychiatry, climaxed in the 1890's and the first decade of the 20th century. A number of psychiatrists, physicians, and lawyers came out defending patients' rights against the arbitrariness of psychiatrists. Flechsig took part in this reaction. One year after Schreber's death, the psychiatric establishment, beleaguered by the public, the *Reichstag* and the press, mounted a counteroffensive. It was documented in a book by a Bavarian psychiatrist Bernhard Beyer (1912), *The Campaign to Reform Psychiatry* (or, for brevity, *Reform*), a 668 page-long treasure trove of case histories, documents, commentaries and debates for and against psychiatrists and the revision of Germany's mental health laws. Among the cases discussed was Schreber's and among the psychiatrists, Flechsig.[52]

While Beyer says that in Schreber's case there was no room for doubt that the patient was crazy and the psychiatrist maligned, the next case in which Flechsig was implicated as a forensic expert was at best an ambiguous one. The case was that of the merchant Feldmann, discussed by psychiatrists Beyer (1912) and Goetze (1896), the former as an adversary, the latter as advocate.[53]

Hermann Feldmann was born in 1831 and became a wealthy merchant and an American citizen. Following a wound to his head, he developed hypochondria and anxiety states. Later ideas of persecution, hallucinations and severe headaches led to two suicide attempts. He believed that the doctors secretly conspired to poison all the rich people in Bonn. He saw hideous animals crawling out of stoves, small horrible little figures sitting on the bedposts, and, "according to Flechsig, he heard the voice of his wife and other people everywhere hurling accusations and threats at him, that 'his sister was his mistress,' etc. . . . he believed he was syphilitic, that his body was rotten inside, that only the outside shell was still intact, that with his syphilis he made his whole family unhappy" (Beyer, pp. 242-243; also in *AZP*, 51:824ff). He was initially treated in a hospital and either was released or absconded.

After a period of relative calm, trouble started again in 1883, when Mrs. Feldmann took up with a lover, a pharmacist and entrepreneur named Hemmerling. For the next decade Feldmann was in and out of hospitals. Two facts were beyond doubt: that Feldmann was disturbed and that Mrs. Feldmann wanted no part of him and openly cuckolded him. Thus in 1886, in anticipation of Feldmann's return home from a stay in Switzerland, a habitual sanctuary for many a German psychiatric and political fugitive, Mrs. Feldmann pleaded with the eminent Bonn psychiatrist Professor Pelman that her husband was still crazy and prevailed upon Pelman to sign a certificate about her husband, sight unseen, which she presented to the police who then committed him to an asylum by force.

When Herr Feldmann was later duly declared mentally incompetent, the wife, as the court appointed guardian, proceeded to squander her husband's fortune in the company of her lover, unhampered by a husband safely under lock and key. Feldmann's vehement letters and protests against the confinement and the shameless exploitation by wife and lover went unheeded until he enlisted the support of two powerful figures on the German psychiatric scene: the lawyer H. Reinartz and the prominent professor of medicine and psychiatry, Carl Finkelnburg.

It is not clear how Feldmann got to Flechsig in 1887, when Flechsig rendered an expert opinion. It appears that it was an opinion favorable to Feldmann, for he bombarded Flechsig with letters and telegrams to be sent the report. Feldmann also pestered the Minister of Justice and court officials. This prompted his new advocate, Finkelnburg, to write letters to him (reproduced in Beyer, pp. 246-247), dissuading him, in his own interest, from threatening Flechsig with complaints to the Ministry. Finkelnburg also pleaded with Feldmann to desist from complaining to all and sundry about being pursued by Freemasons, Jews, Ultramontanists, and spies lest he destroy the efforts he and the lawyer were making on his behalf. Finkelnburg's actions were decried by psychiatrists inimical to Feldmann as an unethical prompting of a patient to disguise his illness and as treasonous to the profession.

There came a time, however, when the lovers themselves ended up being hounded by the public prosecutor and the police: they were arrested, tried as swindlers, and sent to prison, the wife for two, her accomplice for four years. The betrayed husband seemed to be vindicated. Moreover, as a result of Finkelnburg's and Reinartz's advocacy the incompetency ruling was itself overturned and Feldmann was released in 1893. The indignities and horrors suffered by poor Feldmann were laid bare in a brochure by Reinartz (1894), *The Story of an Incompetency Ruling*, with a preface by Finkelnburg, which created a furor in the press.

The *forensic-psychiatric* issue was that even though Feldmann was obviously sick, this in and of itself should not have impugned Feldmann's credibility nor should it have been used as a reason to keep him confined in an asylum indefinitely. This was exactly the point made by none other than Auguste Forel, who became involved in the case in 1894, after the patient again fled to Switzerland. Forel—the outstanding neuroanatomist, a former competitor of Flechsig's for the post in Leipzig and Eugen Bleuler's predecessor as director of Burghölzli—was flooded with letters and telegrams from Germany, including some by Mrs. Feldmann herself, to prevail upon him to lock Feldmann up. However, Forel found that Mr. Feldmann, chronic paranoiac that he was, caused no disturbance in Switzerland. Forel was also impressed that the patient "had a tremendous fear of mental hospitals and an intense desire to have the freedom of movement, that he felt well and happy after he had absconded from the last asylum he was in, even though he had no complaints about it" (Beyer, p. 546). Therefore, he decided that the patient did not need to be in a hospital. Said Forel, "Looked at objectively, this case is rich in lessons. We cannot emphasize enough that it is the duty of the psychiatrist to proclaim loudly that to be mentally sick and to be locked up are two different things" (Goetze, 1896, p. 16). However, Forel was not the only lenient and liberal one. The irony, noted in a follow-up report of the Rhein Province Psychiatric Association, was that "Flechsig made the same determination and recommended that as much as possible one should accommodate the patient, to the extent that this became feasible given his states of hallucinatory confusion. These facts have been partially suppressed in Reinartz's brochure" (*AZP*, 51:825).

The notoriety of the case had forced the psychiatric establishment to take notice; and the affair was formally discussed at two meetings of the Psychiatric Association of the Rhein Province. The psychiatrists were in an uproar. At one of the meetings a letter of clarification and support from Flechsig was read (Beyer, pp. 247-248). In his letter Flechsig sought to clear himself of two accusations. He insisted that he never considered Feldmann entirely healthy, nor did he see him as totally paranoid. He believed the story of the wife's infidelity with one exception: "Mr. Feldmann maintained that one day he asked his wife whether she could possibly have infected him with syphilis and she replied, 'No, I've always picked them healthy.' It was only this statement, underscored by Dr. Reinartz, which I had considered as 'possibly' delusional, which would also suggest that the expression 'possibly' might refer to a fresh delusion. I have believed all the other complaints of Feldmann against his wife" (Flechsig quoted in Beyer, 1912, p. 248). Eventually, following his release, Feldmann did not do so well. He rented rooms from a lady who owned a villa and had an attendant living with him around the clock. He remained depressed and one time attempted to hang himself and was rescued. He continued to suffer from depressions and died not long after having regained his freedom. He presumably starved himself to death under the influence of fears of being poisoned. In a subsequent review of the case, Beyer bemoaned the fact that after the indefatigable psychiatrists finally succeeded to procure for him a tolerable way of living, less experienced people managed to tear him away only to consign him to his old misery.

With respect to Flechsig, the significance of the Feldmann case lies in the demonstration of Flechsig's relative sophistication and judgment. No less perspicacious than Forel, he both accepted the reality of Feldmann's accusations against his wife and recognized that Feldmann's various delusions on other subjects did not necessarily mandate a forced hospitalization.

Flechsig was involved with three more cases. The first concerns the sad story of a man from the lower classes, a shoemaker. The dramatic events took place in Dresden, two years before Paul Schreber's appointment to the high court there and his second admission to Flechsig's. The simple shoemaker Johann Andreas Rodig, born in Erfurt in 1850, was the only son of a weaver from Sebnitz in Saxon Switzerland, thus a contemporary of Paul Schreber. His story appears in two pamphlets: *A Forbes Case in Saxony or How One Can Be Gradually Driven Crazy. The Experiences of J. A. R. from Leipzig-Lindenau* (1895) and *Without Rights in a Constitutional State: A Faithful Representation of the Legal Injustices and Errors By a Victim Thereof J. A. R. or How to Declare Someone Crazy Made Easy as ABC* (1897).[54]

Rodig married in 1877 and settled in Leipzig. The mechanization of labor made him unemployed and penniless. A year later on a visit to Sebnitz, he learned serendipitously from church registries that back in 1854 Dr. J. C. Rodig, a lawyer and judge in Pirna (the site of the Sonnenstein Asylum) to whom Johann Rodig believed himself to be related, died without issue and left an estate of 30,000 thalers, which was divided among several legatees. No official legal notices had been published in the newspapers. By coincidence, that same year there was an attempt on the Kaiser's life by two Social Democrats, Hödel and Nobiling, which led to the outlawing of the Social Democratic party in Germany. Rodig was overheard by an informant of the police discussing these events, handed an expulsion order on false grounds of defamation of the monarchy and membership in the Social Democratic party, and imprisoned. In 1884 Rodig was told to emigrate to America, which he declined and was jailed again as "vagrant and homeless." His wife's pleadings got him released to a marginal life without work, house, or homeland.

Rodig's next misfortune in 1891 was to be falsely denounced as a thief, a charge of which he was cleared. He now "broke down physically, [his] nerves . . . shattered" (Rodig, 1895, p. 20). He consulted Dr. Windscheid,[55] who prescribed a rest cure paid by the state health insurance. "Upon his return to Leipzig, Herr Professor Flechsig and Herr Dr. Teuscher continued to treat me for my nerves, and I have to thank these gentlemen for still having my wits with me" (Rodig, 1897, p. 21).

Rodig persisted in his efforts to obtain the inheritance and compensations from the state. The matter was referred to Minister of Justice Schurig, the same one who would inform Paul Schreber of his appointment to the high judicial post in Dresden two years later. The case was heard in the highest court of appeals of the land, in the First *Civilsenat* of the Dresden *Oberlandesgericht*, and was rejected by the high court and the ministries of justice and of the interior. Rodig was arrested and remanded to the Dresden Municipal Hospital for the Invalids and the Insane for observation. He refused an offer of settlement and the director of the hospital, Dr. Ganser (famous for the syndrome in psychiatry named after him), noted forensic expert and friend of Weber, diagnosed him as suffering from delusions due to litigious paranoia and declared him incompetent and fit to be transferred to a custodial asylum. While all this was going on behind his back, Rodig hoped that "the Dresden Asylum would transfer [him] to the Clinic of Herr Professor Flechsig in Leipzig, of which [he] was not afraid, since Herr Professor Flechsig knew full well that [he] was not psychotic" (Rodig, 1897, p. 35). Instead, Rodig was committed to the custodial asylum Colditz, where Weber had worked as a beginner in psychiatry. The court-appointed guardian rubber-stamped the decision.

Rodig stayed at Colditz for 15 months, unaffected by the roaring and laughing maniacs. He behaved quietly, showed no signs of mental illness, and kept busy making boots for the doctors. Like Schreber, he "wrote a book describing [his] experiences from childhood up until my confinement in the institution . . . hoping that [it would] . . . persuade the hospital director that [he was] mentally normal" (Rodig, 1895, p. 57). Whether it was the manuscript or his behavior, the fact remains that throughout his 15 month stay the doctors were favorably inclined toward him and stated so in writing. Rodig also kept writing letters which showed no trace of mental disturbance to his wife, and the indefatigable woman, supported by the letters of the Colditz psychiatrists, finally prevailed: Rodig was released and the incompetency ruling was annulled. Since he continued to sue for his inheritance, in 1895 he was again examined by psychiatrists. Dr. Popitz of Leipzig diagnosed him as suffering from neurasthenia (*Nervenschwäche*) but emphatically denied having observed any signs of psychosis (*Geisteskrankheit*). The psychiatric court-appointed expert (*Gerichtsarzt*) Dr. Thümler, diagnosed Rodig as "suffering from a variant of chronic craziness [*Verrücktheit*, i.e., paranoia], the litigious insanity [-*Querulantenwahn*]. Amid his continuing woes Rodig found many people in various cities sympathetic to his plight and ready to help out with money. In the epilogue to the story Mr. Rodig was able to remain free and obtain a domicile.

The story illustrates how a simple man made himself into a social nuisance and became a victim of his character, circumstances, and the system. Rodig's story is paradigmatic of the deep social and political problems brewing in Saxony at the turn of the century. While England and France were forging the traditions of democracy, the Germans seemed to be living in the era of the post-Napoleonic reaction. The unprecedented growth of what in England was termed "the lunacy trade" paralleled the rise of industrialization, the bourgeoisie, the proletariat, the party system, and in particular, German socialism and communism in the shape of the Social Democratic Party, which defeated Schreber in the elections of 1884. Pandora's box had been flung open, and social ills of all kinds descended on the land. Institutional psychiatry, armed with its own impressive power in what was otherwise a parliamentary police state, was called upon to serve as an additional bulwark of social order. The crisis in psychiatry was one of the symptoms of the agonies of society as a whole. But in this respect, as a University Professor and a man of the upper class, Flechsig could afford, if he chose, to remain loftily above the fray. Thus, not only did his treatment win Rodig's thanks for helping him keep his "wits," but Flechsig was also willing to contribute privately to the poor man's upkeep thereafter. He thus appears discreetly listed in Rodig's pamphlet in the roster of his benefactors as "Herr Hofrath Prof. F." of "Leipzig" (Rodig, 1895, p. 62). In an age that was still in flux, the imperious Flechsig could still choose private charity as an alternative to official medical-forensic intervention.

Flechsig was involved in two more incompetency cases: Carl Paasch and Karl Albert Petzold. Both cases were brought up as victims of psychiatric abuse in the 1897 session of the *Reichstag*, during which motions to reform the mental hygiene laws of the land were debated and voted upon (Beyer, 1912). Carl Paasch was an example of the political abuse of psychiatry. He was active in German anti-semitic organizations that met in Leipzig. Beginning in 1891 he wrote numerous anti-semitic pamphlets[56] decrying the world domination by the Jews and attacked the behavior of Bismarck's Imperial Envoy to China, the Jew von Brandt,[57] in a pamphlet, *Eine Jüdisch Deutsche*

Gesandtschaft und Ihre Helfer (A Jewish–German Embassy and Its Helpers). He argued that von Brandt must have had connections in the cabinet, since Bismarck's chief financial wizard was the Jew Gerson von Bleichröder. The troublesome Paasch was declared psychotic by the then well-known psychiatry professors Jolly and Siemerling and admitted to an asylum. Later, he was detained on the orders of a police physician as "a madman dangerous to the public order" and again certified to an asylum. Smuggled out by friends and still under threat of being declared incompetent, Paasch stayed voluntarily at Flechsig's in 1894 at the same time as Schreber. He went out on a leave and never came back;[58] on October 2, 1894 he was given a clean bill of health by Flechsig: "The nervous irritability which at the time has required his treatment at the *Psychiatrische Klinik* has disappeared and he appears capable to go back to exercise his former profession."[59]

Karl Albert Petzold was also given a clean bill of health by Flechsig. The Petzold case is of particular interest. The story was told by Representative Lenzmann during the 132nd session of the German *Reichstag* on February 1, 1902, ten months before Schreber's release from Sonnenstein. The factory owner Petzold of Auerbach was believed to be insane by the local authorities; a doctor declared him to be demented before the courts. This misuse of expert opinion was engineered by the mayor of Auerbach. For years the mayor had been embezzling city funds with the collaboration of a fraudulent treasurer. When Petzold blew the whistle, the psychiatric report came in handy as a means of getting rid of the enemy. Petzold solicited a psychiatric opinion from Flechsig, and Flechsig declared him mentally healthy, thus saving him from ignominy and incarceration. Lenzmann also mentioned that the whole affair was described in a pamphlet authored by Flechsig himself. (I was unable to find this pamphlet anywhere. In our attempt to understand the Schreber case, such a pamphlet would be as important as all of Flechsig's writings on the brain.[60])

What the foregoing cases demonstrate is that Flechsig was well versed in the forensic issues pertaining to psychiatric diagnosis and that on the whole his attitude toward what we now call patient rights was both more sophisticated and more liberal than that of many of his colleagues.

Flechsig's involvement with issues of antipsychiatry has not been discussed before in the literature on Schreber. This is of particular importance in understanding the background to the issue of the involuntary hospitalization of Schreber at Sonnenstein, since Flechsig arranged for the transfer. Our interest in the attitude of Flechsig toward Feldmann stems from the fact that both Schreber and Feldmann entered Flechsig's life orbit at the same time and similar themes reverberated in both cases. Moreover, in both cases the wives played prominent roles in their husbands' institutionalizations.

The forensic activities of Flechsig show an aspect of Flechsig that is of considerable relevance to the story of Paul Schreber. Flechsig was well aware that a diagnosis of psychosis could result in a declaration of incompetency and in turn deprive an individual of his civil liberties and rights, ruin his standing in the community, and wreck his career. We can thus appreciate that the diagnosis he initially rendered on Schreber to the Ministry of Justice during his second hospitalization—"sleeplessness"—could have been a way to protect the patient. But then, it is also a fact that the florid delusions did not appear until months after Schreber's second admission to Flechsig's. Furthermore, then as now, a transfer from a teaching hospital setting to a state hospital also meant a stigmatization of the patient as one whose prognosis was poor and thus was unlikely—or legally permitted, as in the case of Schreber—ever to return to his premorbid level of functioning.[61] This brings us to an unanswered question: Why was Flechsig unwilling to be an advocate for Paul Schreber? For Flechsig showed a certain liberal pro-patient attitude not shared by many of his institutional colleagues. It is possible that Flechsig simply thought that Schreber's illness was indeed too grave, his prognosis indeed too poor, to justify a continued stay at his Hospital. And it is certainly likely, that in his own mind he justified his decision along these diagnostic and prognostic lines. But one should also consider the impact on Flechsig of Schreber's deterioration, which occurred in the face, so to speak, of both Flechsig's confident initial pronouncements and his best therapeutic efforts. A patient who gets worse does not thereby endear himself to his doctor. One must consider, too, the impact of the incipient alliance with Schreber's wife. In Sabine, Flechsig had an ally with whom he could share his frustration over this difficult patient; moreover, as a patient in her own right, she proved herself to be responsive to Flechsig's therapeutic interventions, quite unlike the intractable husband. In the absence of more documentation, it is impossible to be sure precisely what interpersonal drama was played out between the three, patient, wife and doctor. The only certainty is that the outcome was psychically lethal to Schreber. But, taking matters from Schreber's point of view, it is a reasonable surmise to think that what he ultimately received from Flechsig was diametrically opposite to what he had expected. Flechsig was known for his relative sensitivity to the forensic issues related to diagnosis, findings of incompetency, and forcible hospitalization, and he had heretofore shown that he could be skillfully protective of Schreber's interests in terms how he diagnosed him. Now, however, Flechsig was willing to transfer him to a state hospital, and thereby to expose him to all the formidable police powers then enjoyed by institutional psychiatry. He sided with Paul's wife and was turned off by Schreber. Either way, the net result was that he banished Paul Schreber to Sonnenstein.

The relationship between Flechsig and Schreber ended on a sour note. The last and only known statement by Flechsig about Paul is in what is marked as "Professor Flechsig's Report from June 25, 1894" (see Appendix). It is unclear how much of the report is direct quotation and how much paraphrase. A diagnosis is not mentioned. In this brief summary Flechsig refers to a number of hallucinations and delusions he termed hypochondriacal (for example, Schreber said he had softening of the brain, that he was dead and decayed), but without noting their depressive connotation. There was one gender and one sex idea: that he was a woman and had to "oppose energetically the Urning[62] [homosexual man] love of certain persons." He also had "persecutory ideas: 'luckily for him, he had been driven crazy.'" In addition, "especially toward the end of his stay at the Leipzig Hospital the references were increasingly to being tortured to death in a gruesome manner. . . . He wanted to convert to the Roman Catholic Church in order to escape from snares and traps [Nachstellungen]."[63] If this is a quote from Schreber himself, which seems likely, it speaks to his sense of entrapment. And putting this psychotic elaboration on the theme to one side, the fact was that Schreber was indeed caught in a medical-forensic trap, one that was partly of his own making. For by alienating Sabine and denying her funds, he had forced her to make her own arrangements. And here must be observed more closely the significance of her own unsuccessful efforts, mentioned earlier but not yet discussed in a way they deserve, to have his paycheck cleared without his signature or consent. When these efforts failed, Sabine was driven to consider her options, and among those options the determination of incompetency naturally loomed largest. That option would allow her to receive the funds she needed to maintain herself and the household without any further need for continuing negotiations with her difficult, manifestly ill husband, who was at that time finding fresh avenues for distancing himself and for violating the terms of their hitherto shared sensibility. Necessarily, Sabine would have discussed the issue of incompetency with Flechsig, just as he would have discussed with her his plan to have Schreber transferred. As the sixth-month deadline approached, Schreber's continued dependency on these two people was becoming progressively more problematic. There were indeed "snares and traps" about, and Schreber did not know how to extricate himself.

The text of Flechsig's report was incorporated into the first of two

hitherto unknown reports by Weber (Schreber's Personal File, Devreese, 1981a), Schreber's next important psychiatrist. The other reports by Weber are reproduced in the *Memoirs*. In this chapter I have
described a hitherto unknown facet of Flechsig, his role as forensic
expert. But Weber was the forensic expert par excellence, and it is to
him that we now turn.

SYNOPSIS OF FLECHSIG'S LIFE AND WORK

1847, June 29: Born in Zwickau, Saxony, to a Protestant minister.

1856-1865: Student at the Zwickau high school (*Lyzeum*).

1865: Graduates from the Zwickau high school and matriculates as
medical student at Leipzig University (except for brief ab-
sences, he was to stay in Leipzig all his life).

1870: Passes exams for his medical degree; graduates as M.D. from
Leipzig University with dissertation on syphilitic meningitis.

1870-1871: Service in the Franco-Prussian war; surgeon-major in
the reserve.

1872: Assistant to Professor Ernst Wagner at the Institute of
Anatomy and Pathology and the Department of Medicine of
Leipzig University.

1873: Assistant at the Physiological Institute of Leipzig University.

1872-1881: First period: papers on the anatomy of structures and
nerve tracts in the brain and spinal cord.

1873: Takes over from Carl Ludwig the direction of the histology
department of the Physiological Institute.

1874-1875: Habilitation as lecturer at Leipzig University with his
work on myelogenesis, which led to his main work on the
subject in 1876: *Conduction Pathways in the Brain and Spinal
Cord on the Basis of Developmental Researches*.

1877: Elevated to professor extraordinarius (associate professor) of
the Department of Medicine of Leipzig University.

1878: Elevated to professor extraordinarius of psychiatry there;
recommended as chair of the Psychiatric Hospital and chair of
psychiatry at Leipzig University.

1877-1882: Study tour of psychiatric facilities from Berlin to Paris.

1882: Director of Psychiatric University Hospital (*Irrenklinik*); reads
inaugural speech "The physical basis of mental disorders."

1882-1893: Second period: writings on neuroanatomy and organic
treatments in psychiatry.

1884: Ordinarius (full professor) of medicine at Leipzig University.

1893-1927: Third period: begins work on the cerebral hemispheres,
writings on organic treatments and brain anatomy.

1894–1895: Serves as Rector magnificus of Leipzig University and reads his inaugural speech "Brain and Soul."

1896: Second enlarged edition of "Brain and Soul" translated into other languages. Named as legal medical officer (*Gerichtsarzt*) of the lower court for the district of the Leipzig University Psychiatric Hospital.

1898: Honorary doctorate from the University of Oxford. Also: honorary member of Dorpat University.

1899: Invited to the United States to lecture at Clark University in Massachusetts but denied leave by the Ministry of Education.

1901: Takes part in congress of physiologists in Turin. Presentation at congress translated into English.

1904: Flechsig in London, one of a number of visits there; contributes to the formation of an international Brain Commission; presented to King Edward VII; honorary doctorate in science from Oxford University

1905: Rome Congress of Psychology, reads "Brain Physiology and Theories of Volition," which is translated into English.

1906: Participates in the meeting of the Brain Commission in Vienna, presented to Kaiser Franz Josef as an "anatomist."

1909: Jubilee of Leipzig University and of the 25th anniversary of his professorship, with publication of Festschrift by his pupils and followers. Receives honorary doctorate in philosophy from Leipzig University.

1914: Invited to lecture at the Illinois University but did not travel because of the war.

1920: Retirement, publication of the first and only volume of *Anatomy of the Human Brain and Spinal Cord on the Basis of Myelogenesis*.

1922, April 24: Second marriage, to Irene Colditz (born 1876), 29 years his junior; last public appearance.

1923: Elected to membership in the Royal Swedish Academy in Stockholm.

1927: On his 80th birthday publishes *Myelogenesis* and is honored by a second Festschrift.

1929, July 22: Death in Leipzig.

NOTES

1. Further data were gathered from Gerda Sachse (1955) and her extensive bibliography (supplied by Dr. Ingrid Kästner from Leipzig), a number of obituaries, Haymaker and Schiller (1970), Meyer (1981). I also discussed and corresponded about Flechsig with Gerd Busse (also see Busse, 1990).

2. This friendship, and its possible homosexual undertones, is discussed by P. Ostwald (1985).

3. Weber was the author of *Annotationes anatomicae et physiologicae*. His *Prolegomenon XX*, of 1833, contains the autobiography of Daniel Gottlob Moritz Schreber (also cited by Israëls).

4. He may be the same Wagner who eleven years earlier performed the autopsy on Moritz Schreber, according to G. Friedrich, in a letter of October 1910, 1983.

5. The previous method of elucidating the course of nerve tracts, that of Türck, was based on tracing patterns of degeneration of nerve fibers. Both methods have their worth and are complementary (Marie, 1929).

6. Fritsch and Hitzig were the first to demonstrate, in 1870, that the brain reacted to electrical stimulation, thus ushering in the era of the modern neurophysiology of the brain.

7. The anterior and posterior limb and knee of the internal capsule, the dorsal spinocerebellar tract and the pyramidal tract (McHenry, 1969, p. 174).

8. According to the most authoritative Freud literature data base in existence today, that of Professor Gerhard Fichtner from the Institute of the History of Medicine of Tübingen University, Flechsig's findings are mentioned 32 times in Freud's neurological works (1844b, 1844d, 1885d, 1886b, 1886c, 1887e, 1888b, 1888c, 1891a, 1891b, 1893b, 1893f, 1897a). I am indebted to Professor Fichtner (1989) for sending me these references, which can be found in the bibliography in Volume 3 of the *Standard Edition*. For example, Freud (1893, p. 15) notes: "Flechsig's findings on the development of the spinal cord—which ushered in a new epoch in our knowledge of the 'localization of nervous diseases'." Freud (1891) was to break with the idea of strict localization in his monograph "On Aphasia," which was the forerunner of the antilocalizational and holistic views of Henry Head (1926) and Kurt Goldstein (1927). He mentions Flechsig in a number of his letters to his bride Martha, for example, on November 4, 1885: "Unhappy with Meynert, he [Darkschewitsch] went to Leipzig to my competitor Flechsig" (Freud, 1873-1939, p. 181). The latter is of interest to our story as well (see footnote 31).

9. Most vocally by the Vogts, Oscar and his wife Cécile. The Vogts are mentioned frequently in Kurt Kolle (1956); Flechsig is not mentioned.

10. Flechsig's interest in the study of tracts and the brain areas into which they led, the projection areas and the association areas, committed him to the domain of localization of brain functions and the elaboration of brain maps. He did not become interested to the same extent in the histologic structure of brain tissue, the way of the future. It fell to others to pursue the microscopic structure of nerve cells and their substructures, or the domain of cytoarchitectonics (the Spaniard Ramón y Cajal, the German-Korbinian Brodmann, also active in Leipzig, and the Englishman Sherrington). Such studies would become important for the future growth of neurophysiology. Of course, the future also belonged to neurochemistry, which was still in an embryo stage in Flechsig's day. Eventually, in spite of his anatomical contributions, Flechsig would end in blind alleys in psychiatry. This was essentially the appraisal of

Henneberg (1929) in his obituary on Flechsig: "the highest mental processes were for him 'an effect of the brain.' That this was a dated point of view, rather than scientific research data, needs no further demonstration" (p. 1491). Nonetheless, he viewed Flechsig as one of the greatest neuroanatomists by virtue of his having inspired many others.

11. According to a typescript by Dr. K. Gilardon of the Karl Sudhoff Institute for the History of Medicine, then Karl-Marx-Universität, Leipzig.

12. Among those considered there were Bernhard von Gudden from Munich, whose fame is secured by the fact that he drowned with his patient, King Ludwig II of Bavaria, in the Starnberg Lake, in 1886; Ludwig Meyer from Göttingen, whose descendant Professor Joachim Ernst Meyer I had the pleasure to discuss Schreber with in Göttingen in 1989; Carl Westphal, from Berlin; Friedrich Jolly, from Strasbourg; Eduard Hitzig, Berlin; and Auguste Forel. All these were prominent men in psychiatry and a number had also made important contributions to neuroanatomy (von Gudden, Forel) and neurophysiology (Hitzig) (Quoted from Flechsig, 1877-1931 and Trenck-mann, 1882, p. 118). Von Gudden (1885-1886) was also known for his contribution to brain and mind.

Auguste Forel, distinguished as a neurologist trained under von Gudden in Munich, subsequently became chief at Burghölzli in Zurich, and the future teacher of Eugen Bleuler.

13. He owed his appointment to Professors Wunderlich, Thiersch, Kussmaul and Ludwig. Sachse (1955, p. 7) quotes from a letter of Flechsig of November 15, 1877 in which he admits to "lacunae" in his knowledge of psychiatry but pledges to fill them prior to assumption of his teaching duties. She quotes Ludwig's retort to Flechsig's detractors, according to Henneberg (1929): "The psychiatrists know nothing about the psyche—at least Flechsig knew something about the brain!"

14. Specifically in regard to Flechsig's famous address "Brain and Soul (1894a); see Bumke, 1931, p. 15; and Bumke, 1938, p. 12.

15. Griesinger's (1868) ideas about the city asylum and its academic counterpart, the university hospital (called *Klinik*), were set forth in his "Mental hospitals and their future development in Germany," in the first issue of the *Archiv für Psychatrie und Nervenkrankheiten*, which he edited.

16. Flechsig must have been indeed hurt by these reactions. By contrast, throughout *Myelogenesis* he takes great pains to mention all the many honors and distinctions he received abroad.

17. H. A. Bunker (1944) translated the title of this address as "A Lecture on the Physical Basis of Insanity" (p. 212). It was anonymously reviewed in the *American Journal of Insanity* (Anonymous, 1882). The reviewer juxtaposed Heinroth, who views "Theories of physical pathogenesis . . . [as] the vain conception of misguided minds [for] insanity . . . is man's own fault [and due to] the soul laden with sin . . . [and] abuse and misuse of freedom'" (pp. 89-90) with Flechsig, who "Places himself exclusively on the solid basis which regards insanity as a symptom of brain disease . . . as evidence of disease of the organ of the mind" (p. 90).

18. Flechsig here goes against his father, who was a man of the cloth, and

Heinroth. To salve any guilt feelings about such a dual betrayal Flechsig adds the following remark:

Even as Heinroth was masterful in creating an impression abroad as well, that his ideas and treatment methods were inspired by an attitude of mildness and upright humaneness, very much like Pinel, 'who removed the chains from the insane of Paris,' Heinroth did not in fact use such mild methods of treatment. There is absolutely *no proof of it* in the documents. Nevertheless, his popularity, and especially in church circles, was so great that at the end of my lecture a committee was formed with the purpose of repairing and adorning Heinroth's grave, which was quickly done. In this way, I effectively increased the fame of my predecessor, which I wish him with all my heart [*Myelogenesis*, p. 26; emphasis Flechsig's].

So much for noble feelings.

19. Flechsig uses the term *"Institute"* as a synonym for asylum (Flechsig, 1888a, p. iv). Paul Schreber states that in the basic language "hospitals for mentally deranged [*Geisteskranke*] were called 'God's nerve-institutions [*Nervenanastalten Gottes*]'" (*M*, p. 24), and more colorfully, the "Institute of the fleeting phantoms" (*M*, p. 54). Could Paul Schreber have read Flechsig's work of 1888?

20. This work, along with Flechsig's other publications, was mentioned in the self-authored entry in Dr. J. Pagel's (1901) *Biographical Dictionary of the Eminent Physicians of the 19th Century*. The same dictionary had an entry by Freud, without his picture. (Flechsig's picture in the entry is probably the likeness seen by Paul at the beginning of his second illness.) In his entry Flechsig also listed: *Conduction Pathways in the Brain and the Spinal Cord of Man Presented on the Basis of Developmental Research* (Leipzig 1876); essays in journals: in *Wagner's Archiv der Heilkunde* XIV, "On Certain Relations Between Secondary Degenerations and Developmental Processes in the Human Spinal Cord" (Flechsig, 1873); "On Variations in the Structure of the Human Spinal Cord" (Flechsig, 1874); "Systemic Diseases of the Spinal Cord" (Flechsig, 1878); "On the Anatomy and Developmental History of the Conduction Pathways in the Human Cerebrum" (Flechsig, 1887); "New Staining Methods of the Central Nervous System and Results Concerning the Relation Between Ganglion Cells and Nerve Fibers" (Flechsig, 1889); "On the Development of Association Systems in the Human Brain" (Flechsig, 1894b); also a series of papers in *Neurologisches Centralblatt*, from 1884 to 1898. Additional references are listed in Haymaker and Schiller (1970) and in Meyer (1981). Flechsig's bibliographies can also be found in Pfeifer (1930), Sachse (1955) and Busse (1990). I have found additional references in the proceedings of scientific meetings reported in German psychiatric journals.

Summaries of Flechsig's papers were published in the annual *Jahresbericht über die Leistungen und Forschritte auf dem Gebiete der Neurologie und Psychiatrie* (Annual Reports on Progress in Neurology and Psychiatry), published by S. Karger in Berlin, beginning with the first volume in 1898: Frontale Associationscentrum und Cingulum (1:45-46); review of epilepsy treatments (1:1117-1118); review of his work on myelogenesis and localization (2:47-48); report on his lecture at the Third International Congress of Psychology in Munich (4:104-105; Flechsig, 1897a); and reviews of two papers on the visual and auditory pathways in the brain (12:48-49).

Flechsig was acknowledged early on in the English language professional literature (Ireland, 1874). A rare honor is bestowed upon him in the classic *Gray's Anatomy* (Johnston & Whillis, 1950), a textbook that shuns mentioning of names: the section on myelination begins with "Flechsig has shown" (p. 1022). He was cited in Sir Charles Sherrington (1906), in J. F. Fulton (1938), and more recently in Alfred Meyer (1971). In the United States early recognition can be found in Ranney (1881, p. 20). His inauguration speech (1882a) was reviewed in the *American Journal of Insanity* (Anonymous, 1882; see footnote 17), and M.A.S. (1884) reviewed his work of 1876. *"Brain and Soul"* (1896a) was received enthusiastically (by L. F. Barker) and critically (by M. P. Jacobi), both in the *Journal of Nervous and Mental Disease* for 1897. Flechsig was also acknowledged by American physiological psychologists, for example, George T. Ladd (1897). Jacoby (1912) discussed Flechsig's localizations (including color illustrations) and used them to explain the screaming behavior of the newborn infant (p. 92). Flechsig's place in the history of neuroanatomy and neurology is given due credit in McHenry (1969); Haymaker and Schiller (1970); G. von Bonin (1960); and E. G. Clarke and C. D. O'Malley (1968). I also found an entry about him in American encyclopedias (e.g., Gilman, Peck & Colby, 1904); it has a few wrong dates and facts but mentions Flechsig's (1888a) *Report* about the "Clinical Institute of Psychiatry and Neurology" and his original work on the spinal cord of 1876. Flechsig is mentioned in the entries on the brain and spinal cord of the 11th edition of the *Encyclopaedia Britannica*. I have not searched as intensively in the French and the Russian literature. He has an entry in the Russian Brockhaus of Efron (1903) and the *Bolshaya Sovetskaya Entsiklopedia* (my letters to the Soviet Academy of Sciences have gone unanswered). Flechsig is cited by Ramón y Cajal (1901-1917).

21. The hospital was bombed out in 1943; everything was destroyed, except the library, which had been moved to the countryside (Sänger, 1963).

22. There was also an agreement between the Ministry of Education and the City Council of Leipzig (a copy was given to me at the Stadtarchiv Leipzig) about making available up to 20 psychiatric beds in the hospital for admissions of citizens of Leipzig, paid for by the city.

23. The bylaws are in the Administrative Files of the Hospital, State Archives, Dresden (which I first read in 1988), both in longhand and printed (Flechsig, 1882b). It is instructive to compare Flechsig's hospital policies with those recommended by Griesinger (1868), the originator of the idea of university asylums, or "clinics." Griesinger's idea was to build small (up to 150 bed) city hospitals that would deal swiftly and efficiently with acute psychiatric emergencies and acute episodes of illness without involving the patient in the cumbersome provincial asylum procedures. However, compared to Flechsig's six months, Griesinger (1868) envisaged stays of up to one year, and even up to a year and a half if necessary, with a median stay of 6 to 9 months (p. 15).

He was for simple architecture and conditions, with no special "isolation wards [*Zellenabtheilungen*]" but with active treatment approaches. He advocated admitting psychiatric patients to general hospitals, on a temporary and emergency basis, because in many cases "it is plain arbitrary whether one claims they have 'mental illness' or 'nervous illness'" (p. 23). Also, he held that "chronic" illness and an "incurable" one were two different things. His superior clinical skills and experience are impressive.

24. In a letter of January 16, 1883, Kraepelin writes: "I hear the wildest stories about Flechsig; the day before yesterday the head male and head female nurse from the Irrenklinik called on me, to my greatest surprise; both of them and countless other attendants are resigning by April 1; it looks like a hopeless madhouse" (in Forel, 1968, p. 162). In connection with a suicide in his hospital Flechsig (1888a) notes this was due to negligence on the part of a female attendant who was at that time on the verge of a psychotic breakdown herself, which indeed occurred days later (*Report*, Footnote 2, p. 16).

25. In a letter of December 31, 1882, Kraepelin recommends to Forel a Dr. Fischer who is "not happy with his position here . . . and as far as I know intends to resign" (Forel, 1968, p. 160).

26. Here Flechsig addresses a polemical remark to Wundt, whose fame at that time exceeded Flechsig's. Wilhelm Wundt (1832-1920), the founder of the first modern experimental psychology laboratory, in Leipzig, was a teacher of Kraepelin, who applied Wundt's psychological methods to the study of mental patients. I believe that the philosophical humanism of Wundt made Kraepelin into the psychologically minded psychiatrist he became.

27. Flechsig's *Report* was reviewed by L. (1888a, *AZP*), who noted that such hospitals as Flechsig's already existed in Heidelberg (Fürstner's) and Halle (Hitzig's). L. was impressed with Flechsig's psychiatric hospital—with its 5 buildings, 7 services, and 15 isolation rooms. L. notes that suicidal patients were not kept in the hospital. There was a staff of 49 persons, and the treatments consisted of bed rest, good diet, narcotics for sleeplessness, and prolonged baths. He also noted the three successful laparotomies that were performed there (see footnote 28). The reviewer was certainly ahead of his time when he took exception to Flechsig's idea that "psychological analysis" was the "most incidental part of treatment."

28. Files of Leipzig University Psychiatric Hospital, State Archives, Dresden (1882-1896). In a report of May 5, 1891, Flechsig asks for "favorable evacuation conditions by the provincial hospitals" and "speedy evacuations" ("*rasche Evacuationen*") in a lengthy report of June 28, 1893. In that letter he expresses the wish to be able to compete favorably with the Private Thonberg Asylum. In a previous report to the Ministry dated March 15, 1893, Flechsig requests more staff physicians because he is overworked. He notes that by virtue of his agreements with the city of Leipzig he has been mainly functioning as a psychiatrist for the city (*Stadtirrenazt*), in addition to being overwhelmed with administrative duties, to the detriment of time left for scientific and teaching pursuits. He complains that compared with other university hospitals his is very busy with admissions which have tripled due to the increase in the population of Leipzig from 150,000 to 400,000 inhabitants.

29. Flechsig (1884, a, b; 1885) was no innovator in treating hysteria with removal of the ovaries (i.e., castration), citing other authorities (e.g., the well known gynecologist Hegar, whose book, "The Connection Between Genital Disorders and Nervous Disorders" was reviewed in the *NC* by psychiatrist Schüle, 1885). He rephrased the ancient belief that hysteria is caused by disorders of the uterus in modern idiom: "The brain symptoms are caused at least in part by the abdominal disorder" (1884b, p. 437). Based on this series Flechsig felt confident in recommending castration in "cases of melancholic, manic and mild paranoid conditions, . . . [and possibly] in cases of progressive psychic degeneration of hysterical women" (p. 468). He gave three case histories. The first case was that of a hysterical woman, aged 32, who suffered from curious fits consisting of "paroxysms of *laughing* and *crying*" (p. 434; emphasis Flechsig's), hallucinations and ideas of persecution restlessness, deep sighing and breathing, and heart symptoms, thus "a presumptive evidence of the connection between sexual disorder and nervous abnormalities" (p. 436). (In the first two years of Schreber's illness Flechsig treated Sabine Schreber for paroxysms of laughing and crying, according to Baumeyer, 1955.) After surgery, the patient was instantly cured and felt reborn. The symptoms returned, but, says Flechsig, that didn't contradict the indication for castration because the recurrence may have been due to an intercurrent cystitis. In the discussion that took place during the presentation at a meeting (1884a), the well-known Professor Mendel, was very critical of the method and felt the same results could be achieved with placebo surgery and bread crumb pills. He feared the gynecologists and felt that the indications were hard to prove. Flechsig retorted that there was no danger, because the genitals of the patients were manipulated under chloroform anesthesia. Von Gudden felt that castration was a significant insult to the physiologically important organ, a view supported by an authority like Winkel from Munich, who was also against this surgery. Flechsig's responses and therapeutic ideas show his inflexible organicist attitude.

30. Flechsig first wrote "On a new method of treating epilepsy" in 1893 (which was the third occasion of his citing a brief clinical vignette); also cited in *CNP*, 18:85 and *DMW*, 20:602-603. This means that by the time Schreber was his patient the second time the method had already been in use. It was followed by another (Flechsig, 1897), also cited in the *MPN*, 2:165. Flechsig's antiepileptic regimen was not an entirely original idea; it was widely discussed in the literature. An early reference was by Otto (1875), "Potassium bromide as treatment for epilepsy." Rabbas (1896) noted that Flechsig "obtained good results in chronic diseases, especially paranoia, using opium in doses of up to one gram per day, discontinuing it suddenly to be replaced with high doses of bromide" (pp. 796-797). However, even this idea had a forerunner in Richard Kohn (1881): "On the aborting of 'fits' in chronic psychoses by means of quinine injections and potassium bromide." A negative review of Flechsig's method was published by Bratz (1897a, b; 1898). Bratz claimed that this was a treatment only suited for inpatients, not outpatients. He noted that there were some positive but transient results but also eight deaths. He felt it was dangerous to discontinue opium and give bromide. Bratz (1898) cited earlier

favorable assessments: Linke (1896), his own (1897a) and the critical one by Paul Pollitz (1897), pointing out that the results were doubtful and the toxic side effects considerable and often lethal, and who recommended that the treatment should be withdrawn.

A critical overview of treatment methods of epilepsy published by Julius Donath (1900), "Therapeutic trials and successes in the field of epilepsy," has a sizable bibliography in which Flechsig is only mentioned once. In the Index-Catalogue of the Surgeon General's Office (second series), volume 5:76-77, there is a separate entry for the treatment of epilepsy with bromides and opium and more references about Flechsig's method.

31. A most illustrious student was the Russian Vladimir M. Bekhterev (the earlier spelling was W. von Bechterew). Another Russian pupil was Darkschewitsch. Freud first met L. O. Darkschewitsch in Vienna and later at Charcot's in Paris (Strachey, *Standard Edition*, 3:237), and the two were close friends. They jointly published a paper (1886) in the *Neurologisches Centralblatt*: "On the relation of the restiform body to the posterior column and its nucleus with some remarks on two fields of the medulla oblongata." This leads us into an interesting side story. In 1894 Flechsig (1894c) published "On a new principle of classification of the cerebral surface." This provoked a riposte from Professor Adamkiewicz (1894) from Vienna and a response from Flechsig (1894d). The debate went back and forth. It may have been read by Schreber, for he referred to a Viennese nerve specialist who was a converted Jew and a rival of Flechsig for domination in various lands and whose name rhymed with that of a Benedictine monk named Starkiewicz (*Memoirs*, pp. 49, 151). Busse (1989) was the first to theorize that this is a reference to the said Adamkiewicz. Dr. Daniel Devreese from Ghent in Belgium believes that the doctor in question is Freud's friend Darkschewitsch, a non-Jew. (For a non-Slavic person, the accent might determine the degree of rhyming and thus the homophony between Starkiewicz and the other two names: accenting the first syllable in STARkiewicz, would more easily rhyme with DARKschewitsch, in spite of the extra consonants, whereas StarKIEwicz rhymes more easily with Adamkiewicz.)

Albert Adamkiewicz is mentioned by Freud (Freud, 1887) but I have not found citations of Freud by Adamkiewicz, who was indeed a celebrated Jewish professor from Poland who lived in Vienna and wrote prolifically in German and Polish on neuroanatomy, neuropathology and medicine. He was later embroiled in theories about the causation of cancer, for which he was discredited. Toward the end of his life he wrote philosophical-psychological works.

This led me to wonder if Schreber could have been aware of Sigmund Freud (Lothane, 1989c); the lead is inconclusive but highly suggestive. One more reference should be added to the ones I mention there: Flechsig's citations of Freud's in *Brain and Soul* (1896a) and in *Localization* (1896c), which could have been read by Schreber. Freud is cited in Jung (1902) and in Kraepelin (1899).

32. The event was called "The change of rectors at Leipzig University October 31,1894. Address of the new rector P. F." The words in the title of Flechsig's speech were already used by Wilhelm Wundt from Leipzig (the Germans call this *Wortplagiat*, plagiarizing someone's words) in his essay

"Brain and Soul" of 1885, cited by Friedrich Paulsen (1892). Flechsig did not mention Wundt's essay, or another essay with the same title by Auguste Forel, at one point a candidate for the chair of psychiatry in Leipzig.

Forel read his lecture, "Brain and Soul" (1894) at the 66th meeting of the *Deutsche Naturforscher und Ärzte* held September 26, 1894, in Vienna. It first appeared in print in 1899 and went through many editions, the 12th in 1914 (Leipzig: Kröner). In spite of his excellent reputation as neuroanatomist and pupil of von Gudden, the tone of Forel's essay was decidedly more philosophical. He invoked "God, a concept of the unfathomable metaphysical omnipotence" (1894, p. 6). He also invoked Kant and Schopenhauer, but also Spinoza, Leibniz and Hartmann, the latter cited by Schreber. Forel said, "There is no brain without a soul and no complex soul like ours without a brain, no more than there is energy without matter or matter without energy" (p. 14). Thus, reductionism is not his way of approaching the mind body problem. I have not found Forel mentioned by Flechsig (Stingelin 1989a, p. 113, cites unpublished letters of Flechsig to Forel), but Forel wrote: "I have not mentioned Flechsig's associations schemata of the tracts in the brain, because they were shown to be incorrect" (p. 40, footnote).

33. The word *Bahnen* means both tracts, as in *Hirnbahnen*, and railroad tracks, as in *Eisenbahnen*, and thus lends itself to the pun.

34. Since the beginning of Flechsig's publications on the brain, his studies have provoked considerable interest and controversy. When Flechsig lectured on "The association fibers of the human brain with anatomical demonstrations" at the Third International Congress of Psychology in Munich, August 4-7, 1896 (Flechsig, 1897a), the discussion among the illustrious participants was "agitated" (as reported by Löwenfeld). The neurological aspects and the psychological correlates of Flechsig's work were given their due, but such correlations shocked an attending philosopher, Professor Lipps, who felt the neuroanatomist, the physiologist, and the psychologist should each remain in his own domain, a view which was forcefully opposed by Forel and Bekhterev.

Flechsig has made a lasting contribution to neuroanatomy (McHenry, 1969; Haymaker and Schiller, 1970; Meyer, 1981). Nevertheless, he was a target of criticism for his brain maps derived on the basis of his myelogenetic method (Sänger, 1963, Meyer, 1981). From the point of view of method of research, Flechsig's myelogenetic method had a rival in the myeloarchitectonic (the Vogts, Brodmann) and cytoarchitectonic methods (Brodmann, Ramón y Cajal, von Economo). Flechsig's method was replicated by his immediate followers in Germany (Pfeifer) and Russia (Yakovlev), but apparently nowhere else. Flechsig was attacked by von Monakow, the Vogts and Déjerine (Sänger, 1963). From the point of view of the conception of brain functioning, Flechsig's rigid localizations were opposed by Freud's conception of the aphasias (1891), which later became the foundation of the holistic notions of Head (1926) and Goldstein (1927). Meyer was impressed how close the relationship between Flechsig's "work on cortical localization with the results of neuroanatomical and neurophysiological research of the last three decades" (Meyer, 1981, p. 101). However, it should be remembered that the new research is in experimental animals, which calls for caveats regarding a too facile homologizing to the human brain and mind.

His earliest translation into English, of excerpts from *Brain and Soul*, is probably by Barker (1897). The authoritative Alfred Meyer (1981), who offers an extensive bibliography, was only aware of later a translation of Flechsig in *Lancet*, in 1901. I found a Russian translation in Berlin (Flechsig, 1897c) and Polish translations in a popular science magazine (Flechsig, 1896 e, f). The French published an omnibus volume of *Brain and Soul, Localization,* and *Boundaries* (Flechsig, 1898a).

35. Of the immediate predecessors the most important are Theodor Meynert (1833-1892), born in Dresden and moved to Vienna as a child, and Carl Wernicke (1848-1905). Meynert was a foremost neuroanatomist and professor of psychiatry and nervous diseases at the Vienna Allgemeines Krankenhaus, a poet and colorful Viennese celebrity who taught Freud in 1883. Flechsig read his work from 1868 on the mammalian brain and borrowed important ideas from Meynert's (1890) textbook of psychiatry, such as the distinction between projection and associations pathways and areas in the brain; the brain as an *Associationsorgan* (organ of association activity); and the brain as an *Organ der Moral* (organ of moral emotions; Meynert, 1890, p. 98). While emphasizing a brain-mind parallelism, Meynert was also dynamic in his approach. Thus, he formulated an ego psychology, distinguishing a "primary ego *(Ich)*, our *infantile* ego, and the *secondary* ego, which as it were develops later alongside the former, becoming joined to it through association. The defensive acts and the aggressive acts of the child have the purpose of defending the cohesion of the personality, whose boundaries are determined by the outside skin" (Meynert, 1890, pp. 11-13). Freud also took from him the delineation of acute paranoia as an acute hallucinatory amentia (Meynert's amentia), that is, an acute traumatic neuro-psychosis of defense, a concept he invoked in his analysis of Schreber's paranoia (Freud, 1894, 1911a). It is important to note that Meynert denied the exclusively hereditary nature of paranoia and connected delusions of persecution to "anxiety feelings [*Angstgefühle*]." Thus, both delusions of persecution and of grandeur were correlated by Meynert with defensive affects and aggressive affects: "The defense-affects are in relation to a feeling of external *influence*, the attack-affects to a feeling of an active external *overpowering*" (Meynert, 1890, p. 143; Meynert's emphasis). Such ideas did not influence Flechsig.

36. Flechsig would have been influenced by the approach in Wernicke's (1880) lecture "On the scientific viewpoint in psychiatry," at the 53rd Meeting of the German Scientists and Physicians in Danzig. In that lecture Wernicke (after whom sensory aphasia is named) invoked Meynert's 1873 lecture "*Zur Mechanik des Gehirnbaues* (The Mechanics of Brain Structure)" and proceeded to set forth a neurophysiological model of psychopathology—taken specifically from the pathophysiology of neurosyphilis (paresis)—as the fundamental model for a scientific, as against a philosophic, psychiatry. Even Griesinger, argued Wernicke, still operated with brain-mind analogies where none existed. Wernicke would replace such analogies with an uncompromising organicism. He stressed that in neurosyphilis there was actual destruc-

tion of memory-pictures (*Erinnerungsbilder*) due to focal lesions caused by processes in nerve cells. A summation of such multiple defects in cells combines to produce the picture of syphilitic dementia. The loss of memory-pictures due to lesions in the affected parts of the brain or their putrefaction (*Fäulniss*, a term frequent in Schreber) is, Wernicke said, the real cause of hallucinations and of mood changes in the paretic. This model also explains the "more acute forms of psychosis [*Wahnsinn*], or, as one now calls it, primary madness [*primäre Verrücktheit*]" (Wernicke, 1880, p. 409), even though the lesion here is merely an alteration, not a destruction, of the nerve cells. At this point the absolute organic model begins to show cracks. But it is the absolute that prevails in the formulations of Flechsig and, later of Weber.

37. It is curious that Flechsig has a slip of the pen: he misspells "cogitation" as "coagitation."

38. It is of interest to compare the lessons that Freud and Flechsig derived from Charcot. The great Frenchman neatly distinguished between organic focal lesions and diffuse functional states which he called dynamic lesions. Thus an organic paralysis, due to a focus of infection or tumor, was an organic lesion, whereas a hysterical paralysis was a dynamic lesion, that is, no lesion at all but an altered dynamic, or functional, state. Of course, a hysterical paralysis was no paralysis at all, either, but only a charade, i.e. dramatic enactment of paralysis. Here there was neither real paralysis nor pseudo-paralysis of a *limb*, but a pseudo-paralytic patient, or one impersonating somebody with a paralysis. While Freud understood the hysterical paralyses as symbolic acts, he continued to use the medical term paralysis to describe such enactments. I believe Charcot's word *dynamique* enabled Freud to understand the metaphorical meaning of the functional lesion and rescued him from that concreteness of localization Flechsig never escaped. It is most interesting that Freud's use of the word 'dynamic' in his writings is rather infrequent, even as his intentions are unmistakable. I am quoting some of the few instances in which he used the word *dynamic*.

Early on, in his anatomo-neurological phase, Freud quoted Charcot's definition (in his annotated translation of the French master's (1887) *Leçons sur les Maladies du Système Nerveux*: "a dynamic or functional lesion," which then evolved into a "a dynamic, hysterical lesion" (Andersson, 1962, p. 59). By 1888 Freud realized that such lesions "in no way represent a picture of the anatomical relations in the nervous system," and that one day in neurosis, "observable changes will be found in the nervous system with the help of more refined anatomical techniques" (Andersson, 1962, pp. 60-61).

In his later writings, discussing the difference between the organically toned views of Janet and his own, Freud states: "We do not derive the psychical splitting from an innate incapacity . . . we explain it dynamically, from the conflict of opposing mental forces and recognize it as the outcome of an active struggling of the two psychical groupings against each other" (Freud, 1910a, p. 26); on comparing psychoanalysis with the "'descriptive psychology of consciousness'" he says: "Up till now, it has differed from that psychology mainly by reason of its *dynamic* view of mental processes." Therefore, it qualifies to be regarded as a "'depth-psychology'" (Freud, 1915,

p. 173; emphasis Freud's). Depth psychology was Bleuler's characterization of psychoanalysis (Freud, 1914a, p. 41). In the *Ego and the Id* (1923) Freud defines the word *unconscious*: "But we have arrived at the term or concept of the unconscious . . . by considering certain experiences in which mental *dynamics* play a part. . . . we restrict the term *unconscious* to the dynamically unconscious repressed" (Freud, 1923b, pp. 14–15; emphasis Freud's). The other difference between Freud and Flechsig is in their understanding of aphasias. Flechsig quotes Freud's monograph on aphasia, Freud's first book, published in 1891. In this work Freud combined the dynamic spirit of Charcot and the ideas of the great Hughlings Jackson, who was both a neurologist and a dynamic psychologist.

Jackson's central idea, later called organo-dynamic, was to discern two phenomena in a combined body and mental state such as a delirium: the negative syndrome and the positive syndrome. In the state of delirium the negative syndrome, caused by fever, resulted in a lowering of higher mental functioning (he called this "disinhibition" and Freud renamed it "regression"), and led to the emergence of the positive syndrome, the dream-like ravings of the delirious person, the content of which reflected his current life situation. The deliria, in the sense of ideas and images (retained in the French *délire*, delusion), were thus facilitated by the state of delirium, but not created by it. This was indeed the approach Freud took toward aphasias. The organic focal lesion was the precondition of the complex disturbances of psychological performance that Freud called alexia, agnosia, and apraxia. Flechsig indeed mentions Freud in his text three times: in *Brain and Soul* (1896a, pp. 46, 47) and in *Localization* (1896c, p. 61), where he refers to Freud's ideas of apraxia and agnosia. I don't believe Flechsig understood Freud's holistic and dynamic conception.

39. Fritz Wittels (1924) writes: "In the nineties, one of Freud's earliest collaborators, Isidore Sadger, sent Freud an essay extolling Flechsig's works. Freud considered the essay bombastic, and since Sadger had previously written upon Ibsen, Freud dreamed of a 'norekdal' style, the adjective being a condensation of 'kolossal'[preposterous], 'Nora,' and 'Ekdal'" (p. 76). I am indebted to Israëls for this citation. Freud was reacting to the ideas of Flechsig in *Brain and Soul* and other works of that period and also possibly to Sadger's ecstatic portrayal of Flechsig in his essay, "The Miracle of the Thinking Eggwhite" (Sadger, 1897), which Wittels may have referred to. It was sent to me by Dr. Angela Graf-Nolde from Zurich.

40. The lecture on localizations (1896b) was followed by a discussion (it was covered in the *CNP* and in the *DMW*, 20:185, in the section *Vereins-Beilage* # 28). Von Monakow objected to Flechsig's schema of the sensory centers, claiming that skin muscle sensations were scattered over a wider area of the cortex. Hitzig acknowledged Flechsig's anatomical side but underscored his undeveloped neurophysiology. He also claimed that the sensory fibers of the corona radiata were spread over a wider cerebral area than allowed for by Flechsig, as proved by the degeneration method. He felt that Flechsig's schema was only valid for a certain phase in development. Various objections were also raised by Sachs, His and Hitzig.

41. These are cited in Sänger (1963, p. 72). Sänger states the year as 1904, but the report of the meeting was published in 1903, according to a reference found by Busse.

42. See footnotes 20 and 34. As noted earlier, the first burst of Flechsig's work on the cerebrum was in the last decade of the 19th century. The second and last round of discussion of Flechsig's neuroanatomical works took place in the first decade and in the beginning of the second decade of this century. Flechsig lectured about these researches at a number of scientific meetings, reported in the journals. His main rivals for fame were the Vogts and Brodmann in Germany and especially Santiago Ramón y Cajal, who in 1906, together with Golgi, became the recipient of the Nobel Prize in medicine.

In 1900, August 2-9, at the 13th International Congress of Medicine in Paris, Flechsig's (1900 a, b, c) lecture on "The projection- and association-centers of the human brain" was read for him. His discussants and critics were Hitzig, Monakow, and O. Vogt, the latter offering "13 dissenting theses" (*MPN*, 8:303). In 1901 Flechsig presented a paper at the International Congress of Physiology in Turin; it was translated into English in *The Lancet*.

Flechsig lectured at the Ninth Meeting of the Association of Middle-German Psychiatrists and Neurologists, held in Leipzig on the 24th and 25th of October of 1903, the year of the publication of the *Memoirs* and Schreber's first year in freedom. Flechsig (1903) offered welcoming remarks and presented a paper entitled "The inner structure of the human fetus born at term" [reported and discussed in the *PNW* (5:375-376; 382; *MPN*, 4:467-468)]. Guido Weber-Sonnenstein was elected chairman of the second session of the meeting (*MPN*, 14:465). Did the good friends Flechsig and Weber mention Schreber?

The tenth meeting of the aforementioned association, held in Halle on the 23rd and 24th of October 1904, attracted a great deal of coverage; much neuroanatomy was discussed. Schreber had been living for more then a year as a free man in Dresden. It was attended, among others, by Dr. Lochner, Director of the Thonberg Hospital, Dr. Stegmann, and Dr. Lehman, director of the new hospital in Dösen. Weber did not come but sent a welcoming telegram. Flechsig did not present but was active as discussant. For example, in one discussion, seconded by his student Hoesel, Flechsig (1904) quibbled with the presenter Foerster, which was declared an unresolved issue by Hitzig. That meeting was covered in the *PNW* (6:329-330; 342-344; 354-355; 369-371), *AP* (39:923-946), *MPN* (vol. 17), *CNP* (vol. 27), *DMW* (30:1831-1832, in the section *Vereinsbeilage*), all of which carried a clinical lecture by Dr. Stegmann (1904, 1905) from Dresden, "On the treatment of neuroses by means of the cathartic method (according to Freud)." The topic must have made some impression. Dr. Binswanger expressed his doubts about the efficacy of the method (p. 1832). Was Flechsig listening?

The year 1905 was a year of glory for both Flechsig and his former patient. The Fifth International Congress of Psychology was held in Rome, April 26-30 and on the program were such luminaries as Flechsig (1905a), on "Brain physiology and theories of volition (Projections)" (*PNW*, 6:498); Professor Sante de Sanctis, the host, from Rome; Professor Richet, from Paris, an expert on *métapsychique*, or occult phenomena; another fellow brain scientist, Professor Bianchi, from Naples; Professor P. Janet, from Paris; James Sully, from London, an expert on psychology and pedagogy; and Th. Flournoy, from Geneva, on "The psychology of religion." Flournoy (1854-1920), a student of Wundt, had created a stir with his book (1900) about a medium, Helen Smith, who spoke in tongues and recalled her past lives, while his note in 1906 on another captivating woman, Frank Miller, inspired Jung's interest and the result was his trailblazing essay of 1912 (Shamdasani, 1990).

At the 13th Meeting of the Association of Middle-German Psychiatrists and Neurologists, held in Leipzig on October 26 and 27, 1907, just one month prior to Schreber's final admission to the new psychiatric facility at Dösen, the opening remarks were offered by Flechsig, with eulogies to Hitzig and Möbius, and Herr Weber-Sonnenstein was elected chairman of the second session (*CNP*, 30:947). Flechsig (1907) held forth on the "Auditory area of the human brain (with demonstrations)," which provoked a lively discussion. The lecture was cited in a number of journals: *DMW* (33:2165-2166, in the section *Vereinsberichte*), and *MPN* (23:88-89; 172-173, thus citing the same meeting twice, the second time as the 14th). The meeting was also covered in the *PNW* (9:354-356; 462-464; 469-471) and *CNP* (30:947-949). Dr. Dehio from Dösen lectured about the advances introduced in the new hospital, one of them being the elimination of isolation cells. Freud's paper "Character and anal erotism" appears on pages 463-467. Was Freud aware of this accidental proximity?

In 1909 Flechsig published a preface to a book by Paul Näcke on the brain in paresis. He used the opportunity to state that the correctness of his association centers theory was proved by the psychopathology of paresis. That year Flechsig's students compiled a festschrift in his honor which was published in the *MPN* and included his famous portrait: Flechsig at age 62, sitting at his desk, with a huge picture of the auditory sphere of the brain behind him on the wall. The portrait, reproduced in Niederland (1974) and Israëls (1989), taken long after the events of the *Memoirs*, was not the face Schreber would have seen during his days at Flechsig's.

At the time of the 17th meeting of the aforementioned association, held on October 21 and 22, 1911, at Flechsig's hospital, Paul Schreber was already dead half a year (at the beginning of the year Freud's essay on him appeared in the *Jahrbuch*). Weber was absent from the meeting. Flechsig's theme was neuroanatomical again (1911). A Herr Wanke gave an enthusiastic lecture "On psychoanalysis" (*MPN*, 31:93-94), comparing it with Vogt's *Kausalanalyse* (causal analysis, a method producing hypnotic hypermnesia in the patient), praising the method of free association and stressing infantile sexuality and infantile trauma; this was criticized by a number of discussants. Was Flechsig paying attention?

In 1912 the 18th meeting of the Middle-German Psychiatrists and Neurologists was held on October 26 in Halle. It was covered in the *AP*, 50(1912-1913):986-1020 and the *PNW*, 14:439-442, 452-454, 462-468,477-481,489-492. By now Weber was retired, and one of the participants was the former associate of Flechsig, Dr. Teuscher, misspelled in the *Memoirs* as Täuscher, then director of the sanatorium Weisser Hirsch. Flechsig (1912) spoke on "The surface anatomy of the human cortex with special consideration of the recently attempted division of the human cortex into cyto-architectonic fields by Brodmann." Times were changing. The new spelling was now being used for the German language and there were new ideas about the structure of the brain. The cell experts, like Brodmann, Ramón y Cajal and Sherrington, were dominating the field and Flechsig's myelogenetic method, while respected, was being left behind. I do not share the view of Liselotte Leibnitz (1977) that this was an important speech.

The last report I found was a presentation by Flechsig at the annual meeting of the German Association for Psychiatry, including Section 23 of psychiatry and neurology, in Leipzig, on September 21 and 22, 1922. Flechsig spoke on September 22nd on the "Localization of Mental Functions," inveighing against the "rampant pessimism concerning localization" and argued against the views of Vogt. Interestingly, he now located "drives and feelings of unpleasure in the medulla oblongata" (p. 322). Flechsig himself stated his last appearance in public was in 1922 at the 100th anniversary meeting of the German Scientists and Physicians (*Myelogenesis*, p. 55). In 1927 another Fest-schrift was published by his followers in the *MPN*.

His work was assessed in a number of obituaries. Among the latter, the most important are by Henneberg (1929), two by his pupil R. A. Pfeifer (1929, 1930) and other Leipzig followers: F. Quensel (1929) and P. Schröder (1930). His death was also noted in the United States [*Journal of Nervous and Mental Disease*, 71(1930):246] and by Pierre Marie (1929) in France. There are additional sources for the present-day assessment of the importance of Flechsig in the history of neuroanatomy and neurology. A rare encomium for being a "starting-point of a great revolution in the conception of mental illness" is expressed by P. Glees (1956). This Flechsig did not do. More accurate are the reviews by Alfred Meyer (1981) and Ulrich Trenckmann (1982).

43. In the letter of January 15, 1894 Flechsig also tells of "having pulled together a new brain map for the Chicago World Fair but not sure if it will be found noteworthy." Flechsig hopes in a new edition of his book Bekhterev will be able to "confirm the principal results of [his] recent researches based on the developmental-historical method" (Letter of October 27, 1896). In a later letter he deplores not being able to take the long journey to come to Moscow for a scientific meeting because his "state of health requires [him] to undertake a water cure"; he can, however, report that his "collection of the slides of the auditory area has grown so much that [he is] now able to demonstrate something worth seeing (Letter of July 28, 1897). Bekhterev published a number of papers in the *Neurologisches Centralblatt*.

44. He was Dr. Shilo, who retired in Tel Aviv and passed on his reminiscences to Niederland in letters of November 24 and 27, 1966, found in the Niederland Papers at the Library of Congress by G. Busse, who kindly sent me a copy.

45. As alleged in Kolle (1956): "[in view of] Flechsig's difficult character [he was] apparently chagrined that Kraepelin at the same time started working in Wundt's laboratory" (p. 183). This opinion is also shared by Sänger.

46. Another impression on record about Flechsig and von Gudden was offered by Auguste Forel, at one point a candidate for the chair of psychiatry in Leipzig and one of the towering psychiatrists of the period: "Saturday Flechsig was here. Gudden has treated him very badly, he ended up asking whether he could come back in June for some time, but only out of politeness, for the last reception and the invitation would have scared even a more brazen person. He said here also he had been searching in vain to find the true psychiatry, whereupon Gudden advised him to discover it himself" (1968, p. 151). [Letter of Melchior Bandorf of June 2, 1879.] Maybe von Gudden inspired him to achieve this, after all?

47. It is of interest to cite Kraepelin's attitude to cerebral localization. An outraged Oscar Vogt writes to Forel on August 15, 1894:

During the same [conversaton] K.[raepelin] expressed views with such vehemence that I could not have imagined existed in the heads of psychiatrists. Thus among others: brain localization has only hurt psychology; brain anatomy will for a long time remain totally worthless for psychology; I know of motor and sensory centers but no psychical ones; all the contemporary clinical observations have no scientific worth because they lack method, i.e., the use of measuring apparatus; as far as I am concerned, as long as I adhere to my present views, I am lost forever for psychology [Forel, 1968, p. 298].

48. Kindly found for me by Professor Martin Unger of the Manuscript Division of the University of Leipzig in 1989.

49. Flechsig quotes from the "First Book On the Cognitive Faculty on Being Conscious of One's Self § 1:

The fact that man is aware of an ego-concept raises him infinitely above all other creatures living on earth. Because of this, he is a person; and by virtue of this oneness of consciousness, he remains one and the same person despite all the vicissitudes which may befall him. He is a being who, by reason of his preeminence and dignity, is wholly different from *things*, such as the irrational animals whom he can master and rule at will. He enjoys this superiority even when he cannot give utterance to this ego, although it is already present in his thought, just as all the languages must think it when they speak in the first person, even if the language lacks a specific word to refer to this ego-concept. This faculty (to think) is understanding [1800, p. 9; emphasis in the original].

50. The second Festschrift in honor of Flechsig was published in volume 45 of the *MPN* for 1927. It included papers by Theodor Ziehen about psychiatry and philosophy, surprising from an old organicist; by Paul Schröder, Flechsig's successor at Leipzig from 1925 to 1939, "*Gehirnlokalisation und Psychiatrie* (Brain Localization and Psychiatry)," in which he concludes that localization is only valid for neurological diseases but contributes nothing to psychiatry; and by Hänsel on depth psychology, free will, and criminality, in which psychoanalysis is discussed. There is no known source in which Flechsig ever mentioned psychoanalysis.

51. In this context it is interesting to quote from an unpublished letter by

Flechsig dated March 7, 1900, kept in the manuscript division in the West Berlin *Staatsbibliothek* and transcribed by Gerd Busse. In that letter Flechsig invokes Plato, Kant, Wilhelm Wundt and Friedrich Paulsen (1846-1908). All four were philosophers who dealt with the mind–body problem and were aware of the brain. The latter two were influenced by both Kant and by G. T. Fechner, who spent most his life in Leipzig.

After invoking Plato and Kant, Flechsig writes:

> The inborn organization of the brain determines the manner and fashion by which we build intuitions and concepts out of impressions-
> . . . Wundt is still unclear about this fact; the immortal soul creates all that is of a higher nature and woe to him who attributes to the brain the capacity to build concepts; what the soul creates hovers above the ganglion cells and can be possibly sought either in the stomach or in the mouth (Paulsen). Why should not vibrations recurring 5000 Million times per second, during the stimulation of our brain, produce an effect on [the star] Sirius, a manifestation of consciousness. This is taught at the leading University [i.e. Berlin, where Paulsen taught] of Germany . . . had I written anonymously, I would have many more followers; the fact that *I* have discovered the association centers causes me to be hated by people. . . . The frontal brain seems to me to be the archive for the emotions—all the joys and the sorrows leave traces there. The great temporal association center is connected to this storehouse of the emotions . . . "I want," says the frontal brain, "No, don't want" . . . [says] the parieto-temporal[brain] . . . [I] will not speak about this fantasy in Paris!" [unpublished letter of March 7, 1900].

This a rare glimpse into Flechsig the staunch yet self-conscious materialistic monist, with his anthropomorphizing of the parts of the brain. Compare this with the idealistic monist Paulsen:

> We shall now attempt to answer the old question concerning the *seat of the soul*. . . . we cannot speak of the seat in the sense of space, or a place in space, in which the soul is supposed to be. . . . It is meaningless to say, a thought or a feelings here or there, and extends through this or that part of space. Thoughts are not in the brain; we might as well say they are in the stomach or in the moon. The one statement is as absurd as the other. Physiological processes occur in the brain, and nothing else. Now if the soul is nothing but the unity of psychical life, it cannot of course be located in space any more than thoughts are [Paulsen, 1892, pp. 132-133; emphasis Paulsen's].

Paulsen may have been an influence on Paul Schreber.

Gustav Theodor Fechner (1801-1887), another son of a protestant minister, had two careers. While he was a professor of physics at Leipzig University, he was concerned with the following subjects: the nature of angels, beings he deemed to be spherical and capable of communicating by means of a language of luminous signs; the soul life of plants; and the notion that earth was a living being of a level higher than man and on a par with angels. Among his works we find *Die vergleichende Anatomie der Engel, eine Skizze* (Comparative Anatomy of Angels, a Draft), 1825; *Nanna, oder über das Seelenleben der Pflanzen* (Nanna [the German Goddess of Vegetation], or the Soul Life of Plants), 1848; *Zend-Avesta, oder über die Dinge des Himmels und des Jenseits* (*Zend-Avesta*, or on The Things of Heaven and the Hereafter), 1851. The latter may have inspired some of Schreber's ideas about the Persian gods and immortality. Ellenberger (1970) noted Fechner's depressive illness from 1840-1843 and his creative transformation from physicist to philosopher. Fechner made a new break-through with *Elemente der Psychophysik* in 1860; this work became an inspiration to Wundt. Fechner is mentioned by Freud via the Weber-Fechner law in the *Beyond the Pleasure Principle*; Fechner (1848) also wrote a work on that subject: *Über das Lustprincip des Handelns* (On the Pleasure Principle in Action).

Wundt published in 1874 his *Grundzüge der physiologischen Psychologie* (Foundations of Physiological Psychology), the basic text of the new discipline and an inspiration for generations of investigators, including his English-born American follower, Edward B. Titchener (1867-1927). In 1875 Wundt founded in Leipzig the Institute for Experimental Psychology, a model for followers of the new science the world over, including William James at Harvard. His psychology was not based on any background in neuroanatomy or neurophysiology and the method was a combination of documenting the content of consciousness and measuring reaction times. Kraepelin, too, was his student in Leipzig. Flechsig acknowledged Wundt toward the end of his life.

52. It was given the imprimatur by the prominent psychiatrist Johannes Bresler, editor of the *Psychiatrisch-Neurologische Wochenschrift* (abbreviated as *Wochenschrift*), a forum for institutional psychiatry and, surprisingly, for dynamic psychiatry as well. Freud's paper "Character and Anal Erotism" appeared in its 9th volume.

53. The case was originally discussed in the *AZP* by psychiatrists Noetel (51:458-476) and Tigge (51:781-843, especially 823ff.), both in the year 1894-1895, as part of two reports: (1) the meeting of the Psychiatric Association of the Rhein Province of June 9, 1894 and (2) the annual meeting that same year of the Association of the German Alienists in Dresden. Beyer reproduced the story from the *AZP* in a somewhat disorganized manner, because the presenter spoke from memory (Beyer incorrrectly identified the volume of *AZP* as 41). It was also discussed during the *Reichstag* debate of 1897 (Beyer, 1912).

54. Both were ghost-written by a staff member of the publisher. The first pamphlet (1895) cost 50 pfennig and the title page bore this announcement: "The proceeds are earmarked for the unhappy Rodig family." The Forbes case, mentioned in the title, refers to a Protestant minister from England who lived in Germany and was committed as insane to the Mariaberg Asylum, run by the Alexianer, a religious order. Gruesome stories about the abuse of patients at Mariaberg hit the newspapers, and in a brochure published by Mellage, Forbes was portrayed as a victim of psychiatric oppression. The case of Forbes is discussed by Beyer. A self-vindicating pamphlet was published by the psychiatrist of the asylum, Dr. Carl Capellmann (1895).

55. It may be the same one who later wrote a review of the *Memoirs* (Windscheid, 1904).

56. Beyer lists some 20 anti-semitic and anti- psychiatry pamphlets. Some representative titles are: Carl Paasch's *To the Germans! For the Struggle Against the Jews! A Patriotic Call to all Germans from the Prince to Poorest Worker* (1892a) and *To the German Anti-Semites! A Pamphlet Against the Representative L. from S."* With the same house Paasch also published an attack on the venerated pathologist Rudolf Virchow, a defender of the Jews (1892b). On his (1893) illness Paasch wrote *"Briefe aus dem Irrenhause* (Letters from a Madhouse) in *Anti-Korruption.* See next note.

57. Von Brandt was attacked in pamphlets by another anti-Semitic critic of the Jewish "domination" of Germany who also shared Paasch's fate of incarceration in mental institutions, the merchant Ewald Krüner. Krüner created a sensation by publishing a number of *Appeals* (Krüner, n.d.), attaching himself to the antipsychiatry campaign launched in a number of influential newspapers, such as the *Kreuzzeitung* #25/1892 and reprinted in the *Frankfurterzeitung.* The latter *Appeal* decried involuntary hospitalization, contained such phrases as "buried in asylums," "the need for protection of the invaluable gifts of reason, civil rights and freedom," "corruption," "protection against brutal force," and was signed by prominent citizens. Krüner also attacked the power of Jewish men of science in the German Reich, in the psychiatric establishment and Bismarck's top financial advisor, the Jew Gerson Baron von Bleichröder, whose relationship with Bismarck has been captured by Stern (1977). Krüner was detained in asylums beginning in 1889 as a sufferer from litigious paranoia (*Querulantenwahn*), which, Goetze (1896) argued, was the psychiatric label stuck on somebody who was simply litigious. Flechsig (1896d) had made a similar distinction. The title of Krüner's 1897 pamphlet was *Modern Torture Chambers. A Popular Book to Throw Light on Prussian-German Justice and New Horrendous Revelations About the Question of Mental Patients by Merchant Ewald Krüner of Haspe in Westphalia Who for Eight Years Was Unjustly Condemned as Psychotic and Kept Prisoner in Asylums.* There were at least five editions privately printed in Westphalia. In the appendix Krüner listed 45 other cases similar to his, including Feldmann, Robert Mayer and Paasch. The appendix also contained a reprint of a report of December 31, 1895 by Dr. Rudolf Goetze about Krüner's mental state in which Goetze rebutted claims that the patient had ever been psychotic. It had five editions.

58. As recorded in Flechsig (1884–1896); Karl Paasch is case #469, admitted on November 8, 1893, with an admission diagnosis of "uncertain psychic condition." All the other data routinely filled out upon admission are missing, the only notation under the rubric "Discharge" is "on leave from March 17, 1894." These dates coincide with Schreber's stay there. Were the two aware of each other?

59. As recorded by Goetze (1896, p. 99). A similar opinion was rendered by psychiatry professor Arndt, from Greifswald.

60. Another reference to Flechsig appears in the brochure *Revelations about Psychiatry and Law* by Robert Lutz, who specialized in antipsychiatry publications:

Another case took place in Leipzig. There an eminent psychiatrist, Professor Fl., testified about the presence of psychotic illness on the basis of every possible alleged fact, about which no evidence was presented. In this case the lawyer had his wits with him: "How have you got to know these alleged facts?" "Well, I have heard about them, they were told to me." "That means, you have not come to know them first hand, you have no proof of them?" "No." "Nonetheless you are ready to attest to them as witness or take your oath as expert?" "Oh, no, that is no way my intention." Following this sharp exchange one no longer doubted either the mental state of the well represented plaintiff or that of the psychiatrist. At least, we get a glimpse how such testimonies come into being [p. 19].

If the story is true, it would have been one more reason for Flechsig to hate jurists.

61. From the beginning of his career as psychiatrist Flechsig was not unaware of the issue of illegal confinement (*Freiheitsberaubung*) and psychiatric abuse of patients. Already in 1888a, in the *Report*, Flechsig boasts, "As the director of the hospital I always personally [*durchaus selbständig*] test the necessity of the psychiatric admissions"; he says in a footnote that he has set free many patients who the asylum doctors felt should be confined and adds: "Obviously, even the Director [i.e. Flechsig] could be in error; the psychiatrist in his domain is just as fallible as any other physician in his. Even the most skilled can err in their diagnoses and bring about 'illegal detentions,' without incurring the risk of being accused of negligence or *mala fides* [bad faith]. Until now such has not occurred in the *Klinik*" (p. 24).

62. In the original: *Urningsliebe*. The term *Urning* for homosexual was coined by Karl Heinrich Ulrichs, an avowed homosexual, whose writings in defense of homosexuality began in 1864 under the pen name Numa Numantius. He is cited in Freud (1905, p. 142). The *Urning*, from the name of the planet Uranos, was a biological variant, a *Zwischenstufe*, an intermediate developmental stage, or a third biological gender. This idea, as well as the writings of Ulrichs, was popularized, beginning in 1898, by Magnus Hirschfeld, a prominent sexologist in Berlin and a homosexual, who organized the "Scientific Humanitarian Committee" for the abolition of Paragraph 175 of the penal code defining homosexuality as a crime. Hirschfeld's committee and the journal he edited, along with issues of homosexuality and Paragraph 175, are discussed in the Freud–Jung letters. Flechsig was not listed in Bloch's (1908) *The Sexual Life of Our Time* among the signatories in favor of the abolition of Paragraph 175. (Flechsig is, however, listed on page 298 as a member of the "Alliance for the Protection of Mothers," a humanitarian body against free love and illegitimate children.) I found an abstract of Weber's statement against abolition in the *AZP*. It is an open question whether Schreber knew the expression *Urning* or whether this is Flechsig's word. See also Arno Press Collection (1975) and Kaarsch-Haack (1911), *The Homosexual life of Primitive Peoples*.

63. In Baumeyer (1956, p. 63) *Nachstellungen* is translated as "persecution," in the singular, and the now-rare sense of the word is lost.

6

GUIDO WEBER AND THE FIRST ANTIPSYCHIATRY

Before . . . Easter 1900 . . . the medical expert only became acquainted with the pathological shell, as I would like to call it, which concealed my true spiritual life.

D. P. Schreber, 1903

The appellant's oft-repeated firm intention of publishing his "Memoirs" must be regarded as pathologically determined and lacking sensible consideration. . . . Every impartial observer particularly the expert would call this . . . both offensive and compromising to the author.

Weber, 1902

Having discussed academic psychiatry, we now consider German institutional psychiatry, its private and public psychiatric hospitals. The year of the founding of the department of psychiatry at Leipzig University, 1811, was also the year proclaiming the foundation of the Royal Public Acute Care State Hospital, or asylum, at Sonnenstein castle in Pirna, near Dresden, the first of its kind in Germany, where Paul Schreber was confined from June 29, 1894 to December 20, 1902. However, before his transfer to Sonnenstein Schreber spent two weeks at Pierson's private asylum, Lindenhof.

Lindenhof, bought by Pierson in 1891, was called a *Heilanstalt für Gemüths- und Nervenkranke*,[1] that is, a facility for the treatment of

260

patients suffering from mood and nervous disorders. "The Asylum itself, a relatively small building in beautiful grounds, gave the impression of being quite new. Everything seemed only just finished; not even the enamel paint on the stairs was fully dry" (M, p. 100). It was "fairly elegantly furnished" (M, p. 118). The designation "mood and nervous disorders" was indeed a euphemistic description of posh Lindenhof's dual nature: a private hospital for wealthy neurotic and an asylum for psychotic patients. The name may have provided Paul with the justification to call himself a *Nervenkranker*, a nervous patient. In 1911 Lindenhof was still being advertised by its original name as a hospital "for the comfort of the higher classes" (PNW, vol. 13).

Dr. R. H. Pierson does not appear in the standard reference works. Were it not for the obituary by Dr. Lehmann (1906),[2] Pierson's successor at Lindenhof, we might have remained in the dark about the details of his life. The son of a music professor Pierson from Edinburgh University and his wife Caroline, said to be a well-known author, Pierson was born in Berlin on November 19, 1846; he was thus four years younger than Paul Schreber. He graduated from a gymnasium in Stuttgart and was educated at the Universities of Tübingen and Würzburg. In 1869 he was an assistant in a private institution, and after a number of months he moved to the Royal Asylum at Colditz, where he was preceded by Weber.

During the Franco-Prussian War, in 1870, Pierson volunteered to serve as army physician, which earned him the second class iron cross. We remember that Flechsig was also active in that war, and so was Paul Schreber. It is anybody's guess if their paths crossed that early on. After additional studies in Leipzig and London, Pierson settled in 1873 in Dresden as a specialist in nervous diseases and electrotherapy.

Pierson's two principal achievements were said to be a textbook on electrotherapy,[3] *Compendium of Nervous Diseases and Electrotherapy*, "as well as numerous[4] publications in scientific journals and membership in many learned societies" (Lehmann, 1906; p. 202), and, of course, the acquisition of the private hospital Lindenhof in Coswig. In 1884 he had acquired the private psychiatric hospital in Pirna (see Footnote 1), which functioned until 1891. That year he bought Lindenhof and merged the two into one. The years in Pirna brought him again in contact with Weber.

The only papers by Pierson of interest to us are "On Certain Forms of Dementia and Their Forensic Significance" (Pierson, 1898) and "On Incompetency Due to Dementia" (1903). The relevance of this specialization of Pierson's will become apparent in the story of Princess Louise, discussed later in this chapter. The first paper was discussed at length by Doctors Weber, Ganser (after whom a psychiatric syndrome is named) and Teuscher (who was the good Dr. Täuscher, assistant to Flechsig, in the *Memoirs*); the second was discussed by Weber (1903a).

In Pierson's obituary, the eulogizer, Dr. Lehmann, praised his humane qualities as doctor and director and his administrative and organizational skills in making Lindenhof an exemplary private institution esteemed by professionals. Pierson was an educated man and a talented musician. After 21 years, in the face of failing health, he gave up the directorship and died in 1906 of a belatedly diagnosed abdominal cancer. He had been ailing from gallstones and a mysterious intestinal affliction that the doctors ascribed to neurasthenia. Upon learning the results of the laparotomy, Pierson said, "Now it will be believed that I suffered."

THE LIFE AND WORK OF GUIDO WEBER

By contrast, Guido Weber, born on June 5, 1837, thus five years older than Paul Schreber, and deceased on January 15, 1914, three years after his famous patient, made it to the hall of fame of the great German institutional psychiatrists. His coworker Georg Ilberg (1914) enshrined him as such in an obituary (*Allgemine Zeitschrift für Psychiatrie*, which I abbreviate as *Zeitschrift* and *AZP*) that became the chapter on Weber in the standard reference work by Theodor Kirchhoff (1924) on the history of German alienists (*Deutsche Irrenärzte*).[5]

Like others before him, Weber appended an autobiographical sketch to his dissertation, *On Hematoma of the Dura Mater*,[6] in which he told the bare bones of his life. He was born in the city of Reval, today Tallinn, in Estonia, then part of Russia, to Eduard Weber, at that time a riding school teacher, and his wife Elisabeth née Becker. Until the age of ten he was tutored at home; he then attended a private school. Subsequently he went to high school for seven years and graduated. In 1854, at the age of 17, he became a student at the University in Dorpat, now Tartu,[7] where he stayed for one year and studied philosophy and natural sciences. There for the first time he became interested in studying medicine. In 1855 he followed his father to Germany and subsequently matriculated at Jena University, where he studied the following for three semesters: anatomy, physiology, theoretical and practical chemistry, zoology and microscopical anatomy, physics, botany, pharmacology, surgery, gynecology and medicine in its two aspects, pathology and therapy. He became an enthusiastic member of the student organization *Burschenschaft Germania*. (Schreber was also a member of this student corps.)[8]

In 1857 Weber moved to Leipzig where he remained until the end of his medical studies. Among his teachers in Leipzig were the respected Wunderlich, professor of special pathology and therapy, and Credé, the professor of obstetrics (those two were among the supporters of Flechsig for the chair of psychiatry), professors Bock and Wagner in pathological anatomy (the former a friend of Moritz Schreber's and the latter the pathologist who performed Moritz Schreber's autopsy), Leubuscher who taught psychiatry (not mentioned in Sänger, 1963), and Sonnenkalb, professor of forensic medicine. Weber took his state examination and the doctor's examinations in obstetric medicine and surgery in Leipzig. He also studied one semester in Vienna, a fact he does not mention himself in his autobiographical sketch. Following work in the city hospitals of St. Jacob and St. Georg, Weber graduated with a dissertation in Latin on hematoma as a result of hemorrhaging into the dura mater, the hard cover of the brain (Weber, 1859). The thesis was done under the aegis of the pathology professor Wagner. Weber reviewed the literature on the subject and described anatomo-pathological findings in twenty-two cadavers of both sexes, from infancy to old age. To Schreber, Weber, like Flechsig, was a "God" who dealt with corpses.

Following graduation, on the second day of 1860, Weber wrote a letter to the Ministry of the Interior, in charge of all the royal public hospitals, to apply for a job.

> As I have learnt, His Majesty's Ministry intends to appoint as resident physician a graduate of a medical school, to serve in the Colditz and in the Sonnenstein Asylums. . . . Having personally learnt about the situation in the Colditz Asylum, I feel hopeful that I will be able to perform the required duties. Conscious of my good will to render those to the best of my abilities, I take the liberty to most humbly request of His Majesty's Royal Ministry, with accompanying attestations, to be accepted for one of the positions in the above named institutions . . . Calleberg near Lichtenstein [Saxony], 2nd of January 1860, your most obedient servant, G. Weber Dr. med. [Weber, 1859-1910].[9]

The letter shows poise and maturity; the style and tone might indicate obsequiousness, as prescribed by the etiquette of the times. The two institutions mentioned appear to be very different from each other. In those days, the Colditz Asylum, situated in the old Colditz castle, functioned as a *Versorganstalt*, or custodial institution, a warehouse for the most hopeless of cases.

On January 13, 1860 Guido Weber was interviewed by the Director of Colditz, Dr. Nauhof, who made the following observations:

> Dr. G. Weber, born in Reval and nationalized in Calleberg, where he followed his father who took over the position of a director of a women

teachers' seminary, . . . graduated November last from Leipzig University, where he pursued special studies in psychiatry [as well as] medical sciences such as microscopy, pathological anatomy and surgery, passing the *examen rigorosum* with high honors [*erste Censur*] [Weber, 1859-1910].

Weber's competitor, mentioned in the same letter by Naufhof, was a Dr. Langenhager, a physician with four years' experience in a Leipzig asylum and proficient as physician and surgeon, who passed his exams with a grade of only "very good" (*zweite Censur*). Both gentlemen made a very good personal impression, and neither was preferred to the other. We do not know what tipped the scale, but on January 28 the Ministry appointed Weber to the position at Colditz. It went into effect on February 2 and on February 9, 1860, Weber was officially sworn in and took over the duties at Colditz. This fact was cited by the superintendent of Colditz at that time, Dr. Voppel (1880).[10]

The 23-year-old Weber did not stay long at Colditz. He felt oppressed and frustrated by the depressive and hopeless atmosphere of the place, and on May 24, 1861, he sent a request to the Ministry of the Interior to be transferred to the prestigious Sonnenstein Asylum, set up as an acute care hospital:

My reasons for the request are . . . to have the opportunity to study the fresher forms [of mental illness] . . . and in this way and through personal experience to acquire a knowledge of a more comprehensive therapy than is available here . . . it was a subjectively felt need to achieve and maintain a true professional satisfaction and more tangible social successes . . . [Weber, 1859-1910].

The director of Colditz supported the request; it was well worth it, even if the pay was lower. The Ministry acted favorably and with dispatch.

On the first of August 1861 Weber arrived in Sonnenstein to be sworn in again, on August 3, as the new assistant psychiatrist. He was to stay there until his dying day.

The Royal Public Asylum Sonnenstein

By 1805 the spread of humanistic ideas under the influence of French psychiatry led to the institutional separation of two kinds of inmates: felons and madmen.[11] Dr. Hayner (1817)[12] wrote the book, *Petition to Governments, Authorities, and Directors of Madhouses for the Abolition of Certain Serious Faults in the Treatment of the Insane* to separate prison inmates and patients and to promote humane treatment of the insane, even though he favored corporal punishment as an effective method of treatment. He also recommended to Minister von Nostitz und Jänckendorf that Sonnenstein Castle in the town of Pirna, an old fortress that originally housed both the criminal and the crazy, be converted from an asylum for the incurable to a place of treatment of acute patients only.[13]

This is how Sonnenstein, the jewel in the crown of Saxon asylums, looked at mid-century to a visitor from the United States, Pliny Earle, M.D. (1853):[14]

> Pirna lies upon the southern banks of the Elbe, ten miles above Dresden. A railroad connects the two cities and as one is passing from the latter to the former, his eye is regaled by a beautiful view up the valley of the river. The romantic district of the "Saxon Switzerland" stretches in fine perspective before him; Koenigstein and Lilienstein lift their precipitous cliffs, each in solitary grandeur from the valley which surrounds them; and the distant mountains of Bohemia lie like clouds, faint, misty, and blue, against the far horizon.
>
> At the eastern extremity of Pirna, [on] a rocky promontory, from one hundred and fifty to two hundred feet in height . . . [which] terminates in an abrupt precipitous declivity . . . the lords of Auld Lang Syne dwelt in their solitary and ferocious grandeur . . . [after many wars]. The river of blood terminated in the clear, broad sea of benevolence, and Sonnenstein, so long the residence of the destroyer, became the dwelling of those whose duty—whose labor is *to save*. . . . "Sonnenstein," says Damerow, "was the morning sun of a new day in the sphere of insanity in Germany. With the mildly illuminating rays which emanated from this high point, came warmth, light and life into the gloom of the institutions for the insane . . . " [pp. 132-133; emphasis Earle's].

At the time of Dr. Earle's visit the superintendent was its founder (in 1811), Dr. Ernst Pienitz,[15] a student of Pinel who married a Frenchwoman, under whose leadership Sonnenstein became a "pioneer of the well-organised curative establishments," attracting students and visiting dignitaries, among them the Russian Empress Maria Fedorovna; there were two other physicians, a resident (*Hülfsarzt*) and an assistant physician. There were two buildings, one for men and one for women, housing a total of some 250 patients. There were three classes of patients and a luxury class—the boarders, who had private apartments and attendants and paid 750 thalers, or five times as much as first class dwellers, per annum. Convalescing boarders took up quarters in a new building, which also housed the physicians. Milieu treatment was the main modality, with emphasis on work on the grounds and in the gardens and the many artisan shops, but the old-fashioned restraints were still in use (Ilberg, 1926; cited in Busse, 1990). The medicinal treatments were limited: opiates for the excited and cathartics and tartar emetic for the melancholics. Protracted baths were also used to calm excitement. The communal spirit was fostered by socialization, playing musical instruments, and an occasional party, especially at Christmas.

WEBER'S CAREER

Weber performed to the satisfaction of his superior and the overseers at Department IV of the Ministry of the Interior. He rose from the position of second assistant physician to that of the first, and by March 1, 1867, he was installed as a tenured second *Anstaltarzt*, or physician of the institution, that is, as the second in command to the director. He functioned in this capacity for the next 16 years, choosing to live with his wife in a service apartment in the nearby town of Pirna.

Twenty-two years after his arrival at Sonnenstein, in 1883, one year before Schreber's first hospitalization at Flechsig's, Weber, at the age of 46, was approached by the Ministry of the Interior to become the new director of Sonnenstein, the third since its founding, upon the resignation of his predecessor, Dr. Lessing. This was an important milestone. Weber was also asked to move back into the hospital precinct and live with his family in the *Pensionsanstalt*, the special building occupied by socially prominent boarders, where Schreber was also to live. In his letter to the Ministry Weber says that after consultations with his wife and Dr. Lessing about the problems of such an undertaking, he felt it "was in the public interest and of the institution as well, to continue the tradition of the *Pensionsanstalt*": "I am willing to consider the possibility of taking over the boarders' building with my wife, and we will try to manage it in the heretofore established manner, to the best of our modest and tried powers" (Weber, 1859-1910, letter of May 3, 1883). This is now the voice of an experienced physician, no longer obsequiously bent over but conscious of his weight and importance. In July 1883 Weber was officially instated as the new director and in August the Ministry raised him to the rank of *Medicinalrath* of the fourth class. His career took off. By 1890 he was *Obermedicinalrath* and by 1896 he rose to the highest rank, that of *Königlicher sächsischer Geheimer Medicinalrath* (privy Saxon medical councillor), like Flechsig; and his top salary was 10,000[16] marks per annum, 1,000 more than the highest director's pay in Saxony (Müller, 1908), 500 less than Schreber and 3,000 more than Flechsig.

In his obituary of his predecessor Lessing, who died in 1886, Weber (1887-1888) eulogized his qualities as a practical and self-taught man who believed in his own experience and his own invincible self-confidence. Lessing eschewed theoretical constructions; he was a conservative man with the greatest respect for authority. However, even though his attitude toward his patients was marked by love, kindness, and respect, he never let go of the use of mechanical restraints, such as the camisole and the famous tranquilizing chair. This was left for Weber to achieve. Weber was indeed progressive in his pursuit of Conolly's[17] idea of no-restraint, called by its English name in the German literature.

By 1883, Weber also became a member of the Royal Saxon *Landes-medizinalkollegium* (health commissioners board for the Kingdom of Saxony). This was a regulatory and supervisory body entrusted with overseeing the professional standards and conduct of psychiatrists of the land. In this capacity Weber also collected the annual reports of the Saxon Asylum directors and published them as part of yearly reports of the entire Saxon medical system, which included the state hospital system.[18]

There are a few personal glimpses of Weber in his personal file, including two self reports of illness. In the first, dated February 7, 1894, Weber tells of an illness that started as a "bronchial catarrh" (not unlike an influenza but not as intensive) and within a short time was followed by a "peculiar, intensive complication with concurrent sleeplessness, and a complete lack of appetite, affecting the lower rectum." Explains Weber:

In the wake of exceedingly strong and continuous pain, aggravated by every movement, I feared the development of an inflammation in this area (a so-called periproctitis), but an old district physician for the insane, Dr.[name illegible], after repeated thorough examinations, assumed that this was a nervous phenomenon, a neuralgia [illegible] and the further course of events confirmed this diagnosis [Weber, 1859-1910].

Within a few days the patient recovered from his bout of nervousness and the psychosomatic rectal disorder. The second illness was longer and entailed Weber's absence from his job from August 19, 1897 to October 5, 1897, including an admission to the Diaconissen Hospital. At a later time, in a letter of 1906 to the Ministry in connection with a forthcoming congress of psychiatrists in Milan, Weber expresses appreciation for the honor and voices concern about his failing health.

Like Pierson at Coswig, Weber devoted his career to expanding the physical plant, tearing down old dungeon-like towers, adding new wings, and thus creating a facility that in 1893 reached a census of 513 patients, nearly four times that of Flechsig's hospital. His goal was to create a modern treatment center (Weber, 1910),[19] a model acute care hospital, not a custodial one. Weber and Sonnenstein became synonymous: he embodied and lived the history of Saxon institutional psychiatry. It is of interest to trace the evolution of Sonnenstein in some of his unpublished statements that can be found in the various files of the Ministry of the Interior.[20] They also offer a glimpse into Weber's policies, his unfulfilled dreams, and shed light on the tragic clash with Schreber during his long years of detention at Sonnenstein.

In its heyday, and during his first decade as director, Sonnenstein's status as an acute care hospital was assured by royal ministerial regulations which gave Weber discretionary powers over admissions and discharges, as described in the "Notice of the Ministry of the Interior of September 26, 1855" (*Behandlung*, 1862). At that time there were three asylums: Sonnenstein and two custodial asylums: Colditz for men and Hubertusburg for women. Sonnenstein operated pretty much like Flechsig's asylum: incurable or dangerous patients were transferred to the custodial asylums. By 1893, ten years into his tenure as director, Weber saw his dream of Sonnenstein as an ideal institution shattered by the changes in the land and, as a result, a changing Sonnenstein population and new directives from the Ministry of the Interior. The Ministry was then pushing for a reorganization of the provincial asylums, Sonnenstein included, into mixed facilities for the treatment of acute (curable) and chronic (incurable) patients alike. What Weber escaped in Colditz was staring him in the face again at Sonnenstein: the "inappropriate elements," that is, droves of unruly, noisy, unsocial, unappealing, raving mad women and men. He was most unhappy and gave muted expression to his frustration in a lengthy, discursive report (Weber, 1898).[21] His dream had been to treat patients as long as there was a "presumption of curability, . . . as long as the illness was still fluid and as long as . . . these patients have not become injurious by their attitudes and behavior to other patients" (Weber, 1898). Otherwise, there was a need to have chronic patients evacuated—a word beloved of Flechsig and Weber (other expressions used by Weber: removed, unburdened, eliminated, and isolated)—to the human warehouses. The mixed-admissions policy filled all hospitals to capacity. But the notion of a "pure" treatment hospital turned out to be a chimera: it was soon flooded with chronic patients and the custodial hospitals had no more space to receive transfers. Thus, Sonnenstein became clogged with "great numbers of the totally hopeless, continuously noisy" inmates, who could "infect entire hospital floors and paralyze doctors' treatment effort," and adversely affect "acutely ill, sensitive patients in need of peace and rest," with the result that it came to "resemble a custodial institution and this impression . . . [affecting] the public so that people . . . no longer [entrusted] their kin to [Sonnenstein] but [looked] for other places, such as city hospitals, private hospitals, those for nervous diseases and for naturopathy" (Weber, 1898).

Weber was caught in a bind ("circulus vitiosus" he called it): on the one hand, the demographic changes in society (rapid industrialization, growth of the workers' class, poverty, disease, a frustrated middle class) were producing legions of the mentally sick; on the other hand, the promoters of the lunacy trade in the psychiatric and legal establishments were locking up more and more people within the walls of asylums. Against this sea of misery were the efforts of a small number of physicians to protect the interests of a few hand-picked "good" patients. Poor noisy and turbulent Schreber, whose screams may have been heard all the way to the director's quarters in the boarders' hospital, fell through the cracks of a failing system.

Weber dreamed of having an arrangement like Flechsig's—nice, well-behaved patients of good social standing—so that he could pursue the lofty goals of science and therapeutic success. The answer was to build more custodial hospitals—more concentration camps for mankind "left to rot" (as Paul Schreber expressed it)—but no rapid relief was in sight.[22]

In other reports Weber reluctantly agrees with a directive from the Ministry to grant therapeutic leaves to "temporarily" admitted patients, having overcome his fears that this should not jeopardize their being returned to the hospital by the families should further care be needed, and having realized that after all, leave may in some cases be equivalent to discharge.[23] This attitude had a bearing on Schreber, for Weber's conservative policy about patients' leaves delayed Schreber's efforts to prove his capacity to function and thus gain a timely release.

Interesting data are furnished by Weber's files concerning his attendants. Here Weber shows himself to be a man devoted to his staff, pleading with the Ministry for consideration of leaves and pension benefits. There are reports of a number of cases of attendants, both male and female, who went psychotic themselves and had to be hospitalized.[24]

These institutional realities were often discussed in the contemporary psychiatric literature. Each year there were more mentally sick at large and in the asylums.[25] The hospitals were understaffed, the workers underpaid.[26] The low morale often resulted in physical abuse of inmates.[27] These serious issues, which had already stirred many protests on the pages of daily newspapers, were being belatedly admitted by the official psychiatric organs.

Weber's conservatism and rigidity stand out in comparison with the new ideas blowing in the wind at the turn of the century, past the stormy days of Schreber in the asylum. There was a growing recognition of the adverse effects of the environment, including prolonged isolation[28]—such as the acquisition by patients of habits resulting from hospital routines—on the course of disorders; the deterioration in patients with the various disorders were now defined as "artifacts of hospitalization" (Kreuser, 1899). The very admission to a psychiatric facility was seen as a "psychic choc" (the French spelling). Finally recognized was the need for "psychotherapy and individualized approaches to the patient," the potential in therapeutic uses of the milieu, and the growing importance of family care (Ohlah, 1900).[29] The pleading for psychotherapy is remarkable for a time when psychiatric hospitals were not even built to include space for holding private and confidential patient–therapist conversations. There was also a growing awareness that attendants were not merely servants but participants in the treatment team:

> The new psychiatry should strive more energetically to rejoin her mother: psychology. . . . The days are over when diets, opium, electricity and gymnastics were the mainstay of therapy: it is solely the influence of the doctor and the environment shaped by him. . . . Psychic *treatment in our institutions should begin with the nursing staff* [Fuhrmann, 1905; Fuhrmann's emphasis].

There was a burgeoning of critical attitudes among psychiatrists toward their own profession, as in discussions of "psychopathic traits in psychiatrists" (Lomer, 1906).[30] There was also a questioning of the effects of hospitalization. Bleuler (1905) in a paper entitled "Early Discharges" argued for this policy for manic-depressive patients, who, he believed, were the best candidates for a cure: "*Hospital treatment* [for them] *is an evil.* . . . The injuriousness stems from the fact that such patients are made worse by repressive measures. The more freedom they have, the better they fare. . . . I demand nothing less than the extension of the No-restraint to include hospitalization itself as a restraint" (p. 442 and footnote; emphasis Bleuler's). This sentiment was echoed by Riklin (1905) in his paper "Improvements Due to Transfers," in which he recommended moving patients from one hospital to another in search of a new environment, to enhance therapeutic movement.[31]

These trends culminated in the first decade of the 20th century in a plea for a new treatment modality like the one practiced

> In the Bloomingdale Hospital (White Plains) . . . [where] special attention [was] given to the search for the psychic causes of certain forms of

mental disorder, to unbalanced affects and psychic conflicts, with their specific reactions and failed adaptation efforts, that lie hidden under the confused web of symptoms, in short, a kind of psychic analysis [*eine seelische Analyse*], whose basic directions, foundation and rich elaboration we owe to a Viennese, Professor Freud, who has found eminent promoters in Bleuler, Jung and others [Bresler, 1908].[32]

Weber was not affected by these new trends. Scientifically, he was said to be a follower of Kraepelin, an authority for Schreber and Freud as well, but he did not have Kraepelin's clinical and dynamic scope and depth. He made no original contribution to clinical psychiatry. However, as dean of the Saxon institutional psychiatrists, he achieved fame as a forensic expert whose opinion was frequently sought by the courts. His interests remained limited to psychiatric paradigms hardened into habit and dogma and to the interface between psychiatry and law. He also acted for the preservation of the power of the psychiatrist vis-à-vis other professionals, physicians and lawyers.[33] Weber was among the founding members of two societies, the *Forensisch-psychiatrische Vereinigung zu Dresden* (Forensic-Psychiatric Association of Dresden) and the *Vereinigung mitteldeutscher Psychiater und Neurologen* (Association of the Middle-German Psychiatrists and Neurologists). The latter had its first meeting at Flechsig's hospital, with Flechsig himself in the chair, which was reported in the first issue of the newly founded journal, the *Monatschrift für Psychiatrie und Neurologie (MPN,* 1:497). He was also a member, and toward the end an honorary member, of the all-German *Verein der deutschen Irrenärzte* (Association of German Alienists, i.e., institutional psychiatrists). It was as a member of these and other societies that Weber found expression for his creative impulses. Almost all of his written output is in the form of abstracts and reports of presentations or discussions in the meetings of these societies, published mainly in the *Zeitschrift*.

WEBER'S SCIENTIFIC PUBLICATIONS

The first publication by Weber that I was able to find is from 1876, the last from 1912. These texts show the orderly and average mind of a judicious functionary, devoid of the spark of originality. In his writings Flechsig projected an aura of a mind in conflict; by contrast, Weber remains placid, stolid, and conventional throughout.

At age 39, in his 15th year at Sonnenstein, Weber (1876) gave a presentation about pregnancy and postpartum psychoses at a scientific meeting. It was a decent clinical and statistical overview, based on patients observed at Sonnenstein. In the discussion a number of colleagues remarked about medications recommended for excitement in these conditions. Of the known agents—opium, bromides, and chloral hydrate—opium was recommended by Weber as the drug of choice, and so was camphor. Bromides and chloral hydrate were not indicated. One wonders if Flechsig was aware of these opinions when he advocated his opium-bromide regimen for epilepsy.

To recreate the atmosphere of such proceedings, let us follow in some detail the events at the founding meeting of the Association of Middle-German Psychiatrists and Neurologists which took place in Leipzig on April 25, 1897, at Flechsig's hospital, with Flechsig in the chair. It was reported both in the prestigious *Archiv für Psychiatrie* for 1896 and in the *Monatschrift für Psychiatrie* for 1897. After Flechsig opened the meeting, Weber was elected as treasurer of the association. The first lecture of the meeting was then given by Weber (1897c). Also present was Dr. Pierson. One might say that, all the conspirators, as Schreber saw them, were here. Weber gave a speech about the history of public psychiatric institutions in Saxony, noting that, at the beginning of the 18th century a need arose in Saxony to deal with the hordes of the poor, the orphaned, the lawless, the homeless, and the insane; the need was satisfied by erecting penal institutions and poorhouses. The mentally sick were housed with the paupers and the criminals. The criminal inmates were made into attendants of the insane, and they controlled the latter by holding them chained to their beds, or chairs, or in manacles. The insane inmates, both men and women, wore a kind of uniform, blue with yellow piping and edgings. Knowing this history, one can appreciate the enlightened reforms promulgated by Dr. Hayner (1817) which also inspired Weber. The goal at Sonnenstein was twofold: separating the insane from the criminal and creating a hospital for the acutely ill, that is, for curable patients. The first was duly achieved, but the second was not, causing Weber long-standing chagrin. Another aspect of the Saxon reforms was the move of asylums from the old and forbidding castles into small modern pavilions, implemented for the first time in 1868 in the Zschadrass Hospital.

Also at this meeting a lecture was given by Dr. Otto Binswanger on the pathogenesis of the so-called exhaustion psychoses. This was discussed by Flechsig (1897d), who pointed out that the clinical picture of such exhaustion states, due to metabolic processes in the brain, could be explained by the precise localization of these processes in the brain. Flechsig also discussed a lecture by his assistant Hösel on "Association and Localization."[34]

From 1896 through 1912, in essence the last period of his life, we find a spate of published statements by Weber on a variety of legal psychiatric problems, the bulk of them talks or remarks made at prior meetings of the Forensic-Psychiatric Association of Dresden. For example, we can read Weber on mental incompetency and the Civil Code (1897a), including incompetency due to alcoholism (1897b). His remarks on stealing due to sexual motives (Weber, 1898b) were interesting in that they offer a glimpse of Weber's views on sexuality. At a meeting of the Forensic-Psychiatric Association of Dresden one discussant pointed out the dangers of a the book *Der Fall Wilde oder das Problem der Homosexualität* (The Case of [Oscar] Wilde and the Problem of Homosexuality), written by one Os. Sero and recently published by Spohr in Leipzig, to which Weber added that "he considered the periodical *Vita Sexualis* "equally dangerous." A year later Weber (1899c) lectured against the abolition of the homosexual penal code.[35]

The fourth annual meeting of the Association of Middle- German Psychiatrists and Neurologists took place in Dresden and was reported in the *Archiv*: "Following a convivial gathering on the eve of the event, the meeting was opened at 9 o'clock in the morning of October 23, 1898, in the board room of the *Landes-Medicinal-Collegium*" (*AP*, 31:911). It was a small gathering. Among the assembled members and guests were Dr. Stegmann from Dresden, later Freud's informant about Schreber; Dr. Pierson from Lindenhof in Coswig; and Dr. Weber from Sonnenstein. Weber spoke on forensic-psychiatric aspects of responsibility and the penal code (Weber, 1899e). Regarding the criminally insane, he argued for not commuting sentences due to mental illness but for replacing prisons with special long-term psychiatrically supervised special correctional-educational facilities and for incompetency determinations to that end.

In a discussion at a meeting of the Forensic-Psychiatric Association of Dresden on May 22, 1897, Weber (1899a) considered the various forms of psychosis in young psychotics (Kahlbaum's and Hecker's hebephrenia, Kraepelin's dementia praecox, and catatonia) and noted, "The form labeled by Kraepelin's Dementia paranoides is not part of the discussion." Historically, we are dealing with the great classificatory breakthrough of Kraepelin with regard to schizophrenia, and the issue is also relevant to the future diagnosis of Paul Schreber.

Of particular interest is Weber's reaction to a burning issue of the day: the 1897 debates in the German *Reichstag* in Berlin concerning the need to enact national mental hygiene legislation to provide for checks and balances to current incompetency statutes that led to railroading people into asylums and depriving them of their civil liberties. Weber expressed his opposition to any idea of reform and to a suggestion that laypersons be part of a board dealing with admission policies: "Only reliable physicians can offer definitive protection against unjustified admissions and delayed discharges" (Weber, 1902a, p. 542). The following year, in 1903, Weber made a presentation of the now publicized

Schreber case anonymously (as Mr. N) from the forensic point of view (Weber, 1905a), which is discussed in full in this chapter. That year he was also concerned with his other forensic case, the sensationalized affair of the Princess of Sachsen-Koburg-Gotha (Weber, 1909a).

Weber (1901) collaborated in the founding of the *Hilfsverein für Geisteskranke* (Charitable Society for Mental Patients). He was director of this organization and frequently acted as chair of the meetings, giving of his time unstintingly for the rehabilitation of indigent mental patients in the community through financial help and job placements.[36]

On June 4, 1907, Weber celebrated his 70th birthday. From near and far came greetings and acclaim for his efforts on behalf of Sonnenstein and of psychiatry in Saxony. In the morning Ministry Director Appelt was on hand to announce his being honored with the title and rank of *Geheimer Rat*, or privy councillor, a rare honor for a Saxon psychiatrist.[37] The king of Saxony, in recognition of his achievements, bestowed upon Weber the Cross of the Knights of Merit, first class; the Officer Cross; and Commander of the Order of Albrecht. In the afternoon, the official festivity was opened by a motet sung by a male choir. Various local dignitaries, as well as former students, came to pay homage, Professor Sterl of Dresden presented Sonnenstein with his masterpiece: a life size oil portrait of the celebrant. Also presented was an artistically crafted commemorative plaque. Then and there the former students set up a Geheimer-Rat-Weber charitable fund to provide assistance for former Sonnenstein patients (*PNW*, 9:108).

In January 1910, in his 73d year and after half a century at Sonnenstein, the golden jubilee of "Guido Weber-Sonnenstein"—the way he used to sign his pieces in the *Zeitschrift*—was marked with a lead article in the *Wochenschrift*, probably written by editor Bresler himself, and accompanied by his portrait (*PNW*, 11:391-393). It shows a patriarchal and Bismarckian-looking Weber, bald on top with mustache and sideburns, a wise expression on his face and in a pose of dignity and self-assurance. In the article Weber was praised for being an excellent family man, friend and colleague. He was kind to his patients and cared for their welfare, and saw to it that their stay in the hospital was only for the purpose of treatment. He was, noted the article, far from regarding any of the modern medications as panaceas. He was very devoted to his staff and students, who revered him. While his wife was alive, the Webers entertained frequently, with Weber excelling as an author of witty and lightly satirical toast speeches. He also wrote poetry. He was a wise and fatherly chief to his subordinates, the article continued, a benevolent and friendly adviser, self-sacrificing and generous. Throughout his life he was interested in politics and was an enthusiastic supporter of the Empire and of Bismarck. He was also chairman of the *Verein zum Schutz der Deutschen im Ausland* (Society for the Protection of Germans Abroad). As a German born abroad, he naturally felt for Germans who were themselves ethnic minorities.

While he functioned as director, Weber lived with his family on the grounds of Sonnenstein. After half a century of devoted service he retired on June 1, 1910, after 45 years and 8 months of civils service, with an 80% pension of his last salary of 10,000, or 8,000 marks annually (Weber, 1859-1914). Later that year he left his Sonnenstein apartment and moved to Dresden. As far as I know, Weber had two children: a daughter (mentioned in Weber, 1912) and a son, who also became a psychiatrist and later wrote to Baumeyer (1956) about Paul Schreber.

On July 4, 1911, on Weber's 74th birthday,[38] about three months after Schreber's death, the 100th anniversary of the Royal Saxon Asylum Sonnenstein was celebrated with great pomp. On the eve of the event a motet was sung and commemorative speeches were made at the cemetery of Sonnenstein, where many of its previous employees were buried. The celebration proper began in the new Sonnenstein church. The buildings were adorned with banners, the main entrance with garlands, and the altar with laurel and flowers. The festivities were attended by the Minister of State and other high officials, nobles, and prominent ladies and gentlemen. Present were directors of other institutions, among them Dr. Lehmann, the director of the Leipzig-Dösen Asylum. Many inspired speeches were heard. The long history of the castle was recalled by Dr. Ilberg, Weber's successor, as well as the glory that was Sonnenstein. The first building went back to Roman times as castrum, or fortified camp, Pirna. The name Sonnenstein was given by the Margrave Wilhelm the One-Eyed in 1409. After a number of turns of fate it finally became the site of the premier Saxon mental institution. It was temporarily occupied by Napoleon in 1813, followed by the forcible evacuation of the inmates, on Napoleon's orders: *Que l'on chasse ces fous* [get these madmen out]."[39] After the liberation from Napoleon, the operations of the hospital were restored, inspired by the enlightened principles of Dr. Hayner and under the leadership of its first director, Pienitz.[40] Dr. Weber recalled his long years of service, praised his predecessors and followers, and gave his blessing to "his beloved old Sonnenstein."[41]

Weber died on January 15, 1914, predeceased by his wife by many years. He was eulogized for the wisdom and benevolence he showed toward patients, colleagues, students, and subordinates. At the request of the Sonnenstein personnel (Weber, 1859-1910), he was buried on the grounds of the institution he had served with so much love and devotion. The passing of Weber marked the end of an era. In August Europe would be engulfed in the First World War.

INSANITY AND INCOMPETENCY

Forensic-psychiatric interests, among them the issue of patient incompetency, were but an incidental activity for Flechsig. In Weber's case these were the heart and soul of his identity as a psychiatrist.

Incompetency belonged to the jurisdiction of the individual states. It was an idea originally alien to Saxon lawmakers, for it was considered a serious interference in an adult person's civil liberties. Saxony was late to follow the other states of the German Empire in adopting it. Incompetency statutes were proclaimed in Saxony in 1881 by King Albert in Decree #30 (*Bestimmungen*, 1879–1890) and made into law in 1882. By law, a declaration of incompetency due to inability to manage one's own affairs was applied to a person certified as a psychotic, a cripple, or a spendthrift, in contrast to one suffering merely from a nervous disorder (*Geistesstörung*), or a *Gemüthskrankheit* in the popular parlance and in the sense used by Paul Schreber. In the case of alleged mental illness, either a district physician (*Kreisphysicus*, i.e. a nonpsychiatrist) or psychiatrists were the legal experts who could certify that the person was mentally ill. A judge of the county court in the county of the person's legal residence could use such expert opinion and declare the person legally incompetent. The diagnosis of psychosis had to be linked to evidence that the allegedly psychotic person was also unable to take care of his affairs and this had to be certified by a physician. In cases of adults, the application for this legal procedure had to be made either by a relative, usually a spouse, if the sick spouse had failed as a provider or homemaker, or by a guardian, or by the public prosecutor, if unlawful acts were committed or the police were involved. The mere presence of psychosis was not sufficient ground for a ruling of incompetency but was, of course, the necessary precondition. In the eyes of the law one could be psychotic and functional at the same time.

It is important to realize the power of those entitled to make the initial application, for situations were known in which a request for a declaration of incompetency by an asylum was denied, whereas a relative's or a guardian's application resulted in an incompetency ruling by the court. The person who had been declared incompetent, or his guardian, had the right to sue to have the declaration rescinded.

Certain words, such as delusions, easily led to a diagnosis of insanity and hospitalization. This was a severe enough complication of a person's life. We have seen this in Schreber's case. Being declared legally incompetent was an additional danger. Incompetency was thus a sui generis legal, not a psychiatric, measure defined by the Civil Code as belonging to the domain of public interest and specifically aimed at curbing the liberty and property rights of the socially dysfunctional, the sick and the spendthrifts. In this way, the prosecutor, the police, the physician (including the psychiatrist), and the power brokers in the ministries of justice and the interior, could exercise control over people for the sake of public order and safety. It also opened the door, as we have already seen in the cases in which Flechsig was involved, to political and private abuses of psychiatry.

An incompetent person was considered by the law as a seven-year-old child. The individual was thus stripped of his civil rights, could not dispose of his property or money, and could only make limited decisions with the approval of a person designated as his legal guardian. This also happened to Schreber. As incompetent before the law, Schreber was also prevented from being discharged from the hospital, thus his status allowed Weber to have a double stranglehold on him, both medical and juridical.

The forensic-psychiatric principles of incompetency rulings were discussed a great deal in the *Wochenschrift* and to a lesser extent in the *Zeitschrift*, and also in the law periodicals and in textbooks of forensic psychiatry (for example, E. Schultze's essay in a textbook edited by A. Hoche, 1909).[42]

The lawmakers warned against premature declarations of incompetency because the procedure was costly and because it could cause injury to a person's career owing to adverse publicity or social consequences. For example, a physician or a pharmacist could regain his right to practice once the incompetency was legally rescinded; a lawyer could not—such a decision doomed him forever. Also once a declaration of incompetency was in place, the patient could not automatically leave the hospital if his condition improved: the incompetency ruling had to be legally overturned first. Upon improvement, such a patient had an inherent right to sue to have the incompetency decision rescinded. However, such a countersuit was difficult, costly, and not routinely done. According to ministry statistics, of an average of 4,000 incompetency rulings annually, only 76 were challenged. In the years 1888-1892 only 16 rescissions per 10,000 were approved at appeals.

THE CASE OF PRINCESS LOUISE

Diagnosis and incompetency were key issues in a cause célèbre in which Weber was involved the same year he lectured on Paul to the Dresden Forensic-Psychiatric Association. The case involved Princess

Louise, the daughter of the King of the Belgians. We will follow her fate as an exemplar of the diagnostic and legal vagaries of the period in order to understand Weber's context and how he subsequently dealt with Paul Schreber.

The previous cause célèbre involving royalty was the case of the extravagant King Ludwig II (1845-1886) of Bavaria, builder of the famous castles and the Richard Wagner Theatre in Bayreuth. He was deposed after having been diagnosed, on the basis of depositions of his servants, as suffering from an incurable disease, paranoia; declared incompetent; and remanded to permanent detention in the Berg Castle on the shores of the Starnberg Lake. This was accomplished by a team of psychiatrists headed by the renowned neuroanatomist and psychiatrist, Professor Bernard von Gudden, the teacher of Forel and Flechsig. Being king, Ludwig could not even be psychiatrically examined: he would have used his body guards to jail the psychiatrists. Thus, a formal psychiatric examination was never performed. One day Ludwig lured von Gudden to take a boat ride with him on the lake, where he proceeded to both drown himself and the psychiatrist.[43]

The trouble with Louise[44] was that at the age of 20 she married a cousin, Count Philipp of Coburg and Gotha and later became a royal Anna Karenina. The marriage was loveless and childless, after a number of miscarriages. In 1895 Louise fell in love with a Croatian army lieutenant named Mattassich. This was clearly not to the liking of her husband, but the princess sued for divorce. The affair lasted for quite some time, and Louise spent considerable amounts of money on her vanity and her luxurious hobbies, which included keeping racehorses. Louise became an undesirable: an unfaithful and rejecting wife. She refused to bow to the will of her husband, and a way to stop the affair was found—putting her away in an asylum.

Acting at the behest of the husband, a number of psychiatrists, among them the most famous Viennese professor of psychiatry at the time, Dr. von Krafft-Ebing himself, came to the conclusion, again without examining the subject herself and on the basis of depositions, that the ill-fated princess suffered from the psychotic disorder called feeble-mindedness, or dementia (Geistesschwäche), essentially indicating a lack of proper moral judgment. Louise was declared incompetent and locked up in 1895 in the private hospital near Vienna run by Professor Obersteiner. It appears that the professor refused to go on indefinitely with what he considered an illegal confinement, so a new place of internment had to be found. After her brief stay elsewhere, it finally dawned on the husband's advisers that the best place for Louise was the private asylum Lindenhof in Coswig, administered by Dr. R. H. Pierson. The transfer to Lindenhof took place in 1898 and there Louise was held captive in a private villa for the next five years. The detention drew fierce criticism in Dahl's (1905) antipsychiatric pamphlet: Pierson was accused of prostituting science for the sake of filthy lucre.[45]

While the scandal around her incarceration continued, the princess was presented for a new evaluation in 1903, completed by September 18, 1903, by an international panel of forensic experts: Professor Jolly of Berlin; the yet-to-become famous Dr. Julius Wagner von Jauregg, at that time already chief of the psychiatric hospital of Vienna; the Belgian Dr. Mellis; and Guido Weber. Weber's was the fourth signature on the psychiatric report dated "3 December 1903" and presented to County Court of the Saxon city of Meissen (Jolly, 1903; Weber, 1903b).[46]

In their report, based on a review of the princess's history of symptoms, again derived from various depositions and reports, the undersigned were impressed with her character traits of selfishness, vanity, and indifference, as well as her profligacy. At least Dr. Pierson had the benefit of having observed her apathy, which later alternated with periods of excitability and anger. She evinced a "groundless hatred toward her husband," was given to "fantastic ideation . . . [and] said she was the holiest and purest virgin that ever was, that she [would] play her role in history like Queen Elizabeth or Mary Queen of Scots" (Weber et al., 1904). The conclusions in the report were (1) that the diagnosis made at the time of the declaration of incompetency stood unchanged and that the princess was therefore incapable of managing her own affairs; (2) that she "had to be kept continuously in a closed institution because of the nature of her illness and for her own good"; and (3) that Dr. Pierson's institution provided the optimal conditions for the treatment of this nobly born patient. Based on this report, the County Court in Meissen declared the princess incompetent and delivered her into the arms of Pierson in perpetuity. As in previous cases, a diagnosis was turned into a court decision. As before, a diagnostic statement became a legal sentence. As before, psychiatric-forensic procedures were used in the service of political persecution.

Like Schreber, the princess dared to disagree with her doctors. After five years of detention she managed to escape from her villa in Pierson's asylum to Paris, where she turned herself over to the care of the respected Parisian professor of psychiatry Dr. Magnan, known for his landmark papers on chronic paranoia. After half a year of friendlier observation and for an honorarium of 15,000 francs (PNW, 7:163)— easily afforded by her father the King of the Belgians and a royal ransom by any standard—doctors Dubuisson and Magnan signed their forensic opinion, on May 23, 1905, stating that it is "clearly evident that the present mental state of Her Royal Highness does not justify either her being declared incompetent or returned to an asylum" (Bresler, 1905). The guardianship was rescinded and the princess regained her liberty.[47]

One cannot escape the impression that in Germany, at the turn of the century, something was seriously the matter with psychiatry as a science if such extremely contradictory conclusions could be reached by experts based on examinations of the same patient. Of course, the problem was, then as now, not so much with psychiatry but with the abuses of psychiatry for political purposes. Weber was beholden to a system that paid his salary and had the right and the power to define his job and function. In his attempt to reconcile the glaring contradictions between the German and the French experts—the latter being the princess's political advocates and the former her antagonists—Bresler endorsed the opinion that the differences were due to the national French virtue of gallantry (as condescendingly remarked in a Viennese newspaper)[48] and to the French way of reasoning psychologically, as opposed to the German way of reasoning pathologically. I am in agreement with the latter part of the judgment. What Bresler did not address was the ethico-political meaning of mental disorder; it was a phenomenon that could not be fully understood without considering its social and cultural context. Pneumonia, both as observable data and as diagnosis, is pretty much the same in every society; paranoia as data and as diagnosis is not. For paranoia is not just a diagnostic label: it is a social transaction, a social stigma, and a social sanction. It is to this aspect of paranoia we now turn.

THE POLITICS OF PARANOIA

The word *paranoia* comes from Hippocrates, who used it to refer to a state of delirium, or mental disorder due to high fever. However, as noted in Cramer's (1895) survey, "The introduction of the term paranoia created a chaos and a multitude of names for the same disease form" (p. 287). Paranoia is a prominent topic in the various editions of Kraepelin's monumental *Lehrbuch,* or *Textbook* (1893), the first edition of which appeared in 1883.[49] This led to the emergence of the so-called paranoia question (*Paranoiafrage*), a protracted diagnostic polemic in the German literature, of which I will note some highlights.

By the time Weber took over as the director of Sonnenstein in 1883, paranoia was classified as one of the endogenous psychoses, that is, an organic, congenitally and constitutionally conditioned disorder of the central nervous system; it was considered to be a neurological disorder with a psychological content—the assorted delusions. These, in turn, were seen as the effects of hallucinations, and hallucinations themselves were conceived as neurological disorders of so-called elementary sensations. Like disturbances of sensation, described in neurology as dysesthesias (altered sensations), hallucinations were pictured as manifestations of sensory disturbance and regarded as a dysesthesia caused by an altered, spastic state of the sensory nerves, defined by the "so-called nervous spasm law" (das sogenannte Nervenzuckungsgesetz).[50]

By the end of the first decade of this century another analogy to neurology was used: a distinction was made between a neuralgia, or a condition of nerve pain, and the condition of neuritis, or nerve inflammation. Thus, the endogenous psychoses were like neuralgias (i.e., due to a neuropathic predisposition) and were differentiated from the exogenous psychoses, which included the toxic psychoses (those due to specific toxins or poisons) and psychoses secondary to diagnosable lesions in the central nervous system (e.g., inflammations, tumors, arteriosclerosis).[51] This conception left no room for any dynamic (i.e., psychogenic) causation of hallucinations. (Some psychiatrists still hold to similar classifications today, and the controversy between the organic and dynamic conceptions of psychoses is still as alive as it was then.) Accordingly, during the psychiatric examination of the patient, one looked for signs of peripheral tremors and spasms, as in any routine neurological examination.[52] This neurological conception of hallucinatory activity was also reflected in the German word for hallucination: Sinnestäuschung, literally, sensory deception, or sensory illusion, as one reads in Strachey's translation of Freud (1911a) quoting Weber.

It was further taught that the sensory illusions are the cause of delusions, a rather mysterious leap from the physical to the mental, delusions being false beliefs and feelings impervious to correction by reason or evidence.[53] Through the linking of hallucinations with delusions, with their obvious absurdity and bizarreness, paranoia became synonymous with craziness (Verrücktheit), the quintessential idea of madness being the presence of crazy ideas, or delusions, with or without sensory-like components (i.e., hallucinations). It was indeed believed that sensory illusions were an integral part of what was then called paranoia, even if they might not be immediately manifested in any given patient.

Kraepelin's critique of the way paranoia became a diagnostic fad in his day was based on principles that are as valid now as they were then. Kraepelin noted that according to the older teachings of Griesinger (1867), craziness followed in the wake of an affective disorder, either mania or melancholia. Beginning in the late 1860s and the 1870s with the writings of a number of German psychiatrists (Sander, Snell, Westphal, Cramer, Ziehen), a "modern" vogue was born: to speak of a separate third disease, a "primary form of madness,"[54] a disorder of reason or ideas in which morbid and incorrigible ideas predominated. Historically, this conception was fashioned by the old, static association psychology, augmented by Herbart's ideas, and reinforced by brain mythology. The result was a *Vorstellungsmechanik*—the static, atomist science of the mechanics of ideas. In this way, paranoia became the "third disease," to be sharply differentiated from mania and melancholia, the classical mood disorders.

In the fifth edition of his *Textbook*, which Schreber cites, Kraepelin (1896) objected to this vogue for two reasons: Such singling out of a target symptom was an example of psychological, not clinical, reasoning, for it was based on an artificial contrast between feeling and thinking and therefore denied the existence of mixed forms, that is, disorders of mood and ideation. Being anticlinical, it also did not sufficiently consider the criteria of onset, course, and outcome of the disorder; it tended to create a diagnostic wastebasket into which all kinds of clinical syndromes, not related to paranoia, were dumped, such that some clinicians were making the diagnosis of paranoia "in 70 to 80 per cent of their case material." The essential connection between emotions and ideas in paranoia was taken up again on the pages of the *Wochenschrift*.[55]

By 1899, in the sixth edition of his *Textbook*, also quoted from by Schreber, Kraepelin introduced his basic descriptive and diagnostic innovation: the concept of dementia praecox.[56] He unified various previously described syndromes of madness under one inclusive generic name, dementia praecox, describing its three main varieties as hebephrenic, catatonic, and paranoid. Later, at Bleuler's suggestion, he added the fourth type, simple. The term *dementia praecox* had a short career. Its main drawback was its unwieldiness and the lack of an adjective. This was supplied by Bleuler by his introducing the words *schizophrenia* and *schizophrenic*. The solution was not only elegant but it also referred to the phenomenon of the split between feelings and ideas, and suggested a defensive operation of the mind, splitting. (The basic conception of psychic splitting, conceived both as a mechanism and as a mode of defense against painful emotions, had established roots in psychiatry and was later to reappear, in various versions, in psychoanalysis.) As the new term, schizophrenia, quickly conquered the old one, it also became necessary to differentiate the old paranoid madness, variously referred to as paranoia, paranoia vera (true paranoia), and paraphrenia, from the newly created entity of paranoid schizophrenia. Some psychiatrists, including Freud (1911a) himself to a degree in the Schreber analysis, tended to subordinate everything to paranoid schizophrenia.

Guido Weber did not follow the clinical ideas of Kraepelin. Being a forensic expert, he shared the criteria accepted among forensic psychiatrists of the day: he was less impressed with the differential diagnosis, such as course and outcome of the disorder and focused more on the current cross-sectional aspects and their legal ramifications: was there a diagnosis of chronic paranoia, defined as a disorder in which there is a system of delusions, predominantly of persecution and of grandeur, not corrigible by common sense, logic or experience and in which there is otherwise preserved cognitive functions and some mood disturbances, with or without hallucinations? Could the diagnosis be related to actual or potential conflicts with the society, the state, and the law, specifically with regard to certain crimes, such as defamation (libel and slander), physical violence to self or other, squandering, litigiousness, and many other social or political conducts deemed antisocial? And, finally, was a finding of paranoia sufficient grounds for declaring the sufferer as legally incompetent to function in society?

PARANOIA AND INCOMPETENCY

As already indicated, in the eyes of the law there was no necessary connection between being psychotic and declared legally incompetent. Somebody had to be interested to have such a ruling imposed, and the court had the jurisdiction to impose it. The authority on incompetency in Hoche (1909) was the coeditor of Hoche's book, E. Schultze, author of the chapters "The Civil Code," whose previous works of 1899 and 1901 are in Hoche's bibliography. Schultze's book of 1899 was reviewed by Weber's coworker Ilberg (1899). Schultze was also one of the early reviewers of the *Memoirs* (Schultze, 1904).

Schultze (1901) accepted the principle that the actual decision was up to the judge, based on the report of the psychiatric expert. Weber wanted greater quasi-juridical authority for the psychiatrist, but the court disagreed with him. Schultze also expressed a number of caveats and criticisms that seemed to apply to Weber's conduct toward Schreber.

One of the most difficult problems then facing forensic psychiatrists, other than evaluating the chronicity of a person's mental illness, was applying the incompetency criterion to paranoiacs. Every clinician knew from his own experience individuals who might easily be diagnosed as paranoid but who were eminently capable of performing both professionally and personally. The delusions of such individuals might be limited to one sphere (e.g., the religious) and not affect their daily lives. Indeed, we might add, such could even be true of some eminent psychiatrists. Thus, as Schreber himself argued, were the paranoiac to

Paul Emil Flechsig, 1906. Photograph by Nichola Perscheid (courtesy National Library of Medicine)

Paul Schreber (courtesy National Library of Medicine)

Guido Weber (reprinted from Baumeyer, 1970)

Sonnenstein (reprinted from Baumeyer, 1970)

Pauline Schreber (courtesy Jung family)

Pauline Schreber and unidentified members of the family (courtesy Jung family)

Paul Schreber and his adopted daughter, Fridoline, ca. 1906 (courtesy Jung family)

Heinrich Eucharius Behr
(courtesy Prof. U. H. Peters)

Franz Petter (courtesy Prof. U.
H. Peters)

Sabine Schreber (courtesy Jung
family)

Pauline Schreber in her widowhood (courtesy Jung family)

Anna and Carl Ferdinand Jung
(courtesy Jung family)

Anna Jung, 1928 (courtesy
Jung family)

Pauline Schreber, ca. 1855 (courtesy Jung family)

Moritz Schreber, ca. 1855 (courtesy Jung family)

become a public nuisance, the intervention of the police would be necessary; otherwise, one was enjoined to be very careful in instituting incompetency proceedings in the case of people with circumscribed delusions.

One reason to challenge a ruling of incompetency was a change in the condition of the patient such that the behavior that was initially the cause for the ruling were no longer present. This was certainly true in Schreber's case. Schultze was of the opinion that in deciding that a patient had improved, the clinician was not expected to state that the patient was completely cured or to be unnecessarily fussy in his expectation that all the morbid manifestations would disappear. Nor did the personal pride or pique of the expert need to influence his judgment just because the patient had complained of bad treatment or of having been kept in the asylum unnecessarily. The patient was entitled to retain a certain amount of "residual delusions," the same way, to use a surgical simile, a patient could retain an aseptically healed foreign body. The expert would not be justified in opposing the rescission of an incompetency ruling with the reasoning that "back then he had made a diagnosis of paranoia in the patient then adjudged as incompetent, and paranoia is an incurable psychosis" (Hoche, p. 296).

That was exactly Schreber's position, argued most cogently in Addendum A to the *Memoirs*, "Under What Premises Can a Person Considered Insane Be Detained in an Asylum Against his Declared Will?" This essay is truly remarkable, the more so if one compares it not only with the reasoning of Schultze in Hoche's (1909) textbook but also with the ideas expressed in his paper of 1901.[57] I submit that Weber may have read Schultze's paper, if not the textbook, but as a forensic expert he did not assimilate the latest thinking in the field. Indeed, Weber remained arrested at the level of an antiquated and obsolete expert.

ANOTHER CASE OF PARANOIA

This narrow forensic-psychiatric approach to incompetency rulings became eminently suited to the politics of paranoia: to enhance the prestige and the power of psychiatry as a profession; to create a new role for the judiciary; and to set both up as watchdogs ever ready to rid society of its lunatics, heretics, deviants, and undesirables. Whereas German psychiatrists prided themselves on being enlightened, and having separated the crazy from the criminals and thus improved the fate of the patients, in actuality politics of paranoia led to a renewal of the propinquity of criminals and mental patients and created conditions conducive to the abuse of psychiatry for personal and political reasons. These developments were reflected in the first antipsychiatry movement in Germany, in which the psychiatrists, the public, and the parliament became sharply polarized. Before discussing this reaction, we first review a case involving an incompetency ruling that came before the law. This case of victimization by the legal system with the connivance of the psychiatric system actually illustrates a much wider web of social, economic and political complexities of the period and this has a bearing on the story of Schreber. We have already discussed a number of cases in which Flechsig was involved; now we turn to Weber.

The case, in which both Flechsig's and Weber's names come up, is that of a coal merchant, F. W. Krumbiegel from Zwickau in Saxony, who published a pamphlet in his defense and at his own expense. If the colorful subtitle of Rodig's (1895) pamphlet spoke of being slowly driven crazy, Krumbiegel's (1893) title speaks of a healthy man railroaded into an asylum, or how a man can be "buried alive [*Lebendigbegrabenwerden*] behind the walls of an asylum" (p. 3). The phrase *buried alive* was also used by Paul Schreber.

The good merchant Krumbiegel became entangled in a number of lawsuits, too complicated to review here. As a result of the actions of the different lawyers, Krumbiegel ended up by accusing his lawyers of fraud, lies, and exploitation. This turned out to cost him a great deal. The lawyers retaliated and sued him for slander. The merchant's countersuits were rejected, as were his witnesses, and on March 23, 1888, he was ordered to appear before the district physician and expert to the courts (*Gerichts-* and *Bezirksarzt*; titles also borne by Weber), Dr. Barth, for the purpose of furnishing a report about his mental state.

This Dr. Barth, who happened to be Krumbiegel's neighbor and was not a psychiatrist, excused himself for having to perform this duty. His conversation with Krumbiegel was a short one, largely about legal circumstances, and ended with Dr. Barth saying, "You're quite healthy, Mr. Neighbor." However, to Mr. Krumbiegel's horror, a panel of judges was presented with a very different statement from Dr. Barth. In that report he stated that "Mr. Krumbiegel belonged to the not-so-rare category of psychotic persons suffering from litigiousness, i.e., those convinced that they are in the right and that they have been dealt an injustice." As a result, such persons spread

slander about the people of the law. . . . In the course of a physical examination one finds in most cases the signs of a brain disease, and in this case we find a fibrillary tremor of the tongue and trembling of the hands. I assume that Krumbiegel is suffering from a persecution psychosis, a subgroup of the so-called paranoia [*Verrücktheit*]. Therefore, he is currently not responsible for his actions and has to be viewed as a psychotic [Krumbiegel, 1893, p. 29].

Parenthetically, a diagnosis of insanity was not always a bad thing. In another case, as Mr. Krumbiegel noted in his pamphlet, a report rendered by Dr. Barth actually became the salvation of the man in question. It concerned a case of a civil servant in Zwickau who fled from family, home, and homeland to live with a prostitute in a remote part of the globe. Dr. Barth declared the love-and-variety-starved globe-trotter psychotic and in this way saved the man's retirement pension: for how can you incriminate a psychotic?

Following the aforementioned events, the court dismissed Krumbiegel's legal action on account of his being psychotic. On August 3, 1888, he was called to the police to be told there that since Dr. Barth had diagnosed him as psychotic, he was a case of incurable litigious paranoia, a danger to public safety, and thus fit to be committed to a custodial asylum. Krumbiegel asked for a respite and journeyed to Berlin to consult Royal *Physikus* Prof. Dr. Lewin, whom he saw daily for long sessions until August 23 and who attested that in his opinion the patient showed no signs of dementia, delusions, or ideas of persecution. Krumbiegel presented this report to the authorities in Zwickau, and it was rejected. He then received a visit at his apartment from a police physician, Dr. Geipel, who performed a new examination and rendered a report dated September 22, 1888, in which he rejected Dr. Barth's diagnosis. Now Krumbiegel hoped that the two reports in his favor would be sufficient to overturn the opinion of Dr. Barth.

When the state prosecutor asked for additional opinions, it occurred to Krumbiegel to solicit an examination and opinion from a "recognized authority in brain pathology," none other than the "asylum director Professor Flechsig." This turned out to be not a very good idea. Professor Flechsig regretfully declined the request owing to conflicts of interest: since the Zwickau-born professor still had an extensive family in Zwickau, he could not in fairness provide an unbiased expert opinion, like the previous doctors. At the same time, he spared no criticism concerning Dr. Lewin and regarded his opinion as well as Dr. Geipel's as of no use. Furthermore, Flechsig advised Krumbiegel to consult a certain legal expert in Zwickau, to have him send the legal papers to Leipzig, and then to admit himself to Flechsig's hospital in Leipzig, whereupon he would be in a position to give him an official report. Mr. Krumbiegel felt he could not in clear conscience accept Flechsig's advice and that Flechsig was indeed not the right person for him in view of his connections with the Zwickau judiciary.

He packed up his documents and bid him a most courteous adieu after having paid a fee of ten marks.

Krumbiegel took the next train to Berlin and sought the opinion of Royal Councillor Prof. Dr. Eulenburg, professor and lecturer for nervous diseases at the University of Berlin, who endorsed the previous opinions of Drs. Lewin and Geipel. He also argued that opinions about a person's mental condition should be backed by a thorough examination. He thus found that the opinion rendered by Barth was based predominantly on data taken from court files and on a very superficial examination. He deprecated the diagnosis of paranoia based on such signs of brain disorder as fibrillary tremor of the tongue and trembling of the hands and he found Krumbiegel free from any suspicion of psychosis or dementia. Still anxious, Krumbiegel also consulted in Berlin the respected Professor Mendel, an authority and the editor of the *Neurologisches Centralblatt*. Professor Mendel reassured him that there was no need for another examination and that he had plenty of documents to convince the Zwickau court of his sanity.

The matter did not stop there. On January 8, 1889, Krumbiegel received a demand to present himself to the State Health Board in Dresden for another examination. He declined with the excuse that he was also a citizen of Berlin and thus would gladly accept an examination by the parallel body in Berlin. This was refused by the authorities, and privately Krumbiegel received the intelligence that he was in the process of being declared legally incompetent and that his court-appointed guardian would be a neighbor by the name of Heidel.

Other conflicts with the law followed, as a result of which Krumbiegel complained to the Ministry of Justice. His complaints were refused, and the refusal bore the signature of the Minister of Justice, Dr. Schurig. Later, in 1891, Krumbiegel continued to importune the Ministry of Justice, again with no results. His claims that he was plaintiff against three lawyers and not a defendant went unheeded. Instead, toward the end of 1891, he was again ordered to present himself for an examination by the Dresden Health Board. As he dragged his feet, he was visited on November 1, 1891, by two marshals of the court and ordered to follow them, with no time to prepare for the trip, to Dresden to face a body of physicians. But instead of this, with no explanation, he was ushered into the office of Herr Direktor Dr. Guido Weber. Dr. Weber emphasized the fact that he was the director of Sonnenstein, pointed to the stack of files on his table, and informed him in a courteous manner that he intended to examine him psychiatrically. Krumbiegel declined since he recognized only the jurisdiction of the Prussian authorities. The two gentlemen had a three-hour-long private conversation, whereupon Dr. Weber invited Krumbiegel to visit his private apartment in the asylum. The latter thanked the doctor for the invitation but never kept his appointment, since he feared for his safety if he stepped into the confines of the asylum; he sent his regrets by cable. In response he received a letter from Weber dated November 15, 1890, in which Weber expressed his regret and his willingness to serve Krumbiegel with whatever advice was necessary concerning his case, an offer Herr Krumbiegel found surprising. In the end he successfully contested his legal incompetency status. In spite of all this, he was later notified by the Zwickau court that on the basis of a report from the State Health Board in Dresden he was considered "mentally not responsible for his actions." Krumbiegel protested to the King and to the Ministry but received no replies.

A case like this provides some insight into the devious relations between psychiatry and the law in those days, which often resulted in abuses of civil liberties. This one also shows Flechsig and Weber to have played a role—perhaps shrewdly, perhaps naively—in the games between individuals and authorities.

THE EMBATTLED PSYCHIATRISTS: THE FIRST ANTIPSYCHIATRY REACTION

Stories like Krumbiegel's are also the voices of protest of citizens trampled by the system, a protest that culminated in the famous debates in the Reichstag in 1892 and again in 1897. The ferment that led up to the debates had been brewing in Germany for a number of decades. There was already a spate of scandals, pamphlets, and books on stories like Krumbiegel's by mid-century,[58] but the late 1880s and the early and mid-1890s witnessed a veritable explosion of this literature, the titles ringing both poignant and provocative.[59] The scandal first erupted while Schreber was still doing his stint in Freiberg. The antipsychiatry reaction and the call for a revision of the national insanity laws erupted on the pages of the daily Kreuzzeitung of July 9, 1892, in an Appeal penned by Pastor Stöcker (Beyer, 1912, pp. 414-415; Irrenfreund, 35:57-60; Krüner, n.d.), in the wake of the debate in the Reichstag about a number of cases of railroading with the help of psychiatric certificates, among them the notorious case of the convert Morris de Jonge, the rebellious scion of a prominent Jewish family. It became a cause célèbre not only because of how colorful the young man himself was but because he had the support of Pastor Stöcker, the anti-semitic preacher to the Imperial Court and later a representative to the Reichstag, a man well known for his reactionary politics and inflammatory speeches. Ironically, the archconservative preacher was a libertarian as far as patients' rights were concerned. Stöcker came out defending the rights of "persons buried in asylums," that is, "imprisoned" as a result of declarations of incompetency and in the absence of any threat of violent or dangerous action (Beyer, 1912, p. 424). This could no longer be ignored by the psychiatric establishment and the Association of German Alienists moved to react to Stöcker's *Appeal*. Among the resolutions adopted at the meeting of the Association in Frankfurt, on March 25-26, 1893, were the following: There was no need to change existing procedures since both patients' needs and civil rights were protected by them; "Admissions to public and private can and should remain independent of a prior declaration of incompetency" (p. 425); such declarations of incompetency were to be decided by medical certificates approved by judges; the legal procedures for rescission of incompetency were sufficient safeguards of individual liberties and there was no need to change the existing laws (Beyer, 1912, pp. 423-425; *AZP*, 50(1894):344-348). The second resolution is of particular importance in regard to Paul Schreber: since he did not oppose his transfer to Sonnenstein, there was no necessity to have him declared temporarily incompetent on November 27, 1894, in order to protect him against himself; and there was even less justification, except for the impact of Weber's reports, to have the temporary declaration changed into a permanent one on April 13, 1901. It also shows that Weber was more conservative than his colleagues.

The protests came not only from former inmates but also from professionals, such as Rudolph Goetze[60] and Eduard August Schroeder, toward whom the author of *Reform*, Beyer (1912), took particular exception, believing their protests to have greatly promoted the antipsychiatry movement. E. A. Schroeder's (1890) *Law and Psychiatry, Critically and Systematically Codified: Based on a Report on Léon Gambetta's Law Proposal* was printed by Füssli, a serious publishing house that could not be as easily dismissed as a "theosophical" house, the way Mutze had been, in the case of Schreber. Schroeder endorsed the libertarian premise of Léon Gambetta (1838-1882), the French statesman and orator, that personal freedom is more important than the pursuit of health. Schroeder identified the main conflict of interest in psychiatry, as in no other profession, whereby the pursuit of law and healing are vested in the same person, who simultaneously acts as physician and judge. The net result is that the physician has acquired untold power, for "the psychiatric diagnosis may become a legal verdict of the greatest importance leading to moral, economic and social death" (Schroeder, 1890, p. 6). Schroeder pointed out some of the most frequent complaints leveled against the psychiatric profession: the shallowness of many a report, simply copied from a textbook; the contradictory diagnoses of different experts; the exclusion of the diagnosis of health; the solidarity of the profession; the social stigma of the psychiatric diagnosis; lack of awareness of the traumatic impact of the hospital setting, the resulting anxiety, and attempts to abscond; the confusion of brain and mind, of brain disorders and mental disorders. The latter is most evident in the reigning somatic-hereditary theory of paranoia, which denies the psychic or traumatic causation of paranoia; thus, when a patient reacts in an agitated and paranoid manner to involuntary confinement in the hospital setting, the conscience of the physician is salved by the somatic theory.

Beyer's counterargument is also enlightening. He believed that Schroeder was not educated enough about psychiatry, "for admission or confinement to a facility do not depend on an exact diagnosis, but on the establishing of the fact that somebody is psychotic. Whether a person is paretic, paranoid or manic-depressive is of no consequence legally speaking" (Beyer, 1912, p. 61). But the diagnosis of psychosis is precisely what begs the question: it is given in the premise, rendered without evidence.

In 1897 a number of Reichstag representatives made public a number of sensationalized psychiatric scandals and demanded that checks and balances be imposed on the existing system in the shape of new state mental hygiene laws and lay commissions. Among the various cases the representatives presented to the *Reichstag* were those in which Flechsig or Weber was involved, some of which I have presented in this book. The embattled psychiatrists struck back. Weber expressed his opinions at the 63d session of the Forensic Psychiatric Association of Dresden, held on March 21, 1901.

In that discussion Weber (1902a) vehemently protested the defamatory portrayals of psychiatrists as untrustworthy and prone to lock healthy people up in asylums so as to remove them or render them "harmless." He was indignant that educated and experienced people overlooked the fact that the profession had been a blessing to patients. There may have been one in a thousand who was admitted to an asylum and not psychotic, but such an event, he insisted, had never happened in the some 12,000 admissions to his institution. Such complaints over the last decades, when advances in science contributed to more humane treatment of the sick, were due, Weber charged, to a press geared toward the sensational and the scandalous. The allegedly healthy detained people who spread their complaints in countless brochures were, claimed Weber, "almost without exception paranoiacs or carriers of psychical degeneration states, who outwardly appear as organized and in full command of their wits. . . . These incurable patients were formerly barely able to come into contact with the outside world, whereas now they are given free play to disseminate their crazy trash literature among the public" (p. 537). Weber viewed such protests as "fighting windmills, nonexistent dangers." Weber also could not imagine an idea more contrary to reason than setting up lay commissions to rule on scientific matters, such as diagnosis and treatment of mental illness, and on issues of legal incompetency. No layman would be able to know much about mental illness, Weber insisted, which from the scientific viewpoint must be regarded as brain illness and thus requires special professional knowledge and experience. Weber did not believe new mental hygiene laws were necessary since the procedures to declare a person mentally incompetent were sufficiently clearly defined by the law. He felt improvements could be obtained by segregating curable patients from incurable ones in separate institutions, a striving in which he found himself personally frustrated throughout his lifetime. He believed that there was a need for better trained directors and medical staffs and that only in these was there hope for better protection against unjustified admissions and delayed discharges of patients.

Given such views, such a complete rejection of all complaints against the system, Weber is revealed as an unbending defender of psychiatric prerogative. He was not the only one: a raw nerve had been touched. The petition for a revision of the existing laws was defeated in the *Reichstag* in 1897. Having provided the historical background to Weber's approaches, we can now more readily understand his psychiatric assessments of Paul Schreber.

WEBER ON SCHREBER: THE FIRST TWO REPORTS

The first report Weber ever wrote about Schreber to the Ministry of Justice, kept in Schreber's personal file (published by Devreese, 1981a), dates from November 24, 1894, half a year after Schreber's transfer to Sonnenstein and five years prior to the first published report of 1899 (*Memoirs*, p. 379ff), when Schreber first set into motion the procedure for his release.

Weber's opening clinical descriptions in essence recapitulate the long paragraph in the clinical chart from Sonnenstein marked "Professor Flechsig's report June 25, 1894" (Appendix). Thus, Weber repeated that Schreber's first episode of 1884-1885 was marked by "severe hypochondria" and that in 1893 there was a recurrence of hypochondriacal complaints, accompanied by "ideas of persecution (*Verfolgungsideen*) . . . based on hallucinations (*Sinnestäuschungen*, sense-deceptions)" (Devreese, 1981a, p. 60). Since Flechsig did not date the onset of the delusions in his report, the impression is maintained by

Weber that they occurred at the same time as the hypochondriacal ideas. Even more emphatically than Flechsig, Weber takes Schreber's hallucinations to be a neurological organic disorder having the nature of a "high-grade hyperesthesia, great sensitivity to light and noise, . . . coupled with disturbances of general sensation [*Gemeingefühl*, or cenesthesia, i.e., the sensation of the body other than the five senses]" (p. 60) and to be the cause of the delusions. After summarizing Flechsig's report Weber goes on to state "In this institution . . . the clinical picture was the same as in Leipzig" (p. 61). Weber then refers to Schreber's inaccessibility, his stiff posture, refusal to eat, and difficulty sleeping. Among the continuing hallucinations and delusions Weber now mentions the

> truly fantastic elaboration of the persecutory hallucinations that haunt him continuously, he feels injured by persons he knew before, whom he believes to be present here, believes the world has been changed by them and disturbed by their speeches, curses, etc, repeatedly demands that the broken 'God's peace' be restored, holds that the people surrounding him are destroying God's omnipotence, drawing thoughts out of his body, complains that the divine rays are withheld, etc. [p. 62].

Weber does not mention Flechsig nor who these other persons were, but he was able to ascertain that "the whole being of the patient is tense and irritated, determined by inner uneasiness, and there was no doubt that he was continuously under the influence of vivid and painful sense-deceptions which were elaborated in a delusional way."
Weber's diagnosis was:

> hallucinatory psychosis (*hallucinatorische Wahnsinn*)[61]. . . . The prognosis of this disorder is dubious; however, as long as these morbid phenomena are still fully fluid [*noch in vollem Flusse*], as in this case, as long as they are accompanied by lively affects, and as long as the delusions have not become fixed and elaborated into a closed system, one should hold on to the expectation that the disease process will have a favorable outcome, and at any rate, one cannot simply exclude the possibility that the Senatspräsident Dr. Schreber might be able to resume all the functions of his office [Devreese, 1981a, p. 64].

Citing this report, Schreber's boss, C. E. Werner, authorized imposing on Schreber a temporary status of incompetency on November 26, 1894.

About a year later, on November 7, 1895, Weber rendered his second crucial—and until recently unknown—report. Now Weber finds the patient somewhat physically and mentally improved:

But the features of the clinical picture have not changed at all; moreover, they have become critically fixated. The delusions, described in the first report, and which determine his entire conduct, have become more monotonous, . . . are not accompanied by stronger affects and are more or less systematized, the reaction to the outside stimuli is not natural but distorted and strange, there is a slight, and instantly vanishing interest in persons and matters that are outside the circle of the delusions . . . In addition, there is constant restlessness and anxiety in the patient, partly due to the lack of sleep, lack of concentration upon an object for any length of time, a being that is both disjointed and bizarre, factors that indicate a certain psychic feebleness [*psychische Schwäche*, a word that suggest feeblemindedness, or dementia]. . . . some improvement may be gained such that he might be able to exist on the outside under proper care and supervision, but we cannot assume in good conscience that the Senatspräsident Dr. Schreber will recover full mental intactness and be capable of performing the duties of his office [Devreese, 1981a, pp. 82, 84].

These clinical descriptions do not contain statements about feelings and life events. This is in contrast to a number of items in the standard psychiatric questionnaire,[62] which Weber followed selectively. Thus, in the questionnaire (*Behandlung*, 1862) there are probes about the patient's "shattering life circumstances (wounds to one's pride, loss of property, unhappy love etc)" (#10). Question #11 explores the patient's moral temperament: "Addiction to pleasure and sensual excesses." Question #37, following one about syphilis and other "disgusting or incurable illnesses," asks about "factors which could be seen as the probable causes of the present illness?" Question #15 deals with "agitation or depression and #17 with suicide attempts. However, there are questions (#20 to #24) that reflect the organicist bias toward the symptom that concerns Weber most, hallucinations.

Does the patient suffer from hallucinations and visions? How are they manifested? How is the mobility and the position of the eyes? Is there an unusual widening or narrowing of the pupil, in one or both eyes? Are the other sense organs affected or is there a disturbance of function? Is there a marked alteration in general sensation (*Gemeingefühl*) and great sensitivity to external stimuli? [And #25]: Is the tongue stuck out straight? Without tremor?

The drift of these questions and their underlying assumptions is clear. Hallucinations are seen as neurological, not psychological, manifestations of a disorder of the sensory organs and the brain. From here it is one step to the diagnosis of paranoia, as a disorder of the nervous system, with its assumed chronicity and incurability. (By the way, such questions were also used to elicit the symptoms of paresis.)

The method of psychiatric examination followed by Weber is described in a lecture by his colleague in Dresden Dr. Ganser (1897), a member of the Dresden Forensic-Psychiatric Association. The premise is that mental illness is a physical illness, due to disease of the cerebral cortex or other body organs. Only a physician is capable of determining such disorders by an examination of the person's mental status, that is, of his fund of information, memory, ideation, judgment, mood, actions and facial expression. The psychiatrist possesses special psychological knowledge of

> certain elementary phenomena. The various groupings of [these phenomena], their degree of their intensity, form the various total pictures of mental illness that always recur in typical ways. By mastering such elementary disturbances and typical disease picture the physician becomes a *psychiatrist*. He who possesses such special skills has a great advantage over many a keener observer who still remains a dilettante. The psychiatrist does not actually require any greater psychological knowledge than any other educated person. All he has to do is to determine whether in a give case there are elementary disturbances, in which group they belong, and what the total picture presented by the examined is all about [Ganser, 1897, p. 585; emphasis Ganser's].

The aforementioned premise and procedure clearly explain not only Weber's method and reasoning about Schreber but also show him to be a narrowly defined specialist and not in the clinical tradition of Kraepelin, who, following a much nobler clinical tradition, laid great stress on psychological understanding of the patient.

In this second report Weber does not describe any specific delusions, as was done by Flechsig, and referred to the description in his previous report. His descriptions do not quite tally with the notations in the chart. In March 1895 Paul is described as "Agitated, talks loudly when by himself and laughs ostentatiously, at night excited. He plays a lot on the piano sent by his wife but bangs it a lot when in a bad mood and excited." In June

> [He] claims his body is completely changed, the lung has all but disappeared, everything he sees around is only a semblance. The world has perished. . . . Periodically quiet again. Plays the piano a lot, even hard pieces rather well. Writes many letters, also in Italian, once signed "Paul the Prince of Hell." One letter was addressed to "Mr. Ormuzd in heaven" [Appendix].

In September the chart reads: "Very excited, nights mostly agitated. Often laughs loudly and piercingly and screamingly repeats the same words. From time to time stands totally still in one spot and stares at the sun and grimaces in the most bizarre way. Usually he stops himself when someone approaches him and speaks to him."

Weber's report essentially portrays Schreber as having began the descent into the kind of affectless, stereotyped, essentially feeble-minded end-state that was thought to characterize the illness and that putatively justified the use of the word "dementia," as in "dementia praecox." But the actual clinical picture is still characterized by a great deal of bizarreness and is altogether stormier and more agitated than Weber's summary implies. Weber's dignified style sounds euphonious but is erroneous. He misses the manic agitation, the iconography of heaven and hell, the continuing sleep disturbances at night. His writing is loaded with cliches that are guaranteed to seal Schreber's fate. It is also noteworthy that Weber does not offer a clear diagnosis, only a negative prognosis. On the basis of this prognosis the Royal Ministry of Justice decided, on November 18, 1895, to retire Schreber permanently as of January 1, 1896, and to reduce his pension to 6,930 marks per annum.

SCHREBER VERSUS WEBER: DAVID AND GOLIATH

Freud (1911a) noted that whereas Schreber "took appropriate steps with a view of regaining control over his own affairs [Strachey blurs the legal meaning given in the original: *"Aufhebung seiner Kuratel*, rescission of his guardianship]. . . . Dr. Weber set himself to prevent the fulfillment of these intentions and drew up reports in opposition to them" (p. 15). Freud did not inquire about the motives of Weber's opposition or how the incompetency ruling affected Schreber's life. Furthermore, Schreber's confrontation was not only with the system but with the personality of Weber, and, as with Flechsig before, it had its reality and transference aspects. As adversary Weber may have helped Schreber to rally to his own self-defense, but this does not alter the fact that Weber was an actual persecutor on two counts: he denied Schreber's personhood, his polite lip service notwithstanding, seeing him at first as a pathological specimen and toward the end as a forensic one; and he used all the power vested in him to deny Schreber his freedom, until he had to bow to the power of the judges in the court of appeals. It is thus another striking fact that Schreber never accused Weber of being his persecutor, even as he never stopped railing at Flechsig. The paradox can be read of course as evidence for the fantastic nature of the charges against Flechsig, but it might be more illuminating to consider the difference in terms of the different relationships the two physicians established with Schreber. Confronting a frank, unequivocal adversary in the person of Weber, Schreber found a way to mobilize his resources and deal with the man both face to face and in the courts. But faced with Flechsig, who presented himself in the guise of medical rescuer and protector only to ultimately betray Schreber's interests, Schreber reacted quite differently.

In his fantasy mood Schreber thought Weber came in to see him on daily rounds, but in actuality Weber misrepresented in his reports the fact that Schreber was placed in the isolation cell for two and a half years running. As Schreber testified, "On the whole I believe I am justified in asserting that the medical expert has only come *to know me really well in the last year,* that is to say since I have taken my meals regularly at his family table" (*M*, p. 424; emphasis Schreber's).

The taking of meals with Weber impressed some people as proof the doctor's benevolence. Actually, it was guaranteed by the hospital by-laws as a privilege of the social class of inpatients to which Schreber belonged.[63] It was to Schreber's credit that he finally was able to control his behavior and thus to enjoy a right that was his. The fact is that Weber did not bestir himself to pay much attention to Schreber until he legally contested his incompetency status and wrote his manifesto, the *Memoirs:* "I have been treated very *much more respectfully in this* Asylum since the contents of my Memoirs became known and my intellectual and moral personality appreciated differently than perhaps had been possible before" (*M*, p. 444; emphasis Schreber's).

It has been said already that it was the text of the *Memoirs,* rather the clinical and personal knowledge of the patient, that were the basis for Weber's vehement opposition to the rescission of the incompetency and Paul's release, and to the publication of the *Memoirs.* This opposition is the locus of intersection of reality and transference. Weber's distaste for Schreber's unabashed talk of "sexual matters" and bodily functions in "'strong language'" (Schreber's flaming words, *Flammenworte,* an echo of Luther), was not far from a similar response by Nordau (1895) to the hypersexualized degeneracy of Friedrich Nietzsche and Richard Wagner.

Schreber could be tolerated at the director's table as "well behaved and amiable during light conversation with the ladies" (*M*, p. 399), but Weber's tolerance extended neither to Schreber's sexual ideas nor even to his more reasonable inquiries about sexual matters in general. Thus, even as Schreber continued to improve clinically, his preoccupations in the sexual sphere still counted against him and Weber could only regard it as a continuing indication of craziness (i.e., paranoia) when Schreber importuned him with the following question:

Does the science of neurology acknowledge the existence of special nerves whose function it is to *conduct the sensation of voluptuousness* (nerves of voluptuousness or sensory nerves—an expression I heard Professor Weber [Ernst Heinrich Weber of Leipzig?] use the other day or whatever the scientific name may be)? . . . do I therefore mention a fact known to neurology or would it be regarded as erroneous in the present state of that science? [*M*, p. 275].

Such receptors were, in fact, mentioned in a contemporary textbook of psychiatry (Arndt, 1883, p. 11): in addition to Krause's end-bodies, Meissner's and Wagner's taste corpuscles, Arndt mentions "Finger's lust corpuscles in the genital parts" [*Wollustkörperchen an den Geschlesttheilen*]." Clearly, Weber was ignorant of Arndt's textbook, and very few people have heard of Finger. Histology today still recognizes corpuscles of Krause and also additional receptors called genital corpuscles (Bloom and Fawcett, 1986, p. 342). Weber was even less likely to know an earlier source, Haeckel's *Anthropogenie* (1874), where Schreber, who cited Haeckel (*M*, Foot Note #36), would have read about sexual receptors, "corpuscles similar [to Pacini's touch corpuscles] found in the penis of man and clitoris of woman" and "sexual nerves" (*Nervi pudendi*)," conductors of sexual sensations (p. 538). Schreber's question was thus more reasonable than Weber grasped, though of course by itself the existence of such "nerves of voluptuousness" would scarcely have all of Schreber's previous elaborations on the theme. But the point here is not that Schreber was on this matter more sophisticated than his doctor, and even less that his question should be taken as evidence of a dramatic turn to sanity, but only that in the dyadic context between doctor and patient his question could not be taken as anything other than a symptom, i.e., with disdain and disparagement. No dialogue could be begun on sexual matters, no matter how carefully Schreber tried to couch his inquiries. In self-defense, Schreber was entitled to exclaim, like Protestant heretic John Hus on the stake: *O sancta simplicitas*, O holy naïveté.

THE SCHREBER DECISION AS PRECEDENT

The legal issues raised by Schreber's appeal could not have been mentioned in the first 1901 edition of Hoche's textbook on forensic psychiatry. Weber (1898b, c) is quoted twice: on pages 587 and 591, respectively. "Schreber, D. P. *Denkwürdigkeiten eines Nervenkranken*. 1903" is cited on page 402, for the decision by the Dresden Court of Appeals in Schreber's case at appeals.

It was not only a personal victory by Schreber over Weber: it also set a legal precedent and was so acknowledged in Hoche's textbook in its second edition, of 1909. The Saxon Ministry of Justice in a decree of December 23, 1899 had already enunciated the principle that the mere presence of psychosis and incompetency were not necessarily connected. The inability to manage one's affairs must be a live issue at the time of the incompetency determination, and the mere suspicion of such incapacity is not sufficient: it has to exist close at hand "and to be made credible by facts (O.L.G. [*Oberlandesgericht*, the Supreme Court of Appeals] Dresden 14.VII.02). Factual observations are required" (Hoche, 1909, p. 233). Accordingly, as already recommended by Bresler (1901a), such facts should be ascertained during trial leaves.

Weber was not able to prove in court that he had made such observations that showed that Schreber was unable to manage his affairs. The judges found in Schreber's favor. That Schreber was still psychotic in the eyes of the judges was not at issue; but that in spite of any such morbid manifestations, by having so brilliantly conducted his own defense he was expected, *a fortiori*, to be able to manage the much simpler affairs of his daily life. Subsequent events proved both the patient and the judges right.

There is an interesting development by the end of 1902, a sign of the times contained in a circular from the Minister of Justice Köber dated October 18, 1902 to the presidents of the German highest appeals courts (Pfausler, 1902). Under the pressure of the public outcry over cases like Schreber's, the Ministry of Justice took an adversary position toward hospital psychiatrists, considering them caught in a conflict of interest in incompetency rulings and recommending that experts to the courts be appointed from among nonpsychiatrists. Pfausler became the spokesman for injured feelings and hefty protests on the part of hospital psychiatrists, who were being scapegoated for failures in social justice that were not of their doing.[64]

The self-defensive reaction of the embattled psychiatrists culminated, as already noted, in the publication of Beyer's *Reform* in 1912, which defended the interests of the psychiatrists and was negative toward the critics. The debates in the Reichstag were renewed in 1912 and reported in the *PNW*, in issue #1 for 1913. The insanity laws in Saxony were revised in 1912 (Hösel, 1912). The laws for Germany were revised in 1923 (Rittershaus, 1927).

WEBER'S EPILOGUE: SCHREBER AS A FORENSIC CASE

Weber's epilogue to the Schreber story came in the form of a presentation of the case that he made to the Forensic-Psychiatric Association of Dresden in 1903 (Weber, 1905a), during Schreber's first year as a free man. The presentation went unnoticed until our own day, probably with the exception of the discussion of Schreber as a case by Beyer (1912).[65] Weber's interest in the case was mainly from the forensic point of view: it was an "interesting incompetency case," which he wanted to impress on the assembled psychiatrists and jurists. Weber began his presentation by stating some biographical details that conform to what is known from Schreber's hospital chart, namely, that the patient was married, childless, with some relatives who were mentally sick and nervous, that he had been an excellent student, who had advanced rapidly in the profession and had tried for candidacy in the Parliament, that he had hypochondriacal ideas at the time of his marriage. Weber noted the hallucinatory stupor, as described in his unpublished reports.

Weber then referred to the course of illness as described in the chart and stressed the dual personality of Schreber: the man ruled by his delusions and the socially functioning, charming, intelligent and educated man. The course of the illness, explained Weber, amounted to a transformation of the hallucinatory psychosis into a paranoid one. The patient's culminating paranoid idea was that he had been changed into a woman and now had female sexual organs, a change linked to the idea of attracting God's nerves, becoming impregnated to produce a new race of man, thus saving mankind. Weber then referred to Schreber's the first legal attempt to regain his freedom in the low court, in 1900, which ended in failure. We learn of a new detail here. It was already stated that Schreber made a poor personal impression on the judge. The new detail is that an unnamed family member expressed reservations, in spite of the patient's good performance in a number of situations, about his ability to manage his affairs, in view of the fact that during one visit he still appeared under the influence of his ideas. The witness chose to defer to the opinion of the doctors. Was the family member Schreber's wife? Very likely, in view of the stated reaction to the visit and her letters to the Sonnenstein administration, cited by Baumeyer. Or was it some other relative?

I believe the testimony and the setback hurt Schreber emotionally and, for a time, legally; also, other families in those days fought back. Weber found justification in the fact that in addition to the aforementioned testimony by the family member, the court ruling against Schreber was based on the report he gave to the court after Paul had offered in evidence the "peculiar memories of his life" (p. 404). That also hurt Schreber.

Weber further noted that following his appeal "Mr. N. [i.e., Schreber] in the meantime [had] left the third institution and that he [Weber] had no knowledge about his present state [although] it [was] reported that marked disturbances had made themselves felt in his affairs" (p. 405). Weber's words here are, to say the least, self-contradictory: he has no knowledge but he does have some, based on rumors. Rumors by whom, about what? We know, on the other hand, that Schreber did rather well until he got sick for the third and last time.

In this presentation Weber revealed that he felt it to be an unconscionable requirement by the high court of appeals that in order to declare a person incompetent the person had to function at the level of a child, unable to take care of *any* of his affairs. He was also critical of the decision of the high court that the welfare of third parties was not a consideration when deciding incompetency. He ignored the legal fact that the judges found that he had failed to produce sufficient evidence to show that Schreber was indeed mentally incompetent and unable to handle his affairs. While agreeing that it was the court's prerogative to decide issues of competence on legal grounds, he thought other psychiatrists might disagree. Also, he believed that a paranoiac might one day come into conflict with the world, although this was not inevitable.

Weber stuck to his guns to the very end, and if it took some bending of the facts to do it, his intent was, after all, to save the patient from himself and the world from the dangers of conflict and risk. Among the discussants were the respected Dresden psychiatrist Ganser, whom we encountered earlier, and three jurists who were involved in the Rodig case. They all agreed with Weber that the law was deficient; while Ganser also opined that Schreber should never have been given his freedom. None of them expressed any feelings of sympathy toward Schreber. Given Weber's good relations with the jurists in Dresden, the decision of the court in favor of Schreber must have been felt by Weber as a rebuff. One can't help seeing him as a sore loser.[66]

Given the nature of mental illness and the interpersonal conflicts that cause it, especially conflicts that lead to rage and interpersonal violence, this tragic clash between personal freedom and professional coercion is endemic to psychiatry as to no other medical specialty. Both Schreber and Weber had their deep reasons to feel injured and mistreated. Both deserve our sympathy, the oppressor and the oppressed alike. However, in spite of its cloak of benevolence, the asylum did become a kind of a concentration camp for undesirables of all kinds. It came to be ruled by an ethical attitude that aimed to save a society and to segregate its rejects—the psychotics and the psychopaths, all those deemed to be dysfunctional, deviant, and despised —but at an incalculable cost to the oppressors and the oppressed. Whether segregated in the asylum or sent back to the community, these truants from reason and decency have never stopped being a problem for society. In spite of progress made, these issues are as alive today worldwide as they were in Schreber's Saxony.

Sonnenstein can still be seen today in all its gloomy grandeur. It was still a psychiatric hospital in World War II. At that time, it was the scene of the Nazi euthanasia program against mentally defective adults and children.[67] Did the dehumanization of psychiatric patients lead logically to the idea of concentration camps and death camps? At the end of the war Sonnenstein was closed down as a psychiatric facility. The last director was under investigation as a war criminal and committed suicide. An austere commemorative plaque in the massive fortress wall reads as follows: "In memory of the victims of fascist crimes committed in the former asylum for acute and chronic patients in the territory Pirna-Sonnenstein 1940-1941."[68]

Today the old Sonnenstein castle, with its adjoining park, is the site of a vocational school.

SYNOPSIS OF WEBER'S LIFE AND WORK

1837, June 5: Born in Reval (now Tallinn, in Estonia).

1854: Student at the University of Dorpat, Estonia; later moves to Jena, becomes member of the student organization *Burschenschaft Germania*.

1859: Graduates as M.D. with the dissertation "On Hematoma of the Dura Mater."

1860-1861: Resident at the Colditz Asylum for the chronically insane.

1861: At his request, transferred to the Sonnenstein Asylum for acute (later acute and chronic) patients, to stay there until his death.

1864, October 7: Officially installed as civil servant.

1876-1912: Various publications in journals, the bulk in the *Allgemeine Zeitschrift für Psychiatrie*.

1883: Appointed as director of the Sonnenstein Asylum and to rank of Medicinal Rath.

1890: Elevated to rank of Obermedicinal Rath.

1896: Elevated to the rank of privy medical councillor (*Geheimer Medicinalrath*).

1899-1902: Fights Schreber's release from Sonnenstein in the courts.

1910, June 1: Official retirement in Dresden.

1914, January 15: Death and burial at Sonnenstein.

NOTES

1. The hospital was described by Pierson in a 34-page monograph, *Hospital for Patients with Mood and Nervous Disorders*. I did not see the monograph, but am quoting from the literature review section of the *AZP* for 1898, 54:188. The founder of the hospital, in 1845, was Dr. G. Bräunlich, a pupil of Hayner (1775-1837), the latter director of the older Colditz Asylum from 1834 to his death. After a number of vicissitudes, the hospital was taken over in 1891 by Pierson. It was built in the style of cottages and villas, situated in a park spread over 60,000 square meters, about 20 acres. Statistics in the review include the following:

> Between 22/10/1891 and 1/7/1895 a total of patients treated, 430 (236 men and 194 women), discharged as recovered or markedly improved, 136 (62 men and 74 women), 165 (96 men 59 women) went to other institutions and home care, 47 (33 men 14 women) patients died, of these 22 men and one woman died from paresis. Thirty-four percent of the men suffered from paresis. This leaves a residue of 91 patients (44 men 47 women) [p. 188].

Pierson published a report about another hospital, *The Private Asylum of Pirna* (Pierson, 1893b). This report was reviewed in the literature review section of the *AZP*, 1894-1895, 51:253. According to the review, this private hospital for the wealthy was founded the same year as Sonnenstein, 1811, in Pirna near Dresden, by the patriarchal first director of Sonnenstein, Dr. E. Pienitz, a student of Pinel. It could treat 45 patients at one time, and between 1884 and 1890 a total of 445 patients were treated, including those suffering from alcoholism, morphinism (including four doctors), general paresis (a fourth of admissions), and ten cases of neurasthenia. In 1891 the place was closed down and merged with Lindenhof, then owned by Pierson. Another report by Pierson (1894-1895), *On the Relation between Syphilis and Syphilitic Dementia*, is reviewed in *AZP*, 51(1894-1895):200. (Syphilis was a a frequent concern of Paul Schreber.)

During one of the sessions of the Forensic-Psychiatric Association of Dresden the participants were invited by Dr. Pierson to visit his Lindenhof in Coswig, to admire the villas, the beautifully appointed rooms, the physical plant and the gorgeous wooded surroundings (*AZP*, 55:170-171).

In the *PNW* Lindenhof was routinely advertised as

> Lindenhof near Dresden, Dr. Pierson's facility for patients with mood and nervous disorders of both sexes. Railway station Coswig, a 20 minute ride from Dresden, modern, built in villa style, in a 10 hectare park. Comfort as required by the upper classes, central heating, electrical lighting. For patients with extraordinary needs separate 3 room apartments, closets, porch. Details in prospectus. Three assistant physicians. Director: Dr. Fr. Lehmann [*PNW*, 11:332].

2. Dr. Fr. Lehmann, who took over Lindenhof in 1906, was the son of the former owner of the private hospital in Pirna, Dr. Gr. O. Lehmann (*PNW*, 7:378). The obituary is in *PNW*, 8:202.

3. *Compendium der Nervenkrankheiten und der Electricitätslehre* may have been the title of the first edition of the work. There was a second edition (1878)— translated into Russian with an Italian one to follow—a third edition (1882), and a sixth edition (1893a).

4. However, the publications of Pierson were not that numerous. I found him mentioned only occasionally in the proceedings of psychiatric meetings, where he appeared in the company of Flechsig and Weber. Thus, we find Pierson (1898) present at the 35th session of the Dresden Forensic Psychiatric Association held on October 29, November 20, and December 17, 1896; he read a paper entitled "On Certain Forms of Dementia and Its Forensic Significance." The case discussed was of a 25-year-old man who would today be labeled a psychopath. After considering cognitive dementia, Pierson went on to discuss moral dementia (or, since the Germans referred to it by its English name, moral insanity). In dwelling on "immoral drives and proclivities," Pierson was echoing similar views by Flechsig, which we already discussed. Such persons, declared Pierson, deserved to be declared incompetent and consigned to an asylum. These views were fully supported by his discussants, Ganser and Weber. Ganser stressed the aspects of moral defect, of unbound selfishness; Weber addressed the pathological weakness of the will. Weber felt that such persons were not to be considered fully legally responsible owing to their defect and that this should not lead to a shortening of their penalty but, on the contrary, to changing the nature of the penal institution, from prison to hospital, where the sufferers could be held for long periods. We find Pierson (1903) mentioned once more in the literature, describing a case, discussed by Weber (1903a), of inborn mental defect and declaration of incompetency due to dementia.

5. The *Verein der deutschen Irrenärzte* had a name change in 1903, when it became the *Deutscher Verein für Psychiatrie* (*MPN*, 1903, 13:641).

6. *De haematomate durae matris. Dissertatio inauguralis anatomico-pathologica quam gratiosi medicorum ordinis auctoritate in Academia lipsiensis ad summos in medicina, chirurgia et arte obstetricia Honores rite capessendos . . . Die XXIV mens Novembris MDCCCLIX . . . publice defendet Guido Weber Revaliensis medicinae baccalareus.* Which means: "On hematoma of the hard cover of the brain, an anatomico-pathological inaugural dissertation which by authority of the gracious members of Leipzig Medical College, in order to bestow properly the highest honors in medicine, surgery, and obstetrical art . . . on November 24, 1859 . . . will be defended by Guido Weber of Reval, bachelor of medicine."

7. This detail is mentioned in what is probably the first published biography of Weber, at the time of the celebration of his golden jubilee in 1910 (*PNW*, 11:391-393). Ilberg's (1914) obituary differs.

8. According to Hirschfeld and Franke (1879), Paul Schreber was also a member until 1863.

9. The letter and the documents cited in subsequent paragraphs of this chapter come from Weber's personal file, entitled "Dr. Guido Weber's Anstellung als Hülfarzt der Anstalt zu Colditz Sonnenstein betr[effend]," Ministry of the Interior; I found it at the State Archives in Dresden in 1988. It is henceforth referred to as Weber, 1859-1910.

10. In his paper entitled "50 year retrospective of a chronic care asylum." Weber is listed there as an "assistant psychiatrist from 1860-1861 (currently in the acute care asylum Sonnenstein)," p. 574.

11. Jetter (1966) documents the birth of the mental hospital, the separation of the psychiatric *Tollhaus* (madhouse) from the *Zuchthaus* (prison) systems in Germany. Heretofore, the indigent, the criminal, and the insane were often literally chastised by the same whip. In 1805 Karl August von Hardenberg, the Prussian minister and later chancellor appointed the physician Johann Gottfried Langersmann to convert the madhouse into a "mental hospital for the mentally ill" (p. 119).

12. Hayner was mentioned in note 1. In the book he pays homage to Jänckendorf for having removed the chains from the insane and converted Sonnenstein into a facility for acute patients. According to Dörner (1969) Jänckendorf made the proposal to convert Sonnenstein into a hospital.

13. In Schumann's (1824) *Lexikon* we read a description of the beginnings of Sonnenstein. The fortress was first used as a prison, then as a home for retired army officers, and then as an asylum, restored after the devastation wrought by the French occupation forces (see Hempel, 1901). At this time it housed 140 to 150 mental patients (*Gemüthskranke*), as well as invalids and criminals, under the supervision of the government. In addition, to the poor and the common, it housed a class of client called distinguished (*distinguirt*), whose quarters were fitted out with a grand piano and other musical instruments for concerts. The disobedient were treated with straitjackets or put in a tranquilizing cabinet. The offenders were supervised by a manager. The treatment and custodial functions were supervised by one physician and one priest. Moneys for the asylum, regarded as one of the best in Germany, came from the government, from a lottery, and from church collections. It was represented in etchings by the famous Italian landscape painter Bellotto, alias Canaletto, who resided in Dresden.

14. Dr. Earle (1809-1892) quotes some interesting statistics. On January 1, 1840, the census was 212 (134 men and 78 women). In the 28 years since Sonnenstein's founding in 1811 "1255 patients were admitted, 264 discharged cured, and 391 removed to other asylums, incurable; 340 died, and, at the close of 1839, 48 were at home, upon trial, but not discharged, a large part of them supposed to be cured" (Earle, 1853, pp. 139-140).

15. According to Dörner (1969), Pienitz's wife was French and took a lively interest in the running of the institution; she aimed to create the atmosphere of one big family. The atmosphere of those days was recreated by Ilberg (1926) (cited in Busse 1990). Pienitz's method followed the French idea of "traitement moral" and socialization.

16. Flechsig's salary on January 1, 1909 was 7,000 a year. In Weber's case, by 1908 this was 1,000 more than the top range in Saxony; the only other place in the realm that paid such a high salary was Frankfurt am Main, with many states paying no more than 6,000 (Müller, 1908).

17. John Conolly (1794-1866), known for his introduction of the humane treatment of the insane at Hanwell Asylum, where he abolished mechanical restraints.

18. See, for example, published annual reports for 1899 (*PNW*, 2:479) and for 1910 (*PNW*, 13:234) in which the details about Sonnenstein are limited to the most essential statistics. Weber maintained an ongoing correspondence with the Ministry of the Interior, kept in the administrative files of Sonnenstein that survive in the Dresden State Archives, but the reports about the hospital he sent on do not compare with the voluminous and elaborately tabulated productions furnished by Flechsig to the Ministry of Education (Flechsig, 1882-1896). Weber's (1893) annual report on Sonnenstein for the year 1893 is quoted in an unsigned review of the *Annual Report of the Landes-Medicinal-Collegium on the State of Medicine in the Kingdom of Saxony for 1893*, 350 pages long, in the literature review section of *AZP*, 53(1897):264-266; that unsigned review is in turn based on a previous review in another psychiatric journal, *Das Irrenwesen* (compare also Weber, 1896). The statistics for 1893 at Sonnenstein were as follows: "Total census, 513; admissions, 241 (103 men, 138 women); departed, 343, remaining, 411. Among the discharged: cured, 81 (32 men, 40 women[sic]); relatively cured or improved 75 (27 men, 48 women); chronic 32 (21 men, 11 women); transferred to other hospitals 130 (78 men, 52 women); died 32 (21 men, 11 women), including one by suicide" (p. 264). Of the cures, 87.6% took place in the first year and only 4.5% at a later time. Of the admissions 26 were cases of "paralysis" (i.e., syphilis), of which 82.5% were cases of less than one year's duration. Among the causes of death listed are syphilis, influenza and tuberculosis. There is also mention of controlling noisy behavior of female patients (by placing them in single rooms), of the opening of an outpatient department, and of plans for a cottage-style building in the future. Another annual report (Weber, 1895) is quoted in the *Irrenfreund* for 1897. In that year the five Saxon asylums had a census of 4674 patients, of which 2116 were men and 2558 women, a higher number according to Bresler (1899a), is shown in footnote 25.

19. Weber's (1910) chapter on the "Sonnenstein Asylum near Pirna," which was also his annual report for 1909, was reprinted in *PNW* in 1911 to coincide with the celebration of the 100th anniversary of Sonnenstein. The article focuses on the various renovations—removal of old dungeon-like towers, erection of new buildings, and extension of gardens and acreage under cultivation. The treatments, briefly listed, included bed rest, diet, and water cures (such as prolonged baths). The statistics for 1909, were as follows: during the year, the total census rose from 620 to 647: total admissions, 138 (68 men and 70 women); discharged as cured or improved, 77 (43 men and 34 women); died 31 (17 men, 14 women). In addition to the director the hospital employs: six psychiatrists (three senior and three junior), four male and four female senior nurses, 140 nurses and attendants, one parson, one teacher, ten office and technical workers, and a number of servants, in part taken from the nursing staff.

20. For example, File #16805 (*Bestimmungen*, 1879-1890), "Provisions about the Admission, Leaves and Discharges of Mentally Ill in the Acute and Custodial Asylums"; Files #16807 and #16808 (*Umgestaltung*, 1883-1893), "Transformation of the Provincial Institutions for the Insane and of Admission Procedures in All the Institutions; Preparatory to Regulations, 1883-

1893"; and File #16809 (*Unterbringungs*, 1897-1902), "Admissions Regulations for Asylums, 1897-1902" of the Ministry of the Interior.

21. Dated October 19, in File #16809, *Das Unterbringungs* (1897-1902). The
letter was in response to a directive from Department IV of the Ministry of the
Interior dated September 15, 1898 urging all the five asylums of the land to
agree to care for a mixed population, with special wards set aside for incurable
patients. Some of Weber's objections had already been stated by him in a
published annual report (Weber, 1895).

22. My comparison of custodial state hospitals to concentration camps may
appear brutal, but one should distinguish between concentration camps, that
is, sites of segregation of the socially dysfunctional, criminal, or politically
persecuted (such as the Gulag under Stalin), and death camps (those created by
Hitler and his henchmen). This comparison has already been made by Dörner
(1969, p. 20). A more benign impression was created by the cottage-style
institutions, or *"kolonialen Irrenanstalten."* The pressure to admit more and
more people for chronic care and the tendency to centralization was relentless:
the new laws of 1912 provided for the admission of the homeless (Hösel,
1912). During the Nazi regime, the state hospitals became the site of euthanasia of the mentally ill.

23. Reports to Department IV of the Ministry of the Interior (dated August
13, 1897, October 28, 1899, November 22, 1901) in *Unterbringungs* (1897-
1902). The number of patients involved was small, 9 men and 14 women, in
the year 1900 and a total of 50 patients in the years preceding, which Weber
saw as "quite considerable."

24. Files #16887 and #16888, "Attendants and Sevice Personnel at Sonnenstein Asylum" (*Krankenwärter*, 1874-1909) of the Ministry of the Interior.

25. The statistic for the German Empire show that there were these totals of
mentally ill persons in the entire population: 55,043 in 1871, 66,345 in 1880,
and 82,850 in 1895. The corresponding figures for Saxony were 4,088; 4,809;
and 5,524. The population of Saxony at that time was about 4.5 million.
Mentally ill persons in asylums, in all of Germany: 11,760 in 1871, 18,894 in
1880, 43,711 in 1895. The corresponding figures for Saxony were 762; 1,338;
and 2,757 (Bresler, 1899a, p. 225). With regard to the doctor-patient ratios for
1897 in Saxony, there were 18 doctors for 2,770 patients and 803 new
admissions, or one doctor per 154 patients and 45 admissions (Hoppe, 1899);
in 1899—21 doctors for 2,800 patients, for 803 admissions, or one doctor for
138 patients and 38 admissions (Hoppe, 1900). The overcrowding of hospitals
is discussed in an unsigned editorial, which one may assume Bresler approved
(1899b), "Psychiatry at the Turn of the Century."

26. In an article signed K. (probably a sign of both daring and caution on the
part of the author) and entitled "The Need for an Organization to Represent
the Interests of German Alienists and Asylums in General," in the *Wochenschrift*
for 1899 (pp. 264-267), the author complains that psychiatrists are underpaid
compared to other civil servants, that the ratios of attendants, supervisors, and
doctors to patients are below par, and that doctors are shamefully underpaid
for writing medical reports on felons admitted for observation: 24 marks per

report, each requiring an enormous amount of work—16 hours at 1.5 mark per hour, a rate lower than that earned by an accountant.

27. Described in an article "Abuses of Asylum Patients by Nursing Personnel," by the editor of the *PNW*, Dr. J. Bresler himself (1909a), are attacks by patients on staff and staff on patients, in small and large facilities, in the years 1895-1909. Such matters were underreported, as stated in a letter by Professor Weber (a different Weber), in his riposte (*PNW*, 1:172-173). The Sonnenstein Hospital Files (#16888) in the Ministry of the Interior contain reports of attendants who became psychotic.

28. Director of the state mental hospital in Lübeck, Dr. Wattenberg (1895-1896) asks the question: "Should we place patients in isolation rooms?" and answers, "No, not as a matter of principle" (p. 929).

29. Ohlah (1900), "Building Bridges Between Life and the Asylum." This was an address read by the Budapest hospital director Ohlah (or Olah, as in other places) at the International Psychiatric Congress held that year in Paris.

30. Lomer (1906) argued that no other profession is susceptible to stimuli that can either impair or instruct the practicing physician, as is psychiatry. The psychiatrist is under constant assault by the noise, filth (both physical and moral), animality and violence of the patients. One consequence is the frequency of pathology among doctors: many become neurasthenics and depressives ("in some rare cases [there is] a most pronounced paroxysmal rise to the point of suicide"). Doctors are often lonely in the pursuit of their profession; the patients often cause frictions among the doctors and unbearable pain, to the point of faultfinding and spying among colleagues. Or, in reaction to the dreadfulness of hospital life, they develop "defense reactions" such as apathy and insensitivity to the point of "institutional dementia." A frequent self-cure, says Lomer, is heavy drinking. The director is often sitting on a powder keg.

31. Riklin mentions his work under Eugen Bleuler at Burghölzli, where this principle was adhered to and described by Bleuler (1905). Riklin was an early adherent of Freud and published psychoanalytic papers in the *Wochenschrift*.

32. The editor of the *PNW*, J. Bresler (1908), in "The present state of psychiatry." In that year the *PNW* also printed by "Prof. Dr. Sigm[und] Freud 'Charakter und Analerotik'", on pp. 465-467. In 1901 *"Ueber den Traum.* Von Sigm. Freud, Wiesbaden, J.F. Bergmann" was reviewed (*PNW*, 1901:430-431). Earlier, in discussing a case of hysteria on the pages of the *AZP*, Bresler (1897) had cited Freud's *Studies on Hysteria*. In that same volume of *AZP*, in the reviews section, Freud (1895) and Freud's paper on obsessions and phobias of 1895 were reviewed (pp. 114, 118-119). The Bloomingdale Hospital still functions today in White Plains as the Westchester Division of New York Hospital, New York City, under the direction of Dr. Otto Kernberg.

33. Thus, in discussing a presentation by Pierson of a case of a man diagnosed as suffering from dementia, who the court allowed to get married in spite of two psychiatric certificates against, Weber cast doubts on the expert opinion of the lawyer (*AP*, 37:1053, *MPN*, 13:156, *PNW*, 4:383). At a meeting of the *Medizinalbeamten* (health care professionals) in Leipzig in 1903 Weber

argued for the power of the psychiatrist, as against physicians, in the treatment of alcoholics and epileptics [*CNP*, 28(1905):822].

34. Interestingly, although Hösel was emphatic in making the association centers all important, Flechsig felt it was "not very helpful to designate all the possible processes in the nervous system as associations."

35. The bulk of Weber's output (except for Weber 1876, and 1887-1888, 1910, and 1912) is compiled in the Index Volume (*Register Band*) of the *Zeitschrift*. I found a number of additional references in other journals. The remaining publications cover the following topics: degeneration signs (Weber, 1898a); a discussion of Dr. Pierson's lecture (Weber, 1898d); the historical background to issues of diminished responsibility (Weber, 1899b); more on legal responsibility and its forensic aspects (1899d), a dysentery epidemic in asylums (Weber, 1900); responsibility for crimes committed while intoxicated (Weber, 1902b); morbid lies of hysterics (Weber, 1902c), a talk given immediately following a presentation by Stegmann (1902); a discussion of a forensic case (1902d); a discussion of Pierson (1903); a discussion of a paper on the testamentary capacity of the insane (1905b); a talk on the legal aspects of the care of invalids (1909b); and a paper on the clinical picture of general paralysis of the insane (1912). I also found Weber mentioned as a discussant in 1846 at the 40th Meeting of the German Scientists and Physicians, section of psychiatry, but could not locate this reference.

36. See under "Charitable Society for Mental Patients" (1901, 1907, 1911). For example, from an account of the meeting in 1907, held on May 27 in Bautzen, we learn that the membership rose to 3,800, and that 6,000 marks were spent on rehabilitation of former inpatients. Officers were elected from among Sonnenstein psychiatrists, and a lecture, "Mental Illness and Crime" was held in an effort to educate the public about psychiatry. J. Bresler also published a monthly organ, under the auspices of the *PNW*, called *Der Irrenschutz* (Defender of the Insane), "dedicated to the members of the Charitable Society for Mental Patients of German-speaking lands and all the friends of mental patients." The first issue of 1901 carried a short notice about the meeting held on May 23 of that year with Weber-Sonnenstein in the chair. In 1911 Weber was still chairman, but was now called Weber-Dresden, since he was now retired and living in Dresden.

37. According to the aforementioned source in the *PNW* and *PNW* 10:391-393, 1910. However, according to Weber (1859-1910) he was bestowed the title of *Geheimer Rath* in 1896, on his 59th birthday.

38. This date may be a mistake. In the Personal File (Weber, 1859-1910) the birthday is consistently recorded as June 5, 1837 in the documents and June 4 on the face sheet; the latter was also copied by Ilberg (1914).

39. Recalled by Weber and also by Felix Hempel, for many years the parson at Sonnenstein, who had written the event up (1901) and also wrote about the therapeutic role of religion in the asylum.

40. The *PNW* also reprinted a story about the festivities entitled "The Centenary Celebration of the Royal Saxon Asylum Sonnenstein near Pirna," based on the newspaper *Dresdner Nachrichten* (1911).

41. As reported by Dr. Serger in the *PNW* for 1911, pp. 166-169.

42. *A Textbook of Forensic Psychiatry*. Professor Alfred Ernst Hoche was one of the early virulent opponents of psychoanalysis, mentioned in the Freud-Jung letters. The first edition was published in 1901, and Schreber may have been familiar with it. I am quoting from the second edition of 1909. Weber is cited twice (on pages 587 and 591).

43. It is very likely that Schreber knew of King Ludwig's fate. The story of Ludwig and von Gudden is told in the *AZP*, 43(1887):163-168 and by Szasz (1963, pp. 48-53; 1973, pp. 82-83). For a modern view see Schnidbauer & Kemper (1986). An anonymous obituary of von Gudden was also published in the *AZP*, 43(1887):177-187.

44. In Germany, the case was discussed in the *Zeitschrift*, the *Wochenschrift*, the antipsychiatry pamphlet by Richard Dahl (1905), *The Bankruptcy of Psychiatry*, and a lot in Vienna (see the following note).

45. After writing this chapter I became aware of the fact that the story of Louise had been the subject of an essay by the Viennese Karl Kraus, the mordant founder and editor of *Die Fackel*, where his essay was published in 1904. Freud may have seen it but did not connect the names Pierson and Weber. Neither did Szasz, who reprinted the essay (Szasz, 1973, pp. 127-137). Kraus, a foe of psychiatry and psychoanalysis, railed against the corruptibility and stupidity of psychiatrists. On the basis of interviews with a number of journalists, Kraus regarded Princess Louise as

> a gracious lady not only in full possession of her faculties, but also a rare, indomitable spirit of great vitality. She adequately, and more than adequately, rebuts every argument of her infamous torturers. Indeed, thanks to the training acquired through six years' suffering, she could now supply a more convincing opinion of the mental states of Doctors Wagner, Jolly, Mellis and Weber, than they could ever of hers. We laymen cease to be impressed by a "science." . . . On the liberated Princess, psychiatry wants to demonstrate to us its latest "discovery"— that insanity can simulate sanity! A feeble mind here offers proof of its weakness by demonstrating strength. But no! Psychiatrists haven't quite yet managed this [Kraus, quoted in Szasz (1973), pp. 134-135].

Has Kraus heard of Schreber?

46. The diagnosis of dementia in a forensic context was made by Weber in connection with an obscure story from the years 1902-1903, about which very little is known except for a few fragments in the administrative files of Sonnenstein. It was in connection with a certain Otto Herrmann from Blasewitz, a lower-court judge who lost his job as a result of a psychiatric diagnosis of dementia (*Schwachsinn*) submitted by Weber to the authorities. On August 7 of 1902 Herrmann placed an advertisement in the local paper in which he claimed he had taken his appeal all the way to the *Reichsgericht*, the supreme appeals court of all Germany, sitting in Leipzig, which allegedly vindicated him against the unnamed psychiatric expert. The unfortunate man lodged complaints against Weber, City Hall of Dresden, and other administrative

bodies and all the complaints were ultimately rejected by the First Chamber of the House of Representatives (File #3489, bearing the same name as *Behandlung*, 1862).

47. The German psychiatrists were also supported by their colleagues in the judiciary. Arnemann, the reviewer of the *Memoirs* (1903), also reviewed the pamphlet of Oberjustizrath Dr. Frese of Meissen (1905), who was critical of the superficial and unscientific character of the French report, in stark contrast to "German thoroughness." Frese countered Dahl's criticisms of German psychiatry (as unscientific, mercenary, and one-sided in its organicism, as exemplified by Meynert, Kraepelin, Flechsig, and Hitzig), expressed in Dahl's antipsychiatry brochure (see note 44), by noting that Dahl himself was a crook who had spent 18 months in jail and was thus an impostor and not to be taken seriously.

Dr. Frese made an appearance at the 101st meeting of the Forensic Psychiatric Association of Dresden in 1905 (Weber, 1909a), presented his views on the two reports about the princess, and stressed that the French legal position was based on the Code Napoléon. The old friends Pierson and Weber joined in the discussion, their last joint appearance; Pierson died the following year. They both reaffirmed the severe pathology of the princess and the correctness of the Austrian and German forensic positions and the treatment administered. Pierson claimed the French overlooked the hereditary loading, namely, that the Belgian King was a genius but an eccentric (a polite euphemism for crazy) and that the Empress of Mexico had been mentally ill. Weber was astonished by the conclusions of the French commission. His stand here was as unbending as that adopted toward Schreber. Pierson and Weber were joined by Ganser, who opined that the authors of the French report were motivated by money. The shoe is often on the other foot.

48. Since the story of Louise was a big sensation in Vienna, due to the connections of the Count of Coburg to the Austro-Hungarian Empire, it is pertinent to recall another legal psychiatric scandal that shook Vienna, in which Wagner von Jauregg was also implicated as forensic expert. It was the sensational affair of the Viennese actor Girardi, whose vindictive wife persuaded Wagner von Jauregg to declare him incompetent and consign him to the asylum. Girardi was saved by the intercession of his friend Mrs. Schratt, also an actress, and mistress of the emperor Franz Josef.

49. Schreber cited the 4th, 5th, and 6th editions of Kraepelin's *Textbook*. In the 4th (1893) we find a recommendation to utilize the depressant virtues of potassium bromide for the treatment of masturbation coupled with patient exhortations (p. 226). Another important topic is litigation regarding mental illness and home care for harmless patients (p. 233), which was of particular interest to Schreber.

Melancholia is divided into "A. Simplex" (simple) and "B. Anxiety melancholia (*Angstmelancholie*)," including abdominal hypochondriasis (*Hypochondria gastrica*). "Psychosis (*Wahnsinn*)," is divided into "A. Hallucinatory psychosis (*Hallucinatorische W.*)," a condition also seen in prison inmates in the form of "prison psychosis" (*Gefangenenwahnsinn*)" and "B. Depressive psychosis (*Depressive W.*)," delusions in a depression. There is also mention of "fever deliria," a functional state associated with fever and, interestingly, with functional symptoms in the heart. Another topic of relevance to Paul is castration in hysterical women, improvements attributed to the "psychical impact of the surgery."

Paranoia is dealt with in chapter "VII. Craziness (*Verrücktheit*) (Paranoia)," divided into "A. Depressive forms, hallucinatory delusion of persecution (*Hallucinatorische Verfolgungswahn*)," and "B. Expansive forms, hallucinatory delusion of grandeur (*Expansive Formen, Halluc. Grössenwahn*)." Chapter VIII treats of "psychic degenerations (*Entartungen*)," which include "A. *Die Dementia praecox, B. Die Katatonie, C. Die Dementia paranoides.*"

In the 5th edition (1896) we have new classifications. In chapter section "II. Phenomena of Insanity" includes "acute confusion (*acute Verwirrtheit (amentia), Meynert's amentia*," confusion and amentia pointing to the same syndrome. Meynert's (1890) name became associated with what was viewed as a special form of paranoia, different from the classical chronic paranoia (without hallucinations or confusion): an acute and fluid delirium-like syndrome of confusion, hallucinations, delusions, and excitement which often ended in a remission. Freud (1894) applied the dynamics of dreams and hysteria to explain it as a defense neuropsychosis. Kraepelin calls persecutory paranoia *combinatory* (which includes ideas of persecution, grandeur, eroticism, and litigiousness), to be distinguished from *fantastic* paranoia (which includes florid fantastic content, sexual delusions of persecution, fantastic ideas of grandeur, and elaboration of systems à la Magnan), which suggests a degree of overlapping. Castration as treatment is again discussed, on p. 747. Of interest is Kraepelin's rudimentary dynamic conception of hallucinations as having "unconscious connections" to "morbid fears and wishes" (p. 105).

In the 6th edition (1899), the diagnoses are in their final shape: the groupings in the earlier category "degenerations" are subsumed in Chapter V under the three basic forms of dementia praecox, hebephrenic, catatonic, and paranoid, the latter also discussed in Chapter X under "*Verrücktheit (Paranoia).*"

50. As enunciated in the preface to Arndt's (1883) *Textbook of Psychiatry for Physicians and Students*. Freud may have read it, too. The book is close to 600 pages long and in its scope it surpasses Kraepelin's 1883 *Compendium der Psychiatrie*, the first edition of his *Textbook*.

51. This was the view of J. Bresler (1909b) in his "Unitary Classification and Division of the Psychoses." According to his schema, the endogenous psychoses included constitutional depression, paranoia, epilepsy, hysteria, and the psychopathic inferiorities, such as compulsive drives, compulsive ideas, moral insanity and related states. The toxic psychoses included amentia, alcoholic disorders, paresis, dementia praecox and senilis, and other toxic conditions, such as thyrotoxicosis and pellagra. The secondary group included all the inflammations of the brain membranes, traumas, and tumors.

52. This bias is still with us; hallucinations are still defined as disorders of perception but as perceptions without an object. But this is a contradiction: if there is no object, there is no perception, only a kind of imagining or dreaming. Therefore, one should instead speak of hallucinations as sui generis dream-like experiences, as I have argued (Lothane, 1982a).

53. There is another internal contradiction here, in defining hallucinations as sense-deceptions, for deception belongs in the category of judgment, not of sensation (true sensory illusions, such as the stick seen as bent in the water, are built into neurocognitive functioning and have nothing to do with the psychological function of judgment). Hallucinations were thus seen as the sensory-organic foundation of delusions, even though delusions are in the combined realm of thought, feeling, and judgment; thus, another manifestation of brain mythology. (This is not to deny the existence of true sensory hallucinations in proven, not hypothetical, organic lesions of the central nervous system.) The psychological and dynamic conception of hallucinations and delusions was well understood by Kant and epitomized by Goethe: senses do not lie, only reason lies. This is also the view expressed by a philosophically informed psychiatrist Robert Neupert (1904) in "The Problem of Delusions." An ethical note of tolerance, in addition to a psychological analysis, was sounded by Paul Näcke (1906) in his "Delusion and Error" (Näcke is cited in Freud, 1914b).

Indeed, the problem is neatly reflected in the German words, which show that there is a relation between *irren* (to err), as in *Irr-tum* (error) and *Irr-sinn* (craziness). *Irrsinn* is extended into *Wahnsinn* (which means both delusion and madness). However, note the ambiguity of the verb *wähnen* (to believe, to think, to fancy, and to rave). Delusion, like illusion, comes from the Latin *ludere* (to play), and delirium—in the sense of delusion, as in the French *délire* — is derived from the *lira* (furrow), expressing the idea of de-ranged.

Earlier Näcke (1900) expressed progressive ideas in support of patients' rights in "To What Extent Do Psychotics Retain the Capacity for Self-Determination and the Choice Where to Stay?"

54. The discussion appears on pages 653 to 658 of the fifth edition of Kraepelin's *Lehrbuch der Psychiatrie* (1896).

55. In his paper "On the Question of Paranoia" (1901b) Bresler discussed a paper published that year by Specht, "Ueber den pathologischen Affekt in der chronischen Paranoia (On the Pathological Affect in Chronic Paranoia)," in a festschrift dedicated to HRH the Prince Regent of Bavaria. Bressler argued that Specht's central thesis, that paranoia was a disorder of ideas (*"Krankheit der Vorstellungen"*) or madness of reason (*"Verstandesirresein"*), had become obsolete. According to Specht, the main unpleasure feeling at the start of paranoia, the suspiciousness, can proceed either to manic delusions of grandeur or to depressive delusions of persecution, but these are the plus and minus aspects of the same emotional disorder originating in a feeling of unpleasure; therefore, the "*'Geisteskranke*' [madman] has again become the '*Gemüthskranke*'[mood man]" (Bresler, 1901b, p.172), a sufferer from a mood disorder, a term more benign, used in Kant's time, and one that Paul Schreber himself preferred (*M*, 376), when he speaks of "*die Unterscheidung zwischen blossen 'Gemüthskranken' und 'Geisteskranken'*," which Macalpine and Hunter render as "mentally ill" and "insane patient" (*M*, 263). For Schreber the differentiation has not only nosological but also important legal implications.

The argument in favor of the role of the emotions was carried by Tiling (1902), one of the experts on paranoia, in his "On the Question of Paranoia." He also stressed the importance of habit and the hardening of paranoid ideas into habits of thought and the fact that the forensic definitions of paranoia in all the German lands disregarded feelings and focused on the ideas. Tiling's conception was again reaffirmed by R. Lehmann (1909) in "Paranoia—Affect—Delusion of Persecution—Delusion of Grandeur." Interestingly, in discussing Specht, Bleuler (1901) in a paper entitled "On the Genesis of Paranoid Delusions" denied the importance of feelings, in particular of mistrust, creating the bridge between paranoia and mood disorders, a viewpoint he later repeated in his monograph of 1906, *Affectivity, Suggestibility and Paranoia*. There is no sign that Weber followed these interesting debates.

56. On the pages of the *Neurologisches Centralblatt* for 1899, *"Zur Diagnose und Prognose der Dementia praecox."*

57. The paper by E. Schultze (1901) is "The Obligation to Discharge Following Dismissal or Rescission of Incompetency." Even as Schultze was a psychiatric-forensic expert defending the profession against undue criticism, he quoted a legal authority, Vierhaus, who delivered a paper at the XXV Meeting of Jurists with the title: "Is There a Need for Legal Regulations as to the Premise Under Which a Patient may be Admitted to an Institution Before Being Declared Incompetent or Detained There Against His Will After Having Been Declared Incompetent?" The title of Schreber's forensic essay (*M*, pp. 363-376), written in "early 1900, at the time of my complete isolation from the outside world, and therefore almost totally without the opportunity of using literary sources" (*M*, Foot Note #121), is very close to Vierhaus's. The same Vierhaus is quoted as enunciating the following premise, close to Schreber's reasoning, the purpose of which is to separate the issues of treatment and incompetency: "there are mental patients who need to be admitted, even if temporarily, without requiring a declaration of incompetency and, obversely, there are patients declared as incompetent whose admission to an institution is not necessary." And also: "The declaration of incompetency is based on legal premises and has legal consequences; admission to an asylum is primarily a practical measure and has no legal consequences" (Schultze, 1901, p. 229). This notion of separation of realms was not well understood by Weber, who wanted to play judge and jury. Even while he paid lip service to judicial authority, he complained that judges did not listen enough to psychiatrists.

58. One of the most famous midcentury cases involved the scientist Robert Meyer, the discoverer of the law of conservation of energy, who according to Dühring (1904), was railroaded into an asylum by defamation spread by his envious colleagues (see chapter 8 footnote 23). Meyer seems to have suffered from bipolar affective disorder. Another famous neglected asylum case was that of Robert Schumann (Ostwald, 1985).

59. The numbers in parentheses following the titles in this note refer to numbered works in Beyer's bibliography: *Of Sound Mind, Incarcerated as Mad for 39 Months!* (6); *A Warning. The Tale of Sorrows of a Doctor Declared Psychotic* (18); *A Military Legal Murder* (23); *A Dreyfus Case in Germany (In the Light of the Pamphlet Class Justice and the Incompetency Mischief)* (25); *How One Tries to Lock Up in a Madhouse a Mentally Healthy Man out of Revenge and In Order to Get His Money* (41); *The Great Madhouse Swindle or the Gruesome Total Destruction of Many Innocent Victims in Madhouses While Knowing Better and By Means of Studied Murder*

in the 19th Century (42); *Black Bands Among Jurists and Doctors in the Newly Unified German Reich* (43); *Witchhunt on People* (47); *Artificial Madness. A Warning Against Mental Hospitals* (53); *Legal Murders. Rape and Incarceration of 24 Healthy Persons in Madhouses with Full Knowledge and Out of Greed* (56); *For Those Buried Alive* (57); *Les Bastilles Modernes* (60); *Robbers of Reason or Mentally Buried Alive For Six Years* (61); *An Act of Modern Torture* (87); *The Domination of German Officialdom* (99); *How One Becomes a Litigious Paranoiac and Gets Into a Madhouse* (110); *The Manufacture of Madmen* (118); *J'accuse* (125); *The Sufferings of an Honorable Lady Under Prussian Legal Bureaucracy Because She Sought Justice* (128); *A Contribution to the New German State Inquisition* (168); *To King and Citizens. Tale of Sorrows of an Innocent Victim of Persecution* (172).

60. According to *Das litterarische Leipzig* (1897, p. 92), in which his other medical publications as well as his contributions to general interest journals were cited, Dr. Rudolf Götze (the spelling there) was born in 1863 in Glauchau. Following graduation he was *Oberarzt* at the psychiatric hospital of the University of Würzburg. In 1893 he moved to Leipzig and became the director of an outpatient clinic for nervous patients (*Nervenkranke*) and of a private hospital for nervous patients. He was active as a member of the Richard Wagner Society. Did Schreber know of this man, did Götze know of Schreber?

61. In his lecture "On Hallucinatory Psychosis (Kraepelin)", Georg Ilberg (1894-5), a coworker of Weber's and later his successor as director of Sonnenstein and the author of his obituary, discusses 40 acute and recovered cases of the disorder. Cases due to intoxicants were excluded. Ilberg notes elementary illusions and hallucinations, followed by delusions—of persecution, poisoning, sinfulness, grandeur, but also of nihilistic, hypochondriacal, and erotic content, often accompanied by refusal of food, attempts to escape, and violence. He notes an incubation period of many days to weeks, a course of four and a half to 15 months, 66% incidence in males between the ages 20-63, in those with hereditary loading and also in previously normal individuals. Those who recovered showed cessation of hallucinations and insight into their delusions. Among etiological factors Ilberg lists prior physical illness, "depressed mood (illness and death of relatives, concerns and worries, unhappy love), mental overstrain (working nights). Many developed [the condition] in prison (solitary confinement!). Hallucinatory psychosis plays a role in periodic and circular psychosis [bipolar affective disorder]. . . . The differential diagnosis [includes] hallucinatory or acute confusional state, paranoia and dementia paranoides." Of interest for our argument is evidence of awareness among clinicians of dynamic etiological connections, as well as the differential diagnosis, which were not considered by Weber.

62. An early sample can be found in File #3488 (*Behandlung*, 1862) and later versions in Files #16805 (*Bestimmungen*, 1879-1890) and #16807 (*Umgestaltung(en)*, 1883-1893). The questions in the last version of the questionnaire (officially approved as of August 8, 1892), compared with the version quoted from in the text, followed the same outline, with some additions, for example: the question about the moral temperament now included alcohol and drug addiction and masturbation; the question about depression included "Exalta-

tion of mood? Anxiety states? Stuporous fixity? Apathy?" These should have led Weber to a consideration of a differential diagnosis.

63. "In addition to the three classes of care, the Sonnenstein Asylum has a special service for wealthy citizens and foreigner called the boarder's quarters (*Pensionsanstalt*). Patients on this service are entitled to a choicer diet and their condition permitting take their meals at the table of the medical director such that they may be observed and supervised in the most particular manner; they also have special quarters separated from other patients and special attendants . . . and the cost per annum is 500–700 thalers" (*Behandlung*, 1862).

64. In his article, "Remarks on the Conflicts of Interest of Institutional Psychiatrists as Experts to the Courts," Pfausler (1902) seeks to defend the institutional psychiatrist's profession from attacks by the public (as in a recent article "Protecting the Public from Psychiatrists") and from the adversarial position of the Ministry of Justice. While admitting that psychiatrists have made some mistakes, Pfausler accuses the judges of many more mistakes and affirms the principle that the responsibility for incompetency decisions lies with the judges and their proper use of the institutional psychiatrist as the best expert witness. The author defends the goodwill of institutional psychiatrists toward their patients and decries the many obstacles in their path: the sick patients themselves, the families that reject their sick relatives, and now the curbs imposed by the Ministry on the authority of the psychiatrists. He invokes the views of Kraepelin from the 6th edition of the *Lehrbuch*, when bureaucracy was nonexistent and psychiatrist was king: the psychiatrist is "*judge in all human affairs, teacher of jurists and theologians, leader of historians and writers*" (Pfausler, 1902, p. 345, emphasis Pfausler's). The *Wochenschrift* was more open to debate from within and without the profession than the *Zeitschrift*. Thus the *PNW* printed a call for reform from a mechanical engineer from Bavaria who echoed the antipsychiatry protests published by the daily "*Kreuzzeitung*," with negative comments by Beyer (1909).

65. Gerd Busse (now Gerhard Busse, PhD) of Berlin found Weber (1905a) first and gave it to me in Berlin in the summer of 1988. Upon my return, I found that article, along with the rest of Weber's output listed in the Index Volume of the *AZP*, in the library of the New York Academy of Medicine. Initially a friendly and collaborative colleague, with whom I exchanged ideas and references, Busse took the liberty of forbidding me to use this reference, even though Weber is in the public domain, and then turned hostile when I went ahead and used it, citing him the first finder. In an attempt to discredit my two published papers on the Schreber case (1989a and b), he sent a letter dated June 5, 1989, and on August 7, 1989, a paper entitled "Schreber, Lothane, and the Second Invention of Gun Powder" (the German equivalent of the English *reinventing the wheel*), both submitted for publication in the *Psychoanalytic Review* and rejected, both containing untruths, exaggerations, and distortions; both letter and paper were sent to me as a professional courtesy by the editor of the *Psychoanalytic Review*, Dr. Martin Schulman.

In his article "Schreber und Flechsig: der Hirnanatom als Psychiater" (Busse, 1989), published in the winter 1989 issue of the *Medizinhistorisches*

Journal, half a year after mine, and discussing views that reflected my influence, Busse only made reference to my "unpublished manuscript" of 1988, even though prior to the publication of his 1989 article, he had already quoted—in the summer of 1989—the final published version of "Schreber, Freud, Flechsig and Weber Revisited: an inquiry into methods of interpretation" in his paper "Schreber, Lothane, and the Second Invention of Gun Powder." I wrote a letter to the editor of the *Medizinhistorisches Journal* requesting a correction of the way I was cited but have not been answered to this day.

In his dissertation (1990, p. 66, footnote 15) Busse characterizes the bibliography to my paper, "Vindicating Schreber's Father: Neither Sadist Nor Child Abuser," as "the worst" and one reference as "leading a wretched existence." Even though I cite Busse gratefully in the text, he quotes the reference in question tendentiously and incompletely. It does not take a scholar to realize that the mistakes in this reference—the only problematic one of the eight by Moritz Schreber—were caused by the type-setter and lack of proof-reading, and the evidence for this is that not only are the German words misspelled but even a simple English word: "Souzce" instead of "Source," omitted here (Busse, 1990). Nor does he acknowledge that I correctly pointed out an inaccuracy in Israëls.

66. The inflexibility of his psychiatric forensic posture stands out even more clearly if we compare his with the views of a contemporary, L. W. Weber (1905), chief psychiatrist of Cramer in Göttingen, eloquently expressed in his paper "Chronic Paranoiacs with Respect to Administrative, Penal and Civil Law." L. W. Weber argued that chronicity of illness and residual symptoms were compatible with the ability to manage one's affairs on the outside and that such patients should not be kept in an institution indefinitely. The patients described in his paper were in some respects similar to Schreber. G. Weber might have been more flexible had he diagnosed melancholia; responding to Ganser (1897), he noted that in mild cases of melancholia, the capacity to handle one's own affairs can remain more intact [*AZP* (1897), 53:588].

67. In the biographies of psychiatrists appended by the editors to Kraepelin's *Memoirs* there is a note on Paul Nitsche, who became director of Sonnestein in 1928 and who "played a considerable role in the persecution of mentally ill patients" (p. 215). Here, persecution, *Verfolgung*, means the crimes committed by Nazi physicians on such patients.

68. In the summer of 1988, during a visit to the Dresden State Archives, Dr. Brichzin, the then director, explained in the presence of Busse and me that in the 1950s, in view of the impending investigation of physicians who were war criminals, many patient files mysteriously disappeared from the State Archives. This dashes hopes of retrieving more pages from Schreber's chart. Let's hope that the new order in Germany will create new opportunities for finding the original documents.

7

How Others Interpreted Schreber

My Memoirs are not written for flappers or High School girls . . . I have not always hit the form of expression which sensitive school matrons think fit for their charges. A person who wishes to pave the way for a new conception of religion must be able if need be to use flaming speech [*Flammenworte*] such as Jesus Christ used against the Pharisees or Luther towards the Pope and the mighty of the world.

D. P. Schreber, 1903

In Schreber's system the two principal elements of his delusions (his transformation into a woman and his favored relation to God) are linked. . . . It will be an unavoidable part of our task to show that there is an essential *genetic* relation between these two elements. Otherwise our attempts at elucidating Schreber's delusions will leave us in the absurd position described in Kant's famous simile . . . We shall be like a man holding a sieve under a he-goat while someone else milks it.

Freud, 1911a

From the very beginning Schreber has been both a paradigm and a person, and the paradigm has regrettably obscured the person. As a paradigm, Schreber the person became the Schreber case, a specimen exhibiting forms of psychopathology and psychodynamics. Of course, the first people who saw Schreber as a person and then treated him as a case were his psychiatrists, specifically Flechsig and Weber. Everyone else merely read the *Memoirs*.

317

SCHREBER AND THE PUBLISHERS

Among the first readers were a number of publishers who considered printing the *Memoirs*. Of course, Schreber could have published his *Memoirs* privately, as did so many other victims of the psychiatric system. He chose to have a certain measure of approval by being published as an author. He does not tell us how he got to Oswald Mutze.[1] Whereas Nauthardt and Fleischer considered publishing the book on commission, that is, with Schreber bearing at least part of the costs, Mutze appears to have bought the book, promoted it through advertising, and offered it to the public at the price of eight marks unbound and ten marks bound, a respectable price for those days.[2]

The house of Oswald Mutze is no more. Some members of the family were killed by the Nazis during World War II and the firm and its holdings were destroyed.[3] Mutze had a strong interest in championing the cause of occultism, as described in his *Prospektus*. However, an unknown interest of Mutze's was the rights of mental patients. Besides the *Memoirs*, Mutze published the book by Rudolf Goetze (1896), mentioned in chapters 5 and 6. In addition to the numerous books, Mutze's interest in occultism was represented by the periodical *Psychische Studien*, which began publication in 1874, described by the publisher as "a monthly primarily devoted to the investigation of little-known phenomena of mental life, founded by [Russian occultist] Alexander Aksakow and edited by Dr. Friedrich Maier." This periodical was the counterpart of a similar publication in England, the *Proceedings of the Society for Psychical Research*, started in 1882, a journal well known to Freud. Other periodicals of this nature were *Nebus* published in St. Petersburg, *Light* in London, *Banner of Light* in Boston, and the *Religio-Philosophical Journal* in Chicago. Advertisements for occult books published by Mutze can be seen on the last pages of the original 1903 edition of the *Memoirs*, itself advertised in the *Psychische Studien*. We don't know who wrote the copy; it could have been Schreber himself, which I suspect. Both intentions of the *Memoirs*, the mystical and the forensic, were underscored.

> Oswald Mutze in Leipzig is the publisher and distributor, as well as through book stores, of *The Memoirs of a Nervous Patient* by Dr. Jur. P. Schreber, *Senatspräsident* of the *Oberlandesgericht* in Dresden, retired. With an addendum about the question: "UNDER WHAT PREMISES MAY A PERSON CONSIDERED INSANE BE DETAINED IN AN ASYLUM AGAINST HIS OR HER DECLARED WILL?" 532 pages. Marks 8, bound Marks 10.
>
> The author, a well-known personality in Saxon law circles, who in recent years was named to high positions in the judiciary and among

others functioned as *Landgerichtsdirector* in Chemnitz and Leipzig and as *Landgerichtspräsident* in Freiberg and as *Senatspräsident* in the Royal *Oberlandesgericht* in Dresden,[4] spent nine years in insane asylums as a result of a nervous illness. During a court case he pursued as plaintiff in two courts to rescind the incompetency decision that was imposed on him he was able to achieve his long-desired discharge from the Sonnenstein Asylum, where he had spent the last eight years.

As a result of his nervous illness, the author believes that *supernatural impressions*, that were vouchsafed to him in great measure, have given him undreamt-of insights into matters divine, the *nature of God, life after death*, etc. The author, who by his own confession counted himself as an out and out *skeptic* in religious matters, portrays these supernatural impressions as well as his personal, often truly depressing, even horrendous, experiences during his nine-year-long stay in asylums.—The Preface contains an "OPEN LETTER TO PRIVY COUNCILLOR PROF. DR. FLECHSIG," under whose care the author has been for a long time.—The work includes a great many stimulating ideas and will therefore be found worthwhile by *theologians, philosophers, physicians, jurists*, particularly *psychiatrists*, and in general all *educated persons interested in questions relating to the hereafter*.

There are also interesting sidelights on the issue of improvements in some procedures in asylums for the insane and the sometimes ruthless treatment in those hospitals. The addenda include three expert opinions of Privy Councillor Dr. Weber, the writ of appeal, and the decision of the Royal *Oberlandesgericht* of Dresden [emphasis in the original].[5]

To be sure, certain portions of Schreber's religious musings do qualify as delusional. As such, they are carriers of meanings and messages personal to Schreber. But this cannot be said about Schreber's very serious intention of addressing the perennial philosophical and religious questions of mankind, those concerning the nature of the deity, the soul, and immortality. Furthermore, the advertisement truly reflects the purpose of the *Memoirs* as an act of self-vindication.

THE FIRST RECEPTION OF THE *MEMOIRS*

So far, we know of no reactions to Schreber's book in the lay press. The work was immediately noted by a number of psychiatrists and reviewed in the professional literature. In those days the reviewers quoted the full title of the *Memoirs*, that is, including the addendum on the question of involuntary hospitalization.

There was an enthusiastic review by Paul Möbius (1903), who compared Schreber's to the famous confessions of Rousseau.[6] Möbius earned a place in the history of neurology and psychiatry. Freud said about him that his studies on suggestion, like those of Liébeault and

Bernheim, ushered in modern psychotherapy (Schiller, 1982), which he practiced in Leipzig. Möbius was the originator of pathography, the application of psychopathology to explain the life of a famous person, which he began with a study of Rousseau in 1889. This was an early model for Freud's essay on Leonardo (1910b) and other early works in applied psychoanalysis.

At the other extreme, the only truly negative review was written by Gustav Aschaffenburg (1903), who later became an opponent of psychoanalysis. Like Weber, Aschaffenburg was mainly interested in the forensic-psychiatric aspects of the case. Like Weber, he believed psychiatrists could not but regret the publication of the Memoirs, a work of an incurable psychotic, incapable of managing his affairs. He also expressed compassion for Schreber's family, who should have been spared the embarrassment and psychological damage that he believed would ensue from the publication of the work.

R. Pfeiffer (1904), another reviewer, felt that in spite of its merits the work might confuse the general public. This was also the opinion of a Leipzig psychiatrist, Windscheid (1904), who focused on Schreber's contention that his confinement at Sonnenstein was unjustified. One anonymous reviewer noted the author's "personal, really depressing, nay, horrendous experiences during his nine year stay in asylums" (Friedreich's Blätter, 1904, p. 239). The book was also reviewed in the Zeitschrift by Pelman, the prominent psychiatrist noted in connection with the Feldmann case. Pelman was impressed with Schreber's self-portrayal as a worthwhile work for psychiatrists, ranking it with the famous self-description in the history of psychiatry by James Tilly Matthews, as presented in Haslam (1810). Pelman described the Memoirs as rising head and shoulders above the thick tomes, mostly self-published, by litigious ex-patients clamoring against their unlawful detentions. Coming at the height of the public outcry of the antipsychiatry movement, this was a very high accolade indeed by a revered representative of the establishment. Pelman (1903) was not only impressed with Schreber's honesty and seriousness of purpose but also with his legal battle: "One will have gained the conviction that it was not the usual kind of opponents that faced each other here but opponents who were each other's equal" (p. 659).[7] Equally sympathetic was Arnemann (1903), writing in the Wochenschrift. He noted that even though the author was a paranoiac whose successful adaptation outside the hospital was doubtful, the book was neither sensation-seeking nor ill-tempered. Another reviewer (Kron, 1903) noted the forensic interest of the case and the fact that Schreber was one of those quiet mental patients who are not a social burden and are even creative. He also noted that Schreber received an assurance from the Dresden Court of Appeals that he would be covered by Paragraph 51 of the Civil Code, that is, legally protected as a mental patient and thus not liable to prosecution for publicly attacking an eminent psychiatrist, namely, Flechsig. One of the champions of this paragraph was the forensic psychiatrist Guido Weber. In this respect Paul Schreber seems to have been able to eat his cake and have it, too.

Two Viennese reviewers (R., 1905, and Infeld, 1905) were also sympathetic toward the *Memoirs* and Schreber: "in the reports characterized as paranoid . . . he is very intelligent, conscientious as far as possible and a seemingly likable personality. Compared to many other productions of similar provenance, the present work is different in its lack of polemical and litigious elements and the endeavor to be fair toward the doctors" (Infeld, 1905).

The other two psychiatrists who discussed the *Memoirs* before Freud did were Guido Weber (1905a), who alluded to "memories" and "this work" (p. 404), and Hoche (1909). No further notice seems to have been taken of the *Memoirs* in the first decade of its publication until it was read by Freud's crown prince, Carl Gustav Jung.

JUNG AND BLEULER ON SCHREBER

Jung would have known of the *Memoirs* through the aforementioned reviews in the literature[8] and possibly also through Oswald Mutze in Leipzig, who published Jung's doctoral dissertation, *On the Psychology and Pathology of So-called Occult Phenomena* (1902a), just one year before the *Memoirs*. Mutze's announcement of the *Memoirs* among new books in print for 1903 would have caught Jung's eye: "a work of the highest interest for physicians, theologians, spiritists and educated readers."[9]

Jung's dissertation is of interest in its own right, not on account of the faked mediumistic phenomena but for his discussion of hallucinations.[10] He gave a thorough review of the literature on the subject and regarded hallucinations on a spectrum from the normal to the morbid, quoting from Freud's *Interpretation of Dreams*. It is an open question whether Schreber read Jung.[11] Later, Jung himself became a promoter of occult notions. One might thus wonder which of the two, Schreber or Jung, had a greater identification with the occult or who was more delusional, Schreber in his day or Jung after his break with Freud and in his later years. Some of the esoteric texts of present-day Jungians might have caused Dr. Weber to raise his eyebrows.[12]

Jung was among the first to apply Freud's seminal idea, by that time expressed in the *Studies on Hysteria* and *The Interpretation of Dreams*, that symptoms have meaning. Jung expressed these ideas in his *Psychology of*

Dementia Praecox, published in 1907.[13] In that work an attempt was made for the first time to look at Schreber's psychotic productions not just symptomatically, as a sign of an organic disorder, but dynamically, as a meaningful content.[14] Accordingly, the individual symptoms were seen as conversions while the total clinical picture, that of dementia praecox, was regarded as an organic-toxic brain disorder. This view makes good sense as a Jacksonian conception of the positive and negative syndromes in delirium.

In the preface to his book Jung acknowledged his indebtedness to Freud's method of studying "daily life, hysteria, and dreams." He expressed reservations about the preponderant role of "sexual trauma in youth" (pp. xix–xx). Jung not only invoked Breuer's and Freud's (1893) "On the Psychical Mechanisms of Hysterical Phenomena," but also his two papers on defense neuro-psychoses (published in the *Neurologisches Centralblatt*, in 1894 and 1896, respectively). In the former, Freud showed that "a hallucinatory delirium originates from an unfulfilled wish, and that this delirium is a compensation for unsatisfied yearnings" (p. 28). In the latter, "the author of the first analysis of paranoia [i.e., Freud]" (p. 31) demonstrated the "transformation mechanism of hysteria" and that the essence of the defense in paranoia is "the repression of painful memories . . . [such] that the form of the symptoms is determined by the content of the repression" (p. 28). The repressed memories "determine the nature of the delusions and hallucinations as well as the whole general behavior" (p. 32).

Jung (1907) held that "the essential basis of our personalities is affectivity" (p. 36), that "the feeling tone of the whole mass of presentations" is the core of what he called "the emotionally accentuated complex" (p. 38). Thus "if the patient, as described by Schreber, perceives other persons in his environment as fleeting shadows [*flüchtig hingemacht*] of men, we can again understand that he is unable to react adequately to the stimuli of reality, that is, he reacts adequately but in his own way" (p. 73). On the purely phenomenological level, Schreber was also used by Jung as an example of "neologisms [that] originate from dreams and especially from hallucinations" (p. 75) and of "voices and delusions [that] degenerate. . . ." (footnote 41: Schreber describes very well how the contents of the auditory hallucinations become grammatically abbreviated" (p. 95). Jung did not offer a differential diagnosis of Schreber.[15] However, the inclusion of Schreber in his book implies a firm diagnosis of dementia praecox, or schizophrenia, and is thus a departure from the diagnosis of paranoia consistently made by Weber.

Schreber also became known to Jung's superior at Burghölzli, Paul Eugen Bleuler. By 1906 Bleuler had already published, one year before

Jung, an important endorsement of Freud, "Freudian Mechanisms in the Symptomatology of the Psychoses," citing his discussions with "colleague Jung."[16] Bleuler also stressed the importance of affectivity and was impressed with the importance of wish fulfillment as a reaction of defense to painful and frustrating reality, the distressed feelings being the stimulus for the transformation of both the reaction and the wish into symbolic thinking. In this conception, there was a transition from the dream to the hallucinations and delusions of the psychotic, since many delusions expressed secret compensatory wishes, especially in the face of frustration: "For in the delusion (*Delir*) and in the dream a person can never totally forget that his wishes are thwarted by obstacles. These, in turn, are symbolized as 'persecutions,' similar to the experience of the healthy to create Ormuzd and Ahriman, God and the Devil" (Bleuler, 1906, p. 323). Bleuler was also impressed that sexual feelings easily develop into anxiety, which can shade into psychopathology should the dream express repressed sexual wishes without disguise. It is clear that Bleuler and Jung saw eye to eye on a number of dynamic issues, especially the feeling-toned complex.

A number of references to Schreber were later made in Bleuler's 1911 *Dementia Praecox or the Group of Schizophrenias*.[17] Bleuler was impressed with a number of Schreber's clinical features, which he classed as schizophrenic, as had already been done by Jung. He noted Schreber's "special language," reflecting his ambivalence. He also addressed Schreber's altered sense of reality, such as his describing the attendants as "miracled up, changeable individuals" (Bleuler's 1911, p. 66, referring to "*flüchtig hingemacht*"), and saw Schreber as given to "negative hallucinations." On the other hand, Bleuler thought Schreber was like many paranoids who "think incorrectly only when their complexes are involved. Schreber could criticize the expert opinions on his tutelage most pertinently at the very time when he was defending his most preposterous delusions" (p. 77). Lastly, Bleuler mentions Schreber's surrender of his masculinity to become a woman. Here, he preceded Macalpine and Hunter by positing that Schreber's wish to become a woman impregnated by God was related to his desire for children. Bleuler also posited a connection between a so-called paranoid sexual transformation (*metamorphosis sexualis paranoica*) and impotence.[18] Bleuler did not, however, offer a differential diagnosis of Schreber's illness.

FREUD ON SCHREBER

Schreber came to the attention of Freud through Jung. During 1910 Jung discussed the *Memoirs* with Freud and from that point on "Schreberisms" frequently pepper their correspondence. In the summer of 1910 Freud was already writing his essay on Schreber while traveling in southern Italy in the company of Ferenczi,[19] who was described as follows: "My travelling companion is a dear fellow, . . . his attitude toward me is infantile. He never stops admiring me . . . He has been too passive and receptive . . . like a woman, and I really haven't got enough homosexuality in me to accept him as one" (McGuire, 1974, p. 212). Freud was highly animated while the work was in progress, as evident in such utterances as "our dear and ingenuous friend Schreber," "our Paul Daniel," "news of our Paul Daniel," and "I am all Schreber" (McGuire, 1974, pp. 368, 369, 377).

The most famous patient in psychiatry and psychoanalysis, in Macalpine and Hunter's characterization, was never seen by Freud in person. This fact needs emphasizing, because many readers fall into the natural assumption that since Freud wrote about Schreber, he must have seen him.[20] He never did, but he was tempted to. On October 1, 1910 he wrote to Jung, "Since the man is still alive, I was thinking of asking him for certain information (e.g., when he got married) and for permission to work on his story. But perhaps that would be risky. What do you think?" (McGuire, 1974, p. 358). What was the risk? We are not told. Be that as it may, one wonders how much Schreber, in the last year of his life, could have told Freud. The more amazing fact is that Freud did not contact either Flechsig or Weber, or say he intended to. He could have learned something from them, too, especially from Weber; for the unexpurgated prepublication copy of the *Memoirs*, which would have contained the cut third chapter Freud so desired to see, was part of the chart (Appendix), or in Weber's possession (*M*, p. 391).

Freud's analysis of Schreber—or, for that matter, anyone else's after Schreber's death—could not be a clinical analysis, employing the *clinical* psychoanalytic method, where a patient can confirm the analyst's interpretations. It was an exercise in *applied* psychoanalysis, of grafting preformed dynamic formulas onto a literary text. Therefore, the applied method was primarily a *hermeneutic* method of decoding universal symbols, or applying assumptions and generalizations derived from psychoanalytic theories. Freud had already employed the hermeneutic method in his analyses of Jensen's *Gradiva* (Freud, 1907a) and Leonardo da Vinci (Freud, 1910b). In the same spirit, the hermeneutic method was applied by Pfister (1910b), an early Swiss follower of Freud, in his analysis of Count Zinzendorf, a pietist active in the 18th century, in which the latter is repeatedly referred to as "the analysand." Of course, the count was an analysand in the Pickwickian, that is, metaphorical, sense only.

Even though he had a predominant interest in creative constructions, Freud was sensitive to historical facts. He claimed he made "use
of no material in this paper that is not derived from the actual text of the
Memoirs." In actuality, Freud did use a few biographical details, a
fraction of an unknown quantity, supplied to him by Dr. Stegmann
from Dresden. The details Freud requested were about both father and
son. Along with these details Stegmann,[21] a colleague of Weber's and
one well acquainted with the social and psychiatric scene in Dresden
and presumably Leipzig, also supplied Freud with the October 1908
issue of the *Freund der Schreber Vereine*, which included articles and
analyses of Moritz Schreber's ideas on education. He also learned from
Stegmann that Paul was 51 at the outbreak of the second illness. He did
not make use of his knowledge of Schreber's third episode of illness
(Strachey, *Standard Edition*, vol. 12, p. 6). The use of these additional
data by Freud marked the beginning, albeit rudimentary, of *historical*
Schreber studies. Based on these additional sources, Freud reached his
conclusions about the stature of Moritz Schreber and the possible effect
he could have had on his son's real and transference feelings.

Freud and the Descriptive

In life, as in science, description, diagnosis and dynamic formulation
are inextricably interwoven, even though they are separated for purposes of presentation and analysis. Thus, a descriptive approach is
necessarily the lowest level of interpretation of data by virtue of its
being selective. It already is a certain perspective on the story, a way of
imposing sense and order onto the blooming and buzzing confusion of
a text, especially one as complex as the *Memoirs.*

On the whole, Freud (1911a) was not very impressed with Schreber's own testimony about his life circumstances. For example, Freud
mentioned Schreber's wife only twice (pp. 13, 45) and his mother not
at all. In the first section of the essay "Case History," Freud selected
only a few facts as told by Schreber, using Weber's report as a source
for the history of the illness, and paid scant attention to the story
Schreber told in factual prose: the conditions of living at Sonnenstein,
the consequences of the involuntary hospitalization, and the factual
chronology of the illness. Freud took note that the "second illness set in
with a torturing bout of sleeplessness" (p. 13), without mentioning the
suicidal attempts. This onset followed a prodrome between "June
1893 . . . [and] October of the same year. . . . Between these two
dates . . . [he] dreamt two or three times that his old nervous disorder
had come back; and this made him . . . miserable. . . . Once, in the
early hours of the morning . . . the idea occurred to him 'that after all it

really must be very nice to be a woman submitting to the act of copulation' ([*M*, p.] 36). This idea was one which he would have rejected with the greatest indignation if he had been fully conscious" (p. 13).

Beyond that, Freud drew upon Weber's first report of 1899 as a source of the major events of the story of the illness and how Schreber "developed an ingenious delusional structure . . . while his personality had been reconstructed" (p. 14). Freud (1911a) quoted Weber (quoting Flechsig) about the initial "hypochondriacal ideas . . . and ideas of persecution . . . already finding their way into the clinical picture," and about Schreber's belief "that there were certain people by whom he thought he was being persecuted and injured," even though Weber only mentioned one persecutor, the " 'soul murderer' Flechsig" (p. 14).

But while Weber's interest was limited to

> the patient's *assumption of the role of Redeemer*, and his *transformation into a woman* . . . the nucleus of religious paranoia . . . [which] may appear to be true or the delusion in its final form, [Freud believed] a study of the *Denkwürdigkeiten* compels us to take a very different view of the matter. For we learn that the idea of being transformed into a woman (that is of being emasculated) was the primary delusion . . . the sexual delusion of persecution . . . later converted in the patient's mind into a religious delusion of grandeur [Freud, 1911a, p. 18].

Thus, early on Freud determined that, for Schreber, transformation into a woman equaled castration, and that castration played a causal role in everything that followed. However, a more careful study of the *Memoirs* shows that, at the level of description, the prodromal disturbing idea of feeling like a woman was *not* one of being emasculated or persecuted, and this is supported by two additional facts, unequivocally stated in the *Memoirs* and cited by Freud himself: the alleged emasculation was caused by Flechsig, and Flechsig was not in the picture yet; and Schreber's conviction of emasculation, as part of soul murder, did not take place until mid-March, thus well into the hospitalization. This contradicts Freud's premise (1911a) turned into conclusion, namely, that "the emasculation phantasy was of primary nature . . . [and that] it appeared during the incubation period of his illness, and before he had begun to feel the effects of overwork at Dresden" (p. 20).

After describing Schreber's many sexual emotions and "his conception of God, this mixture of reverence and rebelliousness" (p. 29), Freud concludes his "case history" with a description of Schreber's feminine transformation:

> If we now recall the dream during the incubation of his illness . . . it will become clear beyond a doubt that his delusion of being transformed into

a woman was nothing else than a realization of the content of that dream. At the time he had rebelled against the dream with masculine indignation . . . and looked upon it . . . as a disgrace with which he was threatened with hostile intention. But there came a time (it was in November of 1895) when he began to reconcile himself to the transformation and bring it into harmony with the higher purpose of God: "Since then, and with full consciousness of what I did, I have inscribed upon my banner the cultivation of femaleness" ([*M*, pp.] 177—178) [p. 33].

I agree that Schreber's cultivation of femaleness was a deep psychological issue, not, in spite of Freud's insistence, one of castration but of identification. It began in the incubation period and indeed found its fullest expression in the redeemer fantasy, but not, however, as a result of castration anxiety in the accepted Freudian sense. Besides, Freud himself was impressed that

> the idea of being transformed into a woman was the salient feature and the earliest germ of his delusional system. It also proved to be the one part of it that persisted after his cure, and the one part that was able to retain a place in his behaviour in real life after he had recovered . . . [e.g., as Schreber says,] "standing before the mirror or elsewhere, with the upper portion of my body bared, and wearing sundry feminine adornments . . ." ([*M*, p.] 429). . . . The Herr Senatspräsident confesses to this frivolity at a date (July, 1901) at which he was already in position to express very aptly the completeness of his recovery in the region of practical life . . . ([*M*, p.] 409). In contrast to the way in which he put his emasculation phantasy into action, the patient never took any steps towards inducing people to recognize his mission as Redeemer, beyond the publication of his *Denkwürdigkeiten* [p. 21].

Freud's clinical appraisal and tolerance are superior to Weber's. Indeed, as Freud notes, Schreber was able to keep his feminine pursuits well under control, proving by his conduct that he was not psychotically driven by his emotions. There is only one descriptive refinement missing: Freud does not consider cross-dressing to be nondelusional, or an activity separate from homosexuality and not caused by castration anxiety, and keeps equating it with the "emasculation phantasy," which has been begging the question all along. However, such a syndrome of feminine identification and cross dressing was already in place in a famous classic on disorders of sexuality, namely, *Psychopathia Sexualis*, which went through numerous editions since its appearance in 1886, by the Viennese professor of psychiatry, sexologist and forensic expert Richard von Krafft-Ebing (1840-1902).[22] The book was cited by Freud and may have been known to Schreber. Krafft-

Ebing described a syndrome of paranoid sexual transformation (*meta-morphosis sexualis paranoica*), classed as a disorder of acquired homosexuality and divided into four stages.[23] For us the relevant stage is the third, the nonpsychotic form of feminine identification. The patient described by Krafft-Ebing, born in 1844 and endowed with "a very active imagination," described himself as having felt as a girl growing up and as a woman in his adult years. He was a physician, remained married and fathered five sons, but often had feelings such as these: "I had felt exactly like a woman with libido. . . . on standing and walking, I felt *vulva* and *mammae* [- breasts]. . . . I feel like a woman in man's form; . . . the skin all over my body feels feminine; it receives all impressions, whether of touch, of warmth, or whether unfriendly, as feminine . . . " (Krafft-Ebing, 1939, pp. 312-318). The patient never succumbed to the temptation to submit to pederasty. At some stressful times he had auditory and visual hallucinations. He was summed up by Krafft-Ebing: "in character and in the sexual act , he felt as a female . . . he felt bodily like a woman . . . he experienced a complete transformation of his former masculine feeling, . . . At the same time, his "ego" [ego in the 1893 edition] was able to control these abnormal psycho-physical manifestations, and prevent descent to *paranoia*" (p. 324).

Freud's differentiation between the frivolity of Schreber's playing at being a woman rather than a dire delusion of being one, coupled with assessment of Schreber as having good overall ego functioning, parallels Krafft-Ebing's classification of the nonpsychotic form of feminine identification and suggests a familiarity with the latter's writing. This appraisal also softens the impact of Schreber's imperative wish to be turned into a woman and the mother of a new race to save mankind.

Freud and the Diagnostic

While in the main pursuing the interests of depth psychology, Freud returned briefly to issues of descriptive and diagnostic psychiatry. He had two diagnoses for Schreber, stated in the title of his essay: paranoia and in brackets dementia paranoides, Kraepelin's (1893, 1899) name for paranoid schizophrenia, thus also equating the two disorders. His diagnosis was thus shaped by Weber, Jung (and, by extension, Bleuler), and Kraepelin. For Weber paranoia meant a crystallized and entrenched chronic delusional system in the presence of a preserved cognitive ability and logical reasoning—the way Weber saw Schreber from early on and certainly toward the end of his stay at Sonnenstein. By that time Kraepelin's newly formed diagnostic consolidation of the various syndromes of schizophrenia under the umbrella term *dementia praecox* was already in place, yet Weber did not apply this to Schreber.

Clinically speaking, Schreber did not behave like a textbook case of either paranoia or schizophrenia. Paranoiac is indeed the most common label affixed to Paul Schreber, an undeserved stigma created initially by Weber's prejudice, while the fantasy content of the *Memoirs*, formerly called paranoia, is now invariably characterized as schizophrenic.

Freud equivocated with Weber's diagnosis of paranoia. Combining the hallucinations of the early phase and the delusions of the later phase into one syndrome and label, Freud amended paranoia to dementia paranoides. But since the picture was not unequivocally that of paranoid schizophrenia either, he invoked another diagnostic label, paraphrenia, also borrowed from Kraepelin, to indicate a syndrome that combined paranoia and schizophrenia. These distinctions between schizophrenia and paraphrenia have not stood the test of time.[24] At any rate, in private Freud was uncertain about dementia praecox. In a letter to Jung he reasoned thus: "I write paranoia and not Dem.[entia] pr.[aecox] because I regard the former a good clinical type and the latter a poor nosographical term" (McGuire, 1974, pp. 120-121). For Freud "clinical type" implied not only the syndrome but also the pivotal paranoid defense mechanism of projection, a new dynamic paradigm he had in place in 1896. Thus, Freud's excursus into nosology was more ritualistic than real: his main interests were dynamic, not diagnostic. Therefore, unlike Jung and Bleuler, he did not regard Schreber's paranoia-cum-schizophrenia as an organic, that is, brain, disorder but as a dynamic disorder. Because of the dynamic-psychological conception he and Jung shared initially, both repeatedly discussed in their letters the similarities and differences between hysteria, by then an established dynamic disorder, and paranoia.

Given such diagnostic leanings and his dynamic conceptions in that period, it is also not surprising that Freud was not impressed with the pervasive mood alterations in Schreber and consequently the possibility of a mood disorder. His awareness of depression as a primary affect of unpleasure and of melancholia as a syndrome were yet to come. Stekel and Abraham were the first to explore manic-depressive illness dynamically.[25] From our perspective it is important to see the phenomenological and characterological difference between schizophrenia and mood disorders without losing sight of the dynamic issues, such as loss and conflict, that may be present in both, for the understanding of Schreber.

An essential distinction to keep in mind is the classical, static, organic conception of mental disorder of German psychiatry in the second half of the 19th century as against Freud's dynamic conception which was influenced by, among others, the teachings of Kant while Freud was still in high school, of Brentano while a medical student, and of Meynert in Vienna and Charcot in Paris. In the German organicist view, mental disorders were static phenomena of heredity and brain lesions. According to Freud, mental disorders were an outcome of a dynamic interplay of forces.

Freud's dynamic view of psychosis led him to invoke his teacher Meynert's delineation of paranoia as an acute syndrome, Meynert's amentia (Freud, 1911a, p. 75). Freud had utilized it in his first paper on defense neuro-psychoses in 1894. The case Freud (1894) described as Meynert's amentia, or acute hallucinatory paranoia, seemed to resemble Schreber's acute hallucinatory phase.[26] In the acute state the patient had experienced hallucinations and delusions that were causally and dynamically a defense against loss, the awareness of painful reality, and a wishfulfillment. While Weber also described Schreber's hallucinatory insanity, the idea of understanding Schreber's psychosis dynamically never occurred to him. Meynert's amentia qualifies as a traumatic psychosis, that is, as an adaptive psychological reaction to a current stress.

Freud's conception was dynamic in recognizing three basic causes of symptoms: (1) the *general* dynamisms (mechanisms) of memory and dream, both with their latent (unconscious) and manifest (conscious) content of force and counterforce, as in psychological conflict, of trauma, defense against traumatic feelings and wish fulfillment; (2) the *special* dynamics based on a particular etiology, such as the sexual etiology of the neuroses; (3) the *specific* personal-historical motives of discrete mental content, intent, and action toward oneself or another person, in the past or in the present. These dynamic concepts of Freud were applied by him to every diagnostic type of mental illness.

In agreement with Dilthey, it can fairly be said that Freud's general and special dynamics serve the aims of explanation while the specific dynamics serve those of understanding, and both are much needed complementary approaches. It is also fair to say that the lion's share of Freud's dynamic readings of Schreber were of the general and the special variety, explaining the pathology rather than understanding the person.

Freud and the Dynamic

A common misconception about Freud is that his interest in paranoia and the elucidation of its dynamics stemmed from the Schreber case (e.g., Swales, 1982). The fact is that the general and special dynamics of paranoia were first described in 1896 in his second paper on neuropsychoses of defense, in a case report of an actual patient of Freud's, who, unlike Schreber, exhibited a classical form of paranoia. Paranoia was the third psychoneurosis, the newcomer beside the two established ones—hysteria (including anxiety hysteria, or phobia) and obsessional neurosis. The dynamics Freud described for this case became the first paradigm of paranoia.

The patient, Frau P, was a 32-year-old woman, depressed for a second time in her life following the birth of a child two years earlier. She was caught in a crossfire between her beloved brother, her husband, and her sister-in-law, who she felt slighted her. While undergoing the water cure in a spa, Frau P was assailed by visual hallucinations of naked women and had sensation in her lower abdomen and genitals, thus suggesting a homosexual preoccupation. This was followed by persecutory voices of scorn, threat, and reproach. By means of the cathartic method of recall Freud unraveled the hallucinations, both visual and auditory, and understood them as disguised (by means of "distortion through compromise") memories of the trauma of infantile seduction, namely, sex play between the patient and her brother. According to Freud, paranoia shared with hysteria the tendency to repression but was closer to obsessional neurosis in the greater use of distortion. Also, it used a new mechanism of defense, projection, while *"interpretative delusions* [led to an] *alteration of the ego"* (Freud, 1896, p. 185; emphasis Freud's). According to a footnote Freud added in 1922, the patient got worse under treatment and had to be admitted to an asylum in a condition of dementia praecox. She recovered, had another child, and was well for another 12 to 15 years, after which she fell ill again when her husband became unable to work and the family she disliked had to support them. She was readmitted to an institution and soon thereafter died of pneumonia. Freud's formulations were approvingly discussed by Jung (1907, pp. 29-31).

For Freud, the general idea that psychosis was a defense (thus a neuropsychosis of defense) against a traumatic experience was the dynamic underlying both forms of disorder, hallucinatory confusion, or Meynert's amentia (1894), and paranoia (1896), the former caused by an adult traumatic situation, the latter traced both to infantile seduction and to current conflicts. Being sensitive to trauma, the affected individual was, Freud believed, compelled to handle the resulting anxiety by means of a defense, hallucinatory confusion in the former, projection in the latter.

The heart and soul of the dynamics of projection as a defense is a disavowal of an unpleasant and alien complex of ideas and feelings and its subsequent externalization. This externalization/projection takes place in the mind only: it is therefore a hallucinating of voices, or a delusion of external influence. It is most important to see the phenom enological identity between projection, hallucination, and delusion. This projection/hallucination/delusion has only psychic reality, not material reality. It is a metaphorical externalization, and yet many, including Freud himself, have often slipped into the fallacy of concretizing the metaphor and speaking of literal (sensory) externalizations that have become literal, i.e., sensory, perceptions. But this is fundamental phenomenological confusion of the functions of perceiving and dreaming (Lothane, 1982a). For if people act *as if* they see or hear, that is, imagine they see or hear, then such "perceptions" are no more true perceptions than the "paralyses" of hysterics are true paralyses. Rather than asking the question, What kind of perceptions are these hallucinations and delusions?—which is really begging the question—we should be asking, Who is the hallucinator and what is he saying, and to whom, through his hallucinations?

Given the above dynamic approach to paranoia, the burning question is, What was the innovation in Freud's approach to paranoia in the Schreber case, or what did Freud add to the already enunciated general and special dynamics of paranoia of 1896?

In the sections "Attempts at Interpretation" and "The Mechanism of Paranoia" of his Schreber analysis Freud deemphasized the aforementioned general dynamics of paranoia and added a new slant to the special etiological role of sexuality, or the libido theory. The net effect was to emphasize infantile sexuality schemata and deemphasize trauma. In Frau P, behind the adult manifest homosexually toned hallucinations lay the latent memory of the traumatic sexual seduction in childhood, reactivated by current conflicts.[27] Guilt-laden self-reproaches were projected or portrayed as delusions of reference. In Schreber, the alleged repressed homosexual desire of the son for the father returned in the form of paranoid delusions of persecution; his desire for Flechsig as a transference from the father was transformed through the mechanism of projection into a delusion of sexual abuse. This new theory was, with few exceptions, applied to male patients. The welling up of such desire was conceived as an intrapsychic (Freud also called it "endopsychic") monadic process, not a dyadic process, that is, unrelated to any conduct on the part of another.

The process, as Freud depicted it, also entailed a phenomenological transvaluation blurring the boundaries between neurosis and perversion, between sexual fantasies and sexual acts. Heretofore, neuroses were defined as the negative of the perversions; that is, neuroses were the inhibited (thus, the covert), disguised, and distorted compromise derivatives of sexual impulses whereas perversions were overt expressions of sexual impulses. If this is given, then Schreber was not a pervert, since at no point, neither as healthy nor sick, was Schreber overtly homosexual. His only perversion was to dress in female attire, that is, to cross-dress in private and to daydream of turning into a woman. Yet, in spite of all the reasons offered, Freud still equivocated about Schreber being a homosexual (p. 43).

Now a new definition was given for homosexuality: having homosexual fantasies. Such fantasies meant a return to an earlier developmental phase, or fixation point, as a result of the undoing of social sublimations and the escape of the component sexual instincts from genital primacy, with regression to infantile polymorphously perverse forms of sexuality. This substitution of fantasy for behavior is reminiscent of the New Testament view of adultery. We see such a confusion lately in this startling statement by Gay (1988): "Like Leonardo, Schreber was a homosexual" (p. 277). Such an assessment is at best a guess, at worst an aspersion.

At the heart of the question is the very definition of homosexuality: overt homosexuality in the flesh versus fantasy only. In general, psychoanalysts are prone to infer or to impute homosexuality based on fantasies alone. An early sexologist and an authority for Freud, Paul Näcke (1911)[28] made a clinical distinction between the true homosexual and the pseudohomosexual: the former has sexual feelings toward persons of the same gender and acts on them, the latter has heterosexual emotions and desires and engages in occasional homosexual acts. Näcke further argued, on clinical grounds, that psychoses are no more frequent among homosexuals than heterosexuals. He viewed inversion neither as illness nor as a degeneration but as a developmental variant and believed homosexual acts observed in asylums were mostly pseudohomosexual ones. The observations of Näcke among hospitalized patients were confirmed in an American study (Klein and Horwitz, 1949). In that study homosexual content was absent in many paranoid cases.

The linkage of paranoia and latent homosexuality has since been challenged as a universally valid special causal theory. Nor was Schreber's paranoia, as foreshadowed by Freud, totally independent of factors such as trauma and interpersonal influences. But then, Freud never really rejected the idea of trauma and external influence.[29] Before long, Freud (1914b) returned, in his great paper on narcissism, to an important feature of his general dynamics—the kernel of historical truth in paranoia, that is, the connection between a stimulus in external reality and its return as a paranoid symptom—reaffirming the role of actual experience and its persistence in memory as an internalization.[30]

Interpreting: Explaining Versus Understanding, Hermeneutics Versus History

Freud's basic project at the time of his writing about Schreber was to establish psychoanalysis as a scientific, dynamic explanatory psychology of the neuroses. When he sought, as a scientist, explanations in the process of "tracing back . . . the nucleus of the delusional structure with some degree of certainty to familiar human motives," he found lurking behind the symptoms "the monotony of the solutions provided by psycho-analysis" (Freud, 1911a, p. 54). Thus, in Schreber's case he found castration anxiety, in the unmanning fantasy and in the erotic desires for Flechsig, the perpetrator of soul murder. Where he tried to use his explanatory psychology to understand, Freud was no longer a historian reading from the text but a hermeneutist reading into it. For science subsumes and generalizes, going from the general to the particular. History individuates: it goes from particular to particular.

For a historical analysis, there was a need for access to a lot more information about Schreber's life circumstances. Freud (1911a) was well aware that he lacked the details of Schreber's life that would have illuminated the source of the delusions:

> Anyone who was more daring than I am in making interpretations, or who was in touch with Schreber's family and consequently better acquainted with the society in which he moved and the small events of his life, would find it an easy matter to trace back innumerable details of his delusions to their sources and so discover their meaning, and this in spite of the censorship to which the *Denkwürdigkeiten* have been subjected. But as it is, we must necessarily content ourselves with this shadowy sketch of the infantile material which was used by the paranoic disorder in portraying the current conflict [p. 57].

We should note Freud's three assumptions: that infantile material is already present in a sketchy form in the content of the neurosis, that there also is a current conflict, and that the current conflict can be explained by the infantile material. Here Freud is pushing the genetic point of view to its very limit by circular reasoning, bypassing any idea of explaining the *current conflict* in terms of *current material*. This strategy is justified by one pivotal assumption: both the adult and the childhood material concern one overriding dynamic factor— erotization, or sexualization, and the castration threat.[31]

Sexualization, Latent Homosexuality, and Paranoia

Freud treated Schreber's statements as pathological material, as manifest content, as a disguise behind which lay hidden the truer fact: Schreber's tendency to sexualization and his homosexual wishes, to which all other emotions became subordinated. With even greater certainty, the manifest sexual fantasies were read as homosexuality. Undoubtedly, some of Schreber's manifest sexual themes are about sexuality, while other themes, such as being homosexually abused, may have had underlying motives other than sexual, let alone homosexual.

For instance, Schreber's lecture on anatomy and psychology in the first chapter of the *Memoirs* struck Freud as meaning that "Schreber's 'nerves' are derived from the sphere of ideas derived from sexuality." However, as applied to Schreber's idea that "the male semen contains the nerve of the father" (Freud, 1911a, p. 22), Freud's imputation of a sexual meaning is spurious, for in Schreber's terminology nerve meant soul, thus suggesting qualities inherited or acquired from father. The remainder of Schreber's didactic exposition was, for Freud, rather "an astonishing mixture of the commonplace and the clever, of what was borrowed and what was original" (p. 21): it came from Moritz Schreber's chapters on anatomy and physiology. It was also rather reminiscent of Freud's own disquisitions in his *Project for a Scientific Psychology*.[32]

Freud (1911a) sexualizes the cause of the second illness:

> During the incubation period of his illness (that is, between June, 1893, when he was appointed to his new post, and the following October, when he took up his duties), he repeatedly dreamt [of] . . . a woman submitting to the act of copulation . . . we . . . infer that at the same time . . . [of] his recollection of his illness, *a recollection of his doctor was also aroused in his mind* and that the feminine attitude which he assumed in the fantasy was from the first directed towards the doctor or it may be that the dream of his illness having returned simply expressed some such longing as "I wish I could see Flechsig again." . . . Perhaps . . . a feeling of affectionate dependence upon his doctor, *which had now, for some unknown reason, become intensified to the pitch of an erotic desire*. . . . the feminine phantasy carried everything before it . . . [we] divine the fact that the patient was in fear of sexual abuse at the hands of his doctor himself. *The exciting cause of his illness, then, was an outburst of homosexual libido*; the object of this libido was probably from the very first his doctor, Flechsig; and his struggles against the libidinal impulse produced the conflict which gave rise to the symptoms [pp. 42-43].

Freud arbitrarily reinterprets the dependent longing for Flechsig as an erotic desire for him, a revival of a late-life transference. Given this perspective, Freud invokes only to dismiss Schreber's real worry, the menacing premonition that his depressive illness had returned.

On the other hand, the idea of changing places with the opposite sex, out of curiosity, is a universal fantasy of mankind, sane or insane; the celebrated Theban prophet Tiresias was in his young age changed by the gods into a woman and lived in marriage. He was later questioned by Zeus and Hera as to who received greater pleasure in intercourse. Speaking from personal experience, Tiresias agreed with Zeus that the pleasure of the woman was greater than that of the man. This drew the wrath of Hera, who was convinced that the male was superior to the woman and caused Tiresias to go blind. To compensate him, Zeus bestowed on him the gift of prophecy.

This tendentious sexualization is also in evidence in Freud's interpretation of Schreber's "decline in my nervous state about the 15th of February of 1894 . . . when my wife . . . undertook a four-day journey to her father in Berlin. . . . Decisive for my mental collapse was one particular night; during that night I had quite an unusual number of pollutions (perhaps a dozen)" (M, p. 44).

> It is easy to understand that the mere presence of his wife must have acted as a protection against the attractive power of the men about him; and if we are prepared to admit that an emission cannot occur in an adult without some mental concomitant, we should be able to supplement the patient's emissions that night by assuming that they were accompanied by homosexual phantasies which remained unconscious [Freud, 1911a, p. 45].

In Freud's analysis of Schreber no thought is given to the role of the wife in Schreber's heterosexual conflicts in the past or in the present. Freud then goes back to discuss an earlier phase: "The question of why this outburst of homosexual libido overtook the patient *precisely at this period* (that is, between the dates of his appointment and his move to Dresden) cannot be answered in the absence of more precise knowledge of the story of his life" (pp. 45–46; emphasis added). But this is precisely the point: without knowing more details about the story of his life we cannot even begin to claim that there was an outburst of homosexual libido, whether before or after February 15th.

Having laid out the aforementioned arguments, it now becomes a blinding glimpse of the obvious for Freud to attribute a sexual character to the pivotal persecutory delusion—soul murder at the hands of Flechsig—extensively quoted by Freud from the *Memoirs* (in Strachey's translation):

> "In this way a conspiracy against me was brought to a head (in about March or April, 1894). . . . my body . . . was to be transformed into a female body and as such surrendered to the person in question [here Freud's footnote: "the person in question . . . was none other than Flechsig"] with a view to sexual abuse, and was then simply to be 'left on one side' ([M, p.] 56)" [p. 19].

Freud interprets that here Schreber is speaking of a fantasy of being castrated and then sexually abused. The sexual abuse is read as a projected sexual wish. He disregards Schreber's dating of the conspiracy and his differentiating psychological and political soul murder from carnal soul murder. He also discounts Schreber's idea of a transformation of his body into a female body, rather than a castration or mutilation. In fact, Schreber describes such a transformation as a reversal of the normal developmental stages of fetal life, that is, a biological regression[33] to a previous stage of female sexual organs, as described in biology textbooks (*M*, p. 53). Furthermore, these facts point to the biological basis of bisexuality not as homosexuality, but as hermaphroditism, the innate presence of both male and female elements in the organism. In translating soul murder as castration Freud employed a psychoanalytic cliché, a universal hermeneutic formula. However, he did not specify who was the source of castration threats to young Schreber. Furthermore, the German *Entmannung*, much like *emasculation*, has the added metaphorical meaning of loss of virile power and pride. Thus, being transformed into a woman also carries the implication of being powerless and helpless and open to abuse by someone more powerful. The converse is expressed in the German word *Ermannung*: regaining strength, self-control, and lifting the mood, as we read in his father's story, "The Confessions of a Former Melancholic" in chapter 3.

Sexualization, Paranoia and the Psychoanalytic Pioneers

Freud was not the first to apply the libido theory to the psychoses: he was preceded in this by Abraham (1908), and Freud gallantly acknowledged his debt to him:

> A paper that I have just finished deals with Schreber's book and uses him as a point of departure to try and solve the riddle of paranoia. As you can imagine, I followed the path shown by your paper on the psychosexual differences between hysteria and dementia praecox [Abraham, 1908]. When I worked on these ideas in Palermo [travelling in the company of Ferenczi] I particularly liked the proposition that megalomania was the sexual over-estimation of the ego. . . . I have of course to plagiarise you very extensively in this paper [Abraham & Freud, 1965, p. 97].

Abraham's inspiration was Freud's *Three Essays on the Theory of Sexuality* (Freud, 1905), but the aforementioned paper was about neither paranoia nor homosexual conflicts but about deeply regressed schizophrenic patients who turn their libido away from the world and sink to the level of autoerotism. From Abraham's paper Freud took

only the part about the differences between the total detachment of
libido from the love object in schizophrenia as against the partial
detachment in paranoia, in the latter due to conflicts regarding homosexual desire. For the rest, Freud propounded quite a novel revision of
the developmental line from narcissism to both heterosexuality and
homosexuality, as compared to the formulations in the *Three Essays* and
in his Leonardo analysis (Freud, 1910b). Heretofore a man's (and
woman's, too) first real love object was the mother and she played a
determining role in the development of male homosexuality; the new
developmental line did not include the mother at all and stressed
narcissism in its original definition of falling in love with one's own
body and genitals.[34]

There was another source of inspiration for the paranoia-
as-homosexuality conception. As averred by Freud: "I can nevertheless call a friend and a fellow-specialist to witness that I had developed
my theory of paranoia before I became acquainted with the contents of
the Schreber book" (Freud, 1911a, p. 79). The fellow-specialist was
Ferenczi, as attested by A. A. Brill (1944). Ferenczi (1911) confirmed
this himself:

> In the summer of 1908 I had the opportunity of opening up the problem
> of paranoia in the course of conversation [in the original: "in lengthy
> conversations"] with Professor Freud, and we arrived at certain
> tentative ideas, which were for the main part developed by Professor
> Freud. . . . We assumed . . . that the paranoiac mechanism stands be-
> tween the opposite mechanisms of neurosis and dementia praecox
> [p. 131].

Ferenczi, on his own, came to this stark conclusion: "in the pathogenesis of paranoia, homosexuality plays not a chance part, but the most
important part, and that paranoia is perhaps nothing else at all than
disguised homosexuality" (p. 135).

However, scientific formulations about paranoia aside, latent homosexuality played a role in Freud and in the relations among the
pioneers themselves: it was both an overt and a covert current in the
early days of the history of the psychoanalytic movement, when it was
an exclusively male club and a mutual admiration—and interpretation—society. The earliest personal linkage between paranoia and
homosexuality was made by Freud himself in relation to Fliess. In the
letter to Ferenczi of October 6, 1910, after their trip to Italy, Freud
says: "Since Fliess' case, with the overcoming of which you recently
saw me occupied . . . [a] part of homosexual cathexis has been withdrawn and made use of to enlarge my own ego. I have succeeded where

the paranoiac fails" (Freud, 1910c).[35] In addition, homosexual concerns repeatedly came up as countertransference in the psychotherapy of male patients.[36] Thus, Freud's attribution of homosexuality to Schreber is, among other motives, a projection onto Schreber of his own sexual conflicts and emotions.

Freud's Own Revision of the Sexual Concept

Nowhere is the libido dogma of Freud more evident than in his interpretation of Schreber's depressively toned "idea of the end of the world" (*M*, pp. 65, 70, 73, 90), which Freud characterized as a delusion (1911a, pp. 68—69). Again, Freud puts a sexualized interpretation on this fantasy. True to his a priori assumption that "in the severe psychosis . . . the feminine fantasy carried everything before it" (p. 42), he concludes that "the end of the world was the consequence of the conflict which had broken out between him and Flechsig, . . . [which is the same as] between him and God" (p. 69).[37]

But to compound the issue, Freud also argues that "the patient has withdrawn from the people in his environment and from the external world generally the libidinal cathexis which he has hitherto directed on them. . . . The end of the world is the projection of this internal catastrophe; his subjective world has come to an end since his withdrawal of *his love from it*" (p. 70; emphasis added). And Freud notes later on that "it is certain that in normal mental life (and not only in periods of mourning) we are constantly detaching our libido in this way from people or from other objects without falling ill" (p. 72), an observation that anticipates what he would soon have to say about the dynamics of mourning and melancholia engendered by personal loss.

One wonders whether in this context love for Freud is broader than libidinal, or sexual, cathexis. Does libidinal here mean interest in sex, love, or life? To confuse us even more, Freud adds to his understanding of Schreber the following footnote: "He has perhaps withdrawn from [the world] not only his libidinal cathexis, but his interest in general— that is, the cathexes that proceed from his ego as well" (p. 70).

Thus it is on the very pages of the Schreber case, as already noted by Strachey, that a major theoretical revision is taking shape: the revolution called ego psychology is blowing in the wind. It was Freud himself who showed the first cracks in the edifice of the libido theory. Small wonder Jung pounced to use the Schreber analysis to dynamite the libido theory. In December 1911, Jung wrote to Freud: "As for the libido problem, I must confess that your remarks in the Schreber analysis . . . have set up booming reverberations, . . . The loss of reality function in D[ementia] pr[aecox] cannot be reduced to repression of libido (defined as sexual hunger)" (McGuire, 1974, p. 287). Freud replied gallantly: "I am all in favor of your attacking the libido question[38] and I myself am expecting much light from your efforts" (McGuire, 1974, p. 472).[39] A year later, after further developments, Jung wrote Freud his "brazen" letter (p. 487ff.), in which he attacks Freud's character and ethics. By April of 1914 it was all over between them.

Return to the Dream Model: Hallucinations as Cause and Cure of Illness

For Weber and for many German psychiatrists hallucinations and delusions were the bedrock—and the scandal—of madness. Instead of romanticizing these fantastic creations of the mind, Weber demonized them under the pseudoscientific cloak of brain and sensory organ pathology. This is where Freud made an ethical and clinical departure. As with dreams, he restored to hallucinations the dignity of a personal redeeming epiphany. This would have been inconceivable for a Weber or a Flechsig.

Freud qualified hallucinations and delusions as fantasies and ideas, thus clearly placing them in the realm of thinking, not perception, and characterized them as pathogenic and nonpathogenic. He departed from the common conception of hallucinations on two essential points, both pregnant in consequences. One was to compare hallucinations to dream psychology: "it is legitimate to judge paranoia on the model of a far more familiar mental phenomenon, the dream." Thus one was justified in speaking of the "intense work of delusion formation [*Wahnbildungsarbeit*]" (Freud, 1911a, p. 38). Since everybody dreams, this conception also approximates paranoia to the spectrum of psychopathology of everyday life. If Freud stayed true to the dream model, he might have said that the projection of internal perceptions into external ones is also a dream phenomenon: it is as if they were external perceptions, without really being so. The connection between dream psychology, hallucinations, and delusions had already been adumbrated in *Delusions and Dreams in Jensen's Gradiva* (Freud, 1907).

The other essential point about hallucinations suggested by Freud is even more revolutionary: far from being a cause of madness, hallucinations and delusions are a cure of madness:

> The end of the world is a projection of this internal catastrophe: his [i.e., the paranoiac's] subjective world has come to an end since his withdrawal of his love from it. And the paranoic builds it again, not more splendid, it is true, but at least so that he can once more live in it. He

builds it up by the work of his delusions. *The delusional formation, which we take to be the pathological product, is in reality an attempt at recovery, a process of reconstruction* [pp. 70-71 and Strachey's footnote 1 on p. 71; emphasis Freud's].

Schreber would have agreed with this paraphrase of his own views.

Paranoia and Rage

In Freud's now famous syllogisms of paranoia that he developed in the third section of his essay, rage is briefly mentioned in connection with love turning into hate. Freud, however, does not dwell on the importance of rage and hatred in Schreber, even though in that same letter to Ferenczi of October 6, 1910, he discussed a source for some of Schreber's anger, also for the particular symptom of bellowing, in Schreber's relation to his physician father:

> What would you say to Doctor S[chreber] senior performing 'miracles' as a physician? But who was otherwise a despot in his household who 'bellowed' [i.e., yelled and scolded] at his son and understood him as little as the 'lower God' understood our paranoiac.

However, Freud does not dwell on the importance of rage and hatred. But he also wrote to Jung later that same month: "in other words, his father bellowed, too" (McGuire, 1974, p. 369).

Brüllen, inarticulate bellowing and roaring, was a prominent piece of behavior during Schreber's hospitalization. At the nonverbal, instinctive emotional level, these are cries of pain and rage. It was impotent rage. One can assume that the rage was directed internally against himself—surely Schreber knew that he was partially to blame for his fate—as well as against others for failing to rescue him. He was to blame but others got him into the mess, too. It is this rage and its reasons, not sex, that Schreber hid from himself and others by qualifying it as a miracle, the bellowing miracle. Freud did the same: he hinted at rage but otherwise said as little about it as Schreber himself.

Freud's public silence is all the more remarkable when we consider that not only did he acknowledge rage in private, personally, but that rage was brought to his attention as a clinical issue by at least three authors: Adler (1908), Maeder (1910), and Pfister (1910a). By 1911, Freud was already witnessing the first secessions from the psychoanalytic movement, those of Stekel and Adler, the latter dismissed as a paranoid in a letter to Jung (McGuire, 1974, p. 373). Freud never lost his respect for Pfister. As for Maeder, he simply chose to ignore his important paper. It is also noteworthy that in print he stated "The present paper I regret to say was completed before I had the opportunity of reading Maeder's work" (1911a, p. 59), whereas in a letter to Ferenczi on October 10, 1910, he admitted that he had read Maeder's paper. He refers to Maeder again on p. 65 and says nothing about him in the postscript published in 1912. Freud's writing on Schreber was completed in December 1910, which followed the publication of Maeder's paper in August 1910 and Freud's receipt of a copy of the *Jahrbuch* in August of 1910, in which Maeder's paper appears back to back with a paper of Freud's. Let the reader judge.

Maeder's was a rich clinical analysis of two patients with delusions of persecution and grandeur. In analyzing their paranoid ideas he took into account the role of repressed and projected homosexuality but also considered other dynamic factors: impotence, contemporary conflicts (*"Jetzheit"*) and their relation to past events (*"Vergangenheit"*) and conflicts in childhood, identification, inferiority, and conflicts between family members, symbolized in both patients as a conflict between God and Satan. As an explanation for delusions of grandeur he posited wish fulfillment in fantasy.

Like Bleuler, Maeder (1910) stressed the reaction to frustration and obstacles to one's wishes. "The *drive* to action . . . is inhibited by an outside *obstacle*. In the ego . . . this is transformed into a *hostile power*" (p. 235; Maeder's emphasis). As a result, persons who disappoint are hated as persecutors and the frustrating person is seen as harboring hostile attitudes. Again, Freud was aware of the importance of frustrating reality in his Schreber essay and took it up again in "Types of Onset of Neurosis" (Freud, 1912b; published in the same year as the postscript to Schreber). He discussed frustration at some length but still did not discuss it in connection with rage.

Other Views of Schreber by Freud

Freud never formally revised his ideas about Schreber. The only other place where Freud (1923) again invoked the dynamics of the boy's castration fears and his feminine attitude toward the father was in "A Seventeenth Century Demonological Neurosis," an essay in which the victim, the painter Christoph Haizmann, depicted the male devil as endowed with large female breasts. Using this image as proof of the "projection of the subject's femininity onto the father substitute," Freud proceeded to draw an analogy to a feminine attitude in Schreber, whose "God—who, incidentally, exhibited distinct traits of his father, the worthy physician, Dr. Schreber—had decided to emasculate him, to use him as a woman, and to beget from him 'a new race of men born from the Spirit of Schreber.' In his revolt against this intention of

God's . . . he fell ill with symptoms of paranoia, which, however, underwent a process of involution in the course of years, leaving only a small residue behind" (Freud, 1923, pp. 90-91; a picture of Haizmann's devil precedes p. 69). Freud did not state what that small residue was and where he got the information.

The latter essay gives evidence of a subtle shift in Freud's thinking. For there the transformation of male into female, which in Schreber's case was seen only as a derivative of repressed homosexual desire, now acquires independent status and rises to a co-equal role in the etiology of the paranoid state. Behind the feminine attitude toward the father, there lurks in Freud's revised formulation an even more telling identification with the mother, expressed by the painter Haizmann by putting huge breasts on the male devil and the dream of impregnation and birth. In the same essay Freud restated his opinion about Schreber's recovery:

> Senatspräsident Schreber found his way to recovery when he decided to . . . accommodate himself to the feminine role cast for him by God. After this he became lucid and calm, was able to put through his own discharge from the asylum and lead a normal life—with one exception that he devoted some hours every day to the cultivation of femaleness, of whose gradual advance towards the goal determined by God he remained convinced [p. 92].

Another change occurred in Freud's views on psychosis. After having fully developed the ego psychology, foreshadowed in the Schreber analysis, he bowed to Jung's timely protest of the narrowness of the libido theory and revised his ideas. "In regard to the genesis of delusions, a fair number of analyses have taught us that the delusion is found applied like a patch over the place where originally a rent has appeared in the ego's relation to the external world" (Freud, 1924, p. 151).

THE LITERATURE ON SCHREBER AFTER FREUD

Almost all the psychiatric literature on Schreber after Freud has been the work of psychoanalysts. The few psychiatrists to refer to the case of Schreber that I could find were Bjerre (1911), Beyer (1912), Bleuler (1912), Jaspers (1913), Kraepelin (1913), Schultz-Henke (1952), and Ahlenstiel and Meyer (1967). Schreber was either invoked as a paradigm in discussions of paranoia and schizophrenia or discussed as his own case. Bjerre, Bleuler, and Schultz-Henke, influenced by Freud, were the only ones to be psychodynamically oriented.

In his *Reform,* Beyer (1912) noted that Schreber's publisher Mutze was oriented toward both theosophy and antipsychiatry (he published, among others, Rudolf Goetze, 1896). This dual appeal of Schreber for Mutze was important. However, Schreber is tarred with the same brush as one Friedrich Krauss, an author who described his psychotic experiences in two lengthy volumes.[40] Beyer's bias shows in his critical attitude toward Goetze, who offered a thoughtful critique of the psychiatric and forensic problems of his day.

As a defender of psychiatry against its detractors, Beyer adduced a series of cases in which all the alleged victims of psychiatrists were indeed mentally sick, justifying their confinement. In *Reform* Schreber is listed as case #25 in chapter 3 ("Some Cases of Alleged 'Unlawful Confinement in an Asylum'"), in the part entitled "The Origins of the Antipsychiatry Movement."

Beyer also praised the *Memoirs* as a "highly interesting book deserving to be read" even by psychiatrists. "One can notice throughout the book that the author is an uncommonly intelligent man of a decent character throughout. It emerges from the entire writing that Schreber believes himself to be a kind of messiah" (*Reform*, p. 313). Beyer reproduced lengthy excerpts from the book to show that Schreber was patently crazy. At the end of his account Beyer noted that Schreber left Sonnenstein on December 20, 1902; "It seems that he then lived for a number of years in Dresden, appearing outwardly normal. On 27 November, 1907, he had to be admitted to the psychiatric hospital in Dösen. I have no details about his stay in that hospital" (p. 321). Beyer doesn't tell us how he got this information, which for us surfaced in 1955 with the publication of Schreber's hospital chart by Baumeyer (1956). The only other published statement about Schreber at that time was from Weber (1905b), who said, "I have no knowledge of the present whereabouts of Mr. N [i.e., Schreber], who has in the meantime left the third psychiatric facility [i.e., Sonnenstein]: it appears that his conduct has shown considerable disturbances" (p. 405). Therefore, Beyer's qualifies as the first correct clinical follow up of the Schreber case. Beyer had nothing to say about Schreber's legal battle and its implications for psychiatry.

Three issues important to the Schreber case have continued to reappear from Bjerre (1911) down to our times: separating the paranoid syndromes from schizophrenia instead of keeping them together in one basket; the differential diagnosis between schizophrenia and affective disorder; and the general and the special dynamics of paranoia. Bjerre's (1911) forgotten paper is unique in that he offered a description of a woman with persecutory paranoia of ten years' duration and her successful psychotherapy. Freud offered an explanation of Schreber's dynamics, but no treatment plan other than to suggest that

Schreber was a case of self-cure. Bjerre argued that paranoia was caused by the emotions and passions of the person and, contrary to Freud's formulation, that repressed homosexuality played no role in his case, for which the editor (i.e., Jung), chided him in a footnote (p. 840). Freud first found the paper "very interesting, though not quite clear" (McGuire, 1974, p. 434) and later qualified it as "Bjerre's piece of confusion . . . it is not very pleasant to have to publish such muddles" (pp. 484-485).

The first American psychoanalyst to endorse Freud's view of Schreber was A. A. Brill, the first translator of Freud and founder of the New York Psychoanalytic Society in 1911. Brill was at the Third International Psychoanalytic Congress in Weimar and heard Freud lecture on Schreber, on September 21, 1911. "We should say," Brill quotes Freud as saying, "that the paranoic character lies in the fact that as a defense against a homosexual wish fantasy, the patient reacts precisely with a delusion of persecution of this kind" (Brill, 1944, p. 104). Note the shift from paranoid psychosis to paranoid character. Brill wrote his own paper on paranoia and also noted Bleuler's (1912) lengthy review of Freud's essay on Schreber and saw the review as entirely positive.

Actually, while praising Freud's essay on Schreber, Bleuler (1912) had some fundamental reservations. Bleuler assessed the first episode of illness as a mild schizophrenic episode and the second as an acute protracted episode of catatonia that developed into a chronic paranoid schizophrenic psychosis, but not paranoia in Kraepelin's sense. In this, then, Bleuler also rejected Weber's diagnosis. He was impressed with the richness of Freud's analysis but could not say that it was a "necessary corollary to the remainder of Freud's psychopathology"; he believed it required much further study. He also questioned the causal role of the homosexual conflict, since he did not observe it in many of his own cases. Thus he "was not sure that the defense against homosexuality caused the disease in Schreber, even as it was prominent in the symptomatology." Bleuler restated his objection in his 1913 lecture; it is time, he reaffirmed, that there was only one disease—schizophrenia, an organic toxic disease of the brain—in which dynamic factors play an important role.[41]

Another early American reaction to the *Memoirs* was the review by van Teslaar (1912). He was negative toward Schreber ("he pleaded his cause with all the cunning and the tact which is characteristic of many paranoiacs"; p. 116) and, like Brill, endorsed all of Freud's dynamic views without reservation. He used the term *obsession* as well as *delusion* to refer to Schreber's ideas about becoming a mother of a new race and a world savior, and endorsed their harmless nature.

Adolf Meyer (1913) cited Freud's Schreber analysis approvingly but he was just as, if not more, impressed, with Freud's 1896 analysis of Frau P and with Bjerre's (1911) analysis of the woman with paranoia, in whom homosexual factors did not seem to play a role. A follower of Bleuler and Forel, Meyer, together with his pupils, played an important role in promoting dynamic psychiatry in the United States and shaped the now-superseded DSM-II, the American Psychiatric Association's diagnostic manual of mental disorders.

Of paramount importance is the far-flung heuristic influence of Freud's Schreber analysis and the effect it had on the spread of dynamic approaches to psychoses among American psychiatrists. This was not the case in Europe, where Kraepelin and Jaspers represented the organic approach and did not embrace Freud. The Europeans were interested in phenomenology and differential diagnosis; the Americans were more interested in dynamic formulations.

In a historical overview of paranoia, Smith Ely Jelliffe (1913) cited Freud's Schreber essay approvingly, as well as Freud's dynamic ideas on projection. He also praised Bjerre's 1911 analysis of the paranoid woman. Charles R. Payne (1913) reviewed Freud's interesting study of the "Memoirs of a Nervous Invalid" (p. 77) and all other writings at that time on the subject of paranoia in the first volume of a new periodical, the *Psychoanalytic Review*, "a journal devoted to the understanding of human conduct." Payne was the first to translate into English a number of quotations from the *Memoirs*. His endorsement of Freud's view of the homosexual genesis of paranoia was echoed in that same volume in a paper by Shockley (1913), including a brief discussion of Schreber: "Freud's views are the result of his accurately scientific analyses and observations, and have not only been supported, but plainly demonstrated in his work" (p. 432).

In that same first volume of the *Psychoanalytic Review* the leadoff original article was the first installment of Jung's 1913 monograph, *The Theory of Psychoanalysis*.[42] In it Jung continued both the private (the letters) and the public (Jung, 1912) challenge to Freud's libido theory and his formulations of Schreber. In the second section of his 1912 work, Jung had quoted an entire passage (pp. 73-75) from the section "The Mechanism of Paranoia" in Freud's (1911a) essay on Schreber, to argue that Freud had himself broadened the concept libido to mean interest in general, that is, the "whole adjustment to reality" (Jung, 1912, p. 174), a harbinger of ego psychology. Moreover, Jung had challenged Freud with Janet's concept of loss of reality function (*fonction du réel*)—which Freud had scoffed at early on only to embrace it in 1924—and had stated that "The Schreber Case was no pure paranoia in the modern sense of the word" (Jung, 1912, footnote 1, p. 174), but rather a case of dementia praecox, as "best shown by Freud's brilliant investigation of Schreber's fantasies" (Jung, 1912, p. 183).

Now, one year later, Jung drove his point home. In this "well-known case of dementia praecox—the so-called Schreber case," wrote Jung (1913), there is demonstrated

> the peculiar phenomenon consisting in a special tendency of these patients to construct an inner world of phantasy of their own, surrendering for this purpose their adaptation to reality. . . . This goes so far that the dream-world is for the patient more real than external reality. [In the] . . . patient Schreber . . . the "end of the world" [is his] loss of reality. . . . [T]he libido withdrew itself more and more from the external world, . . . its original pure sexual meaning being very rarely recalled. In general, the word "libido" is used practically in so harmless a sense that Claparède, in a conversation, once remarked that we could as well use the word "interest" [pp. 34-35].

Two years later Jung (1915) had this to say about Schreber:

> The peculiar delusions the patient had about his doctor, whom he identified with God, . . . Freud was able to reduce in a very ingenious manner to the infantile relationship between the patient and his father. Freud confines himself to pointing out the universally existent foundations out of which we may say every psychological product develops historically. The analytical-reductive method . . . seems to suit hysteria better than dementia praecox [pp. 179-180].

However, applying the synthetic approach of Herbert Silberer, Jung (1915) avers:

> To understand the psyche causally is to understand only one half of it. . . . The causal standpoint merely enquires how this psyche has become what it is, as we see it today. The constructive standpoint asks how, out of this present psyche, a bridge can be built into its own future. . . . Closer study of Schreber's or any similar case will show that these patients are consumed by a desire to create a new world-system, or what we call a *Weltanschauung*, often of the most bizarre kind. . . . This is a purely subjective adaptation at first, but it is a necessary transition stage on the way to adapting the personality to the world in general. . . [pp. 183, 189].

Jung was both right and self-promoting. The germ of constructive synthesis, not only of reductive analysis, was already in the third section of Freud's essay (1911a); Paul Schreber, as Freud showed, was building a bridge to the future and did reestablish, in some measure, an objective connection with life.

Karl Jaspers, whose *Allgemeine Psychopathologie*, written in 1913, has remained one of the most influential texts in psychiatry,[43] would have known of Jung's diagnosis of Schreber, since he quoted the Jung work of 1912 (Jaspers, 1913, p. 278). Jaspers used the *Memoirs* as a paradigmatic text for the study of the so-called primary phenomena of psychosis—hallucinations and delusions—which, he said, cannot be further reduced or analyzed and in the last analysis elude all explanation. Jaspers espoused a purely organic, not a dynamic, notion of *"Wahnarbeit,"* or delusion-work (Jaspers, 1913, p. 89).[44] He adhered to the same monadic-organic approach with regard to delusions of influence, the phenomena of thought-insertion and thought-withdrawal, which he saw as unrelated to real external influence, quoting as an example Schreber's bellowing-miracle (Jaspers, 1973, pp. 103-104). Kraepelin (1913), in a footnote concerning delusions of influence, made only a passing reference to Schreber citing him alongside Haslam (p. 682).

Although the issue of the differential diagnosis between schizophrenia and affective disorder was very much on the mind of Jaspers, Schreber remained for him a classical case of schizophrenia, with no thought about any other diagnosis. Some years earlier, Gruhle (1906) had challenged Paul Möbius's diagnosis of Robert Schumann as suffering from dementia praecox (Möbius, 1906) rather than the melancholic form of paresis, as had been held heretofore. Gruhle argued that artistic sensibility and creativity were more compatible with a diagnosis of manic depressive illness or, better yet, cyclothymic disorder, the latter having an affinity with the traits connected with the sensitive-feminine-artistic disposition. Gruhle (1906) concluded: "Your judgment in this case, as well as in Nietzsche's and others, must be seen as judgments of your personality but not as the definitive views of our science" (p. 810). Gruhle's diagnostic considerations apply to Schreber as well.

In the first two decades after Freud's essay of 1911, psychoanalysts kept on linking paranoia to homosexuality.[45] The first questions on the paradigm were raised by analysts who used Freudian dynamics of anality. It is surprising that Freud did not apply to Schreber some of his own ideas from the cases of Little Hans and the Rat Man.[46]

The next more decisive step was taken by Melanie Klein as early as 1932, while Freud was still writing.[47] Klein viewed paranoia as a basic defense dynamism of the infant in the first months of life, the gist of which is the splitting of the mother into good and bad (i.e., a frustrating mother felt as persecutor). In this reformulation of paranoia Klein also reaffirmed the importance of what Freud had called the "kernel of truth," or the reality residue, in the paranoid reaction.[48] Klein reversed the essential connection between paranoia and homosexuality, placed her concept of the "paranoid position" in the realm of unfulfilled oral desires toward the mother's and father's body and the resulting frustration and rage, deriving homosexuality itself from this paranoid reaction. In 1946 she discussed Schreber in connection with splitting in the ego, linking it with Freud's remarks about Schreber's "abnormal changes in the ego . . . the distinctive characteristic of psychoses" (Freud, 1911a, Riviere's translation):

> Schreber described vividly the splitting of the soul of his physician Flechsig (his loved and persecuting figure). . . . the division of the Flechsig soul into many souls was not only a splitting of the object but also a projection of Schreber's feeling that his ego was split. . . . The conclusion suggests itself that God and Flechsig also represented parts of Schreber's self. The conflict between Schreber and Flechsig, to which Freud attributed a vital role in the World destruction delusion, found expression in the raid by God on the Flechsig souls. In my view this raid represents the annihilation of one part of the self by other parts—which, as I contend, is a schizoid mechanism. . . . the raid which ended in the Flechsig souls being reduced to one or two, was part of the attempt towards recovery. For the raid was to undo, one may say heal, the split in the ego by annihilating the split-off parts of the ego. . . . This attempt . . . was effected by very destructive means used by the ego against itself and its introjected objects [Klein, 1946, pp. 109-110].

In the wake of Melanie Klein's work, the trend was to modify the connection between homosexuality and paranoia. It was continued by the Kleinian Herbert Rosenfeld (1949), who reviewed the preceding literature extensively and concluded homosexuality was a defense against the paranoid position. Hostility as a determinant in the dynamics of paranoia was discussed by Robert Knight (1940) and Karl Menninger (1942, p. 262).[49]

Prior to Niederland, the first step in the revival of interest in Schreber was taken by Maurits Katan in 1949. Katan's reading of the *Memoirs* was purely hermeneutic, relying on sexual formulas derived from Freud. Thus, "the murder of the soul means yielding to the temptation aroused by Flechsig to masturbate with thoughts about him. But he successfully warded off these 'attacks.' . . . A basic masturbatory fantasy is at work in all periods of his illness" (Katan, 1949, in Niederland, 1974, pp. 123-124). Later Katan (1953) correlated actual events in Schreber's life and his relationship with Flechsig. Katan offered two main dynamic formulations. The first, the wish to become a woman, was already operative prior to the first illness, "for the election had aroused in Schreber feelings of feminine nature towards his rival(s)" (p. 44). Schreber's accusations against Flechsig were "projections of an unconscious wish on Schreber's part to be impregnated by Dr. R. or by Professor Flechsig" (p. 45). Whereas the appointment to Senatspräsident placed him "among individuals 'wrecked by success,'" (p. 46), this also "caused his feminine feelings to be aroused . . . at the time of his starting his new position" (p. 47). Later Schreber "split the figure of Flechsig into two parts: one part which stimulated him homosexually, and another which caused his (Schreber's) ego to ward off this feminine urge. When the ego was no longer able to ward off orgastic manifestations, the psychosis began" (pp. 50-51). The second formulation (developed in the second part of Katan, 1959, not reprinted in Niederland, 1974) sought to explain adult soul murder and its roots in childhood. The childhood trauma, and the resulting childhood neurosis, the basis of the transference onto Flechsig, were caused by the older brother Gustav's sexual seduction of Paul, grafted onto his own conflicts about masturbation and a homosexual desire for his father. This seduction by the brother was covered up by mother and sisters, the first conspirators. The fingering of Flechsig as the originator of the adult soul murder was a replay of the childhood scene and was the result of Schreber's being sexually excited by Flechsig.[50] Later Katan would dismiss the importance of historical data adduced by Niederland from Moritz Schreber's writings and other sources (Katan, 1975).

A unique formulation of Schreber was offered by Schultz-Henke (1952), who was the only one to pay significant attention to the role of Schreber's wife. While endorsing in principle the notion of latent homosexuality, he stressed Schreber's adult sexual frustration, due to his wife's "severely disturbed" sexuality marked by her "refusal to gratify" her husband and her worship of Flechsig (p. 262). This caused Schreber to experience a heightened sexual tension, causing him to feel tempted by young girls (symbolized by the miracled birds) and to exhibit other symptoms.

Freud's first rudimentary steps in historical research on Schreber remained a dormant seed until 1951, with the publication of the first paper on Schreber by Niederland, who was the first to show historical data about the precipitating causes of Schreber's first and second illnesses. A year later Franz Baumeyer (1952) announced he had the good luck of finding Schreber's hospital chart. He collected other data that advanced the historical knowledge of the Schreber story and family which he first published in 1955 (in English in 1956), adding new findings in 1973. There are still some additional unpublished data by Baumeyer.[51]

The interpretation of Schreber's dreams and delusions by Macalpine and Hunter in 1953 as pregnancy wishes motivated by unfulfilled desires for progeny does not qualify as a new paradigm, for this idea was already expressed by Freud: "Dr. Schreber may have formed a phantasy that if he were a woman he would manage the business of having children more successfully; and he may have thus found his way back into the feminine attitude towards his father which he had exhibited in the earliest days of his childhood" (Freud, 1911a, p. 58).[52] Macalpine and Hunter researched the story of Schreber historically (1955, 1956) and in 1955, made the first complete English translation of the *Memoirs*.[53]

The paper by Fairbairn (1955) relied on the Oedipus constellation and the reaction to the primal scene as the main hermeneutic formula: "Schreber's homosexuality, at first severely repressed and later barely disguised, represented a means of denying the primal scene and his hatred of his mother as the more significant participant in his eyes, whilst enjoying the sexual excitement which it provoked in him . . . " (p. 125). This did not create much of a reverberation, even though it paid implicit attention to the role of the mother.

The following methodological questions about the linking homosexuality and paranoia were raised by Orville S. Walters (1955): Which fantasy is primary and which derivative, feminization or homosexuality? What is cause and what is by-product in psychosis? What was assumption turned into fact in Freud's formulations? Similar considerations were on the mind of Shulman (1959), reviewing Schreber from the perspective of the psychology of Alfred Adler, who, according to Shulman, had only mentioned Schreber once (p. 187). Shulman viewed Schreber's predicament from the perspective of self-centeredness, the quest for superiority, and the masculine protest (i.e., the conflict over submission vs. dominance, to which Freud alluded dismissively). Shulman (1959) saw a kinship between the views of Sullivan and those of Adler concerning the role of homosexuality (not its libidinal function but its connection to social adaptation and lifestyle).

> Schreber did not become psychotic because he had homosexual impulses . . . [but] because (a) he was isolated from his fellow men, (b) he overvalued the importance of his masculinity, his intellect and his morality, and (c) he felt completely lost when these were threatened when he was in positions of responsibility and faced with perhaps the most severe test of his actual abilities. . . . [He] finds surcease from his unsuccessful struggle to be a significant male by being transformed into a female of supreme significance [p. 191].

A predominantly hermeneutic type of Schreber literature, inspired by Jacques Lacan's (1958) system, began around 1955: textual-literary explications of Schreber, based on Lacan's formulas, themselves derived from Freud, such as father-son dynamics expressed in Lacan's "the name of the father." From France the approach spread to Germany and the United States. Lacan was embraced by authors in comparative literature.[54]

Niederland, the dean of Schreber studies worldwide, created a revolution in the formulations of Schreber: it is fair to divide the entire Schreber literature, psychoanalytic and non-psychoanalytic alike, into two eras: before and after Niederland. He combined psychoanalytic formulas, textual analysis, and historical findings in a series of papers published as a book in 1974 with additions by other authors.[55] In his pioneering paper, "Schreber: father and son" (1959a; see also 1959b), Niederland emphasized the historical Moritz Schreber; since no archive had been found about the *actual* father-son relationship, the latter had to be reconstructed through a hermeneutic interpretation of the father's alleged actions, inferred mostly from a perusal of the *Kallipädie* and the son's alleged reliving of the father's actions in the form of the hallucinations and delusions of his psychosis. Even though I have challenged this reading, its heuristic influence cannot be exaggerated.

The traumatogenic view of the father amounted to a methodological breakthrough and a revision of Freud's analysis in two important respects: (1) it explained Schreber's symptoms as an interactional product of paternal manipulations; (2) it de-emphasized the endogenous erotic component of paranoia linked to passive homosexual desires toward the father. The libido theorem Freud applied to Schreber left no room for any interpersonal influence, because the son's erotic transference to the father, and its repetition in the adult illness, were seen solely as intrapsychic (monadic) processes in the son. Niederland, on the other hand, without saying so, took Ferenczi's view in the Freud-Ferenczi dispute about the traumatogenic impact of parents on children.[56] The problem for Niederland was to reconcile the contradiction between Moritz Schreber's sadism and the son's erotic longings for him. Niederland resolved this by positing a range of seductive manipulations of the son by the father, including enemas; seduction and sadism were seen as equally traumatogenic. Later Niederland further complicated his argument by the unproven assumption that the father also advocated the use of antimasturbation devices, which he did not.[57] Niederland did not confront directly the issue of hostility in either father or son, which was reaffirmed by Carr (1963), citing previous authors.

White (1961, 1963) was virtually alone in the sea of patricentric theories to articulate the mother conflict in Schreber. In 1961 he argued that "the influx of feminine nerves . . . [was] very likely a delusional symbolic oral incorporation of the lost wife-mother, a primitive, delusional effort [that] . . . projected greedy, possessive, and destructive longings to be the sole possessor of the mother . . ." (White, 1961, p. 55). In 1963 White proposed to formulate Schreber's life in terms of Erikson's epigenetic phases.

A very different trend was started in the early sixties by the influential German novelist and essayist Elias Canetti (1960), quoted by Baumeyer: Paul Schreber's paranoia—his feeling persecuted by Flechsig and his fantastic delusions of armies of souls—was equated with, and set up as an explanatory paradigm for, paranoia and power and the deeds of such cruel conquerors as Jenghiz Khan, Tamerlane and Hitler. However, since the first two had not yet been branded as paranoid and Hitler was, it was Hitler's paranoia that Canetti sought to explain by means of lengthy quotations from the *Memoirs*. Such an idea is not just false and preposterous: it is an abuse of a psychiatric diagnosis and an offense to Paul Schreber's memory. It trivializes the complexity of Nazism as a sociohistorical phenomenon by reducing it to a psychiatric formula and negates the historic responsibility of the German masses that supported Hitler and the courage of the many who resisted him, and the lessons from it for all mankind. This paradigm of explaining the Nazi phenomenon in terms of Hitler's pathology, was then used by Heinz Kohut (1971) to equate the alleged psychoses of Hitler and of Moritz Schreber. Kohut hailed Niederland's achievement as epoch-making and regarded Moritz Schreber as "having a special kind of psychotic character structure . . . probably a kind of healed-over psychosis, similar perhaps to Hitler's . . . who emerged from a lonely hypochondriacal phase with the fixed idea that the Jews had invaded the body of Germany and had to be eradicated . . . [and saw Schreber's] *Das Buch der Erziehung an Leib und Seele* [the revised edition of the *Kallipädie*, misdated as 1865] as the expression of a hidden psychotic system" (p. 256).

Even though Canetti did not say a word about Paul Schreber's father, Schatzman doubled his yield by applying Canetti's formula to both Moritz Schreber's educational methods and to the son's psychotic "revelations" (Schatzman, 1973, p. 143) to drive home the idea that both were precursors of Hitler's *Mein Kampf*. Niederland (1974) extrapolated Schreber's paranoia and projection to the Nazi and Stalinist regimes, reducing political persecution and oppression to the psychology of a charismatic leader and ignoring the realities of the totalitarian state. Niederland did not mention Canetti, but having recast Schreber's diagnosis as paranoid personality, he developed similar thoughts about "the paranoid personality's ascent to political leadership" (p. 29) and also believed that "Schreber's biographer Ritter, expressing his admiration for both [Moritz] and Hitler, sees in the former a sort of spiritual precursor of Nazism" (p. 65). Here, I suspect, Niederland simply repeated Kohut's equations and Schatzman's (1973) sweeping misreadings: Ritter said nothing about Hitler nor about Moritz Schreber being a precursor of Nazism. This equating of Paul Schreber with Hitler was also pursued by Krüll (1977). These various assessments are a vilification of Schreber father and son and are based on false analogies: they miss the facts of Hitler's politics and military machine in the service of multi-national genocide; and the religious, racial, economic and political roots of German and European anti-Semitism, which cannot be solely explained by individual pathology and call for an understanding of mass psychology as well (see chapter 2 for a discussion of political anti-Semitism in Germany in the 1880s and 1890s).[58]

In 1971 appeared the first publication on Schreber by Schatzman, which he expanded into a book, *Soul Murder*, in 1973. This popularization in Schatzman's best-seller of Niederland's view of the father as sadistic made the son famous and the father notorious among the wide reading public, the latter an indisputable achievement.[59] It shed little light on Paul Schreber's adult life situation and illness, being marred by the genetic fallacy. Schatzman's mistakes and distortions were discussed earlier.

French studies of Moritz Schreber and his influence on the son, inspired by Niederland, were those by A. Tabouret-Keller (1973), who traced the Schreber family tree and discussed Moritz's works at some length, and of B. This (1973-1974).

Researchers who subjected the text of the *Memoirs* to a computer analysis (Klein, 1976; Laffal, 1976) were impressed that "neither sun, God, nor Flechsig was significantly associated with clusters concerning gender, sexuality or castration" (R. H. Klein, 1976, p. 373). Verdiglione (1976), formulating Schreber with the help of Lacan's idea "that the drama of madness . . . is situated in man's relation to the signifier" (1976, p. 213), connected Schreber's delusions with the role of the image and the semblant, i.e., the appearance and the as-if, as the key to unlock their meaning. He later theorized that in the idea of turning into a woman (Verdiglione, 1980) Schreber meant to indicate that woman, created of man's rib, returned to man. Another discussion of Schreber, inspired by Lacan and Melanie Klein but without any reference to Niederland, is that of André Green (1977). Positing that "Schreber's *delusions* represent the *theory* of Freud," (p. 34), Green drew parallels between the process of writing and creating by Schreber the hallucinator and by Freud the dreamer, that is, between the *Memoirs* and Freud's *Project for a Scientific Psychology* (1950) and *The Interpretation of Dreams*.

Schreber's confinement and the court confrontation were briefly discussed by psychoanalyst Maud Mannoni (1970) as an issue of antipsychiatry. She was impressed that the Dresden judges recognized Schreber's right to madness and to freedom. Szasz (1976) was the only psychiatrist to discuss the issue of Schreber's involuntary hospitalization, chiding Freud for devoting "page after page to speculations about the character and cause of Schreber's 'illness' but not a word to the problem posed by his imprisonment or to his right to freedom" (p. 39). In Strachey's translation, Freud noted that Schreber's efforts to regain his "freedom" and "civil rights" were "crowned with success" (Freud, 1911a, pp. 16-17). In the original, Freud's words were *"Befreiung"* (liberation), *"verhängte Entmündigung"* (imposed incompetency ruling), and *"Triumph,"* a word much more emotion-laden than success.[60]

Breger (1978) accepted Niederland's formulations and took from Freud the notion of delusion as self-therapy. Thus, for Breger, quoting the ideas of Wilden (1972), Schreber's turning into a woman was self-therapy and both a protest against the patriarchal-masculine-authoritarian ideas of the father and the society in which he lived and a move toward the ideals of femininity and motherhood.

The most significant work to develop as a result of Schatzman's writings was the historical research of Israëls, who defended his dissertation in 1980 and first published it privately in 1981. His important documentary, archival and biographical findings are marred by a partisan advocacy of Schatzman and a vilification of Niederland. I have already commented on some aspects of these polemics and I have also discussed them in my review of Israëls (Lothane, 1991b).

Surprisingly, besides Jung himself, few Jungians interpreted the *Memoirs*, as noted by Eigen (1986): "Jungians did not explore the Schreber case to the extent Freudians did. . . . Schreber's basic movement from a male position to death and rebirth through the feminine seems made for Jungian analysis" (p. 254). Among Jung's basic tenets are the self, the animus-anima polarity and the archetypes, used as hermeneutic formulas. Edwards (1978) was impressed with the preoedipal mother motif in the *Memoirs* while Hillman (1986) redefined unmanning as "not emasculation in the narrowest sense, but removal from the category of men" (p. 21), stressing issues of faith and revelation.

In 1979 Prado de Oliveira, whom I met in 1989, edited a volume of French translations of English and American papers on Schreber and wrote an introduction in which he noted that not enough attention had been given to Weber (see footnote 55). A selection of French papers on

Schreber (1973 to 1988), quite a few inspired by Lacan, was offered in a volume edited in 1988 by Allison, Prado de Oliveira, Roberts and Weiss, including additional Schreber documents found by Israëls, which I reviewed (Lothane, 1991a).

In 1980, shortly before his death, the dean of Hungarian psychoanalysts, Imre Hermann, offered some interesting speculations about Schreber's symptoms from the perspective of his own theories. He argued that the symptoms were caused by a regression to infantile clinging-going-in-search, to primitive ego perceptions, and a childhood father-teacher image. The father-teacher transference would explain Paul's hatred for his father, while the bellowing was seen as equivalent to tantrum behavior of a child clinging to his mother. Hermann did not concern himself at all with Schreber's adult relationships.

An important historical discovery for Schreber studies was the publication by Daniel Devreese (1981a) of Schreber's personal file in the Ministry of Justice of Saxony, reissued in French in 1986 (Devreese, Israëls and Quackelbeen). Devreese's formulations about the Schreber case followed the patricentric ideas of Niederland and Lacan (Devreese, 1981b).

The story of Schreber found its way into theatrical productions that were influenced by the *Memoirs* and by the literature inspired by Niederland and Schatzman. A play called *Schreber* with the subtitle "A Piece of the Psychotic World of a 19th Century Judge," by the team Meijer and Rijnders (n.d.), was produced in Amsterdam in the later 1970s. A multimedia event by Richard Zvonar, *Soul Murder*, was produced in Berkeley, California, in 1983. Has the time come for a motion picture on Schreber?

Questions about the diagnosis of Schreber continue to be raised.[61] The diagnosis created by Weber had earlier been emended by Freud as paranoid schizophrenia. This was again modified when Niederland published his collected papers in book form: paranoia became paranoid personality (Niederland, 1974), also questionable. The diagnosis of schizophrenia was questioned by Koehler (1981), using Kraepelin-inspired criteria for differentiating affective from schizophrenic disorders. Koehler saw Schreber's first illness and the first "pre-schizophrenic" (prior to February 15, 1894) phase as an affective syndrome, followed first by a schizoaffective phase and later by a chronic paranoid schizophrenic syndrome. Rejecting the idea of paranoia or paraphrenia, Koehler was aware that diagnostic preferences reflect social and emotional attitudes on the part of the diagnostician. Lipton (1984) argued for bipolar affective disorder, and was brought up short by his critics Kendler and Spitzer (1985). Grotstein (1984-

1985) invoked "paranoia, or 'delusional masochism'"(p. 340), echoing the characteristic diagnosis, paranoid-masochism, already advanced by Nydes (1963).[62] Grotstein also considered Freud's hint about involutional paranoia, tied to climacteric factors, and bipolar affective disorder, in both its depressive and manic manifestations. The term *schizophreniform* was not used by any of these authors. Grotstein (1985) also applied to Schreber the idea of interactional regulation and felt that Schreber was misunderstood by his parents, "ignored by Flechsig, was seemingly misused by God, but . . . himself never forswore his desire to help humanity" (p. 312).

In 1987 Schreiber traced certain statements in the *Memoirs* to texts in contemporary works mentioned by Schreber in his Foot Note #36.[63] By the method of textual analysis and comparison, that is, aligning Schreber's texts with the texts found in the works cited by him, she was able to show how contemporary views on religion, philosophy and science—in sum, the *Zeitgeist* and cultural climate—were reflected in Schreber's stream of consciousness. As a result, she contributed to making Schreber's content both intelligible and not prima facie reducible to psychopathology.

The paper by deMause (1987) was discussed in chapter 4. Porter (1987) entered a plea for shedding more light on Schreber and Flechsig. In view of the importance of Flechsig in Schreber's life, Porter believed this relationship deserved special emphasis. An interesting perspective on Schreber was offered by Louis Sass (1987), inspired by the ideas of Michel Foucault. He aligned Moritz Schreber's alleged punitive methods of upbringing with the idea of the panopticon, Jeremy Bentham's notion of the all-seeing eye created in 1791, that was embodied in the architecture of the modern jail, barrack and hospital. Sass was also respectful of Schreber as a psychologist.

Shengold (1989), writing on Schreber since 1961, applied Schreber's "soul murder" as a term for early childhood parental abuse. He is an example of authors, too many to cite, who followed in Niederland's footsteps and applied this paradigm to Paul Schreber. In 1989 Devreese completed a two-volume erudite doctoral dissertation on Schreber, which is a penetrating linguistic, textual-hermeneutic and historical analysis.

The very first and hitherto unknown author to have concerned himself with the traumatic impact of Flechsig on Paul Schreber was Hungarian psychoanalyst Tibor Rajka (1971). Until now, however, apart from the few remarks by Freud, Niederland (1974) was the one widely known to have focused on the impact of Flechsig, but he did so largely from the perspective that Schreber's relationship with Flechsig was a repetition of his traumatic relationship with his father, calling the latter "patient–doctor relationship" a "transference situation with Dr. Flechsig" (p. 102). In addition, "Schreber's . . . intense castration fear" was tied by Niederland to Flechsig's 1884 paper on the surgical treatment of *hysteria*, in which Flechsig discussed "the use of actual castration . . . *for the cure of serious nervous and psychological ailments.* . . . To be sure, the patients described . . . were *female*; but at no point are the indications limited as to sex or mental condition" (p. 104, emphasis Niederland's). However, this method of curing female hysteria, tied to the age-old belief that hysteria was due to diseases of the uterus, was commonly known and discussed in the psychiatric literature of the day (e.g., Kraepelin's *Textbook*) and was nowhere applied to hysteria in men. But even if actual castration threats played a role in Schreber's childhood, this alone could not account for his concerns as an adult for his reactions to the conduct of his psychiatrists.[64]

Niederland's formulation based on Flechsig's paper about the castration of hysterical women was echoed by Calasso (1974) and by Masson (1982, 1988). Calasso's *The Unholy Madman* is both a historical analysis and a satire suggestive of Swift, Voltaire and Joyce. Flechsig and Schreber were also on the mind of Kittler (1984), who saw Flechsig's language as brain and nerve researcher portrayed in Schreber's delusional nerve-language. Continuing the ideas of Calasso's (1974), Kittler sought connections between Flechsig, Schreber and Freud in the dialectic of soul murder and corpses but enlarged the paradigm by inquiring into issues of control and power.

In 1989 papers on Schreber were published by Busse, Stingelin and me, as well as the English and German versions of the 1981 Israëls' Schreber biography, which I reviewed (Lothane, 1991b).[65] Informed by the theories of Foucault and based on a study of Flechsig's works, Stingelin (1989a) argued that Flechsig was an example of "the medical rationalization of the technological-administrative power" of society over the individual. Comparing Schreber's lecture on the brain and mind with statements from Flechsig's *Brain and Soul,* Stingelin (1989b) showed the parallels and the possible influence and dispelled the impression of pathology from Schreber's remarks. Busse (1989) agreed with me that for Schreber God was a reference to Flechsig, rather than to his father, but was in doubt about my contention that Flechsig was a traumatic influence upon Schreber. Instead of stressing Flechsig's conduct as director of the hospital and Schreber's psychiatrist, that is, Flechsig's "politics of souls"—"*Seelenpolitik*," as Schreber called it—Busse was more impressed with Flechsig's "politics of corpses," that is, his activities as a neuropathologist and neuroanatomist.

Schreber was also an inspiration to a number of authors writing from the perspective of religious and mystical experiences. Rather than dismissing Schreber's religious experiences as delusional and thus unworthy of attention as ideas in their own right, these authors accorded Schreber the status of a religious thinker.[66] The most eloquent was Wilden (1972).[67] At least "in this sense," as Schreber had hoped at the very end of the *Memoirs*, "favorable stars" did "watch over the success of [his] labour" (*M*, p. 294).

NOTES

1. In *Das litterarische Leipzig* there is no mention of Nauthardt, so he must have been in another German city. Friedrich Fleischer, Moritz Schreber's publisher, is described as specializing in "theology, physiology, law, medicine, pedagogics and pamphlets" (p. 279), and Oswald Mutze in "spiritism and related matters, theater, as well as periodicals: *Zeitschrift für Spiritismus, Spiritistisch-rationalistische Zeitschrift, Neue Zeit, Psychische Studien*." Mutze also indicated the house solicited manuscripts in the subjects of "*Spiritus, Okkultismus*" (p. 283).

2. Unfortunately, the actual contract with Mutze could not be found. There was no information available at the Deutsche Bücherei in Leipzig or the Deutscher Börsenverein. Nevertheless, I am contradicting the opinion of Israëls, which I think he derived from one of the reviewers, that the book was published at Schreber's expense.

3. Letter from the Director of the Stadtbibliothek of the City of Leipzig to Mr. Felix von Leppel of April 23, 1959, in the Niederland Collection in the Manuscript Division of the Library of Congress.

4. The biographical data mentioned here constitute a second biographical sketch published in Schreber's lifetime. The first, in 1884, prior to the election, was found by Israëls (1989, p. 161) in the *Chemnitzer Tageblatt* of 1884.

5. Advertisement in *Psychische Studien* facing Issue X for October, 1903, Volume 30. The number of pages indicated, 532, is surprising, because there are only 516 pages in the original edition. Just below the advertisement there are notices about two books by Max Seiling: *Goethe und der Okkultismus*, and *Ernst Häckel und der Spiritismus*. Following p. 516 of the original *Memoirs* are advertisements for a variety of works on occultism, magnetism, and hypnotism, for Jung's doctoral thesis, and for the book by Goetze.

6. Möbius was in private practice of psychiatry in Leipzig. I wonder how Schreber would have fared had he chosen to be a patient of Möbius rather than Flechsig.

7. The other review by Pelman (1904) is also positive but with the reservation that Schreber's confessions are too crazy to be compared with Rousseau's. The *Memoirs* were also briefly and anonymously noted in the special literature supplement of the *AZP* for 1904, 61:99, with the remark that at the time of writing, Schreber, even as he obtained the rescission of the incompetency ruling, was still not cured of his illness and was still preoccupied with supernatural impressions about the nature of God, the survival of the soul, etc. I wonder if Weber, as collaborator with the editorial board of the *AZP*, was not behind this review.

8. According to John Kerr (personal communication, 1990), the members of the Burghölzli staff were required to keep up with the literature.

9. A sizable portion of the catalogues and announcements of Mutze has been kindly sent to me by Dr. Leo Ikelaar, the librarian of the Duits Seminaar at the University of Amsterdam.

10. Mutze advertised Jung's book as follows: "Dr. med. C. G. Jung, first assistant physician at the University Psychiatric Hospital in Zürich. In this interesting book written with great dedication the author presents his thorough investigation results in this controversial field to the development of which his work is an important contribution. His observations at the psychiatric university hospital and the Burghölzli asylum will arouse wide interest not only in university circles, the sites of psychological research, but also among educated laymen" (*Psychische Studien*, 1903, vol. 30, facing p. 64).

11. In my paper on Schreber and Freud (Lothane, 1989c) I do not mention Jung's dissertation. Had Schreber read it, he would have become aware of Freud's *Interpretation of Dreams*. It is in their views of dream psychology that Schreber and Freud touch each other, as recognized by Freud in his letters to Jung (McGuire, 1974, p. 358) and in Jung's (1907) and Freud's views on the analogies between paranoia and hysteria (see also footnote 14).

12. For example, nine years before his death, in his *Answer to Job* (1952), Jung says: "From the ancient Egyptian theology of the divine Pharaohs we know that God wants to become man by means of a human mother, and it was recognized even in prehistoric times that the primordial divine being is both male and female" (p. 188). While Jung located himself in an ancient tradition, I cannot escape the feeling that he had been influenced by Schreber's theology, which, in turn, harks back to ancient beliefs. The myth of the androgyne and of bisexuality appears in Plato's *Symposium,* and in the Kabbalah there is a myth of God as a hermaphrodite. An example of Jungian esoterica is offered by Beverly Zabriskie (n. d.): "In the *Seven Sermons to the Dead* Jung introduced Abraxas, the monstrous Gnostic god with a human body, the head of a rooster, and legs of serpents, carrying a shield in his right hand and a whip in his left . . . (based on Stephan Hoeller) . . . to me Abraxas is the informing presence in its theory of the psyche and its conceptual structure."

Sonu Shamdasani (personal communication, 1990) informed me that he heard it stated by Michael Fordham that in the early 1950s Fordham came upon Jung reading Paul Schreber whereupon Jung reaffirmed that the *Memoirs* was one of the most significant books he had ever read and that a number of Schreber's prophecies have turned out to be true. Shamdasani (1990) researched the story of Frank Miller, a woman whom Jung diagnosed as schizophrenic on the basis of Miller's written productions and concluded that Miss Miller became for Jung "a feminine icon at the head of Jung's *Transformations and Symbols of the Libido,* presiding over the birth of Analytical Psychology" (p. 28). Thus, in the days preceding their dispute over Schreber and the eventual breakup, Jung imitated Freud in that he constructed a theory of psychosis rival to Freud's, one also based on a literary-hermeneutic analysis of a written text without ever having known the author, the real Miss Miller.

Jung (1961) was astonished that he "a psychiatrist, should . . . have run into the same psychic material which is the stuff of psychosis and is found in the insane" (p. 188). In the "darkness" that descended on him after the break with Freud he saw cataclysmic "visions," both before and after the outbreak of World War II. He also heard a voice of

"a woman within me" [who] did not have the speech centers I had. And so I suggested that she use mine. She did . . . She must be the soul . . . "anima". . . . Why was it thought of as feminine? Later I came to see that this inner feminine figure plays a typical, or archetypal, role in the unconscious of man and I called her the "anima" (p. 186).

Is it fair to say that Schreber, too, had a concept of anima, which inspired Jung's?

13. The book was translated as *The Psychology of Dementia Praecox* by Frederick Peterson, M.D., Professor of Psychiatry at Columbia University, and A. A. Brill, the founder (two years later) of the New York Psychoanalytic Society; it was published in New York in 1909, the year of the Freud-Jung visit to America. In their preface the translators hailed Jung's work as a major breakthrough after Kraepelin's descriptive psychiatry: "an individual psychology," a method "absolutely essential for the understanding of the psychosis, just as the microscope is for pathology," in the wake of the discoveries of Breuer and Freud in *The Studies on Hysteria* and Freud's discoveries in *The Interpretation of Dreams*.

14. It is of historical interest that an awareness of the dynamic importance of unconscious processes is also found among some psychiatrists of the period. Thus, Kraepelin himself, according to Jung, "was struck by the resemblance between the speech of dreams and of dementia praecox." Jung quoted from a work by Kraepelin, "*Über Sprachstörungen im Traume* (On Speech Disturbances in Dream)"; *Psychol. Arbeiten*, vol. 5, issue 1, in which Kraepelin referred to "dream paraphrasias," and "metaphoric paralogia" (Kraepelin, p. 62). Kraepelin also used the term *ellipse* as a concept parallel to Freud's notion of condensation. The word *ellipsis* to denote condensation and new word formations in paranoid states was used in the 1880s by Forel. Jung (1907) noted that "It escaped Kraepelin that Freud had already, in 1900, treated dream condensations in a detailed manner" (p. 23). Already in the fifth edition of his *Textbook of Psychiatry* Kraepelin (1896) spoke of "unconscious wishes" (p. 105), and in the sixth edition (1899)—both editions cited by Schreber—he invoked Freud's work on hysteria.

15. From my own diagnostic perspective, Jung erred in not considering the differential diagnosis of melancholia, which he should have done since he was so concerned with affects. In connection with affects and Schreber he cited Forel's (1901) "Autobiography of a Case of Acute Mania" (footnote no. 4 on p. 72). In that paper Forel indeed described florid hallucinations and delusions in a disease that is not schizophrenia. The implication is that hallucinations and delusions as such do not differentiate, certainly not in the acute phase, schizophrenia from affective disorders. Thus, Jung's observations are more pertinent from the point of view of psychodynamics, which applies in equal measure to both psychoses.

16. According to Peter Swales (personal communication, 1991), the earliest published mention of Freud by Bleuler was in 1892. John Kerr called my attention to Masson's (1985, p. 461) citation of Bleuler's positive review of Freud's *Studies on Hysteria* in the *Münchener Medizinische Wochenschrift* of 1896. In the 1906 essay Bleuler refers to the attack on Freud by Aschaffenburg, a bitter critic of Freud, and invokes the importance of Freud's concepts, as expounded by then in the *Studies on Hysteria*, in the *Interpretation of Dreams*, and in the *Psychopathology of Everyday Life*, all appearing by 1901.

17. *Dementia Praecox, oder Gruppe der Schizophrenien* (1911), written around 1908. In the preface Bleuler thanks his "coworkers in Burghölzli of whom [he] mention[s] only Riklin, Abraham, and particularly Jung" (p. 2). The term 'schizophrenia' had already been used by Bleuler in print prior to the publication of the book and it appeared in Freud (1911a) along with Kraepelin's term *dementia praecox*. In this book Bleuler neatly distinguished between the content of the psychosis and its cause. Bleuler reaffirmed Jung's view that the cause of schizophrenia is organic whereas the manifestations and the content are psychological. For a thorough discussion see chapter 26 in Rapaport (1951). This organic conception did not prevent Bleuler from acknowledging Freud's psychodynamics, in the way discussed by Jung, in an essay he published a year later, "*Das autistische Denken* (Autistic Thinking)," published in the *Jahrbuch*, 1912, 4:1–39, one year after the publication in it of Freud's essay on Schreber. This book created one major terminological innovation: it firmly established the renaming of dementia praecox as schizophrenia, thus an adjective form, schizophrenic, a distinct linguistic advantage. The unwieldy name dementia praecox was first coined by Morel in 1860 and then made popular by Kraepelin.

18. Bleuler, 1911, pp. 54, 66, 77, 114, 399, 400. On page 200 he refers to Schreber's bellowing. The *Memoirs* are listed as reference #669.

19. See McGuire, 1974, p. 307. John Kerr told me that at first Freud offered Ferenczi the opportunity to collaborate in the work, but when Ferenczi found out that collaborating meant taking dictation, he politely declined.

20. The confusion about Schreber as Freud's patient stems from the manner in which he is referred to in the literature: he is listed among Freud's cases in the indexes of the *Standard Edition*. Similarly, Schreber is presented as a patient of Freud's in a recent publication, *Freud and His Patients* (Kanzer and Glenn, 1980). Also, in the DSM-III Case Book (Spitzer et al., 1981) Schreber is included among Freud's "historical" cases.

21. Arnold Georg Stegmann, and later his wife, Margarete, were early supporters of psychoanalysis. Stegmann settled in Dresden in 1903 and appears in the group photograph of the participants in the Weimar International Congress in 1911. Early on he published papers and reviews on hypnosis and suggestion, the cathartic method, and alcoholism. In a review of a book, entitled *The therapeutic effects of hypnotic suggestion*, Stegmann (1899) was critical of the author's suspicious attitudes toward hypnosis and suggestion. Stegmann (1903) reported on his own successes in treating alcoholics with suggestion. He also published a paper called "A Clinical Contribution to the Treatment of Neuroses by Means of Freud's Cathartic Method" (1904) and

wrote "The Causes of Alcoholism" (1908). The last publication I found was a lecture in 1912 to the Gesellschaft für Natur- und Heilkunde zu Dresden (The Dresden Society for Nature Sciences and Naturopathy), entitled "Remarks on hysteria from the viewpoint of the teachings of Freud."

22. The old name for cross dressing was *eonism*, after the sensational case of Charles Geneviève Louis Auguste André Timothée Chevalier d'Éon (1728–1810), an aristocrat educated as a lawyer who on a spy mission, disguised in woman's dress, gained the confidence of the Russian empress to become her reader. An English jury ruled he was a woman, and thereafter in France he became the Chevalière d'Éon. In 1810 his true gender was officially established at autopsy. The term *transvestite* was coined by the Berlin sexologist Magnus Hirschfeld (1910), who separated transvestism from homosexuality, a view also espoused in Stekel (1923).

23. I am indebted to John Kerr for reawakening my interest in this matter. The syndrome is introduced in the fifth edition of the *Psychopathia* of 1890 and fully described by the seventh edition of 1892, which was then translated in the United States (Krafft-Ebing, 1893). A later American edition (1939) does not mention the translator, but in the cases relevant to this discussion the text is identical to the 1893 English version. Writing in 1886, Krafft-Ebing was already relying on a vast German and French forensic literature (including Brouardel mentioned in the *Memoirs*, p. 91) dealing with inversion and perversion, going back to the end of the 18th century. The various names of homosexuality were *contrary sexual instinct, uranism,* or *Urning-*[homosexual man] love, the latter term coined by the famous homosexual Ulrichs, alias Numa Numantius (see chapter 5, note 62) and appearing in Schreber's clinical chart. There thus was a prevailing tendency to equate effeminacy and feminine emotions with passive homosexuality. Freud was also heir to this vast literature and did not discover the importance of sexuality in mental disorders only by listening to his patients, as is commonly believed. The progressive stages, or degrees, in the evolution of acquired homosexuality, according to Krafft-Ebing, were: (1) simple reversal of sexual feeling; (2) eviration (emasculation) in men and defeminization in women, terms that indicated reversal of emotions and passive homosexuality but had nothing to do with the Freudian theory of castration as a threat of physical sexual mutilation; (3) a stage of transition to "metamorphosis sexualis paranoica," i.e., paranoid sexual transformation (Krafft-Ebing, 1893, p. 202, case #99, or case #129 in the 1939 edition), a non-psychotic, ambulatory stage; and (4) the psychotic stage of "metamorphosis sexualis paranoica," predominantly a paranoid psychosis, with hospitalization.

24. The difference between paraphrenia and schizophrenia was also disputed by Kurt Kolle (1931) in his monograph *The Primary Psychosis*.

25. The contribution of Stekel (1912, chapter 31), remains unknown and overshadowed by Abraham. Stekel noted Freud's interest in melancholia as early as 1910, in the discussion on suicide at the Vienna Psychoanalytic Society (p. 362). Another early contributor to the paranoia-melancholia problem was Victor Tausk (1916) in his "Diagnostic Considerations Concerning the Symptomatology of the So-called War Psychoses," *Psychoanalytic Quarterly*,

38(1969):382–405. There Tausk is concerned with the mixed picture of "paranoia *cum* melancholia." In an attempt to bridge the dynamics of both disorders, Tausk proposed that

> the melancholic identifies himself with the abandoned love object. ... According to this hypothesis, a predisposition to melancholia should be expected in individuals who make their object choice on the narcissistic pattern and therefore deal with the heterosexual object on a homosexual basis. ... Thus in melancholia, as in paranoia, a regression to the narcissistic stage takes place. ... The identification mechanism peculiar to the narcissistic constellation causes the loss of external love object to appear in the form of loss of self-love, and in melancholia this assumes the pathological dimensions, in the form of total collapse of narcissism, self-love, self-confidence and self-esteem [pp. 398–399].

Freud, of course, knew these ideas of Tausk's, which were repeated in Tausk's (1919) paper for which he is known best, where in footnote 12 he defines "Melancholia [as a] disintegration of psychic narcissism ... the persecution psychosis without projection" (p. 78) and in other places discusses Freud's views about "projection of homosexual libido," without quoting Freud (1911a). Tausk (1919) also pointed out that delusions of influence ("*Beeinflussungswahn*") can appear in "another clinical group, such as depression, mania, paranoia, compulsion neurosis, anxiety hysteria, or amentia; ... " (p. 57). Did Tausk make Freud rethink his ideas about Schreber?

26. The case is mentioned in Section III of Freud's (1894) "The Neuro-Psychoses of Defence," published in the *Neurologisches Centrallblatt*, a journal Schreber presumably scanned for Flechsig's publications:

> The ego has fended off the incompatible idea through flight into psychosis [i.e, an *Überwältigungspsychose*, in which the ego has been overwhelmed] ... but the [ego] is inseparably connected with a piece of reality, so that, in so far as the ego achieves this result, it, too, has detached itself wholly or in part from reality. In my opinion, this latter event is the condition under which the subject's ideas receive the vividness of hallucinations; and thus when the defence has been successfully carried out he finds himself in a state of hallucinatory confusion [Freud, 1894, pp. 59–60].

In this paper Freud does not use the term *amentia*, but in the "Metapsychological Supplement to the Theory of Dreams" he says: "The formation of the wishful phantasy and its regression to hallucination ... the most essential parts of the dream-work ... are also found in two morbid states: in acute hallucinatory confusion (Meynert's 'amentia') [that is, Meynert's name for acute paranoia] and in the hallucinatory phase of schizophrenia" (1917, 229–234). Amentia is also mentioned in Draft K and in Letter 55, in *Extracts from the Fliess Papers* (Freud, 1950). In the important Draft K, "The Neuroses of Defence (A Christmas Fairy Tale)," Freud aligns clinical syndromes with defenses, that is, "pathological aberrations of normal psychical affective states," among which are *"mortification* (paranoia)," and *"mourning* (acute hallucinatory amentia)." Among the preconditions are *"sexuality and infantilism"* (p. 220; emphasis Freud's). The result is an overwhelming of the ego, or "a permanent damage to the ego" (p. 220), or "recovery with a malformation" (p. 222). In Letter 55 Freud speaks of "amentia or a confusional psychosis—a psychosis of overwhelming" (p. 240). However, in the Schreber essay, Freud says that it "cannot be asserted that a paranoic, even at the height of the repression, withdraws his interest from the external world completely—as must be considered to occur in certain other kinds of hallucinatory psychosis (such as Meynert's amentia)" (1911a, p. 75). But is it complete in amentia? We will leave the complexities and Freud's self-contradictions here.

27. Freud states in a letter to Jung (McGuire, 1974, p. 19): "Still, I believe that my case ought to be diagnosed as authentic paranoia." And later (p. 121): "The paranoid form [of dementia praecox] is probably conditioned by restriction to the homosexual component. My old analysis (1896) also showed that the pathological process began with the patient's estrangement from her husband's *sisters"* (Freud's emphasis).

28. Paul Näcke (1851-1913), noted psychiatrist, criminologist, and sexologist, was born in St. Petersburg of a German father and a French mother and settled in Dresden at the age of five. He worked at Sonnenstein and later became director of the custodial Hubertusburg asylum for women. He was credited by Freud with having coined the term narcissism. His obituary (Näcke, 1913-1914) included a bibliography 146 items long, with many contributions in the area of sexuality.

29. I have made this claim in "Love, Seduction and Trauma" (Lothane, 1987a).

30. Of paranoiacs Freud (1914b) wrote that they had "delusions of being *watched* . . . that all their thoughts are known . . . by voices which characteristically speak to them in the third person. . . . This complaint is justified; it describes the truth . . . [it] arose [in the paranoiac] from the critical influence of his parents (conveyed to him by the medium of the voice) . . . to whom were added the innumerable and indefinable host of all the other people in his environment—his fellow men—and public opinion" (1914b, pp. 95-96; emphasis Freud's). This view was reaffirmed in Freud's two other major papers dealing with delusions (1915b, 1937).

31. His interim formulations of Schreber are described in two letters to Jung (McGuire, 1974). In 214F:

I didn't even read half the book in Sicily, but I have fathomed the secret. The case is easily reduced from its nuclear complex. His wife falls in love with the doctor and keeps his picture on her writing-desk for years. He too, of course, but in the woman's case there are disappointments, attempts to have children are unsuccessful; a conflict develops; he ought to hate Flechsig as his rival, but loves him, thanks to his predisposition and his transference from his first illness. The infantile situation is now complete, and soon his father emerges behind Flechsig. Fortunately for psychiatry this father was also—a doctor. One more confirmation of what we found in so many paranoid cases when I was in Zürich; that paranoiacs are unable to prevent the re-cathexis of their homosexual leaning. Which brings the case in line with our theory [p. 358].

So much worse for the theory. In 218F:

One can guess a good deal reading the book. . . . First the father complex: Obviously Flechsig-father-God-sun form a series. The "middle" Flechsig points to a brother who like the father was already "blessed," that is dead, at the time of the illness. The forecourts of heaven or "anterior realms of God" (breasts!) are the women of the family, the "posterior realms of God" (the buttocks!) are the father and his sublimation, God. . . . The castration complex is only too evident. Don't forget that Schreber's father was—a doctor. As such he performed miracles, he miracled. In other words, the delightful characterization of God—that he knows how to deal only with corpses and has no idea of living people—and the absurd miracles that are performed on him are a bitter satire on his father's medical art. In other words, the same use of absurdity as in dreams. The enormous significance of homosexuality for paranoia is confirmed by the central emasculation fantasy, etc. etc. . . . (In other words, his father bellowed too) [p. 368-369].

In the published case Freud omits any reference to father's scoldings and does not allow anywhere that the true object of the bitter satire could have been Flechsig, who actually dealt with corpses, or to Weber (1859), who wrote his dissertation on pathological findings in corpses, in contrast to Moritz Schreber who did not.

32. Thus in his unpublished *Project for a Scientific Psychology* (Freud, 1950a) we find Freud discussing *"Lust"* and *"Unlust"* (pleasure and pain), in the section entitled *"Das Bewusstsein"* (consciousness, p. 396). And so does Schreber. Freud discusses perception and memory (pp. 409, 414) and *"verstanden"* (understanding, p. 416), and Schreber *"Verstandesnerven"*, nerves of understanding. Instead of Schreber's *"Wollustnerven"* (nerves of lust), Freud uses the more neutral *"Befriedigung"* (gratification). But in the diagram in Draft G, Freud (1950a, p. 114) uses *"Wollustleitung"* (nerve pathways conducting lust feelings), translated as "Conduction of voluptuous feelings" (Freud, 1950, p. 204). To be sure, Freud's neuroanatomy is much more sophisticated, but the psychological ideas and concepts are the same.

33. These facts were first described by the Leipzig professor of anatomy and surgery Thiersch. Schreber might have read them in a work by Haeckel (1874, pp. 676-681), including Table #26 which shows the "homologies in the sexual organs of both sexes in mammals" (p. 686), for he cited this author in Foot Note #36.

34. The new revision goes beyond the assumption invoked earlier (Freud, 1911a, p. 46) of the universal predisposition to bisexuality in mankind as the explanation of man-to-man eroticism:

There comes a time in the development of the individual . . . [when] he begins by taking himself, his own body, as his love-object and only subsequently proceeds from this to the choice of some person other than himself as his object. This half-way phase between auto-erotism and object-love may perhaps be indispensable normally. . . . What is of chief importance in the subject's self thus chosen as a love-object may already be the genitals. The line of development then leads on to the choice of external object with similar genitals—that is, to homosexual object-choice—and thence to heterosexuality. People who are manifest homosexuals in later life . . . never emancipated themselves from the binding condition that the object of their choice must possess genitals like their own [Freud, 1911a, pp. 60-61].

Freud continues this argument to posit civilized sublimation of the erotic attachment among men as the basis of all friendship and social instincts. On this assumption, developmentally speaking, all men are created homosexuals and are lucky if they later manage to turn to women.

35. This letter is in E. Jones (1955, pp. 83-84). The words of Freud to Ferenczi became a title and focus in a recent book on Schreber by C. Azouri (1991).

36. In a letter to Freud of October 28, 1907, Jung confessed:

I have a boundless admiration for you as a man and a researcher . . . my veneration for you has something of a 'religious' crush. . . . I still feel it disgusting and ridiculous because of its undeniable erotic undertone. This abominable feeling comes from the fact that as a boy I was the victim of a sexual assault by a man I once worshipped. . . . Another manifestation of it is that I find psychological insight makes relations with colleagues who have a strong transference to me downright disgusting [McGuire, 1974, p. 95].

In a 1908 letter to Jung Freud says in connection with paranoia (referring to his case of 1896): "My one-time friend Fliess developed a dreadful case of paranoia after throwing off his affection for me, which was undoubtedly considerable. . . . Too bad we shall not be exactly undisturbed in Salzburg!" (McGuire, 1974, p. 121). Note Freud's wanting to be alone with Jung. Jung says shortly afterwards: "the Fl.[iess] case helped me greatly in understanding your views, since I always knew what you had in mind. Your line of thought on the paranoia question seems to me very different from mine, so I have great difficulty in following you" (McGuire, 1974, 133). In another letter from Freud we read: "My Schreber is finished, . . . the piece is formally imperfect, . . . it contains the boldest thrust at . . . psychiatry since your [Psychology of] Dem[entia] Pr[aecox]. I am unable to judge its objective worth as was possible with earlier papers, because in working on it I have had to fight off complexes within myself (Fliess)" (McGuire, 1974, pp. 379-380). Both terms of disparagement, homosexuality and paranoia, are later dropped on Adler, not known to have been homosexual: "It is getting really bad with Adler. You see a resemblance to Bleuler: in me he awakens the memory of Fliess, but an octave lower. The same paranoia" (McGuire, 1974, p. 376). Jung had already fallen in with this kind of "wild analysis" (against which Freud inveighs in a paper by that title published in 1910), by saying this about Bleuler:

Bleuler . . . dreamt he was *suckling his child himself*. So now he is becoming a woman. . . . He is dying to be analysed and torments himself
with delusional ideas. . . . He does not feel in the least homosexual.
. . . Consequently, from love of me, he is turning himself into a woman
and wants to behave exactly like a woman, to go along with our Society
only *passively*, to be scientifically *fecundated* since he cannot express
himself *creatively*, is afraid of being violated. So, for the time being, he
won't join chiefly because of homosexual resistance [p. 371; emphasis
Jung's].

Both Freud and Jung freely ascribe sexualized motives and are oblivious of
such other motives as ambition, anger, politics, and power.

In the letters Jung complains a great deal about the homosexual transference
to him of Otto Gross (1887-1920), a psychiatrist and son of Hans Gross, the
noted psychiatric forensic expert and editor of the *AKAK*, in which Weber's
last paper was published. Otto Gross, an author of a paper published in the
PNW (1904), an early supporter of psychoanalysis and quoted a number of
times in Jung (1907), had an affair with Frieda von Richthoffen, who later
married D. H. Lawrence. The Gross affair is told by Russell Jacoby (1983, p.
40ff). Otto Gross wrote papers showing an affinity to Freud's ideas. Jung kept
complaining to Freud how much trouble he was. Another patient Jung and
Freud discussed was the promising young Swiss psychiatrist Honneger, who
committed suicide while in treatment with Jung. In a conversation on February 16, 1988, John Kerr called my attention to Jung's repeated statements to
Freud about Honneger's homosexuality. Jung was stern with Honneger to the
point of brutality, for which Freud duly admonished him. John Hickman
Phillips, who was Jung's student in Zurich for many years, cited Jung's role in
the breakup of Honneger with his fiancée and confirmed Jung's homophobia:
Jung told him he never treated homosexual men and always referred them
elsewhere.

37. Freud is not impressed with Schreber's own explanations of the end of
the world: "I further thought it possible . . . something in the nature of a
wizard had suddenly appeared in the person of Professor Flechsig and . . . this
had spread terror and fear amongst the people" (*M*, p. 91). In addition,
Schreber says in Foot Note #46, "The name of a French Doctor Brouardel was
also once mentioned to me, who was said to have imitated Professor Flechsig." Brouardel (1884, 1887, 1898, 1899) was a French expert in forensic
medicine. In his work of 1884 he deals with the issue of errors in expert
opinions concerning sexual assaults. In a joint work from 1897 he discusses a
classic case by another French forensic expert, Tardieu, on false and simulated
pregnancies and on artificial means employed to provoke an abortion. Was
Schreber's mention of Brouardel a hint about Sabine's abortions? This hinting
may also be suggested by linking Brouardel to Flechsig, himself a childless
man, who is accused by Schreber of acting "in the direction of denying them
[i.e., the Schrebers] offspring. . ." (*M*, p. 27). For more on Brouardel and
Tardieu see J. M. Masson (1984; chapter 2).

38. Freud never stopped appeasing Jung. He was far from being all in favor

of Jung attacking the libido question, not only because of its status as dogma, but because of its value as a safeguard against occultism. In a letter of April 2, 1909 (McGuire, 1974, p. 216 and footnote 4, p. 216) Jung refers to the famous "spookery" incident and discussion when he tried to convince Freud about the truth of precognition and parapsychology. Freud enjoined him on that occasion "that they must make an unshakable bulwark of the sexual theory 'against the black tide of mud of occultism'" (quoted by McGuire from Jung's *Memories*). In his paper of 1912 Jung mentions mystical works, but this is still mild compared to his later occultist views. For a history of Jung's and Freud's occultist views, see Webb (1976). Fichtner (Freud Collection, Library of Congress) documents 1911 as the date Freud became a honorary member of the Society for Psychical Research in London.

39. The light was supposed to come from Jung's 1912 landmark paper *"Wandlungen und Symbole der Libido* (The Transformations and Symbols of the Libido," translated in Jung's *Collected Works* as *Symbols of Transformation* (first published in vol. IV of the *Jahrbuch*, Part II). Jung's points against Freud are of considerable historical interest. Jung quotes the entire third subsection of Section III of Freud's essay on paranoia (1911a, pp. 73-75) in the *Jahrbuch* (3:65ff). He uses Freud's own statements in that subsection as support for his own new "genetic theory of the libido" as a more inclusive theory that also contains the concept of "'desexualized' instinctual energies" (p. 182) used in the service of adaptation to reality, for it is not only the erotic "but the whole reality adaptation" (p. 174) that is lost in paranoia. Jung finds further support in a paper by Sabina Spielrein (1911), a follower of the Zurich School (his patient and lover, and one of the early original analytic writers), "On the Psychological Content of a Case of Schizophrenia (Dementia praecox)," which emphasizes archaic thinking of the schizophrenic; it appeared in the same volume with Freud's Schreber analysis. As to the specific reaction Jung, as editor of the *Jahrbuch*, had to the publication of Freud's Schreber analysis: "It is not only uproariously funny but brilliantly written as well. . . . I must content myself with the invidious role of wishing I had got in first, although that's not much of a consolation" (McGuire, 1974, p. 407). Of course, he had already been there first, but came nowhere near what Freud reached.

40. Friedrich Krauss (1852), *A Cry of Distress of One Poisoned by Magnetism; The Facts, Explained through Unvarnished Description of a Course of 36 Years Accompanied by Proofs and Testimonials. For Instruction and Warning, Especially for Fathers of Families and Merchants*, "privately published by the author." It was followed in 1867 by *A Desperate Continuation of My Cry of Distress Against my Poisoning with Concentrated Vital Ether and the Masked Influence of the Above upon Body and Soul to Create Suspended Animation*. These books are very rare; a complete set can be found in the National Library of Medicine. Excerpts in facsimile are in Ahlenstiel and Meyer (1967). There is a marked difference between Krauss's style and Schreber's: Krauss is full of undefined bizarre neologisms compared to the carefully wrought definitions of concepts in Schreber. Krauss's content reflects the contemporary influence of Mesmer, Schreber reflects the occultists, like du Prel and, to some extent, the varieties of radiation (uranium rays, Roentgen rays, radio waves and cosmic rays) that

were widely talked about after 1895. Some of Paul's descriptions reverberate with those of Krauss: for example, the words *"Leibmord"* (body murder), and *"Seelenmord"* (soul murder) appear in Krauss's 1867 work. Krauss speaks of "effluvia in the form of rays *(strahlenförmige Ausläufe).*" Krauss' enemies, "the Anthropophobes," have brought to bear upon him "an overwhelming influence *(beherrschenden Einfluss).*" They intend to destroy him, and thus, due to "an increase or local withdrawal of the ether [as energy] he has presently been deformed . . . such that, like a whore (*"nach Hurencaprice"*) they completely *own me body and soul"* [emphasis Krauss'] . . . The exalted friend of mankind Alexander forbids *"ownership of body"* [emphasis Krauss's] and even more so the *"ownership of the soul"* [emphasis Krauss's], the all-threatening and all-destroying body- and soul-murder of the better part of mankind" [Krauss, 1867, p. 380; Ahlenstiel and Meyer, p. 105].

41. I cannot give more space to the details of this debate, whose main motifs are still with us. Bleuler was for analysis, in spite of his reservation, while Hoche, the archfiend of the "sect," sarcastically acknowledged Stegmann's defense while morally accusing Bleuler of being the cause of the analysts' success. Bleuler's main problem was with Freud's views on sexuality. In an unpublished letter to Adolf Meyer of November 18, 1912, in response to an invitation to speak at the Psychiatric Hospital in Baltimore, he said: "I cannot speak on the subject of Freud's developmental phases of sexuality because I do not believe in them at all" (kept in the Alan Mason Chesney Medical Archives at Johns Hopkins University).

42. *Versuch einer Darstellung der psychoanalytischen Theorie.* These were nine lectures given in 1912 at Fordham University, published in 1913 in German (in the *Jahrbuch* and by Deuticke) and in the *Psychoanalytic Review.*

43. First published in 1913. I use the ninth unchanged edition (1973, p. 89). Jaspers uses a locution analogous to Freud's *Traumarbeit,* dream work, but with a very different intention.

44. I have pointed out the fallacies and contradictions in Jaspers's phenomenological analysis of hallucinations (Lothane, 1982a).

45. To survey the literature of that first period is beyond the scope of this work. The interested reader should consult the bibliography in Rickman (1926-1927) and Fenichel (1945).

46. Freud's dynamic idea of repressed homosexuality was championed in the United States by A. A. Brill (1911). Another early contribution was Hitschmann's (1913) "Paranoia, Homosexuality and Anal Eroticism." None of the cases in these two papers resembled Schreber. Later, phallic castration became overshadowed by anality. Thus, Stärcke (1920) and van Ophuijsen (1920) viewed intestinal bodily sensations (e. g., the pressure of feces in the rectum), not genital sensations, as engendering feelings of persecution in the person, a view later developed by Annie Reich and Melanie Klein.

47. See Melanie Klein's *Contributions to Psycho-Analysis, 1921-1945* (London: the Hogarth Press, 1948), where she quotes Stärcke and van Ophuisen, and *The Psychoanalysis of Children* (1932). Of interest is that she places her discussion of the paranoid defense mechanism also in the context of "A Contribution to the Psychogenesis of Manic-Depressive States" from 1934. It is noteworthy

that in her two books (1921-1945 and 1932) there is no mention of Freud's Schreber analysis.

48. I do not know of any proof that Freud (1937) was aware of this implication when he wrote his "Constructions in Analysis," an essay in which he acknowledged the historical reality residue in hallucinations and that later became the basis for a paper by Waelder (1951). Of course, in that paper Freud himself provided a perspective on the genesis of paranoid ideas that differs from his views in the Schreber analysis.

49. Similar ideas about paranoia were expressed by McCawley (1971), who noted the role of hatred and aggression in Schreber's paranoia and the connection to mother. While not questioning the diagnosis of paranoia, McCawley was impressed with the strong depressive element and "nihilistic delusions which are classically associated with involutional depression" (p. 1512).

50. Similar ideas, based on sexualization, are found in Katan's work (1959a), too complicated to summarize. According to Katan (1950), 'the little men' are spermatozoa or men to whom Schreber is attracted homosexually. Other papers by Maurits Katan are from 1952, 1954, and 1959b.

51. These are contained in a correspondence file between Baumeyer, the last nephew of Schreber, Felix Jung and others, which is in the possession of Han Israëls, who denied me copies of this file. Part of it is cited in Busse (1990).

52. Male pregnancy and the Schreber case were also linked by M. J. Eisler (1921, p. 274), thus still in Freud's lifetime.

53. Until then, the *Memoirs* were only known in the fragments included in Freud's essay, translated as part of the 1925 five volume Collected Papers, published by Hogarth in London. The French translation of the *Memoirs* appeared in 1932. The first new printings of the German original appeared in 1972 by the Focus Verlag, and in 1973 by the Ullstein Verlag, then in West Germany.

54. Lacan's views can be read in his 1958 *Ecrits* and in *Les Psychoses*, Volume 3 of *Séminaire de Jacques Lacan*, 1981, both published in Paris by Éditions du Seuil. An accessible summary of Lacan's views is offered by Margaret Ganz (1987), who is negative toward Schreber: "Reading . . . Schreber's *Memoirs* . . . does not constitute a literary experience" (p. 37). That is her opinion; I strongly disagree. A sampling of this literature in English is found in Allison et al.(1988), which I reviewed (Lothane, 1991a). Of interest is the Lacanian analysis of S. M. Weber (1973), first written in German for the Ullstein edition of the *Memoirs* and appearing in translation as an introduction to the 1988 English Harvard edition, a reprint of the Macalpine-Hunter translation.

A literary-psychological view of the *Memoirs* as a narrative, is offered by Ernest Kean (1986). Kean's formula is that Schreber's was a cataclysmic narrative whose aim was to "avoid the panic of an acute psychotic crisis" (p. 185).

Schreber has also been studied by historians. Carl Pletsch (1979) did not provide any research of his own but endorsed the findings of Niederland as historical and characterized Schatzman as a popularizer of Niederland's ideas. In an oral presentation (1990), one of Pletsch's central contentions was that historians deal both with collecting facts and hermeneutics, without specifying what kind of hermeneutics. This is also the view of Chabot (1982), a professor of English, who saw a common denominator between the psychoanalytic method and literary criticism. Gay (1988) endorsed Niederland's reading of Schreber's illness but also noted Freud's unpublished remarks about his own conflicts about homosexuality and about Moritz Schreber's aggressive attitudes.

55. In the sixties Niederland worked in archives and libraries in what was then East Germany and also had people doing research for him there, blazing trails for those who came after him. Niederland's works on Schreber include 1959a, 1959b (of which German versions appeared in the *Zeitschrift für Kinderpsychologie und Kinderpsychiatrie* in 1961 and in *Psyche* in 1969); 1960; 1963; 1968; 1972. The last journal publication also included a debate with Schatzman, tendentiously assessed by Israëls (1989) owing to his partisan advocacy of Schatzman, which I have discussed (Lothane, 1991b). The papers were collected in book form that appeared twice: in 1974 and 1984, as *The Schreber Case: a profile of a paranoid personality*, which was translated into a number of languages. Niederland's influence has been worldwide.

56. Niederland inspired a sizable literature on Schreber that pursued the idea of the traumatogenic father, made popular by Schatzman, who then became a target of attacks by psychoanalysts, not always fairly. Among the American followers of the idea the most important is Leonard Shengold (1961, 1974, 1975, 1989). The views of Niederland were discussed in a special symposium, "Reinterpretation of the Schreber Case: Freud's theory of paranoia" organized in 1963 (Kitay, 1963).

The orthodox Freudian commentaries on Schreber in France from the year 1966 did not contribute anything new, since they followed in the footsteps of either Freud or Niederland, or both. The Schreber case, paranoia and homosexuality were discussed in a special issue of *Revue Française de Psychanalyse*, with contributions by Barande (1966), "Reading Schreber's Memoirs"; Chazaud (1966), "A Contribution to the Psychoanalytic Theory of Paranoia"; Chasseguet-Smirgel (1966), "Notes On the Reading of the Revision of the Schreber Case"; and Racamier & Chasseguet-Smirgel (1966), "A Reappraisal of the S. Case: An overview." One should note Deleuze & Guattari (1972), a book that emphasizes Freudo-Marxism and cultural and poltical issues, with incidental mention of Schreber and Niederland's views of the torture machines, which reminds the authors of the the contraption worn by the Countess de Ségur, similar to that of Balsan (1952). Interesting points about Schreber and Flechsig were made by Octave Mannoni (1974, 1978). Schreber has been of special interest to the French analyst Luis Eduardo Prado de Oliveira. In his introduction to the volume he edited (1979b), Prado de Oliveira discusses the Freud–Jung dialectic about Schreber. He also published (1981) "The Liberation of Men or the Creation of Pathogenesis" and "Freud and Schreber, Lectures, Revisions" (Prado de Oliveira, 1986-1989). A French historical study is by Skurnik & Bourguignon (1980), "History, Education and Psychiatry in 19th Century Saxony." The Belgians are represented by Fr. Croufer (1970), "The Life of President Schreber, an ordeal related to paternity?"), by Kris Vermeiren (cited in Busse, 1990), and the many contributions cited in this book by Daniel Devreese. I found two other papers by Italians: Benvenuto (1984) and Marozza (1986). Benvenuto's intepretation of Schreber's text is informed largely by Lacan; Marozza's reflections by Jung, Ricouer and Canetti.

Among analysts, Edoardo Weiss (1960) was alone in championing the views of Paul Federn who interpreted Schreber according to his own ego-psychological views on psychosis and, according to Weiss, "came later to different and in some respects opposite conclusions from those of Freud" (p. 315). For example, Federn believed that Schreber's feeling " 'He does not love me' is felt as 'he hates me' because for a lover no love return is by contrast hatred" (p. 315). Federn also held that in Schreber there was "a decrease in ego cathexis (including ego libido), and for this reason the ego's functions can no longer be dynamically maintained. . . . Federn . . . denies that hallucinations and delusions correspond to unsuccessful attempts at restitution" (p. 316). Peter Swales reminded me to include Federn's views.

57. In the epilogue of the 1984 edition I doubt both these assumptions, the traumatogenic (see Chapter 4) and the masturbatory (see Chapter 4, note 32). First, there is no evidence that the father manipulated the son more than did other caretakers when Paul Schreber was an infant and young child. Second, there is not one mention of antimasturbatory devices in Schreber's work, only injunctions against the unhealthy effects of masturbation, a commonplace of medical wisdom in those days and a view shared by Freud himself.

58. An earlier model for Kohut may have been Treher (1966), representative of the trend of producing pathographies of leaders guilty of crimes against humanity, such as Hitler, in which these criminals are seen as "messianic leaders." Niederland's (1974) impression of Moritz Schreber's "missionary zeal" (p. 59) may have inspired Kohut's (1971) extrapolation that Moritz Schreber was also an example of a "messianic leader" (p. 316 footnote 4). Treher set up occultism as a philosophical cause of Hitler. Has Treher heard of Houston Stewart Chamberlain who married Richard Wagner's daughter and was such an inspiration to Hitler?

59. Schatzman, Israëls's claims notwithstanding, has contributed nothing new to the Schreber father–son problem (Lothane, 1991b). He did, however, expand on the issue of coercive parental education as against an ideal of freedom that he saw incarnated in the socio-analytical writings of Wilhelm Reich, whom Israëls ignored completely. Thus, not unlike Jeffrey Masson, he has made a contribution to the parental trauma literature. I have not seen anything by Freud on coercion and punishment in upbringing. Some of the early psychoanalytic writers on education spoke in favor of love and leniency in education, e.g., Siegfried Bernfeld (1925), in *Sisyphus or the Limits of Upbringing* and Meng (1934), in *Punishment and Upbringing*.

60. Szasz (1976, p. 40) also noted that Freud was himself instrumental in locking up Otto Gross, a drug addict and enfant terrible whom Freud dumped on Jung and of whom he wrote: "Enclosed the certificate for Otto Gross. Once you have him, don't let him out before October when I shall be able to take charge of him" (McGuire, 1974, p. 147).

61. I raised this question in lectures on June 7 and June 24, 1988, at the New

York Academy of Sciences and the History Section of the Payne Whitney Clinic, respectively, both in New York City. I subsequently received from Israëls the reprints of the papers by Grotstein (1984-1985) and Lipton (1984). In a later paper I received from Grotstein (1985), he reverted to the diagnosis of schizophrenia but stressed the aspect of interaction and self-regulation and expressed views sympathetic to Paul Schreber. Through the Wellcome Institute catalog of *Current Work in the History of Medicine* I found the paper by Koehler (1981). McCawley (1971) also raised questions about diagnosis.

62. It was still, however, regarded by Nydes (1963) as a backdrop for his other "schizophrenic symptoms" (p. 210). Nydes was rare in addressing the issue of rage in Schreber. However, Nydes could only speak of the rage against the father of childhood; toward Flechsig, Schreber only had rivalry.

63. She also cited historical sources, about Gustav and Paul Schreber and about Flechsig, from the Leipzig dissertation of Gerda Sachse, who had compiled a comprehensive Flechsig bibliography.

64. Flechsig (1884) can be read in Masson (1988).

65. My papers of 1989b and 1989a were published in the beginning and middle of 1989, respectively; Busse's (1989) at the end of 1989. Busse both incorporated my idea of the traumatic impact of Flechsig and denied its validity. In 1990 I found Martin Stingelin's chapter (1989b) and on March 5 I wrote to his Viennese publisher, who put me in touch with him and I have corresponded with him since. Stingelin sent me Kittler (1984).

66. A skeptical view was offered by philosopher Scharfstein (1973). Even though he believed mysticism to be a genuine phenomenon, and the boundary between mysticism and madness to be often blurred, he relegated Schreber's experiences to the realm of madness.

67. This approach is represented by Lucy Bregman (1977), a professor of religion. She quoted approvingly from Wilden (1972) and saw Schreber "among 'the great mystics and the great utopian socialist philosophers'" (p. 120). The "personal myth" idea was taken from Jung. Podvoll (1979-1980) also placed Schreber in the mystical tradition, claiming for him an affinity with the mystic path described by Evelyn Underhill. A recent contribution is by Merold Westphal (1989), which provides a mixed argument: Schreber is viewed as a repressed homosexual who uses God as an escape from responsibility (by blaming a malevolent deity) and as waging holy war, which is a model for the persecution of the Jews by the crusaders and the Nazis, and for the similar war waged by the Jewish state against the Palestinians, and by the Afrikaner against South African blacks.

8

SCHREBER AS INTERPRETER AND THINKER

I have thus gained insight into the nature of human thought processes
and human feelings for which many a psychologist might envy me.
My experiences . . . will provide the future generations with food for
thought.

D. P. Schreber, 1903

To the welfare of future generations.

D. G. M. Schreber, 1858a, dedication to the Kallipädie

I plan to introduce "basic language" as a serious technical term—
meaning the original wording of a delusional idea which the patient's
consciousness . . . experiences only in distorted form.

Freud to Jung, October 1, 1910

Freud was among a handful of people who considered Schreber a
quotable author. Everybody else regarded him as a madman, to be
diagnosed, decoded, or disposed of. Schreber himself admitted he had
been ill but not a madman and he meant his ideas to be taken *seriously*:
he, too, knew how to "*interpret*" (*M*, p. 82, emphasis Schreber's) and he
was a thinker. As such, he deserves a hearing on his own terms. There
is a need to disentangle his factual from his fantastic (delusional) ideas,
to discover the truths hidden in the "distorted form," and to understand his worthy and memorable reflections on many subjects, in-

375

cluding religion, sexuality, cosmology, biology, philosophy, psychology, education, politics, man and woman in society, and forensic psychiatry. Like his father, he wanted to bequeath to mankind a book that would live in memory.

Although Schreber felt tormented by his visions and voices (they struck him as grotesque gibberish—not the usual statement from a paranoiac), he believed them to be *meaningful* messages. In this he was of the same mind as Freud, whose epochal discovery was that dreams and symptoms have meaning and as such are potentially intelligible and analyzable formations. The difference was in the meanings they both found, and in the methods of interpretation. Today the idea that hallucinations and delusions are both encoded and decodable is fairly well established. In their day Schreber and Freud were among a tiny few who held this view.

Descriptively, the *content* of the *Memoirs* is Schreber's re-creation of the stream of consciousness that filled his long days and nights at Sonnenstein, that is, his thinking, whether hearing his thoughts silently or vocally, in the form of voices, that is, his own voiced thoughts. Thinking is what Schreber did more than anything else, whether we regard it as normal or abnormal, whether we call his thoughts hallucinations, delusions, daydreams—or voices. As *content*, this reportage of his thinking could be likened to Stendhal's *monologue intérieur* or James Joyce's stream of consciousness. As *form*, it was both realistic and fantastic, that is, delusional. The latter presented a problem: the psychiatrists diagnosed it, Freud analyzed it. And so did the author himself. It is with Schreber's own diagnostic and dynamic views that we are concerned here.

A person's thinking during the day may be determined by life's realistic goals, problems, and problem-solving or be preempted by unpleasant themes, such as conflicts, frustrations, and worries, or by pleasant wish-fulfilling daydreams. Schreber was between the ages of 51 and 60 during his life at Sonnenstein. He was an active man, removed from work, home, family, and outlets for sexual hunger. No doubt, a major part of his thinking was taken up with trying to resolve his conflicts about career, family life, and identity, with feelings of anxiety, depression, anger, regret, helplessness, and irony. A lot of time was spent in reminiscences about his past. But he was not living in a vacuum: he also had to cope with the stimuli presented by the brutal conditions of life in the asylum. For the rest, like any other prisoner, he filled the long hours with a rich fantasy life, distracting himself with meditations on the most diverse topics. When he recovered from the depressed, agitated psychotic state, he was also able to enjoy music and read his old books (*M*, p. 84). Another source of reading material was the extensive library at Sonnenstein. Since there is no indication that there was at Flechsig's or at Sonnenstein a well-organized occupational therapy program as we understand it today, apart from drawing, painting and walks in the garden, Schreber used his inventiveness and designed his own: "during *day-time* I occupied myself decently, quietly, and in accordance with my intellectual standing by playing the piano, playing chess, and later reading books and newspapers" (*M*, p. 198; emphasis Schreber's).

In addition to this self-designed, healthy-minded occupational therapy, there were Schreber's morbid-minded productions, the assorted hallucinations and delusions, which, it is most important to realize, as Freud did, were not only the manifestations of his illness but also the method of its cure, a form of self-therapy. Even though supportive and suggestive psychotherapy was recommended by Kraepelin as a method of treatment for institutionalized psychotics, none was offered to Schreber. Above all, it was the composing of the *Memoirs* that became the supreme act of self-analysis, just as gaining his freedom was the supreme act of his self-assertion and self-vindication.

In what follows we discuss Schreber's psychology of thinking and feeling, especially his own image and dream psychology, his religious and cosmological views, and his ideas on sexuality and education. We will also review, one by one, his ideas about his illness and its diagnosis and the nature of soul murder. It is crucial to realize that all these views are a coherent whole, both as a worldview (*Weltanschauung*) and as an attempt to explain his experiences to himself and to others. He also assimilated and debated views of other persons he knew or read, especially his father and his first doctor. Let us now compare his views and theirs.

SCHREBER'S STYLE

Schreber told his story in a counterpoint of the realistic and fantastic modes of representation, the latter based on thinking in analogies, pictures, metaphors, and puns. Even though Schreber puts us on notice about his use of analogical discourse, he more often than not assumes that we remember his caveat and freely mixes, without further warning, straight describing with the analogical style. When the expressions "like," "as if," "it seems that" are missing (at times due to omissions of Macalpine and Hunter), we are abruptly plunged into the thicket of the fantastic mode of representation and left wondering whether we are reading an analogical discourse, one that knows itself as such, or a delusional one and whether Schreber believes his own delusional discourse or is pulling our leg.

Schreber's brusque transitions from the realistic to the fantastic and back have done much to create a global impression of the *Memoirs* as an assemblage of mad productions.[1] What is missed in such global perceptions is that Schreber was indeed a keen observer and psychologist. Furthermore, it is not true that Schreber's style is schizophrenic gibberish or word salad. Neologisms are not only present in a delusional system but in many a scientific and philosophical system. Schreber took great care in giving definitions of his terms, but it takes some effort to remember them as one reads his text. It thus becomes important to separate his fantastic representations of the real from the hardcore delusions and then to try to understand what he meant. Beyond these two kinds of discourse, the analogical and the delusional, Schreber's style is marked by a multiplicity of precise detail and a high degree of pithiness. His book cannot be simply read: it must be studied. It can be likened to a Bach fugue: there is so much on one page, so much polyphony in the many voices heard. That is why Schreber reveals so many different perspectives with every rereading.

Picturing, that is, pictorial representation, is a centerpiece of Schreber's style. However, since the picture is the essential thought form of the dream and the hallucination, we are immediately plunged into Schreber's dream psychology.

PICTURING

Picturing is a translation for Schreber's "*sogenannte Zeichnen*," literally drawing pictures, a Greek metaphor taken from the draftsman's or painter's craft (Plato called imagination the painter, *zoographos*) and Schreber's term for thinking in images, or imagining. This process is both caused by divine inspiration from out there ("because my inner nervous system is illuminated by nerves" or "rays") and is an everyday psychological process. Under picturing or imagining, Schreber, following Kant, subsumes the reproductive imagination, productive imagination, and recollection. He defines it as follows: "To picture [literally, *das Zeichnen*, i.e., drawing with one's imagination] (in the sense of the soul-language) is the conscious use of the human imagination for the purpose of producing pictures [*Bilder*] (predominantly pictures of recollection) in one's head. . ." (*M*, p. 232). He defines further in Foot Note #98:

> imagination (fantasy derived from *phainomai*). The German word [*Einbildungskraft*] indicates clearly the notion of 'something being put into the head or into human awareness,' which is not present outside; hence also the term 'to imagine something' [*Sicheinbilden, Vorgaukeln*] for *morbid*

imagination, conjuring something up before one's eyes (hopes, etc.) which cannot be realized, but is used as a motive for inappropriate and wrong action [emphasis Schreber's].

Picturing is indeed the heart of his dream psychology, in the two fundamental meanings of dream, both cause and cure of sickness. Schreber puts it this way:

> By vivid imagination [*lebhafte Vorstellung*, literally, vivid image] I can produce pictures [*Bilder*] of all recollections of my life, of persons, animals and plants, of all sorts of objects in nature and objects in daily use, so that these images become visible either inside my head or if I wish, outside, where I want them to be seen by my own nerves and by the rays [i.e., God]. I can do the same with weather phenomena and other events; I can, for example, let it rain or let lightning strike—this is a particularly effective form of 'picturing', . . . because the weather and particularly lightning are considered by the rays manifestations of the divine gift of miracles; . . . All this naturally only in my imagination. But in a manner that the rays get the impression [*as if*, omitted by Macalpine and Hunter; emphasis added] these objects and phenomena really exist [*als ob die betreffenden Gegenstände und Erscheinungen wirklich vorhanden wären*]" (M, p. 232).

This activity of drawing pictures in his mind is also applied to his dreams of being changed into a woman: "The picturing of female buttocks on my body—*honi soit qui mal y pense*—has become such a habit that I do it almost automatically when I bend down" (p. 233). It is both horrific and healing, depending on how you look at it. But Schreber's opinion is the one that counts:

> He who has not experienced what I have cannot form any idea in how many ways the ability to 'picture' has become of value to me. It has truly often been a consolation and a comfort in the unending monotony of my dreary life, in the mental tortures I suffered from the nonsensical twaddle of voices. . . . In sleepless nights I often took revenge as it were for the rays' play with miracles, by conjuring up myself all sorts of shapes, serious or humorous, sensuously exciting or fearful, in my bedroom or in the cell; the entertainment I obtained in this way was an essential means to conquer the otherwise unbearable boredom. . . . I sometimes enjoy myself by jokingly "picturing" . . . [pp. 234-235].

Images, whether of sense perception or of imagination, so-called mental images, are of fundamental importance in daily life, psychology, and philosophy. In the latter, they go back at least to Plato's theory of ideas. The concept of the imagination's image, seen in the mind's eye, is preliminary to coming to grips with all the varieties of diurnal and nocturnal dreaming, including hallucinations. In the 19th century, images were on the mind of philosophers, such as Fechner; empirical psychologists, such as Francis Galton; and many others with interests in mysticism and occultism.[2] It properly introduces Schreber's concept of dreaming and the dream state.

SCHREBER'S DREAM PSYCHOLOGY

When Schreber was writing his book at Sonnenstein, he consulted a number of works on psychiatry. He would have seen the name Freud in the sixth edition (1899) of Kraepelin's *Textbook*. Freud's work on hysteria is mentioned on pages 511 and 518 of the *Textbook*, and Freud's German translation of Bernheim's work on hypnosis, suggestion, and psychotherapy is mentioned on page 329 ("Bernheim, *Neue Studien über Hypnotismus, Suggestion und Psychotherapie*, deutsch von Freud, 1893"). I have traced a number of other works by Freud that Schreber could have seen (Lothane, 1989c). Had he read Jung's doctoral dissertation, he would have also seen Jung's reference to Freud's *Interpretation of Dreams*. If he did not, it means that he intuitively and independently developed his own dream psychology.

The term dream psychology embraces images from sleep and wakefulness alike. This view was fully expressed by Freud in *"Delusions and Dreams in Jensen's Gradiva"* (1907a) and in "Creative Writers and Day-Dreaming (*das Phantasieren*)" (1907b):

> Our dreams at night are nothing else than phantasies like these, as we can demonstrate from the interpretation of dreams. [*Freud's* footnote: Cf. Freud, *The Interpretation of Dreams.*] Language, in its unrivalled wisdom, long ago decided the question of the essential nature of dreams by giving the name of "day-dreams" to the airy creations of phantasy [*Phantasierender*, day-dreamers]. . . . May we . . . compare the imaginative writer with the "dreamer in broad daylight," and his creations with day-dreams? [Freud, 1907b, pp. 148-149].

Mostly concerned with daydreams, Schreber is forever fascinated by the emergence in his stream of consciousness of unbidden thoughts and images and other similar experiences. Such unbidden experiences, beyond his voluntary control, were called "divine miracles" by Schreber, hallucinations and delusions by the psychiatrists, and dreams by Freud. In this we are back to Kant's famous aphorism, "Let the dreamer be wide awake, and we have a madman."[3]

This is how Schreber expounds his dream theory:

I have witnessed not once but hundreds of times how human shapes were set down for a short time by divine miracles only to be dissolved again or to vanish. The voices talking to me designated these visions the so-called *fleeting-improvised-men* [fleeting phantoms][4]—some were even persons long ago deceased . . .; there were others also, who had apparently passed through a transmigration of souls, as for instance . . . the Privy Councillor Dr. W.,[5] the lawyer W., my father-in-law and others; all of them *were leading a so-called dream life*, i.e., they did not give the impression of being capable of holding a sensible conversation, just as I myself was at that time also little inclined to talk, mainly because I thought that I *was faced not by real people but by miraculously created puppets*. . . . From this conception it follows that the Dogma of the Ascension of Christ is a mere fable by which His disciples tried to explain the fact that after His death they repeatedly *saw* His person in the flesh amongst them [*M*, p. 4, Foot Note #1; emphasis added].

This description is a window into Schreber's dream conception and religious myth, as well as a demarcation between dream life, waking life, and delusion. In his dream or trance state, existentially a retreat (Freud's decathexis) from an interest in the real world, Schreber sees everything around him as in a dream: fleeting, shadowy, insubstantial. In this state, real people are themselves seen or thought of as living a dream life; they exist only as Schreber's dream thought of them. The notion of the transmigration of souls, a very old belief, is expressed merely as a possibility. As a nonbeliever, Schreber regards as fable the common folk belief in the bodily Ascension of Christ, while the visions of Christ by the faithful were dream representations of it, i.e., religious myths; thus, he implies a connection between dream consciousness and mythical consciousness.

This view of unbidden images erupting in waking consciousness as hypnopompic, hypnagogic and other daydreams was, of course, endorsed by Freud in his Schreber essay and elsewhere. He also said that the structure of delusions, *Wahnbildung*, is completely homologous with *Traumbildung*, the structure of dreams.

The main difference between Schreber's conception of the dream and Freud's is in the understanding of the *dynamic* nature of the dream and the symptom. For Freud, the dream is but the manifest content of a latent unconscious content that lies behind it. There is no dynamic conception of unconscious processes in the *Memoirs*, although Schreber mentions the word *unbewusst* and defines his own manifest content as nonsense (*Unsinn*). Nor does he articulate the method of interpretation of the manifest by exploring the latent content.

From the onset of his hallucinatory-delusional state of mind in mid-March 1894 until 1896 Schreber was in a prolonged dream trance.

During that time, fleeting phantoms appeared as convincing and real as in an ongoing dream. When he awoke from the dream-trance,[6] he could look back and see his experiences for what they were—dreams. As for the latent content, Schreber only recognized that the voices and the miracles were manifestations of divine causation and remained unconscious of his deeper personal motives and conflicts. Nonetheless, he was retrospectively aware that he had been deluded, and that at least some of his delusions frankly reflected his feelings of despair. Thus, he knew that he had "labored under the delusion that when all attempts at cure had been exhausted, one would be discharged—solely for the purpose of making an end to one's life either in one's own home or somewhere else" (*M*, p. 41). He was aware of other things as well: "All kinds of extraordinary symptoms of illness appeared in my body in the course of time, apart from the repeatedly mentioned changes in my sex organs. In discussing them I must return again to the idea of the end of the world . . ." (pp. 90-91). Here again, Schreber is capable of grasping that he is discussing "symptoms" of an "illness," but when he moves to explicate them he turns to a frame of reference, "the idea of the end of the world," that takes the reader deeper into Schreber's own phenomenological interior.

SCHREBER'S DYNAMIC PSYCHOLOGY AND SELF DIAGNOSIS

With regard to the form of the unbidden thoughts and images—in his language, the various voices and visions—that plagued him, Schreber's interpretive stance was informed by his dream psychology. But with regard to interpreting their content, and to establishing their ultimate metaphysical sanction as experiences, Schreber turned instead to his private religion, or personal mythology. The result was a mixture of quasi-literal and metaphorical statements, in which the ground shifted back and forth between subjective self-reports of vivid experiences and metaphysically grounded reflections upon those experiences with a view to understanding what they said about the nature of God and man. In consequence of this, God was put to psychological uses. that is, as an explanation for phenomena understood to be emanating from within, but not experienced as products of the self. In the psychological use of religion, God became the equivalent of the dynamic unconscious: not I but God in me, reminiscent of Homer's heroes, whose actions were portrayed as caused by interventions of the various deities. A lot of what was seen as his paranoia was such a divine personification of impulse, sensation and action. It is sometimes difficult to tell whether Schreber believes in his myths literally or only metaphorically. The delusional religion could also be qualified as Schreber's dream religion, the use of religious ideas in his daydreams.[7]

Under severe emotional stress and in the throes of uncontrollable, incomprehensible, and terrifying sensations, visions, voices, and bellowing, Schreber resorted to the divine as a dynamic explanation. That is why in "ground" or "soul language," Schreber's name for unconscious processes, all unbidden experiences were called miracles. These miracles/hallucinations/delusions fill the bulk of Chapter 11 of the *Memoirs* and are scattered in other places, and include, for example, the lung, chest, and shortness of breath miracles:

> But in the first year of my stay at Sonnenstein the miracles were of such a threatening nature that I thought I had to fear almost incessantly for my life, my health and my reason. The miracles enacted against my organs of the thoracic and abdominal cavities were very multifarious. My lungs were so affected by miracles that for a time I seriously believed that I had to fear a fatal outcome in consequence of pulmonary phthisis. A "lung worm" was frequently produced in me by miracles; I cannot say whether it was an animal-like being or a soul-like creature. I can only say that its appearance was connected with a biting pain in the lungs similar to the pains I imagine occur in inflammation of the lungs. . . . At about the same time some of my *ribs* were sometimes temporarily smashed, always with the result that what had been destroyed was re-formed after a time. One of the most horrifying miracles was the so-called *compression-of-the-chest* miracle [*Engbrüstigkeit*, commonly, shortness of breath], which I endured at least several dozen times; it consisted in the whole chest wall being compressed, so that the state of oppression caused by the lack of breath was transmitted to my whole body . . . it belongs mainly to the second half of 1894 or perhaps the first half of the year 1895 [pp. 148-151; emphasis Schreber's].

In this passage it is important to pay attention to Schreber's own description, because the temptation is so great for an interpreter to change or paraphrase Schreber's words to fit his interpretive scheme. The translators fused the idea of compression of the chest and shortness of breath, and Niederland saw here the effect of Moritz Schreber's orthopedic compressing gadgets. But Paul Schreber's experience is a feeling of oppression and tightness in the chest that causes shortness of breath and spreads to the whole body. Calling it a delusion misses not only the fact that this is a bodily post-perceptual metaphor for anxiety but that anxiety is the essence of the entire here-and-now experience. This was Schreber's description of fears occurring at a time of severe emotional stress, that is, following the transfer to Sonnenstein, which made him feel so threatened. The feelings of terror are depicted by the terrifying bodily metaphors; it is a daymare, and, like its counterpart, the nightmare, anxiety and oppression of the chest are its main features. Furthermore, this experience is a communication: he is telling himself and his imaginary audience—and now a reader—that he was scared.

In yet another description of fear:

> The so-called *frightening miracle* . . . In early years where sometimes appeared when I was in bed—not sleeping but awake—all sort of large, queer, almost dragon-like shapes. . . . The "black bears" and the "white bears". . . which I saw repeatedly in Flechsig's Asylum belong probably to the same category of "frightening miracle". . . . which in certain circumstances could be further condensed to [fleeting phantoms]" [p. 249].

Again, terror depicted by bodily metaphor: "On the other hand, as a result of miracles practiced against me all manner of painful states occur alternately . . . sciatica, cramp in the calves, states of paralysis, sudden attacks of hunger . . . lumbago and toothache . . . almost uninterrupted headaches . . . tearing and pulling pains. . ." (p. 201).

Like Schreber, many patients—and often their physicians as well—cannot fathom how emotions, communicating through the body, can come in such an astounding multifariousness of form and content, earning names like hysteria, hypochondria, or delusion. The daymare, like the nightmare, is both a breakthrough of the anxiety caused by painful reality and an attempt to master that reality. In Schreber's case this is expressed in the idea that divine rays were at first "searing" and in the end "blessing" rays (p. 93).

Schreber regarded picturing as "the real cause" of yet "another interesting phenomenon . . . compulsive thinking (*Denkzwang*)" (p. 231), an important variety of unbidden experience, existing in two forms: one spontaneous and one caused by environmental stimuli.

Compulsive Thinking

Schreber has given us eloquent descriptions of the spontaneous state of mind that the French neuropathologists referred to as automatism and Freud as compulsion neurosis. These descriptions count as a phenomenological contribution to our knowledge of compulsive states, fit for a textbook of psychiatry:

> The nature of compulsive thinking lies in a human being having to think incessantly; [as against] man's natural right to give the *nerves of his mind* [nerves of intellect, *Verstandesnerven*] their necessary rest from time to time by thinking nothing (as occurs most markedly during sleep) . . . a

human being can at certain times as well think of *nothing* as of *thousands of things at the same time* . . . [p. 48; emphasis Schreber's].

The bulk of chapters 16, 17, and 18 concerns compulsive thinking. Schreber not only describes its mechanics, so to speak, but also its dynamics. It is difficult for anybody, sick or healthy, to think nothing. Certain mystics claimed to have been able to empty the mind of thoughts. Schreber stresses the universal compulsion to think something. Lacking the concept of a dynamic unconscious, he feels acted upon by God (the rays): "For instance, I was asked . . . : 'What are you thinking of now?'. . . the above question was answered spontaneously: 'he should' *scilicet* [that is, in Latin] 'think about the Order of the World'; that is to say, the influence of the rays forced my nerves to perform the movements corresponding to the use of these words" (p. 48). Furthermore, "It is the nature of nerves that if unconnected words or started phrases are thrown into them, they automatically attempt to complete them to finish thoughts satisfactory to the human mind" (p. 217). Schreber could have been describing a present-day sentence completion test, a Rorschach response, the Bluma Zeigarnik effect, or the imperative nature of free association. He also speaks of "thoughts of decision," that is, "man's exertion of will to do a certain thing," "wishful thoughts," "thoughts of hope," "thoughts of fear," "the-human-thought-of-recollection," and "thinking-it-over thoughts," the latter "known to psychologists . . . [to] *automatically cause doubts*" (p. 165; emphasis Schreber's).

Compulsive thinking is an "infringement of the freedom of human thinking" (p. 222); it is enforced both from within and from without. The stimuli from within often combine with stimuli from without, as in conversations with people in his environment (Foot Note #96) or owing to "every word spoken around me" (Foot Note #67). "All the noises I hear . . ." he says, "*seem* to speak the words which are talked into my head by the voices and also those words in which I formulate my own thoughts" (p. 236). This creates a counterpoint of causes and effects and he is no longer "master in [his] own head against the intrusion of strangers" (*gegen fremde Eindringlinge*, alien intruders, a double reference to thoughts and persons, Foot Note #96).

A different intrusion occurs on occasions for examining him (p. 244), which may refer to mental status examinations:

It is so obstinately held that I have become stupid to such a degree that day after day one doubts whether I still recognize people around me, whether I still understand ordinary natural phenomena, or articles of daily use or objects of art, indeed, whether I even still know *who I am or have been.* The phrase 'has been recorded' with which I was examined [appears]. . . . For example, when I saw the doctor my nerves immediately resounded with 'has been recorded' [*fand Aufnahme*] [*M*, p. 245-246, emphasis Schreber's].

"Has been recorded" is a mistranslation: it means "was admitted"; for many years and until his release, Schreber was prey to the compulsively and intrusive thought that he was held at Sonnenstein against his will.

At first viewed as a "mental strain" and a "mental torture," compulsive thinking had, Schreber believed, certain advantages:

> I must also mention the mentally stimulating effect compulsive thinking has had on me. Throwing into my nerves unconnected conjunctions expressing causal or other relations ("Why only," "Why because" . . . etc.) forced me to ponder many things usually passed over by human beings, which made me think more deeply . . . stimulated [me] in immeasurably greater degree than other human beings to contemplate the reason or purpose behind them. . . . Being continually forced to trace the causal relations of every happening, every feeling, and every idea has given me gradually deeper insight into the essence of almost all natural phenomena and aspects of human activity in art, science, etc., than is achieved by people who do not think it worthwhile to think about everyday occurrences [pp. 228-229].[8]

Schreber often qualified his enforced thoughts and voices as nonsense. But already years ago he heard the repeated phrase: "All nonsense cancels itself. . . . [for a] human being who . . . can say *that eternity is in his service.* . . . Ultimately a time must come when nonsense exhausts itself [and] . . . ignorance . . . soon gives way to better insight" (pp. 331, 332).

Compulsive Feeling

Schreber's statements about feelings, like those about thinking, are not only descriptive but also inherently didactic: they make the point that something was missing from the concepts used by his psychiatrists, namely, feelings as an integral aspect of a person's life in health and disease.

The frightening and bellowing miracles were Schreber's way of succumbing to overpowering feelings and emotions, the only psychological realm that he has not been able to penetrate. His emotions, especially those of rage, remained a complete mystery to him; he was unaware of any motives for feeling rage. Speaking psychoanalytically, such feelings remained unconscious, or repressed, in two senses of the word: he could not tell himself he was angry (he does not use the word anger in reference to himself at all), nor could he say anything about the causes of his anger. He believed that the roaring and bellowing were caused by divine miracles.

Closely related to anger are irony and contempt—or "bitter scorn," as Freud (1911a, p. 52) put it—and such intent could be expressed in the guise of grotesque hallucinations. Freud was the only one to have considered it: "absurdity in dreams expresses ridicule and derision. Evidently, therefore, it is used for the same purpose in paranoia."[9] I submit that Schreber resorts to both mockery and self-mockery in his text, but that he hides his angry intent from the reader, as he no doubt hid it from himself, by leaving it unclear when he is being serious, and psychotic, and when he is being sardonic. Certainly, the text is full of irony, even bitter irony—consider only the use of the word "miracles" to describe painful bodily experiences—but the reader never knows for sure whether Schreber himself feels how much bitterness is lodged inside himself. Is the same with the sense of irony. If a madman need not be mad at every moment, then what is a reader to do with a madman who allows himself to posture as mad when it suits his purposes? Is the posturing, which conceals a secret superiority even as it discharges it, part of the illness? Or is it the residual protest of a still sane remainder of the personality?

The same goes for another essential emotion, sadness. Here Schreber is more explicit, as we noted earlier in connection with the poem in the *Memoirs;* but as with anger, he cannot fully articulate why he is sad. Neither can he clearly express any feelings of guilt. Both sadness and guilt remain in the realm of the unreflected, the semiconscious, or the unconscious. But if they are not articulated, they are certainly expressed, the way dreams are expressions and not articulations. For Schreber sadness and guilt are expressed in their icons, or signs. Among the most telling are his end-of-the-world fantasies, his statements about reward and punishment, about God and Devil.

End-of-the-World Fantasies

Schreber describes one of his "recurrent nightly visions": "[There is] the notion of an approaching *end of the world*, as a consequence of the indissoluble connection between God and myself. Bad news [*Hiobposten*, literally, Job's tidings] came in from all sides, that even this or that star or this or that group of stars had to be 'given up' (p. 70; emphasis Schreber's). Other expressions of his end-of-the-world fantasy include the following: "I regarded the starry sky largely, if not wholly, extinguished" (p. 72); "I believed the whole of mankind to have perished" (p. 65); "Sodom and Gomorrah were destroyed by a rain of brimstone and fire, although of their inhabitants there were some, even though very few, 'righteous' men" (p. 60); "In such an event, in order to maintain the species, one single human being was spared—perhaps the relatively most moral—called . . . the 'Eternal Jew.' This appellation has therefore a somewhat different sense from that underlying the legend of the same name of the Jew Ahasver; one is, however, automatically reminded of the legends of Noah, Deucalion, and Pyrrha . . . the Eternal Jew (in the sense described) had to be *unmanned* (transformed into a woman) to be able to bear children" (p. 53); "Perhaps God was also able to withdraw partially or totally the warmth of the sun from a star doomed to perish . . .; this would throw new light on the problem of the Ice Age. . . . It is possible that in this sense Cuvier's theory of periodically recurring world catastrophes contains some truth" (p. 53).

In addition to images of giving up, loss, and restoration, Schreber is also is concerned with the issue of sin and punishment, embedded in the reference to Sodom and Gomorrah. Schreber believes sinful mankind is a threat to God; for the purpose of His own self-preservation, God has to destroy sinful mankind and then replenish it with a better kind of mankind, thus the invocation of the mythological motifs of destruction, purification and moral renewal.

The eternal Jew in this context, as Schreber indicates, is Noah. Even though Schreber gives expression to some anti-Semitic sentiments, here he explicitly refers to Noah the righteous, the renewer and redeemer of mankind, and not, says Schreber, Ahasver (the Jew who jeered Jesus on his way to the cross, as a result of which Jews have been damned and suffered throughout history).

The iconography of sin and punishment is also reflected in Schreber's references to plagues and epidemics, like "the peril of a syphilitic epidemic" (p. 74). Or even more specifically:

> In the modern world something in the nature of a wizard had suddenly appeared in the person of Professor Flechsig (the name of a French doctor Brouardel was also one mentioned to me, who was said to have imitated Professor Flechsig). . . . This had spread terror and fear amongst the people, destroying the bases of religion and causing general nervousness and immorality. In its train devastating epidemics had broken upon mankind [p. 91].

We now have a clearer picture of the nature of the sin Schreber is concerned with. Sodom and Gomorrah and syphilis have to do with sins of the flesh. In Biblical times and in Schreber's day (as well as in our own), sexual excesses were believed to be punished by plague and disease: if nerves become black and require purification, before they can be returned to the forecourts of heaven, in Schreber's words, then immoral sexual behavior, is one of the most common and serious causes of such blackening.

There are a number of additional remarks by Schreber about dynamic concepts, which are fundamental for every dynamic psychiatrist and psychologist. The notion of "mental individuality," (p. 7), "personal identity" (Foot Note #9), "consciousness of identity" and "my own ego" [*Identitätsbewusstsein, mein eigenes Ich*; p. 95]. Schreber is also aware of the concept of symbolism (Foot Note #37), for example, "boots . . . an especial symbol characteristic of manliness" (p. 166), and "the symbolic meaning of the act of defecation" (p. 226). He labels some of his mental techniques "methods of defence" (pp. 225, 314).

Schreber on His Differential Diagnosis

The end-of-the-world fantasy is drenched in depressive feelings, but how much did Schreber speak of his illness as a depression? The surprising answer is, not that much and not that clearly, in spite of his eloquent descriptions of his depressed state of mind in the first period of his illness, also reflected in a number of his operatic allusions.[10] At Flechsig's, at the urging of his wife, he played the piano score "I Know That My Redeemer Liveth," from Handel's *Messiah*, "in the certain conviction of it being the last time of my life." In Sonnenstein, he gave expression to his despair and rage through Tamino in the *Magic Flute:* "'Oh, I feel it, it has vanished, gone forever, love's delight,' or 'The vengeance of hell boils in my heart, death and despair flame around me'" (p. 263). The other allusions are to "melancholia [*Schwermuth*]," (p. 368) versus mania and to patients, like himself, suffering from a mood disorder [*Gemüthskranke*] (p. 376) versus those suffering from psychosis (*Geisteskranke*).[11] In his writ to the Dresden Court of Appeals Schreber also made a distinction between the hypochondriacal delusions from which he suffered and true delusions.

Given all these indirect references to hopelessness and depression, it is remarkable that in view of his untiring objections to being called insane, he did not mention depression as a diagnosis in the *Memoirs* (although it was noted in the chart). Instead, he described himself as suffering from hyperirritability, or hyperexcitability, of his nerves, thus a *Nervenkrankheit*. He meant that his was a medical sickness, like any other, not madness. He was using Flechsig's own brain and nerve model of illness to vindicate himself.

The added implication of the concept of hyperexcited nerves is that it is a synonym for emotions—not only depression, but also fear, anxiety, and rage. Just as Schreber is unable to clearly articulate his depression, so he is limited in the ways he can admit to experiencing fear and anxiety. He speaks of frightening miracles and symptoms of illness, but not of the emotions as such and how to trace them to their sources. Either he is following a convention of the times, or else the emotions are under repression. Denial of emotions as a basic clinical fact, as articulated by Kraepelin, was also a convention in the psychiatry of his day.[12] Nothing is as repressed in Schreber as the emotion of rage. It is labeled *"Brüllzustände,"* states of roaring and bellowing that come upon him uncontrollably, out of nowhere, another miracle totally beyond his control: "The attacks of bellowing were very different from the noisy outbursts of *catatonic* patients. Among paranoiacs—to which category I am supposed to belong—they seem to be very unusual; Dr. Weber in his report of 5th April 1902, could only mention one single case where apparently something similar was observed in a paranoiac" (p. 357). Alternately, the outbursts and the compulsion to speak obscenities and other phrases makes one think of depressive and obsessional states and of the rare Gilles de la Tourette's syndrome, or *maladie de tics.*

The issue of diagnosis was no mere pedantry. The words used to diagnose were also used to impose on the diagnosed a potentially lifelong sentence of involuntary incarceration in an asylum. The reason for Schreber's writing the *Memoirs* in the first place was to vindicate himself as a person entitled to his freedom and his civil rights and to fight his way out of Weber's prison. In his view, he was still being held there against his will, essentially because he expressed ideas strange and repugnant to Weber, pejoratively classed as delusions; some of Schreber's most offensive opinions were no doubt his ideas about religion and sex.

SCHREBER'S RELIGIOUS VIEWS

If Schreber was profoundly identified with his father's character and philosophy, in the area of religion he totally rebelled against his father's views. We have discussed the psychological uses of his personal religion; here we examine its cosmological and existential uses.

Schreber's placing religious ideas at the center of his interests raises a question about religious discourse in general:

> I shall try to give an at least partly comprehensible exposition of supernatural matters. . . . I cannot, of course, count upon being *fully*

understood because things are dealt with which cannot be expressed in human language; they exceed human understanding. . . . To make myself at least somewhat comprehensible I shall have to speak much in images and similes [*Bilder und Gleichnisse*]. . . . Where intellectual understanding ends, the domain of belief begins [p. 2].

In this Schreber echoes Kant's distinction between knowledge and belief, as he proposes to enlarge on the immortal soul of religion and the soul of psychology. Invoking images and similes, Schreber addresses the knotty problem of the existence of God and the discourse about God. All we know are approximations and analogies. Kant also believed that the *Ding-an-sich* will remain forever unknowable and elusive, the will-o'-the-wisp of religion and metaphysics.

As an educated professional born in a traditional evangelical Lutheran family, Schreber nevertheless turned out to be a doubter in the matters of Christian faith. Like many in his generation, among them Flechsig and Freud, Schreber was following in the footsteps of such famous 19th century critics of Biblical and Christian dogmas as David Friedrich Strauss, Ludwig Feuerbach, and Joseph Ernest Renan, although he mentions only Luthardt.[13] The doubts raised about miracles as literal revelations of the divine were followed by the shattering influence of Darwin's teachings about evolution. The void created by the demise of traditional religion was waiting to be filled. Schreber, like others in his generation, found a number of solutions.

In his quest for the divine, Schreber returned to the writings of his father, which abound in references to God and the workings of the deity in life upon earth. However, there is no mysticism in Moritz Schreber and his religious sentiment amounts to a philosophico-ethical conception of God (e.g., in the spirit of Fichte). In him piety, spirituality, morality, and a scientific spirit coexist without interference. In the first half of the 19th century the word God is a naturally occurring locution in all kinds of writings in Germany and elsewhere; a few generations later such a use of *God* is neither self-evident nor acceptable.

One of Paul Schreber's solutions was to espouse a spiritual conception of creationism and biology and an individual form of deism as an antidote to the crude materialism of the German *Darwinismus*. Another way to fill the void was to resort to a trend that came to be known as occultism. The migration of American table-rappers (so named because in their seances, spirits of the departed would communicate by making a rapping noise on the table) spawned an upsurge of interest in mediums, levitations, extrasensory perception, "empirical" proofs of life beyond the grave, communications with the dead, and the like.

These topics were hotly and seriously debated and led to two developments: mystical preoccupations and the birth of dynamic psychiatry. Schreber was aware of at least part of the literature surrounding occultism, and it provided him with a ready store of ideas for his meditations on God, the structure of the universe, and the soul.

Schreber and Nineteenth-Century Occultism

In unraveling Schreber's many delusions it is important to consider how much of their content is simply a reflection of the climate of opinion or the *Zeitgeist* (Schreiber, 1987, Stingelin, 1989c).[14] Many of his statements about the soul[15] refer to occultist preoccupations throughout the 19th century, and especially the last decades. Moreover, these occultist beliefs create an aura, a mood that colors much of what Schreber says by way of description and explanation. He refers to these preoccupations in Foot Note #58, where he berates Flechsig for his scientific materialism, "for his tendency to replace the basic language by some modern sounding and almost ridiculous terms. Thus it [i.e., Flechsig's soul] liked to speak of a 'principle of light-telegraphy,' to implicate the mutual attraction of rays and nerves" (p. 117). He hurls the same criticism at Kraepelin.[16]

Schreber condenses a number of issues here, including the issue of influence a person has over another via the combined action of the psychological (rays) and the physical (nerves) and the issue of telepathy, the communication between persons separated by a physical distance—or, as it came to be called later, mental radio.[17] The prefix *tele*, like the prefix *para* ("alongside" or "beyond," as in *paranormal*) is a synonym for the occult. As noted by Max Dessoir (1917), there is but a step from paranormal to paranoia.

In his occultism Schreber was unlike his father, who was steeped in the traditional suspicion medicine has evinced toward the paranormal. Moritz Schreber was a Kantian and thus a rationalist who abhorred any preoccupation with matters mystical or occult, which was in his day (and at other periods as well) characterized by the pejorative connotations of *Schwärmerei* (dreamery). Did not Kant write an essay *Dreams of a Visionary Explained by Dreams of Metaphysics*, ridiculing the *Geisterseher*, or seer of spirits, Swedenborg (1688-1772), an epithet Paul Schreber applied to himself (*M*, pp. 77, 79)?

One of the leading concerns of that period was the overcoming of traditional dualism, the two-substance theory (the duality of mind and body) and the striving toward monism, a one-substance theory. Three kinds of monism came into being: the materialistic monism of the scientists, as exemplified in the brain mind theories of Flechsig; the

idealistic-theistic monism of philosophers, such as Paulsen (1892); and
the mystical, or transcendental spiritualistic, monism of philosophers
such as du Prel, Frederick W. H. Myers (1903) and William James
(1904), a monism that seemed to connect with the more popular
mystical views of the spiritists. The tendency was to see a common
thread in dreams, psychosis, and paranormal phenomena, that is, a
window into a suprasensory order of reality, inaccessible in the ordinary waking state. Schreber was aware of all these varieties of monism.
When he rails against "naked materialism" and the "arrogance of
professors," perhaps he has in mind the hostile stance of official science
to spiritual phenomena.

Some people are certified madmen. But there are also certified saints,
mystics, and mediums. If Schreber's visions were not genuine, then
were Saint Teresa and Swedenborg paranoiacs? Schreber himself argued that believing in spiritism or the like does not justify a person's
being declared mentally incompetent. The point here is not to engage
in validating paranormal phenomena or to romanticize psychopathology but to locate some of Schreber's ideas within the mind-set of
some of his contemporaries who seriously debated such ideas in books,
the press, and on the pages of journals such as *Psychische Studien*,
published in Leipzig and New York; the *Sphinx*, appearing in Berlin;
and the *Proceedings of the Society for Psychical Research*, published in
London.[18] People were drawn to such topics as communication with
the spirits of the dead via mediums, materializations of spirits, immortality, the fourth dimension, magnetism, and dream life. Such topics
became the contents of many of Schreber's waking dreams.

An important influence on Schreber was the philosopher and occultist Baron Karl du Prel, cited in the *Memoirs* four times (*M*, Foot
Note #2 and pp. 64, 115, 253).[19] In a book written in 1892, *The Enigma
of Man: An Introduction into the Study of Occult Sciences*, based on his earlier
lecture published in the periodical *Sphinx*, which would have been
known to Schreber, du Prel summed up his theory of what was later
called by Dessoir "magical idealism." Invoking the authority of Kant,
du Prel claimed that man lives in two worlds, the actual world and the
beyond (*Jenseits*), the realm of the subconscious (*Reich des Unterbewus-
sten*), that is, of the transcendental consciousness. On passing the
threshold of sensation, the other world reveals itself upon earth (*Dies-
seits*) to the realm of sensory consciousness (*Reich des sinnlichen Bewusst-
seins*). The beyond is revealed in such phenomena as sleepwalking,
spiritism, the astral body, and the like, which affect living persons
through their capacity to affect the body. Four papers written by du
Prel stand out on account of their thematic kinship to Schreber's ideas:
"There is a Transcendental Subject" (1889a), "Mysticism in Madness"

(1889b), "What are Premonitions?" (1890) and "Are there Warning Dreams?" (1893), the last appearing the year Schreber became ill.

The nature of dreams proves for du Prel (1889a) that man is split into an earthly and a transcendental subject. Dreams show a "dramatic split of the ego." In the dream, the "dream stage [*Traumbühne*]" is created, says du Prel, by the conditions of the body but the content is either a projection of one's fantasies from within or a perception of influences coming from without, from other beings or other spheres, that is, transcendental ones. The transcendental subject is defined as this transcendental consciousness and by what du Prel called the astral body (*Astralleib*). The latter is an ether-like form of being, our transcendental source and not the same as our bodily form; it put us in touch with other worlds. It is the source from which other worlds and earthly forms come, or it is a form of energy that permeates us in life.[20] These theories were very much in keeping with those of Fechner a generation earlier. For du Prel, they furnished an explanation for clairvoyance, telepathy, prophecy, and the healing power. If we replace the term *transcendental* with *unconscious mental powers and processes*, as du Prel himself did, then the statement might become more understandable to the modern reader.

Mysticism and madness (du Prel, 1889b) would have been fascinating reading for Paul Schreber both before and during his second hospitalization. The affinity between madness and mysticism is as old as mankind. Occultists such as du Prel maintained that mystical capabilities were dormant in the waking state but could often be aroused to action in conditions of physical and mental disorder. In earlier times people claiming mystical powers were taken for witches and warlocks. Nowadays, physicians tend to equate the conditions under which such phenomena are often reported with the causes of their occurrence, that is, with physical and mental disorders. They thus view the phenomena themselves as pathological. To this an occultist like du Prel could reply that such a purely materialist view not only misses the significance of the transcendental subject, that is, the soul, but that it also mistakes conditions with causes. Similarly, Paul claimed that his nerve-illness, his hyperexcited nervous system, was only the condition of his genuine mystical experiences.

Du Prel also compared psychosis to waking dreams, recognizing that the productions of the psychotic are marked by considerable vividness, plasticity and dramatization, as well as condensation of ideas (*Vorstellungsverdichtung*). Du Prel explained the relationship between transcendental phenomena and the brain. The brain, argued du Prel, is the organ of cognition (*Erkenntnissorgan*), necessary for perceiving the world through the senses, and of memory. Transcendental consciousness is independent of the brain but is perceived by the brain. Du Prel reversed the statement of the materialists: it is not the brain that causes the soul, it is the soul that causes the brain.

The transcendental function, according to du Prel (1890), also includes premonitions, manifestations of the capability of prevision—that is telepathy and clairvoyance—and warning dreams (du Prel, 1890). The unconscious self, or soul, has for du Prel been aptly described in the Cabala: "The *Neschamah* [soul, in Hebrew] (the transcendental subject) perceives where the bodily eye does not see; sometimes man is suddenly befallen by fear whose cause he does not know. The reason for this is that the Neschamah sees the disaster; she knows the future and the distant and she is sad as a result" (du Prel, 1890, p. 310).[21]

Premonitions, intuitions whose cause remains unconscious, and warnings frequently appear in dreams, according to du Prel (1893), because the sleep state, the closest to magnetic or somnambulistic sleep, is where the transcendental subject makes contact with the brain and mind of the person. In the usual waking state prevision is under the threshold of consciousness. But the ideas continue to exist as subconscious. In situations fraught with danger for the life of the person or those dear to the person in the environment, the subconscious (*transcendentales Bewusstsein*), stimulated by environmental circumstances and associated ideas, crosses the threshold of perception and erupts into perceptual consciousness (*Gehirnbewusstsein*), in the form of night or day visions and feelings of anxiety or impending disaster or death. The visions (*Visionen*, a word frequently used by Schreber) of people speaking in dreams are personifications of the subconscious according to the law of the dramatic splitting of the ego. The subconscious content can come from various sources: a forgotten prophetic dream, a telepathic message from a loved one, a stimulus from a contemporary event. The psychological processes point to a kinship with auto-suggestion, hetero-suggestion, and post-hypnotic suggestion.

Schreber's second illness was ushered in by anxiety dreams about the return of his previous illness. In chapter 1 of the *Memoirs*, entitled "God and Immortality," in Foot Note #2, Schreber invokes obscurely a work by du Prel that cannot be identified and expresses the belief that upon death the soul is not extinguished but can be reawakened to a new life (p. 7). It is thus plausible to infer that God is for Schreber another name for the origin of ideas in man, akin to transcendental consciousness. Accordingly, God is able to "get into contact (to form 'nerve-contact with them') . . . with highly gifted people (poets, etc.), in order to bless them (particularly in dreams) with some fertilizing ideas about the beyond. But such 'nerve-contact was not . . . the rule . . . [but] in a state of *high grade excitation*" (p. 11). Schreber was struggling with personal, philosophical and religious questions he may have also believed that he was backed by the scientific authority of du Prel, considered by some of his contemporaries as a legitimate investigator.

Schreber's cosmology and existential religion

The fantastic cosmology is a mixture of different strands: occult beliefs, popular ideas about the scientific advances of the day; it is a curious blend of the mundane, the mystical, and the sublime. God the creator, who coexists with modern science (e.g., the "nebular Hypothesis of Kant-Laplace") is, says Schreber, "a living God whose existence has become absolute certainty for me . . . the light and warmth-giving power of the sun, which makes her the origin of all organic life on earth, . . . an indirect manifestation of the living God . . . has for years spoken with me in human words and thereby reveals herself as a living being or as the organ of a still higher being behind her" (pp. 89—90).[22]

Life-sustaining solar radiation is the foundation of many metaphors of the divine. Light is an attribute of divine wisdom, from the pagan Apollo and the Persian Ormuzd to the shining countenance of the Lord of the Bible and the light emanating from the words of the Gospel. According to Schreber, it is the essence of rays, the irradiating stuff God is made of, that is, spirit and light, and the stuff the soul is made of. Rays, his word for nerves, are also a favorite metaphor in his father's writings. But nerves are the modern scientific-medical name for soul, since nerves and the brain are the seat and organ of the soul; this materialistic-scientific view of the mind was, of course, constructed by none other than physicians, especially neuroanatomists and neuropathologists and neuropsychiatrists, like Flechsig. There is thus an equivalence between spirit, soul, rays, and nerves. The following passage from the *Memoirs* can be read substituting *soul* for *nerve* and *nerves*:

God to start with is only nerve, not body, and akin therefore to the human soul but unlike the human body, where nerves are present only in limited numbers, the nerves of God are infinite and eternal. They possess the same quality as human nerves but in a degree surpassing all human understanding. They have in particular the faculty of transforming themselves into all things of the created world; in this capacity, they are called rays, and herein lies the essence of divine creation. An infinite relation exists between God and the starry sky. I dare not decide whether one can simply say that God and the heavenly bodies are one and the same, or whether one has to think of the totality of God's nerves as being above and behind the stars, so that the stars themselves and particularly our sun would only represent *stations*, through which God's miraculous creative power travels to our earth . . . [p. 8].

If we add one more term to this above description, the mystification will diminish even more. That term is energy. God's rays, like the sun's rays, are the reservoir of divine energy, which is transformed into His creation . If we also say with Spinoza that God equals nature, *Deus sive natura*, then we are on the grounds of modern science and the transformations of one form of energy into another. (The law of transformation of energy was discovered in 1842 in Germany by Robert Mayer.)[23]

In Schreber's cosmology, the law of conservation of energy is conceived as follows (in Foot Note #11): Even though God's nerves (soul, energy) are infinite and transformed into His finite creations, both inorganic and organic, human nerves (souls) after death are returned to the eternal reservoir, called the forecourts of heaven or the anterior realms of God. This constitutes the "eternal cycle of things which is the basis of the Order of the World. In creating something, God in a sense divests Himself of part of Himself [*seiner selbst*, his self] or gives a different form to part of his nerves. The apparent loss is restored when after hundreds or thousands of years the nerves of departed human beings . . . return to him as the 'forecourts of heaven'" (p. 19).

Where did Schreber get his equation of soul and nerves? The answer given so far has been that it came from Flechsig and from reading his works. While such an assumption appears plausible, and I do not wish to deny it, I also believe that Schreber, as an intelligent and inquisitive adolescent and adult, already had another prototype in the writings of his own father. These two influences created a dual conflict for him. On one hand, there is Flechsig, who explains soul in terms of brain, has a brain museum next to his office, tells Paul his illness is caused by a nervous disease of the brain. On the other hand, there is his father, also a medical authority, who spoke of the brain in the spirit of Kant, while at the same time decrying mysticism and occultism. Schreber ended by rejecting both learned doctors to espouse a view shaped by the occultists.

The first to draw parallels between Schreber's ideas and Flechsig's was, of course, Niederland (1974). He was impressed with the reverberation of the neuroanatomical term radiation, or *Strahlung*, in Schreber's multiple ray references. Of course, it is the other way around: the name *corona radiata*—to convey the image of the radiating crown of the sensory tracts in the brain coming in from the periphery and fanning out to form relays in the cerebral cortex—was itself suggested by the sun's rays. Thus the words *strahlen* and *strahlend*, frequent in Moritz

Schreber's writings, antedate any influence by Flechsig's neuroanatomical terms *Sehstrahlung* and *Hörstrahlung*. Martin Stingelin (1989b) has drawn parallels between some of Paul Schreber's statements about nerves and statements in Flechsig's (1896a) *Brain and Soul* and related writings.

Two of Moritz Schreber's books are particularly pertinent: *Health* (1839) and *Anthropos* (1859a). Paul would have been able to read them as early as his high school years, while his father was still alive. Both books contain anatomical illustrations, including many of the spinal cord and the brain and its coverings. The text and the illustrations would have been sufficient for an intelligent layman's working knowledge of the brain and its functions.

Let us compare a few statements by father and son. Moritz says: "The nerves are thread like structures spread throughout the entire body. . . . Those delicate little threads. . . . The nervous system is the connecting link between mind and body" (1839, p. 12). Paul says: "The human soul is contained in the nerves of the body; about their physical nature I, as a layman, cannot say more than that they are extraordinarily delicate structures—comparable to the finest filaments—so that the total mental life of a human being rests on their excitability by external impressions" (p. 6).

Moritz: The nerves conduct "excitations, sensation, voluntary acts. . . . Through it [the brain] are mediated the reception, storage and revival of ideas (brain pictures, *Gehirnbilder*) . . ." (1861, pp. 50-52). Paul: "Part of the nerves is adapted solely for receiving sensory impressions . . . ; other nerves receive and retain mental impressions and as the organs of will, give to the whole human organism the impulse to manifest those of its powers designed to act on the outside world" (p. 6).

Moritz: Through the brain we achieve "the feeling of our self (*unserer selbst*), become conscious of all our sensory and mental states." The brain is concerned with "imagination and memory pictures. . . . It can raise our personal existence to high Heaven or plunge it into Hell. Every life-state of which our ego becomes conscious—the highest joy, the most blessed happiness (*das seligste Glück*), as well as the most tormenting pain (physical or mental)—takes place in this organ . . ." (1859, pp. 51-53). Paul: "sensory impressions (nerves of sight, hearing, taste and voluptuousness . . . are . . . capable of the sensation of light, sound, heat and cold, of the feeling of hunger, voluptuousness and pain etc) . . . *every single nerve of intellect represents the total mental individuality of a human being*, that the sum total of recollections is as it were inscribed on each single nerve of intellect" (p. 6; emphasis Schreber's).

Freud and Niederland viewed Paul Schreber's descriptions as belonging in the realm of delusions. Actually, as Freud (1911a) also noted, they are "an astonishing mixture of the commonplace and the clever, of what has been borrowed and what is original" (p. 21). The locution "nerve of intellect" betrays a Kantian influence. Moreover, these ideas represent the outer limit of what anyone at that time could know, or surmise, about the nervous system. For all of Flechsig's neuroanatomy, his brain-mind model is in its essential points the same one described by the Schrebers, father and son.

The similarities and the differences between the theories of Moritz and Paul are instructive. The crucial difference is this: for Moritz the vital functions of nerve and brain cease with death; for Paul, under the influence of the occultists, this is not so.

> Should the body lose its vitality then the state of unconsciousness, which we call *death* and which is presaged in sleep, supervenes for the nerves. This, however, does not imply that the soul is really extinguished; rather, the impressions received remain attached to the nerves. The soul, as it were, only goes into hibernation as some lower animals do and can be re-awakened to a new life" [p. 7; emphasis Schreber's].

His father would not approve, and neither can we.

Is this faith or fantasy? For many, as for Paul Schreber, it has been both. For him it served the purpose of conferring a meaning on his illness and his fate, of promoting cure and self-vindication. For his illness is not *Geisteskrankheit* (psychosis), but *Nervenkrankheit*, a disease of the nerves—not, however, a neurological disease (à la Flechsig), but a moral disease (à la Moritz Schreber). To reconcile these conflicting theories, he converts the energetics in his cosmology into the exegetics of the moral life and his own moral downfall and his eventual victory in his personal battle with God. Moving back and forth between the notions of nerves and the immortal soul, Schreber views his morbid state as a high-grade nervous excitation, that is, both an illness and a precondition for becoming a conduit for divine inspiration and contact with God Himself. As a result of the attraction exercised by him on God, there were "six years of uninterrupted influx of God's nerves into [his] body," a situation which has caused God a loss of the state of blessedness:

> For God's nerves also it is unpleasant and against their will to enter into my body, shown by the continual cries for help which I daily hear in the sky from those parts of the nerves which have become separated from the total mass of nerves. All these losses can however become made good again insofar as *Eternity* exists . . . [pp. 31—32; emphasis Schreber's].

From this there is only one step to the other now- famous idea: to achieve this restoration, Schreber believes, he has to be turned into a woman, but all this "may take thousands of years" (p. 32). Such theories, developed before 1900, are seen differently in 1902; in a Foot Note (#5) added in November of that year Schreber explains that such attraction should no longer be understood purely in mechanical terms "but [as] something like a *psychological motive power*." This suggests that the prior concrete cosmological descriptions were but a metaphor for the psychological. Psychology and psychodynamics have developed in a similar manner.

As nerves become variously degraded in living persons in the course of their morally tainted lives, says Schreber, they have to be purified before being returned to God. At this point, the fantastic cosmology shades into the familiar ideas of purgatory and purification of sins.

> The regular contact between God and human souls occurred in the Order of the World only after death . . . thereby awakening them to new heavenly life . . . the *state of Blessedness* . . . But this did not occur without prior purification and sifting of the human nerves . . . to become in a sense part of Him as "forecourts of heaven." The nerves of morally depraved men are blackened; morally pure men have white nerves . . . an intrinsic property of God's nerves [p. 12].

In this context God is also defined as the "posterior realms of God . . . [which] were (and still are) subject to a peculiar division, a lower God (Ariman) and upper God (Ormuzd). . ." (p. 19). The ancient religion of Zoroaster promulgated the twofold idea of God as a source of both good and evil. The Zoroastrian gods Ormuzd (the Wise Lord Ahura Mazda, source of goodness and light) and his twin antagonist, Ahriman (Angra Mayniu, the Evil Spirit of destruction, the devil), fascinated the educated Europeans early on, but especially after the popularity of Nietzsche's *Zarathustra* in the 1890s (Ellenberger, 1970, p. 272).[24] After death, Ahura Mazda acted as divine judge who separated the wise from the unwise, the virtuous from the wicked, as they crossed the bridge to the bliss of all eternity. These personifications reflect the doctrine of reckoning and the ethical and psychological concerns with merit and guilt.[25] This is also Schreber's personal concern, and in the *Memoirs* the deities come to personify his own moral dilemmas. A case could be made for the heavenly judge being symbolic of his own conflicts as a judge on earth whose task it was to decide issues of guilt and merit, to reward and punish. His own name, the Hebrew name Daniel, means "God is my judge."

Schreber's existential use of religion places him in the vicinity of Job and Jesus. This personal version of religion is a reversal of the Christian position. Until now, mankind suffered when God withdrew His grace from mankind. In Schreber's religion God is made to suffer and cry for help when mankind withdraws love from God, when mankind suffers. This is Schreber-Job-Christ speaking again. He is among those modern writers who have challenged God's justice and put God on trial. In portraying his personal tragedy, like Jesus on the cross, Schreber cries out in anguish, "Eli, Eli lama sabachtani." [26] In a more pugnacious mood Schreber inveighs against "God's egoism" (p. 358). He feels that he "is often forced in self-defence to *mock God* with a loud voice ... " (p. 333). Schreber is ultimately rewarded: "Perhaps the personal misfortunes I had to suffer and the loss of the states of Blessedness" (p. 61—62) were a "kind of recompense for the wrong done to me" (p. 228). In the end God's inherent justice is expressed in "an oxymoron [namely] God himself was on my side in his fight against me, that is to say I was able to bring His attributes and powers into battle as an effective weapon in my self-defence" (Foot Note #35).

Beyond this Schreber conceives his own personal crisis as having engendered a crisis in the universe. The harmonious cycle of cosmic energies described earlier is called by Schreber a "miraculous struc-ture"—(*wundervoller Aufbau*):

> This "miraculous structure" has recently suffered a rent, intimately connected with my personal fate. . . . I want to say by way of introduc-tion that the leading roles in this development, the first beginnings of which go back perhaps as far as the eighteenth century, were played on the one hand by the names Flechsig and Schreber . . ., and on the other hand by the concept of *soul murder* [p. 22; emphasis Schreber's].

This soul murder, which is the Faustian prologue of the *Memoirs*, is Schreber's central interaction with Flechsig.

SCHREBER'S VIEWS ON PLEASURE AND SEX

We have seen how the themes of sexuality, continence, sexual excesses, and obscenity run like a crimson thread in the writings of the Schrebers over a number of generations. For Paul, sexuality had a double-edged significance: as consolation and as a project for sexual reform. Like a new Luther or Huss he wanted to make sexual enjoyment scientifically and religiously (i.e., morally) acceptable and removed from the puta-tive sphere of sin and pathology. But these apologetics of sexuality, under the guise of the latest moral ideal for man—the cultivation of femininity—is double-edged for Schreber in quite another way as well. For in embracing his new ideas, he was departing from his father's views in important ways. While he otherwise needed to maintain a continuity with the father (whose mixture of science and a belief in God was in every way preferable to Flechsig's soul-murdering materialism), the insistence on these ideas requires of Schreber that he both identify with and rebel against his father's repressive ideas about sex. This important subtheme of the *Memoirs* is then played out vis-à-vis Weber as a real and as a transference opponent (i.e., he held the same repressive views as Moritz Schreber).

Schreber's conflicts with sex were importantly connected to his ideas about virtue, vice and sin, and, as we saw earlier, with the iconography of depression. In connection with sin, Schreber hints but does not explain what his conflicts about sexuality are. The only certainty is that initially the idea of a feminine identification caused Schreber nervousness. Beyond this, his fantasy of sexual abuse could be used as a metaphor of personal abuse, degradation, or defeat. Otherwise, Schreber was also concerned, like Freud, with sexuality as a problem of pleasure and unpleasure. In the prodrome of the second illness, Schreber muses about what a woman might feel in intercourse. This is later followed by thoughts and feelings about unmanning as "an intended insult," such as when Schreber is mocked by God's rays as "Miss Schreber" (in English in the original) or told "'You are to be *represented* as given to voluptuous excesses'" (pp. 127-128). By contrast, unmanning for the purpose of restoring mankind and consonant with the Order of the World occurred, says Schreber, when

> female nerves, or nerves of voluptuousness . . . had penetrated my body in great masses. . . . I suppressed every feminine impulse by exerting my sense of manly honour. . . . On the other hand, my will power could not prevent the occurrence, particularly when lying in bed, of a sensation of voluptuousness which as so-called 'soul-voluptuousness' exerted an increased power of attraction on the rays; this expression used by the souls meant a voluptuousness sufficient for souls but felt by human beings only as a general bodily well-being without real sexual excitement [pp. 128-129].

This passage expresses Schreber's approach to the problem of pleasure and pain, or pleasure and unpleasure, *Lust* and *Unlust*, what Freud (1911b) termed the pleasure-unpleasure principle, written at the same time as the Schreber analysis. Whereas Freud defines pleasure as cessation of unpleasure, Schreber defines it both ways, negatively, like Freud, and positively—as pleasure existing on earth and in the beyond in the shape of blessedness. Schreber's word for pleasure is *Wollust*, which is translated by Macalpine and Hunter's as voluptuousness. Since one of the basic meanings of *Wollust* in German is simply sexual pleasure, or lust, Schreber in this respect approaches Freud's (1905) earlier equation of pleasure and sexual excitation in the *Three Essays on the Theory of Sexuality*.[27] As Freud noted humorously (1911a): "Schreber himself speaks again and again as though he shared our prejudice" (p. 31). Schreber, however, distinguishes three varieties of pleasure: sexual pleasure or enjoyment (*Geniessen*); a general sense of well-being of body and mind, called soul-voluptuousness (*Seelenwollust*); and "heavenly Blessedness (*himmlische Seligkeit*)" (pp. 179–180).

For Schreber the unpleasure end of the spectrum consists of feelings of anxiety, unpleasant bodily sensations, and sleeplessness. Against all this he finds solace not in prayer, or in the pursuit of health, like his father, but in fantasies of turning into a woman, or the "cultivation of femininity," which is both "essential and curative," as it leads to *"high-grade voluptuousness* [that] *eventually passes into sleep,"* which is, says Schreber, "the sleep necessary for the recuperation of my nerves." In this he "must follow a healthy egoism, unperturbed by the judgment of other people" (p. 178).

Schreber was convinced of the serious scientific intent of his delving into the nature of human sexuality and enquired about its neurophysiological basis in a letter addressed to Weber on March 26, 1900 (pp. 275–277). We can just imagine the good doctor Weber acting kindly and indulgently toward his patient and encouraging this dialogue on sexuality while keeping his outrage under control. It is, of course, ironic that these explanations by Schreber were meant to convince Weber that he was not psychotic. Weber was polite in his response to Schreber, while sending negative reports to the courts, the purpose of which was to keep Schreber in the asylum.

But Schreber is addressing important issues and prefiguring Freud's *Three Essays on the Theory of Sexuality*. Like Freud, Schreber defined pleasure as sexual and as an end in itself. Until now voluptuousness was "permissible for human beings if sanctified in the bond of marriage . . . [and] reproduction; but in itself it never counted for much. In my relationship to God, however, voluptuousness has become 'Godfearing'" (p. 285), this constituting an oxymoron. Pleasure in the cosmic scheme is sexual-sensual, both as an idea of heavenly bliss and as God's scheme to guarantee a pleasure incentive for procreation. However, says Schreber, sexual pleasure is also important for recreation, as avoidance of pain and as personal enjoyment. This latter use of pleasure requires limits. "An excess of voluptuousness would render man unfit to fulfill his other obligations; it would prevent him from ever rising to higher mental and moral perfection; indeed experience teaches that not only single individuals but also whole nations have perished through voluptuous excesses" (p. 282).

Schreber is heir to both his father's and the contemporary society's guilt attitudes about sexual gratification. Therefore, he protests against a possible imputation of "mere low sensuousness . . . [as] . . . a motive in my case . . . [or] any sexual lust in contact with other people [and that it] has nothing whatever to do with any idea of masturbation or anything like it" (pp. 281-282). In his case sensuous enjoyment is tantamount to "finding a fitting middle course in which both parties, God and man, fare best" (p. 284):

> For me such moral limits to voluptuousness no longer exist, indeed in a certain sense the reverse applies. . . . *I never mean any sexual desires towards other human beings (females), least of all sexual intercourse*, but that I have to imagine myself as a man and a woman in one person having intercourse with myself, or somehow have to achieve with myself a certain sexual excitement etc. [p. 282; emphasis Schreber's].
>
> [Thus] . . . painful sensations will diminish and states of voluptuousness or Blessedness prevail. . . . In my lifetime I will enjoy in advance that Blessedness granted to other human beings after death . . . which for its full development needs the fantasy of either being or wishing to be a female being, which is naturally not to my taste [pp. 336-337].

The combination of voluptuousness, femininity, and soul blessedness (*Seelenwollust*) in Schreber's philosophy of religion and sexuality suggests yet another synthesis: having proclaimed, against father's and his own puritanical attitudes, the redemptive power of sexual pleasure, he uses religion, both occultist and traditional, to make pleasure sacred, allowed, and required. The other synthesis is to bridge blessedness (*Seligkeit*) and happiness (*Glückseligeit*), his father's recurrent sermon and a cure for depression. Such a synthesis of spiritual and sensual happiness had already been suggested in the title of Wilhelm Heinse's (1787) famous Renaissance fantasia, *Ardinghello and the Happy Isles*.

Schreber's ideas were incomprehensible to Weber and would probably have been misunderstood by his own father. Moritz's ideas on mental health, upbringing, and sexuality were very well known to Paul, and it is to their echoes in the *Memoirs* that we now turn.

SCHREBER ON HIS FATHER'S ETHICAL AND EDUCATIONAL IDEAS

Early on Schreber invokes the "Schrebers' spirit" and his "father's soul," a model for imitation and non-imitation and important in shaping his ideas and character in childhood, adolescence and adulthood. Both parents would have molded his essential character, which Schreber describes as follows: "Whoever knew me intimately in my earlier life will bear witness that I had been a person of calm nature, without passion, clear thinking and sober, whose individual gift lay more in the direction of cool intellectual criticism than in the creative activity of an unbounded imagination" (p. 63); and "Anybody who knew me in my former life had the opportunity of observing my cool and sober nature" (p. 162).

One of Moritz's oft-repeated precepts was the importance of truthfulness, and Paul strongly identified with this virtue. "One might of course doubt whether I can or will speak the truth, in other words whether I exaggerate or suffer from self-deception. But I may say— whatever one may think of my mental faculties, that I can claim two qualities for myself without reservation, namely *absolute truthfulness* and *more than usually keen powers of observation*; no one who knew me in the days of health or witnessed my behavior now would dispute this" (pp. 246-247; emphasis Schreber's). He also assures us he has provided a truthful account of events, since he is a "human being of high intellect, of uncommon keenness of understanding and acute powers of observation" (p. 35). I concur with this self-assessment. It does not mean, however, that he was incapable of fooling himself about his own motives. These qualities of character mirror those of Moritz, as expressed in *Gymnastics* (1889), which Paul quoted from; in other works; in the life he lived; and in the lives and personalities of the descendants of his daughter Anna Jung, whom I have interviewed. This basic truthfulness also impressed the judges in the court of appeals, who restored Paul Schreber's freedom to him, and a number of psychiatrists who reviewed the *Memoirs* upon their publication.

We can safely assume that certain ideas in Paul are based on certain ideas in *Gymnastics*, for he quoted from the 23rd edition (revised and enlarged by Rudolf Graefe and printed in 1889, when Paul was 47 years old), around the midpoint between his first illness and second illness. Thus, man's marvelously intimate union of two natures, mental and physical, is echoed in the "miraculous structure" of the universe (p. 22). Paul's concern with evolution and spontaneous generation (*Urzeugung*) may be traced to Moritz's concern with human development passing from a primitive state (*Urzustand*) to an evolved civilized state. But whereas father dwells on the lofty and the sublime, the son finds sublimity and redemption in the raw human physiological functions of the natural body: defecation, urination, and copulation. Father stresses exercising the body to ensure the proper circulation of bodily juices, the renewal of substances (*Stofferneuerung*), the "organic rejuvenation" of the organism, and the prevention of fat deposits. Paul is also concerned with "poison of corpses and other putrid matter [*Fäulniss*]" (p. 129), and he may be thinking of such self-poisoning as a cause of headache when he says, "Apart from my head, pain is also caused in other parts of my body where the poison of corpses is unloaded. All parts of my body are affected" (Foot Note #115). But he viewed his fat deposits as a welcome feminine roundness of limbs and rump.

Some happenings in the asylum reflect father's health prescriptions (M. Schreber, 1842) and the practices in the Schreber household. An example is Moritz's healthy-minded ideas about hardening the body, as in the use of cold water and sunlight, an idea in Kant (1780) and elsewhere and expounded in a book by his father (Schreber, 1842), which, however, was not mentioned by Paul. Although Paul says, "Miracles of heat and cold . . . [were] daily enacted against me during walks in the garden and when I [was] indoors, always with the purpose of preventing the natural feeling of bodily well-being . . . [to] make my feet cold and my face hot" (p. 172), he made use of "cold therapy" to keep himself from going crazy at Sonnenstein: "From youth accustomed to enduring both heat and cold, . . . I put my feet through the iron bars of the open window at night in order to expose them to the cold rain. As long as I did this the rays could not reach my head . . ." (p. 172).[28] In this Schreber was completely misunderstood by the hospital physicians who put wooden shutters on the windows to prevent him from sticking his feet out, and thereby also shrouded his room in such complete darkness, that "even the first light of day in the morning could hardly penetrate . . . [filling him] with a deep and long-lasting sense of bitterness. Light, necessary for every human occupation, had become almost more essential for [him] than [his] daily bread . . ." (p. 173).[29]

Moritz's concern with the "equal balance . . . of excitability and activity . . . as a means of relieving or drawing off the causes of nervous overstrain" may be seen in Paul's belief that nervous overstrain played a major role in causing his second illness. The issue of activity versus passivity also played an important role in his character and the various crises, but practicing therapeutic gymnastics per se was not considered by Paul as an exclusive means leading to a cure. In the end, he did overcome the passive role of inmate and assumed the active role of fighting for his freedom.

Paul indicates his affinity to the wider scope of Moritz's educational ideas by means of a fantastic locution, *Seelenauffassung* (translated as "soul conception" but which may also mean the "conceptual system of souls") to refer to an ideal of a moral philosophy and education:

Fundamentally this contained significant and valuable ideas. In its original meaning soul conception is I think a *somewhat idealized version which souls had formed of human life and thought*. One must remember that souls were departed spirits of erstwhile human beings. As such they had a lively interest not only in their own human past but also in the fortunes of their still living relatives. . . . They were able to express in more or less distinct words some *rules of conduct and attitude to life* [*M*, p. 164; emphasis Schreber's].

Of course, the most important departed soul was that of Moritz himself, a guardian soul with a lively interest in the son's fate on earth. But mother cannot be far behind. The son remembers the prescriptions for right living, but with a touch of irony: these rules, he says, were more idealistic than realistic. These precepts and admonitions shaped character but did not become a bulwark against illness and suffering, as had been hoped by the father—neither for him nor for his two sons.

A number of Paul's ideas are traceable to Moritz's prescriptions in his educational works, notably the *Kallipädie* (1858a), concerning parent-child relations. For example:

Consider the case of parents or teachers being present during a school examination of their children. If they follow the examination attentively they will automatically answer every question in their mind, perhaps only in the form: "I am not at all sure whether the children will know this" (*M*, pp. 219-220).

Note Paul's awareness of the parents' and teachers' concern for—if not anxiety over—the child's performing well.

Of course, there is no mental compulsion for parents or teachers, they have only to divert their attention from the proceeding examination towards something else in their environment to spare their nerves this strain. This is the essential difference between this example and my case [i.e., the conditions of life in the hospital] [p. 220].

In our consideration of the influence of Moritz's ethical and educational ideas on Paul, a number of issues arise: parental anxieties over their methods of upbringing, Paul's inherited and acquired character traits, the stresses that brought about his illness and his ways of coping with them, as well as the stresses of life in a hospital. Thus, Paul notes, "[the] nervous impatience in every human being, not like myself and more and more inventive in using methods of defence, as to make him jump out of his skin; a faint idea of the nervous unrest caused is perhaps the example of a judge or teacher always listening to a mentally dull witness or a stuttering scholar [more correctly, school-boy], who despite all attempts cannot clearly get out what he is asked or wants to say" (p. 223). Note Paul's identification and empathy with the concerned parent or teacher and the possible positive appreciation of the good parenting that he himself may have received. He may also be referring here to nervousness in himself, as in his work as a judge of the conduct of others, which was for him a strenuous profession.

A number of father's precepts of good behavior in the *Kallipädie* (1858a) reverberate with certain statements in the *Memoirs*. For example, Moritz taught that children should be brought up to avoid "*twisting the mouth* in speaking and other *facial grimaces*" (*Kallipädie*, p. 217; emphasis Schreber's). Grimacing was a prominent feature of Paul's behavior in the asylum. Other examples of commands mentioned in the *Memoirs* that may be derived from Moritz's precepts of good behavior are the following:

> "Do not think about certain parts of your body" was a rule of conduct apparently expressing the idea that man in his normal healthy state has no reason to think of particular parts of his body, unless reminded of them by pain. "Not at the first demand" was another phrase indicating that a sensible human being would not allow himself to be led into one or other action by a momentary impulse. "A job started must be finished" was the formula expressing that man should pursue to its ultimate goal what he starts, without being distracted by adverse influences, etc. [pp. 164-165].

For children in the age group of 2 to 7 years Moritz Schreber (1858a) warns against the premature arousal of sensuality, the basis of "the universally prevailing character-trait," for which the recommended counterweight is "small exercises in renunciation" (p. 149). For children between ages 8 and 16 it is a good habit in the morning not to linger in bed after awakening, whether fully awake or half awake, because this is "mostly connected to a seduction toward an unchaste drifting of thoughts" (p. 172; emphasis Moritz Schreber's). Paul had his reverie of a woman yielding to coitus while he was lingering in bed between sleep and wakefulness. Moritz discusses the dangers of the premature arousal of sexual lust, *Wollust*, in boys and girls. This *Wollust*, translated as voluptuousness, fills pages of the *Memoirs*. The word *Ausschweifungen*, sexual excesses, is not Moritz Schreber's but Hennig's, the editor of the later editions of the *Kallipädie*, under the new name, *Das Buch der Erziehung*, which Paul most probably saw. He may have also read his father's reedition of the very popular book of Hartmann (1861b).

The father's concern with joy and happiness are paralleled in the son's recurrent concern with happiness and pleasure as foundations of health; Paul was also concerned with their antagonists—metaphorical putrefaction, melancholy and "moral decay ('voluptuous excesses')" (p. 52). This concern with pleasure and sex marks both an identification with and a departure from Moritz. Paul is the only one who talks of nerves of pleasure, pain, and voluptuousness (i.e., sexual pleasure, or lust); Moritz's may be referring to them in euphemisms. Paul himself connected sexuality with his upbringing and character: "Few people have been brought up according to such strict moral principles as I, and have throughout life practised such moderation especially in matters of sex, as I venture to claim for myself" (p. 281). We recall that such principles of chastity were also embraced by the students during Paul's university years.

When quoting from his "father's *Medical Indoor Gymnastics* (23rd Edition, p. 102)," where Moritz discusses methods of overcoming excessive nocturnal emissions, Paul counters that "physicians themselves do not seem to be informed" about the sleeping positions of men and women and their connection to voluptuous sensations, whereas the souls told him "that a man lies on his side in bed, a woman on her back (as the 'succumbing part,' considered from the point of view of sexual intercourse)" (p. 166).[30] Eventually Paul had to rebel against Moritz and to embrace "inner voluptuousness transfigured and ennobled [*veredelte*] by human imagination" (p. 190). Lust as '*veredelt*' is another oxymoron.

Another precept Paul was unable to follow was Moritz's warning against the attraction to occultism, which can be seen in Moritz's insistence that children between 2 and 7 should be exposed to concepts related to observation through the senses and to "*concepts derived from perceptual ideas that are directly and easily grasped, thus removed from all that is extrasensory and supernatural . . .*" (1858a, p. 154; emphasis Schreber's). Therefore, the child should not be exposed prematurely to religious teachings. Paul's discourse about the natural wonders of the universe reflects the influence of his father, as in the phrase "the eternal cycle of things which is the basis of the Order of the World."[31] Supernatural wonders, on the other hand, are due not to Moritz's influence but to that of Paul's contemporaries, like du Prel. Paul's preoccupation with the supernatural, as with sex, constitute his rebellion against his father's teachings.

Moritz's teachings about the virtues are less easily extended to one important passion: rage. He preached containment of all the negative emotions, especially rage, and saw in the latter the causes of mental illness. Actually, Paul may have contained his anger more than was healthy for him. Rage is the most repressed emotion in Paul, and it erupts in modes barred from self-awareness (*Selbsterkenntnis*), self-analysis (*Handlungen* ... *zerlegen*, to analyze actions), and self-knowledge (*Beweggründe an's Licht zu ziehen*, to bring motives of action to light). (In parentheses are Moritz's concepts on page 244 of 1858a.)

Another theme in Moritz Schreber's writings is "the apparent enigmas and contradictions in the order of the world that appear in the period of the still immature thinking of youth" and the need "to accept the coexistence of contradictions in the world, the beautiful and the ugly, fortune and misfortune, good and evil" (1858a, pp. 260-261). These contradictions caused Paul much grief and reappeared many times in the guise of the Manichaean deities Ahriman and Ormuzd, the dualistic conception that God is the source of both good and evil, compared with Moritz's monistic Judeo-Kantian precept that the deity is good and loving and evil is created by man. Hence Moritz's moral precept: "Be strong and pure like God"; such identification was expected to become a guiding light, the assurance of overcoming life's hurdles and the foundation of the ideal character. Paul did indeed identify with that ideal but, again, in his own style.

One more identification needs to be stressed: like his father, Paul was also concerned with publishing in the field of mental health. In his own view, at any rate, the *Memoirs* are a kind of guide for the perplexed in life and in the murky world of mental illness, that is, a manual of self-help. Father's dedication to the *Kallipädie* (the book to promote the rearing of beautiful and healthy children) echoes in the son's hope he will inspire future generations. Here, too, Paul both followed Moritz and marked a departure from him. He has captured the positive aspects of father's idea of containing the passions through the power of reason and self-control, as well as the limit and failure of that power, namely, its disintegration under the impact of the explosive onslaught of the passions, leading to illness of body or mind, or both. The failure was amply exemplified in the defeats and illnesses suffered by both his father and brother. Hence, there is in the end in Paul an acceptance of the idea of self-control, on one hand, and an insistence on the redemptive power of the passions, on the other.

The analysis of the effect of the parents on the child brings us back to the issue of interpersonal relations. Although during the long years as inmate Schreber's relations with his next of kin approached the vanishing point, his daily existence became filled with relating to the people in the land of the insane—the other inmates, the attendants, and, occasionally, the physicians (Foot Note #111). It is to this relationship we now turn.

SCHREBER ON INTERPERSONAL (DYADIC) DYNAMICS

Interpersonal influence, and dyadic dynamics in general, is a constant determinant of human behavior, a concept that is not readily found in causal theories in psychoanalysis. During his days in the asylums Paul Schreber was the object of innumerable actions that were brought to bear upon him. But in his accounts in the *Memoirs* everything pales in comparison with the influence exercised on him by his first psychiatrist, Paul Flechsig.

Soul murder and being under the influence of Flechsig are indissolubly linked in Paul Schreber's mind. Schreber viewed it as undue influence, a malpractice. According to experts in psychopathology, this was a paranoid delusion of persecution, that is, without a real cause, an unsubstantiated belief in another's influence. But if we take away from this idea its delusional or fantastic portion, what remains is the irreducible residue of interpersonal action and influence. Moreover, reciprocal influence (interaction, transaction) is inseparable from personal relating. An interpersonal determinism posits that in every relation the participants will have an influence on each other and with consequences for both. It is the same with transference. Transference is also influence, with its realistic part and its projective (i.e., unconscious) part, because the patient and the therapist are engaged in an ongoing reciprocal relationship, with its share of perception and fantasy.

Even before Freud, clinicians acknowledged influence in the entity called "induced madness," or folie à deux. Beside group hysteria, the other recognized induced psychosis was paranoia. Flechsig himself (1899a), in a preface to a book on suggestion by his most illustrious pupil, Professor W. M. v. Bechterew (1857-1927),[32] himself spoke of the dangers of hypnotic suggestion as therapy and as a social phenomenon in the emotional epidemics of influence. Had Schreber by any chance seen that preface?

Our focus here is Flechsig's effect on Schreber and Schreber's perception of Flechsig's effect on him, in reality and in fantasy, i.e., transference. This dual reality-fantasy effect of Flechsig is depicted by Schreber in a number of places in the *Memoirs* in fantasies about Flechsig's ability to influence him through direct nerve contact and hypnosis. In his "Open Letter to Professor Flechsig" (written in 1903 and included in the preface, just prior to publication), Schreber, now a free man, presents Flechsig with a legal brief in which he is charged as follows:

For years [you have] exercised a damaging influence on me and still do to this day. You like other people might be inclined at first to see nothing but a pathological offspring of my imagination in this; . . . mere "hallucinations." . . . I think it is possible that you—at first only for therapeutic purposes—carried on some hypnotic, suggestive . . . contact with my nerves . . . out of scientific interest *until you yourself felt uneasy about it and therefore decided to break it off*. But it is possible that . . . [you were] driven by the influence of ruthless self-determination and *lust for power*, without any restraint by something comparable to the moral will power of man. . . . The mild reproach would perhaps remain that you, like so many doctors, could not completely resist the temptation of using a patient in your care as an object for scientific experiments, *apart from the real purpose of the cure*, when by chance, matters of the highest scientific interest arose. One might even raise the question whether perhaps all the talk of voices about somebody having committed *soul murder* can be explained by the soul (rays) deeming it impossible that a person's nervous system should be influenced by another's to the extent of *imprisoning his will power such as occurs during hypnosis*; in order to stress forcefully that this was a malpractice it was called "soul murder," the souls . . . using a term already in current usage and because of their innate tendency to express themselves hyperbolically [pp. viii–xi; emphasis added].

Schreber stresses three aspects of the soul murder: (1) Flechsig's influences on him during the relation; (2) the arbitrary termination of the relation at the end of the statutory six months; (3) its malpractice aspect and its consequences. Hypnotizing is not only Schreber's term for interpersonal influence. Like their mesmeric forerunners *magnetizing* and *magnetic*, the words *hypnotizing* and *hypnotic* were and are still used by people in the metaphorical sense of attracting, having a suggestive influence, or captivating and charming the other. Besides the conscious currents of influence and sympathy people also acknowledge the unconscious and subliminal currents that make such attraction inexplicable and irresistible.

Schreber tied subliminal interpersonal influence to hypnosis and called it *Nervensprache*, nerve-language, which has so far received scant attention. It is different from *Grundsprache*, basic language (also called by Schreber *Seelensprache*, soul language), which Freud wanted to adopt as a technical term for the language of the unconscious in psychoanalysis. Nerve language belongs with "nerve-contact [*Nerevenanhang*]," that is, a way of relating, which "Flechsig kept up" with him (*M*, p. 44). Schreber explains:

Apart from normal human language there is also a kind of *nerve-language* of which, as a rule, the healthy human being is not aware. . . . This is best understood when one thinks of the process by which a person tries to imprint certain words in his memory in a definite order, for instance a child learning a poem by heart. . . . The words are *repeated silently*, . . . Naturally under normal . . . conditions, use of this *nerve language* depends only on the will of the person whose nerves are concerned; no human being as such can force another to use this nerve-language [Foot Note #25: "*Hypnotising* is perhaps an exception.]. . . . In my case . . . since my nervous illness *took the above critical turn* [emphasis added], my nerves have been set in motion *from without* incessantly and without any respite. . . . I myself first felt this influence as emanating from Professor Flechsig . . . [who] in some way knew how to put divine rays to his own use; later, . . . direct divine nerves also entered into contact [*Verbindung*, also relation and communication] with my nerves . . . [from] mostly departed souls who began more and more to interest themselves in me [pp. 46–48; emphasis Schreber's].

While Schreber admits to a number of influences upon his thoughts and feelings (divine rays, departed souls, himself), what concerns us in this passage and the preceding one, is his vulnerability to Flechsig's actions upon him when he was a patient in his hospital, especially at the critical turn of his illness, and, retrospectively, the consequences of these actions, after he had become a prisoner of the legal and psychiatric systems at Sonnenstein. Schreber knew well that the fundamental ways of influencing are by and through the spoken word. Of course, the word goes with the other communicative influences expressed by means of the body, the face, and the gestures of emotion. The main medium of influence for Schreber, being both articulate and literate, is the human voice and the voiced thought. The human voice was seen as a powerful channel for transmitting influence, exhortations, emotions, persuasion, and power.

Schreber says, "[The voices are] spoken into (*hineigeredet*) my nerves innumerable times" (p. 130); they "seemed calculated to instill fright and terror into me" (p. 136). He does not use the other common term of interpersonal influence, *suggestion*, which had become popular in Germany at that time. Instead, he uses the German root word, to speak, in the extended meaning of suggesting by means of speech, or talking someone or oneself into something or out of something.

Schreber's term for hypnotic-suggestive influence, especially of a subliminal and unconscious kind, is expressed through the allusion to hypnotizing, itself a mysterious and highly suspect kind of interaction. Thus, *nerve-language* as Schreber's term for influence is not far from the notion of undue influence, that is, influence with a motive to deceive, to exploit, to abuse (hence the meaning of nerve-language as both conscious and unconscious influence by the other person and Schreber's own vulnerability to the unconscious, secret and dishonest motives of the other—Flechsig, his wife, or whoever else it may be).

During Schreber's first hospitalization Flechsig's influence on Schreber was on the whole positive, even as he felt to have been a victim of Flechsig's white lie: "[when Flechsig] wanted to put down my illness solely to poisoning with potassium bromide" (p. 35). When at the beginning of the second illness he came to consult Flechsig prior to admission, "a long interview followed," says Schreber, "in which I must say Professor Flechsig developed a remarkable eloquence which affected me deeply" (p. 39), promising him a quick cure by means of the new sleeping drugs. Later, when Schreber asked Flechsig about his chances for recovery: "[Flechsig] held out certain hopes, *but could no longer*—at least so it seemed to me—*look me straight in the eye*" (p. 45; emphasis Schreber's).

During his second admission Schreber felt acted upon by Flechsig (and, by extension, by his attendants) in two modes, realistically as a person and fantastically as a soul:

> Naturally such matters were not mentioned by Professor Flechsig when he faced me *as a human being*. But the purpose was clearly expressed in the *nerve-language*, . . . that is in the nerve-contact which he maintained *at the same time as a soul*. The way I was treated externally seemed to agree with the intention announced in the nerve-language; for weeks I was kept in bed and my clothes were removed to make me—as I believed—more amenable to voluptuous sensations. . . . Completely cut off from the outside world, without any contact with my family, left in the hands of rough attendants . . . [who] forced food into my mouth with the utmost brutality. . . . they even ducked my head repeatedly [in the tub] . . . making all sorts of rude jokes. . . . In the contact kept up with Professor Flechsig's nerves I constantly demanded cyanide or strychnine from him in order to poison myself. . . . Professor Flechsig—as a soul in nerve contact with me—did not refuse this demand, but always half promised it, making its handing over . . . in a hypocritical manner conditional. . . . When Professor Flechsig, on his medical rounds as a human being, subsequently came to me, he of course denied all knowledge of these matters [*M*, pp. 57-59; emphasis Schreber's].

Since in Schreber's phraseology nerve and soul are the same, then Schreber's nerve-contact and soul contact are the same: it is a person-to-person contact. Flechsig's interpersonal influence on Schreber is twofold: his overt, polite and correct messages in his capacity as doctor in charge contrasted with his covert, conscious and unconscious, subliminal messages reflecting his subtle withdrawal from the patient, with that withdrawal reflecting either his countertransference, his rejection, or his knowledge of his negotiations with Sabine—or all of the above.[33]

Was Schreber paranoid—that is, giving utterance to a delusion of influence—or was he correctly perceiving a change in Flechsig's attitude toward himself? Relating to the real Flechsig or projecting a psychotic transference derived from infantile sources? Morbidly suspicious or subject to the legal and psychiatric powers at Flechsig's disposal? Beyond his relationship with Flechsig and its consequences, Schreber found the daily impact of others upon him to be either pleasant or painful, hurting or healing, traumatic or tranquilizing, sincere or secretive. Whatever Flechsig's or other persons' influence was, it was a stimulus that had to be absorbed, abreacted, metabolized, worked through, dissipated; until then there was pain and all manner of miracles, including the bellowing miracle.

What Schreber addressed are the influences inherent in moods and emotions (which are said to be infectious, contagious and communicable), the currents of sympathy and antipathy, the flow of like and dislike, which are communicated in words and in silence, overtly and covertly, on the surface and subliminally. What is communicated is not only content but also intent, candor and concealment, truthfulness and treacherousness. I believe Schreber was at least in part trying to give expression to the discrepancy between content and subliminally perceived intent by means of the distinction between normal language and nerve language. He is trying to sort out the different kinds of messages he has received from Flechsig when he spoke to him ever so eloquently, saying one thing and possibly meaning another.

Over and above the psychology of interaction, Schreber was also concerned with Flechsig's having committed "malpractice" (*etwas unstatthaftes, eine Unstatthaftigkeit*, something forbidden or illicit). Although no longer a prisoner in 1903, to avoid the risk of a libel suit, he still felt he had to express himself hyperbolically, using various strategies of indirection. One of them was to keep accusing Flechsig of soul murder, as a result of which his freedom was stolen and his career wrecked.

THE CRISIS IN GOD'S REALMS AND SOUL MURDER

These words, crisis and soul murder, are in the title of chapter 2 of the *Memoirs*. Schreber thus begins his personal story in *medias res*, placing the climax at the beginning.

After having described in chapter 1, in words reminiscent of his father's, "the miraculous structure"[34] of the universe (God's realms and life upon earth), Schreber begins thus: "This 'miraculous structure' has recently suffered a rent, intimately connected with my fate. . . . the leading roles in the genesis of this development . . . were played out . . . by the names Flechsig and Schreber . . . and by the concept of *soul murder*" (p. 22).

The locution soul murder is puzzling: What does it mean to murder a soul? Other questions follow: Is it a schizophrenic neologism, or is it an established word in the language? Is this what Jaspers and German psychiatrists before him called a primary delusion, irreducible and not further analyzable, a sign of the underlying psychosis as fever is a sign of infection? Or is it a meaningful, potentially intelligible creation, deriving from life events and personal motives and purposes? Does it correspond to a verifiable public fact, or is it a hidden private feeling whose exact reference Schreber took to his grave? Is it a literal expression or a metaphorical one, factual or fantastic? Furthermore, was it an unbidden emergence of an unconscious idea, like a dream or delusion, or was it a thought-out, premeditated creation? Did the fantasy rule Schreber, or was he its master, using it ironically, to confuse and amuse his audience, the way Hamlet made believe he was mad to confuse Polonius?

To begin with, soul murder is not a psychotic neologism coined by Schreber; it is a term that has been used in a number of European languages for a number of centuries. It means destroying the soul, or spirit or mind. In English, soul-killing in this sense is a locution in Shakespeare.[35]

After giving the traditional meanings of soul murder, Schreber defines it as an event between Flechsig and himself, as undue influence culminating in an act of malpractice at the time of the crisis of spring 1894:

> The idea is widespread in the folk-lore and poetry of all peoples that it is somehow possible to take possession of another person's soul . . . for example . . . Goethe's Faust . . . the main role is supposed to be played by the Devil . . . the legend motif of soul murder or soul theft gives food for thought. . . . Ever since the beginning of my contact with God (mid-March, 1894) the fact [was stressed] that the crisis[36] that broke out in the realms of God was caused by somebody having *committed soul murder*; at first Flechsig was named as the instigator of soul murder. . . . I myself may have been 'represented' as the one who had committed soul murder. . . . Through further developments, at the time when my nervous illness seemed almost incurable [*einen schwer heilbaren Charakter anzunehmen schien*], I gained the conviction that soul murder had been attempted on me by somebody, albeit unsuccessfully [pp. 22-23; emphasis Schreber's].

The ideas of a breach in the wonderful structure of the universe and of the soul murder fantasy, represented by Goethe's *Faust*, precede

Schreber's mention of a "crisis . . . caused by . . . soul murder" and a crisis like that described in the *Book of Job*. As in the Biblical prologue, so in the prologue to *Faust* God is seduced by Satan to test an innocent human being. Both these works provide the Manichaean answer to the enigma of the existence of evil in the world: evil is allowed by God. In a way, all that had happened from the beginning of Schreber's illness has been a prologue to the crisis at the fateful juncture of mid–March 1894, the time of onset of God delusions and the deterioration in his condition, when it assumed the character of an incurable disease.

In Schreber's eyes, Flechsig, like Satan and Mephistopheles before, had succeeded in prevailing upon God to forsake him, the way He forsook Job to suffer and Jesus to die on the cross. Heretofore God severely tried man's faith in Him, but now the man Schreber was putting God on trial for having abandoned *him*. Heretofore, man had to answer for his sins; now God had to worry when man was afflicted with nervousness.

> I presume that at one time . . . [Professor Paul Theodor Flechsig, p. 24] . . . succeeded in *abusing* nerve-contact granted to him for the purpose of divine inspiration or some other reasons, in order *to retain his hold on the divine rays* [i.e., God]. . . . It seems very probable that contact with divine nerves was granted to a person who specialized in nervous illnesses partly because he would be expected to be a highly intellectual person, partly because everything concerning human nerves must be of particular interest to God, starting with his instinctive knowledge that an increase of *nervousness* among men could endanger his realms. Asylums for the mentally ill were therefore called in the basic language 'God's Nerve Institutes.' If the above-mentioned Daniel Fürchtegott Flechsig was the first to offend against The Order of the World by abusing contact with divine nerves, this would not be contradicted absolutely by the same man being called a *Country Clergyman* . . . because the time when Daniel Fürchtegott Flechsig was supposed to have lived—in the eighteenth century around the time of Frederick the Great—public asylums for the insane were not yet in existence [p. 25; emphasis Schreber's].

The fantastic mode of representation and indirection in the *Memoirs* refers to real processes and events. In reality—and in retrospect— Flechsig had no reason to be particularly loyal to Schreber as his patient and would soon betray his interests instead of continuing the doctor-patient relationship. However, instead of directly accusing Flechsig of soul murder, Schreber directed this charge against Flechsig's fantasy name, Paul Theodor Flechsig, and against a forbear of his from the 18th century, Daniel Fürchtegott. Since Theodor in Greek means "God's gift," the name suggests sarcasm.[37] Schreber also alludes briefly to

Flechsig's career. His father was indeed a clergyman, and Flechsig's career choice, says Schreber, had to do with leaving the realms of the soul to become a nerve specialist in charge of God's Nerve Institutes, which is Schreber's sarcastic double pun on Flechsig playing God and being in charge of his *Irrenklinik/Nervenklinik*, or asylum. Schreber was correct that asylums—and psychiatry as a profession—were founded in the first decades of the 19th century when administrative and legal powers came to be vested in institutional psychiatry. In fact, Dr. Hayner (1817), a theologian turned alienist who played a historical role in the development of psychiatry in Saxony, bore the given name Christian August Fürchtegott (Devreese, 1990b, citing Dörner). Clergymen may exert control over people's souls, but nothing equals the power of the professional armed with the weapons of science, the law, and the methods of constraint as practiced in an asylum, where overpowering of the patient is both physical and mental. Schreber's description of such a professional follows:

> One would therefore have to imagine that such a person, engaged in the practice of nervous diseases [*Nervenheilkunde*, psychiatry]—having perhaps another profession besides—believed he had at some time seen miraculous visions *in a dream* and experienced miraculous things, which he felt an urge to investigate further, either out of ordinary human curiosity or keen scientific interest. . . . Naturally interest was heightened, particularly as the dreamer may have learnt that these communications came from his own forebears, who lately had been outstripped in some way or other by members of the Schreber family. He may then have tried to influence the nerves of his contemporaries by exerting his will power after the fashion of thought readers—such as Cumberland,[38] etc. . . . One can imagine that . . . something like a conspiracy may have arisen between such a person and the elements . . . of God to the detriment of the Schreber race . . . the conspirators . . . have succeeded in *silencing possible scruples about allowing nerve-contact to be made with members of the Schreber family, in an unguarded moment . . . in order also to convince the next higher instance of the hierarchy of God's realms* that one Schreber soul more or less did not matter in the face of danger threatening the very existence of the realms of God . . . [pp. 26-28; emphasis Schreber's, except for the last one].

Again, writing in the fantastic mode, Schreber is taking issue with the rise of materialist explanations in psychiatry as a development at odds with his own philosophical heritage, while casting the resulting clash of worldviews as a multigenerational struggle between the Schreber and Flechsig families. Flechsig's dream was to find a solution to the problems of soul and existence through science. Like the heroes of the Helmholtz school, who also impressed young Freud, Flechsig, who has another profession besides that of nerve specialist (i.e., psychiatrist), that of brain and nerve anatomist, believes in a new redefinition of mind as a function of the brain. For Schreber, caught as he is in his own cosmic drama, Flechsig's materialist views go beyond the sphere of the intellect, the latter defined by philosophers in Kantian terms and espoused, among others, by Moritz Schreber. Assimilating Flechsig's alien scientific views to his own personal experiences, Schreber concludes that Flechsig must himself have seen "miraculous visions in a dream and experienced miraculous things," as Schreber claimed in the "Open Letter to Professor Flechsig" (*M*, pp. xi-xii).[39] Beneath the psychotic projection and beneath the fantastic drama of multigenerational familial conflict, lies Schreber's sense of being secretly superior to Flechsig precisely because he, Schreber, had regained his belief in a transcendental soul with the help of divine grace and revelation. And here a reader is entitled to ask whether Schreber's sense of superiority toward Flechsig might perhaps have reflected a dim intuition concerning Flechsig's own doubts and hidden conflicts as to his chosen metaphysical path, doubts that were to be revealed only in his final writings.

In Schreber's eyes, soul murder by Flechsig was powerfully linked to suggestion (via the allusion to thought-reader Cumberland) and a suspicious power play with its own method, technique and purpose— a recurrent *Seelenpolitik*, a soul politics and policy. It amounted to an unfair use of power: "Wherever the Order of the World is broken, power alone counts, and the right of the stronger is decisive. . . . In my case, moral obliquity lay in God . . . " (p. 60), for "God Himself must have known of the plan, if indeed he was not the instigator, to commit soul murder on me" (p. 59). God-Flechsig is similarly charged: "While I was in the Leipzig Asylum this power of control seemed to be exerted by Professor Flechsig's soul in combination with the real Professor Flechsig, still present as a human being" (p. 112). Thus soul murder was "a clash of interests" (p. 31), of Flechsig having "gained certain technical advantages" (p. 61), of his "*policy of vacillation* . . . [and] half measures" (*System des Lavierens*, also, maneuvering and shifting course; *Halbheit*, or "*Halbschürigkeit*," the latter suggesting annoying or badgering) (*M*, p. 56).

In branding soul murder as malpractice Schreber had two predecessors, law professors at Leipzig University (Devreese, 1990a). In 1832 a Kant-inspired lawyer, P. J. H. Feuerbach, father of the famous philosopher Ludwig, proposed soul murder as a statutory crime in "*Kaspar Hauser, Beispiel eines Verbrechens am Seelenleben*" ("K. H., an Example of a Crime Committed on a Person's Spiritual Life," *Encyclopaedia Britan-*

nica, 11th edition, 13:70) that is, as an example of a crime on a person's soul, as defined in Grimm's lexicon (see footnote 35), in this case perpetrated on the person of Kaspar Hauser, who claimed to have been the abducted, illegally detained and disinherited son of the Prince of Baden. Feuerbach's opponent, legal expert J. F. H. Abegg, claimed that the existing penal code relating to such matters was sufficient and limited soul murder to one situation: the abuse of medical treatment by a physician with harmful consequences for the patient. Devreese (1990a) limited the harmful effects of Flechsig upon Schreber to the doctor's inability to cure the patient's insomnia, to ideas of poisoning by drugs, and emasculation. I believe the greater injury was caused to Schreber as a result of Flechsig's "soul politics," indicated by mentioning together "soul murder" and "being buried alive" (p. 59); his forced transfer to Sonnenstein, and the declaration of incompetency. Schreber had more to say about these matters, but they fell victim to the censorship imposed on him (*M*, Foot Note #118B). Even though both moves were procedures within the law, Schreber felt they constituted a moral crime against him, a lie and a betrayal of his trust in Flechsig, who played both Judas and Pontius Pilate to his Christ.

In Schreber's eyes, Flechsig as perpetrator of soul murder, was aided by other, unnamed, plotters. The "next higher instance" is a possible allusion to the judiciary that conspired with the psychiatrists to declare an "embarrassing Schreber soul" incompetent and put him behind locked doors. Moreover, Schreber believed, the conspirators have managed to influence a member of the family in an unguarded moment, to cooperate with them in this plot. By fingering Flechsig as the main instigator and perpetrator of soul murder, Schreber, in effect, exonerated his wife from having herself played a role in the events that led to his worsening clinical condition, his ultimate transfer to Sonnenstein, and instituting the incompetency proceedings. But could he silence his own scruples about her, the most beloved person in his life after mother and father, the most important dramatis persona in his love drama? We will attempt an answer in the last chapter.

NOTES

1. Says Niederland (1974), "[Schreber's book is a] hopeless tangle of incomprehensible verbiage" (p. 10). From Israëls (1989): "He was completely taken over by delusions and felt that he was being persecuted by supersensible powers" (p. xi), "[he] was mad . . . a mentally deranged man" (p. xii).

2. F. W. H. Myers , an occultist and a keen psychologist, reflecting the climate of opinion about images, spoke of images in a manner reminiscent of Schreber's (1903, vol. 1, p. 124): the "entencephalic sensory faculty," or the "mind's eye," manifests itself in the sleep and dream, and its "interest is really

scientific rather than therapeutic [i.e., pathological]. . . . Baillarger in France and Griesinger in Germany (both about 1845), were among the first to call attention to the vivid images that rise before the internal vision of many persons, between sleep and waking. . . . Mr. Galton has further treated of them." Indeed, Galton (1883) gave questionnaires to many people and found a plethora of mental images in their conscious thinking. In the course of his enquiries he "was greatly struck by . . . informants . . . [who] described . . . ' visions'; . . . [these informants] were sane and healthy . . . [and] in a few cases [the visions] reached the level of hallucinations" (p. 112). This list would be incomplete without mentioning William James (1902). Born the same year as Schreber, James also underwent a depressive illness with hallucinations and panic, disguised in his 1902 book as an episode of a Frenchman (pp. 160-161, in the chapter "The Sick Soul"), from which he emerged armed with religious and mystical faith. This also qualifies as a creative illness. According to John Hickman Phillips, Jung told him that the episode was James's own. The same opinion is expressed by Scharfstein (1973, p. 36), who also notes that "James's crisis resembled an earlier one his father had undergone" (p. 39).

3. In 1764 Kant wrote his "Essay on Diseases of the Head." In Kant (1800, in sections 35 to 43, separately published as 1898b), the editor credits Kant with being the "first psychologist to observe that 'the madman is a waking dreamer'" (p. viii). For a profound reading of Kant and Freud on dream psychology, see Jung's American student, John Hickman Phillips (1962), *Psychoanalyse und Symbolik*. This work, which should be known in English, was cited by Baumeyer in the original 1972 Focus Verlag edition of the *Denkwür-digkeiten*.

4. Although one of the meanings of *hinmachen* is to make something in a careless way, I believe Schreber had something else in mind and insert here my translation of Schreber's *"flüchtig hingemacht,"* instead of "fleetingly-improvised" of Macalpine and Hunter's, or the "cursorily-improvised" of the *Standard Edition*, which is too mechanical, to indicate these experiences of fugitive will-o'-the-wisp visions. *Hingemacht* suggests a fantasy of influence: the rays made him think it (therefore these men are made-up men, i.e., fleeting images). *Hinmachen* resembles *"vormachen"* in Tausk's (1919) description of the "influencing machine," which "makes the patients see pictures" (p. 54).

5. Weber is probably meant here; thus, this is one of the few times that *Geheimer Rath* Dr. Weber is alluded to as a dream creature.

6. The word delirium in English means an acute confusional state, such as caused by fever or intoxication, accompanied by hallucinations and delusions. The French délire has two meanings: *délire-état*, the state of delirium in which *délires-idées*, that is, the hallucinations and delusions, develop. Early on it was Breuer who held that hysterical symptoms develop in what he called a hypnoid state, that is, a trance-like state of consciousness. Early on Freud used the term *Delir* as a synonym for delusion.

7. The issue of revelation versus delusional religion was treated with a respectful I-do-not-know by Niederland and derision by Israëls. Schreber's religious preoccupations have to be located in the context of philosophizing about the nature of God by men of science in his time. He would have known

about Gustav Theodor Fechner, philosopher and mathematician, the scientific precursor of Wundt in Leipzig, cited by Freud in *Beyond the Pleasure Principle*. Fechner talked of God, angels, souls, and life in the hereafter both before and after he published his scientific work, *Elements of Psychophysics* in 1860, for example in his *Zend-Avesta oder über doe Dinge des Himmels und des Jenseits* (Zend-Avesta or Things of Heaven and the Beyond) of 1851 (and a fifth edition in 1922), and *Die drei Motive und Gründe des Glaubens* (The Three Motives and Grounds of Faith) of 1863 (with a second edition in 1910). In his creative illness, a depressive one, Fechner also stared at the sun. Another example of a scientific giant harboring a religious mysticism (for some tastes verging on the delusional), is Sir Isaac Newton, with his *Observations on the Prophecies of Daniel and the Apocalypse of St. John,* his *Lexicon Propheticum,* and a number of other mystical writings.

8. The ideas expressed here and in the omitted portions of the passage bear a striking resemblance to the ideas expressed by D. G. M. Schreber (1858b).

9. In his essay on paranoia (1911a, p. 52), in reference to his earlier *Interpretation of Dreams* (1900, pp. 444–445). For Jung's comments about Freud's analysis see chapter 7.

10. I am indebted to Thomas M. Kemple (1990), who has traced Schreber's musical references to their sources. Handel's text is from the Bible: "I know that my redeemer liveth, and that he shall stand at the latter day upon the earth; and though worms destroy this body, yet in my flesh shall I see God" (Job, 19: 25, 26); "For now Christ is risen from the dead, the first fruits of them that sleep" (1 Cor. 15:20). Note the reference to decaying flesh, seeing God, and the connection between sleep, death, and immortality.

11. Macalpine and Hunter mistranslate *Gemüthskranke* as "mentally ill" (p. 263), which is the now obsolete general term that covers both mood disorders and insanity and misses Schreber's point that patients suffering from mood and nervous disorders, as distinct from the insane or psychotic, often admit themselves voluntarily to hospitals, especially private hospitals. The latter were conventionally and genteelly called *"für Gemüthskranke."*

12. This is the method in the once influential textbook of Ziehen, *Psychiatry for Physicians and Students* (1894), second revised edition in 1902, a blend of association psychology and brain anatomy. Hallucinations were considered neurological disorders of sensation, and depression, anxiety, and paranoia the emotional reactions to the hallucinations.

13. According to the 1897 *Das litterarische Leipzig* (The Literary Leipzig), Christoph Ernst Luthardt, born in 1823, doctor of theology and philosophy, was professor and lecturer at Leipzig University, whom Paul Schreber would have audited. Between 1864 and 1896 he published four volumes of his *Apology of Christianity, Compendium of Theological Ethics* and other works in this spirit; he was also editor of the *Allgemeine evangelisch-luterische Kirchenzeitung* (The Universal Evangelical-Lutheran Church Journal).

14. Schreiber (1987) traced the analysis of Schreber's Zeitgeist to the authors Schreber cites in his Foot Note #36. One of the authors cited is du Prel. I concur with Schreiber's concern not only with du Prel's views about evolution, but with his transcendental views as well. I believe that du Prel's

statements about the occult qualities of the soul and the supernatural realm are much more relevant to Schreber's text than du Prel's views on evolution and nature.

15. Spirit, the translation of the German *Geist*, Greek *pneuma*, and Hebrew *ruakh*, means gas, breath, wind, or the supposed substance of the soul in the context of religion, whether Christian or pantheistic or almost any other. Spiritual refers to the intellect and the higher endowments of the mind; hence *spiritualism* (also a synonym for philosophical or metaphysical idealism) is a view that spirit is all that matters, as against *materialism* which holds that matter is the only reality. Spirit also means ghost; hence *spiritism* is a belief that mediumistic phenomena are caused by the spirits of the dead communicating with the living, usually through mediumistic phenomena (levitations, table rappings, and the like); hence, a "belief that natural objects possess indwelling spirits" (defined by Webster's, 1971), as in *animism*. Thus spiritualism and spiritism tend often to be confused. *Metaphysical* as *philosophical* is often confused with *mystical* (i.e., all that refers to knowledge of, or communion with, God). In religious discourse spirit and God are used synonymously. Schreber often uses the terms *spirit* and *spiritual*, and, of course, soul and God. While debating Kraepelin on the issue of the veracity of hallucinations, he remarks that "so-called spiritualist mediums [*Medien der Spiritisten*, spiritist mediums] may be considered genuine seers of spirits of the inferior kind . . . although self deception and fraud may also play a part" (*M*, p. 79, 80). During the appeals trial in Dresden the judges agree with Schreber's argument that "one does not usually and without further reason declare the adherents of spiritualism [*Spiritismus*, spiritism] as mentally ill . . ." (*M*, p. 481). (In Webster's, 1971, *spiritism* is a separate entry; however, *spiritualism* is also defined as a synonym for *spiritism*.)

16. Schreber mentioned Kraepelin a number of times (*M*, Foot Note #39, p. 78, Foot Note #42, Foot Note #64, pp. 249, 307, 309, Foot Note #113). He argued against Kraepelin's conception of hallucinations in the fifth edition of the *Textbook* as an opinion influenced by "shallow 'rationalistic ideas' . . . considered to have been superseded by theologians and philosophers, and also in science" (*M*, Foot Note #42), and admonished to avoid "unscientific generalization and rash condemnation of such matters . . . and thus tumble with both feet into the camp of naked materialism" (*M*, p. 80). He was convinced that, like "cases of vision-like experiences related in the Bible" (Foot Note #112), or like the Maid of Orleans (Joan of Arc), he was a genuine seer granted supernatural impressions. He also debated Kraepelin's views on hallucinations in the sixth edition of Kraepelin's *Textbook* (Volume 1, pp. 116, 117, 145ff.). On the other hand, it is hard to reconcile Schreber's broad-minded views with the specious and obscure reasoning in the following passage: "my case is characteristically different from similar cases . . . other persons hear *voices only intermittently* . . . since the beginning of my contacts with God . . . —that is for almost seven years—except during sleep—*I have never have had a single moment in which I did not hear voices*" (pp. 309-310; emphasis Schreber's). On one hand, clearly, not all the voices were channels for the supernatural; on the other, there is a seeming self-contradiction in Schreber's claim of not being

psychotic and having had an affective illness and continuously hearing voices. His voices may refer to a number of disparate experiences, thoughts, and hissing or humming noises. This situation changed after the *Memoirs* was completed (Foot Note 118A).

In that volume (Vol. 1, pp. 88-99) Schreber would have also read some enlightened opinions of Kraepelin about the causes of mental illness: the stresses of modern life, the struggle for existence, the role of childhood in character formation and of adolescence in shaping the later fate of the person, especially excessive sternness and pain, which predispose one to selfishness and aloofness.

17. Schreiber (1987, pp. 256-264), cites an undated work by du Prel on "wireless telegraphy." I found du Prel writing about *telegraphieren ohne Draht und die Telepathie* in his book, *Die Magie als Naturwissenschaft* (Leipzig: M. Altmann, 1912), divided into a part called "*magische Physik*" (magical physics) and another, "*magische Psychologie*" (magical psychology). A similarly titled work, *Die Magie als experimentelle Wissenschaft* (Magic as Experimental Science) was published in 1912 by Staudenmaier, whom Dessoir (1917) cited as a serious work, and Jaspers (1913) and Ahlenstiel and Meyer (1967) diagnosed as a paradigmatic schizophrenic alongside Schreber and Krauss.

18. Occultism as an intellectual phenomenon with a history has been masterfully described in James Webb's two books (1974, 1976). Webb was an antioccultist. For a sympathetic German view see Max Dessoir (1917) and Fanny Moser (1935). In the cited periodicals, endorsing as well as critical views were expressed.

19. Baron Carl du Prel (1839-1899). His works in fifteen volumes were published in 1900. A 1885 work, *Die Philosophie der Mystik*, was translated into English as *The Philosophy of Mysticism* and is cited by Freud (1900) in the *Interpretation of Dreams* in a footnote added in 1914: "That brilliant mystic Du Prel . . . declares that the gateway to metaphysics, so far as men are concerned, lies not in waking life but in the dream" (p. 63). Freud does not mention the work for which du Prel won an honorary doctorate from Tübingen: his *Oneirokritikon. Der Traum vom Standpunkte des transcendentalen Idealismus* (1868, The Interpretation of Dreams. The Dream from the Perspective of Transcendental Idealism; printed in the *Deutsche Vierteljahresschrift* in 1869). Schreiber only cites du Prel's *Entwickelungsgeschichte* (The History of Evolution). But since Schreber also mentions the periodical *Die Gegenwart*, he probably knew of du Prel's other works via the cross-reference to another periodical, *Sphinx*, in which occult issues were discussed. Some of du Prel's terms are echoed in Freud's terminology of the dream work. Freud also quoted the authors cited by du Prel: Scherner, Volkelt, Schubert. Moreover, even though Freud, in the name of science and the libido theory, warned Jung against his penchant for the occult, he himself showed a certain weakness for occult matters, such as telepathy, which he discussed in a number of his papers.

20. Schreiber (1987) traces many of Schreber's ideas to German zoologist and philosopher Ernst Haeckel (1834-1919) and philosopher Eduard von Hartmann (1842-1900). However, du Prel saw von Hartmann as his opponent and debated him at length. In my view Schreber is much closer to du

Prel's mystical views than to von Hartmann's, whom du Prel regarded as a materialist. Von Hartmann was opposed to the notion of mind without a body; and du Prel denounced von Hartmann's objection to his theory of the transcendental "astral-body" and deplored that von Hartmann did not endorse the notion of disembodied (transcendental) ideas, owing to the latter's adherence to the then-fashionable trend called nihilism. Similarly, the occultist Max Seiling in 1901 published (with Oswald Mutze) a pamphlet *Ernst Haeckel und der "Spiritismus." Ein Protest* (Ernst Haeckel and "Spiritism," a Dissent), which rebutted Haeckel, "Darwin's bulldog" in Germany, and his attacks on occult phenomena. Seiling, who also published other works with Mutze, including *Goethe as Occultist* (second edition 1919), is cited in the respected history of philosophy by F. U. Ueberweg (reedition, 1951) along with Dessoir (1917).

21. *Neschamah*, or *neshama*, is the Hebrew feminine noun meaning soul or spirit and is etymologically related to *neshima* (breathing). The Latin word for breath and soul is anima, also feminine. In this German text *Neschamah* is in the neuter gender, not feminine.

22. According to Lamm (1922), the mystical conception of the spiritual sun, of the divine as the sun of life and wisdom, is at least as old as Plato. It permeates the philosophical and mystical views of Emmanuel Swedenborg, whose ideas and style are similar to Schreber's, even though there is no direct proof that he read him, except for the use of the term *Geisterseher* (seer), which also appears in Kant's (1766) critique of the occult in which Swedenborg is discussed. Schreber may have wanted to conceal his influences. Swedenborg (1688-1772) had an illustrious career in science and engineering before he turned to theology and mysticism. In his visions and voices he saw and heard Jesus and the angels. His new exegesis of the Scriptures became the foundation of a new religion.

23. The German genius Robert Mayer was himself a victim of psychiatry. When he first published in 1842 his discovery of "The First Law of Thermodynamics," he became the envy of his scientific colleagues. The conspiracy of his peers and his wife resulted in having him committed to an asylum as laboring under the delusion of grandeur of having made a contribution to science. While he was rotting away, Joule in England, who wrote his first essay in 1843, was garnering accolades for the same discovery. The story is told by Dühring in a book of 1880 (*Robert Mayer, der Galilei des neunzehnten Jarhunderts*, published in Chemnitz), and in its second edition of 1904, *Robert Mayer, the Galileo of the Nineteenth Century and the Outrageous Crimes of Scientists Against a Trail-Blazing Great of Science*. The priority dispute is described in the entry "Mayer, Julius Robert (1814-1878) in the 11th edition of the *Encyclopaedia Britannica*.

24. An early scholarly interest in Zoroaster's religion can be found in J. F. Kleuker's *Zend-Avesta. Zoroaster's Living Word Including the Teachings and Opinions of this Lawgiver of God, World, Nature, People, etc.* Ahriman, the symbol of all that is vice, evil, and uncleanliness, is the great destroyer, and foe of Ormuzd, the creator of heaven and earth, the god of light. The sun is Ormuzd's eye. Ahriman is also the god that seduced the virtuous female spirits. Thus life and

light are juxtaposed against darkness, death, and destruction. The moral message in this cosmology is unmistakable.

25. See *Encyclopedia Britannica*, 11th edition, entry "Zoroaster" and J. D. C. Parvy (1929).

26. "God, why hast thou forsaken me?" Psalms 22:1, Matt. 27:40.

27. The English word lust, in the dual sense of sensual desire and delight, is the same as the Latin word libido in the ancient Roman poets, as still reflected in the word *libidinous*. Freud extended lust to all the manifestations of sensuality and sensuousness and subsumed them under the generic concept of sexual. In the Fliess correspondence we see the term *Wollust*, which again connotes desire and gratification (with the added denotation of debauchery). It is later changed into the supposedly more neutral and more scientific term *Befriedigung* (gratification).

28. Israëls has noted this, too, as well as Schatzman's distorted view that the cold water was a torment.

29. Schreber refers both to sunlight and artificial light. Moritz Schreber (1858c) recommended sunbathing as an essential preventive health measure. Schreber's delusional allusions to the sun may also be related to sunlight. We noted earlier the pun between Sonne, and Sonnenstein, literally "sun stone."

30. Father's recommendation to avoid emissions is to "alternate lying on the back with lying on the side." I agree with Schreiber (1987, p. 210) that Schreber used his father's words about voluptuousness–inducing lying on the back to apply to a woman.

31. Schreiber (1987, p. 52) believes that both Moritz and Paul Schreber were influenced by Jacob Moleschott's 1852 book *Der Kreislauf des Lebens* (The Cycle of Life). I believe Schultz-Schultzenstein was a more important influence for Moritz. As for Paul, he indeed assimilated his father's and other people's ideas about the metabolic cycles in the body but he combined them with ancient and contemporary mystical ideas about the flow of all kinds of currents in the universe.

32. The book is *Suggestion and its Social Significance*. In that preface Flechsig refers to certain degenerates who have cast their pathological suggestive influence on crowds. It is the task of science, he says, to free the world from the domination of fantasy-ridden autosuggestion. Should anyone disagree with such a purpose for science, then we should conclude that "a man like Helmholtz was but an error of the Creator." The notion of an active I, capable of free will, has been an abyss for science since Aristotle. The notion that hypnotic experiments would fill this abyss is itself a kind of autosuggestion.

33. None was more articulate in describing such unconscious communicational processes than Searles, as in "The Schizophrenic's Vulnerability to the Therapist's Unconscious Processes" (1958) and "The Effort to Drive the Other Person Crazy—an Element in the Aetiology and Psychotherapy of Schizophrenia" (1959), both in Searles (1965). However, Searles did not apply these ideas to Schreber. He only endorsed White's (1961) view of the role of Schreber's mother (Searles, 1965, pp. 429-433) and offered an interesting formulation about disillusionment in Schreber's relation to Flechsig (pp. 607-610); thus, the latter would have to qualify as a transference developed

in adulthood, such as the dependent transference to Flechsig described by Freud.

34. *"Wundervoller Aufbau"* should have been translated simply as "wonderful structure," the other equivalents of *wundervoll* being "marvelous" and "wondrous," as an expression of marveling and rejoicing in the grandeur of nature and God's handiwork. "Miraculous" belongs with miracles, and is thus associated with miracle-mongering and delusions. *Wundervoller Aufbau* may hark back to the title of his father's book of 1859: *Anthropos: der Wunderbau des menschlichen Organismus* (Man: the Wonderful Structure of the Human Organism). The style of the title was common in those days and is no sign of bombast. It is a capsule statement of the work's content and faithfully reflects Moritz Schreber's view of the wonderful harmony of body and mind, which was a leading principle of his system of anthropology, or science of man, built on the foundation of natural science and philosophy. Another glimpse of the origin of Paul's wording is given in his Foot Note #14, where he discusses the locution *"wundervolle Organisation"* [wonderful organization], spoken in nerve-language, or thought language.

35. Grimm's *Deutsches Wörterbuch* defines it by way of the Italian: "homicidio *spirituale dell'anima"* [the spiritual killing of the soul]. In the entry "Torture" in the *Encyclopaedia Britannica*, 11th edition, we read that Pope Innocent IV in a bull of 1282 "directed the torture of heretics by the civil power, as being robbers and murderers of souls, and thieves of the sacraments of God." At the beginning of chapter 26 of *Point Counter Point* Aldous Huxley says that as a result of the onslaught of the European civilization on the Melanesians, the latter "had their souls suddenly murdered." The first to use soul murder in the sense of soul destruction with reference to Schreber was Schatzman, but he did so only in relation to alleged traumas in Schreber's childhood. In this he was followed by Shengold (1989), who, following Burnham, traced soul murder, or psychic murder, to its appearance in Ibsen and in Strindberg's discussion of Ibsen (1974, 1989). (I discuss this issue in chapter 2 and in Lothane, 1989a.) Having popularized the term also made Schatzman feel proprietary about it.

36. This word, derived from the Greek, has a number of meanings. In the Hippocratic tradition of medicine, it refers to a critical (the adjective of *crisis*) sudden turn in the course of disease, a climax that could end in either resolution and recovery or in death. It now denotes an unsteady state, an imbalance, a state of stress for the individual or the community (e.g., a financial, cultural, religious and social crisis). Webster (1971) connects this with the concept of juncture, a crucial convergence of factors.

37. Interestingly, this fantasy name is used by Niederland (1974) in the caption under the photograph of Flechsig. It also is used as the real name by Schreiber (1987). Busse (1990) found that Flechsig had a cousin named Theodor.

38. Cumberlandism, the skill of thought-reading, or thought-transference, either by direct observation of the face or by telepathy, was popularized in the mid-1880s in Germany by Stuart C. Cumberland. Schreiber (1987, p. 250) traced Schreber's reference to a discussion of the subject by du Prel, who

stressed that the willpower of the sender is crucial in effecting the transmission to the receiver.

39. Flechsig had not described any visions to Schreber, but Freud's 'visions' are described in his essay on aphasia, quoted in Flechsig's *Gehirn und Seele* of 1896 (it may be a far-fetched idea that Schreber went to Freud's essay):

> I remember having twice been in danger of my life, and each time the awareness of the danger occurred to me quite suddenly. On both occasions I felt 'this was the end,' and while otherwise my inner language proceeded with only indistinct sound images and slight lip movements, in these situations of danger I heard the words as if somebody was shouting them into my ear, and at the same time I saw them as if they were printed on a piece of paper floating in the air [Freud, 1891, p. 62].

Jung's visions are described in chapter 7 footnote 12.

9

THE DREAMS AND
DRAMAS OF LOVE

Insight into the true state of divine matters was granted to me. . . . I have had to pay dearly enough for this insight with the loss of my whole happiness in life for a great many years. . . . From it springs also the quiet feeling of good will which I extend even to those who in earlier years unwittingly caused me pain.

D. P. Schreber, 1903

His subjective world has come to an end since his withdrawal of his love from it.

Freud, 1911a

Woe! Woe!
Thou hast it destroyed,
The beautiful world,
With powerful fist!
In ruins 'tis hurled,
By the blow of a demigod shattered!

Goethe, Faust

THE CENTRAL THEMES OF THE *MEMOIRS*: LOVE LOST AND REGAINED

Schreber's poignant lamentation, "*mir wehe getan* (they caused me pain, hurt me)" that corresponds to the cries of woe from the chorus in *Faust*, is lost in translation. I do not know if Freud noticed this correspon-

429

dence, but I would like to believe that in the end, so many interpretations later, since he paraphrased Schreber's idea of resolution of conflict as "reconciliation" (*M*, p. 177 Freud, 1911a, pp. 20, 40), Freud understood the central drama of Schreber's life: love rather than sex; love lost and love regained; life lost and life regained. The restoration of Schreber is portrayed by Freud (1911a, p. 70) through the chorus from *Faust*: "Mightier / For the children of men, / More splendid, / Build it again, / In thine own bosom build it anew!" This is also in keeping with the main phenomenological and dynamic facts of Schreber's illness: loss, rage, and depression, not sexual deviance, deficit or dementia praecox. Freud's understanding of depression, faintly foreshadowed in his essay on paranoia, was yet to come.

As far as the wider circle of readers was concerned, the *Memoirs* were intended as an apologia, an explanation of its author's "religious conceptions, so that they may have some understanding of the necessity which forces me to various oddities of behavior" (p. 1), but Schreber also states, "It was my original motive to acquaint my wife with my personal experiences and religious ideas" (p. 1; "Prefatory Remark"). Schreber's wife Sabine was the most important and the most loved person in his adult life; the *Memoirs*, drafted around the twentieth anniversary of their wedding, was an offering of love and reconciliation to her. In his formulation of Schreber Freud missed the important role of women in Schreber's love and sex life, placing him in an artificially conceived all-male environment, a projection from the all-male psychoanalytic circle of disciples in which Freud himself operated at the time of writing his essay.

Schreber's restoration to health was shattered again with the losses that ushered in his third illness. It shattered the dream expressed as follows: "When my last hour strikes I will no longer find myself in an Asylum, but in orderly domestic life surrounded by my near relatives, as I may need more loving care than I could get in an Asylum" (p. 338).[1] The presence and absence of love, a woman's love, the love of his "Sabchen-Gretchen" in sickness and in health, as well as his family's love, are the hidden subtext of the *Memoirs* that also informs Paul Schreber's life. For love is the life of the soul.

PAUL SCHREBER'S ILLNESS

In early reactions to my work, colleagues expressed the concern that I would argue that Schreber was not sick, or that his illness was a myth.[2] Schreber's illness was no myth, and he himself recognized the severity of his suffering and the need to be helped. But, as I have argued, various myths have been created about the nature of his illness and its causes, nurtured by a variety of scientific and hermeneutic formulas.

From a diagnostic standpoint, Schreber's illness was no ordinary paranoia, while from a hermeneutic standpoint no single etiological formula, most especially neither childhood trauma nor repressed homosexuality, adequately encompasses the rich phenomenology of his changing condition. Accordingly, by way of providing an historical corrective, I have attempted to emphasize two things in particular. First, I have attempted to stress the manifold aspects of Schreber's psychosis that identify his as a most unusual condition from a diagnostic standpoint. In this respect, I have emphasized, among other things, the atypical course, the prominent depressive aspects, and the preservation of at least some intermittent capacity for maintaining intellectual distance from his illness (indicated in his original text by the frequent use of constructions like "as if," or "it seemed to me though"), all of which suggest a clinical condition that was highly idiosyncratic and unusual, and described not at all by the usual labels of "paranoia" or "paranoid schizophrenia." The question is not whether Schreber was for a time psychotic—he most certainly was—but how best to characterize that psychosis.

I have attempted to reexamine the phenomenology of Schreber's delusions and fantasies by trying to contextualize them vis-à-vis the various forms of discourse available to him as he tried to come to some understanding of his illness. As I see it, not only were his father's ideas about health, child rearing, and metaphysics involved, but Schreber's text also took as its point of departure various contemporary ideas ranging from occultists like du Prel to Flechsig's anatomical understanding of the brain. My goal here is not to endorse Schreber's ideas but to see how far his discourse can be made intelligible, this on the basis that intelligibility remains the standard by which any psychosis must be judged. Only insofar as we understand the degree to which Schreber makes sense in context can we then begin to specify which of his ideas go beyond the limits of shared consensual thought and thereby warrant psychodynamic explanation and/or psychiatric classification.

Yet, as the reader has had ample opportunity to ascertain already, neither endeavor is at all easy. Simply put, Schreber does not make things easy for an interlocutor. He is forever stepping just of out of range of being understood. Consider what happens when close attention is paid to Schreber's own factual narrative of the evolution of his illness.

This approach is helpful when close attention is paid to Schreber's own factual narrative of the evolution of his illness. Reading his own clear account one is impressed with the poignant crescendo of anxiety, loss, disappointment, disillusionment, helplessness, and hopelessness, climaxing in depression, despair and death wishes. These serious disturbances of mood, that Schreber described and diagnosed in himself as melancholia, resulted in his having to stop working, leave home and wife, and seek safe haven in Flechsig's asylum for a second time in 1893, this time complicated by intractable sleeplessness. The mood disorder has not sufficiently impressed most previous commentators, who saw in depression not the heart of Schreber's disorder but a peripheral emotional accompaniment to the disorder of ideation, that is, the assorted hallucinations and delusions. Yet, modern research into the neurochemical and behavioral aspects of depression has shown it to be a fundamental psychobiological response to life stress, one that is especially likely to occur among the predisposed in conditions of loss (Siever and Davis, 1985). Thus, if we take into account the history of depressive morbidity in the Schreber pedigree, especially Paul's father and brother—but also his mother—the depressive nature of his first illness, the severe psychotic quality of the depression in the second and third episodes, and the absence of cognitive deterioration between the first and second and between the second and third episodes, then a depressive syndrome of varying grades of severity, possibly a manifestation of manic-depressive traits, is what meets the eye.[3]

But, if one grants the pervasive depressive elements in Schreber's evolving illness, then what is one to do with the further cosmological elaborations on the "realms of God"? What to do, too, with the multiple indications of boundary loss, especially vis-à-vis Flechsig, which finally exceed all poetic and metaphysical license, even granted that Schreber may have had understandable grievances against the Leipzig Professor and that at least some of these may have involved Schreber's subliminal perceptions of Flechsig's impact on him, perceptions that were hard to conceptualize in the absence of a theory of suggestive influence? Certainly, Schreber's assorted hallucinations and delusions deserve to be regarded as schizophreniform, and certainly paranoid features can be detected along with depressive ones, even if the entire syndrome conforms neither to schizophrenia or to paranoia. But how to integrate the schizophreniform features with the other elements of the illness, which are no less prominent?

Let us be clear that phenomenologically, the hallucinations and delusions Schreber described do not fit the typical picture of schizophrenia, as opposed to schizophreniform psychosis. With the idea of soul murder forming an overarching theme, many were so-called nihilistic and depressive fantasies of decay; some expressed waxing and waning states of anxiety; and many others, like the fantasy of turning into a woman, played the role of consolation and restoration; many others were a vehicle for a complex scientific, theological and legal discourse and debate. This complex discourse lends itself to a hermeneutic-textual exegesis and to translation into ordinary language. It also strengthens the impression that in Schreber we encounter an atypical form of madness in which depression is the central core.

A salient clinical fact is that the second illness, in November of 1893, did not start with hallucinations and delusions but with a near-catastrophic breakdown in functioning at work and at home, with tormenting sleeplessness and suicidal depression. The onset of the hallucinations and delusions in mid-March of 1894 (i.e., some four months into the hospitalization) coincided with a significant breakdown of understanding between Schreber and his wife and between himself and Flechsig, which led to the judgment of incurability and the threat of an imminent transfer. The hallucinatory-delusional phase of the depressive syndrome, a psychosis within a psychosis, which could be likened to a prolonged dream state or trance state, continued following the transfer to Sonnenstein. It was over by 1897, at which point Schreber realized that he was living in a real world of people and not one inhabited by fleeting shadowy phantoms.

In 1897 Schreber began a campaign to persuade his wife and his doctors that he was in a condition to return home and to resume a normal life; he felt strong and showed insight into his illness. The struggle to regain freedom, including the court battle, lasted five years. During this time Schreber continued to hear voices, but not the same way as before, and with decreasing intensity. Following his discharge he heard a residual tinnitus-like hissing, but the testimony about this experience is unclear. This could be seen as an incomplete recovery from residual schizophreniform symptoms.

A different difficulty is presented by what Weber claimed was the fully crystallized delusional system of turning into a woman. Here let us again bear in mind that in discussing his transformation into a woman, Schreber regularly if not always uses qualifying statements like "as if" and "it seemed to me as though." His statements thus allow the possibility that being turned into a woman was entertained by him as a fantasy, one that he turned to for consolation and for the access to pleasure that it afforded him. But if it was a fantasy, as opposed to an outright delusion, then its persistence deserves to be characterized differently. Certainly, something pertaining to gender identity changed in Schreber's enduring psychological organization as a result of his experiences. But it is possible, and, one could argue in the absence of better evidence, even likely, that what changed was indeed his subjectively felt identity, and not necessarily an enduring psychotic alteration of his entire personality. The line of demarcation between these two alternatives is of course hard to draw. But against the presumption of psychosis, one must weigh the testimony of so many non-psychotic transvestite and transsexual persons, who are yet ready to claim that "really" they are of the opposite sex. Let us be clear, too, as to the limits of the available record: all it establishes for certain is that toward the end of his stay at Sonnenstein and during his court appearances, Schreber continued to entertain his gender transformation fantasies. To be sure, in their intensity these fantasies seem to have gone beyond the ordinary range of daydreaming—Schreber very much liked to think that he looked different—but they may well have stopped short of either full-blown hallucinatory gratification of the delusional certitude that Weber's formulations suggested. Schreber's behavior around his fantasies supports such a minimalist view of them: he set aside private moments for them, but did not allow them otherwise to interfere with his social adjustment. A cross-gender fantasy that becomes habitual, even to the point of becoming an obsession, is not yet a delusion; even less, is it evidence for the kind of a fully crystallized system that Weber sought to make it.

The issue of diagnosis is no mere hair splitting, for a diagnosis carries the social implication of stigma. Schreber consistently and vehemently denied that he was psychotic or paranoid, not because he denied being ill but because he understood full well both the stigma of such a diagnosis and its legal consequences. As one aspect of his defense and vindication, he deserves to have this diagnosis reappraised.

Over and above the diagnostic debates hovers the important psychological and existential question of meaning. The insight that hallucinations and delusions are dream-like encoded messages opened the gates to a universe of interpretive possibilities, from Freud down to our own time. However, one story of Schreber's was not in code language but was expressed simply and directly: it was about freedom lost and freedom regained.

Schreber's involuntary detention at Sonnenstein was neither hallucination nor delusion. It was a reality which meant "living in almost prison-like isolation" (M, p. IV). It was all the more hurtful because as a responsible person Schreber entered Flechsig's hospital as a voluntary patient; his status was changed in midstream by decisions made by the psychiatric and legal authorities. After 1897 Schreber was justified in claiming he was a victim of an "illegal deprivation of liberty (Freiheitsberaubung)" (p. 366), of "being buried alive" (Lebendigbegraben-werden) (p. 59). These were not paranoid neologisms but blunt statements describing the state of a man who had begun to recover his wits and now discovered himself kept captive in a total institution.[4] Niederland repeatedly called Sonnenstein a "sanatorium," an ironically cruel misnomer. To date, the only psychiatrist who pointed out the injustice in Schreber's confinement in Sonnenstein past the disappearance of his suicidal impulses is Thomas Szasz (1976, p. 39). It is an eternal credit to the judges on the high court in Dresden who gave Schreber his freedom that they understood that madness is a matter of meaning, that Schreber had an inherent right to his madness as the subjective meaning he chose to give to the world he lived in.

THE MEANING OF MADNESS

In developing his revolutionary psychoanalytic method based on his dream psychology, Freud acknowledged Kant's dictum that the madman is the dreamer wide awake. Unraveling the mysteries of the dream is Freud's most important gift to mankind—not in the narrow sense of the dream as wish fulfillment but in the wider sense of the dream and the dream world as consolation for pain caused by living in the real world. Freud's paradigm seemed to be complete when he joined dream dynamics with the dynamics of desire (wish fulfillment) and defense (the varieties of repression) and memory (the dream as a historical record).

Freud saw that the bridge between emotional health and emotional illness is the concept of meaning: people create meanings when they are well and when they are ill. Nowadays we take meaning for granted, so ingrained is it in our way of thinking. Such meaningfulness was self-evident to Schreber, even if it was strictly his meaning. The ability to discern meaning in Schreber's productions eluded Flechsig and Weber. For them delusions were to paranoia what fever is to pneumonia—a sign merely pointing to a morbid essence, not to existence and meaning. Today some people are still caught on the horns of the dilemma between descriptive-biological psychiatry and dynamic psychiatry. It is a false either/or dichotomy, because emotional illness is both; we need both approaches to be effective as healers. A totally organic psychiatry is reduced to neurology. A totally psychological psychiatry forfeits the gains of modern pharmacotherapy.

Meanings we disagree with, like opinions we dislike, are sometimes grandiloquently—and pejoratively—given the name of delusions. However, this amounts to a political, not a poetical, perspective on delusion. Indeed, as commented by Freud (1911a), delusions as such did not—and could not at that time—hold much interest for "the practical psychiatrist [in whose case] marvelling [was] not the beginning of understanding" (pp. 17-18). By comparison, the psychoanalytical perspective on meaningfulness as the unconscious common denominator of all mental life should lead one to see a spectrum, from delusions of everyday life (a book yet to be written, modelled on Freud's 1901 *Psychopathology of Everyday Life*) to certifiable madness. Rather than being viewed as a creative illness, delusion was too hastily condemned by Weber as craziness (*Verrücktheit*), that is, paranoia, thus, a justification for seeing the patient as incurable and holding him in the asylum against his will for life. But surely paranoia is also in the eye of the beholder: it was as much Schreber's as it was Weber's. One man's theory of paranoia easily becomes the reason for another man's persecution.

The conception of the dream as the means for the healing of trauma, the idea that dreams are a vehicle of the healing of illness, was another revolutionary insight by Freud. This idea that dreams—in Schreber's case, religious delusions, sexual daydreams and transsexual fantasies— were both the cause of illness and the cure of illness is Freud's (1911a) most amazing conclusion:

> *The delusional formation, which we take to be the pathological product, is in reality an attempt at recovery, a process of reconstruction.* . . . we may regard the phase of violent hallucinations as a struggle between repressions and an attempt at recovery by bringing the libido back again onto its objects [pp. 71, 77].

I have not seen this seminal idea in any of his predecessors or contemporaries, with the exception of Silberer and Jung, who carried it further.

Schreber intuitively understood some of Freud's ideas, to Freud's amazement and admiration. Not the least of these were ideas about sexuality. Thus "the surprising sexualization of [Schreber's] state of heavenly bliss" suggested to Freud (1911a) a confirmation of his own analytic experience that "the roots of every mental disorder are chiefly to be found in the patient's sexual life," and that "Schreber himself speaks again and again as though he shared our prejudice" (pp. 30–31).

Yet to say that Schreber shared Freud's "prejudice" on the importance of sexuality is not to suggest that Schreber would have agreed with Freud's understanding of his own case. For the fact is that Schreber nowhere speaks of homosexual desire per se, that is to say a desire toward another man. To the contrary, he speaks repeatedly of his wishful belief that he is being turned into a woman; it is the gender of the subject that rules in Schreber's understanding of voluptuousness, not the object of desire. Freud's inference that the fantasy of gender transformation bespeaks homosexual desire—a rather common assumption at that—is precisely that: an inference that must be sustained on other grounds. And beyond the shakiness of those grounds, one must here note that Freud's inference works to foreclose all the other possible meanings that may have inhered in Schreber's transformation fantasy.

One salient fact about the sexual reading Freud put on Schreber is that Freud, given his preoccupations with homosexual conflicts in his own life and in relation to men in his entourage, did not make full use of the insights about human sexuality he had established in his early writings about the neuroses due to sexual frustration (the so-called actual neuroses) and in the *Three Essays*, even though he cursorily mentioned "disappointment over a woman" (1911a, p. 62) in his discussion on the development of paranoia. For any conclusion about Schreber's alleged homosexual wishes, conscious or unconscious, should have been reached only *after* an evaluation of his *heterosexual* conflicts, such as possible issues of impotence in Schreber, frigidity in the wife, jealousy toward her due to suspicions of infidelity, or any other disturbance in their sexual life. Thus, at the time when the voices derided his manly courage, when the attendants manhandled him with cruelty and contempt, Schreber imagined that he "had a thing between [his] legs which hardly resembled at all a normally formed male organ" (*M*, Foot Note #33), while in his hospital chart (see Appendix) it is noted that he feared his penis had been twisted off by a "nerve probe," more indicative of sexual dysfunction than homosexual desires. An evaluation of Schreber's heterosexual conflicts was undertaken neither by Freud nor by any other analytic commentator on Schreber, with the exception of Schultz-Henke (1952).

This discussion about the sexual meaning of madness is not complete without addressing the related issue of the madness of language, that is, the very ways in which words and the use of words can become distorted—Nordau said, "degenerated"—in creating new words or giving new meanings to old words or altering syntax and style. Schreber was acutely aware of the importance of language in his coining of the terms *Grundsprache* and *Nervensprache* and when he invoked Luther's fire or flame words (*Flammenworte*) to get his own new and searing message across. Does not every innovator create flame words? Was not Freud's very use of *sexual* as a synonym for *sensual* such a flame word?

While many creative geniuses across Europe in the late 19th century were experimenting with the artistic form of writing—Rimbaud, Wagner, Ibsen, Nietzsche, Tolstoy and other "degenerates" listed by the medical skeptic Nordau (1895)—it is the liberties taken with the word itself, the disjunction of signifier and signified, the use of unconventional combinations, that was so disturbing to the medically trained degenerate-basher Lombroso, who spoke of the proximity of genius and madness and was translated into German (1887), and his disciple Nordau, who dedicated his book (1895) to Lombroso. Moritz Schreber, in line with the traditional skepticism of physicians, had already expressed himself in a similar vein (1858a). Flechsig and Weber were not far behind. Paul Schreber's writing shows that he was adept in the use of both formal and flaming words.

The dynamiting of the traditional structures of language in the late-19th century was accompanied by the emerging interest in symbols, a harbinger of the future interest in semantics and hermeneutics. A related development was an inquiry into the meaning of history and the validity of historical knowledge.

HISTORY AND HERMENEUTICS, SEX AND LOVE

At the same time that Freud sought to establish the libido theory as the foundation of psychoanalysis as a natural science, he also developed the hermeneutic method of *applied psychoanalysis*, embracing psychoanalytic theories of the most diverse provenance. Accordingly, the individual was subsumed under generic, universal paradigms, applied not from within, as in clinical analysis, but from above. As a result, the correspondence between the thing interpreted and the interpretation was not established by consensual validation but rested solely on the authority of the interpreter. While undoubtedly of heuristic value, applied psychoanalysis, when pushed relentlessly, as Freud himself showed, can easily degenerate into wild analysis and give rise to hermeneutic myths.

The hermeneutic readings of Schreber have given rise to myths that have become legends. Such legends grow as a result of interpretations that are created at given historical moments. One such legend concerning Schreber—that he was a homosexual—was instigated by Freud, whose intention was misunderstood. Another legend—that Schreber's father was a sadist and child abuser—was started by Niederland. Both legends are tantamount to character assassinations.

History occupies an intermediate position between clinical and applied psychoanalysis: like the latter, it deals with a person whom it seeks to understand from within, with a minimum of preformed theories, but without live confirmatory evidence. Disillusioned in the claims of positivist historiography à la Ranke to discover the past *wie es eigentlich gewesen war*, as it really happened, R. G. Collingwood (1946) propounded a historical method of not merely going after archival or archeological facts but of seeking to understand the historical person through a process of psychological reconstruction and identification from within, or, as Jacques Barzun put it, through the imagination of the real.

The clinical method is historical insofar as it focuses on the individual. But it is also scientific and generic insofar as it makes use of class, type, and species and subsumes the subject, i.e. person, under the species. Thus it observes the person as a body and as an agent, as born with certain givens of body and mind and temperament, and as a carrier of symptoms of disorder, of the course and outcome of disorder, so as to arrive at a generic, or scientific, diagnosis. As a clinical discipline, psychiatry has always been both historical and scientific, descriptive and dynamic; it is also a dynamic depth-psychology; but the proportions have varied, depending on the historical climate of opinion.

There can be no clinical psychoanalytic interpretation of Schreber's symptoms because he is dead. Freud realized this limitation and held that, faute de mieux, the printed text is every bit as good as the living word. But the bulk of his interpretations was hermeneutic: he applied "his knowledge of the psychoneuroses" and convinced himself "that even thought-structures so extraordinary as these . . . are nevertheless derived from the general and comprehensible impulses of the human mind" (Freud, 1911a, p. 18).

In linking Schreber's so-called paranoia to homosexuality, Freud ignored the fact he had himself acknowledged, that Schreber was heterosexual, as well as the more common causes of neurotic sexual misery: incompatibility, frigidity, and impotence. Freud did not sufficiently allow for sex in any form (consummated, masturbated or fantasied) as the most common defense strategy for handling frustration or unpleasure from any source. For one, Schreber had plenty of reasons to be frustrated with his life. For another, in his long years of incarceration, he was also subject to the stresses of people in prisons, i.e., barred from the normal outlets for sexual tension. What else could the poor man do but dream about sex?

In linking Schreber's paranoid delusions to homosexuality, Freud elected to minimize the fact that up to this time Schreber had functioned heterosexually; also minimized by Freud was the fact that the onset of Schreber's alleged homosexual inclinations came in the context of sexual frustration caused first by the absence of his wife and then by the prolonged hospitalization. When one considers further the passage of time between Schreber's initial hypnopompic daydream of submitting as a woman to the full elaboration of both the "soul murder" accusation and the ideas of gender transformation, one is forced to ask what other meanings were entailed in Schreber's more florid sexual ideas. The closest Freud came to examining such undercurrent causes, and meanings, was to say that climacteric changes, suggesting a waning of sexual prowess, could have been among the precipitating causes of Schreber's illness. Schreber's worries about sexual abuse by men, meanwhile, do not *prima facie* indicate a homosexual desire, although they do suggest a pseudohomosexual dream scenario portraying Schreber as heterosexually dysfunctional, degraded, and derided. At the time, the interpretive significance of such dynamics were invoked by Maeder (1910), whom Freud denied having read in time for his essay on Schreber, even though evidence suggests he did (Lothane, 1989a). For Schreber's to qualify as a regressively activated homosexual wish, due to a return to an infantile fixation point, the only kind of homosexuality Freud was really talking about, such a wish would have to be corroborated by more information than was available to Freud.

The other dynamic Maeder was concerned with was paranoia as a response to frustration and anger. Freud mentioned hatred only in passing. His omission of anger as a dynamic factor is even more glaring, for two reasons. On one hand, he had already cited Adler's 1908 paper on the role of the "aggressive drive," that is anger, in life and neurosis in discussing Little Hans (Freud, 1909; p. 140) only to minimize its real significance. On the other hand, in a letter to Ferenczi of 1910 he wondered if perhaps "Doctor S. senior . . . was a despot in his household who 'bellowed' [i.e., yelled and scolded] at his son and understood him as little as the 'lower God' understood our paranoiac" (Lothane, 1989a, p. 215) while in a letter to Jung, Freud inferred that Schreber gave vent to "a bitter satire on his father's medical art. . . . (In other words, his father bellowed too)" (McGuire, 1974, p. 369). It did not occur to Freud that the bitter satire could have also been directed to Flechsig's medical art.

It is not just that it is improbable that the reason Schreber fell ill was that he awoke one day with a sexual desire for Flechsig in the guise of a fantasy about what a woman might feel in coitus; but that in addition, in this construction, Freud reduced love, an inclusive concept, to libido, an included concept. This reduction falls apart in the third section of his essay, where ego interests loom as harbingers of his future ego psychology. This nascent ego psychology is pointing to the ego (i.e., nonsexual) interests and, at a further remove, to interpersonal relations (i.e., love writ large). Schreber was disappointed in sex *and* in love. The worshipful love for his wife was complicated by negative emotions, mostly rage, the most powerful passion given vent in many disguises.

As against myth, the central life reality, on the surface and in the depths, is that persons live in love relations, that love and existence are inseparable. This also applies to the doctor–patient relation: it is a love relation of a special kind. Here we are concerned with both aspects of Schreber's love relations: his dramas of love and his dreams of love and desire. This is the hidden text both in Schreber's book and in Freud's essay.

The role of love raises the issue of interpersonal, or dyadic, dynamics in symptom formation, to this day the stepchild of psychoanalytic theoreticians but so well understood by Harry Stack Sullivan. The gist of interpersonal dynamics is that symptoms are an expression of doings in the dyad, of the intentions, emotions, and communications between two people in a relation. Such interactions are either collaborative or conflicted, causing pleasure or pain. Thus, conflict is external and social, as well as internal and subjective. To say that symptoms, such as the content of psychosis, are acts (Freud, 1916–1917, p. 358) is latently interactionist, for acts do not occur in an interpersonal vacuum: acts are by their nature interpersonal. Thus, every so-called mental symptom is an act addressing two audiences: oneself and an other. Just as the meaning of the dream is in the dreamer, the symptom in the subject, so the meaning of the act is in the actor. But since the actor is also an interactor, the meaning of the act is also in the interaction, as happens in speaking and listening. Meanings are being constantly created and recreated between the sender and the receiver, speaker and listener, doer and observer, in the course of their ongoing and evolving interactions.

The other aspect of interpersonal dynamics, in addition to the communication of content and intent, is the communication of emotions. Emotions are powerful stimuli and are communicable: they travel from a sender and *evoke* in the receiver counteremotions that require processes of handling and dissipation. To metabolize psychologically an emotion evoked in you by another person calls forth the reaction of having that emotion experienced, expressed and extinguished, or else it will continue to rankle as a source of ongoing stimulation. It comes to this: Schreber's hallucinations and delusions were speeches, gestures, and cries of anguish and pain, of love unrequited, addressed to himself and to an audience.

Freud was pragmatically dyadic but theoretically monadic. It was left to others (Ferenczi, 1912; Searles, 1965) to spell out the role of such mutual conscious and unconscious dyadic interactions. This was also on the mind of Freeman and associates (1969) when they attributed hallucinations and delusions arising de novo in hospitalized patients to stimulation by the hospital environment. Schreber called such a traumatic impact on him, of a suggestive hypnotic nature, *Nervensprache*. Both at Flechsig's and later at Sonnenstein, Schreber was at all times sensitive to the impingements of the hospital environment, where he was surrounded by "uneducated attendants and lunatics" (Foot Note #107): "[I became involved in] scenes of violence between myself and other patients . . . starting to talk to me or making some other noise near me" (*M*, p. 265). The result was bellowing, feeling "interferences" (I would translate as "disturbances") from the rays, and miracles of "all manner of painful states." Says Schreber, "This rapid change in my condition (*des Befindens*) gives the overall impression of madness. . . the more so as my surroundings are made up mostly of madmen who themselves add to all sorts of mad things happening" (p. 270). This concept also applies to soul murder, the arch symptom and message.

Given the concept of love in relations, it might be timely to add to Freud's famous syllogisms of paranoia. These formulas show that while Freud thought he was speaking the language of sex by saying libido, he, like Molière's M. Jourdain, did not realize that he was in reality talking the language of love and hate. For by 1910 he had already written his first "Contribution to the Psychology of Love," the essay "A Special Type of Choice of Object Made by Men," and thus demonstrated his awareness of love. Therefore, the famous syllogisms are not about sexual desire in the literal sense but about erotization of love in the symbolic sense, as Freud was well aware. I therefore propose to frame the syllogisms as follows: From the point of view of love between two people, the following five possibilities arise for each member in the love dyad: (1) I love him or her; (2) I do not love him or her; (3) we love each other; (4) we do not love each other. The same possibilities apply to relations of hate. From the point of view of self-love, these are the possibilities: (1) everybody loves me; (2) I love everybody; (3) nobody loves me; (4) I only love myself, I am the greatest, the narcissistic-grandiose solution; or, (5) I hate myself because they hate me, the masochistic–persecutory solution. This grid may explain some of the hallucinatory-delusional states of Paul Schreber: his predicament was unrequited love, and the content and mood of the assorted hallucinations and delusions reflected the many fluctuations between elation and depression, self-aggrandizement, and self-abasement.

SCHREBER AS BIOGRAPHY

As a biography the *Memoirs* present a very slim archive indeed, remaining silent about many basic facts of life in the Schreber family. The forever tantalizing censored Third Chapter, which may have contained valuable data, has not been found. Under pressure from the family and to avoid a lawsuit, Schreber made further cuts prior to publication

(Foot Note #118B). He presents no description of the beginning, evolution, and resolution of his life and love dramas. He tells us nothing about the events of his childhood or his school years. Of the student era we know only that he belonged to a student organization. Nothing has survived about the relations between him and his father, who died when Schreber was a youth of 19. Similarly, we know very little about the relations between him and his mother, his brother, and his sisters. We know nothing about Schreber's relations with friends and acquaintances. We do get from him a number of details about his adult career and the crisis related to it.

The Schreber archive remains slim in spite of the recent biographical research, which revealed no new facts that change the story as told in the *Memoirs*. The veracity of Schreber has been upheld, but a number of significant amplifications and additions have been made to our knowledge of him.

We now know that the many years of Schreber's life between his father's death and his marriage were spent in or in the vicinity of his mother's house. Pauline Schreber was not involved with her son during his long stay at Sonnenstein until the very end. A posthumously published poem composed by Schreber (1905) in celebration of his mother's 90th birthday, two years before her death, is a moving testimony of his deep attachment to and reverence for her. Additional support for this assumption comes from what has been learned about his elder sister, Anna Jung, who grew up to resemble their mother in longevity and strength and to continue the tradition of the powerful matriarch. I suspect that the love between mother and son was at least as important in Schreber's character formation as was his love for father. Upon his father's death, the two brothers were surrounded by a household of women: mother, three sisters and an aunt. The feelings Paul had for these women, especially the mother, must hold some clues to his deep reverence for femininity, his fantasy of turning into a woman, and his excessive dependence on a woman transferred from mother to wife. These feelings also shed light on Paul's deep maternal sensibilities in raising his adoptive daughter, Fridoline Schreber-Hammer.[5]

Much has been learned about Schreber's psychiatrists Flechsig and Weber and their treatment philosophies, the missing links in the dyadic decoding of his delusions, particularly soul murder. These facts also illuminate a corner of the Schrebers' marital relationship, his most important adult relationship in health, disease, and recovery. Schreber said that he was both a victim and a perpetrator of soul murder. Marriage is a frequent scene of soul murder, especially in situations involving power and money. The sadomasochistic knots in a marriage are legion, and there were many in Schreber's. These may now be better understood in the light of information that surfaced about Sabine's family thanks to Dr. Uwe Peters (1990) and to facts recorded in Schreber's personal file at the Ministry of Justice (Devreese, 1981a). In his adult life Schreber not only played out the conflicts between father and son, which, as illuminated by Niederland (1974) and Baumeyer (1956) were projected onto his work relationships; there were also the battles between husband and wife, the dramas and trials of love, that are so prominent in the *Memoirs*. It was the rise and fall of Schreber as a hero with a fatal flaw in his character, which the ancient Greeks believed was a person's destiny, that determined the ways in which he handled matters of love, sex—and work—in health and disease. Thus, of all the relations that had an impact on Schreber throughout his life, the three that were uppermost in his mind in the writing of the *Memoirs* are the relations with his wife, and with Flechsig and Weber.

How could Schreber, a prominent judge of the high court, fall so low? He was soul-murdered due to a convergence of causes: his character, with its mixed traits of passive dependence, passive aggression, and masochism; his style of handling conflicts of love, sex, power, anger; his depressive disease, that is, the losses and the breakdown of the defensive strategies he had developed for coping with his conflicts; and by the double stranglehold of psychiatry and law, with the dual sentence of illness and legal incompetency.

PAUL SCHREBER'S CHARACTER AND CONFLICTS

Freud's essay and Niederland's writings about father and son galvanized Schreber studies and proved of immense heuristic value. Nevertheless, the opinions that Schreber's illness was explained by latent homosexuality and that the father tortured his son by means of posture improving appliances, gymnastic regimens, and cruel pedagogics remain unproven and reductive, a genetic fallacy. Freud reduced love to sex, Niederland tragedy to trauma. His father was undoubtedly a towering person; were he simply sadistic, it would have made Schreber simply hate him or himself develop into a hateful and cruel person. The sadistic father formula would also mean confusing discipline and obedience with cruel punishments, an untenable idea. The father of childhood was both authoritarian and loving, which made love for him conflictual, i.e, tragic. As a result, Schreber suffered from the tragic conflict between his love for and identification with his father and his rebellion against his father's authority and ideas. The conflict between father and son, endemic to the Judeo-Christian heritage, cannot be reduced to the use of a few posture-improving gadgets. Schreber's was, rather, a life of evolving identifications and counter-identifications, clashes and conciliations, crises and resolutions. Father was both "God" and "apostle," epithets often ironically applied to doctors, "of [whose] *pathological states* [*Krankheitszustände*, morbid conditions; emphasis Schreber's] in part most peculiar, which can never be taken as throwing any aspersions" (p. 442), Schreber was well aware. But the father was also the wellspring of the "Schreber spirit" and, says Paul, "[of my own] practical turn of mind—a fundamental trait of my own character" (p. 116).

Schreber grew up in a traditional bourgeois home, the middle of five children, the second boy. The household was ruled by strong ethical principles of work, responsibility, respect for parental authority, thrift, truthfulness, duty, discipline, and self-abnegation, upheld by both father and mother. There was strong opprobrium attached to the negative passions, such as rage, envy, fear, which were expected to be actively suppressed within the individual, and there was a strong bias against sensuality, self-indulgence, and softness. The latter were decried as effeminacy, a deplorable character flaw, by such medical authorities as Hufeland, Hartmann, and, of course, Moritz Schreber. Love was preached according to the Gospels and as taught by ethical philosophers, such as Kant and Fichte. In matters of sex the ideal was chastity and continence. Such values, inculcated at home, at school and university, were expected to be carried into adult life and society. But society was replete, then as now, with the realities of brute force, power, money, hypocrisy, deceit, exploitation, class strife, crime, and sexual temptation. There came a time when Schreber got caught in the clash between such contrasting realms of existence.

I do not believe the Schreber household was much different, say, from the Freud household, except for the difference in religious formulas. I am rather impressed with the paradise-lost quality of this house and home, as recalled by Moritz's daughters, by how sheltered their lives were. Paul had lived such a sheltered and orderly life: home, school, university education, career, each phase running its preordained course, first in the protective presence of both parents, later never too far from mother and the world contained within the boundaries of the Saxon motherland: the great social and cultural center that was Leipzig, the provincial cities of Chemnitz and Freiberg (except for his assignment in Strasbourg during the French German war of 1871/72 and the legal stint in Berlin in 1879, the only times Paul wandered away from Saxony). There is no hint here of adolescent rebellion, of a Sturm und Drang period later in life, no tales of torrid love affairs, of adventures and life-endangering scrapes with fate. After

35 years of this apparently placid existence Schreber married, moved from the shelter of his parental home to the sheltered married home. His new life, home and work, was also placid, if we are to believe him rather than the retrospective assessments of Sabine (Baumeyer, 1956). We know of no ongoing or new male friendships, like Fliess' and Freud's, no daring partnerships, no revolutionary movements started. The one and only attempt of an ambitious nature, six years into his marriage, was Schreber's bid for the *Reichstag*, which ended in a fiasco. An honors law student, Schreber had grown up highly educated and extremely well-read, honest, dependable, respectable and respectful, a man not prone to cunning or scheming. The fatal flaw was in his inclination to develop dependent attachments and the fear of losing them: attachments to work, wife, physicians and hospitals, all relationships suggesting mother attachment, or mother-transference. The darker side of Schreber's mother-transference accounts for his child-like regressive behavior during his illness: excessive dependence, exhibitionism, refusal of food, withholding stool, and rageful tantrums. He could be considered a prime candidate for such regressions for yet another reason: softness, tenderness, and effeminacy were taboo in his father's pedagogical canon. When Schreber recovered, he was able once again to express his profound positive mother-identification in a relationship with another person, his daughter, upon whom he bestowed his love and devotion.

In Schreber's parents' world, woman was subjugated to man in accordance with the ethics of productivity and division of labor: careers belonged to men while women devoted their time to cooking, children, and church. Yet Pauline Schreber was not an ordinary woman. She was a person of high culture, a patron of humanities and the arts, born to a family of university professors. She brought connections and money into her marriage, and her role as mother-hen to the boarding children was scarcely unimportant to Schreber's career. Moreover, she very likely became the power behind the throne, mother and matriarch, during the last years of her husband's life, and her influence on her children continued long after his death. Against the fading image of the father, ill for most of Paul's adolescence (alluded to as God who wanted to keep his distance from Schreber, *M*, pp. 183, 264), the mother would have stood as a pillar of strength, even if, according to the mores of the day, her pre-eminence in the household could not be overtly acknowledged. On the positive side, the son likely assimilated the father's idea of overcoming despair by sheer willpower. Although willpower did not ultimately save Moritz himself, it did stand his son in good stead as he persevered in battling his involuntary hospitalization at Sonnenstein.

It was the identification with father's conscientiousness and his ideas about the ethics of love, sex, and work—preached in his books on education and inculcated at home by both parents—that was so crucial in the son's character development and adult conflicts. Paul Schreber grew up to be serious-minded, law abiding, dutiful and honest to a fault, to the point of a nagging, obsessional ruminativeness. At the height of his career he rebelled: he refused to perform. It was no easy matter for a *Senatspräsident* to give up his profession. A character like this with conflicts like these is a prime candidate for feelings of guilt and a resulting depressive illness. The *Memoirs* are rife with the iconography of guilt, depression and punishment: devils, souls blackened with sin requiring purification, the fires of purgatory, syphilis, pestilences and cataclysms visited on a mankind rotten with moral corruption. Plagued by conflicts Schreber escaped into emotional illness, not unlike the character in the case history in his father's *Health* (1839).

Schreber's predisposition to depression also comes from the parents, whether as an inherited biological trait or an acquired characterological trait. It is a predisposition that runs deep in the Schrebers down the generations. Paul's brother had it too, and his mother was also a sufferer. The father's depressive illness in the last decade of his life, his untimely death, and the brother's syphilis, depressions, and suicide may have contributed their share to Paul's survivor guilt. This may be the reason Paul's agitated suicidal depression peaked in 1895, at age 53, when he finally survived the father's year of death and bought himself a new lease on life.

Another prominent motif, predisposing Schreber to depression, was the identification with father's quest for fame and a place in history. The streak of ambition runs in the Schreber men from generation to generation, but also the tragic discrepancy between ambition and achievement and the exquisite sensitivity to frustration and rejection. Paul is identified both with the dream of glory and with the disappointment of failure. He had witnessed the failed ambitions of his father and brother, their trials, despair, and rage. In proud Dresden he felt lonely and fearful of the demands of high office. In his illness he enacted this despair and this rage, theirs and his own. He himself became a tested soul, tried and purified in the purgatory on earth that was Sonnenstein. Paradoxically, both Moritz and Paul achieved the fame they so desired only posthumously, while many others, much more illustrious then they in their lifetime, have vanished into oblivion.

Paul Schreber identified with the parental ideals of sexual expression, gender identity, and morals in marriage. His own marriage rested on the traditional definitions of roles and rules, man the provider, woman the homemaker. But what were the actual marriage politics, especially the politics of power and money, which can easily become the politics of strife and soul murder? Who controlled whom in the marriage of Paul and Sabine? The early pictures of Sabine show a young face unfurrowed by life's cares and worries: she appears ready to play the role of the obedient wife. Raised in the patricentric tradition, Paul would expect such obedience as a matter of course. Thus, whatever emotional imbalances arose between them could only be assimilated under the conventional rubrics defining what a marriage was and should be. Here it should be noted that when the family was finally reconstituted after Paul's discharge from Sonnenstein, his mental health continued to be relatively stable. When after his release in 1902 Schreber finally rejoined his wife, built a new house in Dresden, and adopted the thirteen-year-old girl found by his wife as his own daughter, he was no longer troubled by any supernatural visitations and never mentioned them in conversation. He went about his daily business and raised his adoptive daughter with love. He also sought to find love and reconciliation with his wife.

Moritz Schreber's copious writings about bodily functions and sexual ethics and conduct are amply matched by the prominence of the themes of sexuality, defecation, and urination in the *Memoirs*. Paul both identified with Moritz's injunctions against sexual expression and rebelled against them. The theme of sex is prominent in the *Memoirs* and in Freud's analysis of it. Schreber's candor in discussing sexual pleasure and masturbation, speaking of urination and defecation in four letter words, and mentioning these topics in the same breath with the name of God, was as daring as his private religion. It would be fair to claim that such an undoing of repressions was brought about by the psychotic process, given the repression of sexuality in the Schreber household and the social taboo on such topics in 19th century Saxony. Guilt over sexuality, then, should be seen as an important motif in Schreber's life both in health and in illness.

It can be safely assumed that transference contributed a significant share to the content of the psychosis, but we are at the mercy of conjectures. For most Schreber commentators, under the sway of the patricentric perspective, it was natural to trace everything back to father. The only exception was White (1961), who used the selfsame material to prove a transference derived from the mother. No doubt transference issues entered Paul's relationship with Flechsig, five years his junior, and Weber, five years his senior. But again: was it maternal or paternal, or was it traceable to transferences built up in the later years of life from teachers and friends and not, as psychoanalysts are fond to think, determined exclusively by the remote infantile past?

In one area, in spite of his basic honesty, Schreber wanted to eat his cake and have it, too. In writing a story with a view toward future publication, he sought refuge against a libel suit by Flechsig in the protection offered by the law to the ravings of madmen. He played it safe, but he is not free of the suspicion that it was a hidden masochistic game nonetheless. He may have taken a masochistic position in the games he played with his wife, too.

SCHREBER AND HIS WIFE

Ottilie Sabine Behr came from a theater and opera family and circles and was the third of four children. Her father, judging by his physiognomy in surviving portraits, gives the impression of a powerful paterfamilias; Sabine would have been under his very strong influence. We know nothing about how Sabine and Paul met, how they fell in love, and why they chose each other. When they married in 1878, one year after Gustav Schreber's suicide, Sabine was 21 and Schreber 36.

Can we believe Schreber that he had a "happy marriage" (*M*, p. 293)? The marriage remained childless, and of this he did complain. It later became known that there were six miscarriages (among them a stillborn girl in 1888 and a boy in 1892 in the genealogical records); they are eloquent testimony to Schreber's pain, clearly recognized by Freud, in not being able to continue the Schreber name. I believe this pain may have played a precipitating role in the second illness, which started out with Schreber's dream of feeling like a woman submitting (*unterliegen*) to copulation. This *unterliegen* reverberates a number of the meanings of the word: "to lie under" but also "to be defeated," which in German rhymes with *siegen*, "to be victorious."[6]

We know nothing about the nature of the sexual relations between Paul and Sabine. Paul tells us, "Few people have been brought up according to such strict moral principles as I, and have throughout life practised such moderation [*Zurückhaltung*, reserve] especially in matters of sex, as I venture to claim for myself" (*M*, p. 208). Taken at face value, this would suggest that Schreber remained continent until his marriage. Such an assumption might also be in consonance with his father's ideas on the sanctity of marriage and the importance of male continence.

In the many factual and fantastic references to his wife in the *Memoirs*, and in his unpublished poems, Schreber repeatedly stated that he loved his "dear Sabchen." This idyllic appearance is belied by the testimony of the adoptive daughter confirming the hidden anger in the *Memoirs*' fantastic references and in the bellowing. Schreber himself may not have been the easiest person to live with and made Sabine angry, causing her to suffer in different ways.

Schreber's first illness in 1884 shows the first cracks in the marriage. The *Memoirs* are silent on this but in Schreber's hospital chart entry of April 14, 1884, we read that he expresses suspicions that his wife will be sent away under some pretext and not come back. Is this mild paranoia or had Sabine threatened to leave him? This clue points to signs of distress in the marriage and to an excessive dependence on his wife, rooted in a mother-transference; and, possibly, to a controlling attitude on the part of the wife. It is not known if divorce was used as a threat at that time. The infantile nature of Schreber's regression is suggested by his wanting to be carried and to be photographed many times.

Strains in the marriage may have also been present prior to the second illness. After 15 years of marriage, love and power relations may have shifted in certain ways. The partners had grown older and more familiar with each other; they knew each other's needs, character strengths and weaknesses. Such familiarity creates possibilities for games of cunning and manipulation, ploys for power and overpowering in the battles of wits (battles of brains, Strindberg said) between the sexes, leading even to soul murder within a marriage. Yet we simply have no information as to what the marriage was like prior to Schreber's becoming depressed and sleepless sometime after his appointment to the Court of Appeals in Dresden. And what little hints we get about the marriage after this time come in the context of the continuing crisis brought on by Paul's illness, hardly a good time to assess the basic emotional tone of a marital union. What we do know, or at least have reason to suspect, however, is that Sabine did not fight her battles alone. As the child of Heinrich Behr, she remained devoted to him, enough so that at a crucial juncture she chose to be with him rather than with her husband; we are entitled to suppose, furthermore, that she enjoyed her father's support in the travails that followed, including the legal ones. Sabine also played the lady in distress with Flechsig and Weber, enlisting their support against the husband as well.

Allusions to accusations of Schreber's alleged threats of divorce appeared during the time of his bid to leave the hospital, when Sabine appealed to Weber for protection against her bellowing husband. Schreber denied such threats vehemently.

> I have never played with the idea of *divorce* . . . the correspondence-
> . . . with my wife for years would prove the true love I feel towards her
> and how painful it is for me that she too has been made most unhappy by

my illness and the factual dissolution of our marriage. . . . She had the right according to law to start divorce proceedings because of mental illness persisting longer than three years. I always added that I would regret this very much; . . . in such an eventuality she would naturally have no claim on the interest of my capital nor on the pension to which I am entitled by twenty-eight years in the service of the State.(My wife it is true has money of her own, but the greater part of the interest she draws comes from mine) [*M*, p. 436].

Had Schreber thought of divorcing his wife for not giving him an heir? We do not know. Could negative attitudes toward Paul have played a role in Sabine's miscarriages? Quite possibly. There is yet another possibility for considering divorce: sexual troubles between the spouses, such as indifference, unfaithfulness, sexual frigidity, and impotence. Freud noted that early on Schreber "had been inclined to sexual asceticism" and drew a conclusion shaped by his fixation on homosexuality: "the sexual enjoyment which he had won for himself . . . was not the sexual liberty of man (*männliche Sexualfreiheit*) but the sexual feelings of a woman. He took up a feminine attitude towards God; he felt that he was God's wife" (Freud, 1911a, p. 32), or God's whore. Yet, Freud's homosexual explanation for this change in Schreber's attitude bypasses all the multitudinous possibilities for sexual frustration and sexual rivalry within the marriage; it bypasses, too, the impact on this dependent, masochistic man of the temporary loss of both his wife and, during his hospitalization, of his mother as well. If we cannot decisively improve on Freud's interpretation, for want of the requisite data, we at least owe it to ourselves to note that other constructions are possible and that they have at least as much warrant in the available documents as Freud's own. The truth is that we simply do not have enough information to decide among the many possible meanings of Schreber's dream of turning into a woman. It might be, for example, that Schreber was simply jealous of women for they could cultivate sensuality in ways forbidden to men. To be sure, a clinician might well doubt that such a motive would be enduring enough to produce all the sequelae seen in Schreber's case. But by the same token a clinician should deem unsatisfactory an interpretive line that fails to capture the exact phenomenology of Schreber's transformation, which involves a change in gender as opposed to a change in love object.

The communications between Paul and Sabine during his stay at Sonnenstein were troubled. A difficulty arose between them when Paul tried to make her understand his delusions, for example, when he maintained that the piano strings snapped due to divine miracles and not because of his "senseless banging on the piano . . . [as] was . . . my wife's repeatedly stated opinion, possibly having heard it from the physicians" (p. 170). What would have been the tactful thing for the poor woman to say? To agree with Paul and risk being a hypocrite or to speak the voice of reality? Furthermore, Sabine evinced fear of her husband and hid behind the doctors in refusing to take him home, long before his discharge (Baumeyer, 1956).

It was an even more delicate issue for Paul when it came to telling Sabine about his sexual abuse fantasies, cross-dressing and transformation into a woman. His voices mocked him: "Fancy a person who was a Senatspräsident allowing himself to be f. . . .d" and "Are you not ashamed in front of your wife?" (p. 177). He resolved the conflict as follows (Foot Note #76; which he would quote later in full in his writ of appeal):

> I must use particular discretion with my wife, for whom I retain my former love in full. I may at times have failed by being too frank in conversation or in written communications. It is of course impossible for my wife to understand my trends of thought fully; it must be difficult for her to retain her previous love and admiration for me when she hears that I am preoccupied with ideas of possibly being transformed into a woman. I can deplore this, but am unable to change it; even here I must guard against false sentimentality [p. 179].

In this passage Schreber shows an uncommon combination of delicacy of feeling, dignity, and honesty, although he may be unaware of the anger hidden in the frankness. But it also indicates the intellectual and spiritual gulf between husband and wife. When the passage is reproduced verbatim in the writ of appeal, in the context of explaining his cross-dressing to the court, Schreber adds the following:

> I do not know how one came to assume that I would neglect that tact and fine feelings towards my wife for which everyone praises me. *Natu-rally*—and I have acted accordingly up to now—I would spare my wife any painful sight; *I showed her my female ornaments only with some reluctance when out of forgivable feminine inquisitiveness she insisted upon it* [p. 437; second emphasis added].

We do not know with what combination of bedeviled curiosity and expressed outrage Sabine "insisted"[7] on seeing Schreber's female ornaments. Schreber's locution, "forgivable feminine inquisitiveness," might be a euphemism hiding a reproach of hypocrisy; that is to say, he may have supposed that she derived her own secret voyeuristic pleasure from the occasion. Then again, it is also possible that having been told of his delusion in this regard, she demanded to see concrete proof, no matter what such a potentially humiliating encounter might mean to her husband.

Schreber's long-standing anguish, presumably shared by Sabine as well, over childlessness is in the end mitigated by the adoption of the half-orphaned girl Fridoline, whom Schreber found living with his wife following his release from Sonnenstein. The origins of this child and the circumstances of the adoption remain veiled in mystery. She was born in 1890 in Wilten, now a part of Innsbruck, Austria, and was said to be a daughter of an unknown mother and the tenor Franz Petter. In the 1970s Baumeyer expressed the belief that she was Sabine's own child by another man. This means that Franz Petter, the girl's father, would have had an affair with Sabine in 1890, when he was 21 and she was 33, and that Sabine traveled then to Innsbruck to deliver the child and leave it with his family. If this story were true, it would suggest a hidden cause of Paul Schreber's illness in 1893—rage at his wife during all those years, until he was finally able to forgive her. There is no confirmation of this story so far. Nor is it known at what point Sabine learned of the child, what she explained to her husband when she brought the girl from Austria, or how an understanding was reached between Paul and Sabine while he was still at Sonnenstein. The adoption was formalized by 1906. By that time the child's father, who until then had been singing in the Dresden opera house, had left for Cologne. From 1902 to 1907 Schreber enjoyed the longed-for peace of mind in the company of his women, but the loss of woman's life-sustaining presence struck him again, with the death of his mother and the stroke of his wife, and became the precipitating event of his third and final illness, which started in 1907.

While Schreber does not tell us who the people were that unwittingly hurt him, and while it is an unproven theory that she was an unfaithful wife, Sabine was certainly an agent in the events that led to his transfer to Sonnenstein. In this the wife had the full support of the legal and psychiatric systems. Schreber was caught between his love and his rage at her for what was done to him and it took him many years before he forgave her.

Toward the end of Schreber's stay at Flechsig's a conflict erupted between the spouses over money; its reasons and circumstances remain unknown, but a few significant facts are documented in Schreber's file at the Ministry of Justice. The following account will give us a glimpse into the nature of the dramatic and fateful events that took place at Flechsig's in mid-June 1894, just weeks prior to Schreber's removal to Sonnenstein. On a certain date once a month, Sabine Schreber would visit her husband at Flechsig's to get his signature on a voucher to be presented to the Court of Appeals in order to collect his monthly pay.[8] Now, for reasons unknown, Schreber refused to sign, amidst unpleasant bickering. In view of these scenes, one day Sabine signed the receipt herself and presented it for payment. It didn't work: the bureaucrats insisted on having Schreber's signature. Flechsig was notified of the patient's agitated moods at these times and advised Sabine not to upset Paul any further and to leave him alone. The psychiatric and legal implication of Paul's refusal to sign meant that he was failing in a crucial social responsibility defined by the laws of the land: to manage his affairs and to take care of his wife's financial needs. According to the laws of the Empire, a spouse who was irresponsible or a spendthrift could be reported to the police and the public prose-cutor, whereupon a court appointed physician, not even a psychiatrist, could have the person diagnosed as psychotic, declared incompetent, and committed to an asylum, with forfeiture of his rights to control his assets. It goes without saying that such a procedure could be instituted in the case of persons already hospitalized. This law placed Schreber in serious jeopardy. The suggestion of the temporary incompetency dec-laration and the appointment of a guardian was made by the president of the *Oberlandesgericht*, Carl Edmund Werner, even though he also recommended exceptional temporary arrangements, bypassing Schre-ber's signature, for Sabine to collect the monies.[9] Sabine followed the advice and, as required by law, made the application setting in motion a process that resulted in both these legal consequences for her hus-band.

Did Sabine understand the consequences of her action? Flechsig's stand in the matter remains unknown. But neither was he an innocent bystander. Flechsig's favoring Sabine and possibly protecting Sabine from her husband's fury is suggested by the fact, brought out by Baumeyer, that Sabine was treated by Flechsig for crying and laughing spells:[10] "Flechsig, who treated me, forbade me, in keeping with my father's wishes, to spend so much time together with the patient." Was this a breach of loyalty toward Schreber? The idea of a "therapeutic contract" is a modern notion, but even in those times it was implicit in the doctor-patient relationship that the doctor not act against the interests of the person he was treating. To be sure, when it comes to brokering between the needs of the patient and the needs of the family, inpatient psychiatry is fraught with ethical dilemmas even today. But understanding the difficulties of the situation should not blind us to the impact they can have on the patient. Freud suggested in a letter to Jung (McGuire, 1974, p. 358) that Schreber was jealous of Flechsig's rela-tions with Sabine, a jealousy which Freud quickly interpreted along oedipal lines. Yet, even granting such a putative oedipal element, could not the adult circumstances have been a double cause of Schreber's fury at Flechsig?

Following Schreber's transfer to Sonnenstein and Weber's first report, Schreber's superior, Werner, reported on November 26, 1894, to the Ministry of Justice that he had instituted a temporary judgment of incompetency through the court of first instance, the County Court. He also stated that "according to a reliable source, Frau Dr. Schreber expressed the wish that Clemens Schmidt, *Oberjustizrath* and director of the Leipzig County Court, be appointed as her husband's guardian, and that the supervision of the guardianship be transferred to the Leipzig County Court" (Devreese, 1981a, p. 68). Werner gave the appropriate orders and the request was duly executed. Upon the declaration of incompetency, Sabine and the legally appointed guardian assumed control of all of Schreber's assets. On the 29th of November, 1894, Mr. Schmidt officially began his duties as Schreber's guardian. On December 6 he wrote to the Ministry that he had no objections to Schreber's being temporarily retired from office and replaced. On the 11th of December the Ministry ruled that out of the 10,500 marks of Schreber's annual salary, 6,930 be paid annually as pension. A year later, based on Weber's second report, Schreber was permanently retired.

In an undated entry in the Sonnenstein chart for the month of November 1894 we read: "Complains that Flechsig disturbs him, believes he is able to hear him calling and saying '*Himmeldonnerwetter*'. During the wife's visit he forced her to say the Paternoster with him. Then he sent her away without saying another word to her" (Appendix). It is noteworthy that this is the only entry in the hospital chart in which Schreber is quoted as mentioning Flechsig. Its juxtaposition in the chart with the scene with Sabine may be coincidental, but if we assume that the complaints against Flechsig occurred at approximately the same time as the scene with Sabine, the possibility is raised that the two events were connected. That is to say, the suggestion is that Schreber's coldness toward Sabine—first she must say a prayer with him, then she is treated with silence and sent away—may be informed by his suspicions that she and Flechsig have conspired against him.

Was Sabine down to the last pfennig? Was Paul's refusal to give Sabine his paycheck a result of his illness, revenge for old grievances, or a symbolic expression of a fear of loss of power and sexual potency? Why was it so necessary for Sabine to act with such haste? Prior to these events Sabine was in continuous consultations with her father. At that time Heinrich Behr was a wealthy man, retired in Leipzig (Peters, 1990). We recall that fateful trip Sabine made to Berlin on the 15th of

February, 1894, which marked a serious downturn in Paul's mental state, which Freud interpreted as a breakthrough of unassuaged homosexual libido. However, Schreber would have had other worries on his mind, such as the counsel Sabine was getting in Berlin from her father. Were money matters discussed? What prognosis was given to Sabine and her father by Flechsig, who was aware that the current illness was much more serious than the one nine years earlier? Schreber may have had reasons to feel fear, jealousy, and anger toward his father-in-law. Could he openly express them? I believe that until his death in 1897 Sabine's father stood between her and her husband, at which time Schreber's mental health picked up significantly.

In the negotiations with her husband over money, Sabine had three powerful men behind her: her father, the judge, and the psychiatrist (with Weber later substituting for Flechsig). There was no small amount of truth in Schreber's statement that there was a conspiracy to unman him for he was effectively unmanned insofar as the woman had overpowered him with the assistance of the legal and psychiatric establishments. Yet, granting this, we must ask again why did he not choose a more effective course of action and why, in terms of his later text, he did not phrase himself more directly the points at issue?

SCHREBER AND FLECHSIG

To turn back to Schreber's character is to return once more to his home and upbringing. How to assess the home Schreber grew up in? Certainly it prepared him for great achievement; certainly, too, it equipped him with unusual powers of mind. Then again, it apparently left him characterologically incapable of dealing more effectively with the forces that became arrayed against him as his illness worsened.

Schreber's response to his situation was essentially masochistic. He could have dealt more effectively and more aggressively with the multiple threats of transfer and incompetency. He could have eschewed the role of crucified messiah; he could have played along with the requirements of the system and sought to conceal his delusions (as so many true paranoids have learned to do), enough to get out and to spread his gospel by other means. Instead, he chose the way of masochistic triumph through surrender, of victory through defeat. And here we have to wonder if his style of seeking masochistic victory had been prepared for him at home, either in his relationship to his father and mother or through an identification with them. The gloss that Moritz Schreber may have been something of a domestic tyrant as Freud suspected, but one who cloaked his tyranny in high-minded sentiments, need not be tied to more specific, and historically unlikely, theories about his use of his posture-improving devices as a means of terrorizing his children. A son may be masochistically attached to an ill and "bellowing" parent on other grounds. If, in fact, Schreber did have a masochistic relationship with a powerful parent, and a need to repeat that relationship in a transference situation, he certainly met his match in the persons of Flechsig and Weber as representatives of a paternalistic psychiatric system whose repressiveness was cloaked in hypocritical benevolence.

The transference situation was also partially determined, at least initially, by the reality of what kind of psychiatrist Flechsig was: primarily a neuroanatomist, he was philosophically an organicist psychiatrist functioning as administrator in a university hospital with neither interest in nor feeling for psychodynamics or psychotherapy.

To be sure, Schreber's second bout of depression, in 1893, was a much more severe disorder than the first one, in 1884, and it required much longer than the six statutory months allotted to him at Flechsig's. Flechsig promised Schreber a cure of his sleeplessness, the major symptom of the depression, by means of his pharmacological regimen, a kind of chemical shock treatment. Compared with today's antidepressants, Flechsig's regimen was ineffectual, and this was disappointment enough. Furthermore, the reduction of Schreber's difficulty to a matter of drugs and brain response was, Schreber felt, a white lie: he needed psychological help as well, which Flechsig could not provide. Schreber perceived that Flechsig was now a different person: the professor, on the threshold of his nomination as rector of Leipzig University, was interested mostly in administrative politics, dubbed by Schreber "the politics of souls" (pp. 183, 265) and less with the patient: "one Schreber soul more or less did not matter . . . during my stay at Flechsig's Asylum I heard more than once the expression 'Merely a Schreber soul'. . ." (p. 27, Foot Note #18).

There was a basic misunderstanding here: Schreber viewed Flechsig as his own private doctor, to whom he had earlier paid an honorarium for services rendered and who, by virtue of the therapeutic contract, was expected to remain his loyal agent. Flechsig, however, came to regard Schreber as just another inmate in the asylum, to whom he owed no particular loyalty. The only Schreber who enjoyed such loyalty was Sabine, who was treated by Flechsig as an outpatient, which perhaps caused Paul to feel jealousy and outrage.

Of course, these voices and visions Schreber started to talk to Flechsig about in the beginning of March 1894 did not help either. The professor of psychiatry, who had rebelled against his father's spirituality, developed the identity of a neuroanatomist and held that hallucinations and delusions were a disease in brain cells and brain centers and was not able to understand a man's "intimation about God's relation to human freedom of will" (Foot Note #103), which Schreber claimed God revealed to him. By now it was clear both to himself and to Flechsig that he was in for a long haul. His first depressive episode lasted for a year and a half, an expected length of time. Since his first depression was less severe, he was able to use the six months of treatment allotted to him at Flechsig's and upon discharge to complete the cure at the Ilmenau spa and fully resume his judicial duties in Leipzig on the first day of 1886. In June 1893 it was up to Flechsig to decide whether to make an exception in Schreber's case and keep him for further treatment—and he decided against it. Schreber was too much trouble: he was demanding, agitated, and a headache for the attendants, whose goodwill Flechsig needed more than Schreber's recovery; he made trouble for his wife with the money; and he was crazy as never before. The cards were hopelessly stacked against Schreber. He simply had to go. By omission and commission Flechsig dispatched his patient to hell. This was soul murder, Schreber's way of encoding his reaction to Flechsig's total and specific impact on him and to the long-term effects of the transfer to Sonnenstein.

Schreber was acutely sensitive to Flechsig's overt and subliminal communications. In light of the dyadic dynamics, the two persons in the dyad reciprocally perceive, act and emote toward each other, based on transference and countertransference, with the healthy and psychotic parts of the personality. When expressed in a style that is unconventional, such communications are called symptoms, from neurotic to psychotic. In this adaptation to the environment both dream and dyadic (relational) dynamics play their complementary roles. Schreber called this nerve-language and explained it as hypnotic suggestion. In the 1903 preface to the *Memoirs* he has "a new idea . . . [of] the *first impetus* to what my doctors always considered mere 'hallucinations'. . . . [it] consisted of influences on my nervous system emanating from your nervous system. . . . I think it is possible that you . . . carried out some hypnotic, suggestive contact with my nerves . . ." (*M*, p. IX; emphasis Schreber's). Flechsig reacted to Schreber's theological dreams with a violent rejection. Schreber reacted to Flechsig's rejection by accusing him of soul murder and having caused all his troubles. Both were engaged in emotions of like and dislike, of love and hate, in acts of perception and hallucination, or transference— in Schreber's language, as real human beings and as souls. In the paranoid dream of the other, as Freud outlined in his famous syllogisms of paranoia (I love him—I hate him—he hates me), no such interaction was implied.

SCHREBER AND WEBER

The ultimate act of "soul murder," as Schreber saw his transfer to Sonnenstein, after a detour through Lindenhof, hit him very hard. The disease peaked. His mood could have been best expressed by the inscription on Dante's hell's gate: Leave all hope, ye who enter. The icons of hell were very much on Schreber's mind. Although he called Flechsig "prince of hell," he was himself prince of hell. Schreber had thought Flechsig's was hell and Pierson's was hell's kitchen. Sonnenstein became the devil's own castle.

The move to Sonnenstein was momentous in two respects. For one, Schreber's fate was sealed by the institution of the incompetency status in November 1894, which legally barred Schreber's way out of the asylum: this verdict could only be undone by a countersuit and trial. For another, the stigma of psychosis now became permanently attached to Schreber by virtue of Weber's psychiatric reports and diagnosis. Flechsig's diagnosis was sleeplessness, which was not emended even after the appearance of the hallucinations and delusions; maybe he was trying to protect Schreber from the effect of a diagnosis of psychosis on the officials at the Ministry, a gentle touch lost on the patient. Weber's initial diagnosis, hallucinatory insanity, even though still hopeful, was enough for the Ministry of Justice to have Schreber declared incompetent. A year later came the final damning diagnosis of chronic paranoia and a dire prognosis: the illness was chronic and the patient was not expected to be able to resume his judicial duties. The net result of the forensic and the psychiatric verdicts was an indefinite sentence at Sonnenstein and an end to Schreber's career as a judge. This was in keeping with official policy: a doctor who recovered from insanity could get his job back, a lawyer or a judge could not.

Did Schreber realize what was in store for him in the last days at Flechsig's? He said he did not know why he was being moved, since nobody told him. Was he so unaware? Was he lying to himself? Is he lying to us? I believe Schreber realized full well the importance of these consequences. The attempt to escape from Sonnenstein early on only brought home more acutely the shock of defeat. The stupor he was in at that time could be read as a prison psychosis[11] involving a denial of the gravity of the situation and emotional shock leading to a state of numbness followed by excitement and a paranoid elaboration.

Schreber's bellowing miracles were frequently enacted at Sonnenstein. Whatever the ironies of his text, in his account Schreber consistently plays the role of metaphysical innocent vis-à-vis these and other expressions of his fury. Accordingly, he gives us no clue to what extent he was enraged at himself and to what extent he was reacting to what he saw as the betrayal by others. He also gives us no clue what dynamic relation his bellowing may have had to do with gender transformation fantasies. Yet, whatever their admixture of self-hate, despondency, and rage, the bellowing miracles constituted their own complication, for they continued even after other signs of Schreber's agitated, suicidal depression as well as of his psychotic dream-delirium had cleared. When he wanted to leave the hospital, neither his wife nor his mother nor his sisters were willing to sign the papers for his release so that he could be treated at home, as was done in many similar situations. His mother and his wife were reluctant to receive him until as late as 1902. Their continued reluctance would have made a fresh contribution to Schreber's fury, but is it fair to hold this against the family? Schreber's rage combined with his preoccupations about being turned into a woman to make him appear both repulsive and dangerous to the women and to the husbands of the women. First Schreber had to cool down, to show his wife and others that they had nothing to fear.

The process of cooling down was accomplished by turning to grandiose, compensatory fantasies of being a redeemer. The notion that he had been unmanned, at first declared to be an abandonment and against the order of the world, was now converted into the grand idea of his being unmanned for the purpose of redeeming mankind. Human conflicts and concerns over money and power appeared petty in comparison with the grandeur of God's cosmic purpose for him. Weber argued this was pathological in the highest degree. Freud was clear-sighted to realize that the redeemer dream was a sign of the process of recovery, of reestablishing the contact with the world lost earlier in the end-of-the-world fantasy. For Schreber, the redeemer dream was indeed powerful consolation: *in hoc signo vinces* [in this sign thou shalt win].

In keeping with his grandiose sense of mission, Schreber naturally contested Weber's dismissal of his ideas as symptoms of an organic disorder. Specifically, Schreber argued that "His nervous illness [*Nervenleiden*] was not a disorder of his mental functions" but was a *Nervendepression,* or "a deep affective depression [*gemüthliche Depression*]" (Appendix); if so, he was a patient like many others treated in spas and hospitals voluntarily, not involuntarily as a psychotic. But the forensic viewpoint stamped everything Weber said. How could Weber fathom that Schreber's talk about God, Ariman, Ormuzd, divine rays, a transformation into a woman was rich in metaphorical and symbolic meaning? For Weber, these were persisting pathological and incurable ideas caused by a diseased brain. At least Flechsig was an honest brain anatomist, but Weber invoked the brain as a ritual formula, as an article of faith, as brain mythology. It was Weber who put on Schreber the diagnosis of paranoia and reversed the priorities, representing the depressed mood as the additive to paranoia. In Weber's generation paranoia was deemed the quintessence of craziness (*Verrücktheit*), of the seemingly unbridgeable gulf between insanity and the rest of the human condition. The varieties of paranoia proliferated in this climate of opinion like the demonological entities in Sprenger's and Krämer's (1487?) *Malleus maleficarum* (*The Witches' Hammer*), rumbling with the sonority of Latin polysyllables: paranoia completa, hallucinatoria, dissociativa, religiosa, hallucinatoria, hyponchondriaca, originaria, querulans (Hinsie and Shatzky, 1940). What was left out was "paranoia scientifica" of those ready to see "paranoia" lurking everywhere and to apply this label indiscriminately. Armed with these labels, psychiatrists of the day came to resemble Holy Inquisitors hounding heretics, as for example, a totally obscure Dr. Brosius (1894) in a booklet for the lay public entitled *Pitfalls in Recognizing Insanity*.

Schreber was never a garden variety paranoiac. His hallucinatory and delusional daydreams were mostly about supernatural influences and inspirations, not persecution by hidden enemies operating in secret compact with one another. For, unlike the classical paranoiac described in the textbooks of psychiatry or encountered in clinical practice, he did not begin one day to become increasingly suspicious of people in his family, social milieu or at work, a suspicion that then evolved into a paranoid system concerning an ever-expanding paranoid pseudo-community (Cameron, 1959), which then moved him to engage in antisocial or violent acts toward his imaginary enemies and in frivolous legal suits. His paranoia-as-persecution was mainly (with the exception of a certain v. W) limited to one enemy, Professor Flechsig, the cause, as Schreber saw it, of all the trouble, who, like Satan, managed to prevail on God to persecute him. This Schreber later emended to say that it was God Himself who instigated the persecution. The influences brought to bear on him were all sent by God's nerves, or rays; they were emanations from an indifferent or vengeful God who punished him and abandoned him, as He did Job and Jesus before him.

Not only was Schreber's paranoia circumscribed but it had a rather precise date of onset: it began around March (or April) of 1894, that is, in the fourth or fifth month of his stay at Flechsig's. By this time it was becoming increasingly clear to Schreber that he was not well enough to go home, that the conflict with his wife was not getting resolved, that Flechsig was growing increasingly distant, and that, based on his previous experience, his days at Flechsig's were numbered. Thus, his anxiety was mounting, and the hallucinations of supernatural contacts and soul murder were the result. Schreber's reaction was thus a profound disappointment in Flechsig. It was based on a kernel of truth: the maneuverings taking place behind his back, the abandonment by Flechsig, and the expulsion from his hospital—all events rich in traumatic consequences.

The balance of Schreber's paranoid ideas consisted of fantastic ideas of influence, most of which involved various bodily sensations. Yet, even these differed from what Tausk was later to call the "influencing machine" in that the bodily sensations were not held to be the work of specific enemies capable of exerting their malevolent influence from a distance. Instead, Schreber's antagonist was God himself, a God who alternately exalted and persecuted him. The grandiose elements, brought into sharp focus by Schreber's redeemer fantasy, had an almost manic quality; moreover, rather than serve as explanation for the persecution, which would be the usual paranoid formation, the ideas of a special destiny are seen as the result of the suffering. Because I have suffered, I am equipped to redeem—this is not the usual paranoid delusional structure and it is indicative of a most atypical psychosis. Then, too, we must take into account the variable degree of intellectual distance that Schreber brought to bear on his experiences. Here it must again be noted that at least some of his ideas had self-reflective merit, given that his discourse was limited to the ideas of his age and that he did not have access to a true dynamic psychology of unconsious emotional processes. But beyond that, it must also be noted that Schreber did not seek to discover meaning in every bodily symptom, nor did he seek to glorify all of the images entering his consciousness. While maintaining that many of his visions were genuine experiences, Schreber himself treated the bulk of the divine influences as disturbances, as "fantastic nonsense" (p. 227) and unbidden experiences. One of the classical traits of a true paranoic is that he seeks to fit everything into his system, to give each individual experience its meaning by fitting it into the overall persecutory system. By contrast, Schreber did not truly develop a system that is all-inclusive; his recognition that some of what he experiences is simply "fantastic nonsense" suggests rather a toxic delirium, one in which some experiences are taken seriously while other are dismissed. In this connection, let me mention the opinions of my colleagues Dr. Uwe Peters and Mortimer Ostow (personal communications), who agreed with me that some aspects of Schreber's more florid symptomatology may reflect a toxic psychosis brought on by the very medications that were being used to treat him (see chapter 2). What then to make of it all? We have a psychosis with an unusual course, with a strange admixture of features each of which suggests a different diagnostic handle yet all of which are ultimately combined by the patient in the formation of a changed world-view. However, against the received view begun by Weber that Schreber suffered from paranoia, later emended to paranoid schizophrenia, one must insist that his was no ordinary psychosis. Peters makes the point that taken in its totality the clinical picture in Schreber's case resembles that of no other patient he has even seen.

Let us be clear, too, that not only was Schreber ill, but that he continued to be relatively unstable, even after his more dramatic symptoms had begun to clear. After six years at Sonnenstein, in 1900, when Schreber challenged the legality of his temporary incompetency ruling imposed in November 1894, he was still insufficiently self-possessed to make an effective showing in the lower court, with the result that the lower court converted the temporary incompetency into a permanent one. His fate seemed to be sealed. Up to the declaration of the final victory, which curiously fell on Bastille Day of 1902, that is, for almost two more years, Schreber remained prey to visions, voices, and violent vociferations. Yet, quite apart from the issue of whether there was anything in his current condition that warranted continued internment, the nature of his condition resists easy delineation. The debate with Weber continued during this time, with Schreber maintaining that his voices were caused by rays, while Weber insisted that they were signs of an endogenous brain disorder. But Weber did not himself become included in Schreber's system as yet another soul murderer; so far as possible in a relationship where one man identified the other as mad, the two men managed to continue to agree to disagree. Nor did Schreber deteriorate further; to the contrary, he continued to improve—and to protest against both his diagnosis and his continued confinement.

From the little we know about Flechsig's behavior as a psychiatric expert, it appears that he found a way to take these psychiatric diagnoses lightly, as in the Paasch and Feldmann cases. Weber, on the other hand, took the matter of Schreber's diagnosis very seriously, too seriously for Schreber's good. A diagnosis in medicine describes the condition and prescribes its treatment; a diagnosis in psychiatry can do that, too, if properly handled. If improperly handled, it not only describes the patient, it proscribes him. Yet, the irony was that Weber's handling of the situation became the avenue for Schreber's ultimate recompensation. It was not fair to say that Weber's treatment proved effective; indeed, one may well suppose that Schreber might have recompensated more rapidly had he been placed at a different asylum. Nonetheless, it is true that Schreber ultimately found a way of becoming active, of regaining a small part of his professional identity and most of his wits, in contending against Weber in the courts. In the forensic psychiatrist Weber, the former *Senatspräsident* found an adversary whom he could deal with.

PSYCHIATRIC POLITICS AND THE MIND-BRAIN DIALECTIC

Exactly one hundred years before Schreber died, in 1811, two events marked the founding of institutional and academic psychiatry in Saxony. Sonnenstein, in Pirna near Dresden, was set up to receive acute psychiatric cases, in the wake of the decree about the separation of the two classes of social deviants, the criminal and the insane. At Leipzig University, the soul psychiatrist and Kantian Heinroth, a friend of Moritz Schreber, became the first professor of mental therapeutics. Heinroth shared Moritz Schreber's love for the life of moderation and harmony of physical and mental powers, the basis of orthobiotics and derived from Kant's ethics of self-control and autonomy. As a member of the psychological school of psychiatry called the *Psychiker,* Heinroth saw mental illness as caused by a breach in personal ethics, in turn caused by vice or sin. The terminology was moralistic and religious, but it nonetheless pointed to the ubiquity of moral conflicts. Replace the words *vice* and *sin* with the psychological word *guilt,* and you have traveled from religion to dynamic psychiatry. Heinroth was trained as a physician; yet he saw no contradiction between the spirit of medicine and the moral conception of psychiatry. His death in 1843 was the end of an era. The chair of psychiatry at Leipzig remained empty until Flechsig was appointed in 1877. By that time the history of medicine and of psychiatry had been irrevocably changed by a number of developments around the middle of the 19th century: the manifesto of the Helmholtz school renouncing vitalistic explanations of biological phenomena; the progress of neuroanatomy, neuropathology and neurophysiology; and Virchow's epochal cellular conception of physical illness. The trend toward materialistic explanations was epitomized in Griesinger's aphorism: mental illness is brain illness. But while these developments were essential for the advance of medicine, they did not advance psychiatry in the same way. Indeed, in some respects they temporarily damaged psychiatry in that they worked to obscure for physicians both the psychological roots of mental disorders and the ethical dilemmas involved in forcible hospitalization and treatment. The psyche that Heinroth and other members of his tradition dealt with was at once a moral being and a psychological one; treatment was likewise conceived of as being both a moral and a psychological intervention. The ethical dilemmas were thus met head on, even if they were then decided on grounds of community values that were quite different from those that prevail in contemporary society. But with the rise of brain mythology, both the ethical dilemmas involved in forcible treatment and the importance of the interior psychological drama going on in the patient tended to be eclipsed. In terms of its explanatory models, psychiatry was assimilating itself to medicine generally; many psychiatrists assumed, mistakenly, that their discipline could also take its cue from medicine with regard to the moral issues involved in treatment.

One should not perhaps draw too sharp a contrast between the ethics of medicine and that of psychiatry; the difference between them is more one of degree. Most medical interventions are voluntary; the patient participates, to whatever degree his understanding makes this possible, in making decisions about what is to be done. Given the consent of the patient, the discussion that then occurs is essentially technical. Where medicine runs up against real ethical dilemmas is in the exceptional instances, for example, when the patient is no longer conscious and thus is unable to consent to ever-more exceptional measures to prolong life, and in epidemics, when individual rights become secondary to the rights of the community to protect itself from a real and current menace. But if these two kinds of instances are, on the whole, relatively rare in medicine, they are relatively common in the practice of inpatient psychiatry. Often enough, patients are not competent to decide their need for treatment or even of their need to be protected from doing harm to themselves or others. Often, too, the community, and especially the family, may feel a need to be temporarily protected from its ill member. In neither case is the conversation primarily a technical one.

The same is true for the relative importance of the psychological factor in the two disciplines. In medicine, this factor is acknowledged, but it is not usually made the physician's first priority, whereas in psychiatry psychological factors necessarily come to the fore. Insofar as psychiatry begins to understand itself as a technical specialty and to take as its ethical and psychological benchmarks the usual practice of medicine, to that extent it runs the risk of losing its bearings on both counts. The result will inevitably be the rise of antipsychiatry movements, such as occurred in Germany at the end of the last century and as has occurred in the past two decades in the United States. When positions become extreme, moreover, the resulting confrontation can be a truly heroic clash, such as that between Schreber and Weber. Schreber's personal and ethical position on mental illness should be left to philosophers; whereas Weber, as a representative of institutional psychiatry in parading as the new brain science, took the position that mental illness belonged to psychiatrists, working in conjunction with prosecutors and policemen, as a matter of public interest. Between them they represented poles of opinion that continue to exist today. As Szasz (1970) has commented, "Medicine is a natural science. Psychiatry is not; it is a moral science" (p. 234). Schreber would have agreed. The banished ghost of ethics has been haunting psychiatry ever since.

Ultimately, however, the dilemmas are not caused by the physicians, though they may be compounded by them. Institutional psychiatry, charged with the care of patients whose inpatient status has often been forced upon them by the legal system, is forever trying to wear the more human mask of compassion rather than correction. Yet, no amount of therapeutic sincerity will change the fact that much of what goes under the label of emotional illness contains a stubborn residue of rejection of social norms, rage, rebellion, and violence. The antinomian aspect of mental illness was a problem no less for the soul psychiatrists than it was for the brain psychiatrists. Paradoxically, the soul psychiatrists attuned to moral conflict as an aspect of emotional illness, were the ones who rejected the no-restraint idea of Conolly, since they believed that the rebellious moral reprobate had to be brought back to obedience by harsh discipline. The brain psychiatrists, by contrast, could see in the no-restraint policies a rational accompaniment of their more "scientific" style of treatment. To be sure, Weber, who adopted the no-restraint policy, did not necessarily become a less coercive psychiatrist. Flechsig, on the other hand, who abhorred the coercive treatments of psychiatry, understood well that medicine enjoyed a luxury in being able to confine itself to voluntary patients. Ultimately, the problems of involuntary inpatients that institutional psychiatry must deal with are such that it must either use some forms of coercion or eschew that role and, like the church of yore, deliver the social deviant to the equivalent of the secular arm.

Progress in biological treatment modalities cannot eliminate the ethical dilemmas that inpatient psychiatry must daily confront. Nor do biological treatments obviate the need for psychotherapeutic ones. In today's world, Schreber would have been better diagnosed and no doubt helped by the state-of-the-art antidepressant and antipsychotic medications, perhaps also by electroconvulsive therapy; as a member of the upper class who could afford private hospitalization, he would also have had the benefit of psychotherapy, hospital milieu therapy, and family therapy to help him understand his conflicts and master them. No psychotherapy was available at Flechsig's or Weber's institutions, the showcases of academic and institutional psychiatry at that time, because these psychiatrists had no concept of it. They read neither Freud nor Jung nor Bleuler to know otherwise.

Schreber rightly warned psychiatry not to "tumble with both feet into the camp of naked materialism" (p. 80). Even though he was wrong in his premises (arguing about his hallucinations from the viewpoint of revelation and his personal religion), he, being a highly intelligent and intuitive man, was right in his conclusion: materialism is good for science, but it can be bad for psychiatry, for raw materialism leads to reductionism: of thoughts to things, of mind to machine, of morals to mechanisms. Schreber was right to jeer at Flechsig, who *"did not really understand the living human being and had no need to understand him, because . . . [he] dealt only with corpses"* (*M,* p. 55; emphasis Schreber's).

Today, a century after the events of Schreber's second hospitalization, we are witnessing many problems that faced psychiatry then: the mind and body issue; the spurious dichotomy between the biological and the psychological; how to treat the chronically mentally ill and where to put them; how to protect both the civil liberties of the individual and the stability of society; and the limits of psychotherapy and verbal persuasion in aiding the mentally ill. It is hoped that pondering the story of *Senatspräsident* Daniel Paul Schreber and the profound moral issues with which he grappled will enrich our experience and encourage our reflection on these recurrent problems of the human condition in the modern world.

NOTES

1. The other times the word *love* is mentioned in the *Memoirs* include the following references: Wagner's *Tannhäuser* ("Alas your love overwhelms me", Foot Note #10); Mozart's *Magic Flute* ("it has vanished . . . love's delight"; p. 263); and the title to an obscure painting by Pradilla, *The Round of Love;* p. 255).

2. Did Schreber, in the privacy of his soul, truly believe his delusions or did he know he was making them up, that is, engaging in mythomania? This was indeed suggested by Ellenberger (1970, p. 532).

3. Peters (1990), also impressed that Schreber looks like no schizophrenic he has ever seen, proposed the diagnosis of anxiety or stress psychosis, or *Emotionspsychose,* a diagnosis he also applied to an autobiographical account of a psychosis (Peters, 1989).

4. The concept of total institution was fashioned by Irving Goffman. Szasz spoke of "psychiatric slavery," Foucault of confinement as punishment, and Dörner (1969) of the "the segregation of unreason" resulting in a coercive community, a *"Zwangsgemeinschaft,"* which he and I liken to a concentration camp. In a letter to me of March 26, 1991 Prof. Dörner not only confirmed this comparison between state hospitals and concentration camps, but also noted that initially the Nazi concentration camps were designed to be educational camps (*Umerziehungslager*) and only later acquired their deadly character. At a

time when Auschwitz was being rebuilt as a death camp, according to Dörner, the early trials of gassing were conducted on Russian prisoners of war at Sonnenstein.

5. She is referred to on line 44 of Schreber's 1905 poem: "A child is permitted to accompany us into our new house," the house Schreber built after his release from Sonnenstein. This suburban townhouse, with its garden and trees, at the corner of Angelikastrasse 15a, can still be admired today.

6. "*Siegen oder Unterliegen*" is the Hegelian Max Stirner's (1806–1856) fundamental dichotomy among people at war with each other, described in his most famous work, in praise of selfishness and self-assertion, *Der Einzige und sein Eigentum* (translated as *The Ego and Its Own*, London: Rebel Press, 1982). Schreber would have known of him via E. von Hartmann, who rescued Stirner (alias Johann Kaspar Schmidt) from oblivion.

7. Prado de Oliveira (personal communication, 1990) called my attention to this point.

8. In Devreese (1981, pp. 56, 58, 66, 68, 70, 72, 74). These events are described in a letter to the Ministry of Justice of June, 15, 1894, signed by the president of the Court of Appeals, Carl Edmund Werner, for whom Schreber worked as the director of the Third *Civilsenat*.

9. Is it possible that the abbreviation "v. W.," the other person accused of committing soul murder on Schreber, was Werner? We may never know.

10. Baumeyer (1955, p. 523) and mistranslated in the English version (Baumeyer, 1956, p. 68) where it reads: "his convulsive crying and laughing," meaning Paul, not Sabine.

11. Not dissimilar to what Freud (1894) had in mind in invoking the notion of "'*Überwältigungspsychose*' [a psychosis in which the ego is overwhelmed]" (p. 55). Riklin (1907) wrote at length about the problem, quoting an earlier contribution by Jung.

APPENDIX
THE ORIGINAL HOSPITAL CHART
OF PAUL SCHREBER IN THE
AUTHOR'S TRANSLATION

[The differences between the original hospital chart, Baumeyer's (1955) transcription of it, and the translation of Baumeyer's transcription (Baumeyer, 1956), as well as my own comments, are given in brackets. The dates have been written in modern notation and italicized, where necessary, for uniformity.]

[The following is the chart of Schreber's admission to Dösen in 1907. The first page of the chart shows items checked in a standard admission form and then notations by a number of psychiatrists.]

HISTORY OF ILLNESS (*KRANKHEITSGESCHICHTE*)

of   the Senatspräsident at the Royal Court of Appeals (*Oberlandesgericht*) in Dresden, retired, Dr. jur. Daniel Paul *Schreber*
from   Dresden
Birthdate and birthplace: July 25, 1842, Leipzig
Domicile: Dresden
Profession: Senatspräsident, retired.
Family status: single?
                married?
                widowed?
                divorced?
                children?
Religion: Evangelical–Lutheran
Guardian:

469

Disease form: Paranoia ?
Admitted on: November 27, 1907
Discharged on [Died]: April 14, 1911

[The chart of Schreber's admission to Dösen included the following past history (copied or summarized from the original Sonnenstein chart, now lost) of his second admission to Flechsig's, from November 21, 1893 to June 14, 1894; and his stay at Sonnenstein, from June 29, 1894 to December 20, 1902.]

Anamnesis: (according to the chart from Sonnenstein)
Heredity: The father (originator of the Schreber gardens in Leipzig) suffered from obsessional ideas of murderous impulses.

Mother with mood swings and nervous

1 sister hysterical

1 brother paretic, died by suicide

1 female cousin of the mother at the Leipzig [University] Hospital due to chronic paranoia (1894)

Earlier hypochondriacal ideas.

December 8, 1884—June 1, 1885 at the Leipzig Hospital for Nervous Diseases [his first admission to Flechsig's] due to hypochondriasis, he believed he had to die, imagined he was unable to walk, etc.

He was said to be talented and an excellent student. His character was described as good natured and easy to get along with. Later in life he showed great talent and advanced rather rapidly in his profession. Lately he was *Senatspräsident* at the Dresden *Oberlandesgericht*. His moral conduct was as far as is known totally irreproachable.

Spared physical illness, already at the time of his marriage in 1878 the patient expressed hypochondriacal ideas (therefore in the Leipzig Hospital from the 8th of December 1884 to 1st of June 1885).

[Appended at the end of the 1907 Dösen chart are entries excerpted from the record of the first and second admissions of Schreber to the Leipzig University Hospital (Flechsig's Asylum). They are inserted here for the sake of chronology.]

Excerpt from the Chart of the [Leipzig University] Hospital of December 8, 1884.

Anamnesis. Heredity tainted.

Since October 1884 actively involved in the election campaign. Later treated at Sonneberg [spa, not: "Sonnenstein Asylum," Baumeyer, 1956, p. 61]. In previous weeks took a lot of morphine, chloral and bromides. From Sonneberg admitted to the Hospital [*Klinik*]. Maintained he was incurable.

Speech disturbances.

Mood very labile.

Two suicidal attempts in the asylum.

Severe hypochondriasis.

Treated [*Kur*, missing in Baumeyer, 1955] with potassium iodide due to suspected syphilis. His wife had two miscarriages.

Present Condition.

General health good. Believes could die any moment, indeed, due to a heart attack.

December 10 [1884]. Agitated. 6.0 gram paraldehyde.

December 13. Frequent mood changes. Three times a day 1 gram potassium iodide.

December 22. Eats a lot.

December 29. Feels too weak to walk, asks to be carried.

January 30, 1885. Suicide attempt.

April 3. A ride with his wife.

April 6. Disturbed by the smallest noise. At times mood cheerful. Patient wants to be photographed six times, what for?

April 14. Suspicious that his wife would be sent away under some pretext and not come back. Sleeps with sodium bromide and paraldehyde.

April 17. Gloomy thoughts, the incurability of his illness. Heightened reflex irritability.

May 20. Mood tearful.

May 26. Wants to have photographs taken of himself, says it will be the last time.

June 1. Departure for Ilmenau. Imagined he had lost 30–40 lbs., has put on 2 kgs. Maintains his weight was deliberately falsified.

Second Admission to the [Leipzig] Hospital.

November 21, 1893. Very depressed. Believes that as his luck would have it they made him crazy, that he is suffering from softening of the brain. Inaccessible.

November 24. At night very agitated, screams for help, throws table and chair around. Attempts to hang himself in the isolation cell. Then tearful, promises to be obedient.

February 12. Visual hallucinations.

March 1. Believes he is a young girl, fears indecent assaults.

March 15. Promises attendant 500 marks for digging a grave.

April 16. Suicide attempts in the water of the bathtub.

April 21. Disconnected delusions. During every visit says he is ready to die, demands the glass of potassium cyanide earmarked for him.

May 5. Numerous auditory and olfactory hallucinations. Repeatedly asks for poison. The doctor should immediately go to the hospital and report that there is a patient stricken with plague. He asks whether he has been dead for a long time.

May 22. Clearer and more open in his communications.

May 24. Opium and morphine. Severe hallucinations continue.

June 2. Ignores the doctor completely, stares rigidly in front of him.

June 5. Visit of his wife. Later asks the attendant whether this was his wife in the flesh, believes she arose from the grave.

June 13. On his own initiative visits another patient and plays a board game with him.

June 14. Discharged (to Lindenhof).

[What follows is Flechsig's pre-discharge report at the time of transfer to Sonnenstein.]

On the 21st of November 1893 admitted to the Leipzig Hospital for the second time. At first more hypochondriacal complaints, he said he suffered from "softening of the brain, must soon die," etc., soon, however, mixed with persecutory ideas [*Verfolgungsideen*]: "luckily for him, he had been driven crazy." Also isolated hallucinations that frightened him. However, these were rather rare or else he dissimulated them, which is probable. Presumably at that time severe hyperesthesias [*Angeblich damals starke hyperaesthesien*], was easily dazzled [*war leicht geblendet*], irritated by the slightest noise and was quite unbearable due to his constant complaining about things. Later there was a massive increase in the visual and auditory hallucinations. He believed he was dead and rotting, that he was no longer in a "condition to be buried," that he was "stricken with the plague," presumably as a result of olfactory hallucinations, that his penis has been twisted off with a "nerve probe" and thus he held he was a woman, but he also explained often that he had to oppose energetically the "*Urning* [homosexual man] love of certain persons." All these matters tormented him a lot, so that he wished for his death; he attempted to drown himself in the bathtub and for weeks demanded daily the "glass of potassium cyanide earmarked for him." The auditory and visual hallucinations were often so severe that he became totally inaccessible and with eyes blinking spent hours in the chair or in bed. The hallucinations [*Sinnestäuschungen*] clearly had a very changeable content, but especially toward the end of his stay at the Leipzig Hospital the references were increasingly to being tortured to death in a gruesome manner. He then sank more and more in the [realm of] the mystical-religious: God often spoke to him, he was a play of vampires and devils. He wanted to convert to the Roman-Catholic Church in order to escape from snares and traps [um den Nachstellungen zu entgehen]. Later he saw miraculous apparitions, heard holy music, and in the end believed himself to dwell in the other world. At the very least, he held people around him to be ghosts and his surroundings a world of appearances. His eating was quite uneven: at first he ate with great appetite, later he refused food and had to be force fed. Sleep was often disturbed in spite of heavy doses of narcotics. He screamed quite frequently at night. For a long time he received opium up to 0.3 three times a day. He was then considered by Prof. Flechsig to be dangerous to himself and to others. (Report of Prof. Flechsig of 25th of June 1894.)

[Following are chart entries about his stay at Sonnenstein.]

From the Leipzig Hospital the patient was transferred to the private asylum of Dr. Pierson in Lindenhof near Coswig, and from there, after a 12 day stay, on the 29th of June of 1894 to the Sonnenstein Asylum. His physical condition was at that time, in June of 1894, very good and his complexion somewhat pale. It was striking that beads of sweat were continuously [beständig] seen on his forehead, as well as fibrillary twitching of the face muscles and marked tremor of his hands. He was markedly agitated, at first quite inaccessible, sullen, almost melancholy. He could not stand any conversation. He hallucinated severely, participated very little with other people, but stood motionless with a scared look in his eyes, in the same posture, gazing into the distance for a long while. In the garden it was noticed that he held his hands to his ears as if listening. There were hypochondriacal ideas. Otherwise the patient was proper, clean, and took care of his needs.

July 1894. Made an attempt to escape, he threw his coat away and ran to the gate. Stool sluggish, appetite poor. From time to time clearly molested by voices, but never said anything about them. Once a short fainting fit, which was probably caused by the patient withholding a strong urge to pass stool.

August. Says he wants to be by himself, that the attendant hinders "God's omnipotence." He wants "*God's peace.*" Does not do a thing, does not read a thing.

November. Altogether somewhat more lively, writes in shorthand and draws figures on paper, from time to time, among others, also occupied with puzzles. With the doctors curt and inaccessible. Complains that Flechsig disturbs him, believes he can hear him calling and saying "*Himmeldonnerwetter*."

During his wife's visit he forced her to say the Paternoster with him. Then he sent her away without saying another word to her.

January 1895. Resisting and inaccessible. At night intermittent sleeping medicines.

March 1895. Agitated, talks loudly [*spricht, wenn er allein ist laut*, not: *spuckt*, "spits," as transcribed (1955) and translated (1956), in Baumeyer] when by himself and laughs ostentatiously, at night excited. He plays a lot on the piano sent by his wife but bangs it a lot when in a bad mood and excited.

June 1895. The excitement mounted more and more. Creates quite a disturbance with his laughing day and night. Almost every evening sulfonal, often without any adequate effect. Completely under the influence of delusions. Claims his body is completely changed, the lung has all but disappeared, everything he sees around is only a semblance. The world has perished.

Repeatedly scolds the doctor loudly: "be off, be off," because the question "whether he considers him (the doctor) to be among the living" was answered by the doctor in the affirmative. He called him [the doctor] a "liar," [told him] "he should go back to his master." Periodically quiet again. Plays the piano a lot, even hard pieces rather well. Writes many letters, also in Italian, once signed "Paul the Prince of Hell." One letter was addressed to "Mr. Ormuzd in heaven."

September 1895. Very excited, nights mostly agitated. Often laughs loudly and piercingly and screamingly repeats the same words. From time to time stands totally still in one spot and stares at the sun and grimaces in the most bizarre way. Usually he stops himself when someone approaches him and speaks to him.

December 1895. Still excited. Nevertheless, he allows [himself] to be drawn into conversations on indifferent topics. Plays the piano, chess, reads again. Nothing can be found out about his delusional ideas. Often at night shouts and roars [*brüllend*] loudly near the window always the same curse-words or "I am the Senatspräsident Schreber."

February 1896. Laughs and roars loudly, bangs upon the piano.

April 1896. During doctors' rounds engages in some small talk, but it is an effort for him to control himself.

June 1896. Since sleep medicine in large doses proved ineffectual and the patient was very agitated, he was put in *isolation* during the night, which the patient vehemently protested at first, then *obeyed* [emphasis in the original].

July 1896. The attacks of laughing and bellowing are less frequent, but more severe and last longer.

The patient shows more interest in his surroundings, at times converses with another patient. He neglects his external appearance, dressed incompletely, shows the doctor his bared chest, "now he has almost a woman's breasts." The only actual change is a more pronounced fatty deposit, as the patient has gained a lot of weight. Is very much under the sway of sexual ideas, eagerly scans illustrated periodicals for nude pictures and makes drawings of those. In a letter to his wife written in Italian he says that the nights are very pleasant because he always experiences "*un poco di* [or die] *volupte* [or *volupta*] *feminae*" [in Italian or French, from Latin *voluptas*, both desire and gratification; the meaning is here ambiguous: a little bit of lust as felt *by* a woman, or lust *for* a woman, not: "'un pou die volupte feminae' habe" in Baumeyer 1955, p. 517, and "has 'un peu de volupté feminae'" in Baumeyer 1956, p. 64, left untranslated in both versions]. At night still in isolation.

September 1896. Not quieter. Thunders on the piano and bellows still, at times really obscene words. "The sun is a whore," or "the good Lord is a whore." At night in isolation.

November 1896. More talkative and approachable, reads more.

February 1897. Mood more cheerful, even though he still roars through the window with great vehemence.

June 1897. Lively correspondence with wife and relatives, written quite properly and without any trace of morbidity. Apparently speaks with full insight about his illness. Still shows the old "bellowing states," banging on the piano. With the doctors correct, polite, often self-confident and haughty. At night still in isolation.

October 1897. Reads a lot, plays a great deal and well both piano and chess. During longer conversations cannot always control himself, even during visits of his wife he often has to go to the window and roar out and laugh, and then, resume the conversation as if nothing happened. Continually isolated at night.

January 1898. The same proper and reasonable behavior with frequent intercurrent episodes of excitement; has no sensitivity for the disturbance he causes.

March 1898. Amiable upon approach, even though quite reserved and aloof, well oriented about current events, reads a lot and discusses legal issues. Excellent memory, writes many letters. Along with it still occasional screaming and bellowing and grimacing. Religious delusions. Adorns himself with multicolored ribbons, at times engages in really petty games.

July 1898. Same behavior. Often naked in his room in front of a mirror, laughing and screaming and adorned in colorful ribbons.

November 1898. Nights still in isolation. Writes to his wife, who is planning to move from Dresden and has been busy traveling, often in a more friendly, if more resolute, manner, that he has a right to being taken care of by her, or else he will not be able to let her dispose of the moneys that actually belong to him.

December 1898. Following many requests and representations the patient given back his former bedroom. At night controls himself bearably.

January 22, 1899. For the first time writes a detailed letter to his wife in which he describes his delusions. One is struck by the clarity and logical acuity with which he develops his system. The behavior of the patient unchanged. Writes a letter to his "Ministerial Director Geheimrat Jahn" and requests his opinion about legislative matters, as is customary among other prominent retired jurists. "His nervous illness" was not a disorder of his mental functions but was a deep affective depression.

April 1899. Condition not materially changed. Continues to be occupied with womanly crafts (pasting, sewing, adorning with colored ribbons). The attack-like screaming continues. Nights are somewhat better.

October 1899. Writes another letter to his wife about his delusions. He does not breathe a word about it to his doctors or his other relatives. In mid-September he inquired if he had been declared incompetent and wrote twice to his guardian Herr Schmid president of the lower court [*Amtsgerichtspräsident*] in Leipzig. He stressed in his letters that it was against the law to let a temporary declaration of incompetency stand for five years; the state prosecutor had the duty to either rescind the temporary incompetency status or to make application to the court for a definitive declaration of incompetency and the appointment of a guardian. On the 9th of October personal discussion with his guardian, at which time he tendered a paper he had written about his incompetency status, whose skillful and strongly logical form is brilliant in many ways. At the same time, he is not shy to display his delusions and shows complete lack of insight. It is particularly striking that he has no understanding of the reasons for having been placed in isolation all these years, whereas in fact he screamed and raged so loud that almost all the patients were disturbed in their sleep. Thereupon the procedure for declaring him incompetent was instituted.

November 1899. Predominantly preoccupied with thoughts about rescinding his guardianship. Outward behavior has changed little; at best, he has better self-control during conversation. When alone, has fits of bellowing, laughing and thundering on the piano.

[Not in Baumeyer, 1955:] The rest is missing from the Sonnenstein chart until entry of October 1, 1902.

In the period from February to September 1900 S. wrote his "Memoirs of a Nervous Patient" (published by Oswald Mutze, Leipzig, 1903).

The postscripts were written during the period October 1900 to June 1901 and the second series of postscripts at the end of 1902. See there for further details; the "Memoirs" are appended to the chart.

On March 13,1900, Herr Präsident Schreber was declared incompetent by the Dresden Amtsgericht. On July 14, 1902, this incompetency was rescinded by the *Oberlandesgericht* in Dresden.

[Notation on the margin] Continuation of the "Sonnenstein" chart.

On October 1, 1902 it is recorded in the "Sonnenstein" chart [these words missing in Baumeyer, 1955]: Has a fervent wish to leave the asylum. Visits his wife weekly in Dresden, goes on frequent trips. Also calmer during the day, only from time to time he can be heard "roaring" and playing the piano loudly.

November 10, 1902. Returned satisfied from an eight-day leave in Leipzig, took sleep medicine only twice at night.

December 20, 1902. Discharged from the asylum upon his request.

[Here end the excerpts from the Sonnenstein chart and the record of the admission to Leipzig-Dösen resumes.]

Admitted to Dösen on November 27, 1907. Information from the patient's sister.

In 1902, following the discharge the patient lived with his mother, his outward conduct was normal throughout. He was occupied with administration of buildings, went on frequent walks, was active in the chess association, also wanted to be employed by the Ministry but got no work. Frequently did private jobs that were always faultless.

During the first year he still often screamed at night, also during a journey away from home. Gradually this disappeared completely and he only screamed occasionally in his sleep. Also he slept without sleep medicines. After mother's death he busied himself with many calculations of the many bequests, was somewhat overworked and therefore [*daher*, missing in Baumeyer, 1955] slept poorly some nights.

The voices never completely disappeared. But he did not speak at all about the illness. When questioned, he said there was a spot at the back of his head where he experienced a constant buzzing noise, as if a thread were pulled. The voices were now only an unintelligible noise. He said nothing about his delusions, did not even mention them once to his wife.

The wife fell ill on November 14. A stroke. Was speechless for 4 days. He immediately had sleepless nights, was very exhausted, he felt he got sick again, heard "noises" again and with greater severity. He deteriorated rapidly. During the first illness he was also very sensitive to noises, was more melancholy. The recovery was a complete one.

November 27, 1907. Physical findings cannot be determined due to the complete inaccessibility of the patient and refusal to cooperate. The pallor of the face is striking, the drawn features. The eyes are kept closed. Only rarely does he open his eyelids following insistent questioning. From time to time a peculiar twitching is seen in the corners of the mouth and in the highly arched eyebrows. The forehead is wrinkled.

Temperature 36.5 *Weight* 84.5 *Head measurements* 19, 15, 12

Urine free of albumen and sugar.

Psychological findings. The pronounced inaccessibility of the patient is striking. The body posture and gait are stiff, the movements are rigid and angular. The patient is domineering and haughty toward the attendants. Oriented to time and place. Impossible to find anything out about what happened recently. The patient lies in bed, melancholy, with the above described facial expression. When asked how he is feeling in general he gives brief and appropriate answers, obviously unhappy about being importuned. Sleep is presumably good. Appetite only moderate. Takes only a few of the things brought along by the sister.

November 30, 1907. Pt. is out of bed★ for a few hours [★ marks an additional text, possibly accidentally missing from the copy of the chart given to me, but found in Baumeyer 1955, p. 519], sits stiffly in the same posture for one half to one hour then gets up suddenly and paces up and down the room, his movements angular. His eyes are almost completely closed. He goes for a while into the garden. On the whole unchanged, inaccessible, and refusing. Mostly refuses to take part in conversation. Frequently will refuse to answer altogether. Apparently he is hallucinating severely and very much adversely affected by his delusions.

December 1, 1907. Uses the toilet only at the strong urging of the attendant, but almost irritated with the attendant. He says he would like to be brought to a place, a cell or an extra room, where he would not be a burden on anyone. He believes something might happen that would be highly unpleasant for the people around him. Then he murmurs something about "The odor of corpses, rotting," from which one concludes that he is totally under the influence of his delusions.

December 5, 1907. Food intake very limited. He maintains he has no stomach any more, that he lost an intestine in a "miraculous way" [*auf wunderbare Weise*]. It will happen that "the body will begin to rot" while "the head will keep on living." These statements are made in a brusque and definitive manner. He refuses to answer further questions. "I cannot express any opinion about that now." "You will not be able to understand this."

December 8, 1907. During a walk in the garden he pulls toward the lake and can be led by the attendant the other way when force is used. In the evening he asks the doctor how deep the lake is. Repeatedly demanded to be given a single room. He would not be responsible if something happened. Evidently he means the "forthcoming rotting."

December 11, 1907. Writes a letter to Herr Obermedizinalrat [the director] in which he requests that his "instructions about his burial" be followed.

December 12, 1907. States he is not in Dösen but in an "Colony of the Monist Confederacy." Yawns a lot and visibly [*augenscheinlich*] at times breathes uncontrollably with his mouth open, which was not noticed before.

December 20, 1907. The condition on the whole little changed; inaccessible, uncommunicative. Says nothing about his obvious hallucinations, he refuses to give answers altogether. At times pulls toward the door, once he pushed the attendant aside with great force in order to gain access to the door leading to the garden, from where he had to be brought back with the use of force. At times at night incontinent of urine, smears feces due to unpleasant sensations in the anus. Creates great difficulties when it comes to the daily bath, irritated with the attendants. Defecation is difficult, refuses enemas, "that is not necessary." Appetite changeable: now poor, now good food intake.

January 6, 1908. Lately unclean with urine a lot. Refuses to go out, gets stubborn and sullen when asked to do so. Allows to be washed reluctantly. Once urinated into a cuspidor of another patient, irritated and angry when this was pointed out to him. Sleeps rather well. Appetite lately moderately good. Defecation difficult, it seems as if the patient holds it in deliberately. At night the patient attacked the night help and urgently demanded the key to the outdoors. Says nothing about his hallucinations. Close-lipped as before, totally inaccessible. During a conversation of the Obermedizinalrat with another patient (Lorenz) he was asked to offer an opinion about matters of guardianship and responded, more or less, that "he is no longer able to render opinion about this question."

January 25, 1908. Frequently incontinent. It seemed a few times that he soiled his bed deliberately, perhaps under the influence of hallucinations. Attacked an attendant, demanded the key urgently and loudly, wanted out. Goes on regular walks with 1-2 attendants. Has a tendency to want to get away.

February. Uncooperative, inaccessible. Always utters only single words. A few days ago he started intermittently to emit tones like "Ha-ha-ha" when spoken to. Stands on his feet a lot, rigidly, the eyes closed. Seldom occupies himself with something, sometimes plays chess with the chief attendant. Greets the doctor on morning rounds with: *Apage satanas* [recorded in Greek characters: Get thee hence, Satan!]. Then speaks unintelligible, unconnected words in French.

March. Says he is "disturbed by voices." Lately due to his disturbing calls of Ha-ha was kept in the single room 2I. Asks the doctor out of the blue: "When was the reign of Gustav Adolf? 1611-1632, isn't it?" (1611—1632 +). Tried to jump out of the window.

April. On the whole unchanged. The suddenly uttered "Ha-ha," especially in the presence of other persons, has become louder. Food intake really bad, says "it won't work" with the food. He has no stomach, cannot digest anything.

May. Believes has not slept for three months, is at times more accessible, is more outgoing; eats better again, stands about a lot in the garden, suddenly lies down on the lawn, the vest and shirt opened over the chest. Cannot be moved to go on walks. Says to the doctor one morning he wants to be in another building and another room. Is forced to eat.

June. No change. At times the uncontrollable screaming and moaning very disturbing. At night sleeps poorly.

July 22. Says to the doctor: "Why haven't the other satans come along, why you alone?" Cannot be moved to say more, just emits his Ha-ha.

Looks very pale and suffering. Spontaneous food intake very limited, has to be fed, which he at times opposes vehemently.

August. Eats almost nothing spontaneously. Strongly rejects all attempts to be fed. Emits a lot of "Ha-ha" in a tortured manner. This is often disturbing. Does not do anything. Never plays the piano that was moved into his room. During the day dons and doffs his clothing repeatedly. Lies down and then stands up and then sits rigidly for hours in the armchair clad in a shirt. Pays little attention to his appearance, washes himself unwillingly, takes a bath now and then for one minute. Makes an impression of someone continually under the influence of tormenting hallucinations. One day says to the doctor: "If you want to kill me, do it already." Then says almost nothing, lifts his hands in resistance and shows the doctor out shouting "Ha-ha." At night sleeps poorly.

September 3. This morning says explosively all of a sudden: "I cannot comprehend how a person could be led to what I have done in the last hours." Then falls silent, grimacing vigorously, it seems as if he is trying to say something more, but only emits "Ha-ha."

October/November. On the whole unchanged. Lately gained some weight. Time and again very disturbing with his "Ha-ha." Speaks only very rarely with the doctor, and then only that he is being tortured with the food that he cannot eat, etc. Continually under the tormenting influence of his hallucinations. Sleep at night mostly poor. Moans, stands in bed, stands rigidly in front of the window with eyes closed and an expression of listening on his face.

January 20, 1909. Up until now fairly even-tempered, restless on rare nights. The body weight is maintained evenly. After patient has been standing about a lot during the last days, today an attack of weakness, repeated a few days later. Eats with great difficulty, bruised his left knee a bit. Very agitated during the examination. Except for the marked dampening of the heart sound and a big soft regular pulse there is no finding. Urine albumin free. Can be kept in bed only with the help of an attendant. Digitoxin 3 times daily 10 drops for 3 days, which the patient at first refuses, then by enema. Then pulse slower, fuller. All the attempts to feed the patient more fail.

February 1, 1909. Almost continually in bed. Has recuperated somewhat after a time when he looked completely down. Wants at times to have his body examined, then refuses. Writes in almost illegible letters about "miracles" (when asked about the cause of his moaning), or "grave" or "not eat."

February 15. Since there is drop in the strength and fullness of the pulse, once again digitoxin solution 10 drops five times a day.

March. The pulse holds well in response to pine-needle-CO_2 baths. Eats with great difficulty, now only with the help of two attendants. Body weight stable, sleep mostly sufficient. Once complaints evidently due to a congestion of the bladder, which emptied easily after an enema.

April. Lies continually in bed, in fair weather is driven in a wheelchair. At times restless, leaves the bed and pulls to go out. Moans uninterruptedly—often during the night—his loud "Ha-ha" and swallows air copiously, so that stomach and intestine are taut with air. Has to be given laxatives.

May 10, 1909. Leaves the bed often, wanders around aimlessly in the room, pulls to go to the cellar, kept in bed with difficulty.

May 20. Calmer, stays in bed. All food has to be given by two attendants.

June 1909. Psychically unchanged. In fair weather the patient is walked or driven in the garden.

July 1909. Spends most of the day out of bed. Looks at different newspapers, apparently without much interest. Tries to express his wishes in illegible written signs. Really disturbing due to his moaning and his calls of Ha-ha!

October. Pine needle baths twice a week.

October 13. Psychically unchanged, continually under the influence of auditory hallucinations that wax in intensity. Food intake leaves a lot to be desired, everything has to be served to him, accepts it under strong opposition.

December 5, 1909. The right hand swells suddenly at times, very tender to pressure, and to passive and active finger movements as well. Bandages of liquid aluminum acetate and spiritus camphoratus remove the swelling. Mild weight gain.

April 1910. Has had a few restless nights. At times writes something on his note pad, but the writing is far removed from anything resembling written characters.

July. Mostly quiet, anxious and restless only when getting up, eating, bathing etc, fends off hallucinations with stereotyped syllables.

December. Psychically unchanged. Pulse most often quite slow, but full.

March, 1911. Angina with a markedly disturbed general feeling. Local treatment with pyocyanase. Rapid improvement, but for two walnut sized axillary side lymph nodes. Recurrent temperature elevations, redness and swelling of the tonsils.

April 10. Dullness [of the heart sounds] and weakened breathing.

April 12. Increased dullness, pulse small, irregular. Improves with digitalis.

April 13. Pleural puncture produces a purulent, cloudy whitish strongly malodorous exudate.

April 14. Death with signs of dyspnea and heart failure.

[The chart contains a detailed autopsy report, of which the following is the diagnostic summary.]

April 15, 1911. Anatomo-pathological diagnosis:

Pleuritis exsudativa chronica [left chronic exudative pleuritis]
Pyothorax sinister [left pyothorax]
Shrinking of the left lung
Atelectasis of the left upper lung lobe
Pericarditis fibrinosa acuta [acute fibrinous pericarditis]
Myodegeneratio cordis [degeneration of the heart muscle]
Sclerosis of the coronary arteries
Multiple hemorrhages in the pons.

[The other documents appended to the chart were temperature charts; Paul Schreber's declaration of December 11, 1907; the letter of Dr.

Rössler, cited in Chapter 2; a number of notes scribbled by Schreber on separate pieces of paper; the autopsy report.]

[At the Dösen Hospital a running log of admissions was kept called the *Grundbuch*. In the log Schreber is case #1726 and contains the following notation:]

Schreber, Daniel Paul, admitted November 27, 1911; born July 27, 1842; married; [religion] Evangelical-Lutheran; *Senatspräsident*, retired; [address] Dresden Neustadt [new suburbs] Angelika Street 15

Endogenous causes: father suffered from obsessional ideas (the well-known Drr. Schreber)

Mother nervous and with mood swings
Sister hysteric
Brother died by suicide (paretic)
A cousin of the mother D[ementia] pr[aecox]

Exogenous causes:
Illness of the wife about 14 days
Duration of illness: 13 years
P[ension] Kl[asse, boarders' class of accommodations]
L[eipzig] December 8, 1884–June 1, 1885; November 21, 1893–June 16, 1894 [should be: June 14]
Pierson 14 days
Sonnenstein 1894–1902? Paranoia
Died April 14, 1911 of lung gangrene

REFERENCES

Abraham, H. C. & Freud, E. L., eds. (1965), *A Psychoanalytic Dialogue: The Letters of Sigmund Freud and Karl Abraham, 1907-1926*, trans. H. C. A. & B. Marsh. New York: Basic Books.

Abraham, K. (1908), Die psychosexuellen Differenzen der Hysterie und der Dementia Praecox. *CNP*, 9:521-533. Trans.: The psycho-sexual differences between hysteria and dementia praecox. In: *Selected Papers of Karl Abraham M.D.* London: Hogarth Press, 1949.

Ackerknecht, E. H. (1955), *A Short History of Medicine.* New York: Ronald Press.

───── (1968), *A Short History of Psychiatry.* New York: Hafner. (Translation of *Kurze Geschichte der Psychiatrie*, Stuttgart: Enke, 1957.)

Ackermann, E. (1895), *Die häusliche Erziehung.* 2te Aufl. Langensalza: Beyer.

Adamkiewicz [A.] (1894), Zu Herrn Prof. Flechsig's Mittheilung: Ueber ein neues Eintheilungsprincip der Grosshirnoberfläche. *NC*, 13:807-809.

Adler, A. (1908), Der Aggressionstrieb im Leben u. in der Neurose. *Fortschritte der Medizin*, 19:577-584.

Ahlenstiel, H. and Meyer, E. J. Eds. (1967), *Selbstschilderungen eines Geisteskranken.* Leverkusen: Bayer.

Ahlwardt, H. (n.d.), *Der Verzweiflungskampf der arischen Völker mit dem Judentum.* Berlin: Dewald.

Ahrens, A.(1891), *Anti-Vernunft.* Beweisstücke für den jetztigen ungenügenden Irrengesetze. Hamburg: Verlag des Verfassers. Former work: *Ein Appell an Hamburg's Bürger*, 1890.

A. L. (1938), "Alt zu werden kann schön sein!" Letzte Tochter Dr. Schreber wird 98 Jahre alt. *LNN*, December 30, 1938.(Source: Renate Jung.)

───── (1939), Die letzte Tochter Schreber steht um 99. Lebensjahr. In: G. Richter (1939).

486   REFERENCES

_____ (1940), Eine hundertjährige Leipzigerin. *LNN*, December 30, 1940.

Allison, D. B., Prado de Oliveira, E., Roberts, M. S. & Weiss, A. S. (1988), *Psychosis and Sexual Identity: Toward a Post-Analytic View of the Schreber Case.* Albany: State University of New York Press.

Andersson, O. (1962), *Studies in the Prehistory of Psychoanalysis.* Svenska Bokvörlaget /Norstedts.

Angerstein, E. F. (1859), *Ruf zum Turnen.* Offene Briefe eines Turners an Jedermann. Stade: Fr. Steudel. (Commission A. Lax in Hildesheim.)

_____ & E. Bär (1861), *Gedenkbuch zur Erinnerung an das 2. allgemeine deutsche Turn- and Jubelfest zu Berlin, an den 10., 11., 12. August 1861.* Zwickau: Bär.

_____ (1897), *Grundzüge der Geschichte und Entwicklung der Leibesübungen.* Zweite, veränderte und erweiterte Auflage, besorgt von Dr. Otto Kurth. Wien und Leipzig: A. Pichler's Witwe und Sohn.

_____ & Eckler, C. (1887), *Haus-Gymnastik für Gesunde und Kranke. Eine Anweisung fur jedes Alter und Geschlecht, durch einfache Leibesubungen die Gesunden zu erhalten und zu kraftigen sowie kranhafte Zustände zu beseitigen.* 2te vermehrte Auflage. Berlin: Enslin.

Anonymous (1843), *Recept zu einem gusunden und langen Leben oder kurze und deutliche Anweisung eine Gesundheit zu erhalten und geringe Störungen derselben durch einfache Hausmittel zu beseitigen.* Mit einem Unterricht für Lebensrettung Verunglückter und einem Anhange über Gymnastik im Allgemeinen und Zimmergymnastik im Besondern. Von einem praktischen Arzte. Leipzig: Teubner.

Anonymous (1882), Review of Flechsig (1882a). *American Journal of Insanity*, 39:89–92.

Arlow, J.(1979), Metaphor and the psychoanalytic situation. *Psychoanal. Quart.*, 48:363–385.

Arlow, J. & Brenner, C. (1964), *Psychoanalytic Concepts and the Structural Theory.* New York: International Universities Press.

Arndt, R. (1883), *Lehrbuch der Psychiatrie für Ärzte und Studirende.* Leipzig u. Wien: Urban & Schwarzenberg.

Arnemann (1903), [Review of] D. P. Schreber (1903). *PNW*, 5:422–423.

_____ (1905), [Review of] Dr. Frese's *Prinzessin von Sachsen-Coburg und Gotha geb. Prinzessin von Belgien. PNW*, 7:192.

Arno Press Collection (1975), *Documents of the Homosexual Rights Movement in Germany, 1836–1927.* New York: Arno Press.

Aschaffenburg (1903), [Review of] D. P. Schreber (1903). *CNP*, 26:500. (Source: Han Israëls.)

Azouri, C. (1991), *J'ai réussi là où le paranoïaque échoue.* Paris: Denoël.

Bach & Eulenburg (1891), *Schulgesundheitslehre.* Berlin.

Baginsky, A. (1898–1900), *Handbuch der Schulhygiene zum Gebrauche für Ärzte, Sanitätsbeamte, Lehrer, Schulvorstände und Techniker.* 3te Aufl. Stuttgart: Enke.

Balsan, C. V. (1952), *The Glitter and the Gold.* New York: Harper.

Barande, I. (1966), La lecture des 'Mémoires' de Schreber. *RFP*, 30:27–39.

Bardeen, C. W. (1901), *Note Book of the History of Education.* Syracuse, N.Y.: Bardeen.

Barker, L. F. (1897), The sense-areas and association-centers in the brain as described by Flechsig. *J. Nerv. Ment. Dis.*, 24:325–356. (Source: G. Busse.)

Barnard, H. (1872), *Systems Institutions and Statistics of Public Instruction in Different Countries. Part 1. Europe—German States.* New York: Steiger.

Bauer, E (1891), *Der Fall Bleichröder.* Leipzig: Germanicus.

Baumeyer, F. (1952), New insights into the life and psychosis of Schreber. *Internat. J. Psycho-Anal.*, 33:262.

———— (1955), Der Fall Schreber. *Psyche*, 9:513–536.

———— (1956), The Schreber case. *Internat. J. Psycho-anal.*, 37:61–74.

———— (1970), Noch ein Nachtrag zu Freuds Arbeit über Schreber. *Zeitschrift für Psychosomatische Medizin u. Psychoanalyse*, 16:243–245.

Beeck, Manfred in der (1982), Denkwürdigkeiten eines Nervenkranken Ein Fall Schreber in Sachsen und in Kamerun. *Deutsches Ärzteblatt-Ärztliche Mitteilungen*, 79:74–81.

Beers, C. W. (1908), *A Mind That Found Itself.* An Autobiography. Garden City, NY: Doubleday, 1962.

Behandlung der Geisteskranken vor ihrer Unterbringung in den Irrenanstalten (1862), File #3488, Ministry of the Interior, Staatsarchiv Dresden.

Benvenuto, S. (1984), Un contributo sul Presidente Schreber. *Giornale Storico di Psicologia Dinamica*, 8:99–120.

Bernfeld, S. (1925), *Sisyphos oder die Grenzen der Erziehung.* Leipzig: Internationaler Psychoanalytischer Verlag.

Bestimmungen über Aufnahme Beurlaubung und Entlassung Geisteskranker in den Heil- und Versorganstalten (1879–1890), File #16805, Ministry of the Interior, Staatsarchiv Dresden.

Bethge, R. (1981), Daniel Gottlob Moritz Schreber—zum 175. Geburtstag am 15.10.1881. *Beiträge zur Orthopädie und Traumatologie*, 28:577–582.

Beyer, B. (1909), Die Zentrale für Reform des Irrenwesens. *PNW*, 11:335–338.

———— (1912), *Die Bestrebungen zur Reform des Irrenwesens.* Material zu einem Reichsgesetz. Für Laien und Ärzte. Ergänzungsband zur *PNW*. Halle: Marhold.

Biedermann, K. (1883), *Die Erziehung zur Arbeit: eine Forderung des Lebens an die Schule* von K.B. 2te völlig umgearbeitete Auflage. Leipzig: Matthes.

Bircher, E. E. (1868), *Die Freiübungen zum praktischen Gebrauch: geordnet für Schulen und Turnvereine.* Leipzig: Weber.

Bjerre, P. (1911), Zur Radikalbehandlung der chronischen Paranoia. *JPPF*, 3:795–847.

Bleuler, E. (1901), Zur Genese der paranoischen Wahnideen. *PW*, 3:254–257.

———— (1905), Frühe Entlassungen. *PNW*, 6:441–444.

———— (1906a), Freud'sche Mechanismen in der Symptomatologie von Psychosen. *PNW*, 8: 34:316–318, 35:323–325, 36:338–340.

———— (1906b), *Affektivität Suggestibilität und Paranoia.* Marhold: Halle.

———— (1911), *Dementia Praecox, oder Gruppe der Schizophrenien.* Leipzig: Deuticke. Translated as: *Dementia praecox or the group of schizophrenias*, New York: International Universities Press, 1950.

———— (1912), Review of Freud 1911: Psychoanalytische Bemerkungen ueber einen autobiographisch beschriebenen Fall von Paranoia (Dementia Paranoides). *Zentralblatt für Psychoanalyse und Psychotherapie*, 2:343–348.

_____ (1913), Kritik der Freudschen Theorien. *AZP*, 70:665-718; 780-784.

Bloch, I. (1908), *Das Sexualleben unserer Zeit*. Berlin: Marcus.

Bloom, W. and Fawcett, D.W. (1986), *A Textbook of Histology*. 11 ed. Philadelphia: Saunders.

Bock, C. E. (1855), *Das Buch vom gesunden und kranken Menschen*. Leipzig: Keil.

_____ (1871), *Ueber die Pflege der körperlichen und geistigen Gesundheit des Schulkindes. Eine Mahnung an Eltern, Lehrer und Schulbehörden*. Leipzig: Keil.

_____ (1891), *Bau, Leben und Pflege des menschlichen Körpers in Wort und Bild* nach vorheriger Begutachtung durch Schulmänner für Schüler herausgegeben von C. E. Bock, 16te Auflage, neu durchgesehen von Dr. med. M. von Zimmermann. Leipzig: Keil's Nachfolger.

Bonin, G. von (1960), *Some Papers on the Cerebral Cortex*. Springfield, IL.: Thomas.

Bornstein, Dr. Karl (1931), Dr. Daniel Gottlieb Moritz Schreber, ein Kämpfer für Volkserziehung. *Zeitschrift für ärztliche Fortbildung*, 28:798.

Bratz (1897a), Ueber die Behandlung der Epilepsie mit Opium-Bromkalim nach Flechsig. *AZP*, 53:970-971.

_____ (1897b), Ueber die Behandlung der Epilepsie mit Opium-Bromkalium (Flechsig Kur) (reported by Edel). *CNP*, 20:66-67.

_____ (1898), Zum Opium-Brombehandlung der Epilepsie nach Flechsig. *AZP*, 54:208-220.

Brauchle, A. (1933), *Handbuch der Naturheilkunde auf wissenschaftlicher Grundlage*. Sechste Auflage. Leipzig: Reclam, 1942.

_____ (1937), *Naturheilkunde in Lebensbildern*. Leipzig: Reclam.

Breger, L. (1978), Daniel Paul Schreber: from male to female. *J. Am. Acad. Psychoan.*, 6:123-156. Also in: *Freud's Unfinished Journey*, London: Routledge & Kegan Paul, 1981.

Bregman, L. (1977), Religion and madness: Schreber's *Memoirs* as personal myth. *J. Relig. and Health*, 16:119-135.

Brenner, C. (1939), On the genesis of a case of paranoid dementia praecox. *J. Nerv. Ment. Dis.*, 90:483-488.

Bresler, J. (1897), Culturgeschichtlicher Beitrag zur Hysterie. *AZP*, 53:333-376.

_____ (1899a), Die Bedeutung einer Reichs-Irrenstatistik. *PW*, 1:224-225.

_____ (1899b), Die Jahrhundertswende in der Psychiatrie (Unsigned editorial). *PW*, 1:377-379.

_____ (1901a), Anordnung der Entlassung aus der Anstalt im Entmündigungsverfahren. *PW*, 3:189-190.

_____ (1901b), Zur Paranoiafrage. *PW*, 3:170-172.

_____ (1905), Das Pariser Gutachten über die Prinzessin Luise von Koburg. *PNW*, 7:109-111.

_____ (1908), Gegenwärtiger Stand des Irrenwesens. *PNW*, 10:253-262.

_____ (1909a), Über Misshandlungen von Anstaltsgeisteskranken durch Pflegepersonen. *PNW*, 11:141-142.

_____ (1909b), Einheitliche Bezeichnung und Eintheilung der Psychosen. *PNW*, 11:367-369, 380-382, 386-388.

Breuer, J. & Freud, S. (1893), On the psychical mechanism of hysterical phenomena. In: S. Freud, *Studies in Hysteria*, 2. *Standard Edition*, London: Hogarth Press, 1955.

Brill, A. A. (1911), Psychological mechanisms of paranoia. *New York Med. J.*, 94:1209–1213.

―――― (1944), *Freud's Contribution to Psychiatry*. New York: Norton.

Brockhaus, F. A. (1898), *Konversations-Lexikon*. 14te Auflage. Leipzig, Berlin u. Wien: F. A. Brockhaus.

―――― (1954), *Der Grosse Brockhaus*. Leipzig: Brockhaus.

―――― & Efron, I. A., eds. (1903), *Entsiklopedicheskii Slovar*. St. Petersburg: the Brockhaus-Efron Society, 39A:854.

Brosius (1894), *Die Verkennung des Irreseins*. Leipzig: Friesenhahn.

Brouardel, P. (1884), *Des Causes d'Erreurs dans les Expertises relatives aux Attentas à la Pudeur*. Paris: Ballière.

―――― (1887), *Le Secret Medical*. Paris: Ballière.

―――― (1898), *La Responsabilité Medicale*. Paris: Ballière.

―――― (1899), *L'Exercise de la Medecine et le Charlatanisme*. Paris: Balliere.

Brouardel, Thoinot et Maygrier, eds. (1897), of the fifth editions of Ambroise Tardieu, 1855, *Etude Médico-légale sur l'avortement suivie d'une note sur l'obligation de déclarer à l'état civil de foetus mort-nés et recherches pour servir à l'histoire médico-légale des grossesses fausses et simulées.* Cinquième edition revue et augmentée de rapports sur l'affaire Boisleux et la Jarrige par Mmes. B. T. et M. Paris: Ballière.

Bumke, O. (1931), *Die Psychoanalyse*. Berlin: Springer.

―――― (1938), *Die Psychoanalyse und ihre Kinder*. 2. Auflage. Berlin:J. Springer.

―――― (1941), *Gedanken über die Seele*. Berlin: Springer.

―――― (1953). *Erinnerungen und Betrachtungen. Der Weg eines deutschen Psychiaters.* 2te Aufl. München: Pflaum.

Bunker, H. A. (1944), American psychiatric literature during the past one hundred years. In: American Psychiatric Association, ed., *One Hundred Years of American Psychiatry*. New York: Columbia University Press.

Burgerstein, L. (1887), *Gesundheitsplfege in der Mittelschule. Hygiene des Körpers nebst beiläufigen Bemerkungen*. Wien: Alfred Hölder.

Busse, G. (1989), Letter of 2/15/1989.

―――― (1989), Schreber und Flechsig: der Hirnanatom als Psychiater. *Medizin-historisches Journal*, 24:260–305.

―――― (1990), *Schreber, Freud und die Suche nach dem Vater*. Inaugural-Dissertation. Freie Universität, Berlin.

Calasso, R. (1974), *L'Impuro Folle*. Milano: Adelphi. German translation: *Die geheime Geschichte des Senatspräsidenten Dr. Daniel Paul Schreber*, Frankfurt: Suhrkamp, 1980.

Cameron, N. (1959), Paranoid conditions and paranoia. In: *American Textbook of Psychiatry*, ed. S. Arieti. New York: Basic Books.

Canetti, E.(1960), Der Fall Schreber. In: *Masse und Macht*. Hamburg: Claassen. Translated as *Crowds and Power*, London: Gollancz, 1962.

Capellmann, C. (1895), *Mariaberg*. Aachen: Rudolf Barth.

Carr, A. C. (1963), Observations on paranoia and their relationship to the Schreber case. *Internat. J. Psycho-Anal.*, 44:195–200.

Chabot, C. B. (1982), *Freud on Schreber: Psychoanalytic Theory and the Critical Act.* Amherst: University of Massachusetts Press.

Charitable Society for Mental Patients (1901), Meeting of May 23, 1901. *Der Irrenschutz*, 1:12. Also in: *PNW*, 3:126. (See Weber, 1901.)

_____ (1907), Meeting of May 27, 1907. *PNW*, 9:97-98.

_____ (1911), Meeting in 1911. *PNW*, 13:115-116.

Chasseguet-Smirgel, J. (1966), Notes de lecture en marge de la revision du cas Schreber. *RFP*, 30:41-61.

Chazaud, J. (1966), Contribution à la théorie psychanalytique de la paranoia. *RFP*, 30:93-119.

Clarke, E. G. & O'Malley, C. D. (1968), *The Human Brain and Spinal Cord.* Berkeley: University of California Press.

Clias, B. H. (1829), *Kalisthenie oder Übungen zur Schönheit und Kraft für Mädchen*, mit Vorwort von A. Meckel, Professor der Anatomie in Bern. Bern: C. A. Jennt.

Collingwood, R. G. (1946), *The Idea of History.* London: Oxford University Press.

Compayre, G. (1889), *Histoire de la Pédagogie.* Paris: Delaplane.

Cotta, C. (1902), *Leitfaden für den Unterricht in der Turngeschichte.* Achte, vermehrte Auflage. Leipzig: Voigtländer, 1931.

Cramer, A. (1895), Abgrenzung und Differenzial-Diagnose der Paranoia. *AZP*, 51:286-369.

Croufer, F. (1970), La vie du Président Schreber, une ordalie relative à la paternité? *Les Feuillets Psychiatriques de Liège*, 3:214-251.

Current Work in the History of Medicine. London: Wellcome Institute.

Cyriax, E. F. (1909), *Bibliographia Gymnastica Medica.* London: Wörishofen.

Dahl, R. (1905), *Der Bankerott der Psychiatrie.* Wien und Leipzig: Coën.

Das litterarische Leipzig (1897), *Illustriertes Handbuch der Schriftsteller- und Gelehrtenwelt, etc.* Leipzig: Fiedler.

Deleuze, G. & Guattari, F. (1972), *Anti-Oedipus / Capitalism and Schizophrenia.* Minneapolis, MN: University of Minnesota Press, 1977.

deMause, L. (1987), Schreber and the history of childhood. *J. Psychohistory*, 15:423-430.

Deputirten der Berliner Lehrer-Vereine und der Hufeland'schen medicinisch-chirurgischen Gesellschaft (1869), *Das Turnen nach medicinischen und pädagogischen Grundlagen.* Berlin: Loewenstein.

Dessoir, Max (1917), *Vom Jenseits der Seele Die Geheimwissenschaften in kritischer Betrachtung.* Vierte und fünfte Aufl., Stuttgart: Enke, 1920.

Devreese, D. (1981a), Schreber-Dokumenten/Documents Schreberiens. *Psycho-analytische Perspektieven*, 1:17-97.

_____ (1981b), Adelstolz und Professorenduenkel, *Psycho-analytische Perspektieven*, 1:99-164.

_____ (1986a), Éleménts nouveaux sur Daniel Paul Schreber: sa carrière de magistrat et l'histoire de sa maladie à la lumière de son dossier personnel. In: D. Devreese et al. (1986b).

_____ Israëls, H., & Quackelbeen, J. (1986b), *Schreber Inédit.* Paris: Éditions Du Seuil.

_____ (1989), *De waan lezen.* Doctoral dissertation. Leuven: Katholieke U.

Leuven, 2 vols.

––––– (1990a), Anatomy of soul murder, family romance and structure of delusion in the Memoirs of D. P. Schreber. *Psychoanal. Rev.,* in press. An abridged version of chapters from Devreese, 1989.

––––– (1990b), Oct. 24, D. P. Schreber's "Realms of God" (Gottesreichen) and the structure and history of Saxonian psychiatry. Poster, unpublished.

Dieckhöfer, K. and Thiem, J. H. (1990), Grundgedanken einer früher Preventivmedizin im Werk des "pädagogischen" Mediziners Daniel Gottlob Moritz Schreber (1808-1861). *Medizinische Klinik,* 85:102-106. (Source: H.U. Peters.)

Donath, J. (1900), Therapeutische Leistungen und Bestrebungen auf dem Gebiete der Epilepsie (1896-1900). *PW,* 2:79-82, 85-89, 93-98.

Dörner, K. (1969), *Bürger und Irre.* 2. ed., Frankfurt: Athenäum, 1984.

Dresdner Anzeiger (1911), Hundertjahrfeier der Königlich Sächsischen Heilund Pflegeanstalt Sonnenstein. *PNW,* 13:166-168.

Dresdner Nachrichten (1911), Hundertjahrfeier der Königl. Sächsischen Landesheilanstalt Sonnenstein bei Pirna. *PNW,* 13:114-115.

dt (1939), Besuch bei einer Neunundneunzigjährigen. *Neue Leipziger Zeitung,* 30.12.1939. (Source: R. Jung.)

Dühring, E. (1880), *Robert Mayer der Galilei des nenzehnten Jahrhunderts und die Gelehrtenunthaten gegen bahhbrechende Wissenschaftengrössen.* Zweite, verbesserte und vermehrte Auflage. Leipzig: Naumann, 1904.

Earle, P. (1853). *Institutions for the Insane in Prussia, Austria and Germany.* In: *American Psychiatrists Abroad,* New York: Arno Press, 1976.

Edwards, A. (1978), Schreber's delusional transference—a disorder of the self. *J. Psychoanal. Psychol.,* 23:242-247.

Ehrenwald, J. (1963), *Neurosis in the Family and Patterns of Psychosocial Defense.* New York: Harper & Row.

Eigen, M.(1986), *The Psychotic Core.* New York: Aronson.

Eisler, M. J. (1921), A man's unconscious phantasy of pregnancy in the guise of traumatic hysteria: A clinical contribution to anal erotism. *Internat. J. Psycho-Anal.,* 2:255-286.

Eisler, R. (1928), *Wörterbuch der philosophischen Begriffe.* Berlin: E.S. Mittler u. Sohn. 4th edition.

Ellenberger, H. (1964), La notion de maladie créatrice. *Dialogue, Canadian Philosophical Review,* 3:25-41.

––––– (1970), *The Discovery of the Unconscious.* New York: Basic Books, Inc.

Ernst, M. (1886), *Das Buch der richtigen Ernährung Gesunder und Kranker.* Ein Kochbuch. Supplement zu Bock's *Buch vom gesunden und kranken Menschen.* Leipzig: Ernst Keil's Nachfolger, vol. 1, p. 685.

Eulenburg, A. (1880-1911), *Real-Encyclopädie der gesammten Heilkunde. Medicinisch-chirurgisches Wörterbuch für practische Ärzte.* First edition: 1881; second expanded edition: 1887; third edition, totally revised: 1896. Leipzig, Wien: Urban & Schwarzenberg.

Euler, C. (1894-1896), Herausgeber, *Encyklopädisches Handbuch des gesamten Turnwesens und der verwandten Gebiete,* in Verbindung mit zahlreichen Fachgenossen. Wien: Pichler's Witwe.

Faber, O. (1859), *Das Turnen in seinen Beziehungen zu Staat un Volk. Eine*

Zeitfrage. Offenes Sendschreiben an Freunde und Gegner. Zum Besten des Jahn-Denkmals in der Hasenhaide von O.F., Vorturner des Allgemeinen Turn-Vereins zu Leipzig. Berlin: Bieler.

Fairbairn, R. (1955), Considerations arising out of the Schreber case. *Br. J. Med. Psychol.*, 29:113–127.

Faust, B. C. (1791), *Wie der Geschlechtstrieb der Menschen in Ordnung zu bringen und wie die Menschen besser und glücklicher zu machen sind* (quoted in Faust, 1794).

_____ (1794), *Gesundheits-Katechismus zum Gebrauche in den Schulen und beym häuslichen Unterrichte.* Bückeburg: Althaus.

_____ (nd), *A New Guide to Health.* Compiled from the Catechism of Dr. Faust with additions and improvements, selected from the writings of men of eminence, following observations of Prof. Hufeland of Jena. Designed for the use of schools and private families. Newburyport: Gilman.

Fechner, G. T. (1905), *The Little Book of Life after Death.* Trans. M. C. Wadsworth. Boston: Little & Brown.

_____ (1910), *Die drei Motive und Gründe des Glaubens.* Zweite Auflage [first edition: 1863]. Leipzig: Breitkopf & Härtel.

Fenichel, O. (1945), *The Psychoanalytic Theory of Neurosis.* New York: Norton.

Ferenczi, S. (1911), On the part played by homosexuality in the pathogenesis of paranoia. In: *Contributions to Psycho-Analysis* (trans. E. Jones), Boston: Badger, 1916.

_____ (1912), Transitory symptom-constructions during the analysis (transitory conversion, substitution, illusion, hallucination, "character-regression" and "expression–displacement"), chapter 7 in: *First Contributions to Psycho-Analysis,* New York: Bruner-Mazel, 1980.

Fichte, J. G. (1806), *Die Anweisung zum seeligen Leben oder auch die Religionslehre. In Vorlesungen gehalten zu Berlin im Jahre 1806.* Zweite, unveränderte Ausgabe, Berlin: Reimer, 1828.

_____ (1808), Addresses to the German Nation, trans. R. F. Jones and G. H. Turnbull. Chicago: Open Court, 1922.

Fichtner, G. (1989), Letter of June 11.

Fischer, M. (1904), Die Benennung der Krankenhäuser für Geisteskranke. *PNW*, 6:281–284; 289–292.

Flechsig, P. E. (1870), *Bemerkungen ueber Meningitis luetica u. einem dahin zu stellenden Fall.* Leipzig: Fr. Andrae's Nachfolger.

_____ (1873), Über einige Beziehungen zwischen secundären Degenerationen und Entwickelungsvorgängen im menschlichen Rückenmark. *Wagner's Archiv der Heilkunde,* vol. 14.

_____ (1874), Über Varietäten im Bau des menschlichen Rückenmarks. *Centralblatt f. d. Medic. Wissenschaften.*

_____ (1876), *Die Leitungsbahnen im Gehirn und Rückenmark des Menschen auf Grund entwickelungeschichtlicher Untersuchungen dargestellt.* Leipzig: Engelmann.

_____ (1877-1878), Über Systemerkrankungen im Rückenmark. *Wagner's Archiv der Heilkunde,* vols. 18/19.

_____ (1877-1931), Personalakte, Ministerium für Volksbildung, File

10281/142, Staatsarchiv Dresden.

_____ (1882-1896), *Acta der psychiatrischen und Nervenklinik der Universität Leipzig.* Files 10166/7-10166/11, volumes III-VII, Ministerium für Volksbildung, Staatsarchiv Dresden.

_____ (1882-1885), *Monatsrapporte der psychiatrischen und Nervenklinik der Universität Leipzig.* Ministerium für Volksbildung, File 10166/20, Staatsarchiv Dresden.

_____ (1882a), *Die Körperlichen Grundlagen der Geistesstörungen.* Vortrag gehalten beim Antritt des Lehramtes an den Universität Leipzig am 4. März, 1882. Leipzig: Veit.

_____ (1882b), *Auszug as dem Statut für die Irrenklinik der Universität Leipzig.* Bestimmungen über die Aufnahme, Verpflegung und Entlassung der Kranken enthaltend. Leipzig: Frankenstein und Wagner. Staatsarchiv Dresden.

_____ (1883), *Plan des menschlichen Gehirns.* Leipzig: Veit. (Source: I. Kästner.)

_____ (1884a), Zur gynäkologischen Behandlung hysterischer Personen. Presentation at the Annual Meeting of the Society of German Alienists in Leipzig. *CNP,* 7:437-440. Also in: *AZP,* 41 (1884):616-636; review of, *AZP,* 42(1885):122-123.

_____ (1884b), Zur gynaekologischen Behandlung der Hysterie. *NC,* 3:433-439, 457-468; discussion 3:452-453.

_____ (1885), Zur gynäkologischen Behandlung hysterischer Personen. *AP,* 16:559-561.

_____ (1887), Zur Anatomie und Entwickelungsgeschichte der Leitungsbahnen im Grosshirn des Menschen. *Arch. f. Anat. u. Physiolog. Anatom. Abt.*

_____ (1888a), *Die Irrenklinik der Universität Leipzig und ihre Wirksamkeit in den Jahren 1882-1886.* Leipzig: Veit.

_____ (1888b), Demonstration von Präparaten aus dem Gehirne choreatischer. *Verhandl. d. Congress f. innere Medicin, Wiesbaden.* Vol. 7, p. 452.

_____ (1889), Über neue Färbungsmethode des Centralen Nervensystems und die Ergebnisse bezüglich des Zusammenhangs von Ganglienzellen und Nervenfasern. *Berichte der k. sächs. Ges. der Wiss., Math.-Phys. Kl.*

_____ (1891), Ueber die patologische Anatomie der Tabes dorsalis. Presentation at the 64th Meeting of the Deutsche Naturforscher und Ärzte in Halle a. S., September 21-25.

_____ (1892-1894), *Monatsrapporte der psychiatrischen und Nervenklinik der Universität Leipzig,* Ministerium für Volksbildung, File 10166/23.

_____ (1893), Über eine neue Behandlungsmethode der Epilepsie, *NC,* 12:229-231.

_____ (1893-1899), Letters to V. M. Bekhterev, unpublished. Bekhterev Collection, St. Petersburg State Archives.

_____ (1894a), Rectoratswechel an der Universität Leipzig/am 31. October 1894. Rede des antretenden Rectors Dr. med. Paul Flechsig: *Gehirn und Seele.* Leipzig: Alexander Edelmann, Universitäts-Buchdrucker.

_____ (1894b), Zur Entwickelungs der Associationssysteme im menschlichen Gehirn. *Berichte der k. sächs. Ges. der Wiss., Math.-Phys. Kl.*

_____ (1894c), Ueber ein neues Eintheilungsprincip der Grosshirn-

Oberfläche. *NC*, 13:674–676.

———(1894d), Bemerkungen zu den vorstehenden Mittheilung des Herrn Prof. Adamkiewicz [1894]. *NC*, 13:809.

———(1895), Rede am Rectoratswechsel an der Universität Leipzig am 31. October 1895. Leipzig: Edelmann.

———(1896a), *Gehirn und Seele.* Zweite Auflage, 1896, Leipzig: Veit.

———(1896b), Die Localisation der geistigen Vorgänge. Lecture held on September 23, 1896 at the 68th Meeting of the Deutsche Naturforscher und Ärzte in Frankfurt a. M. *CNP*, 19:556–557; discussion, 558–560.

———(1896c), *Die Localisation der Geistigen Vorgänge insbesondere der Sinnesempfindungen des Menschen.* Leipzig: Veit.

———(1896d), *Die Grenzen geistiger Gesundheit und Krankheit.* Rede gehalten zu Feier des Geburtstages Sr. Majestät des Königs Albert von Sachsen am 23. April 1896. Leipzig: Veit.

———(1896e), O granicach pomiędzy psychicznym zdrowiem a chorobą. Polish trans. of Flechsig (1896c). *Wszechświat*, 15:609–615; 627–634.

———(1896f), O anatomicznych podstawach teoryi umiejscowień mózgowych. Polish trans. of Flechsig (1896a). *Wszechswiat*, 15:53–57; 67–79.

———(1897a), Ueber die Associationsfasern des menschlichen Gehirns mit anatomischen Demonstrationen. *CNP*, 20:125. (Löwenfeld, reporter.)

———(1897b), Zur Behandlung der Epilepsie. *NC*, 16:50–53.

———(1897c), *Predely Dušhevnago Ravnovesiya.* Russ. trans. of Flechsig (1896d). Odessa.

———(1897d), Discussant of Binswanger, *AP*, 29:982–983.

———(1898a), *Études sur le Cerveau.* Traduction L. Levi. Paris: Vigot.

———(1898b), Neue Untersuchungen über die Markbildung in den menschlichen Grosshirnläppen. *NC*, 17:977–996.

———(1899a), Vorwort. In: W. v. Bechterew, *Suggestion und ihre Soziale Bedeutung.* Leipzig: Georgi.

———(1899b), Vorwort.In: S. Ramon y Cajal, *Die Structur des Chiasma Opticum, nebst einer allgemeinen Theorie der Kreuzung der Nervenbahnen.* Leipzig: Barth.

———(1899c), Demonstration and discussion at the 5th Meeting of the Mid-German Psychiatrists and Neurologists in Leipzig. *PW*, 1:338–341.

———(1900a), Frage der Projections- und Associationscentren. *MPN*, 8:298–303.

———(1900b), Sur les centres de projection et de l'association du cerveau humain. In: *13ème Congrès International de Médecine. Rés. d. Rapports, Sect. Neurol.,* pp. 9–11.

———(1900c), Die Projections- und Associations- Centren des menschlichen Gehirns. *CNP*, 23:501–506. (Including discussions by Hitzig and v. Monakow.)

———(1901), Developmental (myelogenetic) localisation of the cerebral cortex in the human subject. *The Lancet* (October 19):1027–1029.

———(1903), Die innere Ausbildung des Gehirns der rechtzeitig geborenen menschlichen Frucht. (Mit Demonstrationen.) *MPN*, 14:467–468. Also in: *PNW*, 5:375–376.

_____ (1904), Discussant of a presentation by Foerster at the 10th Meeting of the Middle-German Psychiatrists and Neurologists. *AP*, 39:928-929.

_____ (1905), Hirnphysiologie und Willenstheorien. *Ostwald's Annalen der Naturphilosophie*, 4:475-498. (Source: Dr. Kästner.) Trans. "Brain physiology and theories of volitions" in von Bonin (1960).

_____ (1905b), Einige Bemerkungen über die Untersuchungsmethoden der Grosshirnrinde, insbesondere des Menschen. *Arch. f. Anatom. und Entwickelungsgeschichte*, pp. 337-444.

_____ (1907), Ueber die Hörsphäre des menschlichen Gehirns (mit Demonstrationen). *CNP*, 30:947-948. Also in *MPN*, 23:88-90 (the same title cited as the 14th meeting, *MPN*, 23:172-173); *PWN*, 9:454-455; *DMW*, 33:2165-2166.

_____ (1909), Vorwort. In: P. Näcke, *Die Gehirnoberfläche von Paralytischen*. Leipzig: Vogel.

_____ (1911), Ueber das hintere Längsbündel. *MPN*, 31:92-93; *AP*, 49:649-651.

_____ (1912), Flächengliederung der menschlichen Grosshirnrinde unter spezieller Berücksichtigung der neuerdings von Brodmann versuchten Einteilung in zyto-architektonische Felder. *AP*, 50(1912-1913):987-988. Also in: *MPN*, 33:179-180; *PNW*, 14:440-441.

_____ (1920), *Anatomie des menschlichen Gehirns und Rückenmarks auf myelogenetischer Grundlage*. Leipzig: Thieme.

_____ (1922), Die Lokalisation der geistigen Funktionen. *AZP*, 79:319-322.

_____ (1927), *Meine myelogenetische Hirnlehre mit biographischer Einleitung*. Berlin: Springer.

Flounoy, T. (1900), *Des Indes à la Planète Mars*. Paris: Éditions Du Seuil, 1983.

Forel, A. (1886), Zur Heilung der Hysterie durch Castration. *Correspondenz-Blatt f. Schweiz. Aerzte*, 16:1-4

_____ (1894), *Gehirn und Seele*. 7th and 8th edition, Bonn: Strauss, 1902.

_____ (1901), Selbst-Biographie eines Falles von Mania acuta. III. Hallucinationen, Illusionen, Wahnideen und dergl. *AP*, 34:980-997.

_____ (1935), *Mémoires*, Neuchatel: Editions de la Baconniere, no date, a French version of the original German edition, Zurich: Europa-Verlag, 1935.

_____ *Briefe Correspondance 1864-1927*. H. H. Walser, Hg. Bern: Huber, 1968.

Freeman, T., Cameron, J. L. & McGhie, A. (1969), *Chronic Schizophrenia*. New York: International Universities Press, 1958.

Freud, S. (1873-1939), *Briefe 1873-1939*. Frankfurt: Fischer, 1960.

_____ (1887), [Review of] Adamkiewicz's "Monoplegia anaesthetica." *NC*, 6:131-133.

_____ (1891), *On Aphasia*, New York: International Universities Press, 1953.

_____ (1893), Charcot. *Standard Edition*, 3:11-23. London: Hogarth Press, 1962.

_____ (1894), The neuro-psychoses of defence. *Standard Edition*, 3:45-61. London: Hogarth Press, 1962.

_____ (1895), On the grounds for detaching a particular syndrome from neurasthenia under the description "anxiety neurosis." *Standard Edition*, 3:90-115. London: Hogarth Press, 1962.

496   REFERENCES

_____ (1896), Further remarks on the neuro-psychoses of defence. *Standard Edition*, 3:162-185. London: Hogarth Press, 1962.

_____ (1900), *The interpretation of dreams. Standard Edition*, 4, 5. London: Hogarth Press, 1953.

_____ (1905), Three essays on the theory of sexuality. *Standard Edition*, 7:135-243. London: Hogarth Press, 1953.

_____ (1907a), Delusions and dreams in Jensen's *Gradiva. Standard Edition*, 9:7-95. London: Hogarth Press, 1959.

_____ (1907b), Creative writers and day-dreaming. *Standard Edition*, 9:143-153. London: Hogarth Press, 1959.

_____ (1909), Analysis of a phobia in a five-year-old boy. *Standard Edition*, 5:5-149. London: Hogarth Press, 1955.

_____ (1910a), Five lectures on psycho-analysis. *Standard Edition*, 11:7-55. London: Hogarth Press, 1957.

_____ (1910b), Leonardo da Vinci and a memory of his childhood. *Standard Edition*, 12:63-137. London: Hogarth Press, 1957.

_____ (1910c), Two letters to Ferenczi, October 6 and 10. Library of Congress, manuscript file #19,042). (Source: Busse.)

_____ (1911a), Psycho-analytic notes on an autobiographical account of a case of paranoia (dementia paranoides). *Standard Edition*, 12:9-79. London: Hogarth Press, 1958.

_____ (1911b), Formulations on the two principles of mental functioning. *Standard Edition*, 12:218-226. London: Hogarth Press, 1958.

_____ (1912a), Postscript. *Standard Edition*, 12:80-82. London: Hogarth Press, 1958.

_____ (1912b), Types of onset of neurosis. *Standard Edition*, 12:231-238. London: Hogarth Press, 1958.

_____ (1914a), On the history of the psycho-analytic movement. *Standard Edition*, 14:7-66. London: Hogarth Press, 1957.

_____ (1914b), On narcissism: an introduction. *Standard Edition*, 14:73-102. London: Hogarth Press, 1957.

_____ (1915b), A case of paranoia running counter to the psycho-analytic theory of the disease. *Standard Edition*, 14:263-272. London: Hogarth Press, 1957.

_____ (1916), Some character types met in psychoanalytic work. *Standard Edition*, 14:311-333. London: Hogarth Press, 1957.

_____ (1916-1917), Introductory Lectures of Psycho-Analysis. *Standard Edition*, 16. London: Hogarth Press, 1963.

_____ (1917), Metapsychological supplement to the theory of dreams. *Standard Edition*, 14:222-235. London: Hogarth Press, 1957.

_____ (1923c), A seventeenth century demonological neurosis. *Standard Edition*, 19:72-105. London: Hogarth Press, 1961.

_____ (1924), Neurosis and psychosis. *Standard Edition*, 19:149-153. London: Hogarth Press, 1961.

_____ (1926), Letter to Marie Bonaparte, September 13, 1926. In: Jones, E. (1955), *The Life and Work of Sigmund Freud.* New York: Basic Books, vol. 3, p. 447.

_____ (1933), New Introductory Lectures. *Standard Edition*, 22. London: Hogarth Press, 1964.

_____ (1937), Constructions in analysis. *Standard Edition*, 23:257-269. London: Hogarth Press, 1964.

_____ (1950), *Extracts from the Fliess Papers* [including] *Project for a Scientific Psychology. Standard Edition*, 1. London: Hogarth Press, 1966.

_____ (1950a), *Aus den Anfängen der Psychoanalyse*. London: Imago.

_____ & Darkschewitsch, L. O. (1886), Über die Beziehungen des Strickkörpers zum Hinterstrang und Hinterstrangskern nebst Bemerkungen über zwei Felder der Oblongata. *Neurologisches Centralblatt*, 5:121ff.

Friedrich, E. (1855), *Die Heilgymnastik in Schweden und Norwegen: nach eigener Anschauung für Aerzte und Turnlehrer*. Dresden: Adler und Dietze.

_____ (1859). Review of Schreber's *Anthropos. NJT*, 5:143-152.

_____ (1860),[Review of] Schreber's *Ueber Volkserziehung. NJT*, 6:125-134.

Friedrich, G. (1932), Genealogical table of the Schreber family, with annotations. Unpublished. (Source: Dieter Jung.)

Fromm, B. (1887), *Die Zimmergymnastik*. Anleitung zur Ausübung activer, passiver oder Widerstands-Bewegungen ohne Geräthe nebst Anweisung zur Verhütung von Rückgrats Verümmungen. Berlin: August Hirschwald.

Fuhrmann, M. (1905), Ueber Bildung unseres Pflegepersonals. *PNW*, 7:313-315.

Fulton, J. F. (1943), *Physiology of the Nervous System* (2d ed.). London: Oxford University Press.

Galton, F. (1883), *Inquiries into Human Faculty and Its Development* (2d ed.). London: Dent, 1907 (reprinted 1911).

Ganser, Dr. (1897), Ueber die Methode der psychiatrischen Untersuchung. *AZP*, 53:584-585; discussant, *AZP*, 53:588.

Ganz, M. (1987), Schreber's *Memoirs of My Mental Illness*: Art proscribed. In: *Psychoanalytic Approaches to Literature and Film*, ed. M. Charney & J. Reppen, pp. 37-58. Rutherford, NJ: Fairleigh Dickinson University Press.

Gay, P. (1988), *Freud: A Life for Our Time*. New York: Norton.

Georgii, A. (1847), *Kinésithérapie, ou Traitement des Maladies par le Mouvement, Sélon la Méthode de Ling*. Paris.

Gilman, D. C., Peck, H. T., & Colby, F. M., eds. (1904), *The New International Encyclopedia*. New York: Dodd & Mead.

Glees, P. (1956). The emergence of medical psychiatry. *Oxford Med. Sch. Gazette*, 8:21-23.

Goetze, Dr. Rudolf (1896), *Pathologie und Irrenrecht*. Leipzig: Mutze.

Goldstein, K. (1927), Die Lokalisation in der Grosshirnrinde. In: *Handbuch der Normalen und Pathologischen Physiologie* (cited in Meyer, A., 1981).

Gräfe, H. (1845), *Allgemeine Pädagogik*. Leipzig: Brockhaus.

Grashey (1886), Bernhard von Gudden, Nekrolog. *AP*, 17:I-XXIX.

Green, A. (1977), Transcription d'origine inconnue. *Nouvelle Revue de Psychanalyse*, 16:27-63.

Griesinger, W. (1867), *Pathologie und Therapie der psychischen Krankheiten*. Stuttgart: A. Krabbe. Second edition.

_____ (1868), Über Irrenanstalten und deren Weiter-Entwickelung in Deutschland. *AP*, 1:8–43.

Gross, Otto (1904), Zur Differentialdiagnostik netativistischer Phenomene. *PNW*, 6:345–353; 357–363.

Grotstein, J. S. (1984–1985), The Schreber case: A reappraisal. *Internat. J. Psychoanal. Psychother.*, 10:321–375.

_____ (1985), The Schreber case revisited: Schizophrenia as a disorder of self-regulation and of interactional regulation. *Yale J. Biol. Med.*, 58:299–314.

Gruber, L. (1862), *Die Heilgymnastik als Orthopädie im Vergleich mit der Maschinen-Orthopädie . . . .* Regensburg: Pustel.

Gruhle (1906), Brief über Robert Schumann's Krankheit an P. J. Möbius. *CNP*, 29:805–810.

Gudden, B. von (1885), Über die Frage der Localisation der Functionen in der Gronsshirnrinde. *AZP*, 42:478–499.

Haeckel, (1874), *Anthropogenie oder Entwickelungsgeschichte des Menschen.* 2te Aufl. Leipzig: Engelmann.

Hartmann, Ph. C. (1814), *Theoria morbi, seu pathologia generalis, quam praelectionis publicis accomodavit* P.C.H. Vindobonae: Huffer et Wimmer.

_____ (1820), *Der Geist des Menschen in seinen Verhaltnissen zum physischen Leben, oder Grundzuge zu einer Physiologie des Denkens.* Für Ärzte, Philosophen und Menschen im höhern Sinne des Wortes. Von Ph.C.H. Doktor und offentl. ordentl. Professor der Medicin an der U. zu Wien. Wien: Gerold. Second edition, same, 1832.

_____ (1838), *Allgemeine Therapie. Nach seinen öffentlichen Vorlesungen.* Herausgegeben von einem praktischen Arzte. Aus dem Lateinischen. Leipzig: Boss.

_____ (1841), *Glückseligkeitslehre für das physische Leben des Menschen, oder die Kunst, das Leben zu benutzen und dabei Gesundheit, Schönheit, Körper- und Geistesstärke zu erhalten und zu vervollkomnen.* Dritte verbesserte Auflage. Leipzig: Boss.

Hartung, D. (1907), Trauerrede beim Begräbnis der Frau verw. Dr. Schreber, Leipzig, 17. Mai 1907.

Haslam, J. (1810), *Illustrations of Madness, Exhibiting a Singular Case of Insanity, and a No Less Remarkable Difference in Medical Opinion Developing the Nature of Assailment and the Manner of Working Events with the Description of the Tortures Experienced by Bomb-Bursting, Lobster-Cracking, and Lengthening the Brain.* London: Hayden. Reissued with an introduction by Roy Porter (London: Routledge), 1988.

Hauschild, E. I. (1851), Pestalozzi über den Staat: Rede, bei der Feier des Pestalozzi-Festes am 12. Januar 1851 zu Leipzig gehalten bei der Gelegenheit des dritten Berichtes über das Moderne Gesammtgymnasium in Leipzig, veröffentlicht von Dr. E. I. H., Director. Leipzig: Staritz.

_____ (1858), *Die leibliche Pflege der Kinder zu Hause und in der Schule.* Leipzig: Brockhaus.

_____ (1865), *Dreissig pädagogische Briefe.* Leipzig: Prieber.

Haymaker, W. and F. Schiller (1970), *The Founders of Neurology.* Second edition. Springfield: Thomas.

Hayner (1817), *Aufforderung an Regierungen, Obrigkeiten, und Vorsteher der Irren-*

häuser zur Abstellung schweren Gebrechen in der Behandlung der Irren. Leipzig: Göschen.

H. B. (1940), Schrebers Tochter wird 100 Jahre alt. (Source: R. Jung.)

Head, H. (1926), *Aphasia and Kindred Disorders of Speech.* Cambridge University Press.

Heindl, J. B. (1859), *Galerie berühmter Pädagogen, verdienter Schulmänner, Jugend- und Volksschriftsteller und Componisten aus der Gegenwart in Biographien und biographischen Skizzen.* München: Finsterlin. Bd.2, pp. 396-398.

Heinroth, J. C. A. (1838), *On Education and Self-Formation Based upon Physical, Intellectual, Moral, and Religious Principles.* (From the German.) London: Schloss.

Heinse, W. (1787), *Ardinghello und die glückseeligen Inseln. Eine Italiänische Geschichte aus dem sechzehnten Jahrhundert.* Stuttgart: Reclam, 1978.

Hempel, F. (1901), Die Besetzung des Sonnenstein durch die Franzosen im Jahre 1813. *PW,* 2:405-408.

Henneberg (1929), Paul Flechsig. *Med. Klinik,* 25:1490-1492.

Herbart, J. F. (1824-1825), *Psychologie als Wissenschaft, neugegründet auf Erfahrung, Metaphysik und Mathematik.* Reprint of the later 1850 edition, Amsterdam: Bonset, 1968.

Hermann, I. (1980), Some aspects of psychotic regression. A Schreber study. *Internat. Rev. Psycho-Anal.,* 7:2-10.

Hillman, J. (1986), *On Paranoia.* The Eranos Lecture Series. Dallas: Spring, 1988.

Hinsie, L. E. & Shatzky, J. (1940), *Psychiatric Dictionary.* London: Oxford University Press.

Hirsch, A., hg. (1887), *Biographisches Lexikon d. hervorragenden Ärzte aller Zeiten und Völker.* Wien & Leipzig: Urban & Schwarzenberg.

Hirsch, J. (1845), *Die Orthopädie in ihrer speciellen Beziehung zu den Gebrechen der Haltung und des Wuchses nebst ihren speciell-gymnastischen und mechanischen Behelfen* von Dr. J.H.Professor der Medicin und Chirurgie, Gründer der ersten gymnastisch-orthopadischen Institutes zu Prag. Prag: Kronberger und Řziwnatz.

Hirschfeld, A. & Franke, A. (1879), *Geschichte der Leipziger Burschenschaft Germania,* 1859-1879. Leipzig: Naumann.

Hirschfeld, M. (1910), *Die Transvestiten: Eine Untersuchung über den erotischen Verkleidungstrieb.* Berlin: Pulvermacher.

Hirth, G. (1860), *Wie ist das Turnwesen zur echten Volksthümlickkeit zu erheben?*: eine dringende Zeitfrage, allen Turnenden, Turnvereinen und Turnfreunden von Neuem an's Herz gelegt von einem Mitglied des Gothaer Turnvereins. Gotha: In Commission bei Thienemann.

——, ed. (1865), *Das gesammte Turnwesen: ein Lesebuch für Deutsche Turner:* 133 abgeschlossene Muster-Darstellungen von den vorzüglichsten älteren and neueren Turnschriftschtellern. Leipzig: Keil.

History of Education Catalog, (1987-1989), Research Publications, Woodbridge, CT, Reading, England.

Hitschmann, E. (1913), Paranoia, Homosexualität und Analerotik. *Internationale Zeitschrift f. ärztliche Psychoanalyse,* 1:251-254.

500   REFERENCES

Hoche, A. (1909), *Handbuch der gerichtlichen Psychiatrie*. 2te Auflage. Berlin: Hirschwald.

Hoppe (1899), Die Zahl der Aerzte in den preussischen Provinzial-Irrenanstalten. *PW*, 1:250-251.

_____ (1900), Die Zahl der Aerzte an den öffentlichen Anstalten des Deutschen Reiches. *PW*, 1:436-438.

Hösel (1912), Über das neue Irrenfürsorgegesetz und die Neuordnung des Irrenwesens im Königreich Sachsen vom Jahre 1912. *AZP*, 69:369-688.

Hufeland, C. W. (1793), *Bemerkungen uber die natürlichen und geimpften Blattern*, zu Weimar, im Jahr 1778. 2te Auflage. Leipzig: Göschen.

_____ (1796), *Makrobiotik, oder die Kunst das menschliche Leben zu verlängern*. Stuttgart: Hippokrates, 1958.

_____ (1797), *The Art of Prolonging Life* (2 vols.). London: Bell.

_____ (1836), *Guter Rath an Mütter über die wichtigsten Punkte der physischen Erziehung der Kinder in den ersten Jahren nebst einem Unterrichte für junge Eheleute die Vorsorge für Ungeborene betreffend*. Basel und Leipzig: Rottmann; Wien: Gerold.

Ilberg, G. (1899), [Review of] Schultze (1899). *PW*, 1:43-44.

_____ (1894-5), Ueber halluzinatorischen Wahnsinn (Kraepelin). *AZP*, 51:835-836.

_____ (1914), Obituary of Guido Weber, 1837-1914. *AZP*, 71:800-802.

_____ (1926), Von der Gründung der Irrenanstalt Sonnenstein im Jahre 1811 und der Behandlung der Seelenkranken daselbst vor 100 Jahren. *AZP*, 84:237-267.

Index Medicus (1880), *Current Medical Literature of the World* (compiled under the supervision of J. S. Billings & R. Fletcher). New York: Index Medicus Publications Office. Index-Catalogue of the Library of the Surgeon General's Office of the U.S. Army (1st and 2nd Series). Washington, DC.

Infeld (1905), Review of D. P. Schreber (1903). *Wiener Medizinische Presse*, #34, p. 1660.

Ireland, W. W. (1874), Review of Flechsig's presentation at the Psychiatrisches Verein in Leipzig (reported in *AZP*, vol. 30). *J. Mental Science*, 20:128, 1875.

Israëls, H. (1981), *Schreber: Father and Son*. Doctoral Dissertation. Trans. H. S. Lake. Amsterdam: privately published.

_____ (1988), The new Schreber texts. In D. B. Allison, et al., eds. (1988).

_____ (1989), *Schreber: Father and Son*. New York: International Universities Press.

Jacobi, M. P. (1897), Considerations on Flechsig's "Gehirn und Seele." *J. Nerv. and Ment. Dis.*, 24:747-768.

Jacoby, G. W. (1912), *Suggestion and Psychotherapy*. New York: Scribners.

Jacoby, R. (1983), *The Repression of Psychoanalysis* (New York: Basic Books.

James, W. (1902), *The Varieties of Religious Experiences*. New York: Penguin Books, 1987.

_____ (1904), Introduction to Fechner, G. T. *The Little Book of Life after Death*. Boston: Little & Brown, 1905.

Jaspers, K. (1913), *Allgemeine Psychopathologie*. Heidelberg: Springer, 1973.

Jelliffe, E. S. (1913), A summary of the origins, transformations, and present-day trends of the paranoia concept. *Medical Record*, 83:599–605.

Jetter, D. (1966), *Geschichte des Hospitals. Band I Westdeutschland von den Anfängen bis 1850*. Wiesbaden: Steiner.

Johnston, T. B. & Whillis, J., eds. (1950), *Gray's Anatomy*. 30th ed. London: Longmans, Green.

Jolly, F., J. W. Ritter von Jauregg, L. Mellis & Guido Weber (1904), Der Geisteszustand der Prinzessin Luise von Koburg. *PNW*, 6:257–259; 277–278.

Jones, E. (1955), *The Life and Work of Sigmund Freud*, vol. 2. New York: Basic Books.

Jung, C. G. (1902a), *Zur Psychologie und Pathologie sogenannter okkulter Phänomene. Eine psychiatrische Studie*. Leipzig: Mutze.

───── (1902b) *On the psychology and pathology of so-called occult phenomena. Collected Works*, London: Routledge & Kegan Paul, 1957, 1:3–88.

───── (1907), *The Psychology of Dementia Praecox*, trans. F. Peterson & A. A. Brill. New York: Journal of Nervous and Mental Disease Publishing Co., 1909.

───── (1912), Wandlungen und Symbole der Libido. *JPPF*, 4:162–464.

───── (1913), The theory of psychoanalysis. *Psychoanal. Rev.*, 1:1–40.

───── (1915), On psychological understanding. In: *The Psychogenesis of Mental Illness*, Bollingen Series 20. New York: Pantheon, 1960.

───── (1952), *The Answer to Job*. New York: Meridian Books, 1967.

───── (1961), *Memories, Dreams, Reflections*. Ed. A. Jaffé. New York: Vintage Books, 1973.

Jung, R. (1989), Interview on August 19, 1989 in Kühren.

Kaarsch-Haack, F. (1911), *Das gleichgeschlechtliche Leben der Naturvölker*. München: Reinhardt.

Kant, I. (1764), *Versuch über die Krankheiten des Kopfes*. Berlin: Cassirer, 1922.

───── (1766), *Träume eines Geistersehers, erläutert durch Träume der Metaphysik*. Stuttgart: Reclam, 1976.

───── (1779–1782), *Lectures on Ethics*, translated by Louis Infeld, New York: Harper & Row, 1963.

───── (1798a), *Von der Macht des Gemüths durch den blossen Vorsatz seiner krankhaften Gefühle Meister zu sein*. Herausgegeben und mit Bemerkungen versehen von C. W. Hufeland. Sechste verbesserte Auflage. Leipzig: Geibel, 1852.

───── (1798b), The Classification of Mental Disorders. Trans. & ed. C. T. Sullivan. Doylestown, PA: Doylestown Foundation, 1964.

───── (1800), *Anthropology from a Pragmatic Point of View*. Trans. V. L. Dowdell, Carbondale, IL: Southern Illinois University Press, 1978.

Kanzer, M. & Glenn, J., eds. (1980), *Freud and His Patients*. NY: Aronson.

Katan, M. (1949), Schreber's delusion of the end of the world. In Niederland (1974), pp. 121–125.

───── (1950), Schreber's hallucinations about the "little men." *Internat. J. Psycho-Anal.*, 31:32–35.

───── (1952), Further remarks about Schreber's hallucinations. *Int. J. Psycho-Anal.*, 33:429–432.

───── (1953), Schreber's prepsychotic phase. *Internat. J. Psycho-Anal.*, 34:43–51.

_____ (1954), The importance of the non-psychotic part of the personality in schizophrenia. *Int. J. Psycho-Anal.*, 35:119-128.

_____ (1959a), Schreber's hereafter: Its building-up (*Aufbau*) and its downfall. *The Psychoanalytic Study of the Child*, 14:314-382. New York: International Universities Press.

_____ (1959b), Introduction to discussion of Freud's article on Schreber; Freud's Article on Schreber (D. Silverman, reporter). *Bull. Phila. Assn. Psychoanal.*, 9:102-103, 112-113.

_____ (1975), Childhood memories as contents of schizophrenic hallucinations and delusions. *The Psychoanalytic Study of the Child*, 30:357-374. New Haven: Yale University Press.

Kean, E. (1986), Paranoia and cataclysmic narratives. In: *Narrative Psychology*, ed. T.R. Sarbin. New York: Praeger, 1986, pp. 174-190.

Kemple, T. M. (1990), *Schreber on Trial*. Unpublished manuscript.

Kendler, K. S. & Spitzer, R. L. (1885), A reevaluation of Schreber's Case (Letter to the Editor). *Amer. J. Psych.*, 142:1121-1122. (Source: Han Israëls).

Kesting, J. (1987), *Die Krankheitslehre des Psychiaters J. C. A. Heinroth (1773-1843) und deren Bedeutung für die Formierung der Psychiatrie als medizinischer Disciplin in Deutschland*. Medical dissertation, Leipzig. (Source: Stingelin.)

Kilian, G. W. & Uibe, P. (1958), Daniel Gottlob Moritz Schreber. *Forschungen und Fortschritte*, 32:335-340.

Kirchhoff, T. (1924), *Deutsche Irrenärzte*. (2 vols.). Berlin: Springer.

Kitay, P. M. (1963), Freud's theory of paranoia. *Internat. J. Psycho.-Anal.*, 44:191-194; 222-223.

Kittler, F. (1984), Flechsig/Schreber/Freud Ein Nachrichtennetzwerk der Jahrhundertwende. *Der Wunderblock*, Nr. 11/12: 56-68.

Klatt, E., Roy, D., Klatt, G. & Messinger, H. (1983), *Langenscheidt's Standard German Dictionary*. New York: Langenscheidt.

Klein, M. (1946), Notes on some schizoid mechanisms. *Internat. J. Psycho-Anal.*, 27:99-110.

_____ (1921-1945), *Contributions to Psycho-Analysis*. London: Hogarth Press, 1948.

Klein, R. H. (1976a), A computer analysis of the Schreber Memoirs. *J. Ment. Nerv. Dis.*, 162:373-384.

_____ (1976b), A reply to comments on "A computer analysis of the Schreber Memoirs." *J. Ment. Nerv. Dis.*, 162:394-400.

Klein, H. R. & Horwitz, W. A. (1949), Psychosexual factors in the paranoid phenomena. *Amer. J. Psychiat.*, 105:697-701.

Kleine, H. O. (1942), *Ärzte kämpfen für Deutschland*. Stuttgart: Hippokrates Verlag Marquardt.

Kleuker, J. F. (1776), *Zend-Avesta. Zoroasters legendiges Wort worin die Lehren und Meinungen dieses Gesetzgebers von Gott, Welt, Natur, Menschen, etc*. Riga: Hartknoch.

Kloss, M. (1860), *Hantel-Büchlein fur Zimmerturner. Ein Beitrag zur praktischen Gesundheitspflege*. Zweite Auflage. Leipzig: Weber.

_____ (1861), *Das Turnen im Spiel oder lustige Bewegungen fur muntere Knaben*.

Eine Auswahl der einfachsten Jugend- und Turnspiele zur geistigen und körperlichen Erholung des jüngeren Alters. Als Festgeschenk und als Beitrag zu einer naturgemässen Jugenderziehung bearbeitet. Dresden: Schonfeld.

———— (1862), Dr. med. D.G.M. Schreber, geb. den 15. Oktober 1808, + den 10 November 1861. *NJT*, 8:10-16.

———— (1873), *Anleitung zur Ertheilung des Turn-unterrichtes. Zunächst für die Elementarschulen des Königreichs Sachsen.* Zweite vemehrte and verbesserte Aufl. Dresden: Schönfeld (Werner).

———— (1887), *Katechismus der Turnkunst.* Leipzig: Weber.

———— (1889), *Die Weibliche Turnkunst.*

Kneschke, E. H. (1898), *Neues Allgemeines Deutsches Adels-Lexicon.* Leipzig: Voigt, 8:335.

Knight, R. P. (1940), The relationship of latent homosexuality to the mechanism of paranoid delusions. *Bull. Menn. Clin.*, 4:149-159.

Koch, C.F. (1830), *Die Gymnastik aus dem Gesichtspuncte der Dietätik und Psychologie, nebst einer Nachricht von der gymnastischer Anstalt zu Magdeburg.* Magdeburg: Creuss.

Koehler, K. G. (1981), The Schreber case and affective illness: A research diagnostic reassessment. *Psychol. Med.*, 11:689-696.

Kohn, R. (1881), Ueber Coupirung von "Anfällen" chronisch Geisteskranker durch Chinin-Injectionen und Bromkali. *AP*, 11:636-648.

Kohut, H. (1971), *The Analysis of the Self.* New York: International Universities Press.

Kolle, K. (1931), *Die Primäre Verrücktheit.* Leipzig: Thieme.

———— (1956), *Grosse Nervenärzte.* Stuttgart: Thieme.

Kraepelin, E. (1893), *Psychiatrie. Ein kurzes Lehrbuch für Studirende und Aerzte.* Leipzig: A. Barth (the fourth edition of the *Textbook*).

———— (1896), *Psychiatrie. Ein Lehrbuch für Studirende und Aerzte* (5th ed.). Leipzig: A. Barth.

———— (1899), *Psychiatrie.* Sixth ed. Leipzig: Barth.

———— (1913), *Psychiatrie.* Volume 3, part 2. 8th edition. Leipzig: Barth.

———— (1856-1926), *Memoirs.* Ed. H. Hippius, G. Peters & D. Ploog, trans. C. Wooding-Deane. Berlin: Springer, 1987.

Krafft-Ebing, R. (1889), Ueber Neurosen und Psychosen durch sexuelle Abstinenz. *Jahrbucher für Psychiatrie*, 8:1-6.

———— (1893), *Psychopathia Sexualis, with Especial Reference to Contrary Sexual Instinct: A Medico-Legal Study* (7th ed), trans. C. G. Chaddock. Philadelphia: Davis.

———— (1939), *Psychopathia sexualis. A medico-forensic study* (12th ed.). New York: Pioneer, 1950.

Krankenwärter und Dienstleute bei der Anstalt Sonnenstein (1874-1909), Files #16887 and #16888, Ministry of the Interior, Staatsarchiv Dresden.

Kraus, K. (1904), Irrenhaus österreich. *Die Fackel*, October issue. Trans. as "The Case of Louise von Coburg," in Szasz (1973).

Krauss, Friedrich (1852), *Nothschrei eines Magnetisch-Vergifteten; Thatbestand, erklärt durch ungeschminkte Beschreibung des 36jährigen Hergangs, belegt mit allen*

Beweisen und Zeugnissen. Zur Belehrung und Warnung besonders für Familienväter und Geschäftsleute. Stuttgart: Im Selbstverlag des Herausgebers.

_____ (1867), *Nothgedrungene Fortsetzung meines Nothschrei gegen meine Vergiftung mit Concentrirtem Lebensäther und grüundliche Erklärung der maskirten Einwirkungsweise desselben auf Geist und Körper zum Scheinleben.* Stuttgart: Im Selbstverlag des Herausgebers.

Krayatsch (1899), Ein Beitrag zum Geschlechtsleben Geisteskranker in der Irrenanstalten. *PW*, 1:145–146.

Kretschmar, Fr. (1891), *Die Unvollkommenheit der heutigen Psychiatrie und die Mangelhaftigkeit der deutschen Irrengesetzgebung mit Entwurf einer neuen Irrenprocessordnung.* Ein Wort an Laien, Aerzte und Juristen. Leipzig: Rudolf Uhlig.

Kreuser, (1899), Anstaltsartefakte. *PW*, 1:50–52.

Kron, H. (1903), Review of D. P. Schreber (1903). *Deutsche Medizinal-Zeitung*, 24:918.

Krüll, M. (1977), Adolf Hitler—Daniel Paul Schreber: zwei familiendynamische Studien im Vergleich. *Familiendynamik*, 2:229–242.

Krumbiegel, F. W. (1893), *Gesund in's Irrenhaus! Prozesse des Kohlenexpediteur F. W. Krumbiegel in Zwickau i. S.* Ein Beitrag zur Beleuchtung der sächsischen Gerichtspflege. Im Selbstverlage des Verfassers. Zwickau: Trognitz.

Krüner, E. (n.d.), *Aufruf!* Erfurt: "Der Thüringer."

_____ (1897), *Moderne Folterkammern. Ein Volksbuch zur Aufklärung über preussichdeutsche Justiz und neue empörende Enthüllungen zur Irrenfrage von dem acht Jahre unschuldig geistig verurteilten und in Irrenanstalten eingekerkert gewesenen Kaufmann Ewald Krüner aus Haspe i. Westphalen.* Zürich: Schmidt.

L. (1888), Review of Flechsig (1888). *AZP*, 45:265–269.

Lacan, J. (1958), On a question preliminary to any possible treatment of psychosis. In: *Écrits*, New York: Norton, 1977.

Ladd, G. T. (1897), *Elements of Physiological Psychology,* New York: Scribner's.

Laffal, J. (1976), Schreber's Memoirs and content analysis. *J. Nerv. Ment. Dis.*, 162:385–390.

Lamm, M.(1915), *Swedenborg. Eine Studie über seine Entwicklung zum Mystiker und Geisterseher.* Aus dem Schwedischen von Ilse Meyer-Lüne. Leipzig: Meiner, 1922.

Lazarus (1867), Ueber eine eigenthümliche Form von Hallucinationen. *AP*, 1:208–209.

Lehmann (1906), Dr. Pierson. *PNW*, 22, 8:202.

Lehmann, R. (1909), Paranoia—Affekt—Verfogungswahn—Grössenwahn. *PNW*, 11:321–323.

Leibnitz, L. et al. (1977), Von Paul Flechsig zum P.-F.-Institut für Hirnforschung. Die Entwicklung der Hirnforschung an der Karl-Marx-Universität. *Psychiat. Neurol. med. Psychol. Leipzig*, 29:231–239.

Leipzig Communalgarde (1843), Bestandliste der Communalgarde zu Leipzig vom 2. April 1843.

Lewis, D. (1862), *The New Gymnastics for Men, Women and Children: With a Translation of Prof. Kloss's Dumb-Bell Instructor and Prof. Schreber's Pangymnastikon.* Boston: Ticknor & Fields.

_____ (1883), *The New Gymnastics for Men, Women, and Children* (19th ed.).

New York: Clarke Brothers (25th ed., New York: Fowler & Wells, 1891).

Liebreich, O. (1896-1900), *Encyklopaedie der Therapie*. Heraugegeben von O. L. Berlin: A. Hirschwald.

Lindner, G. A. (1884), *Encyclopädisches Handbuch der Erziehungskunde mit besonderer Berücksichtigung des Volksschulwesens*. 2. u. 3. unver. Aufl. Wien: A. Pichler's Witwe & Sohn.

Linke (1896), Zum Brombehandlung der Epilepsie. *AZP*, 52:753-771.

Lion, sen. Dr. (1863), Die Hygiene der Schule. *Deutsche Klinik (Beilage, Monatsbl. med. Statist. öff. Gesundheitspflege)*, pp. 9-12, 17-23.

Lipton, A. A. (1984), Was the "nervous illness" of Schreber a case of affective disorder? *Amer. J. Psychiat.*, 141:1236-1239. (Source: H. Israëls.)

Lochner, Dr. (1891), Irren-Heil- und Pflegeanstalt Thonberg (Für Privatkranke), In: Festschift, see Mittenzwey (1891).

Lombroso, C. (1887), *Genie und Irrsinn*. German trans. A. Courth. Leipzig: Reclam.

Lomer, Georg (1906), Psychopathische Züge bei Irrenärzten. *PNW*, 8:179-181.

Lothane, Z. (1981), A perspective on Freud and psychoanalysis. *Psychoanal. Rev.*, 68:348-361.

———— (1982a), The psychology of hallucinations—a methodological analysis. *Br. J. Med. Psychol.*, 55: 333-348.

———— (1982b), Dialogues are for dyads. *Issues in Contemp. Ego Psychol.*, 5:19-24.

———— (1883), Reality, dream, and trauma. *Contemp. Psychoanal.*, 19: 423-443.

———— (1987a), Love, seduction, and trauma. *Psychoanal. Rev.*, 74: 83-105.

———— (1987b), The primacy of love: love ethics versus hermeneutics. *Academy Forum*, 31:3-4.

———— (1989a), Schreber, Freud, Flechsig and Weber Revisited: an inquiry into methods of interpretation. *Psychoanal. Rev.*, 76:203-262.

———— (1989b), Vindicating Schreber's father: neither sadist nor child abuser. *J. Psychohistory*, 16:263-385.

———— (1989c), Schreber, Freud e Flechsig rivisitati. Un'inchiesta sui metodi d'interpretazione. *La Cifra*, 3:201-205.

———— (1991a), Review of the D.P. Schreber's *Memoirs* and of Allison, Prado de Oliveira, Roberts, and Weiss (1988). *Psychoanal. Books*, 2:52-58.

———— (1991b), Review of Han Israëls' *Schreber father and son*. *Psychoanal. Books*, 2:466-481.

Lückerath, M (1901), Chloradhydratvergiftung. *PNW*, 3:339-342.

Lutz, R. (1895), *Enthüllungen aus dem Bereiche des Irrenwesens und der Rechtspflege*. Stuttgart: Selbstverlag.

Macalpine, I. and Hunter, R. A., trans. & eds. (1955), *Memoirs of My Nervous Illness*. London: Dawson. (Reissued by Harvard University Press, 1988.)

———— (1956), *Schizophrenia, 1677*. London: Dawson.

Maeder, A. (1910), Psychologische Untersuchungen an Dementia praecox-Kranken. *JPPF*, 2:185-245.

Mangner, Eduard (1876), Dr. D.G.M. Schreber, ein Kämpfer fur Volkerziehung (Abdruck von der "Cornelia"). Leipzig: Selbstverlag des Verfassers.

_____ (1884), *Spielplätze und Erziehungsvereine*. Praktische Winke zur Forde-rung harmonischer Jungenderziehung nach dem Vorbilde der Leipziger Schrebervereine. Mit dem Porträt Dr. Schrebers. Leipzig: Fleischer.

_____ (1889?), *Ueber die Bedeutung der Jugendspiele und ihre Einführung an Mittel-und Volksschulen*. No. 138 der Sammlung gemeinnütziger Vorträge. Prag: Deutscher Verein zur Verbreitung gemeinnütziger Kentnisse.

Mannoni, Maud (1970), *La Psychiatrie, son "Fou" et la Psychanalyse*. Paris: Éditions du Seuil.

Mannoni, Octave (1974), Président Schreber, Professeur Flechsig. *Temps Modernes*, 30:624-641.

_____ (1978), Schreber als Schreiber. In: *Clefs pour l'Imaginaire ou l'Autre Scène*. Paris: Éditions du Seuil.

Marie, P.-L. (1929), Paul Flechsig (1847-1929). *Presse Médicale*, 4 December 1929, p. 1584.

Marozza, M. I. (1986), Esperienza delirante ed esperienza intepretativa. Rif-flessioni sul caso Schreber. *Giornale Storico di Psicologia Dinamica*, 10:105-120.

M. A. S. (1884), Review of Flechsig's *Plan of the Human Brain*. *Amer. J. Neurol. Psychiat.*, 3:1-8. (Reprint, New York: Strittner, Lambert.)

Masson, J. M. (1982), Schreber and Freud. Unpublished manuscript.

_____ , trans. & ed. (1985), *The Complete Letters of Sigmund Freud to Wilhelm Fliess 1887-1904*. Cambridge: Bellknap Press of Harvard University Press.

_____ (1988), *A Dark Science. Women, Sexuality and Psychiatry in the Nineteenth Century*. New York: Farrar, Straus & Giroux.

McCawley, A. (1971), Paranoia and homosexuality: Schreber reconsidered. *NY State J. Med.*, June 15, 1971, pp. 1506-1513.

McGuire, W., ed. (1974), *Freud-Jung Letters*. Princeton, NJ: Princeton University Press.

McHenry, L.C. (1969), *Garrison's History of Neurology*. Springfield, IL: Thomas.

Meijer, M. & Rijnders, G. (n.d.), *Schreber een stuk over de waanwereld van een 19de. eeuwse rechter*. Theater program and notes. Amsterdam: Fact.

Meng, H. (1934), *Strafen und Erziehen*. Bern: Huber.

Menninger, Karl A. and Menninger, J. L. (1942), *Love AgainstHhate*. New York: Harcourt & Brace.

Meyer, Adolf (1913), The treatment of paranoic and paranoid states. In: *Modern Treatment of Nervous and Mental Diseases*, ed. W. A. White and S. E. Jelliffe. Philadelphia: Lea & Febiger, pp. 614-661.

Meyer, Alfred (1971), *Historical Aspects of Cerebral Anatomy*. Oxford: Oxford University Press.

_____ (1981), Paul Flechsig's system of myelogenetic cortical localization in the light of recent research in neuroanatomy and neurophysiology, *Can. J. Neurol. Sci.*, 8:1-6; 95-104.

Meynert, T. (1890), *Klinische Vorlesungen über Psychiatrie auf wissenschaftlichen Grundlagen für Studierende und Aerzte, Juristen und Psychologen*. Wien: Brau-müller.

Miller, A. (1986), *Thou Shalt Not Be Aware*. New York: New American Library.

Mittenzwey, L. (n.d.), *Die Pflege des Bewegungsspieles*. Leipzig: Strauch.

_____ (1891) Die Schrebervereine. In: *Die Stadt Leipzig in hygienischer Beziehung*. Festschrift f. die Theilnehmer der XVII. Versamlung des Deutschen Vereins f. öffentliche Gesundheitspflege. Leipzig: Duncker & Humblot.

Möbius, P. J. (1899), Psychiatrie und Litteraturgeschichte. *PW*, 1:17-19.

_____ (1903), Review of D. P. Schreber (1903). *SJIAGM*, 279:105.

_____ (1906), *Ueber Robert Schumann's Krankheit*. Halle: Marhold.

Monroe, P. (1918), *A Cyclopedia of Education*, Vol. 3. New York: Macmillan.

Moser, F. (1935), *Der Okkultismus. Täuschungen und Tatsachen*. München: Reinhardt.

Müller, H. (1908), Gehalt und Anstellungsbedingungen der Ärzte in den Irrenanstalten. *PNW*, 9:405-413.

Muret-Sanders (1897), *Enzyklopädisches Deutsch-Englisches Wörterbuch*. Berlin: Langenscheidt.

Mutze, O. (n.d.), *Prospektus* aller in meinem Verlage erschienenen Werke über Psychismus, Magnetismus, Hypnotismus, Statupolismus, modernen Spiritualismus und Spiritismus, sowie verwandte Fächer. (Source: L. Ikelaar.)

Myers, F. W. H. (1903), *Human Personality and Its Survival of Bodily Death*. London: Logman's, Green, 1939.

Näcke, P. (1900), Inwieweit ist bei Geisteskranken die Fähigkeit der freien Selbstbestimmung bei der Wahl des Aufenthaltortes erhalten? *PW*, 2:381-385.

_____ (1906), Wahnidee und Irrthum. *PNW*, 7:433-436, 444-446.

_____ (1911), Homosexualität und Psychose. *AZP*, 68:295-311.

_____ (1913-1914).Obituary. *PNW*, 15:307-312.

Nemiah, J. (1961), *Foundations of Psychopathology*. New York: Oxford University Press.

_____ (1976), Parsing Schreber: Reflections on Dr. Klein's "Schreber Memoirs." *J. Nerv. Ment. Dis.*, 162:391-392.

Neumann, A. C. (1852a), *Kurze Darstellung des Wesens der Schwedischen Heilgymnastik und ihrer Anwendung in den meisten chronischen Krankheiten, namentlich in Brust- und Unterleibsleiden*. Fur gebildete Nichtärzte. Leipzig: Foerstner.

_____ (1852b), *Die Heilgymnastik, oder die Kunst der Leibesübung* [sic] *angewandt zur Heilung von Krankheiten*, . . . Ein Bericht nach einer auf Kosten des Preussischen Staats und im Auftrage des Herrn Ministers der Medicinal-Angelegenheiten nach Stockholm, London und St. Petersburg unternommenen Reise, Berlin.(2te Aufl.: *Therapie der chronischen Krankheiten u.s.w.*, Leipzig: Foerstner, 1857.

_____ (1855), *Das Muskelleben der Menschen in Beziehung auf Heilgymanstik und Turnen*. Berlin: Schroeder.

_____ (1856), *Lehrbuch der Leibesübungen des Menschen* . . . Berlin: Schroeder.

_____ (1859a), *Haus-Gymnastik. Eine Anwendung durch diätetische, täglich anzustellende, in jeder Stube leicht ausführbare Gliederbewegungen und Athmungsübungen sich bis in's Alter an Leib und Seele gesund zu erhalten, und von vielen Krankheiten zu heilen*. Leipzig: Amelang.

_____ (1859b), *Die Athmungskunst des Menschen*, Leipzig: Volckmar.

Neupert, R. (1904), Das Wahnproblem. *PNW*, 6:299-302.

Niederland, W. G. (1951), Three notes on the Schreber case. *Psychoanal. Quart.*, 20:579-591.

_____ (1959a), Schreber: father and son. *Psychoanal. Quart.*, 28:151-169.

_____ (1959b), The 'miracled-up' world of Schreber's childhood. *Psychoanal. Study of the Child*, 14:383-413. New York: IUP.

_____ (1960), Schreber's father. *J. Amer. Psychoanal. Assn.*, 8:492-499.

_____ (1963), Further data and memorabilia pertaining to the Schreber case. *Internat. J. Psycho-Anal.*, 44:201-207.

_____ (1968), Schreber and Flechsig: a further contribution to the 'kernel of truth' in Schreber's delusional system. *J. Am. Psychoanal.. Assn.*, 16:740-748.

_____ (1969), Interviews with Fridoline Schreber-Hammer. Niederland Papers, now owned by the author.

_____ (1970), A note on research in psychoanalysis. *Bull. N. J. Psychoanal. Soc.*, 2:1.

_____ (1972), The Schreber case: sixty years later. *Internat. J. Psychiatry*, 10:79-84.

_____ (1974), *The Schreber Case: Psychoanalytic Profile of a Paranoid Personality*. New York: Quadrangle.

_____ (1984), *The Schreber Case. Psychoanalytic Profile of a Paranoid Personality. An Expanded Edition*. Hillsdale, NJ: The Analytic Press.

Nordau, M. (1895), *Degeneration* (translation of 2nd ed.). New York: Appleton. (First edition: *Entartung*, Berlin: Duncker, 1892-1893.)

Nothnagel, H. & Rossbach, M. J. (1894), *Handbuch der Arzneimittellehre*. Siebente Auflage. Berlin: Hirschwald.

Nydes, J. (1963), Schreber, parricide, and paranoid-masochism. *Internat. J. Psycho-Anal.*, 44:208-212.

Ohlah, G. (1900), Die Ueberbrückung zwischen dem Leben und der Irrenanstalt. *PW*, 2:205-208.

Ophuisen, J. H. W. van (1920), On the origins of the feelings of persecution. *Internat. J. Psycho-Anal.*, 1:235-239.

Ostow, M. (1989), Discussion of presentation of Z. Lothane's "The Schreber Case Revisited," at the New York Freudian Society meeting of February 3, 1989.

Ostwald, P. (1985), *Schumann: Inner Voices of a Musical Genius*. Boston: Northeastern University Press.

Otto, A. (1875), Ueber Bromkalium als Mittel gegen Epilepsie. *AP*, 5:24-59.

Ovesey, L. (1969), Pseudohomosexualty, the paranoid mechanism, and paranoia: an adaptational revision of a classical Freudian theory. In: *Homosexuality and Pseudohomosexuality*. New York: Science House.

Paasch, C. (1891), *Offener Brief an Se. Excellenz den Herrn Reichskanzler von Caprivi*. Leipzig: Minde.

_____ (1892a), *Auf Deutsche! Zum Kampf gegen das Judentum! Ein patriotischer Aufruf für sämmtliche Deutsche vom Fürst bis zum geringsten Arbeiter*. Leipzig: Minde.

_____ (1892b), *Geheimrath Professor Dr. Rudolph Virchow aus Schivelbein. Unser grosser Gelahrter. Eine psychologische Skizze.* Leipzig: Minde.

——— (1895), *An die deutschen Antisemiten! Flugblatt gegen den Abg. Liebermann von Sonnenberg.* Zürich: Schabelitz.

Pagel, J. (1898), *Einführung in die Geschichte der Medizin.* 2te Auflage, Berlin: Karger.

——— (1901), *Biographisches Lexikon hervorragender Ärzte des neunzehnten Jarhhunderts.* Berlin, Wien: Urban & Schwarzenberg.

Parvy, J. D. C. (1929), *The Zoroastrian Doctrine of a Future Life from Death to the Individual Judgment* (2d ed.). New York: Columbia University Press.

Paulsen, F. (1892), *Introduction to Philosophy* (2d American ed.), trans. F. Thilly (preface by William James). New York: Holt, 1907.

Payne, C. R. (1913), Some Freudian contributions to the paranoia problem. *Psychoanal. Rev.,* 1:76-93, 187-202, 308-321, 445-451; 2:93-101, 200-202.

Peiper, Albrecht (1957), *Chronik der Kinderheilkunde.* Leipzig: Thieme, 1966.

Pelman, [C. W.] (1903), Review of D. P. Schreber (1903). *AZP,* 60:657-659.

——— (1904), Review of D. P. Schreber (1903). *Literaturbeilage der DMW,* 30:563.

Perceval, J. T. (1838-1840), *A Narrative of the Treatment Experienced by a Gentleman, During a State of Mental Derangement; Designed to Explain the Causes and the Nature of Insanity, and to Expose the Injudicious Conduct Pursued Towards Many Unfortunate Sufferers Under That Calamity.* Ed. by G. Bateson as *Perceval's Narrative.* New York: Morrow, 1974.

Pestalozzi, J. H. (1807), *Über Körperbildung; als Einleitung auf den Versuch einer Elementar-Gymnastik in einer Reihenfolge körperlichen Übungen.*

Peters, U. H. (1989), Biographie und Psychose. Eine Neuinterpretation des Falles Martha Schmieder. In *Biographie und Krankheit,* ed. W. Blankenburg. Stuttgart: Thieme, pp. 101-134.

——— (1990). Presentation at the panel "The Schreber Case—New Insights," chair and discussant Z. Lothane, at the 34th Annual Meeting of the American Academy of Psychoanalysis, New York City, May 12.

Pfausler, Dr. (1902), Einiges über die Befangenheit der Anstaltärzte als gerichtliche Sachverständige. *PNW,* 4:341-347.

Pfeifer, R. A. (1929), Obituary of Paul Flechsig. *AZP,* , 91:505-506.

——— (1930), Nekrolog Paul Flechsig. *SANP,* 26:258-262. (Source: G. Busse.)

Pfeiffer R. (1904), Review of D. P. Schreber (1903). *DZN,* 27:352-353.

Pfister, O. (1910a), Analytische Untersuchungen über die Psychologie des Hasses und der Versöhnung. *JPPF,* 2:134-178.

——— (1910b), *Die Frömmigkeit des Grafen Ludwig von Zinzendorf. Schriften zur angewandten Seelenkunde #8.* Vienna: Internationaler Psychoanalytischer Verlag.

Phillips, J. H. (1962), *Psychoanalyse und Symbolik.* Bern: Huber.

Pierson, R. H. (1878), *Kompendium der Electrotherapie.* 2te Aufl. Leipzig: Abel.

——— (1880), Die Lage des Sehcentrums nach den neusten Experimente von Ferrier mitgetheilt von R. H. P. *CNP,* 3:393-395.

——— (1882), *Compendium der Electrotherapie.* III Auflage. Leipzig: Abel.

——— (1883), Ueber Polyneuritis acuta. Volckmann's Sammlung Klinischer

Vortrage #229. *CNP*, 6:269.

_____ (1886), Zur Therapie des Hydrops articulorum intermittens. *CNP*, 9:129-131.

_____ (1893a), *Compendium der Electrotherapie.* 6te Auflage, bearbeitet von Dr. Sperling, Leipzig: Abel.

_____ (1893b), *Bericht über die Privat-Heilanstalt für Gemüths- und Nervenkranke in Pirna (jetzt Lindenhof bei Coswig in Sachsen für die Jahre 1884-1891.* Dresden.

_____ (1894-1895), *Über die Beziehungen zwischen Lues und Dementia paralytica. Bericht über die Privatheilanstalt für Gemüths- und Nervenkranke in Pirna, jetzt Lindenhof by Coswig.* Dresden. *AZP*, 51:200.

_____ (1896), *Lindenhof, Heilanstalt für Gemüths- und Nervenkranke Lindenhof.* Leipzig. *AZP*, 54:188.

_____ (1898), Ueber gewisse Formen von Schwachsinn und ihre forensische Bedeutung. *AZP*, 55:188-189.

_____ (1903), Ueber Entmündigung wegen Geistesschwäche. Read at the 8th Meeting of the Middle-German Psychiatrists and Neurologists. *AP*, 37:1052; also reported in *PNW*, 4(1902):385 and *MPN*, 13(1903):156.

Pletsch, C. (1979), A note on the adaptation of the psychoanalytic method to the study of historical personalities: psychoanalysts on Schreber. *Psychohistory Review*, 8:46-50.

_____ (1990), Presentation at the panel "The Schreber Case—New Insights," chair/discussant Z. Lothane, at the 34th Annual Meeting of the American Academy of Psychoanalysis, New York, May 12.

Podvoll, E. M. (1979-1980), Psychosis and the mystic path. *Psychoanal. Rev.*, 66:571-590.

Politzer, L. M. (1862), Obituary of D. G. M. Schreber. *JKPE*, Beilage, 5:1-7.

Pollitz, P. (1897), Kritische Betrachtungen über die Opium-Brombehandlung der Epilepsie. *AZP*, 53:377-392.

Porter, R. (1987), *A Social History of Madness.* NY: Weidenfeld & Nicholson.

Prado de Oliveira, E., ed. (1979a), *Le Cas Schreber.* Paris: Presses Universitaires de France.

_____ (1979b), Introduction à l'invention de Schreber. In: E. Prado de Oliveira, ed. *Le Cas Schreber*, Paris: Presses Universitaires de France, 1979.

_____ (1981), La libération des hommes ou la création de la pathogenèse. *Cahiers Confrontation, # 6*, Aubier Flammarion.

_____ (1986-1989), Freud et Schreber, Lectures, Ratures. *Coq Héron*, #99(1986):53-76; #101(1987):25-29, 73-82; #111/112:99-107.

Prel, Baron Carl du (1889a), Es giebt ein transcendentales Subjekt. *Psychische Studien*, 16:7-13; 55-61; 120-126; 174-179.

_____ (1889b), Mystik im Irrsinn. *Psych. Stud.*, 16:313-321; 366-371; 414-419; 462-467; 508-514; 553-560 (also 1886 in the science section of the *Wiener Allgemeine Zeitung* for 1886).

_____ (1890), Was sind Anhungen? *Psych. Stud.* 17:201-208; 257-261; 305-310.

_____ (1892), *Das Rätsel des Menschen.* Einleitung in das Studium der Geheimwissenschaften. Leipzig: Reclam.

_____ (1893), Gibt es Warnungsträume? *Psych. Stud.*, 20:242-250; 299-306;

346-354; 396-405; 438-448; 488-496.

Protokolle der Sozialdemokratischen Arbeiterpartei (1971). Reprint edition of the Verhadlungen des Allgemeinen Deutschen sozial-demokratischen Arbeiterkongresses zu Eisenach am 7, 8 und 9 August 1869; Coburg, 1874; Gotha, 1875, 1877). Glasshütten: D. Auvermann KG, Bonn: Neue Gesellschaft Gmbh.

Quensel, F. (1929), Paul Flechsig. *DZN*, 110:161-165.

R. (1905), [Review of] D. P. Schreber (1903). *Wiener Med. Wochenschrift*, #2, p. 105.

Rabbas (1896), Zur Epilepsiebehandlung nach Flechsig. *AZP*, 52:796-805.

Racamier, P.-C., & Chasseguet-Smirgel, J. (1966), La révision du cas Schreber: revue. *RFP*, 30:3-26.

Rajka, T. (1971), Az orvos szemelyisege es a koros folyamat kibontakozasa a "Schreber-eset"-ben. *Orvosi Hetilap*, 112:1143-1148.

Ramón y Cajal, S. (1901-1917), *Recollections of My Life*. Cambridge, MA: M.I.T. Press, 1966.

Ranney, A. L. (1881), *The Applied Anatomy of the Nervous System*. New York: Appleton.

Rapaport, D. (1951), *Organization and Pathology of Thought*. New York: Columbia University Press.

Rein, W. (1895), *Encyklopädisches Handbuch der Pädagogik*, vol. 3. Langensalza: Beyer 1895.

Reinartz, H. (1894). *Geschichte einer Entmündigung. Rückblicke auf den Prozess Feldmann-Hemmerling*. Düsseldorf: Schmitz & Olbertz.

_____ (1895), *Zur Reform des Irrenrechts*. Barmen.

Revesz, B. (1914), *Geschichte des Seelenbegriffes und der Seelenlokalisation*. Stuttgart: Enke, 1917. Reprinted by Bonset, Amsterdam, 1966.

Richter, G. (1925), *Das Buch der Schreberjugendpflege*. Leipzig (later edition of the same in 1930). Leipzig.

_____ (1939), *Geschichte des ältesten Schrebervereins 1864-1939*. Festschrift zum 75jahrigen Bestehen des Kleingärtnervereins Dr. Schreber Leipzig C1 (früher Schreberverein der Westvorstadt). Leipzig.

Richter, H. E. (1845), *Die schwedische nationale und medicinische Gymnastik*. Dresden und Leipzig.

_____ (1850), Gymnastische Kuren. In: *Organon der physiologischen Therapie*. Leipzig.

Rickman, J. (1926-1927), A survey: The development of the psychoanalytic theory of the psychoses. 1894-1926. In: J. Rickman, *Selected Contributions to Psychoanalysis*. New York: Basic Books, 1957.

Riklin, F. (1905), Ueber Versetzungsbesserungen. *PNW*, 7:153-158; 165-170; 179-182.

_____ (1907), Über Gefängnispsychosen. *PNW*, 9:269ff.

Ritter, Alfons (1936), *Schreber, das Bildungsystem eines Arztes*. Inaugural-Dissertation. Erlangen: Friedrich-Alexander-Universität.

Rittershaus, E. (1927), *Die Irrengesetzgebung in Deutschland nebst einer vergleichenden Darstellung des Irrenwesens in Europa*. Berlin u. Leipzig: de Gruyter.

Rodig, J. A. (1895), *Ein Fall Forbes in Sachsen oder Wie Jemand nach und nach wahnsinnig werden kann. Erlebnisse des J. A. Rodig in Leipzig-Lindenau.* Chemnitz: Hager.

_____ (1897), *Rechtlos im Rechtsstaate oder irrsinning erklären ist keine Hexerei. Eine getreue Darstellung rechtmässiger Ungerechtigkeiten und Irrtümer dargestellt von deren Opfer J. A. R.* München und Leipzig: Schupp.

Rosenbaum, J. (1845), *Geschichte der Lustseuche im Althertume, nebst ausfürhlichen Untersuchungen über den Venus- und Phalluscultus.* Halle: Sippert und Schmidt. Trans. *The Plague of Lust*, Frederick Publications, 1955.

Rosenfeld, H. (1949), Remarks on the relation of male homosexuality to paranoia, paranoid anxiety and narcissism. *Internat. J. Psycho-Anal.*, 30:36-47. (Also in: *Psychotic States*, ed. H. Rosenfeld. New York: International Universities Press, 1966.)

Rothstein, H. (1847), *Die Heilgymnastik* (3. Abschnitt der *Gymnastik nach dem Ling'schen Systeme*). Berlin.

Sachse, G. (1955), Paul Flechsig. Unpublished. Inaugural-Dissertation, Karl Sudhoff Institut, Leipzig. (Sources: G. Busse, Dr. Ingrid Kästner.)

Sadger, I. (1897), Das Wunder vom denkenden Eiweis. *Deutsche Revue*, 22/2:93-110.

Sänger, K. (1963), *Zur Geschichte der Psychiatrie und Neurologie an der Leipziger Universität.* Inaugural-Dissertation. Karl Marx Universität Leipzig, unpublished typescript.

Sass, L. A. (1987), Schreber's panopticism: psychosis and the modern soul. *Soc. Res.*, 54:101-147.

Scharfstein, B. (1973), *Mystical Experience.* Oxford: Blackwell.

Schatzman, M. (1971), Paranoia or persecution: the case of Schreber. *Fam. Process*, 10:177-207.

_____ (1973), *Soul Murder: Persecution in the Family.* New York: New American Library, Signet, 1974.

Scheinert, J. (1845-1846), *Erziehung des Volkes.* Königsberg: Vornträger.

Schildbach, C. H. (1848). *De Partu Facie Praeversa.* Lipsiae: E. Stangii.

_____ (1859), [Review of] Doctor Neumann's *Haus-Gymnastik. NJT*, 5:135-138.

_____ (1861), *Bericht über die gymnastisch-orthopädische Heilanstalt der DD. Schreber und Schildbach zu Leipzig*, Zeitzer Str. 43. Leipzig: Hinrichs.

_____ (1862a), Schreber [obituary]. *Deutsche Turn-Zeitung*, 7:4-6.

_____ (1862b), Nachtrag zu Schreber's Nekrolog von Dr. S. *NJT*, 8:16-18.

_____ (1862c), *Beobachtungen und Betrachtungen bei der Skoliose.* Amsterdam.

_____ (1865), Bericht über neuere Heilgymnastik und Orthopädie. *SJIAGM*, 127:113-127; 232-276; 327-349.

_____ (1872a), *Die Schulbankfrage und die Kunze'sche Schulbank.* Leipzig: Weber.

_____ (1872b), *Die Skoliose: Anleitung zu Beurtheilung und Behandlung der Ruckgrathsverkrümmungen.* Leipzig: Veit.

_____ (1877), *Orthopädische Klinik. Mittheilungen aus der Praxis der gymnastisch-orthopadischen Heilanstalt zu Leipzig.* Leipzig: Veit.

_____ (1880), *Kinderstubengymnastik.* Leipzig.

_____ (1886), Die Behandlung der Skoliose im elterlichen Hause. *JKPE*, 25:351-356.

Schiller, F. (1982), *A Möbius Strip/Fin-de-Siècle Neuropsychiatry and Paul Möbius*. Berkeley: University of California Press.

Schilling, K. (1950), Dr. Schreber und der Schrebergarten. *Kleingärtner Jahrbuch*, Hamburg: Konsumgenossenschaft Produktion, Christen and Co., pp. 33-39. (Source: W. G. Niederland.)

———— (1960), Letters to Dr. Niederland of March 6, May 4, September 27, October 30, 1960. Niederland Collection, Manuscript Division, Library of Congress, Washington, DC.

———— (1964), Dr. D. G. M. Schreber und wir: Ein Leben für die Jugend und ein offenes Wort an alle. *Der Fachberater für das deutsche Kleingartenwesen*, Juni 1964, 1-23. (Source: Dr. U. H. Peters.)

Schmid, K. A. (1881-1887), *Encyklopädie des gesammten Erziehungs- und Unterrichtswesens bearbeitet von einer Anzahl Schulmänner und Gelehrten*. Gotha: Besser, Leipzig: Fues.

———— (1883-1885), *Pädagogisches Handbuch für Schule und Haus. Auf Grundlage der Encyklopädie des gesammten Erziehungs- und Unterrichtswesens, vornehmlich fur die Volks-, Bürger-, Mittel- und Fortbildungsschulen*. 2te unveränderte Stereotyp Aufl. Leipzig: Fues.

Schmidt, K. v. & C. E. Schulze, (1891), *Allgemeine Deutsche Biographie*, 32:464-465, D. G. M. Schreber; J. C. D. Schreber, 32: 465-466. Leipzig: Duncker & Humblot.

———— (1896), *Allgemein Deutsche Biographie*, 40:435-440 (1896). C. J. S. von Wächter. Leipzig: Duncker & Humblot.

Schnidbauer, W. & Kemper, J. (1986), *Ein ewiges Rätsel will ich bleiben mir und anderen. Wie krank war Ludwig II. wirklich?* Munchen: Bertelsmann.

Scholz, Fr. (1896), *Ueber Reform der Irrenpflege*. Leipzig: Meyer.

Schreber, Daniel Gottfried (1764), *Rede von den Schäden und Nachtheilen die als Folge der vernachlässigten economischen Wissenschaften auf Universitäten anzusehen sind*. In: *Neue Sammlung verschiedener in die Cameralwissenschaften einschlagender Abhandlungen und Urkunden und auch andrer Nachrichten*. 8 Theile. Bützow und Wismar, 1762-1765.

Schreber, Danielis Gottlobus Mauritius [Daniel Gottlob Moritz] (1833a), *De tartari stibiati in inflammationibus organorum respirationis effectu atque usu*. Lipsiae: ex. off. G. Naumanni.

———— (1833b), Autobiographical note. In: E. H. Weber, *Annotationes anatomicae et physiologicae*. Prolegomenon XX, Lipsiae.

———— (1839), *Das Buch der Gesundheit: Eine Orthobiotik nach den Gesetzen der Natur und dem Baue des menschlichen Organismus*. Leipzig: Volckmar.

———— (1840), *Die Normalgaben der Arztneimittel. Zum Gebrauche für praktische Ärzte und Kliniker übersichtlich dargestellt*. Leipzig: Volckmar.

———— (1842), *Die Kaltwasser-Heilmethode in ihren Grenzen und ihrem wahren Werthe*. Leipzig: Hermann.

———— (1843), *Das Turnen vom ärztlichen Standpunkte aus, zugleich als eine Staatsangelegenheit dargestellt*. Leipzig: Mayer & Wigand.

———— (1846), *Die Verhütung der Rückgrathsverkrümmungen oder des Schiefwuchses: Ein wohlgemeinter Rath an Aeltern, Lehrer und Erzieher*. Leipzig: Reclam.

———— (1852a), *Kinesiatrik oder die gymnastische Heilmethode. Für Ärzte und gebildete Nichtärzte nach eigenen Erfahrungen dargestellt.* Mit 210 Abbildungen. Leipzig: Fleischer.

_____ (1852b), *Die Eigenthümlichkeiten des kindlichen Organismus im gesunden und kranken Zustande. Eine Propedäutik der speciellen Kinderheilkunde.* Leipzig: Fleischer.

_____ (1853), *Die schädlichen Körperhaltungen und Gewohnheiten der Kinder nebst Angabe der Mittel dagegen: Für Aeltern und Erzieher.* Leipzig: Fleischer. (Copy supplied by Busse).

_____ (1855a), *Ärztliche Zimmergymnastik oder Darstellung und Anwendung der unmittelbaren—d.h. ohne Geräth und Beistand, mithin stets und überall auszuführbaren—heilgymnastischen Bewegungen für jedes Alter und Geschlecht und für die verschiedenen speciellen Gebrauchszwecke als ein einfach natürliches System entworfen.* Leipzig: Fleischer.

_____ (1855b), [Review of] E. Friedrich (1855). *NJT*, 1:85–90.

_____ (1855c), Ueber Heilgymnastik im Allgemeinen. *NJT*, 1:105–111.

_____ (1855d), [Review of] Bock (1855). *NJT*, 1:171–172.

_____ (1855e), [Review of] Neumann (1855). *NJT*, 1:289–292.

_____ (1855f), Wahres und Falsches bei der Radicalcur der Unterleibsbrüche auf gymnastischem Wege, *NJT*, 1:334–337.

_____ (1856a), *Illustrated Medical In-door Gymnastics, or a System of Medico-Hygienic Exercises Requiring No Mechanical or Other Aid, and Adapted to Both Sexes and All Ages, and for Special Cases.* Trans. H. Skelton. London: Williams & Norgate.

_____ (1856b), [Review of] *Erster Jahresbericht des Instituts für Orthopädie und Heilgymnastik zu Bonn. NJT*, 2:249–250.

_____ (1857), Ueber den gesundheitlichen und pädagogischen Werth des Schlittschuhlaufens und Stelzengehens. *NJT*, 3:285–286.

_____ (1858a), *Kallipädie oder Erziehung zur Schönheit durch naturgetreue und gleichmässige Förderung normaler Körperbildung, lebenstüchtiger Gesundheit und geistiger Veredlung und insbesondere durch möglichste Benutzung specieller Erziehungsmittel: für Aeltern, Erzieher und Lehrer.* Leipzig: Fleischer. (Copy supplied by Israëls.)

_____ (1858b), *Ein ärztlicher Blick auf das Schulwesen in der Absicht: zu heilen, und nicht: zu verletzen.* Leipzig: Fleischer.

_____ (1858c), Ueber Anwendung der Sonnebäder zu Heilzwecken, insbesondere gegen gewisse chronische Krankheiten des kindlichen Alters. *JKPE*, 1:169–171.

_____ (1858d), Die Turnanstalt als Schule der Männlichkeit. *NJT*, 4:169–170.

_____ (1859a), *Anthropos. Der Wunderbau des menschlichen Organismus, sein Leben und seine Gesundheitsgesetze. Ein allgemein fassliches Gesammtbild der menschlichen Natur für Lehrer, Schüler, sowie für Jedermann, der nach gründlicher Bildung und körperlich geistiger Gesundheit strebt.* Leipzig: Fleischer.

_____ (1859b), Supplement zum "*Anthropos*" (1859a). Entwickelungsleben des menschlichen Organismus, pp. 139–150.

_____ (1859c), *Die planmässige Schärfung der Sinnesorgane als eine Grundlage und leicht zu erfüllende Aufgabe der Erziehung, besonders der Schulbildung.* Leipzig: Fleischer.

_____ (1860a), Die Jugendspiele in ihrer gesundheitlichen und pädagogischen Bedeutung und die Nothwendigkeit ihrer Beachtung von Seite der Schulerziehung. *JKPE*, 3:247-254. (Source: Israëls.)

_____ (1860b), *Ueber Volkserziehung und zeitgemässe Entwickelung derselben durch Hebung des Lehrerstandes u. durch Annäherung von Schule u. Haus. Eine dringende Lebensfrage der Culturstaaten.* Leipzig: Fleischer.

_____ (1861a), *Das Buch der Gesundheit oder die Lebenskunst nach der Einrichtung und den Gesetzen der menschlichen Natur.* Leipzig: Fries.

_____ (1861b), *Glückseligkeitslehre fur das physische Leben des Menschen. Ein diätetischer Führer durch das Leben. Von Ph. Karl Hartmann.* Vierte Auflage, gänzlich umgearbeitet von Moritz Schreber. Leipzig: Geibel.

_____ (1861c), *Der Hausfreund als Erzieher und Führer zu Familienglück, Volksgesundheit und Menschenveredlung für Väter und Mütter des deutschen Volks.* Leipzig: Fleischer.

_____ (1861d), An ein Hohes Staatsministerium des Cultus und Erziehungswesens. Leipzig: January, 1861. (Source: Miss Renate Jung.)

_____ (1862), *Das Pangymnastikon oder das ganze Turnsystem an einem einzigen Geräthe ohne Raumerforderniss als einfaches Mittel zur Entwickelung höchster und allseitiger Muskelkraft, Körperdurchbildung und Lebenstüchtigkeit: Für Schulanstalten, Haus-Turner und Turnvereine.* Leipzig: Fleischer.

_____ (1882), *Das Buch der Erziehung am Leib und Seele.* 2. ed. Leipzig: Fleischer.

_____ (1885), *Die Wasser-Heilmethode in ihren Grenzen und ihrem wahren Werthe.* Nach des Summe der bis jetzt gelieferten Resultate wissenschaftlich-praktisch geprüft. 2te Aufl. umgearbeitet und herausgegeben von Gustav Voigt. Leipzig.

_____ (1889), *Ärztliche Zimmergymnastik oder System der ohne Gerät und Beistand überall ausführbaren heilgymnastischen Freiübungen als Mittel der Gesundheit und Lebenstüchtigkeit für beide Geschlechter und jedes Alter entworfen von Dr. med. D.G.M. Schreber.* Dreiundzwanzigste Auflage durchgesehen und ergänzt von Dr. med. Rudolf Graefe. Leipzig: Fleischer.

_____ (1891), *Das Buch der Erziehung an Leib und Seele. Fur Eltern, Erzieher and Lehrer.* Dritte, stark vermehrte Auflage. Durchgearbeitet und mit Rücksicht auf die Erfahrung der neueren Kinderheilkunde erweitert von Dr. Carl Hennig. Leipzig: Fries.

_____ (1899), *Medical Indoor Gymnastics or a System of Hygienic Exercises for Home Use to Be Practised Anywhere Without Apparatus or Assistance by Young and Old of Either Sex for the Preservation of Health and General Activity* (rev. & suppl. R. Graefe), trans. from 26th ed. by H. A. Day. London: Williams & Norgate (Leipzig: Fleischer, New York: Stechert).

_____ (n.d.), *Hilfsbuch zum verbesserten tragbaren Turnapparat nach System Dr. D.G.M. Schreber.* Leipzig.

Schreber, D. G. M. & Neumann, A. C. (1858), *Streitfragen der deutschen und schwedischen Heilgymnastik: Erörtert in Form myologischer Briefe.* Leipzig: Felix.

Schreber, D. P. (1888), Mein lieben Sabchen am zehnjährigen Hochzeitstage 6ten Februar 1888 gewidmet von ihrem Paul. In: Busse, 1990, pp. 334-335.

_____ (1889), *The 26th of July 1889* ("Poem for the Silver Wedding Anniversary of his Sister Anna"). In: Israëls, 1988b.

———— (1893), Court decisions. Files of the Saxon Justizministerium. Court cases of 14, 21, 24 and 28 of October and 4, 11, and 14 November of 1893.

———— (1903), *Denkwürdigkeiten eines Nervenkranken nebst Nachträge und einem Anhang über die Frage:"Unter welchen Voraussetzungen darf eine für geisteskrank erachtete Person gegen ihren erklärten Willen in eine Heilanstalt festgehalten werden?"* Leipzig: Mutze.

———— (1903), *Mémoires d'un névropathe avec des compléments et un appendice sur la question "A quelles conditions une personne jugée alienée peut-elle être maintenue dans un établissement hospitalier contre sa volonté évidente?"* Trans. P. Duquenne & N. Sels. Paris: Éditions du Seuil, 1975.

———— (1903), *Memoirs of My Nervous Illness*, Trans. & ed. I. Macalpine & R. A. Hunter. London: Dawson, 1955. (Reissued with an introduction by S. M. Weber by Harvard University Press, 1988.)

———— (1904), ("Christening Speech for a Granddaughter of His Sister Anna"). (In: Israëls, 1988b.)

———— (1905), *Zum 29. Juni 1905* ("Poem for His Mother's Ninetieth Birthday"). (In: Israëls, 1988b.)

———— (1907), *Seinem lieben Sabchen zum nenzehntem Juni 1907 gewidmet von Ihrem Paul* ("Poem for the Fiftieth Birthday of His Wife"). (In: Israëls, 1988b.)

Schreber, J. C. D. (1770), *De phasco observationes, quibus genus muscorum vindicatur atque illustratur.* Lipsiae: apud S. L. Crusium.

———— (1782), *Mantissa editioni quartae Materiae medicae B. Eqv. a Linné adiecta.* Erlangae: Symtibus W. Waltheri.

———— (1855), *Die Säugethiere in Abbildungen nach der Natur und mit Beschreibungen. Eine Zusammenstellung der neuesten Entdeckungen auf dem Gebiete der Säugethierkunde, bearb. von Dr. Johann Andreas Wagner.* Leipzig: T. O. Weigel.

Schreber, J. D. (1688), *De Libris obscoeniis, . . .* Lipsiae.

———— (1736), *Lineae Doctrinae Fidei, e.h. Articuli Theologiae theticae, ut ex compendio Hutteriano facilius . . . capiantur, certis justae paediae lineis adumbrati.* Editio novissima. Chemnicii, 1736.

Schreberverein der Nordvorstadt Leipzig (1903), Dr. M. Schreber und die Leipziger Schrebervereine.

Schreiber, E.(1987), *Schreber und der Zeitgeist.* Berlin: Matzke Verlag DiA.

Schröder, P. (1930), Obituary of Paul Flechsig. *Archiv für Psychiatrie u. Nervenkrankheiten,* 91:1-8.

Schroeder, E. A. (1890), *Das Recht im Irrenwesen kritisch, systematisch und kodifiziert. Mit Benützung einer Nachricht über den Gesetzentwurf Leon Gambettas.* Zürich & Leipzig: Füssli.

Schüle (1885), [Review of] Alfred Hegar *Der Zusammenhang der Geschlechtskrankheiten mit Nervösen Leiden,* Stuttgart: Enke. *NC,* 4:112-120.

Schultz-Henke, H. (1952), *Das Problem der Schizophrenie analytische Psychotherapie und Psychose.* Stuttgart: Thieme.

Schultz-Schultzenstein, C. H. (1842), *Über die Verjüngung des menschlichen Lebens und die Mittel und Wege zu ihrer Kultur.* Berlin: Hirschwald.

Schultze, E. (1899), *Die für die gerichtliche Psychiatrie wichtigsten Bestimmungen des Bürgerlichen Gesetzbuches und der Novelle der Civilprocessordnung.* Heft 1 der 3

Bandes der Sammlung zwangloser Abhandlungen aus dem Gebiete der Nerven- und Geisteskrankheiten. Halle: Marhold.

_____ (1901), Entlassungzwang und Ablehnung oder Wiederaufhebung der Entmündigung. *PNW*, 3:219-223, 227-230, 235-245.

Schultze, Ernst (1904), Review of D. P. Schreber (1903). *ZPPS*, 37:469.

Schumann, August (1824), *Vollständiges Staats- Post- und Zeitungs- Lexikon von Sachsen*. Zwickau: Gebrüder Schumann.

Schwarz. G. S. (1973a), May 17, Letter to the editor of the *London Sunday Times*.

_____ (1973b), Devices to prevent masturbation. *Med. Aspects Hum. Sexual.*, May issue, pp. 141-153.

Schwarz, K. M. (1896), *Wie erhalten wir unsere Jugend bei geradem Wuchse und bewahren sie vor den habituellen Verkrümmungen des Rückgrats?* Eine Mahnung an die Eltern, Lehrer u. Erzieher der Jugend überhaupt. Erweiterter Sonder-Abdruck aus der "Zeitschrift für Schulgesdunheitspflege." Hamburg u. Leipzig: Voss.

Searles, H. F. (1965), *Collected Papers on Schizophrenia and Related Subjects*. New York: International Universities Press.

Seiling (1919), *Goethe als Okkultist*. 2te Auf. Berlin: Baum.

Shamdasani, S. (1990), A woman called Frank. *Spring 50*, pp. 26-56, Dallas: Spring Publications.

Shengold, L. (1961). Chekhov and Schreber. *Internat. J. of Psycho-Anal.*, 42:431-438.

_____ (1974), Soul murder: A review. *Internat. J. Psychoanal. Psychother.*, 3:366-373.

_____ (1975), An attempt at soul murder: Rudyard Kipling's early life and work. *The Psychoanalytic Study of the Child*, 30:683-724.

_____ (1989), *Soul Murder The Effects of Childhood Abuse and Deprivation*. New Haven: Yale University Press.

Sherrington, C. (1906), *The Integrative Action of the Nervous System*. Cambridge: Cambridge University Press, 1947.

Shilo, Dr. (1966), Letters of 24 and 27 November to Dr. Niederland, the Niederland Collection, Manuscript Division, Library of Congress Washington, DC.

Shockley, F. M. (1913), The role of homosexuality in the genesis of paranoid conditions. *Psychoanal. Rev.*, 1:431-438.

Shulman, B. H. (1959), An Adlerian view of the Schreber case. *J. Indiv. Psychol.*, 15:180-192.

Siegel, Richard (1909), Interessante Berichte der Töchter Dr. Schrebers über ihren Vater (Zusammenstellung von Richard Siegel, *Freund der Schreberve-reine*, vol. 5, 1909, issue X). Also, typescript, Niederland Collection, Manuscript Division, Library of Congress, Washington, DC.

Siever, L. & Davis, K. L. (1985), Overview toward a dysregulation hypothesis of depression. *Am. J. Psychiat.*, 142:1017-1031.

Skurnik, N. & Bourguignon, A. (1980), Histoire, pedagogie et psychiatrie en Saxe au XIXe siècle. *Annales Méd.-Psychol.*, 138:1-17.

Specht, F. & Schwalbe, P. (1904), *Die Reichstagwahlen von 1867-1903*. 2te

Auflage. Berlin: Heymans Verlag (typescript extracts). (Source: Niederland.)

Spielrein, S. (1911), Über den psychologischen Inhalt eines Falles von Schizophrenie (Dementia praecox). *JPPF*, 3:329-400.

Spiess, A. (1840a), *Die Lehre der Turnkunst.* Basel: Schweighauser.

_____ (1840b), *Das Turnen in den Freiübungen für beide Geschlechter.* Basel: Schweighauser.

_____ (1842), *Gedanken über die Einordnung des Turnwesens in das Ganze der Volkserziehung.* Basel: Schweighauser.

Spitzer, R. L., Skodol, E. A., Gibbon, M. & Williams, J. B. W. (1981), *DSM-III Case Book.* Washington: American Psychiatric Association.

Sponholz (1867), Ueber Bromkalium. Sitzung 28. Mai 1867, Berliner medicinisch-psychologische Gesellschaft. *AP*, 1:209.

Sprenger, J. & Krämer, H. (1487?), *Malleus Maleficarum.* Trans. as *Witches Hammer* by Rev. Montague Summers, 1928.

Stärcke, A. (1919), The reversal of the libido-sign in delusions of persecution. *Internat. J. Psycho-Anal.*, 1:231-234 (1920).

Stegmann (1899), Review of Tatzel: Die hypnotische Suggestion und ihre Heilwirkungen. Leipzig: J. A. Barth, 1899. *PW*, 1:227-228.

_____ (1902), Ein ungewöhnlicher Fall von hysterischen Dämmerzustand. *AZP*, 59:777-778.

_____ (1903), Ueber suggestivbehandlung von Trinkern. *MPN*, 13:156.

_____ (1904), Casuistischer Beitrag zur Behandlung von Neurosen mittelst der kathartischen Methode (nach Freud). *AP* 39:945-946. Also in: *CNP*, 27:770-771; *PNW*, 6:370-371; *DMW*, 30:1832.

_____ (1905), Behandlung der Neurosen nach der katartischen Methode (nach Freud). *MPN*, 17:84.

_____ (1908), Die Ursachen der Trunksucht. *Die Alkoholfrage*, 5:1-8.

_____ (1912), Einiges über Hysterie vom Standpunkt der Lehren S. Freuds. *MMW*, 2 Januar, 59:48-49.

Steiger, E. (n.d.). *Catalog*: Pädagogik, New York.

Stekel, W. (1912), *Nervöse Angstzustände und ihre Behandlung.* Vorwort von Siegmund (sic) Freud [1908]. 2te Aufl. Berlin, Wien: Urban & Schwarzenberg.

_____ (1923), *The Phenomena of Fetishism in Relation to Sex.* New York: Liveright, 1940. Vol. 2, p. 312.

Stephany, Albert von (1848), *Gymnastisches Merkbüchlein.* Wien: Gerold.

Stern, F. (1977), *Gold and Iron: Bismarck, Bleichröder and the Building of the German Empire.* New York: Knopf.

Stingelin, M. (1989a), Die Seele als Funktion des Körpers/ Zur Seelenpolitik der Leipziger Universitätspsychiatrie unter Paul Emil Flechsig. In: Kittler, F.A, M. Schneider and S. Weber, eds., *Diskursanalysen 2 Institution Universität.* Opladen: Westdeutscher Verlag, GmbH.

_____ (1989b), Paul Emil Flechsig/ Die Berechnung der menschlichen Seele. In: Clair, J., Pichler, C. & Pichler, W. eds., *Wunderblock. Eine Geschichte der modernen Seele.* Wien: Löcker, 1989.

_____ (1989c), Gehirntelegraphie. Die Rede der Paranoia von der Macht der

Medien 1900. In: Kittler, F. A. & Tolen, C., eds., *Arsenale der Seele Literatur- und Medienanalyse seit 1870*. München: Fink.

Strindberg, A. (1887), Psychic murder (Apropos "Rosmersholm"), An essay in *"Vivisektioner"*, English translation in *The Drama Review*, vol.13 #2(142), pp. 113-118, 1968.

Sudhoff, K. (1922), *Kurzes Handbuch der Geschichte der Medizin*. Dritte und vierte Auflage, J. L. Pagel (1898). Berlin: Karger.

Swales, P. J. (1982), Freud, Fliess, and fratricide: The role of Fliess in Freud's conception of paranoia. New York: privately published. In: L. Sperling, ed., *Sigmund Freud: Critical Assessments*, Vol. 1, London: Routledge, 1989.

Szasz, T. (1963), *Law, Liberty, and Psychiatry: An Inquiry into the Social Uses of Mental Health Practices*. New York: Macmillan.

_____ (1970), *Ideology and Insanity*, New York: Anchor Books.

_____ Ed. (1973), *The Age of Madness*. New York: Aronson, 1974.

_____ (1976), *Schizophrenia The Sacred Symbol of Psychiatry*. Syracuse, NY: Syracuse University Press.

_____ (1976), *Anti-Freud. Karl Kraus's Criticism of Psychoanalysis and Psychiatry*. Syracuse, NY: Syracuse University Press, 1990.

(Tabouret-Keller, A.) (1973), Une étude: la remarquable famille Schreber. *Scilicet*, #4, pp. 287-321.

Tausk, V. (1919), "On the Origin of the 'Influencing Machine' in Schizophrenia." In: R. Fliess, ed., *The Psychoanalytic Reader*, New York: International Universities Press, 1948.

Teslaar, J. S. van (1912), Review of Freud, 1911a. *Amer. J. Psychol.*, 23:115-122.

This, B. (1973-1974), La race Schreberienne ou Scilicet: "du meurtre d'âme." *Le Coq-Héron*, #37/38, 40, 41/42.

Thom, A. (1987), Carl Wigand Maximilian Jacobi (1775-1858) und der Formierungsprozess der medizinischen Betreuung psychisch Kranker in Deutschland. *Beiträge zur Hochschul- und Wissenschaftsgeschichte Erfurts*, 21:149-159.

Tiling, T. (1902), Zur Paranoiafrage. *PW*, 3:431-435, 442-445.

Trall, R. T. (1857), *The Illustrated Family Gymnasium; Containing the Most Improved Methods of Applying Gymnastic, Calisthenic, Kinesipathic and Vocal Exercises to the Development of the Bodily Organs, the Invigoration of Their Functions, the Preservation of Health, and the Cure of Diseases and Deformities*. New York: Fowler & Wells.

Traugott, J. (1850), *Das Turnen Geisteskranker im Allgemeinen und insonderheit in der kön. sächs. Heil- und Verpflegungsanstalt Sonnenstein bei Pirna*. 2te Aufl. Leipzig.

Treher, W. (1966), *Hitler, Steiner, Schreber*. Oknos Broschüre.

Trenckmann, U. (1982), Der Leipziger Beitrag zur Entwicklung theoretischen Denkens in der Psychiatrie. *Wiss. Z. KMU Leipzig, Math.-Nat. Reihe*, 31:115-130. (Source: Busse and Prof. Thom.)

Turnbull, G. H. (1926), *The Educational Theory of J. G. Fichte*. The University Press of Liverpool Limited/ London: Hodder and Stoughton Ltd.

Ueberweg, F. (1951), *Grundriss der Geschichte der Philsophie*. Basel: Schwabe.

Uhle, M., & Trenckmann, U. (1982), Zur Entwicklung der Betreuungspraxis psychisch Kranker durch die Leipziger Universitätspsychiatrie.*Wiss. Z. KMU Leipzig, Math.-Nat. Reihe*, 31:92-114.

Uhle, P. (1893), (Hrsg.) *Festschrift zum 750 Jubiläum der Stadt Chemnitz*. Im Auftrage des Vereins für Chemnitzer Geschichte. Chemnitz: Commissionsverlag von O. May (E. Röder).

Uibe, P. (1959), Schreber als Orthopäde. *Hippokrates*, 30:216-218.

Umgestaltung(en) der Landesirrenanstalten *und des Aufnahmeverfahrens in sämmtlichen Landespflegeanstalten (Vorarbeiten zum Regulativ)* (1883-1893). Files #16807 & #16808, Ministry of the Interior, Staatsarchiv Dresden.

Unterbringungs-Regulativ für die Heil- und Pflegeanstalten (1897-1902). File #16809, Ministry of the Interior, Staatsarchiv Dresden.

Valentin, B. (1961), *Geschichte der Orthopädie*. Stuttgart: Thieme.

Verdiglione, A. (1976), La drogue du Président. In: *La Psychanalyse, Cette Aventure Qui Est la Mienne*. Paris: Union Générale d'Éditions, 1979.

_____ (1980), Quell'autore dei dramme di Shakespeare. In: *La Paranoia, l'Antropologismo*. Milano: Spirali.

Verwaltung des Landgerichts Chemnitz (1881), File #1493, Ministry of Justice, Dresden State Archives.

Vogel, August (1877), *Geschichte der Pädagogik als Wissenschaft*. Gütersloh: Bettelsmann.

_____ (1881), *Systematische Encyklopädie der Pädagogik*. Ein Wegweiser durch das gesammte Gebiet der Erziehung mit ausführlichen Angabe der Literatur. Eisenach: Bachmeister.

Voppel (1880), Rückblicke auf 50 Jahre einer Irren Pflegeanstalt. *AZP*, 36:564-596.

Wächter, C. G. von (1835), *Abhandlungen aus dem Strafrechte*. Erster Band. Die Verbrechen der Entführung an der Notzucht, nebst einer Erörterung der s.g. Fleischverbrechen im engeren Sinn. . . . Leipzig: Weidmann.

Waechter, O. von (1881): *Carl Georg von Waechter, Leben eines deutschen Juristen*. Leipzig.

Waelder, R. (1951), The structure of paranoid ideas: A critical study of various theories. *Internat. J. Psycho-Anal.*, 32: 167-177.

Walters, O. S. (1955), A methodological critique of Freud's Schreber analysis. *Psychoanal. Rev.*, 42:321-342.

Watson, M. J. (1864), *Watson's Manual of Calisthenics: a Systematic Drill-Book Without Apparatus, for Schools, Families, and Gymnasiums. With Music to Accompany the Exercises*. New York: Schermerhorn & Bancroft.

Wattenberg (1895-1896), Sollen wir isoliren? *AZP*, 52:928-959.

Webb, J. (1974), *The Occult Underground*. La Salle, IL: Open Court.

_____ (1976), *The Occult Establishment*. La Salle, IL: Open Court.

Weber, Guido (1859), *De haematomate durae matris*. Dissertatio. Lipsiae: Sturm & Koppe (Dennhardt).

_____ (1859-1910), *Personalakte* (personal file), Dresden State Archives.

_____ (1876), Schwangerschafts- und Puerperalpsychosen. *Jahresbericht der Gesellschaft für Natur- und Heilkunde in Dresden*, 131-143. Dresden: Kaufmann.

_____ (1887-1888), Necrolog Dr. Lessing. *AZP*, 44:608-614.

_____ (1893), Report of Weber on Sonnenstein for 1893. In: [review of] *Bericht des Landes-Medicinal-Collegium über das Medicinalwesen im Königreiche Sachsen pro 1893. AZP*, 53(1897):264-266.

_____ (1896), Report of Weber on Sonnenstein for 1895. In: [Review of] *Das Irrenwesen im Königreich Sachsen im Jahre 1895*. Separatabdruck aus dem 27. *Jahresberichte des Landes-Medicinal-Collegium über das Medicinalwesen im Königreiche Sachsen auf das Jahr 1895*. Leipzig. *Der Irrenfreund*, 39:25-26, 1897.

_____ (1897a), Die Voraussetzungen der Entmündigung nach dem 1.u. 2. Entwurf des Bürgerlichen Gesetzbuches f. das Deutsche Reich. *AZP*, 53:590.

_____ (1897b), Entmündigung wegen Trunksucht zwangweise in Trinkerasyl laut Para. 14. *AZP*, 53:591; 597-598.

_____ (1897c), Zur Geschichte des sächsischen Irrenwesens. *AP*, 29:976-978. (Also in *MPN*, 1:497.)

_____ (1898a), Report of October 19, in *Unterbringungs* (1897-1902).

_____ (1898b), Ueber die Bedeutung der Degenerationszeichen. *AZP*, 55:164-165.

_____ (1898c), Diebstahl aus sexuellen Motiven. *AZP*, 55:177.

_____ (1898d), Discussion of Pierson (1898). *AZP*, 55:190-191.

_____ (1899a), Discussion of May 22, 1897 on dementia praecox. *AZP*, 56:445.

_____ (1899b), Historische Einleitung zur Besprechung der verminderten Zurechnungsfähigkeit. *AZP*, 56:445-446.

_____ (1899c), Die Petition um Abänderung des Para. 175 des Strafgesetzbuches. *AZP*, 56:447.

_____ (1899d), Discussant, Jahresversammlung des Vereins der deutschen Irrenärzte in Halle, 21, 22 April, 1899. *PW*, 1:26-28.

_____ (1899e), Ueber die Aufnahme von Bestimmungen u. verminderte Zurechnungsfaehigkeit in's Strafgesetzbuch. *AP*, 31:912-918.

_____ (1900), Ueber ruhrartige Darmerkrankungen in Irrenanstalten. *MPN*, 8:476; also: *CNP*, 23:722-723; *PW*, 2:363.

_____ (1901), Der Hilfsverein für Geisteskranke im Königreich Sachsen, meeting of May 23, 1901. *PNW*, 3:126. Also in: *Der Irrenfreund*, 42:16-24.

_____ (1902a), Über die Frage eines Reichsirrengesetzes. *AZP*, 59:535-542.

_____ (1902b), Zurechnungsfähigkeit für Delikte die im Rausch begangen worden sind. *AZP*, 59:768-774.

_____ (1902c), Krankhafte Lügen der Hysterischen. *AZP*, 59:779.

_____ (1902d), Discussion of "Remarks on the Rüger Case" by Judge Döhn. *AZP*, 59:766-767.

_____ (1903a), Discussion of Pierson (1903). *AP*, 37:1053; also *MPN*, 13:156.

_____ (1903b), Co-Signatory of psychiatric report of Jolly et al. (1903). *PNW*, 6:257-558, 277-278.

_____ (1905a), Ein interessanter Entmündigungsfall. *AZP*, 62:402-406.

_____ (1905b), Discussion of "Die Errichtung von Testamenten seitens Kranker" by Judge Dr. Weltz. *AZP*, 62:210-211.

_____ (1909a), Discussion of Frese's "Über den Fall der Prinzessin Luise von Sachsen-Koburg-Gothageb. Prinzessin von Belgien." *AZP*, 66:884-885.

_____ (1909b), Vosrausetzungen der Pflegschaft. *AZP*, 66:886.

_____ (1910), Die Heil- und Pflegeanstalt Sonnenstein bei Pirna. In: J. Bresler (1910), *Deutsche Heil- und Pflege-Anstalten für Psychischkranke in Wort und Bild*. Halle: Marhold. Reprinted in: *PNW*, 13:127-133, 1911.

_____ (1912), Über Dementia paralytica vom klinischen Standpunkte aus. *AKAK*, 45:304-334.

Weber, L. W. (1905), Chronische Paranoiker in verwaltungs-, straf- und zivilrechtlicher Beziehung. *AZP*, 62:1-30.

Weber, S. M. (1973), Introduction to the 1988 edition of the *Memoirs*. See D. P. Schreber, above.

Webster's (1971), *Third International Dictionary of the English Language*. Springfield, MA: Merriam.

Werner, J. A. L. (1834), *Das Ganze der Gymnastik, oder, Ausführliches Lehrbuch der Leibesübungen nach den Grundsätzen der besseren Erziehung zum öffentlichen und besonderen Unterricht*. Meissen: Goedsche.

_____ (1836), *Zwölf Lebensfragen, oder ist das Glück eines cultivirten und wohlgeordneten Staates allein durch eine geregelte geistige Beziehung zu begründen, oder muss nicht unbedingt auch die physische damit verbunden werden? Zu Beherzigung gestellt und anatomisch-physiologisch beleuchtet für Jeden den das Wohl der künftiger Geschlechter wahrhaft am Herzen liegt*. Dresden und Leipzig: Arnold.

_____ (1837), *Amona, oder, Das sicherste Mittel, den weiblichen Körper für seine naturgemässe Bestimmung zu bilden und zu kräftigen*. Dresden: Arnold.

_____ (1838), *Medicinische Gymnastik oder die Kunst, verunstaltete und von ihren natürlichen Form- und Lageverhältnissen abweichende Theile des menschlichen Körpers nach anatomischen und physiologischen Grundsätzen in die ursprünglichen Richtungen zurückzuführen und darin zu kräftigen, mit 100 Figuren erläutert*. Dresden und Leipzig: Arnold.

_____ (1843), *Die gymnastisch-orthopädische Heilanstalt zu Dessau*. Dessau: Eigenthum des Verfassers.

Wernicke,[C.] (1880), Ueber den wisseschaftlichen Standpunkt in der Psychiatrie. *PMW*, 5:407-410. Also in: *Wiener Medizinische Presse*, vol. 21, 1880.

Westphal, M. (1989), Paranoia and piety: Reflections on the Schreber case. In *Psychoanalysis and Religion*, ed. J. H. Smith and S. A. Handelman. Baltimore: Johns Hopkins University Press, pp. 117-135.

White, R. B. (1961), The mother-conflict in Schreber's psychosis. *Internat. J. Psycho-Anal.*, 42:55-73.

_____ (1963), The Schreber case reconsidered in the light of psychosocial concepts. *Internat. J. Psycho-Anal.*, 44:213-221.

Wienstein, B. (1989), Interview of August 29, 1989 in Hamburg-Volksdorff.

Wilden, A. (1972), Critique of phallocentrism: Daniel Paul Schreber on women's liberation. In: *System and Structure: Essays in Communication and Exchange*. London: Tavistock.

Windscheid, B. (1880), *Carl Georg von Waechter*. Leipzig: Duncker & Humblot.

_____ (1904), Review of D. P. Schreber (1903). *MPN*, 15:399.

Winternitz, D. (1860), Ph. C. Hartmann's Leben und Wirken, *Ausserordentliche Beilage zu Nr. 14 der österr. Zeitschrift für practische Heilkunde*, pp. 1-8,

Wittels, Fritz (1924), *Sigmund Freud: His Personality, His Teaching, & His School*, trans. E. Paul & C. Paul. New York: Dodd & Mead.

_____ (1931), *Freud and His Time*. New York: Liveright.

Zabriskie, B. (n. d.). "The Jungian Analyst" (typescript).

Ziehen, Th. (1894), *Psychiatrie für Ärzte und Studirende*. Leipzig: Hirzel.

Zvonar, R. (1983), *Soul Murder*. Produced during the Theater Festival of New Music by the Berkeley Stage Company, September, 1983.

INDEX

A

Abegg, J.F.H., 420
Abraham, H.C., 366n
Abraham, K., 329, 337, 362n, 363n
Abraxas, 360n
Abuse
  psychiatric, 259, 269, 285, 335–337,
    357, 420
  sexual, 4, 96n, 322, 350; *See also sub*
    Schreber, Paul (fantasies of)
Ackerknecht, E.H. 158, 186n, 189n
Ackermann, E., 191n
Adamkiewicz, A., 247n
Adler, A., 341, 351, 367n, 440
Aggression, 221, 249n; *See also* Rage; *sub*
    Schreber, Moritz; Schreber, Paul
Ahlenstiel, H., 343, 369–370n, 424n
Ahlwardt, H., 102n
Ahriman, 63, 66, 172, 218, 323, 400, 410,
    425n, 460
A.L., 96n
Albert, King of Saxony, 41, 213–214, 276
Allgemeine Zeitschrift für Psychiatrie und ihre
    Grenzgebiete or *Zeitschrift* (*AZP*),
    230, 232, 245n, 257n, 259n, 262,
    271, 274, 277, 289, 301, 302n,
    305n, 307–309n, 315n, 320, 359n,
    372n

Allison, D.B., 356, 371n
Althaus, J.F., 187n
Amentia (Meynert's), 249n, 311n, 330n,
    331, 364–365
American Academy of Psychoanalysis, 98n
American Psychiatric Association, 223,
    228, 346
Amsterdam University, 360n
Anacreon, 110
Anality, 348, 370
Andersson, O., 205, 250n
Anger, 152–153, 160, 368; *See also sub*
    Schreber, Paul; Schreber, Sabine
    Ottilie
Angerstein, E.F., 120, 132, 140n, 144n,
    190n
Anima, 355, 361n, 425n, 427n
Antipsychiatry, 9, 200, 236, 258n,
    260–316, 320, 344, 355, 465
  Reichstag debates on, 222, 230,
    235–236, 257n, 273, 288, 290–291,
    298
Anti-semitism, 100–102n, 235–236, 258n,
    354, 374n
Anxiety, affect of, 29, 160, 217, 249n, 290,
    315n, 395, 422n
  castration, 327, 334, 342, 363n
  depression, 36, 38, 95n, 310n
  hypochondriacal, 43, 239

524

hysteria, 62, 331, 364n
neurosis, 161
See also sub Schreber, Paul
Apollo, 396
Appliances
gymnastic, 141n, 144n, 154
orthopedic, 4, 123–126, 129, 143,
181–182
straight-holder, 125, 179–180, 196n
"torture machines," 178–182, 195–196n,
372n, 383, 444
Archiv für Psychiatrie und Nervenkrankheiten
or *Archiv*, 242–243n, 272–273
Aristophanes, 110
Aristotle, 150, 175, 214, 426n
Arndt, R., 258n, 297, 311
Arnemann, Dr., 320
Arno Press, 258n
Aschaffenburg, G., 320, 362n
Association for Popular Literature, 201
Association of German Alienists, 257n,
271, 289
Association of Middle-German
Psychiatrists and Neurologists,
252–253n, 271–273
Association of Turn Teachers (Berlin), 120,
187n
Asylum, 243n
attendants; See sub Schreber, Paul
city, 205, 234
discharge policies of, 129, 258
inmates of, 128, 221, 236, 264, 268–269,
272, 275, 289, 312n, 314n, 410
private, 271
staff, 35, 195n, 307n; See also sub
Flechsig; Weber, G.
transfers to, 209, 211, 234, 236–237,
268, 270, 278; See also sub Schreber,
Paul
See also Charité Hospital; Dresden
Municipal Hospital; Colditz;
Leipzig-Dösen; Leipzig University
Hospital; Lindenhof; Mariaberg;
Sonneberg Spa; Sonnenstein;
Thonberg; Zschadrass
Athletics (bodily exercises), 107, 113, 118,
119, 154
ban on, 112, 120
debates about in Germany, 120–121,
140–141n
medical precepts of Hufeland, 187

Second All-German Turning Festival
and Jubilee (Berlin), 132, 134
See also Gymnastics
Austria, 22, 40, 202, 206
Austrian-Prussian War, 202
Austro-Hungarian Empire, 123, 310
Autopsy, 55, 132, 146n, 241n, 263, 363n,
482–483
Autoerotism, 367n
Autosuggestion, 395, 426n
Azouri, C., 367n

B

Baginsky, A., 190n
Balsan, C.V., 195n, 372n
Bamberger, L., 101n
Bär, E., 132
Barande, I., 372n
Bardeen, C.W., 145n
Barker, L.F., 244n, 249n
Barnard, H., 191n
Barzun, J., 439
Basedow, J. B., 118, 154, 165, 175
Bauer, E., 101n
Baumeyer, F., 14, 27–29, 39, 40, 44, 68,
85, 88, 94–96n, 98n, 102–104n,
246n, 259n, 275, 299, 344, 350,
353, 371n, 421n, 444, 446,
452–454, 468n, 469–471, 474–478
Bautzen (Saxony), 23, 27, 92, 96n, 97n,
308
Beeck, M. i. d., 108
Beers, C.W., 2
Behandlung, 268, 293, 310n, 314–315n
Behr, Albertine, See Rückel, Albertine
Behr, Heinrich Eucharius, 15, 27–31,
92–93, 99n, 381, 450, 455–456
Behr, Heinrich B. Jr., 28
Behr, Heinrich Eucharius, 28–31
Behr, Ottilie (née Benedix), 30
Behr, Ottilie Sabine, See Schreber, Sabine
Ottilie
Behr, Therese Emilie, 28, 98n
Bekhterev, V.M., 224, 247–248n, 254n
Bell, C., 214
Benedix, O., 30
Benedix, R., 30
Bentham, J., 357
Benvenuto, S., 373n
Berlin Court Opera, 30

Berlin Medical Society, 120
Berlin Teacher Associations, 187n
Berlin TurnerVerein, 120
Berlin University, 256n
Bernfeld, S., 373n
Bestimmungen, 276, 305n, 314n
Bethge, R., 136n, 196n
Beyer, B., 230–233, 235, 257–258,
    288–290, 298–299, 313n, 315n,
    343–344
Beyer, H., 191n
Bianchi, L., 253n
Biedermann, K., 121, 133, 140n
Binswanger, O., 272
Bipolar disorder, 313–314n, 329, 356–357
Bisexuality, 360n, 366n
    biological, 337
Bismarck, O. v., 20, 22, 32–33, 42,
    100–101n, 138n, 235–236, 258n,
    275
Bjerre, P., 343–346
Bleichröder, G. v., 101n, 236, 258n
Blessedness, 194n; *See also sub* Schreber,
    Moritz; Schreber, Paul
Bleuler, E.
    on dementia praecox, 282, 362n
    on hospitalization, 270, 307n
    on paranoia, 313n, 323, 342, 367–368n
    and psychoanalysis, 251n, 271, 346, 362n
    See also sub Schreber, Paul
        (interpretations of)
Bloch, I., 110, 259n
Bloom, W., 297
Blow, S.E., 190–191n
Blum, H., 21
Blum, I., 21
Blum, R., 21
Board of Health Commissioners (Saxony),
    208, 267, 273, 305n
Bock, C.E., 121, 133, 140–141, 142n, 263
Bonin, G. v., 244n
Bornstein, K., 135n
Bourguignon, A., 27, 372n
Brain
    cerebral cortex of, 212, 214–216, 219,
        228–229, 239, 247n, 251n, 255n,
        294, 397
    holistic concept of function, 229, 241n,
        248n, 251n
    lesions, etiology of, 48, 216, 250–251n
    mythology, 58, 72, 205, 213, 282, 312n,
        340, 419, 422n, 461, 464–465
    metabolism, 12n, 272
    organic disease of, 37, 46, 80, 88, 152,
        285–287, 292, 311–312n, 322,
        329–330, 345, 348, 362, 460
    projection/association centers of,
        215–219, 221, 229, 241n, 243n,
        248–249n, 252–253n, 256n
    somatosensory area of, 215, 217, 218,
        220
    trauma, 7, 209, 311n
    writings, 9, 200–202, 204, 206–207,
        209–211, 212–215, 218–219,
        222–224, 228–229, 239–240,
        242–245n, 247n, 249, 251n, 254n,
        259n, 358, 398
    See also sub Flechsig; Freud, S.; Jung,
        C.G.; Mind (localization); Schreber,
        Moritz; Schreber, Paul (fantasies of);
        Weber, G.
Brain Commission, 223, 240
Brandt, von, 235–236, 258n
Bratz, Dr., 246n
Brauchle, A., 136n, 141n
Braun, V., 110
Breger, L., 355
Bregman, L., 374n
Brentano, F., 329
Bresler, J., 257n, 271, 274, 280, 298,
    305–308n, 311–312n
Breuer, J., 322, 361n, 421n
Brichzin, Dr., 316n
Brill, A.A., 11n, 338, 345, 361n, 370n
Broca, P., 214
Brockhaus, F.A., 32, 56, 99, 103n, 135n,
    144n, 190n, 244n
Brodmann, K., 241n, 248n, 252n, 254n
Bromides, 34, 36–38, 44, 48, 212, 226,
    246–247n, 272, 310n, 414, 471
Brosius, Dr., 461
Brouardel, P., 363n, 368n, 388
Bumke, O., 102n, 205, 213, 228, 242n
Bunker, H.A., 242n
Burdach, K.F., 214
Burgerstein, L., 190n
Burghölzli (Zurich), 232, 242n, 307n, 332,
    360n, 362n
Burschenschaft Wartburg (Germania)
    Fraternity, 20–21, 262, 301

Busse, G., 12n, 21, 27, 35, 39–40, 94n,
    96n, 103n, 137n, 204, 240n, 243n,
    247n, 252n, 254n, 256n, 266,
    315–316, 358, 371–372n, 374n,
    427n
Byron, G.G., 138n

C

Calasso, R., 358
Calleberg (Saxony), 263
Cameron, J.L., 441
Cameron, N., 461
Canaletto, A., 304n
Canetti, E., 197n, 353, 373n
Capellmann, C., 257n
Caprivi, L. Graf v., 101n
Carr, A.C., 352
Carus, E.A., 117, 129, 133
Carus Orthopedic Institute, 117, 141n,
    145n; See also Orthopedic Institute
    (Leipzig)
Casati, G., 100–101n
Castration, 246n, 311n, 370n
    See also Emasculation; sub Anxiety;
        Schreber, Paul (unmanning)
Catholics, 32, 87, 100–101n, 137–138n,
    238, 473
Catullus, 110
Causality, 78
Celsus, 119
Centralblatt für Nervenheilkunde und
    Psychiatrie (CNP), 34, 246n,
    251–253
Chabot, C.B., 372n
Chamberlain, H.S., 373n
Charcot, J.M., 206, 247n, 250–251n, 330
Charitable Society for Mental Patients,
    274, 306n, 308n
Charité Hospital (Berlin), 211
Chasseguet-Smirgel, J., 372n
Chazaud, J., 372n
Chemnitz (Saxony), 6, 24, 33, 39, 45, 82,
    100n, 319, 425n, 445
    See also County court; District court
Chemnitzer Tageblatt und Anzeiger, 23,
    32–33, 99n, 102n, 369n
Chernigov (Russia), 114
Chloral hydrate, 34, 45, 47, 49–50, 272,
    470

Clark University, 240
Clarke, E.G., 244n
Clias, B.H., 187n
Coburg (Germany) State Archives, 96n
Coccius, A., 200, 204
Colby, E.M., 187, 244
Colditz Asylum, 76, 104n, 240, 261,
    263–264, 268, 301–303n
Colditz, I., 234, 240
Collingwood, R.G., 5, 438
Cologne (Saxony), 29, 30, 40, 67, 453
Cologne Opera House, 87, 105
Cologne Theater Museum, 98–99
Comenius, J.A., 138n
Communalgarde (Leipzig), 121, 133
Compayre, G., 188n
Compulsion, 139n, 311n
    See also Obsession; sub Schreber, Paul
Confinement, involuntary, 1, 59, 62,
    76–84, 231, 234, 259n, 278, 290,
    314n, 467; See also sub Schreber,
    Paul
Conflict
    homosexual, 345
    of interest, 289, 298, 300, 466
    interpersonal, 195, 300, 441, 444
    intrapsychic, 4, 60–61, 250, 271,
        329–330, 335, 351–352, 365n,
    See also sub Schreber, Paul
Conolly, J., 35, 210, 267, 304n, 466
Conservative Party, 33
Coswig (Saxony), 267; See also Lindenhof
    Asylum
Cotta, C., 119, 141n, 190n
Counteridentification, 130
County court
    Chemnitz, 27, 99n, 276
    Dresden, 70, 72, 76, 93
    Leipzig, 56, 230, 455
    Meissen, 279
    See also District court
Court of Appeals, Dresden
    employer of Paul Schreber, 42, 450, 453,
        468–469
    judgment of on Paul Schreber, 76,
        82–84, 92, 99n, 234, 295, 297–298,
        300, 389, 405
Cramer, A., 280–281, 316n
Credé, C., 200, 204, 263
Cross-dressing, 67, 71, 327, 363n, 452

See also Transvestitism
Croufer, F., 193n, 372n
Cumberland, S.C., 427n
Cyriax, E.F., 125, 143–145n

D

Dahl, R., 279, 309–310n
Dannenberg, Dr., 88
Darkchewitsch, L.O., 241n, 247n
Darwin, C.R., 149, 202, 391, 425n
Das litterarische Leipzig, 21, 314n, 359n,
    422n
Davis, K.L., 432
Daydream, 12n, 13, 58, 75, 394, 436
Daymare, 384
Defense, 43, 249n, 307n, 311n, 322–323,
    330–331
  See also Projection; Repression; Splitting;
    sub Schreber, Paul
Dehio, Dr., 253n
Déjerine, J., 248n
De Jonge, M., 288
Deleuze, G., 372n
Delusions, 361n, 421n
  of grandeur, 249, 342, 364n, 425n
  and incompetency, 276
  of influence, 348, 364, 369–370
  of persecution, 230, 223, 246n, 249n,
    280–286, 310–314n, 322–323n,
    342n, 345, 365, 370–371n, 374n,
    436, 442, 461, 462
  treatment of 159
  See also sub Schreber, Daniel Gustav;
    Schreber, Moritz; Schreber, Paul;
    Sexuality
deMause, L., 185, 357
Dementia praecox, 273, 348, 361
  See also Paranoia; Psychosis; Schizo-
    phrenia; sub Bleuler; Freud, S.; Jung,
    C.G.; Schreber, Paul (diagnoses)
D'Eon, C.G.L.A.A.T., 363n
Depression
  diagnosis of, 139n
  paranoia and, 219, 281–282, 293, 311n,
    314n, 329, 361–364n, 371n
  treatment of, 34, 246n
  See also sub Anxiety, Schreber family;
    Schreber; Daniel Gustav; Schreber,
    Moritz; Schreber, Paul; Schreber,
    Pauline

Deprivation, childhood, 77, 169,
Dessoir, M., 392, 393, 424–425n
Deucalion and Pyrrha, 388
Devil, 12n, 343, 416
  See also Ahriman; Satan; sub Schreber,
    Paul
Devreese, D., 21, 27, 39, 57, 94n, 96n,
    138n, 239, 247n, 291–292,
    356–357n, 373n, 418–420, 444,
    468n
Diaconissen Hospital, 267
Diagnosis
  differential, 344, 348
  forensic, 236–238n, 258n, 273n,
    276–277, 279, 289–290, 293,
    309n
  See also sub Schreber, Paul
Dietetics, 124, 141–143n, 147–149,
    191n; See also Hygiene
Dilthey, W., 330
District court
  Bautzen, 23
  Chemnitz, 26–27, 32, 91–92
  Dresden, 75, 93, 99n
  Freiburg, 92
  See also County court; Court of Appeals
District physician (Germany), 142, 267,
    276, 285
Divorce, 278; See also sub Schreber, Paul
Doctor-patient relationship, 3, 35, 306n,
    417, 440, 454
Donath, J., 247n
Dörner, K., 158, 189n, 304n, 306n, 418,
    467–468n
Dorpat University, 240, 262
Dream
  homosexual, 440
  interpretation, 376, 380–381
  latent content of, 43, 381–382
  manifest content of, 43, 330, 334, 381
  work, 370n
  See also sub Psychology; Schreber,
    Moritz; Schreber, Paul
Dresden courts; See sub County court;
    Court of Appeals; District court
Dresden Hofoper, 105n
Dresden Municipal Hospital for the
    Invalids and the Insane, 234
Dresden Pedagogical Institute, 1139n
Dresden Society for Natural Sciences and
    Naturopathy, 363n

Dresden State Archives, 6, 39, 96, 102n, 305n, 316n
Dresden Surgical-Medical Academy, 140n
Dresden TurnVerein, 140n
Dresdner Nachrichten, 308n
Drives
  aggressive, 440
  compulsive, 311n
  immoral, 303n,
  sexual, 172, 216–221
  unpleasure, 254n
Dt, 97n
Dühring, E., 313n, 425n
Dynamics
  dyadic, 297, 332, 411, 413, 441, 443, 458
  interpersonal, 5, 333, 352

E

Earle, P., 265, 304
Eckler, C., 140n, 190n
Economo, v., 248n
Edinburgh University, 261
Education, history of, 7, 119, 138n, 145n, 147, 164, 178, 190n, 194n
Edwards, A., 355
Efron, I.A., 32, 56, 99, 103, 135n, 144, 190, 244
Ego
  active, 165, 191n
  conscious, 162, 255n
  function, 328, 331, 337, 339, 342–343, 373n
  perception, 356
  split in, 349–350, 394–395
  structure, 180–181, 215, 364–365
  See also sub Psychology; Schreber, Moritz; Schreber, Paul
Ehrenwald, J., 195n
Eigen, M., 355
Eiselen, E.W.B., 120
Eisler, M.J., 371
Eisler, R., 191
Ellenberger, H., 19, 97n, 127, 159, 205, 257n, 400, 467n
Emasculation, 115, 117, 326–327, 337, 355, 363n, 366n, 420
  See also Castration; *sub* Schreber, Paul (unmanning)

Emin Pasha, 101n; *See also* Schnitzer, E., 235, 258n
Emotions
  disorder of, 129, 189n, 212, 221, 281, 435, 219–220, 282, 312–313n, 344, 348, 361n, 364n, 393, 424n; *See also sub* Flechsig
  homosexual, 333, 363n
  paranoia and, 345
  See also Mood; specific emotions
Enervation, 49, 50
Enlightenment, ideals of, 118, 153, 165, 189n, 191n
Eonism, *See* Cross-dressing; Transvestitism
Epilepsy, 128, 153, 209, 211–212, 221, 244, 246–247, 272, 311n
  treatment of, 48, 272
Erasistratos, 214
Erdmann, Prof., 22, 200
Erikson, E.H., 353
Ernst, M., 143n
Ethics, 192n
  educational, 108, 118, 165–166, 464
  psychiatric, 72, 219, 221, 300, 312n, 340, 454, 465–466
  religious, 198n
  sexual, 220, 448
  See also sub Schreber family; Schreber, Moritz; Schreber, Paul
Eudaimonics, 149–150, 152, 154, 187n
Eulenburg, A., 127, 136n, 143–144n, 287
Euler, C., 190n
Evolution, theory of, 202, 391, 405, 422–424n
Examination
  bar, 21, 26, 91
  medical board, 113, 263
  neurologic, 281
  orthopedic, 126, 156
  psychiatric, 69, 227, 234, 278, 285–287, 294, 386
  school, 407
Exhaustion, 31, 50, 153, 161, 210, 217
  See also sub Psychosis

F

Faber, O., 120
Fairbairn, R., 351

Fantasy
  homosexual, 333, 345
  masturbation, 349
  sadomasochistic, 402, 427n
  sexual, 66, 68, 153, 475
  sexual transformation, 326, 328
  wish-fulfillment, 342
  See also sub Schreber, Paul
Father-son dynamics, 362 *See also sub*
    Schreber, Paul
Faust, B.C., 149, 187
Fawcett, D.W., 297
Fechner, G.T., 10–11n, 189n, 256–257n,
    380, 394, 422n
Federn, P., 373n
Feldmann, H., 230–233, 236, 258n, 320,
    463
Fenichel, O., 370n
Ferenczi, S., 106, 324, 337–338, 341–342,
    352, 362n, 367n, 440–441
Feuchtersleben, E. v., 191n
Feuerbach, L., 391, 419–420
Fichte, J.G., 119, 165, 175–176, 189n,
    191–198n, 391, 445
Fichtner, G., 241n, 369n
Finger, Dr., 297
Finkelnburg, C., 231
Fischer, M., 245n
Flechsig, E., 201, 241n
Flechsig, P.E., 9–10, 26, 244n, 249,
    254–255n, 324
  administrative power of, 208, 228, 235
  attendants and, 210, 227, 245n
  on brain anatomy, 199–229, 392,
    396–297, 419, 431, 457, 460 *See also
    sub* Mind (localization)
  character of, 224–229
  citations of in literature, 244n, 249n,
    254–255n
  emotional disorder in, 200, 226
  as forensic expert, 215–219, 221,
    224–237, 258–259n
  hospital administrator, as 13, 31,
    99–103n, 208–209, 304–305n,
    377, 441, 470
  on intellect, 220–221, 223
  at Leipzig University, 200–205,
    223–224, 239–240, 247n, 457,
    464
  life history of, 200–208, 239–240
  marriage of, 224, 240

  on natural/supernatural phenomena, 199,
    217
  presentations at meetings of, 203, 206,
    213, 218, 222–223, 240–241, 244,
    248, 251–254n
  projection and association centers,
    215–219, 221, 229, 241n, 243n,
    248n, 249n, 252–253n, 256n
  psychiatric politics and, 271–272,
    276–278, 285–286, 288, 290–292,
    294, 303, 308n, 310n, 315–317, 463
  on psychological functions, 172–175,
    201, 203, 213–215, 223, 257n, 438;
    See also sub Psychology (medical)
  religious views of, 201, 206, 213
  scientific contributions of, 212–224
  sleeplessness of, 206
  students and, 225–226
  writings of, 202, 206, 212, 214, 223,
    239–240
    dissertation, 202, 239
    Boundaries, 214, 219, 222, 223,
      229–230, 249
    Brain and Soul, 9, 213–215, 218–219,
      223, 240, 242n, 244n, 247n, 249n,
      251n, 358, 398
    Myelogenesis, 200–201, 204, 206–207,
      212–213, 224, 228–229, 240,
      242–243n, 244, 254n
    Physical Basis of Mental Disorders,
      206–207, 239, 242n
    *Report on Psychiatric Hospital of Leipzig
      University*, 207, 209–211, 244–245n,
      259n
    See also sub Schreber, Sabine; Schreber,
      Paul
Fleischer, F., 141n, 318, 359n
Fliess, W., 338, 367n, 446
Flournoy, T., 253n
Fordham, M., 360n
Forel, A., 103n, 204, 210, 225, 228,
    232–233, 242n, 245n, 248n, 255n,
    278, 346, 361
Forensic Psychiatric Association of
    Dresden, 271–273, 277, 290, 294,
    298, 302–303n, 310n, 377
Forensic-Psychiatric Association of
    Göttingen, 316n
Francke, A.H., 138n
Franco-Prussian War, 21, 25–26, 30, 91,
    202, 239, 261

Frank, J.P., 151, 186n, 189n
Franke, A., 21, 96n, 259n, 303n, 363
Franz Augustus II, 138n
Franz Joseph, Emperor, 240n, 310n
Free association, 253n, 385
Freeman, T., 441
Freiberg (Saxony), 6, 39, 41–42, 92, 103n,
    288, 319, 445
Freiburg-im-Breisgau (Germany), 98n,
    103n
Freiberger Anzeiger und Tageblatt, 39, 42, 102
Frese, Judge, 310n
Freud, E.C., 366n
Freud, S., 101n
    on aphasia, 214, 241n, 248–250n, 428n
    on brain anatomy, 247n, 253n
    on compulsion, 384
    on dementia praecox, 282, 309n, 311n,
        328–329, 331, 337–338
    on dreams, 9, 43, 340–341n, 380–381,
        421n, 424n, 435–436
    on drives, 149, 161–163, 216
    dynamic psychiatry and, 164, 194n,
        202–206, 250–251n, 329, 441
    hallucinations of, 428n
    on hysteria, 104n, 307n
    Jung, C.G. and, 321–323, 340, 361n,
        368–369n
    on infantile seduction, 331
    on latent homosexuality and paranoia, 2,
        183–185, 259n, 330–370n *passim*,
        387, 437–442
    on libido theory, 2–3, 332, 339, 352.
        369–370n, 402–403, 426n, 438, 440
    occult and, 318, 369n
    psychoanalysis and, 252n, 271, 319–320,
        333
    on psychosis, 281, 312n, 331, 337, 339,
        343, 441, 468n
    religion and, 100n, 257n, 391, 445
    on sublimation, 190n, 220
    on unconscious, 12n, 251n, 330, 412
    See also sub Schreber, Moritz; Schreber,
        Paul (interpretations of)
Friedrich, E., 122, 132, 142n
Friedrich, G., 24–25, 95n, 97n, 110, 114,
    136–137n, 146n, 241n
Friedrich, H., 108, 194n
Friedrich, U., 103n, 194n
Fritsch, G.T.F., 241
Fritzsche, H., 108, 194n

Froebel, F.W.A., 165, 191–192n
Fromm, B., 144n
Frustration, 323, 342, 349, 437, 447; *See
    also sub* Schreber, Paul
Fuhrmann, M., 270
Fulton, J.F., 244n

G

Galen, 119
Galimberti, C., 100n
Gall, F.J., 214
Galton, F., 380, 421n
Gambetta, L., 289
Ganser, Dr., 234, 262, 294, 300, 303n,
    310n
Ganz, M., 371n
Gay, P., 333, 372n
Geiser, B., 32, 99n, 102n
General Leipzig Turnverein, 120
Georgii, A., 141n
German Association for Psychiatry,
    254n
German Physicians and Scientists
    Association, 203, 214, 223,
    249n, 254n, 308n
Gesell, K., 108, 194n
Gibbon, M., 356, 362n
Gilardon, K., 135n, 242n
Gilles de la Tourette syndrome, 390
Gilman, D.C., 187n, 244n
Girardi, 310n
Glees, P., 254n
Glenn, J., 362
Glisson, Dr., 144n
Gobineau, J.A., 101n
God, views on, 2, 11n, 159, 188,
    191–192n, 197n, 242, 248n, 360n
    See also sub Schreber, Moritz; Schreber,
        Paul ("nerves")
Goethe, J.W., 1, 312n, 359n, 416–417,
    425n, 429
Goetze, R., 230, 232, 258n, 289, 318, 344,
    359n
Goldstein, K., 241n, 248n
Golgi, C., 252n
Gonorrhea, 24, 54
Göttingen University, 22
Gräfe, H., 194n
Graefe, R., 188n, 405

Gratification, 216, 366n, 426n,
    sexual, 24, 219, 425n, 475
    See also sub Schreber, Moritz; Schreber,
        Paul
Green, A., 107, 354
Griesinger, W., 205, 242n, 244n, 249n,
    281, 421n, 464
Gross, O., 368n, 373n
Grotstein, J.S., 356–357, 374n
Gruber, L., 143n
Gruhle, Dr., 348
Guattari, F., 372n
Gudden, B. von, 225, 227, 242n, 246n,
    248n, 255, 278, 309n
Guilt, 159, 167, 332, 464
Güntz, E., 210
Güntz Hospital, 35
Guts Muths, J.C., 118–120, 154
Gymnastic-Orthopedic Institute (Prague),
    143n
Gymnastics
    as bodily exercises, 125–127, 139–145n,
        149, 160, 169, 177, 181, 191n
    history of, 123, 140n, 144n
    nocturnal emissions and, 161, 163
    therapeutic, 121–123, 129, 142n, 144n
Gynecology, 193n, 262

H

Haase, Wilhelm A., 15, 133
Haeckel, E.H., 203, 297, 366n, 424–425n
Haizmann, C., 342–343
Hallucinations, 199, 216–217, 223, 230,
    246n, 280–283, 311–313n, 321,
    348, 364n, 370–371n, 373n, 380,
    422n, 436
    auditory, 322, 331, 365, 425n
    olfactory, 55
    visual, 293, 328, 331, 421n, 423n, 425n
    See also sub Freud, S.; Jung, C.G.;
        Psychosis; Schreber, Paul
Happiness, 150–151, 194n; See also sub
    Schreber, Moritz; Schreber, Paul
Hardenberg, K. A. v., 304n
Hartmann, E.v., 424–425n, 468n
Hartmann, C.P., 134, 148, 151–154,
    188–189, 191n, 248n, 408,
    424–425n, 445
Hartung, D., 15, 95n, 97n
Haslam, J., 320, 348

Hate, 153, 159, 279, 342, 371n, 440; See also
    sub Schreber, Moritz; Schreber, Paul
Hauschild, E.I., 108, 135–137n, 144n,
    146n, 194n
Hauser, K., 420
Haymaker, W., 225, 240n, 243–244n,
    248n
Hayner, C.A.F., 264, 272, 275, 302n,
    304n, 418
H. B., 97n
Head, H., 241n, 248n
Hebephrenia, 273, 282, 311
Hegar, Dr., 246n
Heidelberg University, 22
Heindl, J.B., 135n, 164, 190n, 193n
Heinroth, J.C.A., 113, 117, 148, 158–159,
    164, 175–176, 185–186n, 189n,
    204, 206, 242–243n, 464
Heinse, W., 404
Helmholtz, H.L.L. v., 202–203, 224, 419,
    426n, 464
Hemmerling, Mr., 230
Hempel, F., 304n, 308n
Henneberg, Dr., 242n, 254n
Hennig, C., 82, 193n, 196n, 400
Hennig, M., 21, 91
Hera, 335
Heraclitus, 2
Herbart, J.F., 166, 176, 192n, 194n, 282
Hermann, I., 356
Hermaphroditism, 337, 360n
Hermeneutics, 333, 371–372n, 438
Herrmann, O., 309n
Hillman, J., 355
Hinsie, L.E., 461
Hippocrates, 150
Hirsch, A., 114, 135–136, 187–189n
Hirsch, J., 123, 143n
Hirsch, W., 254n
Hirschfeld, A., 21, 96n, 303n
Hirschfeld, M., 259n, 363
Hirth, G., 121, 141–142n, 190n
His, W., 251n
Hitler, A., 102n, 197–198n, 206n,
    353–354, 373n
Hitschmann, E., 370n
Hitzig, E. 203–204, 241–242n, 245n,
    251–263n, 310n
Hoche, A., 56, 83, 85, 277, 283–284,
    297–298, 309n, 321, 370n
Hödel, Mr., 233

Hoeller, S., 360n
Homosexuality, 79, 138n, 259n, 273, 324,
    363n, 372n
  biological, 259
  latent, 444
  latent and paranoia; See sub Freud, S.
  narcissism and, 333, 338
  See also sub Libido; Schreber, Paul
Honneger, J.J., 368n
Hoppe, Dr., 306n
Horace, 110, 163
Horwitz, W.A., 333
Hösel, Dr., 272, 298, 308n
Hostility, 68, 349, 352
Hufeland, C.W., 148–152, 154–155, 157,
    186–189n, 191n, 445
Hunter, R.A., 10–12n, 70, 73, 103–104n,
    188, 312n, 323–324n, 350–351,
    371, 377, 379, 403, 421–422n
Huschke, E., 214
Huss, Jan, 78, 111, 138, 297, 401
Hutten, E.v., 42
Hutter, U.v., 111
Huxley, A., 427n
Hygiene, school, 193n, 196n See also sub
    Schreber, Moritz
Hypnosis, 221–222, 362n, 380, 411–412
Hypochondria, 34–36, 126, 128, 150–151,
    153, 218, 230, 310n, 314n, 384
  See also sub Anxiety; Schreber, Moritz;
    Schreber, Paul
Hysteria, 41, 153, 221, 307n, 311n, 329,
    337, 347, 360–361n, 380, 384
  group, 411
  surgical treatment of, 212, 246n, 358
  See also sub Anxiety; Schreber, Moritz

I

Ibsen, H., 41, 97n, 251, 427n, 437
Idealism, 10n, 202, 393, 423, 424
Ideler, K.W., 142n
Identification, 342, 364, 438
  feminine, 64–65, 327–328, 402
  See also sub Schreber, Paul
Identity
  disorder of, 216
  gender, 433, 447
  self-, 219
  theory of, 152
  See also sub Schreber, Paul

Ikelaar, L., 360n
Ilberg, G., 262, 266, 275, 283, 314n
Illinois University, 240
Illusion, 216, 281, 312n, 314n
  sensory, 312n
  See also Hallucination
Ilmenau Spa, 37–38, 92, 458, 471
Incompetency, 8, 231, 234–235, 261, 273,
    276–280, 283–289, 303n, 315n See
    also sub Schreber, Paul
Incorporation, oral, 353
Infeld, L., 321
Innsbruck (Austria), 98n, 103n, 105n; See
    also Wilten
Insomnia, See Sleeplessness
Instinct
  self-preservative, 154, 186n
  sexual, 152, 172, 218–220
Institute for Experimental Psychology
    (Leipzig), 257n
Institute for Orthopedics and Therapeutic
    Gymnastics (Leipzig), 109
Institute for Therapeutic Gymnastics
    (Berlin), 142n
Intellect, 423; See also sub Flechsig;
    Schreber, Moritz; Schreber, Paul
International Congress of Psychology, 244,
    248, 252
International Psychiatric Congress, 307n
International Psychoanalytic Associations,
    11n
International Psychoanalytic Congress
    (Weimar), 345, 362n
Interpretation, 5–6, 107, 178
  See also sub Dreams; Schreber, Paul
Ireland, W.W., 244
Israëls, H., 5, 7, 20–22, 25–26, 34, 39–40,
    84, 88, 94–101n, 104–105n, 107,
    109, 112–114, 132, 135–137n,
    139–141n, 144–145n, 190–191n,
    193–194n, 198n, 241n, 251n, 253n,
    316n, 355–356, 358, 359n,
    371–374n, 420–421n, 426n

J

Jackson, H., 251n
Jacobi, M.P., 244n
Jacoby, K.W., 244
Jacoby, R., 368

Jahn, F.L., 118, 120, 130, 132, 134, 141n, 154, 476
Jahrbuch für psychoanalytische und psychopathologische Forschungen, 11, 253n, 342, 362n, 369–370n
Jakobi, M.M., 138n
James, W., 10–11n, 257n, 393, 421n
Janet, P., 250n, 253n, 346
Jaspers, K., 343, 346, 348, 370n, 416, 424n
Jelliffe, E.S., 346
Jena University, 262
Jenner, E., 187n
Jesuits, 138n
Jesus Christ, 158, 422n, 425n
    See also sub Schreber, Moritz (on God);
        Schreber, Paul (identifications with)
Jetter, D., 304n
Jews, 31–33, 138, 247, 288, 388; *See also*
        Anti-semitism
Johns Hopkins University, 370n
Johnston, T.B., 244n
Jolly, F.J.W., 210, 236, 242n, 279, 309–310n
Jones, E., 367
Joule, J.P., 425n
Joyce, J., 358, 376
Jung, C.G., 11, 259, 367n, 375, 380, 421n, 436, 440
    on brain, 322
    on dementia praecox, 309n, 359–362n, 365n, 369n
    Freud and, 2, 321, 324, 328–329, 331, 339–341, 343, 345–347, 373n, 422n, 424n
    hallucinations of, 361n, 428n
    and the occult, 253n, 321, 369n, 374n, 424n
    psychoanalysis and, 271
    See also sub Schreber, Paul (interpretations of)
Jung family
    Anna (née Schreber), 6, 112, 121, 405, 443
        character of, 19, 24–26, 97n
        death of, 104n
        life of, 14, 32, 39, 91, 94n, 133
        relations with mother, 16
        relations with Paul Schreber (brother), 40, 82–83, 443
        religiosity of, 111, 193–194n
    Carl-Ferdinand (Karl), 25–26, 82–83, 91

Carl-Heinz, 94n, 97n
Dieter, 94n, 97n
Felix, 39–40, 94n, 99n, 371n
Friedrich (Fritz), 26, 94n, 98–99n
Friedrich Moritz Heinrich, 94n
Helene, 94n, 98–99n
Karl, 82–83, 91
Otto Karl, 95n
Paula, 94n, 99n
Renate, 26–27, 94n, 97n
Ruth, 94n, 97n
Wilhelm, 94n, 99n
See also Friedrich, G.; Friedrich, U.; Röder; Wienstein
Juvenal, 110, 119

K

K., 306n
Kaarsch-Haack, F., 259n
Kabbalah, 360n
Kaiser Wilhelm I, 32, 233, 240n
Kant, I., 124, 139n, 151, 159, 165, 185n, 187–189n, 191n, 193n, 204, 248n, 256n, 312n, 317, 329, 378, 380, 391–393, 396–397, 406, 419, 421n, 425n, 435, 445
    See also sub Philosophy
Kanzer, M., 362n
Karl Marx Universität (Leipzig), 193n, 242n
Karl-Sudhof Institute (Leipzig), 135n
Katan, M., 349–350, 371
Kean, E., 371n
Kemper, J., 309n
Kempis, T. à, 25, 194n
Kemple, T.M., 422n
Kendler, K.S., 356
Kernberg, O.F., 307n
Kerr, J., 11n, 360n, 362–363n, 368n
Kesting, J., 117, 158
Kilian, G.W., 136n
Kirchhoff, T., 262
Kitay, P.M., 372n
Kittler, F., 358, 374n
Klatt, E. & G., 135n
Klein, H.R., 333
Klein, M., 167, 348–349, 370n
Klein, R.H., 354
Kleine, H.O., 114, 136n, 140–141n
Kleuker, J.F., 425n

Kloss, M., 109, 130, 132, 135n, 137n, 141–142n, 144–145n, 190n
Klumpp, Prof., 120
Kneschke, E.H., 139n
Knight, R.P., 39, 349
Koch, C.F., 120, 139n, 141n, 186
Kochendorf, R, 144–145
Koehler, G.K., 356, 374n
Kohn, R., 246n
Köher, Minister of Justice, 298
Kohut, H., 353–354, 373n
Kolbe, Prof., 200
Kolle, K., 215, 241n, 254n, 363n
Kotzebue, A.F.F. von, 113
Kraepelin, E., 212, 223, 257n, 280, 345, 356, 361–362n, 377, 380, 390, 392
  influence on Flechsig, 210, 227–228, 245n, 254–255n
  influence on Freud, 328–329, 345–346
  influence on Weber, 271, 273, 281–283, 294, 310–312n, 314–316n
  Textbook, 191, 212, 280, 312, 315
  See also sub Schreber, Paul (interpretations of)
Krafft-Ebing, R., 278, 327–328, 363n
Krakow University, 138, 143
Krämer, H., 461
Krankenwärter und Dienstläute, 306–307n
Kraus, K., 309n
Krause, Klara (née Schreber), 14, 16, 19, 24–25, 45, 95n, 133
Krause, Theodor, 16, 24, 45, 82, 95, 297
Krauss, F., 344, 369–370n, 424n
Kreuser, Dr., 270
Kreuzzeitung, 258n, 288, 315n
Kron, H., 320
Krüll, M., 354
Krumbiegel, F.W., 285–288
Krüner, E., 258n, 288
Kulturkampf, 42, 100–101n, 138n
Kunde, Dr., 144n
Kussmaul, Prof., 242n

L

L., 245n
Lacan, J., 103n, 195n, 351–352, 354, 356, 371n, 373n
Ladd, G.T., 244n
Ladies' Sanitary Association, 131
Laffal, J., 354

Lamm, M., 425n
Landry, N., 123, 143n
Langersmann, J.G., 304n
Language, *See sub* Schreber, Paul
Lasker, E., 101n
Lawrence, D.H., 368n
Lehmann, Dr. Fr., 261–262, 275, 302n
Lehmann, R., 313n
Leibnitz, L., 254n
Leibniz, G.W., 6, 248n
Leipzig City Council, 244n
Leipzig Historical-Theology Society, 192n
Leipzig Municipal Theater, 30
Leipzig School of Music, 30
Leipzig Turnverein, 121, 133
Leipzig University, 96–97n, 158, 185n, 256n, 260, 264, 422n
  Hospital for Psychiatric and Nervous Diseases, 1, 10n, 92–93, 207, 228, 230, 239, 245n, 419, 470; *See also sub* Flechsig; Schreber, Paul
  Orthopedic Hospital, 118, 145n
  School of Medicine, 15, 114
Leipzig-Dösen Asylum, 14, 89–90, 93, 94n, 275, 478
Leppel, F., 359n
Leprosy, 104n
Lessing, Dr. v., 266–267
Leubuscher, R., 263
Lewis, D., 145n
Libido, 161, 328
  homosexual, 11n, 183, 238, 335–336, 363–364n, 368n, 456
  theory, 337–340, 343, 346–347, 373n, 424n, 436, 442; *See also sub* Freud, S.
Liebreich, O., 24, 34, 37, 55
Lindenhof Asylum, 57, 260–262, 273, 278, 302n, 460, 473–474
Lindner, G.A., 191n
Ling, P. H., 122–123, 126–127, 129, 141n, 144n
Linke, 247n
Linné, C., 111
Lion, Dr., 190, 196n
Lion, J.C., 190
Lion, R., 190
Lipps, T., 248n
Lipton, A.A., 356, 374n
Little Hans, 348, 440
Lochner, Dr., 35, 102n, 252n
Locke, J., 119, 165

Lombroso, C., 220, 438
Lomer, G., 270, 307n
Lorinser, Dr., 135n
Lothane, Z., 5, 41, 136–137n, 139n, 144n, 194–196n, 247n, 311n, 315–316n, 332, 355–356, 358, 360n, 365n, 370–374n, 380, 427n, 440
Louise of Saxe-Coburg, 261, 277–278, 309–310n
Love, 11, 14, 16, 18, 97, 149, 152–154, 159–160, 198n, 267, 293, 314n, 338–339, 364–368, 389, 401, 429, 439–453, 464; See also sub Schreber, Moritz; Schreber, Paul
Löwenfeld, Prof., 248n
Ludwig, C., 200, 202, 213, 224, 239
Ludwig, King of Bavaria, 242n, 278, 309n
Luthardt, C.E., 391, 422n, 456
Luther, M., 110, 203, 296, 317, 401, 437
Lutherans, 25, 87, 111, 138n, 391, 422n, 469n, 483
Lutz, R., 258n

M

Macalpine, I., 10–12n, 70, 73, 103–104n, 188n, 312n, 323–324, 350–351, 371n, 377, 379, 403, 421–422n
Macrobiotics, 148–151, 191n
Madness, 139n; See also Psychosis
Maeder, A., 341–342, 440
Magendie, F., 214
Magic Flute, 389, 467n
Magoun, H.W., 193n
Mariaberg Asylum, 257n
Mangner, E., 108, 135–137n, 194n
Mannoni, M., 355, 372n
Mantius, E., 30
Marriage See sub Flechsig; Schreber, Moritz; Schreber, Ottilie Sabine; Schreber, Paul; Schreber, Pauline
Marozza, O., 373n
Marx, K., 31–32, 372
M.A.S., 244n
Masochism, sexual, 153, 183 See also sub Schreber, Paul
Massmann, Prof., 141n
Masson, J.M., 144n, 212, 358, 362n, 368n, 373–374n

Masturbation, 96n, 190n, 310n, 314n, 350, 373, 404, 448 See also sub Schreber, Moritz; Schreber, Paul
Materialism, 10n, 42, 102n, 131, 174, 199, 202, 213, 391–393, 402, 423n, 467
Matthews, J.T., 320
Mayer, R., 258n, 397, 425n
Mayor, M.L., 196n
McCawley, A., 371n, 374n
McGhie, A., 441
McGuire, W., 324, 329, 340–341, 345, 360n, 362n, 365n, 367n, 369n, 373n, 440, 454
McHenry, L.C., 241n, 244n, 248n
Meckel, A., 187n
Medicine
  history of, 12n, 109, 147, 203–204, 464
  holistic, 7, 123, 136n, 161
Megalomania, 337
Meijer, M., 356
Meissen (Saxony), 110; See also sub County court
Melancholia, See Depression; Bipolar disorder
Mellis, L., 210, 236, 242n, 279, 309n
Mendel, Prof., 246n, 287
Mendelssohn-Bartholdy, F., 30
Meng, H., 373n
Mennonites, 138n
Messiah, 61, 389, 422n
Messinger, H. 135n
Metternich, K., 112–113
Meyer, Adolf, 228, 346
Meyer, Alfred, 242n, 243–244n, 248–249n, 254n
Meyer, E.J., 343, 369–370n
Meyer, J.E., 103n, 189n, 242n
Meyer, L., 210, 242n
Meyer, R., 33n
Meyerbeer, G., 30
Meynert, T., 203, 214–215, 241n, 249n, 310–311n, 330–331, 364–365n
Miller, A., 11–12n
Miller, F., 253n, 350n
Milton, J.L., 190n
Mind, 2, 12n, 423n, 439, 467
  integration with body, 425n
  localization of, 9, 211, 213–220, 228, 241–242n, 244n, 247–251, 254–255n, 272

See also sub Schreber, Moritz; Schreber, Paul

Ministry of Coburg (Germany), 22

Ministry of Education, 131, 193, 204, 208, 211, 223–225, 228, 240, 244n

Ministry of Justice, 287, 295, 298, 315n, 468; *See also sub* Schreber, Paul

Ministry of the Interior, 263–264, 266, 268, 303n, 305–307n

Miracles, 159; *See also sub* Schreber, Paul

Mittenzwey, L., 108, 135–137n, 194n

Möbius, P.J., 253n, 319–320, 348, 359n

Moleschott, J., 214, 426n

Molière, 442

Monakow, C.v., 248n, 251–252n

Monatschrift der Psychiatrie und Neurologie (MPN), 246n, 252–255n, 271–272, 303n, 307n

Money, politics of, 56, 443, 445, 448

Monism, 11n, 392–393

Monroe, P., 119

Mood, 294, 337
  disorders of, 102n, 261, 282–283, 302n, 313n, 329, 389, 442n; *See also sub* Emotions
  See also sub Schreber, Paul

Morphine, 34, 45, 54–55, 64, 470, 472

Moser, F., 424n

Moufang, Dean, 32, 100n

Müller, H., 266, 304n

Municipal Theater (Leipzig), 30

Munk, H., 214–215, 217

Mutze, O., 289, 318, 321, 343–344, 359–360, 425n, 477

Myelogenesis, 203, 215, 224–225, 229, 239, 244, 248

Myers, F.W.H., 393, 420n

Mysticism, 41, 152, 229, 374n, 380, 391, 393–394, 397, 422n, 424–425n; *See also* Occultism

N

Näcke, P., 253n, 312n, 333, 365n

Napoleon, 101n, 112, 192n, 275

Napoleonic Code, 310n

Narcein, 54

Narcissism, 364–365, 442
  See also sub Homosexuality

Narcotics, 53, 221, 474, 477

See also Bromides; Chloral hydrate; Morphine; Narcein; Opium; Potassium iodide

National-Liberal Party, 100n, 102n

Naturalism, 164, 165

Nature
  concept of, 158, 189n, 423n
  laws of, 150
  See also sub Flechsig; Schreber, Moritz; Schreber, Paul

Nauhardt, Mr., 82

Nauhof, Dr., 263

Nazis, 192n, 194n, 197n, 301n, 306n, 316n, 318n, 353–354, 374n, 462

Nekzin, 54, *see* Narcein

Nerves, 188n, 281; *See also sub* Schreber, Moritz; Schreber, Paul

Neue Jahrbücher für die Turnkunst (NJT), 122, 132, 137n, 141–142n

Neumann, A.C., 109, 122, 134, 142n

Neupert, R., 312n

Neuroanatomy, 204, 206, 214, 224, 241–244n, 254n

Neurologisches Centralblatt (NC), 243, 246n, 247, 254, 287, 313n, 322, 364

Neurosis, 35, 55, 145n, 189n, 245n, 250n, 267, 276, 299, 330, 334, 338, 342, 402, 408, 417, 439–440, 458
  infantile, 350
  obsessional, 331, 384
  perversion and, 332
  treatment of, 261
  See also sub Anxiety

Nesper, J., 98

Neurology, 214, 254n, 281, 297, 319, 435

Neurosciences, 229

Newton, I., 422n

New York Academy of Medicine, 195n

New York Psychoanalytic Association, 345

Niederland, W.G., 4–5, 7, 10–12n, 14, 23, 28, 39, 62, 84–85, 87–89, 94–101n, 104–105n, 107–108, 112, 115, 117, 125, 132, 135n, 137n, 139n, 140n, 178–183, 189–190n, 193n, 195–196n, 212, 253–254, 349–350, 352–359, 371–373n, 383, 397–398, 420–421n, 427n, 438, 444

Nietzsche, F., 41, 97n, 197n, 296, 348, 400, 437

Noah, 388

Nobiling, K., 233
Nordau, M., 31, 41–42, 220, 296, 437–438
Nothnagel, H., 34, 54
Nydes, J., 357, 374n

O

Obedience, 444, 448; *See also sub* Schreber, Moritz
Object love, 338–340, 364n, 366–367n, 373n, 429
Obsession, 345, 359, 368n, 373n, 380, 434
   See also Compulsion; *sub* Schreber, Moritz
Occultism, 2, 122, 152, 165, 253, 318, 321, 391–393, 396–397, 409, 423–425n; *See also* Mysticism
Oedipus complex, 2, 183, 351, 454
Ohlah, G., 270, 307n
Ohlenroth, 194n
O'Malley, C.D., 244n
Ophuisen, J.H.W., 370n
Opium, 48, 54–55, 212, 246–247, 270, 272, 472–473
Organs, sexual, 217
   male, 198n, 297
   female, 212, 299, 297, 246n
   See also sub Schreber, Paul, fantasies of
Ormuzd, 66, 172, 218, 294, 323, 396, 400, 410, 425, 460, 474
Orthobiotics, 148, 158, 185n, 464
Orthopedic Institute (Leipzig), 16, 18, 117–118, 124, 126, 128, 143–144n, 180
Orthopedics, 7, 19, 108–110, 114, 118, 123–126, 136n, 138–145n, 180–182, 195n
   See also Appliances, orthopedic
Ostow, M., 95n, 462
Ostwald, P., 241n, 313n
Otto, A., 246n
Ovid, 110
Oxford University, 240

P

Paasch, C., 100–101n, 235–236, 258n, 463
Pacini, Dr., 297
Pagel, J., 12n, 136n, 243n
Pain, 61, 183, 366n, 383, 424n, 435, 441; *See also sub* Schreber, Paul

Paranoia
   diagnosis of, 280–287, 295, 346, 353, 371n, 459, 461, 463
   dynamics of, 246n, 249n, 278–287, 290, 293, 311–314n, 322, 326, 329–357, 360, 363–367n, 387, 392, 422n, 440, 442,
   latent homosexuality and, 2, 327–328, 333–339, 342, 345, 348–351, 366–372n, 431, 439–440, 444, 451
   litigious, 222, 234–235, 258n
   nosology of, 312, 329
   politics of 280, 284
   rage and, 341–342, 460
   schizophreniform, 357, 432–433
   See also Dementia praecox; Psychosis; Schizophrenia; *sub* Schreber, Paul
Paresis, 202, 208, 249n, 253n, 294, 302n, 311n, 348
   See also Syphilis; *sub* Schreber, Daniel Gustav
Parvy, J.D.C., 426n
Paulsen, F., 11n, 193n, 248n, 256n, 393
Payne, C.R., 346, 374n
Peck, H.T., 187, 244
Peiper, A., 136n, 192n
Pelman, C.W., 231, 320n, 359n
Perception, 213
   extrasensory, 169, 391, 409
   sensory, 332, 393, 398
Perceval, J.T., 2
Persecution, 184, 195n, 259n, 279, 316n
Perversion, 332
Pestalozzi, J.H., 119, 165, 191n
Peters, U.H., 27, 40, 50, 87, 94n, 98–99n, 105n, 444–455, 462–463, 467n
Petronius, 110
Petter, F., 40–41, 87, 105n, 453
Petzold, K.A., 235–236
Pfausler, Dr., 298, 315n
Pfeifer, R.A., 224, 226, 243n, 248n, 254n
Pfeiffer, R., 320
Pfister, O., 138n, 324, 341
Pharaoh, 360n
Philipp, Count of Coburg, 310n
Phillips, J.H., 368n, 421
Philosophy
   history of, 425n, 447
   Kantian, 117, 152–153, 158, 160, 162, 171, 174–175, 193, 215–216, 219, 221, 228–229, 392, 399, 419, 464

of religion, 188–189n, 464
Pienitz, E., 265, 275, 302n, 304
Pierson, R.H., 15, 57–60, 92, 106, 260–262, 267, 272–273, 278–279, 302–303, 307–310n, 459, 473, 483
Pisani, P., 35
Plato, 175, 186n, 192n, 214, 256n, 360n, 378–379, 425n
Pleasure, 150, 194n, 366n, 433, 441
  See also sub Schreber, Paul
Pleasure principle, 257n
Pletsch, C., 371n
Podvoll, E.M., 374n
Politics
  German, 42, 100–101n, 235, 288, 354, 368
  soul, 358, 419–420, 457
  See also sub Money; Paranoia; Power; Psychiatry; Schreber, Daniel Gustav; Schreber, Paul; Weber, G.
Politzer, L.M., 135n, 137n, 177
Pollitz, P., 247n
Porter, R., 357
Potassium iodide, 34–35, 48, 471
Power
  fear of loss of, 455
  healing, 394
  judicial, 72, 276–277,
  lust for, 412
  motive for, 368n, 412, 460
  politics of, 353–354, 113, 427n, 446, 448
  psychiatric, 271, 284, 289, 295, 308n, 418–419
  See also sub Flechsig; Schreber, Moritz; Schreber, Paul
Pradilla, 467n
Prado de Oliveira, L.E., 103n, 355–356, 371–372n, 468n
Prel, C. du, 369n, 393–396, 409, 422–425n, 427n, 431
Premonition, 335, 394–395
Prevention; 107–108, 123–125, 134, 139, 144, 148–149, 151, 154, 162–164, 177, 186–187; See also Schreber, Moritz on Hygiene
Prichard, Dr., 220
Primal scene, 351
Projection, 3, 217, 329, 331–332, 342, 364n; See also sub Schreber, Paul
Promiscuity, 24, 90, 150, 153, 389

Pseudohomosexuality, 333, 440
Psychiatrisch-Neurologische Wochenschrift (PNW), 223, 252–253n, 257n, 261, 274, 277, 279, 282, 298, 302n, 305–309n, 315n, 320, 362n, 368n
Psychiatry
  dynamic, 164, 205, 218–219, 249–250n, 384, 392, 439, 464
  forensic, 74–77, 222–223, 228–239, 276–277, 284, 320–321, 328–330, 360n, 368n
  German, 2, 7–9, 12n, 53, 202, 215–216, 241–244n, 248–259, 325
  history of, 2, 8–9, 272, 319–320, 338, 464
  organic, 3, 9, 12n, 46, 95n, 72, 158–159, 199, 211–213, 216, 218, 239, 246, 249–251n, 255n, 293, 310, 330, 346, 435, 447, 457, 464–467
  politics of, 3, 166, 178, 271, 284, 289, 295, 308n, 418–419, 464–468
  soul, 142n, 158, 169, 185n, 189, 204–205, 464, 466
  See also Antipsychiatry
Psychiatric Association of the Rhine Province, 232, 257n
Psychiatrists, pathologies of, 270, 307n
Psychische Studien, 318, 359–360n, 393
Psychoanalysis
  applied, 320, 324, 438
  history of, 2–3, 229, 255n, 309n, 341, 352, 368n, 430, 438
    See also sub Bleuler; Freud, S.; Jung, C.G.
  method, 5, 253n, 324, 372n, 435, 439, 441
  reconstruction, 438, 440
  theory, 4, 169, 252n, 370n, 411–423
Psychodynamics, 361–362n, 400; See also sub Schreber, Paul
Psychology
  child, 166
  of consciousness, 250n
  depth, 255n, 328, 439
  dream, 311n, 322–323n, 340, 420–421n, 434–435, 458
  dynamic, 194n, 251n
  ego, 4, 249–250n, 339, 343, 346, 440
  experimental, 227, 245n, 257n
  faculty, 228–229
  mass, 354

medical (organic), 205, 215–219, 229,
    240–249n, 252–254n, 256n, 272,
    282, 422n
of religion, 253n
See also sub Schreber, Moritz; Schreber,
    Paul
Psychosis
    diagnosis of, 7, 38, 219, 329, 361n
    endogenous, 280
    etiology, 362n, 411
    exhaustion, 272
    forensic diagnosis of, 222–236,
        258–259n, 278, 286–287, 290, 298,
        307n, 313n, 344, 454
    hallucinatory, 71, 310n, 314n, 365, 459
    institutional, 307n
    nosology of, 139n, 189n, 311n, 348,
        351, 360n, 394, 422n, 458
    paranoid, 345, 363n
    persecution, 285
    postpartum, 271
    stress, 467n
    syphilitic, 202, 249–250n
    toxic, 281
    traumatic, 330
    treatment of, 53, 209–210, 212, 234,
        245–246, 261, 273
    See also Dementia praecox; Paranoia;
        Schizophrenia;
    sub Freud, S., Schreber, Moritz;
        Schreber, Paul
Punishment, corporal, 265; See also sub
    Schreber, Moritz; Schreber, Paul

Q

Quackelbeen, J., 356
Quensel, F., 254n
Quillet, C., 192n

R

R., 321
Rabbas, Dr., 246n
Racamier, P.-C., 372n
Rage, affect of, 160, 171, 349, 445, 466
    See also sub Paranoia; Schreber, Paul
Rajka, T., 357
Ramon y Cajal, S., 241n, 244n, 248n
Rampolla del Tindaro, M., 100n
Rank, R., 94n

Ranke, L., 438
Ranney, A.L., 244n
Rapaport, D., 362n
Rasumovsky, Count, 189n
Rationalism, 82, 152
Rat Man, 348
Rays (radiation), 265, 369–370n, 392,
    396–397, 412–413; See also sub
    Schreber, Moritz; Schreber, Paul
    (delusions)
Reason, 153, 192, 216, 220–221, 282,
    312n, 423n; See also sub Schreber,
    Moritz; Schreber, Paul
Regression, 3, 38, 56, 251, 333, 337, 356,
    364, 446, 450
Reich, A., 370n
Reich, W., 373n
Reichstag, 21, 32
    See also sub Antipsychiatry; Schreber,
        Paul
Rein, W., 138n, 191–192n
Reinartz, H., 231–232
Religion, therapeutic role of, 421n
    See also Catholics; Jews; Lutherans;
        Mennonites; Zoroaster; sub Flechsig;
        Jung, Anna; Philosophy;
        Psychology; Schreber, Moritz;
        Schreber, Paul
Renan, J.E., 391
Repression, 2, 12n, 322, 331, 339,
    364–365n, 369n, 387, 390,
    435–436, 448
Reval (Estonia), 262, 263, 301, 303
Revesz, B., 214
Richter, A., 19
Richter, Dr., 34
Richter, E., 99n
Richter, G., 95n, 108, 113, 132, 194n
Richter, H.E., 140–141n
Richthoffen, F.v., 368n
Rickman, J., 370n
Ricoeur, P., 373n
Rijnders, G., 356
Riklin, F., 270, 307n, 362n, 468n
Rimbaud, A., 437
Ritter, A., 108, 112, 136–137, 175, 178,
    189n, 194n, 354
Rittershaus, E., 298
Roberts, M.S., 356, 371n
Röder, Ilse (née Jung), 94n
Röder, Reinhardt, 94n, 96–97n

Rodig, J.A., 233–235, 257n, 285, 300
Rome Congress of Psychology, 240
Römer, 94n
Rosenbaum, J., 104n
Rosenfeld, H., 349
Rossbach, M.J., 34, 54
Rothstein, H., 141n
Rousseau, J.-J., 119, 154, 165–166, 186n, 188n, 191n, 319–320, 359n
Roy, D., 135n
Royal Central Turn Institution, 141n
Royal Gymnastic Central Institute, 122
Royal Health Board for Kingdom of Saxony, 208, 267, 273, 305n
Royal Opera House, Dresden, 87
Royal Physical Education Teachers Training Institute (Dresden), 142n
Royal Swedish Academy, 240
Rückel, Albertine (née Behr), 28–29, 67
Rückel, Dr., 29
Rückert, F., 154

S

Sachse, G., 225, 226, 240n, 242–243n, 374n
Sadger, I., 251n
Sadism, 4–5, 7, 107, 168–169, 178, 183, 352, 354, 444
Saint Augustine, 25
Saint Theresa, 393
Salpêtrière Hospital, 206
Sand, C.L., 113
Sand, R., 194n
Sänger, K., 117, 159, 189n, 244n, 248n, 252n, 254n, 263
Sass, L.A., 357
Satan, 110, 342, 417, 461, 480
Scharfstein, B., 374n, 421n
Schatzman, M., 4, 5, 7, 11–12n, 107, 125, 137n, 140n, 178–179, 181–185, 192n, 194–198n, 353–356, 371–373n, 426–427
Schaudinn, F., 37
Scheinert, J., 192n
Schelling, 152, 189n, 191
Schildbach, C.H., 12n, 113–114, 118, 121–122, 127–130, 132, 134, 135n, 137n, 142n, 144–145n, 191n
Schiller, F., 225, 240n, 243–244n, 248n, 320

Schilling, K., 16–17, 19, 39, 94n, 96–97n, 108, 112–114, 118, 135n, 137–138n, 140n, 193n
Schizophrenia, 273, 282, 329, 338, 344, 361–364n, 369n, 426n
diagnosis of, 345, 356–357
See also Dementia praecox; Paranoia; Psychosis; sub Schreber, Paul
Schmid, K.A., 141–142, 190n, 476
Schmidt, C.v., 79, 135, 136, 185, 190, 455, 468
Schnidbauer, W., 309n
Schnitzer, E., see Emin Pasha
Schopenhauer, A., 215–216, 218, 248n
Schratt, Mrs. 310n
Schreber Associations, 88, 107–109, 134–135n, 137n, 194n
Schreber family
depression in, 15, 95n
ethics of, 18, 25, 194n, 407, 445–447
spirit of, 25, 98n, 104n, 193n, 342, 424, 445
Schreber family members
Anna, See sub Jung family
Barbara, 110
Daniel Gottfried, 14, 111–112, 138n, 304
Friedrich Gustav, 112, 133
Gustav (Daniel Gustav), 374n
betrothal, question of, 96n
birth of, 14, 113, 117, 133, 185n, 204
character of, 19
depression in, 24
delusions of, 24
education of, 20
Leipzig, life in, 26
paresis of, 24, 37, 48, 97n
politics of, 22
seduction of Paul by, 350
suicide of, 16, 22–24, 27, 92, 97n, 447, 449, 483
Hans, 110
Johann Christian Daniel, 14, 111, 136n, 138n
Johann David, 110
Johann Gotthilf Daniel, 112, 133
Klara, See Krause
Louise (née Haase), 14
Martha Maria (née Jakobi), 138n
Moritz (Daniel Gottlob Moritz)
aggression of, 372n

in Berlin, 109, 123, 133
on blessedness, 18, 174, 398
on brain, 153, 162, 170, 172–174, 193n, 398–399
on child psychology, 172, 176–177
on conflict resolution, 46, 164, 430,
death of, 91, 130–134
deformities, on
    childhood prevention of, 123–125
    treatment of, 129, 141n, 143n, 149, 182, 187n
delusions of, 180, 116
depression of, 14, 91, 114–115, 117, 121, 127, 130, 134
on depression, 153, 160, 329, 422n
on dreams, 175
on education, 325, 447
on education, national, 131, 134, 165, 175–178, 192n
on ego, 174–175
on emissions, noctural, 152, 156, 161, 409, 426
on emotions, development of, 156–158, 166, 168
on ennoblement, 162, 175, 190, 220
on ethics, 111, 131, 154, 157–158, 162–164, 172, 175, 407–410
on excess, lustful/sexual, 155–156, 161, 408–409
on forgiveness, 157, 183
Freud on, 106–107, 112, 135n, 177, 372n
on gastrointestinal illness, etiology of, 162
on God, 18, 20, 116, 147, 154, 165, 169, 171–172, 175–176, 193n, 391, 410, 427n
on gratification, sexual, 111, 169,
guilt of, 115
on happiness, 115–116, 174, 398, 409
on hate, 160, 175, 186
on hygiene, 18, 107–108, 131, 147–148, 151–152, 155–156
    mental, 139n, 144n, 154, 160–161, 162–164, 177
hypochrondria of, 154, 157, 160, 162–163, 353
on hysteria, 120, 163
imagination of, 115, 153, 156, 168, 174, 398
on infertility, etiology of, 156

on intellect, 131, 160, 174
life history of, 9, 14, 95n, 106–146
on love and sex, 110–112, 152, 155, 157–160, 198n
on love of learning, 170, 176
on love, parental, 112, 149–150, 156, 166–168, 170–171, 186n
marriage of, 109, 133
on marriage, 150, 153–155
on masturbation, 135n, 150, 153, 155, 158, 161, 195n
on mental illness, etiology of, 115, 153, 158, 160, 163
on mind/body integration, 107, 119, 124–125, 129, 131, 136n, 142n, 147–148, 410, 427n
on natural phenomena, 123, 154, 156, 162, 164–167, 175, 385, 405, 409, 427
on nerves, 126, 153, 163, 172–173, 219
on obedience, 128–129, 157, 165, 168–171
obsessive ruminations of, 15, 94n, 115, 117, 139n
on pain, 169, 174, 186, 398
on passion, control of, 152–153, 157, 159–160, 171, 345, 405, 409–410, 445
on prevention, 186, 406; *See also* Dietetics; Hygiene
on psychosis, 126
on punishment, 188n, 192n, 196n, 373n
on rays, 160, 168, 198n
on reason, 154, 159–160, 164–165, 169, 174, 410
on religion, 112, 138, 153, 159, 165, 172, 193–194n
    Judeo-Christian precepts of, 410, 444
self, concept of, 157, 164, 173–175
on self-development, 175
on selfishness, 157, 160, 167, 171, 176
on sensuality, 155, 169, 176, 408, 445
on softness, 17
on soul, 164, 172–173
on spirit, 131, 170–171
on students, 177, 184
suicidal feelings of, 117

on supernatural phenomena, 165, 171, 409
trauma, head, 5, 14, 110, 127, 134
as university student, 133, 152
in Vienna, 109, 123, 133
on vision, exercising of, 184
on voluptuousness, 111, 156
on will-power, 117, 119, 126, 130, 151, 160, 163–164, 168, 171, 187n, 191n, 402, 410, 428n
writings of:
Anthropos, 134, 142n, 172–173, 176, 193n, 398, 427
Book of Health, 14, 114, 117, 130, 133–134, 147–149, 154–159, 166, 172–173, 398, 447
Kallipädie, 4, 17, 22, 82, 112, 130, 134–135, 136n, 140n, 156, 166–172, 175–176, 178–180, 189, 192–193n, 196n, 198n, 352–353, 375, 407–408, 409, 410
Kinesiatrics, 125, 127, 144n
Medical Indoor Gymnastics, 34, 83, 102n, 104n, 121, 127, 134, 135n, 141n, 144–145n, 160–161n, 189n, 405, 409
Medical Perspective on School Affairs, 134, 189, 191n
National education, 134, 142n, 175–177
Scoliosis, 118, 124–125, 149, 181, 196n
Pangymnastikon, 127, 132, 137, 145, 191
Turning, 119–120, 133
Paul (Daniel Paul)
aggression of, 371n, 444
analogy, use of, 377, 391
anger of, 444, 452, 456; See also Rage
anxiety of, 44–50, 62, 74, 90, 293, 383–384, 390, 403, 407, 432, 461
feminine anxiety of, 64
attendants, relations with, 410, 437, 442
at Dösen, 89, 478–481
at Leipzig University Hospital, 48–49, 53–57, 60, 414, 458
at Sonnenstein, 63–64, 68–69

bellowing of, 67, 70–78, 82, 85, 170, 341, 348, 356, 383, 386–387, 390, 415, 442, 449, 457, 459–460, 463, 474–477
in Berlin, 26–27, 43, 92, 99n
biology, concept of, 229, 337, 376, 391
on blessedness, 66, 80, 163, 366n, 399–404
on body functions, 389, 405, 448
body sensations of, 6, 12n, 383, 403, 462; See also voluptuousness
case history of, 325–326, 333–334, 372n, 469–483
compulsive thinking of, 382–384
confinement of, involuntary, 320, 344, 355, 434–435, 463
conflicts
current, 13, 53, 334, 342
with Flechsig, 54, 339, 349, 419,
with Sabine, 51, 452, 453, 461
sexual, 28, 43, 437, 445, 447–448
death of, 14, 91, 93, 94n, 470, 483
defense, means of, 345, 439, 444
delusions of, 8, 107, 178, 352, 354, 376, 383, 431–443, 451–452, 459, 467n
brain, softening of, 47–48, 55, 238, 250n, 472
corpses, 89, 163, 207–208, 263, 358, 366, 406, 467, 478
drug-induced, 34, 457
father's illness, 95n
grandeur, 63, 90, 283, 311–314n, 326, 342, 460
influencing machine, 421n, 462
persecution, 3–6, 8–9, 11n, 48–49, 67, 71, 291–292, 326, 332, 336, 344, 353, 411, 435, 462–463, 472
"rays of God," 61–63, 160, 250n, 292, 378–379, 384–385, 402, 417, 421n, 442, 460–461, 463
religious, 53–54, 68, 77–78, 172, 188n, 347, 353, 427n, 436, 461
syphilis, 55, 388, 447
See also fantasy; hallucination
depression in, 37–38, 43–51, 55, 61, 64, 389–390, 402, 404, 430, 432–433, 442, 447, 457–458, 460, 476
psychotic, 69–70, 89–90, 376

devil, concept of, 117, 387, 447, 459, 473

Devil's Castle, 57, 59, 459

diagnoses of
    dementia praecox, 7, 295, 322–323, 347, 430
    differential, 219, 322
    forensic, 237–238, 284, 320, 322–323, 350–352, 371n, 403, 415–416, 424n
    hallucinatory psychosis, 292, 299
    homosexuality, 7, 439
    hypochondria, 24, 27, 38, 40, 92, 219, 291, 295, 389, 470–473
    paranoia, 7, 329, 353, 371n, 459, 461, 463
    psychosis, 4, 29, 51–52, 77, 431–434, 448, 460, 462–463
    schizophrenia, 38, 51, 322–323, 328, 345, 348, 356, 374n, 431–432, 463, 467n
    self-, 43, 47–50, 69, 158, 328–329, 377, 382–390, 434

divorce, threats of, 29, 68, 75, 450–451

Dösen, stay at, 14, 89–91, 93, 94n, 419, 469–483

dream psychology of, 8–9, 13, 29, 42, 360, 377–382, 393–396, 419

dream of being woman in intercourse, 43, 326–327; See also sub fantasy

Dresden, life in, 44–45, 85, 87–88, 98n,

on education, 376–377, 389, 406, 445

on ego, 5, 55, 97n, 173–174, 389, 397–398

on emissions, noctural, 336

emotions, lability of, 88–89, 217, 334

on emotions, 327, 386, 413, 415

on eternity, 386, 388, 396–397, 399–400, 409

on ethics, 391, 400, 404, 407

etiology of illnesses, 46, 361, 453, 455

factual vs. fantastic in, 8–9, 47, 52, 79, 168, 256, 325, 375–378, 399, 411, 416–417, 421n, 426n, 431, 449, 451, 462

fantasies of
    castration, 212, 326, 337, 354, 358, 366n

end of the world, 54–55, 329, 339–340, 347, 368n, 382, 387–389

Flechsig, 22, 59–62, 66, 71, 185, 193, 319, 332, 334–336, 339–340, 350, 353–354, 368n, 384, 388–392, 396–399, 402, 426–428, 431–432, 440; See also soul murder
    homosexual abuse, 43, 52–53, 64, 185, 337, 402, 440, 452
    organs, female, 337n, 437
    power of attraction, 63–64, 336–337
    redeemer, 327, 460, 462
    turning into a woman, 64–65, 67, 317, 326–328, 333, 335, 337, 351, 354–356, 403–404, 432–434, 436–437, 440, 443, 451–452, 460 See also unmanning
    See also delusions; hallucinations

father, relations with, 5, 347, 352, 373; See also sub transference

father-in-law, relations with, 15, 381, 456

fear in, 38, 383–384, 390

femaleness, sense of, 327, 343

Flechsig, relations with, 6, 34–38, 80, 83, 92–93, 106, 295–296, 321, 357, 359n, 372n, 374n, 433, 449, 456, 461; See also sub transference

on forensic psychiatry, 68, 70–71, 76–80, 93, 104n, 313n, 411–412, 434, 463, 475

frustration, sexual of, 350–351, 376, 439–440, 451

on gratification, sexual, 111, 404

guilt of, 24, 90, 387, 400, 404, 447–448, 464

hallucinations of, 8, 72–74, 291–292, 330, 441–442, 467, 479–482
    auditory, 51, 53, 55, 59, 60, 73, 75, 84–85, 376, 379, 381–383, 385, 386, 412–413, 423–424n, 433, 437, 452, 457, 463, 472–473, 477, 480, 482
    etiology of, 352, 357, 432–434, 458, 461
    negative, 323
    olfactory, 472
    religious, See miracles

visual, 51, 54–55, 62–63, 75, 376,
    381–383, 393, 395, 457,
    462–463, 471
    See also delusions; fantasy
happiness, on, 40, 63, 404, 409, 429
hate for father, 444, 356
identifications with
    brother, 23–24, 48
    father, 130, 146, 163, 409–410,
        444, 447, 456
    Jesus Christ, 61, 317, 381, 401,
        417, 420,
    Job, 44, 54, 61, 387, 400–401,
        417
    mother, 16, 65, 343, 446, 456
    teachers, 408
identity of, 128, 376, 389, 463
incompetency status of, 8, 56–57,
    70–84, 92–93, 237–238, 291–292,
    295–300, 313n, 319, 355, 359n,
    420, 444, 454–456, 459, 463,
    476–477
on influence, 30, 46, 78, 385, 392, 408,
    411–420, 432, 462
on own intellect, 405
interpersonal relations of, 410–414,
    440–441
interpretations of, 316–317n,
    319–374, 438–439, 451, 454, 456
    by Bleuler, 7, 322, 328–329, 343,
        345, 362n, 370n, 466
    by Flechsig, 40, 216–218, 326,
        233–238, 249n, 335, 340, 355,
        436, 443, 472–473
    by Freud, 1–7, 10–11n, 13, 16,
        43–44, 138n, 273, 295, 317,
        323–341, 347, 350–358
    by Jung, 7, 62, 104n, 321–323,
        346–348, 355, 361n, 368n, 372n,
        422n
    by Kraepelin, 343, 348
    by Weber, 71–74, 281, 291–294,
        299
irony, use of, 80, 376, 387, 407, 463
on Kraepelin, 392, 423–424n
languages of
    basic, 8, 61, 243n, 376, 413, 438
    "flame words," 296, 317, 437
    nerve, 52–53, 412–415, 437–438,
        441–442, 458
    soul, 8, 383–384, 412–413

as law student, 20–21, 99n, 419
leave of absence of, 45, 92
leaves from asyla of, 29, 83, 458
Leipzig University Hospital, stay at,
    45–57, 482–474
life history of, 13–93
Lindenhof Asylum, stay at, 37–58
love
    and hate issues for, 3, 341, 373n,
        442, 458
    on love and sex, 401–404, 438–449
    for Sabine, 27–29, 40, 60, 79,
        86–87, 420, 450–456
marriage of, 27–31, 39–41, 44, 85–86,
    92, 299, 403, 443, 446–451, 470
masochism of, 357, 442, 444, 451,
    456–457
Memoires, publication of, 319–321
on mind/body integration, 392
Ministry of Justice, employment at,
    26, 39, 44, 56, 85, 91, 96n
Ministry of Justice, reports to by
    Weber, 93, 237, 291, 455, 459
miracles of, 8, 12n, 74, 78, 90, 379,
    481
    bellowing, 348, 386–387, 390,
        415, 442, 459–460
    God's realms, 61, 70, 380–381,
        415
    shortness of breath, 179, 383
mood lability of, 37–38, 57, 64, 80,
    432, 459, 470–471, 474–475, 483
"nerves" of, 335, 386, 390, 409
    father-in-law, 30
    feminine, 353
    Flechsig, 51
    God, 52, 69, 366n, 396–400, 403,
        406, 418
    intellect, 398–399
    spirit, 173
    voluptuousness, 297
    wife, 60
on natural phenomena, 2–13, 89, 379,
    385–386
nervous illness of, 33, 42, 50, 52, 70,
    319, 325, 413, 416, 460, 476
pain in, 402–403, 408–409, 415,
    429
    chest, 34, 45
    head, 75, 406
    psychic, 33, 64, 341, 449

paranoia of, 7, 38, 67, 71–72, 77, 80,
    82, 195n, 197n, 296, 382, 411,
    430–432, 435–437, 450, 458, 470,
    483
picturing of, 377–380, 384
pleasure of
    masochistic, 449
    sexual, 53, 80, 152–153, 163, 172,
        188, 217–218, 297, 366, 398,
        402–404, 408–409, 414, 426n,
        436
    soul, 64–65, 163, 403–404
    voyeuristic, 457
politics of, 20, 376
power, sense of, 413
projection by, 349, 353, 419,
projection by analysts onto, 198n,
    339–340, 430
on promiscuity, 105n, 152, 303,
    401–402
psychodynamics of, 219, 317, 431,
    457
on psychology, 9, 10–11n, 376,
    381–392
psychosis of, 276, 292, 314–315n,
    434, 439, 459; See also sub diagnoses
on punishment, 387–388, 447
rage of, 12, 59–60, 95, 300, 374,
    386–390, 409–410, 430, 447
    at Sabine, 51, 56, 440, 453
on reason, 60, 72, 78, 386
Reichstag, electoral run for, 58, 92,
    99n, 121, 446
on religion, 3, 10, 88, 391–392, 423n
    cosmology of, 376, 396–401, 410,
        426n
    existential religion of, 319, 359n,
        374n, 382–383, 388, 390,
        396–401, 404, 421n, 434, 448,
        467
on sadness, 387
self, sense of, 121, 349, 351, 405–406,
    463–464
self-analysis of, 67, 377, 382–390,
    462
self-consciousness of, 68
self-cure of, 64–65, 117, 345, 355,
    377, 399
self-diagnosis of; See sub diagnoses
self-hate of, 460
on selfishness, 75

as Senatspräsident, 7, 41, 43, 90, 92,
    350n, 447, 452, 469–470
on sensuality, 404
sexuality of, 54, 377, 401–404, 409,
    430, 436
    See also sub conflict
on sexuality, 26, 408
sleeplessness of, 37–38, 44–51, 54, 89,
    237, 294, 295, 325, 403, 420n,
    432–433, 457, 459, 473–478, 481
Sonnenberg Spa, stay at, 34, 37, 92,
    470–471
Sonnenstein, stay at, 14–15, 22, 52,
    56–84, 88–90, 92–93, 172,
    178–179, 223, 236, 238, 301, 319,
    377, 434–435, 447, 459, 470,
    473–477; See also sub transfers
on soul murder, 52, 56, 67, 349, 377,
    401, 411–420, 439, 458–459, 461,
    468n
suicidal feelings of, 34, 44, 47, 49,
suicide attempts of, 54, 470–472
on supernatural phenomena, 13, 24,
    34, 43, 51, 82, 199, 319, 390
syphilis, treatment for, 34–35, 37, 48,
    471; See also sub delusions
torture, mental of, 61, 386
transfers of
    to Lindenhof, 15, 56–57
    to Sonnenstein, 59, 61, 260, 289,
        291, 383, 420, 433, 453,
        455–456, 458–459, 472
transferences with
    father, 352, 356,
    Flechsig, 107, 332, 335, 350, 358,
        415, 434, 448, 457–458, 462
    mother, 446, 450
    Weber, 402
traumata of
    brother's suicide, 24
    childhood, 4, 62, 182, 195, 350,
        357–358, 373n, 427n, 431
    transfer, 59, 441
    wife's absence, 50–51
unconscious, on, 381, 383, 385, 387,
    412–414,
unmanning
    emasculation fantasy of, 117, 334,
        355
    religious fantasy of, 64–65, 355,
        402

transformation fantasy of, 43, 52, 64–65, 75

Weber, relations with, 6–7, 15, 56–93 *passim*, 239, 291–301, 317, 390, 402–404, 421n, 433–436, 438, 443–444, 448, 455–464; *See also sub* transference

writ of appeal of, 76–84, 93, 109n, 297–298, 312n, 319, 389

Pauline (née Haase), 14–16
  character of, 16, 95n, 97n, 443, 446
  death of, 88, 93
  depression in, 16, 19
  marriage of, 14, 91, 109, 114, 133
  widowhood of, 25, 443

Sabine, Ottilie (née Behr)
  abortions of, 368n
  adoption of Fridoline by, 40–41, 85–88, 98n, 103–104n, 448, 453
  Berlin, visit to, 40, 50–51
  collaboration with psychiatrists of, 45, 56, 74–75, 93, 450, 452–455
  death of, 91, 93
  Flechsig and, 28–29, 200, 237–238, 246n, 450, 457
  illnesses of, 88–89, 246n, 453
  marriage of, 27–31, 92, 444, 446, 448–455
  miscarriages of, 27, 39, 449, 451
  Vienna, visit to, 28
  Weber and, 28–29, 299, 450, 456

Sidonie, 14, 16, 19, 24, 133

Schreber gardens, 14, 108–109, 135–137n, 194n, 470

Schreber-Hammer, Fridoline, 40–41, 84–89, 93, 95n, 97n, 103–105n, 443, 453

Schreiber, E., 20, 22, 94n, 96n, 189n, 357n, 392, 422n, 424n, 426–427n

Schröder, P., 214, 254–255n

Schroeder, E.A., 289–290

Schüle, Dr., 246n

Schultheiss M., 94n, 97n

Schultz-Henke, H., 343, 350, 437

Schultz-Schultzenstein, C.H., 126, 151, 188n, 426n

Schultze, C.E., 79, 135–136n, 185, 190, 455, 468

Schultze, E., 277, 283, 284, 313

Schultze-Strelitz, 105n

Schumann, A., 304n

Schumann, R., 201, 373n, 348

Schurig, Minister of Justice, 42, 234, 287

Schwalbe, P., 100n, 312–313n

Schwarz, G.S., 139, 190, 195–196n

Searles, H.F., 426n, 441

Seiling, M., 359n, 425n

Self, 5, 97, 173–174, 189n, 255–256n, 397–398
  -awareness, 219, 410
  -determination, 72, 76, 78, 81, 298, 312n, 412
  -hate, 460
  -love, 159, 364n, 442
  -regulation, 374n, 410
  See also sub Schreber, Moritz; Schreber, Paul

Selfishness, 303, 424, 468n; *See also sub* Schreber, Moritz; Schreber, Paul

Sensation, 163, 173, 213–215, 218, 251, 293n, 331, 370
  disorders of, 281, 292, 422n
  See also sub Schreber, Paul

Sense-deception, 287, 292, 312n

Sensuality, 403, 426n, 451; *See also sub* Schreber, Moritz; Schreber, Paul

Serger, Dr., 309n

Sero, Dr., 273

Sexuality
  anal/oral, 185
  delusions of, 311n, 326
  disorders of, 327
  infantile, 2, 253n, 332–334, 440
  neurosis and, 330, 334n
  See also sub Schreber, Moritz; Schreber, Paul; Weber, G.

Sexualization, 334, 337, 371n, 436, 442
  of Moritz Schreber's writings, 184–185, 198n
  of Paul Schreber's writings, 335–336, 339, 368n, 437

Shamdasani, S., 253n, 360n

Shatzky, J., 461

Shengold, L., 357, 372n, 427n

Sherrington, C., 241n, 244n, 254n

Shilo, Dr., 227, 254n

Shockley, F.M., 346

Shulman, B.H., 351

Siegel, R., 17, 95–96n, 137n, 108, 193–194n

Siegfried, 87

Siever, L., 432

Silberer, H., 347n, 436
Skodol, E.A., 356, 362n
Skurnik, N., 27
Sleep, 395, 399, 422n
  disorders, 210, 212, 245n
Sleeplessness, *See sub* Flechsig; Schreber,
  Paul; Weber, G.
Smers, H., 94n
Socialism, 31–33, 42, 99–101n, 201, 235,
  374
Society for Garden Architecture, 188n
Society for Protection of Germans Abroad,
  275
Society for Psychical Research (London),
  318, 369n, 393
Society for Science and Therapeutics, 139n
Sodom and Gomorrah, 388
Sonnenberg Spa (Thuringia), 34, 37, 92,
  470–471
Sonnenkalb, Prof., 200, 263
Sonnenstein Asylum, 98n, 101–102n, 126,
  208–209, 233, 263–275, 280, 287,
  302–309n, 314n, 464
  Pensionsanstalt (boarders' quarters) at,
    266, 315n
  See also sub Schreber, Paul
Soul, concepts of, 2, 10n, 119, 142–149,
  159–160, 381, 394–396
  See also sub Politics; Psychiatry; Schreber,
    Moritz
Soul murder, 2, 4, 41, 54, 61, 83, 90, 326,
  334, 336–337, 350, 354, 356–358,
  370n, 427n, 432, 442–444, 448,
  450, 463; *See also sub* Schreber, Paul
Specht, F., 100n, 312–313n
Spener, P.J., 138
Spielrein, S., 369n
Spiess, A., 118, 154
Spinoza, B., 165, 248n
Spirit, concept of, 2, 10n, 174, 190,
  396–397, 416, 423–425n; *See also*
  sub Schreber family; Schreber,
  Moritz; Schreber, Paul
Spirits, 391, 400; *See also* Anima
Spitzer, R.L., 356, 362n
Splitting, 250, 282, 348–349, 395, 434 *See*
  also sub Ego
Sprenger, J., 461
Stanley, H.M., 101n
Stärcke, A., 370n
Staudenmaier, L., 424n

Stegmann, A.G., 106, 252, 273, 308n, 325,
  362, 370n
Steiger, E., 149, 191n
Stekel, W., 329, 341, 363n
Stephany, A. von, 186n
Stern, F., 258n, 368n
Stingelin, M., 248n, 358, 374n, 392, 398
Stirner, M., 468
Stöcker, Pastor, 102n, 258–259n, 288–289
Strauss, D.F., 391
Strauss, R., 105n
Strindberg, A., 41, 427n, 450
Structural theory, 4
Student Union, 55, 113
Sublimation, 2, 190n, 220, 333, 366–367
Sudhoff, K., 12n, 136n, 242n
Suggestion, 41, 191, 221–222
Suicide, 31, 95n, 245, 301, 305n, 363n,
  368n,
  attempt, 150, 230, 293, 307n
  See also sub Schreber, Daniel Gustav;
    Schreber, Moritz; Schreber, Paul
Sullivan, H. S., 351, 441
Supernatural, *See sub* Flechsig; Schreber,
  Moritz; Schreber, Paul
Swales, P.J., 330, 362n, 373n
Swedenborg, E., 392–393, 425n
Swedish Medical Association, 122
Swift, J., 358
Symbolism, 389
Syphilis, 24, 97n, 101n, 155, 202, 213,
  230, 232, 293, 302n, 305n
  See also Paresis; *sub* Schreber, Paul
Szasz, T., 195n, 309n, 355, 373n, 435,
  466–467

T

Tabouret-Keller, A., 94n, 110–111,
  137–138n, 145n, 354
Tannhäuser, 65, 87, 467n
Tardieu, A., 368n
Tausk, V., 363–364n, 421n, 462
Teschner, T., 30
Teslaar, J.S. van, 345
Thiersch, Prof., 200, 242n
Theology, 10n, 110, 201, 359–360n, 422n,
  425n
Thom, A., 158
Thomasschule, 20, 22, 91, 112–113, 133

Thonberg Asylum (Leipzig), 35, 211, 245n, 252n
Thought
   compulsive; *See sub* Schreber, Moritz; Schreber, Paul
   mechanisms of, 219, 282
   symbolic, 323, 389
Thümler, Dr., 235
Tiling, T., 312–313n
Tiresias, 335–336
Titchener, E.B., 257
Titchmann, E.B., 247n
Tolstoy, L., 437
Torture, 101n, 107, 119, 427n
   See also sub Appliances; Schreber, Paul
Transcendentalism, 393–395, 419, 422n, 424–425n
Transference, 2, 46, 295–296, 325, 411
   dependence, 200, 426–427n
   homosexual, 367–368
   See also sub Schreber, Paul
Transfers, *See sub* Asylum; Schreber, Paul
Transsexualism, 434
Transvestism, 363n, 434
Traugott, J., 126
Trauma, 64
   infantile, 249n, 253, 322, 330–333, 436, 444
   See also sub Brain; Psychosis; Schreber, Moritz; Schreber, Paul
Treher, W., 373n
Treitschke, H.v., 21
Trenckmann, U., 99n, 227–228, 242n, 254n
Tübingen University, 241n, 261, 424
Turck, Prof., 241n
Turnbull, G.H., 192n, 197–198
Turnverein, 16, 117–120, 127, 136n, 141n

U

Ueberweg, F., 425n
Uhle, M., 99n
Uibe, P., 123, 136n, 143n
Ulrichs, K.H., 259n
Umgestaltung der Landesirrenanstalten, 305n, 314n
Unconscious
   dynamic, 361, 382

mental mechanisms of, 9, 12n, 43, 78, 205, 219, 311n, 336, 350, 395, 411, 416, 426n, 441
   theory of, 162, 251, 330, 435, 437
Underhill, E., 374n
Unger, M., 255n
Unterbringungs-Regulativ, 306n

V

Valentin, B., 110, 118, 139n, 143n, 195n
Venel, J.-A., 196n
Verdi, G., 105n
Verdiglione, A., 354
Vermeiren, K., 372n
Verwaltung des Landgerichts Chemnitz, 27
Vienna (Austria)
   Brain Commission meeting in, 240, 248
   psychiatric politics in, 309–310n
   uprisings in, 21
Vienna Allgemeines Krankenhaus, 249n
Vienna Psychoanalytic Society, 363n
Vienna University, 152
Virchow, R., 188, 258n, 464
Vogel, A., 187n, 191n
Vogt, C., 241n, 248n, 252n
Vogt, O., 214, 225, 252–255
Voltaire, 101n, 358
Voppel, Dr., 264

W

Wächter, C.G. v., 20, 96n
Waechter, O. v., 96n
Waelder, R., 371n
Wagner, E., 132, 200, 203–204, 239, 241n, 243n, 263, 297, 309n
Wagner, J.v., 279, 310n
Wagner, R., 30, 41, 105n, 278, 296, 314n, 373n, 437
Walters, O.S., 351
Watson, M.J., 145n
Wattenberg, Dr., 307n
Webb, J., 369n, 424n
Weber, E., 200
Weber, E.H., 22, 241n, 257n, 297
Weber, G., 9, 25, 91, 95n, 106, 227, 234, 250n, 257, 355
   antipsychiatry and, 290

attendants and, 265, 269–270, 272, 274,
    305–307n, 315
on brain, 263, 290–291, 293, 303n,
    460–461, 463–466
children of, 275
discharge policies, 269
dissertation, 262, 302n
as forensic psychiatrist, 72, 277–291,
    303n, 307n, 309–310n, 313–315n,
    319–330, 340, 344–345, 356, 359n,
    365–366
life of, 262–264, 266, 269, 271,
    274–276, 331
reports to Ministry of the Interior, 257,
    263, 268
on sexuality, 273, 296
sleeplessness of, 267
students and, 274–275
in Vienna, 263
writings and presentations of, 262,
    271–273, 298–299, 303n, 305n,
    307–308n, 310n
See also sub Schreber, Sabine; Schreber,
    Paul
Weber, L.W., 316n
Weber, S.M., 317n
Wehlen (Saxony), 15, 81
Weir-Mitchell treatment, 210
Weiss, A.S., 356, 371n
Weiss, E., 373n
Welcker, P.H., 42
Wenck, J.E., 15, 133
Wenck, P.W., 15
Werner, C.E., 56, 92–93, 120, 292,
    454–455, 468n
Werner, J.A.L., 92, 100n, 139–140n
Wernicke, C., 214, 249–250n
Westphal, C., 242n, 281, 374n
Whillis, J., 244n
White, R.B., 352–353, 426n
Wienstein, Brigitte (née Jung), 26, 85,
    94–95n, 97n, 103n, 194n

Wilde, O., 41, 273
Wilden, A., 355, 359n, 374n
Wilhelm, Margrave, 275
Williams, J.B.W., 356, 362n
Willmann, O., 191n
Wilten (Austria), 87, 453
Windscheid, B., 96n, 234, 258n, 320
Winkel, Dr., 246n
Winternitz, D., 152, 189n
Wish
    oral, 349
    sexual, 323, 337
Wittels, F., 251n
Wöhler, F., 22
Wolf, v., 39
Wolff, H.A.W. v., 99n
Women and Children Institute (Leipzig),
    193n
World War I, 223, 276
World War II, 94n, 301, 318, 361
Wroclaw University, 136n
Wunderlich, C.A., 200, 204, 242, 263
Wundt, W.M., 227–228, 245n, 247–248n,
    253n, 256–257n, 422n

Y

Yakovlev, 248n

Z

Zabriskie, B., 360n
Zeus, 335
Ziehen, T., 255n, 281, 410, 422n
Zinzendorf, Count, 25, 138n, 194n, 324
Zoroaster, 400, 425–426
Zschadrass Asylum, 272
Zvonar, R., 356
Zwickau (Saxony), 26, 120, 200–201, 239,
    285–288